WITHDRAWN

COWPER

COWPER, William. Cowper; Verse and Letters, ed. by Brian Spiller. Harvard, 1968. 1018p tab (Reynard Library). 9.50

This selection of Cowper's poems and letters is probably the most extensive and convenient so far available in one volume. The poetic half of the edition is the weaker: it is hard to see on what basis texts were chosen or how they improve on Milford's standard Oxford edition of the *Poetical Works* (4th ed., 1934), and on the crasser level of reading pleasure and easy reference one misses line numbers in long poems like *The Task* and the didactic poems of 1782. The rich 450 pages of letters, however, are clearly better edited than in Wright's two collections; they would alone make the book a bargain for college libraries, at least until Ryskamp's complete edition is ready.

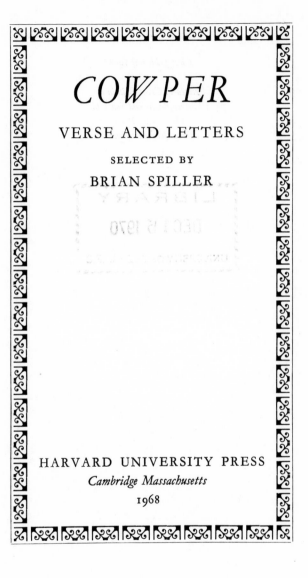

COWPER

VERSE AND LETTERS

SELECTED BY

BRIAN SPILLER

LIBRARY

DEC 15 1970

HARVARD UNIVERSITY PRESS

Cambridge Massachusetts

1968

First published 1968

Printed in Great Britain by
Ebenezer Baylis and Son Ltd
The Trinity Press
Worcester, and London

LIBRARY

DEC 1 5 1970

UNIVERSITY OF THE PACIFIC

228471

CONTENTS

CONTENTS

CONTENTS

CONTENTS

CONTENTS

CONTENTS

CONTENTS

INTRODUCTION

WILLIAM COWPER was the foremost poet in England for a decade or two after the publication of *The Task* in 1785. In his capacity as the chief exponent in poetry of the moral and humanitarian values of the Evangelical Revival, his work enjoyed, well into the middle years of the Victorian era, a far wider readership than he had ever known in his lifetime. The long-delayed reaction then set in; and, apart from a half-dozen anthology pieces, and almost as many hymns regularly sung in the English-speaking churches, his poetry is not much read now. But if Cowper is out of fashion, this hardly affects his merits, for who now reads Dryden or Pope?

The success of Lord David Cecil's biography, *The Stricken Deer*, illustrates the enduring interest in what Cowper called 'the strange and uncommon incidents of my life'. He inherited some flaw in his composition which made him subject to recurring periods of severe depression. His personal tragedy enriched English literature, because if he had been sane, we should never have heard of him. The fear of madness made him turn to writing poetry as a form of mental discipline, and isolation from the great world and from his own kind helped him to become the most enchanting of letter-writers. The letters, written without the slightest thought of publication, form a sort of patchwork autobiography, in which he reveals his character, his thoughts and his ultimate despair with the candour reserved for the most intimate friends. And few scenes of domestic life have been so vividly described, in such exact, telling detail, as the microcosm of Olney and Weston Underwood.

Cowper, who lived from 1731 to 1800, was very much the product of his age and of a particular class. He was born a Christian, a gentleman, and a Whig, and brought up in the two traditions, now rejected, that moulded the minds of the educated classes of Britain for four centuries, the reformed

15

Christian faith and classical humanism. His father was the rector of a country town, Berkhamsted in Hertfordshire, but most of his family were members, active or passive, of the political, legal and church Establishments. They had, or enjoyed the fruits of, 'interest', that valuable eighteenth-century commodity which enabled the heads of families to 'provide for' less fortunate relatives. The interest of the younger branch originated from the successful career of William's grandfather, Spencer Cowper, whose monument in Hertingfordbury Church, a graceful early work by Roubiliac, portrays him in his judge's robes, flanked by the figures of Faith and Justice, above an epitaph describing him as: 'Cheif Justice of Chester in the Reign of King George the First; and Attorney General to His Royal Highness George Prince of Wales, who, on his Accession to the Throne, as a Reward for his unshaken Constancy and Fidelity, further promoted him to be one of his Justices of the Court of Common Pleas; which Offices were united in him by the Peculiar Indulgence of his Royal Master, who was pleas'd thus to distinguish his Superior Merit. These Honours, so fleeting, vain, and unsatisfactory, he soon, too soon, Alas! for his Friends, his Family and his Country, resign'd in Hope of a Blessed Immortality by departing this Life December the 10th, 1727'.

The highest honours were achieved by Spencer's brother, William, third baronet and first Earl Cowper, last Lord Keeper of the Great Seal, first Lord Chancellor of Great Britain after the Act of Union with Scotland, a Lord Justice Regent between the death of Queen Anne and the arrival of King George, Lord High Steward and a member of the oligarchy until he fell out with the new master of Whig politics, Walpole. Spencer's son, the Rev. John Cowper, predictably decided that one of his own sons should follow the law and emulate the career of his great namesake. He had always intended, William wrote in later life, to beget a Lord Chancellor, but had begotten a poet instead: 'it is impossible for the effect to differ more from the intention'. The boy was therefore sent to Westminster School, the cradle of Whig lawyers and Parliament-men, and entered, when still there, in the Society of the Middle Temple, where his great-uncle, grandfather and

16

two uncles had preceded him. After leaving school, he spent three years in the house of a London solicitor, where one of his fellow pupils was Edward Thurlow, who did in fact become Lord Chancellor. Cowper already knew that he was temperamentally unfitted for success at the Bar. He was unwilling, just the same, to thwart the wishes of 'a most indulgent father'. In the event, he compromised by complying with the minimal requirements of the Middle Temple, and by devoting his time to social and literary amusements. His days were spent at the house of his uncle Ashley Cowper, 'constantly employed from morning till night in giggling and making giggle, instead of studying the law'. Here there was a magnet in the shape of three attractive cousins: Elizabeth, who married Sir Archer Croft of Croft Castle, Harriot, who married Sir Thomas Hesketh, and Theadora, to whom he became deeply attached. The early poem 'On Himself' describes how, under her formative influence, the bashful youth became a polished young man about town:

> At length, improv'd from head to heel,
> 'Twere scarce too much to say,
> No dancing bear was so genteel
> Or half so dégagé.

She was not put off by his lack of means. 'If you marry William Cowper, what will you do?' her father asked. 'Do, sir?' she answered, 'wash all day and ride out on the great dog at night.' In 1752 and 1753, Theadora later told Lady Hesketh, 'we saw each other *daily*'. Towards the end of the latter year Cowper, now twenty-one, moved into a set of chambers in the Middle Temple. Here, for the first time, he was on his own. Shortly afterwards, he was 'struck...by such a dejection of spirits, as none but they who have felt the same can have the least conception of. Day and night I was upon the rack, lying down in horror and rising up in despair.' This first severe depression lasted for about a year. At some time during that period Ashley Cowper made it known that he would not consent to the marriage. It was not the act of the heavy father of convention. Ashley Cowper himself suffered from 'nervous fevers', as William described them, and may well have detected unmistakable signs of instability in Theadora, for she too became a victim of melancholy. Besides, she had no fortune; William had none, and showed small signs of making a living. The decision was accepted. The two never met again, never corresponded, never married; but the passage of time failed to efface the pain of their separation. Theadora never ceased to love her William, re-entering his life many years after as 'dear Anonymous', the source of gifts secretly transmitted through Lady Hesketh. She was much distressed to read the evidence in his poetry of his deep affection for Mrs Unwin, and by the thought that she herself 'had only prepared the way for an attachment more solid and more lasting.'

It is probable that Cowper suffered a permanent loss of emotional security with the death of his mother when he was six years old. The wreck of his hopes of private happiness, coupled with the knowledge that the stability of his mind was insecure, must have sapped the remnants of his fortitude. His uncle's house could no longer be his second home; a few years later, he lost the home of his boyhood too. Until his father died, 'it had never occurred to me that a parson has no fee-simple in the house and glebe he occupies. There was neither tree, nor gate, nor stile, in all that country to which I did not feel a relation, and the house itself I preferred to a palace...Then and not till then, I felt for the first time that I and my native place were disunited for ever; I sighed a long adieu to fields and woods from which I once thought I should never be parted.' He had no reason to feel at home in the Middle Temple. As soon as he had discharged his obligations, he bought a set of chambers in another Inn, acquiring the title that he used from then on to denote his rank in society: 'William Cowper, of the Inner Temple, Esq.' Even at this time, a contemporary recalled, he could hardly be described as a 'Temple-haunting martlet', for the summer was more likely to find him at Tewin Water, the house of the future General Spencer Cowper, or in the shrubberies of Cole Green, Lord Cowper's seat, in Hertfordshire. He read much, and talked much about literature—Latin, Greek, French and Italian, as well as English, for he was an excellent scholar. At Westminster he had read the *Iliad* and *Odyssey* with a classmate;

now he read them again with a fellow Templar. There was also some gadding about town with a group of writers who called themselves the Nonsense Club, especially George Colman and Bonnell Thornton, the joint editors of a lively journal, *The Connoisseur*, to which Cowper contributed five essays. All this was much more fun than grinding away at the law. To keep himself in money, he applied himself from time to time, but in the long run, 'lost a legion of attorneys...by never doing their business'.

By 1763, when he was thirty-two, most of his friends were established in their professions, were married or about to marry; yet he had made no progress, and was increasingly left alone, a prey to introspection. His father's legacy was almost spent. Ashley Cowper came to his rescue by offering him two posts on the staff of the House of Lords, to which he held the right of nomination as Clerk of the Parliaments, a lucrative sinecure which Spencer Cowper, the judge, had bought for his elder sons. William eagerly accepted, then took fright at his 'incapacity to executive the business of so public a nature'; so he was nominated instead for the Clerkship of the Journals, where his work could be done in private. The jealousy of other clerks provoked accusations of jobbery, and he was summoned to appear before the bar of the House to be publicly examined on his qualifications. The news set him into a turmoil of agitation. 'Oh, my good cousin!' he wrote to Lady Hesketh, 'if I was to open my heart to you, I could show you strange sights; nothing, I flatter myself, that would shock you, but a great deal that would make you wonder. I am of a very singular temper, and very unlike all the men that I have ever conversed with. Certainly I am not an absolute fool, but I have more weakness than the greatest of all the fools I can recollect.' A holiday at Margate failed to calm his nervous excitement. On the eve of his public examination by the House of Lords, Cowper made two attempts to take his life. He sent for his Uncle Ashley, who told him to consult the celebrated Dr Heberden, who advised him to retire to the country; he sent for a cousin, the Rev. Martin Madan, who urged him to throw himself upon God's mercy; he sent for his brother John, who consulted other relatives about what should be done. They decided that he should be removed to a private hospital at St Albans kept by Dr Nathaniel Cotton, noted for his enlightened methods in the treatment of the insane. Here he remained for eighteen months. Madan's homily had taken root in his mind, and he experienced a sudden, ecstatic conversion. He had become an Enthusiast.

When he emerged again, there was no question of returning to London or of earning a living; for his 'disorder of mind', he believed, had 'unfitted me from all society'. So his brother, a Fellow of Corpus Christi College, was asked to find lodgings near Cambridge. In 1765 he settled at Huntingdon, where he wrote the first of his hymns, 'Retirement', to mark the beginning of a new life:

> *Far from the world, O Lord, I flee*
> *From strife and tumult far;*
> *From scenes, where Satan wages still*
> *His most successful war...*

He had not, however, renounced the desire to be enabled 'to live as my connections demanded'. Within the first three months, 'by the help of good management and a clear notion of economical matters, I contrived to spend the income of a twelvemonth'. A letter from Ashley Cowper apprised him that the family was 'not a little displeased' to learn that he not only kept a manservant, but maintained a destitute boy. Warned in the gentlest way that their indignation might prejudice his sources of income, William remained 'inflexible'. Colonel Spencer Cowper thereupon convened a family council, stated in Foot Guard fashion that he did not propose to support a dependant 'who knew so little how to make a right use of their bounty', and recommended the rest to withdraw their contributions. Sir Thomas Hesketh doubled his own, but the damage was done. The exalted tone of Cowper's letters at this time probably widened the breach with his richer relatives, except Maria Cowper, Madan's sister and also a fervent Evangelical. Communication with them now devolved on Joseph Hill, a close friend and a rising solicitor who frequented Ashley Cowper's house. 'Dear Sephus' took over the management of Cowper's finances for the rest of his life, silently making up the gap between income and expenditure out of his own pocket.

While these exchanges were taking place, Cowper had been adopted by another family. He had struck up a warm friendship with William Unwin, a candidate for orders, whose religious opinions accorded with his own. Unwin's father was a clergyman who prepared resident pupils for the Universities. One of these had just gone up to Cambridge; and Cowper, beset by loneliness and the need for economy, arranged to fill the vacancy as a boarder. Always convinced that whatever happened to him was providential, he believed the Unwin household to be 'a place of rest prepared for me by God's own hand'. In Mrs Unwin, seven years older than himself and twenty years younger than her husband, he found a second mother. She was to be his companion for the rest of her life. When the Rev. Morley Unwin died in 1767, the family resolved to move to a parish—any parish—where they were assured of hearing 'the glad Tidings of Salvation'. Within days, Cowper met the Rev. John Newton, once the captain of a slave-ship, now a minister of the Church Militant, engaged in warfare against the world, the flesh and the devil. He was only too glad to enlist them as auxiliaries, and in September they settled at Olney, Bucks. Here, at Orchard Side, a building likened by Mr Betjeman to a three-storied tram-car, they lived for nineteen years.

In the early years at Olney, Cowper applied himself diligently—perhaps too diligently—to helping Newton as a parish worker. They collaborated in composing *Olney Hymns*, until Cowper was struck down by a third attack of severe depression, again accompanied by attempts to commit suicide. He believed that all his food was poisoned, that everyone hated him, and nobody more than Mrs Unwin. Samuel Greatheed, who was not there at the time, thought it 'not unlikely' that the attack was triggered off by anxiety about his marriage to Mrs Unwin, which had been arranged to take place within a few months and had to be postponed indefinitely.[1] According

[1] *Memoirs of the Life and Writings of W.C.*, London, 1814, p. 30.

to Newton's memorial sermon of 1800, Cowper believed that God had commanded him 'to offer up himself as Abraham his son. He verily thought he ought to do it.' Consequently Mrs Unwin and the Newtons 'left him not an hour for seven years.' The climax of the attack seems to have been a dream which convinced him that his disobedience had cut him off from God's mercy and damned him eternally. This central delusion remained with him, mad or sane, for the rest of his life; and although his basic relief in the Christian dispensation remained otherwise unaltered, he never again attended public worship. When prayers were offered at table, he remained seated, taking his knife and fork in hand, to make it plain that grace was denied to him alone.[1]

After his recovery, he tried a number of expedients to occupy his mind. 'As soon as I became capable of action,' he wrote afterwards to Lady Hesketh, 'I commenced carpenter, made cupboards, boxes, stools. I grew weary of this in about a twelvemonth, and addressed myself to the making of birdcages. To this employment succeeded that of gardening, which I intermingled with that of drawing, but finding that the latter...injured my eyes, I renounced it and commenced poet.' He found 'writing, and especially poetry, my best remedy'. In the words of Goethe's Tasso, a merciful God had given him the power, denied to ordinary men, to articulate his distress, and so to accept it:

> Und wenn der Mensch in seiner Qual verstummt,
> Gab mir ein Gott, zu sagen, wie ich leide.

Acceptance of suffering by trust in divine providence is the theme of his most famous hymn, 'God moves in a mysterious way', composed, according to Greatheed, during a solitary walk in the fields near Olney, when he had a presentiment of the attack of 1773. Resignation, unrelieved by faith, is the mood of the exquisitely sad stanzas of 'The Shrubbery', written in that 'time of affliction'. The verses 'To Mr Newton, on his return from Ramsgate' recall the autumn holiday

[1] *Letters from the Rev. John Newton to the Rev. W. Bull*, ed. T. P. Bull, London, 1847, p. 57.

Cowper had spent on the Kentish coast in a vain effort to disperse the onset of the attack of 1763:

> *To me the Waves that ceaseless broke*
> *Upon the dang'rous Coast*
> *Hoarsely and ominously spoke*
> *Of all my Treasure lost.*
>
> *Your Sea of Trouble you have past;*
> *And found the peaceful Shore.*
> *I, tempest-tost, and wreck'd at last,*
> *Come home to port no more.*

This image of himself as the doomed ship driving before the storm is replaced in 'Alexander Selkirk' by that of the castaway from the Church, but there is a sure hope of mercy at the end. There were also exercises in light verse in which the outward-looking side of Cowper's nature found a happy expression. A stanza from 'Friendship' illustrates his mastery of the technique:

> *The man that hails you Tom or Jack,*
> *And proves by thumps upon your back*
> *How well he knows your merit,*
> *Is such a friend that one had need*
> *Be very much his friend indeed,*
> *To pardon or to bear it.*

Writing verse became 'one of my principal amusements', but did not really satisfy him. He wanted to serve in the household of faith, and that meant writing with a serious purpose. Convinced that he had a natural talent which it would be wrong to bury or neglect to improve, he 'ventured on the only path that at so late a period was yet open to me... For in this only way is it possible for me, so far as I can see, either to honour God, or to serve man, or even to serve myself.' At the end of 1780, Cowper began work on 'The Progress of Error', the first of eight sermons in verse. Mrs Unwin approved the project, though at first she feared that the strain of prolonged composition might be too much for him. They were published, with shorter pieces in Cowper's simpler, spontaneous manner, as *Poems*, 'by William Cowper, of the Inner Temple, Esq.', in 1782.

The reception of this volume was favourable enough to confirm his belief that he had found his vocation. With the arrival of Lady Austen, an iridescent butterfly on the Olney water-meadows, he had entered a period of great creative fertility. The charm of this lively widow animated his spirits and her sparkling conversation stimulated the flow of his ideas. She had the gift of suggesting subjects which inspired some of his most successful poems, including 'The Loss of the Royal George' and the enormously popular 'John Gilpin'. Recognising that he was capable of producing a masterpiece, she gave him the theme of 'The Sofa', which turned into *The Task*. Its publication in 1785 raised Cowper out of obscurity into the front rank of living poets and led, no less happily, to the renewal of relations with his family. Lady Hesketh wrote to say how much she had enjoyed 'John Gilpin'. This was the signal for the beginning of a twice-weekly correspondence which gave us some marvellous letters, and gave him the constant reassurance of her deep affection, material support, and a link with the great world of London.

'How very extraordinary it is!' Maria Cowper wrote to her sister. 'That worthy Creature so many years buried in shades, is now the *conversation* as well as *admiration* of the highest Ranks of people! All the wits and best writers of this age are eager to be introduced to him—but that cannot be. He shuns them all. "Where does he live? Who is he? How can I come at him? Why will he not come amongst us?" &c are perpetually ask'd—which not seldom leads those who are connected and related into some dilemma. But 'tis all the Lord's doing, and therefore right, that this unforeseen *development* of his obscurity and wonderful genius and character should be *forc'd* if I may so say, into Public. He now corresponds very frequently with Lady Hesketh, and the Letters (which I am promis'd the sight of, and have heard some) are a most delightful treat indeed...'[1]

The success of *The Task*, though enduring, was not to be

---

[1] Falconer Madan, *The Madan Family*, Oxford, 1933, pp. 129-30.

repeated. As soon as it had gone to press, Cowper began work
on the translation of Homer which he hoped would bring him
financial security and crown his work as a poet. Lady Hesketh
busied herself with drumming up subscriptions from the
nobility and gentry. Cowper had some qualms about justifying
his preoccupation with this pagan epic to Newton, who was
already disturbed by local reports of rural rides in Lady
Hesketh's carriage to fashionable (and Papist) neighbours, the
Throckmortons of Weston Underwood, who became close
friends after his move to the neater, more cheerful house they
offered him in that still delightful village. '*Olney Hymns and
Olney Homer!*' was Newton's comment to the Rev. William
Bull. Work on the translation absorbed most of Cowper's
working life for the next six years, interrupted only by another
severe depression in 1786. Its publication in 1791 brought him
a clear profit of a thousand pounds, and was followed by a
proposal that he should undertake a new edition of Milton,
in which he would choose the text, supply critical notes and
translate the Latin and Italian poems. Then William Hayley,
who had been commissioned to write a life of Milton, wrote a
letter disclaiming stories in the newspapers that he was setting
himself up as a rival. They took to one another at once. A
warm friendship was sealed by Hayley's visit to Weston and a
return visit to Eartham. It came at a time when Cowper had
great need of moral support, because in 1791, and again
between the two visits, Mrs Unwin had a paralytic stroke. As
she sank gradually into second childhood, he became more
and more alarmed by her condition, felt incapable of work,
and heard the voices of 'nocturnal monitors' who told him
that he was damned. By 1794 Cowper and Mrs Unwin were no
longer able to look after themselves. Lady Hesketh took
charge of the household, but almost broke down under the
strain. A young cousin and fervent admirer, the Rev. John
Johnson, offered them a place in his house in Norfolk. Here,
in a state of inert despair, Cowper remained for the rest of his
life. A year before he died, he read a passage in Anson's
Voyages about a seaman who was swept overboard, and drew
a parallel with his own situation in his last original poem,
The Cast-away:

No voice divine the storm allay'd
No light propitious shone;
When, snatch'd from all effectual aid,
We perish'd, each alone;
But I beneath a rougher sea,
And whelm'd in deeper gulfs than he.

He died in the first spring of the new century. His two
volumes of poetry, which had sold steadily, now began to sell
even better. Henry Crabb Robinson heard in 1812 that they
had earned the publisher a profit of at least £10,000. Mrs
Norma Russell's recent bibliography lists well over a hundred
editions in the British Isles, and forty-eight in the United
States, printed between 1782 and 1837, the date of the final
volume of Southey's edition of Cowper's collected works. She
makes the significant point that this edition, prepared by an
established professional, sold only six thousand copies, compared with thirty-two thousand for the rival compilation
produced for the Evangelical market by an incompetent, the
Rev. T. S. Grimshawe. In 1812 an Edinburgh Reviewer had
estimated the size of the new middle-class reading public at a
figure of at least 200,000, compared with 20,000 for the pre-
sumably more sophisticated upper class. No doubt Carlyle
had the former category in mind when he wrote to Goethe in
1829 that Cowper was still a great favourite 'with the religious
classes', after implying that poets of the new school had
eclipsed his reputation among the literati. Edition after
edition, cheaply printed or ornately produced for presentation,
commanded wide sales for another two generations, until the
image of the Evangelical Revival, made noble by the heroic
stature of Wesley, the reforming zeal of Wilberforce and the
saintliness of Simeon, had been tarnished in the public mind
by the bigotry and bossiness of Mrs Proudie and the loathsome
unction of the Rev. Obadiah Slope.

'Cowper is less read than he deserves to be,' Dean Farrar
noted in 1883, 'but he has this glory, that he has ever been the
favourite poet of deeply religious minds; and his history is
peculiarly touching, as that of one who, himself plunged in
despair and madness, has brought hope and consolation to a

thousand other souls.' There is evidence of this cathartic power in Anne Brontë's poem 'To Cowper', in Elizabeth Barrett Browning's 'Cowper's Grave', and in Sainte-Beuve's *Notes Intimes*: 'venez à moi, mes chères Muses, mes morts chéris en qui je me réfugie avec transport contres les injures du présent, Théocrite, Parny, Cowper, vous qui avez souffert aussi, consolez-moi.'[1] This intense sympathy, to the point of self-identification, could hardly have been felt in Cowper's lifetime, when the facts of his biography and the vivid self-revelation of the letters were still unknown. It was left to later generations to discover that the letters are a gloss on the poems, and vice versa. Taken together, they form connected fragments of a continuing autobiography of almost total self-revelation. Both are immediate reflections of a minutely observed, deeply felt, experience of life. Hippolyte Taine made one point with admirable economy: 'son talent n'est que l'image de son caractère, et ses poèmes ne sont que l'écho de sa vie,' and Sainte-Beuve supplies the necessary corollary on the letters: 'c'est là surtout qu'on apprend à le connaître et à pénétrer dans les mystères de son esprit ou de sa sensibilité.' Another French admirer of a later generation, Teodor de Wyzewa, staked a larger claim: 'Encore cette lumineuse et charmante gaîté n'est-elle pas l'unique attrait de la correspondance de William Cowper. La littérature anglaise a l'enviable privilège de posséder deux œuvres infiniment originales, qui, l'une et l'autre, nous permettent de pénétrer jusque dans l'intimité la plus familière d'une vie humaine; et il n'importe guère d'ajouter, après cela, que l'une de ces deux œuvres a pour auteur un sot, la seconde un fou. La première est cette bizarre et merveilleuse biographie de Samuel Johnson par Boswell où s'est conservée toute vivante et parlante—plus réelle pour nous que les figures de nos plus proches amis—l'immortelle figure d'un personnage extraordinaire...L'autre ouvrage, ce sont ces lettres de Cowper.'[2]

One of the objects of the present edition is to bring together, in a single volume, a generous selection from the poems, long

[1] *Œuvres*, ed. M. Leroy, 1949, I, p. 18.

[2] Review of Sir J. G. Frazer's ed. of Cowper's letters, *Revue des Deux Mondes*, July 15, 1914, p. 467.

or short, grave or gay, and a representative choice of the letters. The other is to reproduce, so far as possible, the text that Cowper himself wrote, unmutilated by careless or bowdlerizing editors. The selections have been grouped in eight sections, each furnished with a separate introduction. The choice of the letters has presented some difficulties. Cowper wrote to each of his correspondents within the framework of a particular relationship, and this posed the problem of keeping a balance between the aspects of his personality and the different interests which are thus exposed. Some weight has been attached to continuity of the narrative, and some preference, but not much, given to letters which were known to be complete. The major problem, as I have set out to explain in the introduction to that section, is the fragmentary and corrupt text of many of the letters printed in any of the collected editions. As some of the letters in this volume have been reproduced from Cowper's manuscript, and others from printed versions which I have been unable to compare with the originals, I have felt myself obliged to follow Southey's practice by modernizing spelling and capitalization, and by modifying the punctuation, of letters in the former category.

Of the 204 letters chosen, 130 have been reproduced from manuscripts in Cowper's hand. Fourteen of these have not previously been published, and thirty-three contain a substantial proportion of new material. Nineteen more letters have been printed from contemporary or early copies in another hand; one of these has not previously been published, and five contain new material. The remaining fifty-five letters have been reproduced from printed sources; a few are now collected for the first time, and some have been redated in the light of the late Kenneth Povey's researches or of my own. Two verses are also printed for the first time; an epigram on Lord Thurlow (p. 951) and the epitaph on Sir Thomas Hesketh (p. 572). I must add that all the foregoing claims are made subject to the qualification: 'so far as I have been able to ascertain'. If any of this material has in fact been printed, or should be printed before this volume appears, I offer my apologies. There are other labourers in this vineyard.

I gladly acknowledge my debt to the authors of several post-war studies from which I have learnt much. They are, in order of date, Mr Norman Nicholson's *William Cowper* (John Lehmann: 1951), a critical appreciation written with the insight of a practising poet; Professor Maurice Quinlan's *William Cowper: A Critical Life* (University of Minnesota Press: 1953), which draws on sources of published material overlooked by earlier biographers; Professor Charles Ryskamp's *William Cowper of the Inner Temple, Esq.* (Cambridge University Press: 1959), a fully documented biography, based on original research, which has immeasurably increased the sum of information about his early life; Professor Lodwick Hartley's *William Cowper: The Continuing Revaluation* (University of North Carolina Press: 1960), a review of his reputation, in the light of critical and biographical studies published since 1895, supplemented by an extensive bibliography; and Mrs Norma Russell's *A Bibliography of William Cowper to 1837* (Oxford Bibliographical Society Publications: 1963), an exemplary work of scholarship and a mine of information.

I also wish to express my thanks, for permission to use the text of manuscript letters of Cowper in their possession, to the Trustees of the British Museum, the Victoria and Albert Museum, the Pierpont Morgan Library, the Cowper Museum, Olney; to the Hon. Lady Salmond and the County Record Office, Hertford, in the case of letters deposited in the Panshanger Collection; to Mr Kenneth Povey, Miss Mary Barham Johnson, Miss Anne and Miss Catharine Cowper Johnson. I am grateful to Professor Charles Ryskamp, to the editor of *The Princeton University Library Chronicle*, to the editor of *The Yale University Library Gazette*, for authority to reprint the texts of letters which were first published in those periodicals, and to the respective Libraries which own the originals; to The Times Publishing Company for permission to publish texts of letters which were first printed in *The Times* in articles by the late Mr Povey; to Mr John Betjeman and John Murray (Publishers) Ltd for permission to use a passage from *First and Last Loves*; to Mr John Sparrow for the translation of Latin and Greek quotations and for constant, ill-rewarded encouragement; to Mr L. S. Dowson, Mr Oliver

Millar, Mr W. T. O'Dea, Mr Brian Petrie, Mr Paul Rogers, Dr Abbot E. Smith and Professor J. R. Strayer, for special services; and to my wife and family for much help and patient long-suffering.

The responsibility for any errors of fact, interpretation or transcription is entirely mine.

BIOGRAPHICAL TABLE

1731 November 15 (Old Style) November 26 (New Style)	William Cowper born at Berkhamsted rectory, Hertfordshire: the son of the Rev. John Cowper, and of Anne, daughter of Roger Donne of Ludham Hall, Norfolk.
1737 November 13	Death of his mother.
(?) 1738 to (?) 1740	At Dr Pittman's boarding school at Markyate Street, Herts.
(?) 1740 to (?) 1742	A boarder in the house of Mrs Disney, 'an eminent oculist', in London.
1742 April	Entered Westminster School
1748 April 29	Admitted to the Middle Temple.
1749 May	Left Westminster School, to spend nine months at Berkhamsted.
1750 to (?) 1753	Articled to a London solicitor, Chapman, in whose house Edward Thurlow was a fellow pupil. Both spend much time in the company of Theadora and Harriot (later Lady Hesketh), the daughters of Ashley Cowper, the poet's uncle.
(?) 1753 or 1754	Abandonment of the hope of marriage with Theadora Cowper.
1753 November	Moves to chambers in the Middle Temple, where he experienced his first breakdown, which lasted for a year.
1754 June	Called to the Bar.
1756 July 9	Death of his father.
1757 April 15	Admitted to the Inner Temple.
1763	Three offices in the patronage of his uncle Ashley Cowper fell vacant: the Clerkship of the Journals of the House

of Lords, the Reading Clerkship and the Clerkship of the Committees. Cowper was nominated to the second and third offices; but he was allowed to exchange them for the first; its duties, though less profitable, were performed in private. The right of nomination was contested and Cowper was summoned to appear for examination at the bar of the House of Lords. After a minor breakdown, he was sent on holiday.

August or September	Return to work at the House of Lords. Renewal of mental agitation.
November	A committee of the House of Lords set up to investigate Cowper's exchange of offices, which had aroused a suspicion of corruption. The findings were wholly favourable, but in the interval Cowper twice attempted to commit suicide.
December	Third attempt at suicide on the eve of his examination. Resignation of the clerkship. On medical advice removed to Dr Cotton's *Collegium Insanorum*, a clinic at St Albans.
1764 July	Recovery and conversion to Evangelicalism.
1765 June	Left St Albans and settled at Huntingdon in lodgings.
c. September	First acquaintance with the Unwin family.
November 11	A boarder with the Unwins, Huntingdon.
1767 July	Death of the Rev. Morley Unwin.
October 14	Arrival of Cowper and Mrs Unwin at Olney, where the Rev. John Newton had offered to find a house for them.
1768 February 15	Move to Orchard Side, Olney.

1769		The Rev. William Unwin appointed rector of Stock in Essex.
1770	March 20	Death of his brother John.
1771		*Olney Hymns* begun, in collaboration with Newton.
1772		Engaged to Mrs Unwin.
1773	January	Severe depression. Engagement broken off.
	February	Visited by a dream 'before the recollection of which all consolation vanishes, and it seems to me, must always vanish' (Letter to Newton, 16.10.1785) in which, he believed, he was cut off from God's mercy. Third breakdown follows.
	April	Moved to Olney Vicarage, under the care of Newton.
	October	Another attempt to commit suicide.
1774	May 23	Return to Orchard Side.
1778	June	Thurlow appointed Lord Chancellor.
1779	February	*Olney Hymns*, by Cowper and Newton, published.
	December 10	Newton inducted as vicar of St Mary Woolnoth in the City of London.
1780	December	*The Progress of Error* and *Truth* begun.
1781	January–March	*Table Talk* and *Expostulation* written.
	Spring	*Charity* written.
	July	First acquaintance with Lady Austen.
	August	*Retirement* begun.
1782,	March 1	*Poems, by William Cowper, of the Inner Temple, Esq.*, published.
	October	*John Gilpin* written.
1783	(?) October	*The Task* begun.
1784	Spring	Final breach with Lady Austen.
	May	First acquaintance with the Throckmortons.
	October	*The Task* completed.
	November	*Tirocinium* completed. The translation of Homer begun.

1785	July	*The Task* published.
	October	Resumption of correspondence with Lady Hesketh, followed by financial help from her and from 'Anonymous' (her sister Theadora Cowper).
1786	June–November	Lady Hesketh tenant of Olney vicarage.
	November	Move to The Lodge, Weston Underwood, at the invitation of the Throckmortons.
	November 29	Death of the Rev. William Unwin.
1787	January	First acquaintance with Samuel Rose.
	January–June	The fourth breakdown.
1788	September	Translation of the *Odyssey* begun.
1790	January	First acquaintance with his cousin, John Johnson.
	September 8	Translation of the *Odyssey* sent to press.
1791	July	Translation of *Homer* published.
	September	Translation of Milton's Latin and Italian poems begun (finished in March 1792).
	December	Mrs Unwin's first paralytic stroke.
1792	May	Mrs Unwin's second paralytic stroke. First visit from William Hayley.
	August 1 to September 17	Visit of Cowper, Mrs Unwin and John Johnson to Hayley at Eartham Place, Sussex.
	Autumn	Renewed depression.
1793	Autumn	Further deterioration in Mrs Unwin's health. *To Mary* written.
	November	Arrival of Lady Hesketh to take charge of Cowper and his household.
1794	January	Beginning of the fifth breakdown, from which Cowper never wholly recovered.
	April	A pension of £300 a year granted by the King.
	May 17	Mrs Unwin's third paralytic stroke.

1795	July 28	Cowper and Mrs Unwin removed by John Johnson to his house at East Dereham.
1796	December 17	Death of Mrs Unwin.
1797	November	Revision of translation of Homer begun.
1799	March 8	Revision of Homer completed.
	March 19	*The Cast-away* begun.
1800	January 31	Treated for dropsy.
	February 22	Confined to his rooms.
	April 25	Death of Cowper.
	May 2	Buried in the parish church of East Dereham.

A LIST OF EDITIONS

OLNEY HYMNS, IN THREE BOOKS. *Book I. On select Texts of Scripture. Book II. On occasional Subjects. Book III. On the Progress and Changes of the Spiritual Life*...London: 1779.

POEMS BY WILLIAM COWPER, OF THE INNER TEMPLE, ESQ.... London: 1782. [Contents: *Table Talk, The Progress of Error, Truth, Expostulation, Hope, Charity, Conversation, Retirement,* and thirty-five shorter poems and translations.]

THE TASK, A POEM, IN SIX BOOKS. BY WILLIAM COWPER, OF THE INNER TEMPLE, ESQ....To which are added, *By the same Author, An Epistle to Joseph Hill, Esq. Tirocinium, or a Review of Schools, and the History of John Gilpin.* London: 1785.

The 1782 and 1785 volumes were subsequently reprinted together as *Poems by William Cowper, Of the Inner Temple, Esq. in two volumes.* The 2nd ed. of 1786 has some verbal changes and many corrections of spelling and punctuation. The 3rd ed. of 1787, the 4th of 1788 and the 5th of 1793 are reprints of the 2nd, with minor errors; the 5th ed. also adds Newton's preface, suppressed from most copies in 1782. The 6th and last of the numbered eds. (vol. I is dated 1794, vol. II, 1795) adds nine new or uncollected poems. The two pott, the fcp. 8° and 12° eds. of 1798 add two new poems (*The Dog and the Water-Lily,* and *On the Receipt of my Mother's Picture*) which had been published as a pamphlet in the same year. The foolscap 8° ed., with ten plates after T. Stothard, was the first to be illustrated. A 'new' ed. of 1799 is a re-issue of the pott ed. of 1798. Three editions dated 1800 were issued after Cowper's death in that year: demy 8°, fcp. 8° and 12°, followed by a pott 8° ed. dated 1801; all add, in varying amounts, much new or uncollected material: up to twenty poems, Cowper's prose essay on his hares, and the Latin originals of some translations from Vincent Bourne; of these, the demy 8° ed. is easily the most handsome printed to date. The 1806 ed., of one volume in 4º, adds for the first time Cowper's translations from Mme Guyon and sixty-six pieces from *Olney Hymns*, including two by Newton. The two 8º eds., and the Stereotype (crown 18º) ed. of 1808 add three new poems to the canon.

THE ILIAD AND ODYSSEY OF HOMER, TRANSLATED INTO ENGLISH BLANK VERSE, BY W. COWPER, OF THE INNER TEMPLE, ESQ. IN TWO VOLUMES. London: 1791. Royal and demy 4º. 2nd ed., in four volumes: royal and demy 8º, with a preface by the Rev. J. Johnson, 1802.

POEMS *Translated from the French* OF MADAME DE LA MOTHE GUION, BY THE LATE WILLIAM COWPER, *Esq. Author of the* TASK. TO WHICH ARE ADDED SOME ORIGINAL POEMS *Of Mr Cowper*, NOT INSERTED IN HIS WORKS. Newport Pagnell: 1801. (With a preface by the Rev. W. Bull). Quoted as *Bull*.

THE LIFE, AND POSTHUMOUS WRITINGS, OF WILLIAM COWPER, ESQR....BY WILLIAM HAYLEY, ESQR....Chichester: 1803. Two vols., demy and royal 4º. Volume III followed in 1804, and SUPPLEMENTARY PAGES TO THE LIFE OF COWPER in 1806.

This is the first edition of Cowper's letters, of which Hayley printed (too often in a mutilated or garbled form) 473 in the 1803–06 series, adding others in the 1809 and 1812 reprints. He also published a large number of new or previously uncollected poems and verse translations. Quoted as *Hayley*.

POEMS, BY WILLIAM COWPER, OF THE INNER TEMPLE, ESQ. IN THREE VOLUMES. VOL. III. CONTAINING HIS POSTHUMOUS POETRY, AND A SKETCH OF HIS LIFE. BY HIS KINSMAN, JOHN JOHNSON...London: 1815. Only Volume III was in fact published. It contains nearly all the verse first published by Hayley, and was designed to provide, with the two volumes already published, a complete edition of Cowper's poetry. It adds thirteen unpublished original poems and seven verse translations. Cowper's *Olney Hymns* and his translations from Mme Guyon are omitted. Quoted as *1815*.

PRIVATE CORRESPONDENCE OF WILLIAM COWPER, ESQ. *with several of his most intimate friends. Now first published from the originals in the possession of his kinsman, John Johnson...*Two vols. London: 1824. This ed. adds 221 new or almost wholly new letters.

POEMS, THE EARLY PRODUCTIONS OF WILLIAM COWPER; NOW FIRST PUBLISHED FROM THE ORIGINALS IN THE POSSESSION OF JAMES CROFT. London: 1825. [Twenty-four unpublished early poems, including the series addressed to Theadora Cowper, after whose death in 1824 they came to her nephew, Croft.]

THE WORKS OF WILLIAM COWPER, ESQ. *Comprising his Poems, Correspondence, and Translations. With a Life of the Author, by the Editor, Robert Southey...*15 vols. London: 1835–36.
[The most complete edition ever published, containing almost everything accessible at the time, except the Autobiographical Memoir. Quoted as *Southey*.]

THE POETICAL WORKS OF WILLIAM COWPER. *With notes and a memoir by John Bruce.* 3 vols. London: 1865. The Aldine edition. [Variant readings and annotations. Quoted as *Bruce*.]

THE POETICAL WORKS OF WILLIAM COWPER. *Edited with notes and biographical introduction by William Benham.* London: 1870. The Globe Edition. [Quoted as *Benham*.]

THE UNPUBLISHED AND UNCOLLECTED POEMS OF WILLIAM COWPER. *Edited by Thomas Wright.* London: 1900.

THE CORRESPONDENCE OF WILLIAM COWPER, *arranged in chronological order with annotations by Thomas Wright.* 4 vols. London: 1904. [The largest collection of Cowper's Letters. Quoted as *Wright*.]

THE POEMS OF WILLIAM COWPER. *Edited with an introduction and notes by J. C. Bailey.* London: 1905. [The text has modernized spelling and punctuation. Thirty-five unpublished or partly published letters, and fragments of others, are included. Quoted as *Bailey*.]

THE POETICAL WORKS OF WILLIAM COWPER. *Edited by H. S. Milford*. London: 1905. [The standard edition: introduction, variant readings and notes. Quoted as *Milford*. 4th ed., with corrections and additions by Norma Russell, 1967.]

THE UNPUBLISHED AND UNCOLLECTED LETTERS OF WILLIAM COWPER. *Edited by Thomas Wright*. London: 1925.

NEW POEMS BY WILLIAM COWPER. London: 1931. Edited by Falconer Madan.

WILLIAM COWPER OF THE INNER TEMPLE, ESQ., by Charles Ryskamp, Cambridge, 1959. The appendices contain unpublished letters and verse. Quoted as *Ryskamp*.

COWPER, ILLUSTRATED BY
A SERIES OF VIEWS

(This is the title of a charming little book of plates, drawn and engraved by J. S. and H. S. Storer, and J. Greig, of scenes 'in or near the Park of Weston Underwood,' 1803)

Now that I talk of authors, how do you like Cowper? Is not *The Task* a glorious poem? The religion of the *Task*, bating a few scraps of Calvinistic divinity, is the religion of God and Nature, the religion that exalts, that ennobles man.
ROBERT BURNS: *letter to Mrs Dunlop, of Dunlop,* 15*th December,* 1793.

I have been reading the *Task* with fresh delight. I am glad you love Cowper. I could forgive a man for not enjoying Milton, but I would not call that man my friend, who should be offended with the 'divine chit-chat' of Cowper.
CHARLES LAMB: *letter to S. T. Coleridge,* 5*th December,* 1796.
(The words 'divine chit-chat' are quoted from Coleridge.)

[Hayley's biography] will contain Letters of Cowper to his friends, perhaps, or rather certainly, the very best letters that ever were published.
WILLIAM BLAKE: *letter to Thomas Butts,* 11*th September,* 1801.

I have all Cowper's works on my table. I mostly read his letters. He is an author I prefer to almost any other, and when with him I always feel the better for it.
JOHN CONSTABLE: *letter to Maria Bicknell,* 15*th June,* 1812.

Cowper was no poet.
LORD BYRON: *letter to Miss Milbanke,* 10*th November,* 1813.

I assure you that, with the exception of Burns and Cowper, there is very little of recent verse, however much it may interest me, that sticks to my memory (I mean which I get by heart).
WILLIAM WORDSWORTH: *letter to R. P. Gillies, 22nd December,* 1814.

In the more sustained and elevated style, of the then living poets, Bowles and Cowper were, to the best of my knowledge, the first who combined natural thoughts with natural diction; the first who reconciled the heart with the head.
S. T. COLERIDGE: Biographia Literaria, 1817.

Her [Jane Austen's] favourite moral writers were Johnson in prose, and Cowper in verse.
HENRY AUSTEN: *Biographical Notice of the Author, prefixed to* Northanger Abbey *and* Persuasion, *1818.*

There is an effeminacy about him, which shrinks from and repels common and hearty sympathy...Still, he is a genuine poet, and deserves all his reputation. His worst vices are amiable weaknesses, elegant trifling. Though there is a frequent dryness, timidity, and jejuneness in his manner, he has left a number of pictures of domestic comfort and social refinement, as well as of natural imagery and feeling, which can hardly be forgotten but with the language itself.
WILLIAM HAZLITT: Lectures on the English Poets, 1818.

The *Cowper's Poems* you are to accept from me as a New-year's gift, the value of which must lie chiefly in the intention of the giver. Cowper was the last of our Poets of the Old School; a man of pure genius, but limited and ineffectual...He is still a great favourite, especially with the religious classes; and bids fair to survive many a louder competitor for immortality.
THOMAS CARLYLE: *letter to J. W. von Goethe, 22 Dec. 1829.*

The forerunner of the great restoration of our literature was Cowper. His literary career began and ended at nearly the same time with that of Alfieri...They both found poetry in its lowest

state of degradation, feeble, artificial, and altogether nerveless. They both possessed precisely the talents which fitted them for the task of raising it from that deep abasement. They cannot, in strictness, be called great poets. They had not in any very high degree the creative power, 'the vision and the faculty divine', but they had great vigour of thought, great warmth of feeling, and what, in their circumstances, was above all things important, a manliness of taste which approached to roughness...The intrinsic value of their poems is considerable. But the example which they set of mutiny against an absurd system was invaluable. The part which they performed was rather that of Moses than that of Joshua. They opened the house of bondage; but they did not enter the promised land.
T. B. MACAULAY: *reviewing Moore's* Life of Byron, Edinburgh Review, *June* 1831.

I am glad you have taken to Cowper. Some of his little poems are affecting beyond anything in the English language: not heroic, but they make me cry.
EDWARD FITZGERALD: *letter to W. M. Thackeray,* 11*th October,* 1831

> Young was I, when from Latin lore and Greek
> I play'd the truant for thy sweeter Task,
> Nor since that hour hath aught our Muses held
> Before me seem'd so precious; in one hour,
> I saw the poet and the sage unite,
> More grave than man, more versatile than boy!

WALTER SAVAGE LANDOR: The Last Fruit off an Old Tree, *Poems, ccvii,* 1853.

Where is the poem that surpasses the 'Task' in the genuine love it breathes, at once towards inanimate and animate existence—in truthfulness of perception and sincerity of presentation—in the calm gladness that springs from a delight in objects for their own sake, without self-reference...? No object is too small to prompt his song—not the sooty film on the bars, or the spoutless tea-pot holding a bit of mignonette that serves to cheer the dingy town-lodging with 'a hint that

Nature lives'; and yet his song is never trivial, for he is alive to small objects, not because his mind is narrow, but because his glance is clear and his heart is large.

GEORGE ELIOT: *'Worldliness and Other-Worldliness'*, Westminster Review, 1857.

There is much mannerism, much that is unimportant or of now exhausted interest in his poems; but where he is great, it is with that elementary greatness which rests on the most universal human feelings. Cowper is our highest master in simple pathos.

F. T. PALGRAVE: *note in* The Golden Treasury, *1861*.

A poet, for example, might perhaps tell us, though a prosaic person cannot, what is the secret of the impression made by such a poem as the 'Wreck of the Royal George'. Given an ordinary newspaper paragraph about wreck or battle, turn it into the simplest possible language, do not introduce a single metaphor or figure of speech, indulge in none but the most obvious of all reflections—as, for example, that when a man is once drowned he won't win any more battles—and produce as the result a copy of verses which nobody can ever read without instantly knowing them by heart. How Cowper managed to perform such a feat, and why not one poet even in a hundred can perform it, are questions which might lead to some curious critical speculation.

LESLIE STEPHEN: *'Cowper and Rousseau,'* Cornhill Magazine, 1875.

The Comic Spirit is not hostile to the sweetest songfully poetic. Chaucer bubbles with it: Shakespeare overflows: there is a mild moon's ray of it (pale with super-refinement through distance from our flesh and blood planet) in 'Comus'. Pope has it, and it is the daylight side of the night half obscuring Cowper.

GEORGE MEREDITH: On the Idea of Comedy, *1877*.

Mr Stopford Brooke's Cowper is excellent, but again there seems to me to be some want of sobriety in the praise given.

44

Philanthropy, no doubt, animated Cowper's heart and shows itself in his poetry. But it is too much to say of the apparition of Cowper and of his philanthropy in English poetry: 'It is a wonderful change, a change so wonderful that it is like a new world. It is, in fact, the concentration into our retired poet's work of all the new thought upon the subject of mankind which was soon to take so fierce a form in Paris.' Cowper, with his morbid religion and lumbering movement, was no precursor, as Mr Stopford Brooke would thus make him, of Byron and Shelley. His true praise is, that by his simple affections and genuine love of nature, he was a precursor of Wordsworth.

MATTHEW ARNOLD: *reviewing Brooke's* Primer of English Literature *in* The Nineteenth Century, *1877*.

After reading Cowper's 'Poplar Field' [Tennyson said]: 'People nowadays, I believe, hold this style and metre light; I wish there were any who could put words together with such exquisite flow and evenness.' Presently we reached the same poet's stanzas to Mary Unwin. He read them, yet could barely read them, so deeply was he touched by their tender, their almost agonizing pathos. And once when I asked him for the 'Lines on my Mother's Portrait', his voice faltered as he said he would, if I wished it; but he knew he should break down.

F. T. PALGRAVE: *'Personal Recollections' in* Tennyson: A Memoir, *by Hallam Tennyson,* 1897.

The letters of Cowper, though they rank high in English literature, do not require much comment. As far as they go, they are perfect, but they hardly go anywhere at all. Their gold is absolutely pure; but it is beaten out into the thinnest leaf conceivable. They are like soap-bubbles—exquisite films surrounding emptiness, and almost too wonderful to be touched. Cowper had nothing to say, and he said it beautifully; yet it is difficult not to wish that he had had something more to say, even at the expense of saying it a little less well. His letters are stricken with sterility; they are dried up; they lack the juices of life. In them, the vast and palpitating eighteenth century seems suddenly to dwindle into a quiet and well-appointed grave. The wheel had come full circle: the flute of Addison was echoed at last by the flute of Cowper; perfection had returned upon itself.

LYTTON STRACHEY: *'Gray and Cowper', written in* 1905 *and first printed in* Characters and Commentaries.

The bicentenary of Cowper's birth was celebrated last November with fitting mildness. Perhaps there have been too many anniversaries lately, perhaps the autumn of 1931 was an unfortunate period. At any rate, Cowper attracted little attention, as he himself would have expected...For who reads Cowper today? This is surely his last appearance on the general stage. Wordsworth (to mention a spiritual kinsman) still keeps his place; in the general holocaust of literature that is approaching he will survive for a little. Cowper perishes. His magic is too flimsy to preserve him, and his knowledge of human nature is too much overshadowed by fears of personal damnation to radiate far down the centuries...It is not an unsuitable moment for him to perish, for England is perishing, and he was English...

E. M. FORSTER: *'William Cowper: Englishman'*, The Spectator, 16 *January*, 1932.

...His letters preserve this serenity, this good sense, this sidelong, arch humour embalmed in page after page of beautiful clear prose. As the post went only three times a week, he had plenty of time to smooth out every little crease in daily life to perfection...'The very stones in the garden walls are my intimate acquaintance,' he wrote. 'Everything I see in the fields is to me an object, and I can look at the same rivulet, or at a handsome tree, every day of my life with new pleasure.' It is this intensity of vision that gives his poetry, with all its moralising and didacticism, its unforgettable qualities. It is this that makes passages in *The Task* like clear windows let into the prosaic fabric of the rest. It was this that gave the edge and zest to his talk. Some finer vision suddenly seized and possessed him...

VIRGINIA WOOLF: *'Cowper and Lady Austen' in* The Common Reader, second series, *1932*.

Meaning is of the intellect, poetry is not. If it were, the eighteenth century would have been able to write it better. As matters actually stand, who are the English poets of that age in whom pre-eminently one can hear and recognise the true poetic accent emerging clearly from the contemporary dialect? These four: Collins, Christopher Smart, Cowper, and Blake. And what other characteristic had these four in common? They were mad. Remember Plato: 'He who without the Muses' madness in his soul comes knocking at the door of poesy and thinks that art will make him anything fit to be called a poet, finds that the poetry which he indites in his sober senses is beaten hollow by the poetry of madmen.'

A. E. HOUSMAN: The Name and Nature of Poetry, *Leslie Stephen Lecture*, 9 *May*, 1933.

Every winter I read *The Task* by William Cowper, and twice or thrice those wonderful books in it where he describes a Winter Evening, a Winter Morning and a Winter Walk at Noon. The frost blades of North Buckinghamshire, the snowed-over woodlands, the dog that gambolled in the snow, the bells and post horns, the cups of tea, melted, dead, silenced, evaporated for nearly two hundred years, come to life again. And if the next morning is nippy and white with frost, then Cowper's magic power of description gives an eternal look to the cold and sparkling scene so that even this duller landscape in which I live might be the gentle undulations round Cowper's Olney, Bucks, or it might be something earlier still, a frost-bound Dutch landscape by Breughel.

JOHN BETJEMAN: First and Last Loves, *1952*.

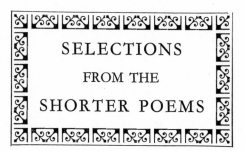

SELECTIONS

FROM THE

SHORTER POEMS

COWPER began to write poetry when he was a schoolboy at Westminster. But he did not write regularly until he reached the age of forty-nine, and even then he turned poet only as a means of distracting his mind from thoughts that led to despair. Some of his verses were first printed in *The Gentleman's Magazine* and in other periodicals. These early texts sometimes differ from those published in the collected editions. Cowper devoted much time and trouble to revision and hardly ever revised without making improvements. The difficulty lies in deciding whether the alterations made in the later editions of the *Poems* had Cowper's sanction. It is known that he corrected, carelessly enough, the proofs of *Poems*, 1782, and of *The Task*, 1785 (subsequently reprinted as *Poems*, volume two). The first of the reprints which obviously received some editorial attention was the sixth of 1794–95 which contained, besides a number of new readings, nine additional poems. Although Cowper was almost certainly too ill to have seen this edition through the press, he had apparently worked on it, with John Johnson as his amanuensis, in the winter of 1792–1793.[1] More new poems, or substantially different texts of poems already collected, appeared in the editions of 1798, 1800 and 1808, in Hayley's *Life*, and in the third volume, containing the 'posthumous poems', edited by John Johnson, of 1815.

For the most part the texts of the poems selected here are those of the editions where they first appeared. But where I have satisfied myself that the later text was the better one, and could conceivably have been printed from a manuscript revised by Cowper himself, I have preferred it. For example,

[1] P. M. Zall, *The Huntington Library Quarterly*, vol. 25, 1961/62, pp. 253–6. The evidence is supplied by three small manuscript notebooks in the Library. These contain 75 poems copied 'with meticulous care', of which 60 are in the handwriting of John Johnson, including two with corrections in Cowper's hand.

the new texts of *The Faithful Bird, On the Death of Mrs Throck-morton's Bulfinch, On the Receipt of my Mother's Picture,* and of *The Dog and the Water Lily,* first given in the 1808 editions, not only excise errors in the earlier versions but seem to me to be more finished products. The same argument applies with greater force to *The Poplar Field.* The text first collected in the editions of 1800 differs materially from, and is incomparably superior to the earliest printed version in *The Gentleman's Magazine* for January 1785. In the case of a number of poems first published or first collected after Cowper's death, the text of a manuscript in his hand has been preferred to the version of the early editions.

The text from which each poem is printed is given in a footnote. Reprinted editions of the *Poems* are referred to by the date of year in which they were published: e.g. 1786. Other editions are quoted by the name of the editor, e.g. *Croft.* A key to the editions and to the abbreviations used will be found in the 'List of Editions' on pages 37–40. One last word of explanation. Cowper's early verse was written, in all probability, without a thought to publication. Where I have known or suspected that the title was supplied by an editor, I have enclosed it within squared brackets. Throughout this edition, I have altered Cowper's spelling, his punctuation, and the heavily stopped punctuation of his early editors, wherever I thought that it presented an unnecessary obstacle to the enjoyment of present-day readers.

[OF HIMSELF]

WILLIAM was once a bashful youth,
　　His modesty was such,
That one might say (to say the truth)
　　He rather had too much.

Some said that it was want of sense,
　　And others, want of spirit,
(So blest a thing is impudence)
　　While others could not bear it.

But some a different notion had,
　　And at each other winking,
Observed that though he little said,
　　He paid it off with thinking.

Howe'er, it happen'd, by degrees,
　　He mended and grew perter,
In company was more at ease,
　　And dress'd a little smarter.

Nay now and then would look quite gay,
　　As other people do;
And sometimes said, or try'd to say
　　A witty thing or two.[1]

He eyed the women, and made free
　　To comment on their shapes,
So that there was, or seem'd to be,
　　No fear of a relapse.

The women said, who thought him rough,
　　But now no longer foolish,
The creature may do well enough,
　　But wants a deal of polish.

[1] *two*: *Bruce. Croft* has *so.*

At length improved from head to heel,
   'Twere scarce too much to say,
No dancing bear was so genteel,
   Or half so dégagé.

Now that a miracle so strange
   May not in vain be shown,
Let the dear maid who wrought the change
   E'er claim him for her own.

[1752]

TEXT: *Croft.* This poem is addressed to his cousin Theadora
Cowper (1731–1824).

[LINES WRITTEN UNDER THE INFLUENCE OF DELIRIUM]

HATRED and vengeance, my eternal portion,
Scarce can endure delay of execution,
Wait with impatient readiness to seize my
        Soul in a moment.

Damned below Judas; more abhorred than he was,
Who for a few pence sold his holy Master!
Twice-betrayed Jesus me, the last delinquent,
        Deems the profanest.

Man disavows, and Deity disowns me,
Hell might afford my miseries a shelter;
Therefore Hell keeps her ever-hungry mouths all
        Bolted against me.

Hard lot! encompassed with a thousand dangers;
Weary, faint, trembling with a thousand terrors,
I'm called, if vanquished, to receive a sentence
        Worse than Abiram's.

Him the vindictive rod of angry Justice
Sent quick and howling to the centre headlong;
I, fed with judgment, in a fleshly tomb, am
                    Buried above ground.

TEXT: *Bailey*. These lines were first printed, and claimed as
Cowper's, in the surreptitiously published *Memoirs of...the Life
of W.C.* 1816 (the scarcer, clumsier version printed by Cox):
the source of Southey's assertion that they were written 'in
the interval between his attempt of suicide and his removal to
a private madhouse', i.e. in 1763. Evidence deployed by Mrs
Russell points to an origin in C.'s severe depression of 1773–
1774. (*Poetical Works*, 4th Ed., Oxford, 1967, p. 660).

THE SHRUBBERY

WRITTEN IN A TIME OF AFFLICTION

O happy shades! to me unblest,
    Friendly to peace, but not to me,
How ill the scene that offers rest,
    And heart that cannot rest, agree!

This glassy stream, that spreading pine,
    Those alders quiv'ring to the breeze,
Might sooth a soul less hurt than mine,
    And please, if any thing could please.

But fixt unalterable care
    Foregoes not what she feels within,
Shows the same sadness ev'rywhere,
    And slights the season and the scene.

For all that pleas'd in wood or lawn,
    While peace possess'd these silent bow'rs,
Her animating smile withdrawn,
    Has lost its beauties and its pow'rs.

The saint or moralist should tread
   This moss-grown alley, musing slow,
They seek like me the secret shade,
   But not like me, to nourish woe.

Me fruitful scenes and prospects waste
   Alike admonish not to roam,
These tell me of enjoyments past,
   And those of sorrows yet to come.

[1773]

TEXT: *1782*

VERSES, SUPPOSED TO BE WRITTEN BY ALEXANDER SELKIRK, DURING HIS SOLITARY ABODE IN THE ISLAND OF JUAN FERNANDEZ

I AM monarch of all I survey,
   My right there is none to dispute,
From the center all round to the sea,
   I am lord of the fowl and the brute.
O solitude! where are the charms
   That sages have seen in thy face?
Better dwell in the midst of alarms,
   Than reign in this horrible place.

I am out of humanity's reach,
   I must finish my journey alone,
Never hear the sweet music of speech,
   I start at the sound of my own.
The beasts that roam over the plain,
   My form with indifference see,
They are so unacquainted with man,
   Their tameness is shocking to me.

Society, friendship, and love,
   Divinely bestow'd upon man,
Oh had I the wings of a dove,
   How soon wou'd I taste you again!
My sorrows I then might assuage
   In the ways of religion and truth,
Might learn from the wisdom of age,
   And be cheer'd by the sallies of youth.

Religion! what treasure untold
   Resides in that heav'nly word!
More precious than silver and gold,
   Or all that this earth can afford.
But the sound of the church-going bell
   These vallies and rocks never heard,
Ne'er sigh'd at the sound of a knell,
   Or smil'd when a sabbath appear'd.

Ye winds that have made me your sport,
   Convey to this desolate shore,
Some cordial endearing report
   Of a land I shall visit no more.
My friends do they now and then send
   A wish or a thought after me?
O tell me I yet have a friend,
   Though a friend I am never to see.

How fleet is a glance of the mind!
   Compar'd with the speed of its flight,
The tempest itself lags behind,
   And the swift winged arrows of light.
When I think of my own native land,
   In a moment I seem to be there;
But alas! recollection at hand
   Soon hurries me back to despair.

But the sea fowl is gone to her nest,
   The beast is laid down in his lair,
Ev'n here is a season of rest,
   And I to my cabbin repair.

There is mercy in ev'ry place,
    And mercy, encouraging thought!
Gives even affliction a grace,
    And reconciles man to his lot.

TEXT: *1782*[1]

HUMAN FRAILTY

WEAK and irresolute is man;
    The purpose of today,
Woven with pains into his plan,
    Tomorrow rends away.

The bow well bent and smart the spring,
    Vice seems already slain,
But passion rudely snaps the string,
    And it revives again.

Some foe to his upright intent
    Finds out his weaker part,
Virtue engages his assent,
    But pleasure wins his heart.

'Tis here the folly of the wise
    Through all his art we view,
And while his tongue the charge denies,
    His conscience owns it true.

[1] The date of this poem has not been established. Cowper's source was possibly Steele's paper in *The Englishman* for December 3, 1713, or a derivative of it. Some of the images and phrases may echo the description of Tierra del Fuego in Cook's account of his second voyage, and more particularly in Forster's (p. 697, *n.*). The latter describes birds 'unacquainted with men' and 'so tame, as to let our boat's crew come among them with clubs and staves' on Staten Land. C. was reading both books for the first time in July, 1777.

Bound on a voyage of awful length
  And dangers little known,
A stranger to superior strength,
  Man vainly trusts his own.

But oars alone can ne'er prevail
  To reach the distant coast,
The breath of heav'n must swell the sail,
  Or all the toil is lost.

[1779]

TEXT: *1782*

THE LOVE OF THE WORLD REPROVED:

OR, HYPOCRISY DETECTED

THUS says the prophet of the Turk,
Good Mussulman, abstain from pork;
There is a part in ev'ry swine
No friend or follower of mine
May taste, whate'er his inclination,
On pain of excommunication.
Such Mahomet's mysterious charge,
And thus he left the point at large.
Had he the sinful part express'd
They might with safety eat the rest;
But for one piece they thought it hard
From the whole hog to be debarr'd,
And set their wit at work to find
What joint the prophet had in mind.
  Much controversy strait arose,
These chuse the back, the belly those;
By some 'tis confidently said
He meant not to forbid the head,

While others at that doctrine rail,
And piously prefer the tail.
Thus, conscience freed from ev'ry clog,
Mahometans eat up the hog.
   You laugh—'tis well.—the tale apply'd
May make you laugh on t'other side.
Renounce the world, the preacher cries—
We do—a multitude replies.
While one as innocent regards
A snug and friendly game at cards;
And one, whatever you may say,
Can see no evil in a play;
Some love a concert or a race,
And others, shooting and the chase.
Revil'd and lov'd, renounc'd and follow'd,
Thus bit by bit the world is swallow'd;
Each thinks his neighbour makes too free,
Yet likes a slice as well as he,
With sophistry their sauce they sweeten,
'Till quite from tail to snout 'tis eaten.

[1779]

TEXT: *1782.* 'It may be proper to inform the reader that this piece has already appeared in print, having found its way, though with some unnecessary additions by an unknown hand, into the Leeds Journal, without the author's privity'. [C] The 'unnecessary additions' were said by Southey to be lines 9–14; if so, it is difficult to see why Cowper included them in 1782. They are cited by the *Oxford English Dictionary* as a possible source of the phrase 'to go the whole hog'.

THE MODERN PATRIOT[1]

REBELLION is my theme all day,
  I only wish 'twould come
(As who knows but perhaps it may)
  A little nearer home.

[1] See the letter on p. 580.

Yon roaring boys who rave and fight
　　On t'other side the Atlantic,
I always held them in the right,
　　But most so, when most frantic.

When lawless mobs insult the court,
　　That man shall be my toast,
If breaking windows be the sport
　　Who bravely breaks the most.

But oh! for him my fancy culls
　　The choicest flow'rs she bears,
Who constitutionally pulls
　　Your house about your ears.

Such civil broils are my delight,
　　Tho' some folks can't endure 'em,
Who say the mob are mad outright,
　　And that a rope must cure 'em.

A rope! I wish we patriots had
　　Such strings for all who need 'em—
What! hang a man for going mad?
　　Then farewell British freedom.

[1780]

TEXT: *1782*

THE NIGHTINGALE AND GLOW-WORM

A NIGHTINGALE that all day long
Had cheer'd the village with his song,
Nor yet at eve his note suspended,
Nor yet when eventide was ended,

Began to feel as well he might
The keen demands of appetite;
When looking eagerly around,
He spied far off upon the ground,
A something shining in the dark,
And knew the glow-worm by his spark,
So stooping down from hawthorn top,
He thought to put him in his crop;
The worm aware of his intent,
Harangu'd him thus right eloquent.

   Did you admire my lamp, quoth he,
As much as I your minstrelsy,
You would abhor to do me wrong,
As much as I to spoil your song,
For 'twas the self-same pow'r divine,
Taught you to sing, and me to shine,
That you with music, I with light,
Might beautify and cheer the night.
The songster heard his short oration,
And warbling out his approbation,
Releas'd him as my story tells,
And found a supper somewhere else.

   Hence jarring sectaries may learn
Their real int'rest to discern:
That brother should not war with brother,
And worry and devour each other,
But sing and shine by sweet consent,
'Till life's poor transient night is spent,
Respecting in each other's case
The gifts of nature and of grace.

   Those Christians best deserve the name
Who studiously make peace their aim;
Peace, both the duty and the prize
Of him that creeps and him that flies.

[February 1780]

TEXT: *1782*. See p. 581.

THE DOVES[1]

REAS'NING at every step he treads,
   Man yet mistakes his way,
While meaner things whom instinct leads
   Are rarely known to stray.

One silent eve I wander'd late,
   And heard the voice of love,
The turtle thus address'd her mate,
   And sooth'd the list'ning dove.

Our mutual bond of faith and truth
   No time shall disengage,
Those blessings of our early youth
   Shall cheer our latest age.

While innocence without disguise,
   And constancy sincere,
Shall fill the circles of those eyes,
   And mine can read them there,

Those ills that wait on all below
   Shall ne'er be felt by me,
Or gently felt, and only so,
   As being shared with thee.

When light'nings flash among the trees,
   Or kites are hov'ring near,
I fear lest thee alone they seize,
   And know no other fear.

[1] This poem was C's preliminary answer to Martin Madan's book advocating polygamy. See *n.* p. 590.

63

'Tis then I feel myself a wife,
   And press thy wedded side,
Resolv'd an union form'd for life,
   Death never shall divide.

But oh! if fickle and unchaste
   (Forgive a transient thought)
Thou couldst become unkind at last,
   And scorn thy present lot,

No need of light'nings from on high,
   Or kites with cruel beak,
Denied th' endearments of thine eye
   This widow'd heart would break.

Thus sang the sweet sequester'd bird
   Soft as the passing wind,
And I recorded what I heard,
   A lesson for mankind.

[Summer 1780]

TEXT: *1782*

ON A GOLDFINCH STARVED TO DEATH IN HIS CAGE

TIME was when I was free as air,
The thistle's downy seed my fare,
   My drink the morning dew;
I perch'd at will on ev'ry spray,
My form genteel, my plumage gay,
   My strains for ever new.

But gawdy plumage, sprightly strain,
And form genteel were all in vain
   And of a transient date,
For caught and caged and starved to death,
In dying sighs my little breath
   Soon pass'd the wiry grate.

Thanks, gentle swain, for all my woes,
And thanks for this effectual close
   And cure of ev'ry ill!
More cruelty could none express,
And I, if you had shewn me less,
   Had been your pris'ner still.

[1780]

TEXT: *1782*

A COMPARISON

ADDRESSED TO A YOUNG LADY[1]

SWEET stream that winds through yonder glade,
Apt emblem of a virtuous maid—
Silent and chaste she steals along
Far from the world's gay busy throng,
With gentle yet prevailing force
Intent upon her destin'd course,
Graceful and useful all she does,
Blessing and blest where'er she goes,
Pure-bosom'd as that wat'ry glass,
And heav'n reflected in her face.

[1780]

TEXT: *1782*

[1] Elizabeth Shuttleworth, sister of Mrs William Unwin.

ON OBSERVING SOME NAMES OF LITTLE NOTE RECORDED IN THE BIOGRAPHIA BRITANNICA[1]

O fond attempt to give a deathless lot
To names ignoble, born to be forgot!
In vain recorded in historic page,
They court the notice of a future age,
Those twinkling tiney lustres of the land,
Drop one by one from Fame's neglecting hand,
Lethæan gulphs receive them as they fall,
And dark oblivion soon absorbs them all.
   So when a child, as playful children use,
Has burnt to tinder a stale last year's news,
The flame extinct, he views the roving fire,
There goes my lady, and there goes the 'squire,
There goes the parson, oh! illustrious spark,
And there, scarce less illustrious, goes the clerk.

[1780]

TEXT: *1782*

TO MR. NEWTON,

ON HIS RETURN FROM RAMSGATE

THAT ocean you have late survey'd,
   Those rocks I too have seen;
But I, afflicted and dismay'd,
   You tranquil and serene.

---

[1] *Biographia Britannica: or, the Lives of the most eminent Persons*: enlarged ed., 1778.

You from the flood-controlling steep
   Saw stretch'd before your view,
With conscious joy, the threat'ning deep,
   No longer such to you!

To me the waves, that ceaseless broke
   Upon the dang'rous coast,
Hoarsely and ominously spoke
   Of all my treasure lost.

Your sea of trouble you have passed
   And found the peaceful shore;
I, tempest-toss'd, and wreck'd at last,
   Come home to port no more.

[October 1780: see letter, p. 601]

TEXT BM Add. MSS 30, 803B; copied in a letter of July 28, 1802, from Hayley to Lady Hesketh.

THE YEARLY DISTRESS, OR TITHING TIME AT [STOCK]

COME, ponder well, for 'tis no jest,[1]
   To laugh it would be wrong,
The troubles of a worthy priest
   The burthen of my song.

This priest he merry is and blithe
   Three quarters of the year,
But oh! it cuts him like a scythe
   When tithing time draws near.

[1] Mrs Russell points out that the first line echoes that of a song in *The Beggar's Opera*.

He then is full of frights and fears
   As one at point to die,
And long before the day appears
   He heaves up many a sigh.

For then the farmers come jog, jog,
   Along the miry road,
Each heart as heavy as a log,
   To make their payments good.

In sooth, the sorrow of such days
   Is not to be express'd,
When he that takes and he that pays
   Are both alike distress'd.

Now all unwelcome, at his gates
   The clumsy swains alight,
With rueful faces and bald pates—
   He trembles at the sight.

And well he may, for well he knows,
   Each bumpkin of the clan,
Instead of paying what he owes
   Will cheat him if he can.

So in they come, each makes his leg
   And flings his head before,
And looks as if he came to beg,
   And not to quit a score.

'And how does miss and madam do,
   'The little boy and all?'
'All tight and well and how do you,
   Good Mr. What-d'ye-call?'

The dinner comes, and down they sit,
   Was e'er such hungry folk!
There's little talking and no wit,
   It is no time to joke.

One wipes his nose upon his sleeve,
   One spits upon the floor,
Yet, not to give offence or grieve,
   Holds up the cloth before.

The punch goes round, and they are dull
   And lumpish still as ever,
Like barrels with their bellies full,
   They only weigh the heavier.

At length the busy time begins,
   'Come, neighbours, we must wag—'
The money chinks, down drop their chins,
   Each lugging out his bag.

One talks of mildew and of frost,
   And one of storms of hail,
And one of pigs that he has lost
   By maggots at the tail.

Quoth one, 'A rarer man than you
   In pulpit none shall hear;
But yet, methinks, to tell you true,
   You sell it plaguy dear.'

Oh why are farmers made so coarse,
   Or clergy made so fine!
A kick that scarce would move a horse
   May kill a sound divine.

Then let the boobies stay at home,
   'Twould cost him, I dare say,
Less trouble taking twice the sum
   Without the clowns that pay.

[? October 1780]

TEXT: B.M. Add. MSS. 24, 155, forming a letter to William
Unwin postmarked 'Oct. 30.'

BOADICEA

AN ODE

WHEN the British warrior queen,
  Bleeding from the Roman rods,
Sought with an indignant mien,
  Counsel of her country's gods,

Sage beneath a spreading oak
  Sat the Druid, hoary chief,
Ev'ry burning word he spoke,
  Full of rage and full of grief.

Princess! if our aged eyes
  Weep upon thy matchless wrongs,
'Tis because resentment ties
  All the terrors of our tongues.

Rome shall perish—write that word
  In the blood that she has spilt;
Perish hopeless and abhorr'd,
  Deep in ruin as in guilt.

Rome for empire far renown'd
  Tramples on a thousand states,
Soon her pride shall kiss the ground—
  Hark! the Gaul is at her gates.

Other Romans shall arise,
  Heedless of a soldier's name,
Sounds, not arms, shall win the prize,
  Harmony the path to fame.

Then the progeny that springs
  From the forests of our land,
Arm'd with thunder, clad with wings,
  Shall a wider world command.

Regions Cæsar never knew
  Thy posterity shall sway,
Where his eagles never flew,
  None invincible as they.

Such the bard's prophetic words,
  Pregnant with celestial fire,
Bending as he swept the chords
  Of his sweet but awful lyre.

She with all a monarch's pride,
  Felt them in her bosom glow,
Rush'd to battle, fought and died,
  Dying, hurl'd them at the foe.

Ruffians, pitiless as proud,
  ` Heav'n awards the vengeance due,
Empire is on us bestow'd,
  Shame and ruin wait for you.

[1780]

TEXT: *1782*

TO THE REV. MR. NEWTON:

AN INVITATION INTO THE COUNTRY

THE swallows in their torpid state[1]
  Compose their useless wing,
And bees in hives as idly wait
  The call of early spring.

[1] It was widely believed in the eighteenth century that swallows became torpid and spent the winter in holes, crevices, etc. 'Swallows certainly sleep all the winter,' Dr Johnson informed Boswell, 'a number of them conglobulate together by flying round and round, and then all in a heap throw themselves under water, and lie in the bed of a river.' Even Gilbert White, though well aware of the evidence for migration, believed that at least some swallows hibernated in England.

The keenest frost that binds the stream,
   The wildest wind that blows,
Are neither felt nor fear'd by them,
   Secure of their repose.

But man all feeling and awake
   The gloomy scene surveys,
With present ills his heart must ache
   And pant for brighter days.

Old winter halting o'er the mead,
   Bids me and Mary mourn,
But lovely spring peeps o'er his head,
   And whispers your return.

Then April with her sister May,
   Shall chase him from the bow'rs,
And weave fresh garlands ev'ry day,
   To crown the smiling hours.

And if a tear that speaks regret
   Of happier times appear,
A glimpse of joy that we have met
   Shall shine, and dry the tear.

[?]

TEXT: *1782*

TO A LADY IN FRANCE[1]

MADAM,
   A stranger's purpose in these lays
Is to congratulate, and not to praise.

---

[1] An Englishwoman, who had gone to France with Lady Austen, married an elderly Frenchman and turned Roman Catholic. The marriage was unhappy; she lost her new-found faith and came under Evangelical influence.

To give the creature the Creator's due,
Were sin in me, and an offence to you.
From man to man, or ev'n to woman paid,
Praise is the medium of a knavish trade,
A coin by Craft for Folly's use design'd,
Spurious, and only current with the blind.

The path of sorrow, and that path alone,
Leads to the land where sorrow is unknown.
No trav'ller ever reach'd that blest abode,
That found not thorns and briers in his road.
The world may dance along the flow'ry plain,
Cheer'd as they go by many a sprightly strain,
Where Nature has her mossy velvet spread,
With unshod feet they yet securely tread,
Admonish'd, scorn the caution and the friend,
Bent all on pleasure, heedless of its end.
But he, who knew what human hearts would prove,
How slow to learn the dictates of his love,
That, hard by nature and of stubborn will,
A life of ease would make them harder still,
In pity to the souls his grace design'd
To rescue from the ruins of mankind,
Call'd for a cloud to darken all their years,
And said, 'Go spend them in the vale of tears.'
O balmy gales of soul-reviving air,
O salutary streams that murmur there!
These flowing from the fount of grace above,
Those breath'd from lips of everlasting love,—
The flinty soil indeed their feet annoys,
Chill blasts of trouble nip their springing joys,
An envious world will interpose its frown
To mar delights superior to its own,
And many a pang, experienc'd still within,
Reminds them of their hated inmate, Sin;
But ills of ev'ry shape and ev'ry name,
Transform'd to blessings, miss their cruel aim;
And ev'ry moment's calm, that sooths the breast,
Is giv'n in earnest of eternal rest.

Ah, be not sad! although thy lot be cast
Far from the flock, and in a boundless waste;
No shepherd's tents within thy view appear,
But the chief Shepherd even there is near;
Thy tender sorrows and thy plaintive strain
Flow in a foreign land, but not in vain;
Thy tears all issue from a source divine,
And ev'ry drop bespeaks a Saviour thine—
So once in Gideon's fleece[1] the dews were found,
And drought on all the drooping herbs around.

[1781]

TEXT: BM. Add. MSS 24, 154, in a letter to Unwin of 15
December 1781: 'I send you on the other side some lines I
addressed last summer to a lady in France, a particular friend
of Lady Austen. A person much afflicted, but of great piety,
and patience. A Protestant.—They are not for publication.'
C. gave the verses no title.

THE COLUBRIAD[2]

CLOSE by the threshold of a door nail'd fast
Three kittens sat; each kitten look'd aghast.
I passing swift, and inattentive by,
At the three kittens cast a careless eye;
Not much concern'd to know what they did there;
Nor[3] deeming kittens worth a poet's care.
But presently a loud and furious hiss
Caus'd me to stop, and to exclaim 'what's this?'
When lo! upon the threshold met my view,
With head erect, and eyes of fiery hue,
A viper, long as Count de Grasse's[4] queue.

[1] Judges, vi, 37.
[2] The poem is based on an incident described in a letter, pp. 664–65.
[3] *Nor*: 1815 has *not*.
[4] The commander of the French navy at the time of the War of American Independence. Caricaturists made the most of the tail of his wig.

Forth from his head his forked tongue he throws,
Darting it full against a kitten's nose;
Who having never seen, in field or house,
The like, sat still and silent as a mouse:
Only projecting, with attention due,
Her whisker'd face, she ask'd him, 'who are you?'
On to the hall went I, with pace not slow,
But swift as lightning, for a long Dutch hoe:
With which well arm'd I hasten'd to the spot,
To find the viper, but I found him not.
And turning up the leaves, and shrubs around,
Found only, that he was not to be found.
But still the kittens sitting as before,
Sat watching close the bottom of the door.
'I hope,' said I, 'the villain I would kill,
Has slipp'd between the door, and the door sill;
And if I make dispatch, and follow hard,
No doubt but I shall find him in the yard;'
For long ere now it should have been rehears'd,
'Twas in the garden that I found him first.
Ev'n there I found him, there the full-grown cat
His head, with velvet paw, did gently pat;
As curious as the kittens erst had been
To learn what this phenomenon might mean.
Fill'd with heroic ardour at the sight,
And fearing every moment he would bite,
And rob our household of our only cat,
That was of age to combat with a rat;
With outstretch'd hoe I slew him at the door,
And taught him NEVER TO COME THERE NO MORE.

[August 1782]

TEXT: *1815*

ON THE LOSS OF THE
ROYAL GEORGE[1]

[WRITTEN WHEN THE NEWS ARRIVED]

To the March in Scipio[2]

TOLL for the brave!
   The brave that are no more!
All sunk beneath the wave,
   Fast by their native shore!

Eight hundred of the brave,
   Whose courage well was tried,
Had made the vessel heel,
   And laid her on her side.

A land breeze shook the shrouds,
   And she was overset;
Down went the Royal George,
   With all her crew complete.

Toll for the brave!
   Brave Kempenfelt is gone;
His last sea-fight is fought;
   His work of glory done.

It was not in the battle;
   No tempest gave the shock;
She sprang no fatal leak;
   She ran upon no rock.

[1] The *Royal George* sank at her moorings in Portsmouth Harbour on
August 29, 1782, with the loss of over 500 lives. See p. 691.
[2] *Scipio:* Handel's opera.

76

His sword was in its sheath;
　His fingers held the pen,
When Kempenfelt went down,
　With twice four hundred men.

Weigh the vessel up,
　Once dreaded by our foes!
And mingle with our cup
　The tear that England owes.

Her timbers yet are sound,
　And she may float again,
Full-charg'd with England's thunder,
　And plough the distant main.

But Kempenfelt is gone,
　His victories are o'er;
And he and his eight hundred,
　Shall plough the wave no more.

[1782 or 1783]

TEXT: *1815*

THE DIVERTING HISTORY OF
JOHN GILPIN,

SHEWING HOW HE WENT FARTHER THAN HE
INTENDED AND CAME HOME SAFE AGAIN

JOHN Gilpin was a citizen
　Of credit and renown,
A train-band[1] Captain eke was he
　Of famous London town.

[1] *train-band*: the London militia, composed of substantial house-holders.

John Gilpin's spouse said to her dear,
  Though wedded we have been
These twice ten tedious years, yet we
  No holiday have seen.

To-morrow is our wedding-day,
  And we will then repair
Unto the Bell at Edmonton
  All in a chaise and pair.

My sister and my sister's child,
  Myself and children three
Will fill the chaise, so you must ride
  On horseback after we.

He soon replied, I do admire
  Of womankind but one,
And you are she, my dearest dear,
  Therefore it shall be done.

I am a linnen-draper bold,
  As all the world doth know,
And my good friend the Callender
  Will lend his horse to go.

Quoth Mrs. Gilpin, That's well said;
  And for that wine is dear,
We will be furnish'd with our own,
  Which is both bright and clear.

John Gilpin kiss'd his loving wife,
  O'erjoy'd was he to find
That, though on pleasure she was bent,
  She had a frugal mind.

The morning came, the chaise was brought,
  But yet was not allow'd
To drive up to the door, lest all
  Should say that she was proud.

So three doors off the chaise was stay'd,
    Where they did all get in,
Six precious souls, and all agog
    To dash through thick and thin.

Smack went the whip, round went the wheels,
    Were never folk so glad,
The stones did rattle underneath,
    As if Cheapside were mad.

John Gilpin at his horse's side
    Seiz'd fast the flowing mane,
And up he got in haste to ride,
    But soon came down again.

For saddle-tree scarce reach'd had he,
    His journey to begin,
When turning round his head he saw
    Three customers come in.

So down he came, for loss of time,
    Although it griev'd him sore,
Yet loss of pence, full well he knew,
    Would trouble him much more.

'Twas long before the customers
    Were suited to their mind,
When Betty screaming came down stairs,
    'The wine is left behind!'

Good lack! quoth he, yet bring it me,
    My leathern belt likewise
In which I bear my trusty sword
    When I do exercise.

Now Mistress Gilpin, careful soul,
    Had two stone bottles found,
To hold the liquor that she loved,
    And keep it safe and sound.

Each bottle had a curling ear
    Through which the belt he drew,
And hung a bottle on each side,
    To make his balance true.

Then over all, that he might be
    Equipp'd from top to toe,
His long red cloak well brush'd and neat
    He manfully did throw.

Now see him mounted once again
    Upon his nimble steed,
Full slowly pacing o'er the stones
    With caution and good heed.

But finding soon a smoother road
    Beneath his well-shod feet,
The snorting beast began to trot,
    Which gall'd him in his seat.

So fair and softly, John he cried,
    But John he cried in vain,
That trot became a gallop soon
    In spite of curb and rein.

So stooping down, as needs he must
    Who cannot sit upright,
He grasp'd the mane with both his hands,
    And eke with all his might.

His horse who never in that sort
    Had handled been before,
What thing upon his back had got
    Did wonder more and more.

Away went Gilpin neck or nought,
    Away went hat and wig,
He little dreamt when he set out,
    Of running such a rig.

The wind did blow, the cloak did fly,
　　Like streamer long and gay,
'Till loop and button failing both
　　At last it flew away.

Then might all people well discern
　　The bottles he had slung,
A bottle swinging at each side
　　As hath been said or sung.

The dogs did bark, the children scream'd,
　　Up flew the windows all,
And ev'ry soul cried out, well done,
　　As loud as he could bawl.

Away went Gilpin—who but he;
　　His fame soon spread around—
He carries weight, he rides a race,
　　'Tis for a thousand pound.

And still as fast as he drew near,
　　'Twas wonderful to view
How in a trice the turnpike-men
　　Their gates wide open threw.

And now as he went bowing down
　　His reeking head full low,
The bottles twain behind his back
　　Were shatter'd at a blow.

Down ran the wine into the road,
　　Most piteous to be seen,
Which made his horse's flanks to smoke
　　As they had basted been.

But still he seem'd to carry weight,
　　With leathern girdle brac'd,
For all might see the bottle necks
　　Still dangling at his waist.

81

Thus all through merry Islington
   These gambols he did play,
And till he came unto the wash
   Of Edmonton so gay.

And there he threw the wash about
   On both sides of the way,
Just like unto a trundling mop,
   Or a wild-goose at play.

At Edmonton his loving wife
   From the balcony spied
Her tender husband, wond'ring much
   To see how he did ride.

Stop, stop John Gilpin!—Here's the house—
   They all at once did cry,
The dinner waits and we are tir'd,
   Said Gilpin—so am I.

But yet his horse was not a whit
   Inclin'd to tarry there,
For why? his owner had a house
   Full ten miles off at Ware.

So like an arrow swift he flew,
   Shot by an archer strong,
So did he fly—which brings me to
   The middle of my song.

Away went Gilpin, out of breath,
   And sore against his will,
Till at his friend's the Callender's
   His horse at last stood still.

The Callender amaz'd to see
   His neighbour in such trim,
Laid down his pipe, flew to the gate,
   And thus accosted him.

What news, what news, your tidings tell,
　　Tell me you must and shall—
Say why bare headed you are come,
　　Or why you come at all.

Now Gilpin had a pleasant wit,
　　And lov'd a timely joke,
And thus unto the Callender
　　In merry guise he spoke.

I came because your horse would come,
　　And if I well forebode,
My hat and wig will soon be here,
　　They are upon the road.

The Callender right glad to find
　　His friend in merry pin,
Return'd him not a single word,
　　But to the house went in.

Whence strait he came with hat and wig,
　　A wig that flow'd behind,
A hat not much the worse for wear,
　　Each comely in its kind.

He held them up, and in his turn,
　　Thus show'd his ready wit,
My head is twice as big as yours,
　　They therefore needs must fit.

But let me scrape the dirt away
　　That hangs upon your face,
And stop and eat, for well you may
　　Be in a hungry case.

Said John, it is my wedding-day,
　　And all the world would stare,
If wife should dine at Edmonton
　　And I should dine at Ware.

So turning to his horse, he said,
   I am in haste to dine,
'Twas for your pleasure you came here,
   You shall go back for mine.

Ah luckless speech, and bootless boast!
   For which he paid full dear,
For while he spake a braying ass
   Did sing most loud and clear.

Whereat his horse did snort as he
   Had heard a lion roar,
And gallop'd off with all his might
   As he had done before.

Away went Gilpin and away
   Went Gilpin's hat and wig;
He lost them sooner than at first,
   For why? they were too big.

Now, Mistress Gilpin when she saw
   Her husband posting down
Into the country far away,
   She pull'd out half a crown.

And thus unto the youth she said
   That drove them to the Bell,
This shall be yours when you bring back
   My husband safe and well.

The youth did ride, and soon did meet
   John coming back amain,
Whom in a trice he tried to stop
   By catching at his rein;

But not performing what he meant
   And gladly would have done,
The frighted steed he frighted more,
   And made him faster run.

Away went Gilpin, and away
   Went post-boy at his heels,
The post-boy's horse right glad to miss
   The lumb'ring of the wheels.

Six gentlemen upon the road
   Thus seeing Gilpin fly,
With post-boy scamp'ring in the rear,
   They rais'd the hue and cry.

Stop thief, stop thief—a highwayman!
   Not one of them was mute,
And all and each that pass'd that way
   Did join in the pursuit.

And now the turnpike gates again
   Flew open in short space,
The toll-men thinking, as before,
   That Gilpin rode a race.

And so he did, and won it too,
   For he got first to town,
Nor stopp'd 'till where he had got up
   He did again get down.

Now let us sing, long live the king,
   And Gilpin long live he,
And when he next doth ride abroad,
   May I be there to see!

[October 1782]

TEXT: *1785*. See letters, pp. 677, 735–6, 745–6, 751, 780.

EPITAPH ON A HARE

HERE lies, whom hound did ne'er pursue,
　　Nor swifter greyhound follow,
Whose foot ne'er tainted morning dew,
　　Nor ear heard huntsman's hollo.

Tiney, the surliest of his kind,
　　Who, nurs'd with tender care,
And to domestic bounds confin'd,
　　Was still a wild Jack-hare.

Though duly from my hand he took
　　His pittance ev'ry night,
He did it with a jealous look,
　　And when he could, would bite.

His diet was of wheaten bread,
　　And milk, and oats, and straw;
Thistles, or lettuces instead,
　　With sand to scour his maw.

On twigs of hawthorn he regal'd,
　　Or pippins' russet peel,
And when his juicy salads fail'd,
　　Slic'd carrot pleas'd him well.

A Turkey carpet was his lawn,
　　On which he lov'd to bound,
To skip and gambol like a fawn,
　　And swing his rump around.

His frisking was at ev'ning hours,
　　For then he lost his fear,
But most before approaching show'rs,
　　Or when a storm drew near.

Eight years and five round-rolling moons
　　He thus saw steal away,
Slumb'ring out all his idle noons,
　　And ev'ry night at play.

I kept him for old service' sake,
　For he would oft beguile
My heart of thoughts, that made it ache,
　And force me to a smile.

But now beneath this walnut-shade
　He finds his long last home,
And waits, in snug concealment laid,
　'Till gentler Puss shall come.

She, still more ancient, feels the shocks,
　From which no care can save,
And, partner once of Tiney's box,
　Must soon partake his grave.

[March 1783]

TEXT: BM. Add. MSS. 24, 155. Included in a letter to Unwin
of March 30, 1783.

SONG

WRITTEN AT THE REQUEST OF LADY AUSTEN[1]

Air—'The Lass of Pattie's Mill'

WHEN all within is peace,
　How nature seems to smile!
Delights that never cease,
　The live-long day beguile.
From morn to dewy eve,
　With open hand she showers
Fresh blessings to deceive,
　And soothe the silent hours.

---

[1] 'The musical talents of Lady Austen induced C. to write a few songs
of peculiar sweetness and pathos, to suit particular airs that she was
accustomed to play on the harpsichord.' *Hayley.*

It is content of heart
   Gives nature power to please;
The mind that feels no smart,
   Enlivens all it sees;
Can make a wintry sky
   Seem bright as smiling May,
And evening's closing eye
   As peep of early day.

The vast majestic globe,
   So beauteously array'd
In nature's various robe,
   With wond'rous skill display'd,
Is to a mourner's heart
   A dreary wild at best;
It flutters to depart,
   And longs to be at rest.

[Summer 1783]

TEXT: *1815*

THE FAITHFUL BIRD

THE greenhouse is my summer seat;
My shrubs displac'd from that retreat
   Enjoy'd the open air;
Two goldfinches, whose sprightly song
Had been their mutual solace long,
   Liv'd happy pris'ners there.

They sang as blithe as finches sing,
That flutter loose on golden wing,
   And frolic where they list;
Strangers to liberty, 'tis true,
But that delight they never knew,
   And therefore never miss'd.

But nature works in ev'ry breast
With force not easily suppress'd;
   And Dick felt some desires,
That, after many an effort vain,
Instructed him at length to gain
   A pass between his wires.

The open windows seem'd t' invite
The freeman to a farewell flight;
   But Tom was still confin'd;
And Dick, although his way was clear,
Was much too gen'rous and sincere
   To leave his friend behind.

So settling on his cage, by play,
And chirp, and kiss, he seem'd to say,
   You must not live alone.—
Nor would he quit that chosen stand,
Till I, with slow and cautious hand,
   Return'd him to his own.

Oh ye, who never taste the joys
Of Friendship, satisfied with noise,
   Fandango, ball, and rout!
Blush, when I tell you how a bird
A prison with a friend preferr'd
   To liberty without.

[? August 1783]

TEXT: *1808*. The first printed text, in 1795, is called 'The
Faithful Friend', and has a variant of the fifth stanza. See pp.
692–3.

THE VALEDICTION

FAREWELL, false hearts![1] whose best affections fail,
Like shallow brooks which summer suns exhale;
Forgetful of the man whom once ye chose,
Cold in his cause, and careless of his woes;
I bid you both a long and last adieu!
Cold in my turn, and unconcern'd like you.
 First, farewell Niger![2] whom, now duly proved,
I disregard as much as I have loved.
Your brain well furnished, and your tongue well taught
To press with energy your ardent thought,
Your senatorial dignity of face,
Sound sense, intrepid spirit, manly grace,
Have raised you high as talents can ascend,
Made you a peer, but spoilt you for a friend!
Pretend to all that parts have e'er acquired;
Be great, be fear'd, be envied, be admired;
To fame as lasting as the earth pretend,
But not hereafter to the name of friend!
I sent you verse, and, as your lordship knows,
Back'd with a modest sheet of humble prose,
Not to recall a promise[3] to your mind,
Fulfill'd with ease had you been so inclined,
But to comply with feelings, and to give
Proof of an old affection still alive.
Your sullen silence serves at least to tell
Your alter'd heart; and so, my lord, farewell!
 Next, busy actor on a meaner stage,
Amusement-monger of a trifling age,

[1] These verses were addressed by C. to the friends of his youth: Edward Thurlow, now Lord Chancellor, and the dramatist George Colman. C. was grieved by their failure to acknowledge presentation copies of his *Poems*.

[2] Thurlow.

[3] C. maintained that Thurlow, when a fellow student of the law, had promised to provide for him if, as C. predicted, he became Lord Chancellor.

Illustrious histrionic patentee,
Terentius,[1] once my friend, farewell to thee!
In thee some virtuous qualities combine,
To fit thee for a nobler post than thine,
Who, born a gentleman, hast stoop'd too low,
To live by buskin, sock and raree-show.
Thy schoolfellow, and partner of thy plays,
When Nichol[2] swung the birch and twined the bays,
And having known thee bearded and full grown,
The weekly censor of a laughing town,[3]
I thought the volume I presumed to send,
Graced with the name of a long-absent friend,
Might prove a welcome gift, and touch thine heart,
Not hard by nature, in a feeling part.
But thou it seems, (what cannot grandeur do,
Though but a dream?) art grown disdainful too;
And strutting in thy school of queens and kings,
Who fret their hour and are forgotten things,
Hast caught the cold distemper of the day,
And, like his lordship, cast thy friend away.

Oh Friendship! cordial of the human breast!
So little felt, so fervently profess'd!
Thy blossoms deck our unsuspecting years;
The promise of delicious fruit appears:
We hug the hopes of constancy and truth,
Such is the folly of our dreaming youth;
But soon, alas! detect the rash mistake,
That sanguine inexperience loves to make;
And view with tears the expected harvest lost;
Decay'd by time, or wither'd by a frost.
Whoever undertakes a friend's great part
Should be renew'd in nature, pure in heart,
Prepared for martyrdom, and strong to prove
A thousand ways the force of genuine love.
He may be call'd to give up health and gain,

---

[1] Colman, who had published a successful translation of Terence.

[2] The headmaster of Westminster School.

[3] As joint editor of *The Connoisseur*: see p. 377.

To exchange content for trouble, ease for pain,
To echo sigh for sigh, and groan for groan,
And wet his cheeks with sorrows not his own.
The heart of man, for such a task too frail,
When most relied on, is most sure to fail;
And, summon'd to partake its fellow's woe,
Starts from its office, like a broken bow.
    Votaries of business, and of pleasure, prove
Faithless alike in friendship and in love.
Retired from all the circles of the gay,
And all the crowds that bustle life away,
To scenes where competition, envy, strife,
Beget no thunder-clouds to trouble life,
Let me, the charge of some good angel, find
One who has known and has escaped mankind;
Polite, yet virtuous, who has brought away
The manners, not the morals, of the day:
With him, perhaps with *her*, (for men have known
No firmer friendships than the fair have shown,)
Let me enjoy, in some unthought-of spot,
(All former friends forgiven, and forgot,)
Down to the close of life's fast fading scene,
Union of hearts, without a flaw between.
'Tis grace, 'tis bounty, and it calls for praise,
If God give health, that sunshine of our days;
And if he add, a blessing shared by few,
Content of heart, more praises still are due:—
But if he grant a friend, that boon possess'd
Indeed is treasure, and crowns all the rest;
And giving one, whose heart is in the skies,
Born from above, and made divinely wise,
He gives, what bankrupt nature never can,
Whose noblest coin is light and brittle man,
Gold, purer far than Ophir ever knew,
A soul, an image of himself, and therefore true.

[November 1783]

TEXT: *Southey*

AN EPISTLE

TO JOSEPH HILL, ESQ.

DEAR JOSEPH—five and twenty years ago—
Alas! how time escapes—'tis even so—
With frequent intercourse and always sweet
And always friendly, we were wont to cheat
A tedious hour—and now we never meet.
As some grave gentleman in Terence says,
('Twas therefore much the same in ancient days)
Good lack, we know not what to-morrow brings—
Strange fluctuation of all human things!
True. Changes will befall, and friends may part,
But distance only cannot change the heart:
And were I call'd to prove th' assertion true,
One proof should serve, a reference to you.

Whence comes it then, that in the wane of life,
Though nothing have occurr'd to kindle strife,
We find the friends we fancied we had won,
Though num'rous once, reduc'd to few or none?
Can gold grow worthless that has stood the touch?
No: Gold they seem'd, but they were never such.
Horatio's servant once, with bow and cringe
Swinging the parlour-door upon its hinge,
Dreading a negative, and overawed
Lest he should trespass, begg'd to go abroad.
Go, fellow!—whither?—turning short about—
Nay. Stay at home; you're always going out.
'Tis but a step, sir, just at the street's end—
For what?—An please you sir, to see a friend.
A friend? Horatio cried, and seem'd to start—
Yea marry shalt thou, and with all my heart.—
And fetch my cloak, for though the night be raw
I'll see him too—the first I ever saw.
I knew the man, and knew his nature mild,
And was his play-thing often when a child,

But somewhat at that moment pinch'd him close,
Else he was seldom bitter or morose:
Perhaps, his confidence just then betray'd,
His grief might prompt him with the speech he made,
Perhaps 'twas here good-humour gave it birth,
The harmless play of pleasantry and mirth.
Howe'er it was, his language in my mind,
Bespoke at least a man that knew mankind:
But not to moralize too much, and strain
To prove an evil of which all complain,
(I hate long arguments, verbosely spun)
One story more, dear Hill, and I have done:
Once on a time an Emp'ror, a wise man,
No matter where, in China or Japan,
Decreed that whosoever should offend
Against the well-known duties of a friend,
Convicted once, should ever after wear
But half a coat, and show his bosom bare.
The punishment importing this, no doubt,
That all was naught within, and all found out.
Oh happy Britain! we have not to fear
Such hard and arbitrary measure here.
Else could a law like that which I relate,
Once have the sanction of our triple state,
Some few that I have known in days of old,
Would run most dreadful risk of catching cold.
While you, my friend, whatever wind should blow,
Might traverse England safely to and fro,
An honest man, close-buttoned to the chin,
Broad-cloth without, and a warm heart within.

[November 17, 1784]

TEXT: *1785*. Joseph Hill: see n., p. 554.

THE POPLAR-FIELD

THE poplars are fell'd, farewell to the shade
And the whispering sound of the cool colonnade,
The winds play no longer, and sing in the leaves,
Nor Ouse on his bosom their image receives.

Twelve years have elaps'd since I last took a view
Of my favourite field and the bank where they grew,
And now in the grass behold they are laid,
And the tree is my seat that once lent me a shade.

The blackbird has fled to another retreat
Where the hazels afford him a screen from the heat,
And the scene where his melody charm'd me before,
Resounds with his sweet-flowing ditty no more.

My fugitive years are all hasting away,
And I must ere long lie as lowly as they,
With a turf on my breast, and a stone at my head,
Ere another such grove shall arise in its stead.

'Tis a sight to engage me, if any thing can,
To muse on the perishing pleasures of man;
Though his life be a dream, his enjoyments, I see,
Have a being less durable even than he.

[1784]

TEXT: *1800*. See p. 794.

THE NEGRO'S COMPLAINT

To the tune of Hosier's Ghost

FORC'D from home and all its pleasures,
    Afric's coast I left forlorn;
To increase a stranger's treasures,
    O'er the raging billows borne;

Men from England bought and sold me,
  Paid my price in paltry gold;
But though theirs they have enroll'd me,
  Minds are never to be sold.

Still in thought as free as ever,
  What are England's rights, I ask,
Me from my delights to sever,
  Me to torture, me to task?
Fleecy locks and black complexion
  Cannot forfeit nature's claim;
Skins may differ, but affection
  Dwells in white and black the same.

Why did all-creating Nature
  Make the plant for which we toil?
Sighs must fan it, tears must water,
  Sweat of ours must dress the soil.
Think, ye masters iron-hearted,
  Lolling at your jovial boards;
Think, how many backs have smarted
  For the sweets your cane affords.

Is there, as ye sometimes tell us,
  Is there one who reigns on high?
Has he bid you buy and sell us,
  Speaking from his throne, the sky?
Ask him, if your knotted scourges,
Fetters, blood-extorting screws,
Are the means that duty urges
  Agents of his will to use?

Hark! he answers—Wild tornadoes,
  Strewing yonder sea with wrecks,
Wasting towns, plantations, meadows,
  Are the voice with which he speaks.
He, foreseeing what vexations
  Afric's sons should undergo,
Fix'd their tyrants' habitations
  Where his whirlwinds answer—No.

By our blood in Afric wasted,
  Ere our necks receiv'd the chain;
By the mis'ries which we tasted,
  Crossing in your barks the main;
By our suff'rings since ye brought us
  To the man-degrading mart;
All sustain'd by patience, taught us
  Only by a broken heart:

Deem our nation brutes no longer
  Till some reason ye shall find
Worthier of regard and stronger
  Than the colour of our kind.
Slaves of gold! whose sordid dealings
  Tarnish all your boasted pow'rs,
Prove that *you* have human feelings,
  Ere you proudly question ours.

[March 1788: see p. 880]

TEXT: MSS. Cowper Museum, Olney.

GRATITUDE

ADDRESSED TO LADY HESKETH

THIS cap, that so stately appears,
  With ribbon-bound tassel on high,
Which seems by the crest that it rears
  Ambitious of brushing the sky:
This cap to my cousin I owe,
  She gave it, and gave me beside,
Wreath'd into an elegant bow,
  The ribbon with which it is tied.

This wheel-footed studying chair,
    Contriv'd both for toil and repose,
Wide-elbow'd, and wadded with hair,
    In which I both scribble and dose,
Bright-studded to dazzle the eyes,
    And rival in lustre of that
In which, or astronomy lies,
    Fair Cassiopeïa sat:

These carpets, so soft to the foot,
    Caledonia's traffic and pride!
Oh spare them, ye knights of the boot,
    Escap'd from a cross-country ride!
This table and mirror within,
    Secure from collision and dust,
At which I oft shave cheek and chin,
    And periwig nicely adjust:

This moveable structure of shelves,
    For its beauty admired and its use,
And charged with octavos and twelves,
    The gayest I had to produce;
Where, flaming in scarlet and gold,
    My poems enchanted I view,
And hope, in due time, to behold
    My Iliad and Odyssey too:

This china, that decks the alcove,
    Which here people call a buffet,
But what the gods call it above,
    Has ne'er been reveal'd to us yet:[1]
These curtains, that keep the room warm
    Or cool as the season demands,
Those stoves that for pattern and form,
    Seem the labour of Mulciber's hands.

---

[1] *as yet* in *1815* is clearly a printer's error.

All these are not half that I owe
    To One, from our earliest youth
To me ever ready to show
    Benignity, friendship, and truth;
For time, the destroyer declar'd
    And foe of our perishing kind,
If even her face he has spar'd,
    Much less could he alter her mind.

Thus compass'd about with the goods
    And chattels of leisure and ease,
I indulge my poetical moods
    In many such fancies as these;
And fancies I fear they will seem—
    Poets' goods are not often so fine;
The poets will swear that I dream,
    When I sing of the splendour of mine.

[April 1788]

TEXT: *1815*

PAIRING TIME ANTICIPATED

A FABLE

I SHALL not ask Jean Jacques Rousseau,[1]
If birds confabulate or no;
'Tis clear that they were always able
To hold discourse, at least, in fable;
And ev'n the child, who knows no better,
Than to interpret by the letter,

---

[1] It was one of the whimsical speculations of this philosopher, that all fables which ascribe reason and speech to animals should be withheld from children, as being only vehicles of deception. But what child was ever deceived by them, or can be, against the evidence of his senses? [C]

A story of a cock and bull,
Must have a most uncommon skull.

   It chanc'd then, on a winter's day,
But warm and bright, and calm as May,
The birds, conceiving a design
To forestall sweet St. Valentine,
In many an orchard, copse, and grove,
Assembled on affairs of love,
And with much twitter and much chatter,
Began to agitate the matter.
At length a Bulfinch, who could boast
More years and wisdom than the most,
Entreated, op'ning wide his beak,
A moment's liberty to speak;
And, silence publicly enjoin'd,
Deliver'd briefly thus his mind.

   My friends! be cautious how ye treat
The subject upon which we meet;
I fear we shall have winter yet.

   A Finch, whose tongue knew no control,
With golden wing and satin pole,
A last year's bird, who ne'er had tried
What marriage means, thus pert replied.

   Methinks the gentleman, quoth she,
Opposite in the apple-tree,
By his good will, would keep us single
Till yonder heav'n and earth shall mingle,
Or (which is likelier to befall)
Till death exterminate us all.
I marry without more ado;
My dear Dick Redcap, what say you?

   Dick heard, and tweedling, ogling, bridling,
Turning short round, strutting and sideling,
Attested, glad, his approbation
Of an immediate conjugation.
Their sentiments so well express'd,
Influenc'd mightily the rest,
All pair'd, and each pair built a nest.

   But though the birds were thus in haste,

The leaves came on not quite so fast,
And destiny, that sometimes bears
An aspect stern on man's affairs,
Not altogether smil'd on theirs.
The wind, of late breath'd gently forth,
Now shifted east and east by north;
Bare trees and shrubs but ill, you know,
Could shelter them from rain or snow,
Stepping into their nests, they paddled,
Themselves were chill'd, their eggs were addled;
Soon ev'ry father bird and mother
Grew quarrelsome, and peck'd each other,
Parted without the least regret,
Except that they had ever met,
And learn'd, in future, to be wiser,
Than to neglect a good adviser.

INSTRUCTION
Misses! the tale that I relate
    This lesson seems to carry—
Choose not alone a proper mate,
    But proper time to marry.

[?]

TEXT: *1794/5*

THE DOG AND THE
WATER-LILY

NO FABLE

THE noon was shady, and soft airs
    Swept Ouse's silent tide,
When 'scap'd from literary cares,
    I wander'd on his side.

101

My spaniel, prettiest of his race,
　　And high in pedigree,
(Two nymphs[1] adorn'd with ev'ry grace
　　That spaniel found for me)

Now wanton'd lost in flags and reeds,
　　Now starting into sight
Pursued the swallow o'er the meads
　　With scarce a slower flight.

It was the time when Ouse display'd
　　His lilies newly blown;
Their beauties I intent survey'd,
　　And one I wish'd my own.

With cane extended far I sought
　　To steer it close to land;
But still the prize, though nearly caught,
　　Escap'd my eager hand.

Beau mark'd my unsuccessful pains
　　With fix'd consid'rate face,
And puzzling set his puppy brains,
　　To comprehend the case.

But with a cherup clear and strong,
　　Dispersing all his dream,
I thence withdrew, and follow'd long
　　The windings of the stream.

My ramble ended, I return'd:
　　Beau, trotting far before,
The floating wreath again discern'd,
　　And plunging left the shore.

[1] Sir Robert Gunning's daughters [C]. It was the nymphs who found the spaniel: see p. 859. Beau's exploit is described in prose on p. 898.

I saw him with that lily cropp'd
   Impatient swim to meet
My quick approach, and soon he dropp'd
   The treasure at my feet.

Charm'd with the sight, the world, I cried,
   Shall hear of this thy deed:
My dog shall mortify the pride
   Of man's superior breed;

But chief myself I will enjoin,
   Awake at duty's call,
To show a love as prompt as thine
   To him who gives me all.

[August 1788]

TEXT: *1808*

ON

THE DEATH

OF MRS. THROCKMORTON'S BULFINCH

Ye nymphs! if e'er your eyes were red
With tears o'er hapless fav'rites shed,
   O share Maria's grief!
Her fav'rite, even in his cage,
(What will not hunger's cruel rage?)
   Assassin'd by a thief.

Where Rhenus strays his vines among,
The egg was laid from which he sprung,
   And though by nature mute,
Or only with a whistle blest,
Well-taught he all the sounds express'd
   Of flagelet or flute.

103

The honours of his ebon poll
Were brighter than the sleekest mole,
    His bosom of the hue
With which Aurora decks the skies,
When piping winds shall soon arise,
    To sweep away the dew.

Above, below, in all the house,
Dire foe alike of bird and mouse,
    No cat had leave to dwell;
And Bully's cage supported stood
On props of smoothest-shaven wood,
    Large-built and lattic'd well.

Well-lattic'd—but the grate, alas!
Not rough with wire of steel or brass,
    For Bully's plumage sake,
But smooth with wands from Ouse's side,
With which, when neatly peel'd and dried,
    The swains their baskets make.

Night veil'd the pole: all seem'd secure:
When led by instinct sharp and sure,
    Subsistence to provide,
A beast forth sallied on the scout,
Long-back'd, long-tail'd, with whisker'd snout,
    And badger-colour'd hide.

He, ent'ring at the study-door,
It's ample area 'gan explore;
    And something in the wind
Conjectur'd, sniffing round and round,
Better than all the books he found,
    Food chiefly for the mind.

Just then, by adverse fate impress'd,
A dream disturb'd poor Bully's rest;
    In sleep he seem'd to view
A rat fast-clinging to the cage,
And, screaming at the sad presage,
    Awoke and found it true.

For, aided both by ear and scent,
Right to his mark the monster went—
    Ah, muse! forbear to speak
Minute the horrours that ensu'd;
His teeth were strong, the cage was wood—
    He left poor Bully's beak.

O had he made that too his prey;
That beak, whence issu'd many a lay
    Of such mellifluous tone,
Might have repaid him well, I wote,
For silencing so sweet a throat,
    Fast stuck within his own.

Maria weeps—The Muses mourn—
So, when by Bacchanalians torn,
    On Thracian Hebrus' side
The tree-enchanter Orpheus fell,
His head alone remain'd to tell
    The cruel death he died.

[? November 1788]

TEXT: *1808.*

ON A MISCHIEVOUS BULL,

WHICH THE OWNER[1] OF HIM SOLD AT THE AUTHOR'S INSTANCE

Go—Thou art all unfit to share
    The pleasures of this place
With such as its old tenants are,
    Creatures of gentler race.

[1] The owner was probably John Throckmorton and the scene Weston Park. See p. 716 for a note on the Throckmorton family.

The squirrel here his hoard provides,
   Aware of wintry storms,
And wood-peckers explore the sides
   Of rugged oaks for worms;

The sheep here smooths the knotted thorn
   With frictions of her fleece;
And here I wander eve and morn,
   Like her, a friend to peace.

Ah—I could pity thee exil'd
   From this secure retreat—
I would not lose it to be styl'd
   The happiest of the great.

But thou canst taste no calm delight;
   Thy pleasure is to show
Thy magnanimity in fight,
   Thy prowess—therefore go.

I care not whether east or north,
   So I no more may find thee;
The angry muse thus sings thee forth,
   And claps the gate behind thee.

[? 1788]

TEXT: *1808*

CATHARINA[1]

ADDRESSED TO MISS STAPLETON

SHE came—she is gone—we have met—
   And meet perhaps never again:
The sun of that moment is set,
   And seems to have risen in vain.

[1] She married George Courtenay Throckmorton, of Weston Park, as
C. hoped. See n., pp. 952–53.

Catharina has fled like a dream—
  (So vanishes pleasure, alas!)
But has left a regret and esteem
  That will not so suddenly pass.

The last evening ramble we made,
  Catharina, Maria,[2] and I,
Our progress was often delay'd
  By the nightingale warbling nigh.
We paus'd under many a tree,
  And much she was charm'd with a tone
Less sweet to Maria and me,
  Who had witness'd so lately her own.

My numbers that day she had sung,
  And gave them a grace so divine,
As only her musical tongue
  Could infuse into numbers of mine.
The longer I heard, I esteemed
  The work of my fancy the more,
And ev'n to myself never seem'd
  So tuneful a poet before.

Though the pleasures of London exceed
  In number the days of the year,
Catharina, did nothing impede,
  Would feel herself happier here;
For the close-woven arches of limes,
  On the banks of our river, I know,
Are sweeter to her many times
  Than all that the city can show.

So it is, when the mind is endued
  With a well-judging taste from above,
Then, whether embellish'd or rude,
  'Tis nature alone that we love.

[2] Mrs John Throckmorton.

The achievements of art may amuse,
    May even our wonder excite,
But groves, hills, and vallies, diffuse
    A lasting, a sacred delight.

Since then in the rural recess
    Catharina alone can rejoice,
May it still be her lot to possess
    The scene of her sensible choice!
To inhabit a mansion remote
    From the clatter of street-pacing steeds,
And by Philomel's annual note
    To measure the life that she leads.

With her book, and her voice, and her lyre,
    To wing all her moments at home,
And with scenes that new rapture inspire
    As oft as it suits her to roam,
She will have just the life she prefers,
    With little to wish or to fear,
And ours will be pleasant as hers,
    Might we view her enjoying it here.

[May 1789]

TEXT: *1794/5*

ON THE RECEIPT OF MY MOTHER'S PICTURE OUT OF NORFOLK,

THE GIFT OF MY COUSIN ANN BODHAM

O THAT those lips had language! Life has pass'd
With me but roughly since I heard thee last.
Those lips are thine—thy own sweet smile I see,
The same, that oft in childhood solac'd me;

Voice only fails, else how distinct they say,
'Grieve not, my child, chase all thy fears away!'
The meek intelligence of those dear eyes
(Blest be the art that can immortalize,
The art that baffles Time's tyrannic claim
To quench it) here shines on me still the same.

Faithful remembrancer of one so dear,
O welcome guest, though unexpected here!
Who bidd'st me honour with an artless song,
Affectionate, a mother lost so long.
I will obey, not willingly alone,
But gladly, as the precept were her own:
And, while that face renews my filial grief,
Fancy shall weave a charm for my relief,
Shall steep me in Elysian reverie,
A momentary dream, that thou art she.

My mother! when I learn'd that thou wast dead,
Say, wast thou conscious of the tears I shed?
Hover'd thy spirit o'er thy sorr'wing son,
Wretch even then, life's journey just begun?
Perhaps thou gav'st me, though unfelt, a kiss;
Perhaps a tear, if souls can weep in bliss—
Ah that maternal smile! it answers—Yes.
I heard the bell toll'd on thy burial day,
I saw the hearse, that bore thee slow away,
And, turning from my nurs'ry window, drew
A long, long sigh, and wept a last adieu!
But was it such?— It was—Where thou art gone
Adieus and farewells are a sound unknown.
May I but meet thee on that peaceful shore,
The parting word shall pass my lips no more!
Thy maidens, griev'd themselves at my concern,
Oft gave me promise of thy quick return.
What ardently I wish'd, I long believ'd,
And, disappointed still, was still deceiv'd.
By expectation ev'ry day beguil'd,
Dupe of *to morrow* even from a child.

Thus many a sad to morrow came and went,
Till, all my stock of infant sorrow spent,
I learn'd at last submission to my lot,
But, though I less deplor'd thee, ne'er forgot.

Where once we dwelt our name is heard no more,
Children not thine have trod my nurs'ry floor;
And where the gard'ner Robin, day by day,
Drew me to school along the public way,
Delighted with my bauble coach, and wrapp'd
In scarlet mantle warm, and velvet cap,
'Tis now become a hist'ry little known,
That once we call'd the past'ral house[1] our own.
Shortliv'd possession! but the record fair,
That mem'ry keeps of all thy kindness there,
Still outlives many a storm, that has effac'd
A thousand other themes less deeply trac'd.
Thy nightly visits to my chamber made,
That thou mightst know me safe and warmly laid;
Thy morning bounties ere I left my home,
The biscuit, or confectionary plum;[2]
The fragrant waters on my cheeks bestow'd
By thy own hand, till fresh they shone and glow'd;
All this, and more endearing still than all,
Thy constant flow of love, that knew no fall,
Ne'er roughen'd by those cataracts and breaks,
That humour interpos'd too often makes;
All this still legible in mem'ry's page,
And still to be so to my latest age,
Adds joy to duty, makes me glad to pay
Such honours to thee as my numbers may;
Perhaps a frail memorial, but sincere,
Not scorn'd in Heav'n, though little notic'd here.

Could Time, his flight revers'd, restore the hours,
When, playing with thy vesture's tissu'd flow'rs,

[1] Berkhamstead Rectory.
[2] A boiled sweet.

The violet, the pink, and jessamine,
I prick'd them into paper with a pin,
(And thou wast happier than myself the while,
Wouldst softly speak, and stroke my head, and smile)
Could those few pleasant days again appear,
Might one wish bring them, would I wish them here?
I would not trust my heart—the dear delight
Seems so to be desir'd, perhaps I might.—
But no—what here we call our life is such,
So little to be lov'd, and thou so much,
That I should ill requite thee to constrain
Thy unbound spirit into bonds again.

   Thou, as a gallant bark from Albion's coast
(The storms all weather'd and the ocean cross'd)
Shoots into port at some well-haven'd isle,
Where spices breathe, and brighter seasons smile,
There sits quiescent on the floods, that show
Her beauteous form reflected clear below,
While airs impregnated with incense play
Around her, fanning light her streamers gay;
So thou, with sails how swift! hast reach'd the shore,
'Where tempests never beat nor billows roar,'[1]
And thy lov'd consort on the dang'rous tide
Of life long since has anchor'd by thy side.
But me, scarce hoping to attain that rest,
Always from port withheld, always distress'd—
Me howling blasts drive devious, tempest-toss'd,
Sails ripp'd, seams op'ning wide, and compass lost,
And day by day some current's thwarting force
Sets me more distant from a prosp'rous course.
Yet O the thought, that thou art safe, and he!
That thought is joy, arrive what may to me.
My boast is not, that I deduce my birth
From loins enthron'd, and rulers of the Earth;[2]

[1] Garth [C] Sir Samuel Garth, *The Dispensary*, 1699, canto lii, 1: 'Where
billows never break, nor tempests roar.'

[2] 'His mother was descended...by four different lines from Henry the
Third...' (Johnson, *Sketch of the life of C.*, in *1815*).

But higher far my proud pretensions rise—
The son of parents pass'd into the skies.
And now, farewell—Time unrevok'd has run
His wonted course, yet what I wish'd is done.
By contemplation's help, not sought in vain,
I seem t' have liv'd my childhood o'er again;
To have renew'd the joys that once were mine,
Without the sin of violating thine;
And, while the wings of Fancy still are free,
And I can view this mimic show of thee,
Time has but half succeeded in his theft—
Thyself remov'd, thy pow'r to soothe me left.

[February 1790]

TEXT: *1808*. The letter on p. 917 refers.

INSCRIPTION

FOR A STONE ERECTED AT THE SOWING OF A GROVE OF OAKS AT CHILLINGTON, THE SEAT OF T. GIFFARD, ESQ. 1790.

OTHER stones the era tell,
When some feeble mortal fell;
I stand here to date the birth
Of these hardy sons of Earth.

Which shall longest brave the sky,
Storm and frost—these oaks or I?
Pass an age or two away,
I must moulder and decay,
But the years that crumble me
Shall invigorate the tree,
Spread its branch, dilate its size,
Lift its summit to the skies.

Cherish honour, virtue, truth,
So shalt thou prolong thy youth.
Wanting these, however fast
Man be fixt, and form'd to last,
He is lifeless even now,
Stone at heart, and cannot grow.

[June 1790]

TEXT: *1815*

ANOTHER,

FOR A STONE ERECTED ON A SIMILAR OCCASION AT THE SAME PLACE IN THE FOLLOWING YEAR

READER! behold a monument
That asks no sigh or tear,
Though it perpetuate the event
Of a great burial here.
                    Anno 1791.

TEXT: *1815*

THE NEEDLESS ALARM

A TALE

THERE is a field through which I often pass,
Thick overspread with moss and silky grass,
Adjoining close to Kilwick's echoing wood,
Where oft the bitch-fox hides her hapless brood,
Reserv'd to solace many a neighb'ring 'squire,
That he may follow them through brake and briar,
Contusion hazarding of neck or spine,
Which rural gentlemen call sport divine.

A narrow brook, by rushy banks conceal'd,
Runs in a bottom, and divides the field;
Oaks intersperse it, that had once a head,
But now wear crests of oven-wood instead;
And where the land slopes to its wat'ry bourn,
Wide yawns a gulph beside a ragged thorn;
Bricks line the sides, but shiver'd long ago,
And horrid brambles intertwine below;
A hollow scoop'd, I judge in ancient time,
For baking earth, or burning rock to lime.

    Not yet the hawthorn bore her berries red,
With which the fieldfare, wint'ry guest, is fed;
Nor autumn yet had brush'd from ev'ry spray,
With her chill hand, the mellow leaves away;
But corn was hous'd, and beans were in the stack,
Now, therefore, issued forth the spotted pack,
With tails high mounted, ears hung low, and throats
With a whole gamut fill'd of heav'nly notes,
For which, alas! my destiny severe,
Though ears she gave me two, gave me no ear.

    The sun, accomplishing his early march,
His lamp now planted on heav'n's topmost arch,
When, exercise and air my only aim,
And heedless whither, to that field I came,
Ere yet with ruthless joy the happy hound
Told hill and dale that Reynard's track was found,
Or with the high-rais'd horn's melodious clang
All Kilwick[1] and all Dingle-derry[1] rang.

    Sheep graz'd the field; some with soft bosom press'd
The herb as soft, while nibbling stray'd the rest;
Nor noise was heard but of the hasty brook,
Struggling, detain'd in many a petty nook.
All seem'd so peaceful, that from them convey'd
To me, their peace by kind contagion spread.

    But when the huntsman, with distended cheek,
'Gan make his instrument of music speak,
And from within the wood that crash was heard,

[1] Two woods belonging to John Throckmorton, Esq. [C]

Though not a hound from whom it burst appear'd,
The sheep recumbent, and the sheep that graz'd,
All huddling into phalanx, stood and gaz'd,
Admiring, terrified, the novel strain,
Then cours'd the field around, and cours'd it round again;
But, recollecting with a sudden thought,
That flight in circles urg'd advanc'd them nought,
They gather'd close around the old pit's brink,
And thought again — but knew not what to think.

The man to solitude accustom'd long,
Perceives in ev'ry thing that lives a tongue;
Not animals alone, but shrubs and trees,
Have speech for him, and understood with ease;
After long drought, when rains abundant fall,
He hears the herbs and flowers rejoicing all;
Knows what the freshness of their hue implies,
How glad they catch the largess[1] of the skies;
But, with precision nicer still, the mind
He scans of ev'ry loco-motive kind;
Birds of all feather, beasts of ev'ry name,
That serve mankind, or shun them, wild or tame;
The looks and gestures of their griefs and fears
Have, all, articulation in his ears;
He spells them true by intuition's light,
And needs no glossary to set him right.

This truth premis'd was needful as a text,
To win due credence to what follows next.

Awhile they mus'd; surveying ev'ry face,
Thou hadst suppos'd them of superior race;
Their periwigs of wool, and fears combin'd,
Stamp'd on each countenance such marks of mind,
That sage they seem'd, as lawyers o'er a doubt,
Which, puzzling long, at last they puzzle out;
Or academic tutors, teaching youths,
Sure ne'er to want them, mathematic truths;
When thus a mutton, statelier than the rest,
A ram, the ewes and wethers, sad, address'd.

[1] *largeness*: *1795*.

Friends! we have liv'd too long. I never heard
Sounds such as these, so worthy to be fear'd.
Could I believe, that winds for ages pent
In earth's dark womb have found at last a vent,
And from their prison-house below arise,
With all these hideous howlings to the skies,
I could be much compos'd, nor should appear
For such a cause to feed the slightest fear.
Yourselves have seen, what time the thunders roll'd
All night, me resting quiet in the fold.
Or heard we that tremendous bray alone,
I could expound the melancholy tone;
Should deem it by our old companion made,
The ass; for he, we know, has lately stray'd,
And being lost, perhaps, and wand'ring wide,
Might be suppos'd to clamour for a guide.
But ah! those dreadful yells what soul can hear,
That owns a carcase, and not quake for fear?
Dæmons produce them doubtless, brazen-claw'd
And fang'd with brass the dæmons are abroad;
I hold it, therefore, wisest and most fit,
That, life to save, we leap into the pit.

   Him answer'd then his loving mate and true,
But more discreet than he, a Cambrian ewe.

   How? leap into the pit our life to save?
To save our life leap all into the grave?
For can we find it less? Contemplate first
The depth how awful! falling there, we burst;
Or should the brambles, interpos'd, our fall
In part abate, that happiness were small;
For with a race like theirs no chance I see
Of peace or ease to creatures clad as we.
Meantime, noise kills not. Be it Dapple's bray,
Or be it not, or be it whose it may,
And rush those other sounds, that seem by tongues
Of dæmons utter'd, from whatever lungs,
Sounds are but sounds, and till the cause appear,
We have at least commodious standing here;
Come, fiend, come, fury, giant, monster, blast

116

From earth or hell, we can but plunge at last.
　　While thus she spake, I fainter heard the peals,
For reynard, close attended at his heels,
By panting dog, tir'd man, and spatter'd horse,
Through mere good fortune, took a diff'rent course.
The flock grew calm again, and I, the road
Following that led me to my own abode,
Much wonder'd that the silly sheep had found
Such cause of terror in an empty sound,
So sweet to huntsman, gentleman, and hound.

MORAL

Beware of desp'rate steps. The darkest day
(Live till to-morrow) will have pass'd away.

[before 1792]

TEXT: *1794/5*

EPITAPH ON MRS HIGGINS

LAURELS may flourish round the conqu'ror's tomb,
But happiest they who win the world to come.
Believers have a silent field of fight,
And their exploits are veil'd from human sight;
They in some nook, where little known they dwell,
Kneel, pray in faith, and rout the hosts of Hell.
Eternal triumphs crown their toils divine,
And all those triumphs, Mary! now are thine.

[1791]

TEXT: The memorial tablet to Mary Higgins in the parish church of Weston Underwood, Bucks., according to which she died on June 4, 1791.

THE RETIRED CAT

A POET's Cat, sedate and grave
As poet well could wish to have,
Was much addicted to inquire
For nooks to which she might retire,
And where, secure as mouse in chink,
She might repose, or sit and think.
I know not where she caught the trick—
Nature perhaps herself had cast her
In such a mould PHILOSOPHIQUE,
Or else she learn'd it of her Master.
Sometimes ascending, debonnair,
An apple-tree, or lofty pear,
Lodg'd with convenience in the fork,
She watch'd the gard'ner at his work;
Sometimes her ease and solace sought
In an old empty wat'ring-pot,
There wanting nothing, save a fan,
To seem some nymph in her sedan
Apparell'd in exactest sort,
And ready to be borne to court.

But love of change it seems has place
Not only in our wiser race,
Cats also feel, as well as we,
That passion's force, and so did she.
Her climbing, she began to find,
Expos'd her too much to the wind,
And the old utensil of tin
Was cold and comfortless within:
She therefore wish'd instead of those
Some place of more serene repose,
Where neither cold might come, nor air
Too rudely wanton with her hair,
And sought it in the likeliest mode
Within her master's snug abode.

A draw'r, it chanc'd, at bottom lined
With linen of the softest kind,
With such as merchants introduce
From India, for the ladies' use,
A draw'r impending o'er the rest,
Half open in the topmost chest,
Of depth enough, and none to spare,
Invited her to slumber there;
Puss with delight beyond expression
Survey'd the scene and took possession.
Recumbent at her ease ere long,
And lull'd by her own humdrum song,
She left the cares of life behind,
And slept as she would sleep her last,
When in came, housewifely inclined,
The chambermaid, and shut it fast,
By no malignity impell'd,
But all unconscious whom it held.

Awaken'd by the shock, (cried Puss)
'Was ever cat attended thus!
'The open draw'r was left, I see,
'Merely to prove a nest for me,
'For soon as I was well composed
'Then came the maid, and it was closed.
'How smooth these 'kerchiefs and how sweet!
'Oh what a delicate retreat!
'I will resign myself to rest
'Till Sol declining in the west
'Shall call to supper, when, no doubt,
'Susan will come and let me out.'

The evening came, the sun descended,
And puss remain'd still unattended.
The night roll'd tardily away,
(With her indeed 'twas never day)
The sprightly morn her course renew'd,
The evening grey again ensued,

And puss came into mind no more
Than if entomb'd the day before.
With hunger pinch'd, and pinch'd for room,
She now presaged approaching doom,
Nor slept a single wink or purr'd,
Conscious of jeopardy incurr'd.

That night, by chance, the poet watching,
Heard an inexplicable scratching;
His noble heart went pit-a-pat,
And to himself he said—'What's that?'
He drew the curtain at his side,
And forth he peep'd, but nothing spied;
Yet, by his ear directed, guess'd
Something imprison'd in the chest,
And, doubtful what, with prudent care
Resolv'd it should continue there.
At length, a voice which well he knew,
A long and melancholy mew,
Saluting his poetic ears,
Consoled him, and dispell'd his fears;
He left his bed, he trod the floor,
He 'gan in haste the draw'rs explore,
The lowest first, and without stop
The rest in order to the top.
For 'tis a truth well known to most,
That whatsoever thing is lost,
We seek it, ere it come to light,
In ev'ry cranny but the right.
Forth skipp'd the cat, not now replete
As erst with airy self-conceit,
Nor in her own fond apprehension
A theme for all the world's attention,
But modest, sober, cur'd of all
Her notions hyperbolical,
And wishing for a place of rest
Any thing rather than a chest.
Then stepp'd the poet into bed.
With this reflexion in his head.

MORAL

Beware of too sublime a sense
Of your own worth and consequence.
The man who dreams himself so great,
And his importance of such weight,
That all around in all that's done
Must move and act for Him alone,
Will learn in school of tribulation
The folly of his expectation.

[1791]

TEXT: *1815*

YARDLEY OAK

SURVIVOR sole, and hardly such, of all
That once liv'd here, thy brethren, at my birth,
(Since which I number threescore winters past,)
A shatter'd vet'ran, hollow-trunk'd perhaps,
As now, and with excoriate forks deform,
Relicts of Ages! Could a mind imbued
With truth from Heaven created thing adore,
I might with rev'rence kneel, and worship thee.

It seems idolatry with some excuse,
When our forefather Druids in their oaks
Imagined sanctity. The conscience, yet
Unpurified by an authentic act
Of amnesty, the meed of blood divine,
Lov'd not the light, but gloomy into gloom
Of thickest shades, like Adam after taste
Of fruit proscrib'd, as to a refuge, fled.

Thou wast a bauble once, a cup and ball
Which babes might play with; and the thievish jay,
Seeking her food, with ease might have purloin'd

The auburn nut that held thee, swallowing down
Thy yet close folded latitude of boughs
And all thine embryo vastness at a gulp.
But Fate thy growth decreed. Autumnal rains
Beneath thy parent tree mellow'd the soil
Design'd thy cradle; and a skipping deer,
With pointed hoof dibbling the glebe, prepar'd
The soft receptacle in which secure
Thy rudiments should sleep the winter through.

So Fancy dreams. Disprove it, if ye can,
Ye reas'ners broad awake, whose busy searce
Of argument, employ'd too oft amiss,
Sifts half the pleasures of short life away.

Thou fell'st mature; and, in the loamy clod
Swelling with vegetative force instinct,
Didst burn thine egg, as theirs the fabled Twins,[1]
Now stars; two lobes, protruding, pair'd exact;
A leaf succeeded, and another leaf,
And, all the elements thy puny growth
Fost'ring propitious, thou becam'st a twig.

Who liv'd when thou wast such? Oh, couldst thou
      speak
As in Dodona[2] once thy kindred trees
Oracular, I would not curious ask
The future, best unknown, but at thy mouth
Inquisitive, the less ambiguous past.

By thee I might correct, erroneous oft,
The clock of history, facts and events
Timing more punctual, unrecorded facts
Recov'ring, and mistated setting right—
Desp'rate attempt, till trees shall speak again!

[1] Castor and Pollux: the offspring of Zeus and of Leda, after she had assumed the form of a swan.

[2] The oracle of Zeus at Dodona in Epirus spoke from an oak.

Time made thee what thou wast, king of the woods;
And Time hath made thee what thou art—a cave
For owls to roost in. Once thy spreading boughs
O'erhung the champaign; and the num'rous flock
That graz'd it stood beneath that ample cope
Uncrouded, yet safe shelter'd from the storm.
No flock frequents thee now. Thou hast outliv'd
Thy popularity, and art become
(Unless verse rescue thee awhile) a thing
Forgotten as the foliage of thy youth.

While thus through all the stages thou hast push'd
Of treeship—first a seedling, hid in grass;
Then twig; then sapling; and, as century roll'd
Slow after century, a giant bulk
Of girth enormous, with moss-cushion'd root
Upheav'd above the soil, and sides emboss'd
With prominent wens globose—till at the last
The rottenness, which time is charg'd to inflict
On other mighty ones, found also thee.

What exhibitions various hath the world
Witness'd of mutability in all
That we account most durable below!
Change is the diet on which all subsist,
Created changeable, and change at last
Destroys them. Skies uncertain, now the heat
Transmitting cloudless, and the solar beam
Now quenching in a boundless sea of clouds—
Calm and alternate storm, moisture and drought
Invigorate by turns the springs of life
In all that live, plant, animal, and man,
And in conclusion mar them. Nature's threads,
Fine passing thought, e'en in her coarsest works,
Delight in agitation, yet sustain
The force that agitates not unimpair'd;
But, worn by frequent impulse, to the cause
Of their best tone their dissolution owe.

Thought cannot spend itself, comparing still
The great and little of thy lot, thy growth
From almost nullity into a state
Of matchless grandeur, and declension thence,
Slow, into such magnificent decay.
Time was, when settling on thy leaf, a fly
Could shake thee to the root—and time has been
When tempests could not. At thy firmest age
Thou hadst within thy bole solid contents
That might have ribb'd the sides or plank'd the deck
Of some flagg'd admiral; and tortuous arms,
The shipwright's darling treasure, didst present
To the four-quarter'd winds, robust and bold,
Warp'd into tough knee-timber, many a load.[1]
But the axe spar'd thee. In those thriftier days
Oaks fell not, hewn by thousands, to supply
The bottomless demands of contest wag'd
For senatorial honours. Thus to Time
The task was left to whittle thee away
With his sly scythe, whose ever-nibbling edge,
Noiseless, an atom and an atom more,
Disjoining from the rest, has, unobserv'd,
Achiev'd a labour which had, far and wide,
By man perform'd, made all the forest ring.

Embowell'd now, and of thy ancient self
Possessing nought but the scoop'd rind that seems
An huge throat calling to the clouds for drink,
Which it would give in rivulets to thy root,
Thou temptest none, but rather much forbidd'st
The feller's toil, which thou couldst ill requite.
Yet is thy root sincere, sound as the rock,
A quarry of stout spurs and knotted fangs
Which, crook'd into a thousand whimsies, clasp
The stubborn soil, and hold thee still erect.

---

[1] Knee-timber is found in the crooked arms of oak which by reason
of their distortion are easily adjusted to the angle formed where the
deck and the ship's sides meet. [C.]

So stands a kingdom whose foundations yet
Fail not, in virtue and in wisdom laid,
Though all the superstructure, by the tooth
Pulveriz'd of venality, a shell
Stands now, and semblance only of itself.

Thine arms have left thee. Winds have rent them off
Long since, and rovers of the forest wild
With bow and shaft, have burnt them. Some have left
A splinter'd stump bleach'd to a snowy white;
And some, memorial none where once they grew.
Yet life still lingers in thee, and puts forth
Proof not contemptible of what she can,
Even where death predominates. The Spring
Thee finds not less alive to her sweet force
Than yonder upstarts of the neighbour wood,
So much thy juniors, who their birth receiv'd
Half a millennium since the date of thine.

But since, although well qualified by age
To teach, no spirit dwells in thee, nor voice
May be expected from thee, seated here
On thy distorted root, with hearers none
Or prompter save the scene, I will perform
Myself the oracle, and will discourse
In my own ear such matter as I may.

One man alone, the father of us all,
Drew not his life from woman; never gaz'd,
With mute unconsciousness of what he saw,
On all around him; learn'd not by degrees,
Nor ow'd articulation to his ear;
But, moulded by his Maker into man
At once, upstood intelligent, survey'd
All creatures, with precision understood
Their purport, uses, properties, assign'd
To each his name significant, and, fill'd
With love and wisdom, render'd back to Heav'n
In praise harmonious the first air he drew.

125

He was excus'd the penalties of dull
Minority. No tutor charg'd his hand
With the thought-tracing quill, or task'd his mind
With problems. History, not wanted yet,
Lean'd on her elbow, watching Time, whose course
Eventful should supply her with a theme;...

[1791]

TEXT: MSS. Cowper Museum, Olney. The poem was not completed. Milford prints 22 additional lines cancelled in the MS.

TO

THE NIGHTINGALE

WHICH THE AUTHOR HEARD SING ON
NEW YEAR'S DAY, 1792[1]

WHENCE is it, that amazed I hear
    From yonder wither'd spray,
This foremost morn of all the year,
    The melody of May?

And why, since thousands would be proud
    Of such a favour shown,
Am I selected from the crowd,
    To witness it alone?

[1] C. wrote to John Johnson on March 11, 1792: 'You talk of primroses that you pulled on Candlemas Day; but what think you of me who heard a nightingale on New Year's Day? Perhaps I am the only man in England who can boast of such good fortune.' Nightingales winter in tropical Africa; and no British record later than November 10 is admitted by *The Handbook of British Birds*. Song-thrushes, which sing in mid-winter, and occasionally at night, are sometimes mistaken for nightingales.

Sing'st thou, sweet Philomel, to me,
   For that I also long
Have practis'd in the groves like thee,
   Though not like thee in song?

Or sing'st thou rather under force
   Of some divine command,
Commission'd to presage a course
   Of happier days at hand?

Thrice welcome then! for many a long
   And joyless year have I,
As thou to day, put forth my song
   Beneath a wintry sky.

But Thee no wintry skies can harm,
   Who only need'st to sing,
To make ev'n January charm,
   And ev'ry season Spring.

[January 1792]

TEXT: *1815*

EPITAPH

ON A FREE BUT TAME REDBREAST,
A FAVOURITE OF MISS SALLY HURDIS[1]

THESE are not dew-drops, these are tears,
   And tears by Sally shed
For absent Robin who, she fears
   With too much cause, is dead.

[1] A sister of C.'s friend, the poet James Hurdis.

One morn he came not to her hand
  As he was wont to come,
And, on her finger perch'd, to stand
  Picking his breakfast-crumb.

Alarm'd she call'd him, and perplext
  She sought him, but in vain;
That day he came not, nor the next,
  Nor ever came again.

She therefore rais'd him here a tomb,
  Though where he fell, or how,
None knows, so secret was his doom,
  Nor where he moulders now.

Had half a score of coxcombs died
  In social Robin's stead,
Poor Sally's tears had soon been dried,
  Or haply never shed.

But Bob was neither rudely bold
  Nor spiritlessly tame,
Nor was, like theirs, his bosom cold,
  But always in a flame.

[March 1792]

TEXT: *1815*

EPIGRAM

PRINTED IN THE NORTHAMPTON 'MERCURY'

To purify their wine some people bleed
A lamb into the barrel, and succeed:
No nostrum, planters say, is half so good
To make fine sugar, as a *negro*'s blood.

Now *lambs* and *negroes* both are harmless things,
And thence perhaps this wond'rous virtue springs.
'Tis in the blood of innocence alone—
Good cause why planters never try their own.

[April or May 1792]

TEXT: *1815*

EPITAPH ON FOP

THOUGH once a puppy, and though Fop by name,
Here moulders one whose bones some honour claim:
No sycophant, although of spaniel race,
And though no hound, a martyr to the chace.
Ye squirrels, rabbits, leverets, rejoice,
Your haunts no longer echo to his voice;
This record of his fate exulting view,
He died worn out with vain pursuit of you.
'Yes,' the indignant shade of Fop replies,
'And worn with vain pursuits Man also dies.'

[August 1792]

TEXT: *Cowper Illustrated by a Series of Views*, whose authors (see p. 41) transcribed it from an inscription on an urn in Weston Park, Bucks. Fop was Lady Throckmorton's dog. A second urn held the remains of her husband's pointer, Neptune.

EPITAPH ON NEPTUNE

HERE lies one, who never drew
Blood himself, yet many slew;
Gave the gun its aim, and figure
Made in field, yet ne'er pull'd trigger.

Armed men have gladly made
Him their guide, and him obey'd;
At his signified desire,
Would advance, present, and fire.
Stout he was, and large of limb,
Scores have fled at sight of him;
And to all this fame he rose
By only following his nose.
Neptune was he call'd; not he
Who controls the boist'rous sea,
But of happier command,
Neptune of the furrow'd land;
And, your wonder vain to shorten,
Pointer to Sir John Throckmorton.

[1792]

TEXT: *Cowper Illustrated.*

STANZAS[1]

SUBJOINED TO A BILL OF MORTALITY FOR THE PARISH OF ALL SAINTS, NORTHAMPTON, ANNO DOMINI 1792

Felix, qui potuit rerum cognoscere causas,
Atque metus omnes et inexorabile fatum
Subjecit pedibus, strepitumque Acherontis avari!—
Virgil, *Georgics*, ii, 458

Happy the mortal, who has trac'd effects
To their First Cause; cast fear beneath his feet,
And death, and roaring hell's voracious fires!

THANKLESS for favours from on high,
Man thinks he fades too soon;
Though 'tis his privilege to die,
Would he improve the boon:

---

[1] These, and similar verses of 1787, 1788, 1789, 1790 and 1793, were composed at the request of the parish clerk: see p. 856.

But he, not wise enough to scan
 His best concerns aright,
Would gladly stretch life's little span
 To ages, if he might.

To ages in a world of pain—
 To ages, where he goes
Gall'd by affliction's heavy chain,
 And hopeless of repose.

Strange fondness of the human heart,
 Enamour'd of its harm!
Strange world, that costs it so much smart,
 And still has pow'r to charm!

Whence has the world her magic pow'r?
 Why deem we death a foe?
Recoil from weary life's best hour,
 And covet longer woe?

The cause is Conscience—Conscience oft
 Her tale of guilt renews;
Her voice is terrible, though soft,
 And dread of death ensues.

Then, anxious to be longer spar'd,
 Man mourns his fleeting breath;
All evils then seem light compar'd
 With the approach of Death.

'Tis Judgment shakes him; there's the fear,
 That prompts the wish to stay;
He has incurr'd a long arrear,
 And must despair to pay.

Pay!—Follow Christ, and all is paid;
 His death your peace ensures:
Think on the grave where he was laid,
 And calm descend to yours.

[1792]

TEXT: *Bull*

131

ON A SIMILAR OCCASION

FOR THE YEAR 1793

De sacris autem hæc sit una sententia, ut conserventur.—
Cicero, *De Legibus*
But let us all concur in this one sentiment, that
things sacred be inviolate.

HE lives who lives to God, alone,
    And all are dead beside;
For other source than God is none
    Whence life can be supplied.

To live to God, is to requite
    His love as best we may;
To make his precepts our delight,
    His promises our stay.

But life, within a narrow ring
    Of giddy joys compris'd,
Is falsely nam'd, and no such thing,
    But rather death disguis'd.

Can life in them deserve the name,
    Who only live to prove
For what poor toys they can disclaim
    An endless life above?

Who, much diseas'd, yet nothing feel,
    Much menac'd, nothing dread;
Have wounds which only God can heal,
    Yet never ask his aid?

Who deem his house an useless place,
    Faith, want of common sense;
And ardour in the Christian race
    An hypocrite's pretence?

Who trample order, and the day
    Which God asserts his own,
Dishonour with unhallow'd play,
    And worship chance alone?

If scorn of God's commands, impress'd
    On word and deed, imply
The better part of man unbless'd
    With life that cannot die,

Such want it; and that want, uncur'd
    Till man resigns his breath,
Speaks him a criminal, assur'd
    Of everlasting death.

Sad period to a pleasant course!
    Yet so will God repay
Sabbaths profan'd without remorse,
    And mercy cast away.

[1793]

TEXT: *Bull*

TO MRS UNWIN

MARY! I want a lyre with other strings,
    Such aid from Heav'n as some have feign'd they drew,
    An eloquence scarce giv'n to mortals, new
And undebas'd by praise of meaner things,
That ere through age or woe I shed my wings,
    I may record thy worth with honour due,
    In verse as musical as thou art true,
And that immortalizes whom it sings.

133

But thou hast little need. There is a book
　　By seraphs writ with beams of heav'nly light,
On which the eyes of God not rarely look,
　　A chronicle of actions just and bright;

There all thy deeds, my faithful Mary, shine,
And, since thou own'st that praise, I spare thee mine.

[May 1793]

TEXT: *1815*

ON A SPANIEL, CALLED BEAU, KILLING A YOUNG BIRD

A SPANIEL, Beau, that fares like you,
　　Well-fed, and at his ease,
Should wiser be than to pursue
　　Each trifle that he sees.

But you have kill'd a tiny bird,
　　Which flew not till to-day,
Against my orders, whom you heard
　　Forbidding you the prey.

Nor did you kill that you might eat
　　And ease a doggish pain,
For him, though chased with furious heat,
　　You left where he was slain.

Nor was he of the thievish sort,
　　Or one whom blood allures,
But innocent was all his sport
　　Whom you have torn for yours.

My dog! what remedy remains,
　　Since, teach you all I can,
I see you, after all my pains,
　　So much resemble Man?

134

BEAU'S REPLY

Sir, when I flew to seize the bird
  In spite of your command,
A louder voice than yours I heard,
  And harder to withstand.

You cried—forbear—but in my breast
  A mightier cried—proceed—
'Twas nature, Sir, whose strong behest
  Impell'd me to the deed.

Yet much as nature I respect,
  I ventur'd once to break
(As you perhaps may recollect)
  Her precept for your sake;

And when your linnet on a day,
  Passing his prison door,
Had flutter'd all his strength away,
  And panting press'd the floor,

Well knowing him a sacred thing,
  Not destin'd to my tooth,
I only kiss'd his ruffled wing,
  And lick'd the feathers smooth.

Let my disobedience then excuse
  My disobedience now,
Nor some reproof yourself refuse
  From your aggriev'd Bow-wow;

If killing birds be such a crime
  (Which I can hardly see),
What think you, Sir, of killing Time
  With verse address'd to me?

[July 15, 1793]

TEXT: *1815*.

ON FLAXMAN'S PENELOPE[1]

THE suitors sinn'd, but with a fair excuse,
Whom all this elegance might well seduce;
Nor can our censure on the husband fall,
Who, for a wife so lovely, slew them all.

[September 1793]

TEXT: *1815*.

TO MARY

THE twentieth year is well nigh past,
Since first our sky was overcast;[2]
Ah would that this might be the last!
                    My Mary!

Thy spirits have a fainter flow,
I see thee daily weaker grow—
'Twas my distress that brought thee low,
                    My Mary!

Thy needles, once a shining store,
For my sake restless heretofore,
Now rust disus'd and shine no more,
                    My Mary!

For though thou gladly wouldst fulfil
The same kind office for me still,
Thy sight now seconds not thy will,
                    My Mary!

[1] A series of illustrations of Homer, drawn by Flaxman at Rome, excited much admiration in 1793. Engravings by Pirelli were brought back by the Throckmortons to C.

[2] *Overcast*: by Cowper's third severe depression, in 1773.

But well thou play'dst the housewife's part
And all thy threads with magic art
Have wound themselves about this heart,
                    My Mary!

Thy indistinct expressions seem
Like language utter'd in a dream,
Yet me they charm, whate'er the theme,
                    My Mary!

Thy silver locks, once auburn bright,
Are still more lovely in my sight
Than golden beams of orient light,
                    My Mary!

For could I view nor them nor thee,
What sight worth seeing could I see?
The sun would rise in vain for me,
                    My Mary!

Partakers of the sad decline,
Thy hands their little force resign;
Yet gently prest, press gently mine,
                    My Mary!

And then I feel that still I hold
A richer store ten thousandfold
Than misers fancy in their gold,
                    My Mary!

Such feebleness of limbs thou prov'st
That now, at every step, thou mov'st
Upheld by two; yet still thou lov'st,
                    My Mary!

And still to love, though prest with ill,
In wintry age to feel no chill,
With me is to be lovely still,
                    My Mary!

But ah! by constant heed I know
How oft the sadness that I show
Transforms thy smiles to looks of woe,
                                    My Mary!

And should my future lot be cast
With much resemblance of the past,
Thy worn-out heart will break at last,
                                    My Mary!

[Autumn 1793]

TEXT: MSS. Cowper Museum, Olney.

THE CAST-AWAY[1]

OBSCUREST night involv'd the sky,
    Th' Atlantic billows roar'd,
When such a destin'd wretch as I
    Wash'd headlong from on board,
Of friends, of hope, of all bereft,
His floating home for ever left.

[1] This was the last original poem written by Cowper. It was inspired by a passage in Richard Walter's *A Voyage Round the World by...George Anson*, 1748. John Johnson was a subscriber to the edition of 1798 and read it to Cowper. The incident described happened when Anson's ship, the *Centurion*, was rounding Cape Horn in a violent storm, on March 24, 1741: 'As we dared not venture any sail abroad, we were obliged to make use of an expedient, which answered our purpose; this was putting the helm a-weather and manning the fore-shrouds; But though this method proved successful, yet in the execution of it, one of our ablest seamen was canted overboard; and notwithstanding the prodigious agitation of the waves, we perceived that he swam very strong, and it was with the utmost concern that we found ourselves incapable of assisting him; and we were the more grieved at his unhappy fate, since we lost sight of him struggling with the waves, and conceived from the manner in which he swam, that he might continue sensible for a considerable time longer, of the horror attending his irretrievable situation.' [ed. 1798, Bk. I, ch. 8.]

No braver chief could Albion boast
   Than he with whom he went,
Nor ever ship left Albion's coast
   With warmer wishes sent.
He lov'd them both, but both in vain,
Nor him beheld, nor her again.

Not long beneath the whelming brine
   Expert to swim, he lay;
Nor soon he felt his strength decline
   Or courage die away;
But wag'd with death a lasting strife
Supported by despair of life.

He shouted: nor his friends had fail'd
   To check the vessels' course,
But so the furious blast prevail'd
   That, pitiless perforce,
They left their outcast mate behind,
And scudded still before the wind.

Some succour yet they could afford;
   And, such as storms allow,
The cask, the coop, the floated cord
   Delay'd not to bestow.
But he, they knew, nor ship nor shore,
Whate'er they gave, should visit more.

Nor, cruel as it seem'd, could he
   Their haste, himself, condemn,
Aware that flight in such a sea
   Alone could rescue *them*;
Yet bitter felt it still to die
Deserted, and his friends so nigh.

He long survives who lives an hour
   In ocean, self-upheld:
And so long he with unspent pow'r
   His destiny repell'd:
And ever as the minutes flew,
Entreated help, or cried—'Adieu!'

139

At length, his transient respite past,
    His comrades, who before
Had heard his voice in ev'ry blast,
    Could catch the sound no more:
For then, by toil subdued, he drank
The stifling wave, and then he sank.

No poet wept him, but the page
    Of narrative sincere
That tells his name, his worth, his age,
    Is wet with Anson's tear;
And tears by bards or heroes shed
Alike immortalize the dead.

I, therefore, purpose not or dream,
    Descanting on his fate,
To give the melancholy theme
    A more enduring date;
But mis'ry still delights to trace
Its semblance in another's case.

No voice divine the storm allay'd,
    No light propitious shone;
When, snatch'd from all effectual aid,
    We perish'd, each alone;
But I, beneath a rougher sea,
And whelm'd in deeper gulfs than he.

[March 20, 1799]

TEXT: *The Cast-away*: the Text of the Original Manuscript, ed. by C. Ryskamp, Princetown, N.J., 1963.

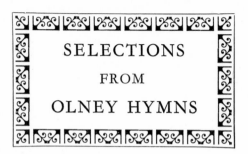

SELECTIONS

FROM

OLNEY HYMNS

ALMOST ALL the *Olney Hymns* were written for use at the evening prayer-meetings conducted by the Rev. John Newton at the Great House in Olney: hence the title. Of the 348 pieces in the collection, 282 were written by Newton; the remaining 66 were contributed by Cowper, for the most part in 1771 and 1772. 'A desire of promoting the faith and comfort of sincere Christians, though the principal, was not the only motive to this undertaking,' Newton wrote in the preface to the volume. 'It was likewise intended as a monument to perpetuate the remembrance of an intimate and endeared friendship...We had not proceeded far upon our proposed plan, before my dear friend was prevented, by a long and affecting indisposition, from affording me any further assistance.' Thus, after Cowper's third attack of madness in January 1773, Newton 'for some time thought myself determined to proceed no further without him'. Later, he continued the task of writing hymns alone, and was at last persuaded by friends to 'overcome the reluctance I long felt to see them in print, while I had so few of my friend's hymns to insert in the collection'. Newton saw the book through the press, distinguishing Cowper's hymns 'by prefixing the letter C. to each of them'.

Olney Hymns, published in 1779, had an immediate and far-reaching success. Mrs Russell's bibliography lists thirty-seven editions up to 1836; and not a few of the hymns were reproduced in other collections. These hymn-books were the instruments by which the Evangelicals introduced the practice of hymn-singing into the Anglican Church service. Before their time, the singing of metrical psalms only had been permitted, and these were generally regarded as an interlude in the service, being sung by the choir alone, or by the clerk, while the congregation remained in their seats, making conversation or taking a nap. The Evangelicals set themselves the task of getting the congregation to stand and join in, as a corporate act of worship. This entailed giving them something worth singing. The metrical psalms, whether in the translation of 1562 by Thomas Sternhold and John Hopkins, or in the New Version of 1696 by Nahum Tate and Nicholas Brady, were antiquated in their language and measures. They could not be adapted to the purpose of inspiring an audience with the Gospel of the Good News, personal salvation by Christ Crucified. Many leading Evangelicals, therefore, wrote hymns themselves, or compiled and published collections. In the early years of the Evangelical Revival, hymns were more often sung at extra-parochial gatherings or at weekday prayer-meetings than at the set Sunday services. It was only gradually, and in the teeth of stubborn opposition from churchmen of other schools, that the hymns of the old masters—Watts, Doddridge, the Wesleys, Cowper and Newton—displaced Sternhold and Hopkins in church and chapel.

The text, except where obvious printer's errors have been corrected and noted, is that of the first edition. Footnotes inserted by Newton in that edition are indicated by the letter N within brackets.

WALKING WITH GOD

Genesis, v, 24.

OH! for a closer walk with GOD,
    A calm and heav'nly frame;
A light to shine upon the road
    That leads me to the Lamb!

Where is the blessedness I knew
    When first I saw the LORD?
Where is the soul-refreshing view
    Of JESUS, and his word?

What peaceful hours I once enjoy'd!
    How sweet their mem'ry still!
But they have left an aching void
    The world can never fill.

Return, O holy Dove, return,
    Sweet messenger of rest;
I hate the sins that made thee mourn
    And drove thee from my breast.

The dearest idol I have known,[1]
    Whate'er that idol be;
Help me to tear it from thy throne,
    And worship only thee.

So shall my walk be close with GOD,
    Calm and serene my frame;
So purer light shall mark the road
    That leads me to the Lamb.

[1767]

[1] This hymn was written when Mrs Unwin was so ill that C. almost despaired of her recovery (letter to Judith Madan, December 10, 1767).

WISDOM

Proverbs, viii, 22–31.

Ere God had built the mountains,
  Or rais'd the fruitful hills;
Before he fill'd the fountains
  That feed the running rills;
In me, from everlasting,
  The wonderful I AM[1]
Found pleasures never wasting,
  And Wisdom is my name.

When, like a tent to dwell in,
  He spread the skies abroad;
And swath'd about the swelling
  Of ocean's mighty flood;
He wrought by weight and measure,
  And I was with him then;
Myself the Father's pleasure,
  And mine, the sons of men.

Thus wisdom's words discover
  Thy glory and thy grace,
Thou everlasting lover
  Of our unworthy race!
Thy gracious eye survey'd us
  Ere stars were seen above;
In wisdom thou hast made us,
  And dy'd for us in love.

And couldst thou be delighted
  With creatures such as we!
Who when we saw thee, slighted
  And nail'd thee to a tree?
Unfathomable wonder,
  And mystery divine!
The voice that speaks in thunder,
  Says, 'Sinner I am thine!'

---

[1] Exodus, iii, 14: 'And God said unto Moses, *I am that I am.*'

THE CONTRITE HEART

Isaiah, lvii, 15.

THE LORD will happiness divine
　　On contrite hearts bestow:
Then tell me, gracious GOD, is mine
　　A contrite heart, or no?

I hear, but seem to hear in vain,
　　Insensible as steel;
If aught is felt, 'tis only pain,
　　To find I cannot feel.

I sometimes think myself inclin'd
　　To love thee, if I could;
But often feel another mind,
　　Averse to all that's good.

My best desires are faint and few,
　　I fain would strive for more;
But when I cry, 'My strength renew,'
　　Seem weaker than before.

Thy saints are comforted I know,
　　And love thy house of pray'r;
I therefore go where others go,
　　But find no comfort there.

O make this heart rejoice, or ache;
　　Decide this doubt for me;
And if it be not broken, break,
　　And heal it, if it be.

THE FUTURE PEACE AND GLORY
OF THE CHURCH

Isaiah, lx, 15–20.

HEAR what GOD the LORD hath spoken:
O my people, faint and few,
Comfortless, afflicted, broken,
Fair abodes I build for you:
Thorns[1] of heart-felt tribulation
Shall no more perplex your ways;
You shall name your walls Salvation,
And your gates shall all be Praise.

There, like streams that feed the garden,
Pleasures, without end, shall flow;
For the LORD, your faith rewarding,
All his bounty shall bestow:
Still in undisturb'd possession,
Peace and righteousness shall reign;
Never shall you feel oppression,
Hear the voice of war again.

Ye no more your suns descending,
Waning moons no more shall see;
But, your griefs, for ever ending,
Find eternal noon in me:
GOD shall rise, and shining o'er you,
Change to day the gloom of night;
He, the LORD, shall be your glory,
God your everlasting light.

[1] *Thorns*: themes, 1779.

EPHRAIM REPENTING

Jeremiah, xxxi, 18–20.

My God! till I receiv'd thy stroke,
    How like a beast was I!
So unaccustom'd to the yoke,
    So backward to comply.

With grief my just reproach I bear,
    Shame fills me at the thought;
How frequent my rebellions were!
    What wickedness I wrought!

Thy merciful restraint I scorn'd,
    And left the pleasant road;
Yet turn me, and I shall be turn'd,
    Thou art the Lord my God.

Is Ephraim banish'd from my thoughts,
    Or vile in my esteem?
No, saith the Lord, with all his faults,
    I still remember him.

Is he a dear and pleasant child?
    Yes, dear and pleasant still;
Tho' sin his foolish heart beguil'd,
    And he withstood my will.

My sharp rebuke has laid him low,
    He seeks my face again;
My pity kindles at his woe,
    He shall not seek in vain.

PRAISE FOR THE FOUNTAIN OPENED

Zechariah, xiii, 1.

THERE is a fountain fill'd with blood
    Drawn from EMMANUEL's veins;
And sinners, plung'd beneath that flood,
    Lose all their guilty stains.

The dying thief rejoic'd to see
    That fountain in his day;
And there have I, as vile as he,
    Wash'd all my sins away.

Dear dying Lamb, thy precious blood
    Shall never lose its pow'r;
Till all the ransom'd church of GOD
    Be sav'd, to sin no more.

E'er since, by faith, I saw the stream
    Thy flowing wounds supply;
Redeeming love has been my theme,
    And shall be till I die.

Then in a nobler sweeter song
    I'll sing thy power to save;
When this poor lisping stammering tongue
    Lies silent in the grave.

LORD, I believe thou hast prepar'd
    (Unworthy tho' I be)
For me a blood-bought free reward,
    A golden harp for me!

'Tis strung, and tun'd, for endless years,
    And form'd by pow'r divine;
To sound in GOD the Father's ears,
    No other name but thine.

LOVEST THOU ME?

John, xxi, 16.

HARK, my soul! it is the LORD;
'Tis thy Saviour, hear his word;
JESUS speaks, and speaks to thee;
'Say, poor sinner, lov'st thou me?

I deliver'd thee when bound,
And, when wounded, heal'd thy wound;
Sought thee wand'ring, set thee right,
Turn'd thy darkness into light.

Can a woman's tender care
Cease, towards the child she bare?
Yes, she may forgetful be,
Yet will I remember thee.

Mine is an unchanging love,
Higher than the heights above;
Deeper than the depths beneath,
Free and faithful, strong as death.

Thou shalt see my glory soon,
When the work of grace is done;
Partner of my throne shalt be,
Say, poor sinner, lov'st thou me?'

LORD it is my chief complaint,
That my love is weak and faint;
Yet I love thee and adore,
Oh for grace to love thee more!

[1768]

ON OPENING A PLACE FOR SOCIAL PRAYER[1]

JESUS, where'er thy people meet,
There they behold thy mercy-seat;
Where'er they seek thee thou art found,
And ev'ry place is hallow'd ground.

For thou, within no walls confin'd,
Inhabitest the humble mind;
Such ever bring thee, where they come,
And going, take thee to their home.

Dear Shepherd of thy chosen few!
Thy former mercies here renew;
Here, to our waiting hearts, proclaim
The sweetness of thy saving name.

Here may we prove the pow'r of pray'r,
To strengthen faith, and sweeten care;
To teach our faint desires to rise,
And bring all heav'n before our eyes.[2]

Behold! at thy commanding word,
We stretch the curtain and the cord,[3]
Come thou, and fill this wider space,
And help us with a large encrease.

Lord, we are few, but thou art near;
Nor short thine arm, nor deaf thine ear;
Oh rend the heav'ns, come quickly down,
And make a thousand hearts thine own!

[1769]

[1] This hymn was specially written for the opening of a room in the
Great House at Olney for prayer meetings. See letter, p. 1003.

[2] The line is from Milton: *Il Penseroso*, 166.

[3] Isaiah, liv. 2. [N].

EXHORTATION TO PRAYER

WHAT various hindrances we meet
In coming to a mercy-seat!
Yet who that knows the worth of pray'r,
But wishes to be often there.

Pray'r makes the dark'ned cloud withdraw,
Pray'r climbs the ladder Jacob saw;
Gives exercise to faith and love,
Brings ev'ry blessing from above.

Restraining pray'r, we cease to fight;
Pray'r makes the christian's armor bright;
And Satan trembles, when he sees
The weakest saint upon his knees.

While Moses stood with arms spread wide,
Success was found on Israel's side;[1]
But when thro' weariness they fail'd,
That moment Amalek prevail'd.

Have you no words? ah, think again,
Words flow apace when you complain;
And fill your fellow-creature's ear
With the sad tale of all your care.

Were half the breath thus vainly spent,
To heav'n in supplication sent;
Your cheerful song would oft'ner be,
'Hear what the LORD has done for me!'

[1] Exodus, xvii, 11 [N].

LIGHT SHINING OUT OF DARKNESS[1]

GOD moves in a mysterious way,
  His wonders to perform;
He plants his footsteps in the sea,
  And rides upon the storm.

Deep in unfathomable mines
  Of never failing skill,
He treasures up his bright designs,
  And works his sov'reign will.

Ye fearful saints, fresh courage take;
  The clouds ye so much dread
Are big with mercy, and shall break
  In blessings on your head.

Judge not the LORD by feeble sense,
  But trust him for his grace;
Behind a frowning providence
  He hides a smiling face.

His purposes will ripen fast,
  Unfolding every hour;
The bud may have a bitter taste,
  But sweet will be the flower.

Blind unbelief is sure to err,[2]
  And scan his work in vain:
GOD is his own interpreter,
  And he will make it plain.

---

[1] According to Samuel Greatheed's memorial *Sermon*, 1800, C. 'conceived some presentiment' of the breakdown of January 1773 'as it drew near, and during a solitary walk in the fields, he composed a hymn', identified as this. Greatheed did not meet C. until 1785.

[2] John, xiii, 7 [N].

TEMPTATION

THE billows swell, the winds are high,
Clouds overcast my wintry sky;
Out of the depths to thee I call,[1]
My fears are great, my strength is small.

O LORD, the pilot's part perform,
And guide and guard me thro' the storm;
Defend me from each threatning ill,
Control the waves, say, 'Peace, be still.'

Amidst the roaring of the sea,
My soul still hangs her hope on thee;
Thy constant love, thy faithful care,
Is all that saves me from despair.

Dangers of ev'ry shape and name
Attend the follow'rs of the Lamb,
Who leave the world's deceitful shore,
And leave it to return no more.

Tho' tempest-toss'd and half a wreck,
My Saviour thro' the floods I seek;
Let neither winds nor stormy main
Force back my shatter'd bark again.

LOOKING UPWARDS IN A STORM

GOD of my life, to thee I call,
Afflicted at thy feet I fall;[2]
When the great water-floods prevail,
Leave not my trembling heart to fail!

[1] Psalm cxxx, 1.
[2] Psalm lxix, 15 [N].

Friend of the friendless, and the faint!
Where should I lodge my deep complaint?
Where but with thee, whose open door
Invites the helpless and the poor!

Did ever mourner plead with thee,
And thou refuse that mourner's plea?
Does not the word still fix'd remain,
That none shall seek thy face in vain?

That were a grief I could not bear,
Didst thou not hear and answer prayer;
But a pray'r-hearing, answ'ring GOD,
Supports me under ev'ry load.

Fair is the lot that's cast for me!
I have an advocate with thee;
They whom the world caresses most,
Have no such privilege to boast.

Poor tho' I am, despis'd, forgot,[1]
Yet GOD, my GOD, forgets me not;
And he is safe and must succeed,
For whom the LORD vouchsafes to plead.

PEACE AFTER A STORM

WHEN darkness long has veil'd my mind,
And smiling day once more appears;
Then, my Redeemer, then I find
The folly of my doubts and fears.

Strait I upbraid my wandering heart,
And blush that I should ever be
Thus prone to act so base a part,
Or harbor one hard thought of thee!

[1] Psalm xl, 17 [N].

Oh! let me then at length be taught
What I am still so slow to learn;
That GOD is love and changes not,
Nor knows the shadow of a turn.

Sweet truth, and easy to repeat!
But when my faith is sharply try'd,
I find myself a learner yet,
Unskilful, weak, and apt to slide.

But, O my LORD, one look from thee
Subdues the disobedient will;
Drives doubt and discontent away,
And thy rebellious worm is still.

Thou art as ready to forgive,
As I am ready to repine;
Thou, therefore, all the praise receive,
Be shame, and self-abhorrence, mine.

SUBMISSION

O LORD, my best desire fulfill,
    And help me to resign
Life, health, and comfort to thy will,
    And make thy pleasure mine.

Why should I shrink at thy command,
    Whose love forbids my fears?
Or tremble at the gracious hand
    That wipes away my tears?

No, let me rather freely yield
    What most I prize to thee;
Who never hast a good withheld,
    Or wilt withhold from me.

Thy favor, all my journey thro',
  Thou art engag'd to grant;
What else I want, or think I do,
  'Tis better still to want.

Wisdom and mercy guide my way,
  Shall I resist them both?
A poor blind creature of a day,
  And crush'd before the moth!

But ah! my inward spirit cries,
  Still bind me to thy sway;
Else the next cloud that veils my skies,
  Drives all these thoughts away.

RETIREMENT

FAR from the world, O LORD, I flee,
  From strife and tumult far;
From scenes where Satan wages still
  His most successful war.

The calm retreat, the silent shade,
  With pray'r and praise agree;
And seem by thy sweet bounty made,
  For those who follow thee.

There if thy Spirit touch the soul,
  And grace her mean abode;
Oh with what peace, and joy, and love,
  She communes with her GOD!

There like the nightingale she pours
  Her solitary lays;
Nor asks a witness of her song,
  Nor thirsts for human praise.

Author and Guardian of my life,
  Sweet source of light divine;
And (all harmonious names in one)
  My Saviour, thou art mine!

What thanks I owe thee, and what love —
  A boundless, endless store —
Shall echo thro' the realms above,
  When time shall be no more.

[1765]

I WILL PRAISE THE LORD
AT ALL TIMES

WINTER has a joy for me,
While the Saviour's charms I read,
Lowly, meek, from blemish free,
In the snow-drop's pensive head.

Spring returns, and brings along
Life-invigorating suns:
Hark! the turtle's plaintive song,
Seems to speak his dying groans!

Summer has a thousand charms,
All expressive of his worth;
'Tis his sun that lights and warms,
His the air that cools the earth.

What! has autumn left to say
Nothing, of a Saviour's grace?
Yes, the beams of milder day
Tell me of his smiling face.

Light appears with early dawn,
While the sun makes haste to rise,
See his bleeding beauties, drawn
On the blushes of the skies.

Ev'ning, with a silent pace,
Slowly moving in the west,
Shews an emblem of his grace,
Points to an eternal rest.

SELECTIONS

FROM THE

TRANSLATIONS

F

Cowper occupied himself with translation in youth, as a distraction from idleness; in middle and later life, as a discipline to keep his mind on an even keel. When still in the Temple, he collaborated with his brother and others in turning Voltaire's *Henriade* into English, and was one of the contributors to Duncombe's translation of Horace. Between 1779 and his death he translated the bulk of Vincent Bourne's Latin verse, many poems from the French of Madame de la Motte Guyon, the whole of the *Iliad* and the *Odyssey*, *The Battle of the Frogs and Mice*, many epigrams from the Greek, nearly all of Milton's Latin and Italian poems, G. B. Andreini's *Adamo* from the Italian (in collaboration with Hayley) and the letters written to Newton in Latin by H. R. van Lier, a minister of the Dutch Reformed Church, published under the title *The Power of Grace Illustrated*. In the last months of his life he busied himself with turning some of Gay's *Fables* into Latin. He was, for his time, an excellent classical scholar.

The translations from Vincent Bourne (1695–1747) are among the happiest, in both senses of the word, that Cowper ever made. Bourne's *Poemata Latine partim reddita, partim scripta*, was first published in 1734. Cowper knew and loved the man as the slovenly, dirty, and good-natured under-master of the fifth form at Westminster School.[1] He over-estimated the poet, as did Lamb, whose verse includes nine translations from Bourne. Cowper's are free translations which, consciously or otherwise, transmute Bourne's paganism into Christian sentiment. Three of the pieces given here are reprinted from *Poems*, 1782; 'The Snail' is from Johnson's edition, 1815.

Cowper's translations from Madame de la Motte Guyon are also free. His letter to Unwin of August 3, 1782,[2] describes how he came to translate thirty-seven of the poems

[1] This edition, pp. 617–18.
[2] This edition, pp. 663–6.

163

written during her imprisonment in the Bastille between 1695 and 1702. A letter written exactly a year later[1] gave Bull authority to do as he judged fit with the translations. In the preface to the little volume which he printed at Newport Pagnell in 1801, Bull warned readers that 'to infer that the peculiarities of Madam Guyon's theological sentiments were adopted either by Mr C. or by the Editor would be almost as absurd as to suppose the inimitable Translator of Homer to have been a pagan'. Bull's text has been used for the three pieces reproduced in this edition.

The translation from Horace is reproduced from John Johnson's edition of Cowper's 'posthumous poems', 1815, where it was first printed. Maurice Baring, a good judge of such things, singled it out 'as an instance of what seems to me a successful translation—successful in the sense that the reader would in reading the poem admire it in itself, whether he knew the original or not, and those who knew the original would not be unsatisfied'. (*Have You Anything to Declare?*, 1936, pp. 68–9.)

Although Milford, in his preface of 1905 to the Oxford Cowper, pronounced that 'the translation of Homer is dead', I hope that the three extracts reproduced here may suggest that it holds beauties to reward the diligent reader. The text is that of the first edition, 1791; the headings are mine.

[1] pp. 689–90.

TRANSLATIONS FROM THE LATIN OF VINCENT BOURNE

THE GLOW-WORM

Beneath the hedge, or near the stream,
  A worm is known to stray;
That shews by night a lucid beam,
  Which disappears by day.

Disputes have been and still prevail
  From whence his rays proceed;
Some give that honour to his tail,
  And others to his head.

But this is sure—the hand of might
  That kindles up the skies,
Gives *him* a modicum of light,
  Proportion'd to his size.

Perhaps indulgent nature meant
  By such a lamp bestow'd,
To bid the trav'ler, as he went,
  Be careful where he trod:

Nor crush a worm, whose useful light
  Might serve, however small,
To shew a stumbling stone by night,
  And save him from a fall.

Whate'er she meant, this truth divine
  Is legible and plain,
'Tis power almighty bids him shine,
  Nor bids him shine in vain.

Ye proud and wealthy, let this theme
  Teach humbler thoughts to you,
Since such a reptile has its gem,
  And boasts its splendour too.

THE JACKDAW

THERE is a bird who by his coat,
And by the hoarseness of his note,
  Might be suppos'd a crow;
A great frequenter of the church,
Where bishop-like he finds a perch,
  And dormitory too.

Above the steeple shines a plate,
That turns and turns, to indicate
  From what point blows the weather;
Look up—your brains begin to swim,
'Tis in the clouds—that pleases him,
  He chooses it the rather.

Fond of the speculative height,
Thither he wings his airy flight,
  And thence securely sees
The bustle and the raree-show
That occupy mankind below,
  Secure and at his ease.

You think no doubt he sits and muses
On future broken bones and bruises,
  If he should chance to fall;
No: not a single thought like that
Employs his philosophic pate,
  Or troubles it at all.

He sees that this great roundabout
The world, with all its motley rout,
  Church, army, physic, law,

Its customs and its businesses
Is no concern at all of his,
 And says, what says he? Caw.

Thrice happy bird! I too have seen
Much of the vanities of men,
 And sick of having seen 'em,
Would chearfully these limbs resign
For such a pair of wings as thine,
 And such a head between 'em.

THE CRICKET

LITTLE inmate, full of mirth,
Chirping on my kitchen hearth;
Wheresoe'er be thine abode,
Always harbinger of good,
Pay me for thy warm retreat,
With a song more soft and sweet;
In return thou shalt receive
Such a strain as I can give.

Thus thy praise shall be exprest,
Inoffensive, welcome guest!
While the rat is on the scout,
And the mouse with curious snout,
With what vermin else infest
Ev'ry dish and spoil the best;
Frisking thus before the fire,
Thou hast all thine heart's desire.

Though in voice and shape they be
Form'd as if akin to thee,
Thou surpassest, happier far,
Happiest grasshoppers that are,
Theirs is but a summer's song,
Thine endures the winter long,
Unimpair'd and shrill and clear,
Melody throughout the year.

Neither night nor dawn of day,
Puts a period to thy play,
Sing then— and extend thy span
Far beyond the date of man—
Wretched man, whose years are spent
In repining discontent;
Lives not, aged tho' he be,
Half a span compar'd with thee.

THE SNAIL

To grass, or leaf, or fruit, or wall,
The Snail sticks close, nor fears to fall,
As if he grew there, house and all
    Together.

Within that house secure he hides,
When danger imminent betides
Of storm, or other harm besides
    Of weather.

Give but his horns the slightest touch,
His self-collecting power is such,
He shrinks into his house, with much
    Displeasure.

Where'er he dwells, he dwells alone,
Except himself has chattels none,
Well satisfied to be his own
    Whole treasure.

Thus, hermit-like, his life he leads,
Nor partner of his banquet needs,
And if he meets one, only feeds
    The faster.

Who seeks him must be worse than blind,
(He and his house are so combin'd)
If, finding it, he fails to find
    Its master.

THREE TRANSLATIONS FROM THE FRENCH OF MADAME DE LA MOTTE GUYON

THE NATIVITY

Poème Héroïque.— Vol. 4, Cantique 4.

'Tis Folly all— let me no more be told
Of Parian porticos, and roofs of gold;
Delightful views of Nature dress'd by Art,
Enchant no longer this indiff'rent heart;
The Lord of all things, in his humble birth,
Makes mean the proud magnificence of Earth;
The straw, the manger, and the mould'ring wall,
Eclipse its lustre; and I scorn it all.
  Canals, and fountains, and delicious vales,
Green slopes, and plains whose plenty never fails;
Deep-rooted groves, whose heads sublimely rise,
Earth born, and yet ambitious of the skies;
Th' abundant foliage of whose gloomy shades
Vainly the sun in all its pow'r invades;
Where warbled airs of sprightly birds resound;
Whose verdure lives while winter scowls around;
Rocks, lofty mountains, caverns dark and deep,
And torrents raving down the rugged steep;
Smooth downs, whose fragrant herbs the spirits cheer;
Meads, crown'd with flow'rs; streams musical and clear,
Whose silver waters, and whose murmurs, join
Their artless charms, to make the scene divine;
The fruitful vineyard, and the furrow'd plain,
That seems a rolling sea of golden grain;
All, all have lost the charms they once possess'd;
An infant God reigns sov'reign in my breast;
From Bethl'em's bosom I no more will rove;
There dwells the Saviour, and there rests my love.

Ye mightier rivers, that with sounding force
Urge down the valleys your impetuous course!
Winds, clouds, and lightnings! and ye waves whose heads
Curl'd into monstrous forms, the seaman dreads!
Horrid abyss, where all experience fails,
Spread with the wreck of planks and shatter'd sails;
On whose broad back grim Death triumphant rides,
While havock floats on all thy swelling tides,
Thy shores a scene of ruin, strew'd around
With vessels bulged, and bodies of the drown'd!

Ye Fish, that sport beneath the boundless waves,
And rest, secure from man, in rocky caves;
Swift darting sharks, and whales of hideous size,
Whom all th' aquatic world with terror eyes!
Had I but Faith immoveable and true,
I might defy the fiercest storm, like you:
The world, a more disturb'd and boist'rous sea,
When Jesus shows a smile, affrights not me;
He hides me, and in vain the billows roar,
Break harmless at my feet, and leave the shore.

Thou azure vault, where, through the gloom of night,
Thick sown, we see such countless worlds of light!
Thou Moon, whose car, encompassing the skies,
Restores lost nature to our wondering eyes;
Again retiring when the brighter Sun
Begins the course he seems in haste to run!
Behold *him* where he shines! His rapid rays,
Themselves unmeasur'd, measure all our days;
Nothing impedes the race he would pursue,
Nothing escapes his penetrating view,
A thousand lands confess his quick'ning heat,
And all he cheers, are fruitful, fair, and sweet.

Far from enjoying what these scenes disclose,
I feel the thorn alas! but miss the rose;
Too well I know this aching heart requires
More solid good to fill its vast desires;
In vain they represent his matchless might
Who call'd them out of deep primaeval night;
Their form and beauty but augment my woe:

I seek the Giver of those charms they show;
Nor, him beside, throughout the world he made,
Lives there, in whom I trust for cure or aid.
   Infinite God, thou great unrivall'd One!
Whose glory makes a blot of yonder sun;
Compar'd with thine, how dim his beauty seems,
How quench'd the radiance of his golden beams!
Thou art my bliss, the light by which I move;
In thee alone dwells all that I can love;
All darkness flies when thou art pleas'd t' appear,
A sudden spring renews the fading year;
Where e'er I turn, I see thy power and grace,
The watchful guardians of our heedless race;
Thy various creatures in one strain agree,
All, in all times and places, speak of thee;
Ev'n I, with trembling heart and stammering tongue,
Attempt thy praise, and join the gen'ral song.
   Almighty Former of this wondrous plan,
Faintly reflected in thine image, Man,—
Holy and just,—the greatness of whose name
Fills and supports this universal frame,
Diffus'd throughout th' infinitude of space,
Who art thyself thine own vast dwelling-place;
Soul of our soul, whom yet no sense of ours
Discerns, eluding our most active pow'rs;
Encircling shades attend thine awful throne,
That veil thy face, and keep thee still unknown;
Unknown, though dwelling in our inmost part,
Lord of the thoughts, and Sov'reign of the heart!
   Repeat the charming truth that never tires,
No God is like the God my soul desires;
He at whose voice heav'n trembles, even He,
Great as he is, knows how to stoop to me;
Lo! there He lies,—that smiling Infant said,
'Heav'n, Earth, and Sea, exist!'—and they obey'd.
Ev'n He whose Being swells beyond the skies,
Is born of woman, lives, and mourns, and dies;
Eternal and Immortal, seems to cast
That glory from his brows, and breathes his last.

Trivial and vain the works that man has wrought,
How do they shrink and vanish at the thought!
    Sweet Solitude, and scene of my repose!
This rustic sight assuages all my woes—
That crib contains the Lord whom I adore;
And Earth's a shade, that I pursue no more.
He is my firm support, my rock, my tow'r,
I dwell secure beneath his shelt'ring pow'r,
And hold this mean retreat for ever dear,
For all I love, my soul's delight, is here.
I see th' Almighty swath'd in infant bands,
Tied helpless down, the Thunder-bearer's hands!
And in this shed that mystery discern
Which Faith and Love, and they alone, can learn.

    Ye tempests, spare the slumbers of your Lord!
Ye zephyrs, all your whisper'd sweets afford!
Confess the God that guides the rolling year;
Heav'n, do him homage; and thou Earth, revere!
Ye shepherds, Monarchs, Sages, hither bring
Your hearts an off'ring, and adore your King!
Pure be those hearts, and rich in Faith and Love;
Join in his phrase, th' harmonious worlds above;
To Bethl'em haste, rejoice in his repose,
And praise him there for all that he bestows!

    Man, busy Man, alas! can ill afford
T' obey the summons, and attend the Lord;
Perverted reason revels and runs wild,
By glitt'ring shows of pomp and wealth beguil'd;
And, blind to genuine excellence and grace,
Finds not her Author in so mean a place.
Ye unbelieving! learn a wiser part,
Distrust your erring sense, and search your heart;
There, soon ye shall perceive a kindling flame
Glow for that Infant God from whom it came;
Resist not, quench not that divine desire,
Melt all your adamant in heavenly fire!

    Not so will I requite thee, gentle Love!
Yielding and soft this heart shall ever prove;
And ev'ry heart beneath thy power should fall,

172

Glad to submit, could mine contain them all.
But I am poor, oblation I have none,
None for a Saviour, but Himself alone;
Whate'er I render thee, from thee it came;
And if I give my body to the flame,
My patience, love, and energy divine
Of heart and soul and spirit, all are thine.
Ah vain attempt, t' expunge the mighty score!
The more I pay, I owe thee still the more.

Upon my meanness, poverty, and guilt,
The trophy of thy glory shall be built;
My self-disdain shall be th' unshaken base,
And my deformity its fairest grace;
For destitute of Good and rich in Ill
Must be my state and my description still.

And do I grieve at such a humbling lot?
Nay, but I cherish and enjoy the thought.
Vain pageantry and pomp of Earth, adieu!
I have no wish, no memory for you;
The more I feel my mis'ry, I adore
The sacred Inmate of my soul the more;
Rich in his Love, I feel my noblest pride
Spring from the sense of having nought beside.

In thee I find wealth, comfort, virtue, might;
My wand'rings prove thy wisdom infinite;
All that I have, I give thee; and then see
All contrarieties unite in thee;
For thou hast join'd them, taking up our woe,
And pouring out thy bliss on worms below,
By filling with thy grace and love divine
A gulph of Evil in this heart of mine.
This is indeed to bid the valleys rise,
And the hills sink—'tis matching earth and skies!
I feel my weakness, thank thee, and deplore
An aching heart that throbs to thank thee more;
The more I love thee, I the more reprove
A soul so lifeless, and so slow to love;
Till, on a deluge of thy mercy toss'd,
I plunge into that sea, and there am lost.

LIVING WATER[1]

Vol. 4, Cantique 81

THE fountain in its source,
  No drought of summer fears;
The farther it pursues its course,
  The nobler it appears.

But shallow cisterns yield
  A scanty, short supply;
The morning sees them amply fill'd,
  The ev'ning finds them dry.

JOY IN MARTYRDOM

Vol. 3, Cantique 94

SWEET tenants of this grove!
  Who sing, without design,
A song of artless love,
  In unison with mine;
These echoing shades return
  Full many a note of ours,
That wise ones cannot learn,
  With all their boasted pow'rs.

Oh thou! whose sacred charms
  These hearts so seldom love,
Although thy beauty warms
  And blesses all above;
How slow are human things
  To choose their happiest lot!
All-glorious King of Kings,
  Say, why we love thee not?

[1] John, iv, 10–14.

This heart that cannot rest
　　Shall thine forever prove;
Though bleeding and distress'd,
　　Yet joyful in thy Love:
'Tis happy, though it breaks
　　Beneath thy chast'ning hand;
And speechless, yet it speaks
　　What thou canst understand.

A TRANSLATION FROM THE LATIN OF HORACE

Odes, Book 1, xxxviii[1]

Boy, I hate their empty shows,
　　Persian garlands I detest,
Bring not me the late-blown rose
　　Ling'ring after all the rest:

Plainer myrtle pleases me
　　Thus out-stretch'd beneath my vine,
Myrtle more becoming thee,
　　Waiting with thy master's wine.

[1] The original is given for comparison:

> Persicos odi, puer, apparatus;
> Displicent nexae philyra coronae;
> Mitte sectari, rosa quo locorum
> 　　Sera moretur.
>
> Simplici myrto nihil allabores
> Sedulus curae: neque te ministrum
> Dedecet myrtus, neque me sub arcta
> 　　Vite bibentem.

TRANSLATIONS
FROM THE GREEK OF HOMER

THE TROJAN ARMY ENCAMPED

Iliad, VIII, 640–55.

Big with great purposes and proud, they sat,
Not disarray'd, but in fair form disposed
Of even ranks, and watched their num'rous fires.
As when around the clear bright moon, the stars
Shine in full splendour, and the winds are hush'd,
The groves, the mountain-tops, the headland-heights
Stand all apparent, not a vapour streaks
The boundless blue, but aether open'd wide
All glitters, and the shepherd's heart is cheer'd;
So num'rous seem'd those fires the bank between
Of Xanthus, blazing, and the fleet of Greece,
In prospect all of Troy; a thousand fires,
Each watch'd by fifty warriors seated near.
The steeds beside the chariots stood, their corn
Chewing, and waiting 'till the golden-thron'd
Aurora should restore the light of day.

TELEMACHUS SETS SAIL
FROM ITHACA

Odyssey, II, 533-53.

Then, led by Pallas, went the prince on board,
Where down they sat, the Goddess in the stern,
And at her side Telemachus. The crew
Cast loose the hawsers, and, embarking, fill'd
The benches. Blue-eyed Pallas from the West

176

Call'd forth propitious breezes; fresh they curled
The sable Deep, and, sounding, swept the waves.
He, loud-exhorting them, his people bade
Hand, brisk, the tackle; they, obedient, reared
The pine-tree mast, which in its socket deep
They lodg'd, then strain'd the cordage, and with thongs
Well-twisted, drew the shining sail aloft.
A land-breeze fill'd the canvas, and the flood
Roar'd as she went against the steady bark
That ran with even course her liquid way.
The rigging, thus, of all the galley set,
Their beakers crowning high with wine, they hail'd
The ever-living Gods, but above all
Minerva, daughter azure-eyed of Jove.
Thus all night long the galley, and till dawn
Had brighten'd into day, cleaved swift the flood.

ULYSSES KILLS THE FIRST
OF THE SUITORS

Odyssey, XXII, 89–98.

...Thus saying, he drew his brazen faulchion[1] keen
Of double edge, and with a dreadful cry
Sprang on him; but Ulysses with a shaft
In that same moment through his bosom driv'n
Transfix'd his liver, and down dropp'd his sword.
He, staggering around his table, fell
Convolv'd in agonies, and overturn'd
Both food and wine; his forehead smote the floor;
Woe fill'd his heart, and spurning with his heels
His vacant seat, he shook it 'till he died.

---

[1] Sword.

THE LONGER
POEMS
OF 1782

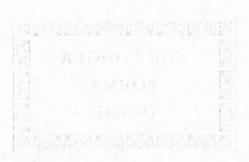

THE EIGHT LONG POEMS which formed the bulk of Cowper's first volume were written between December 1780 and October 1781, when the war against the American colonists was pursuing its catastrophic course and when public opinion was shocked by scandals in the government of India. They were written as a series, and have been termed for convenience the 'Satires', or, since they do not conform to the general conception of satire, the 'Moral Satires'. But Cowper did not apply this or any other description to them. Although he wrote in the couplets that Dryden and Pope had used, he did not imitate their manner or their matter. Satire of the Juvenalian kind was not his bent, and he knew it; he was writing partly *pour se faire la main*, but mainly (as he told Newton) 'in hopes to do good' by criticizing the manners of society in his own way. Newton believed that literature should be the handmaiden of religion; and Cowper's first essay in satire, *Anti-Thelyphthora*, was his response to the pressure exerted on him to write a rebuttal of Martin Madan's theological arguments in favour of re-introducing polygamy.[1] Newton arranged for it to be published anonymously, to avoid unnecessary pain to Cowper's Madan relatives, and told him on December 8th, 1780, that '*Anti-Thelyphthora*, tho' not quite *ad captum plebis*, will please persons of taste like yourself.'[2] Thus encouraged, Cowper answered on the 21st: 'You have bestowed some commendations on a poem now in the press...it will not be long, perhaps, before you will receive a poem called *The Progress of Error*. That will be succeeded by another, in due time, called *Truth*.' The final outcome was a series of eight Calvinist sermons written in easily-flowing verse.

[1] See C.'s letters of February 27 and July 12, 1780.
[2] BM. L. Egerton MSS. 3662.

Table Talk, in so far as it has a subject, is a tract on the necessity of righteousness in public men, clergymen and poets. The title of *The Progress of Error* explains itself; it was the first of the series to be written. *Truth* preaches justification by faith as against justification by works. *Expostulation* compares the history of the English with that of the Jews, and admonishes the nation to remember the fate of heedless Israel. *Hope* sounds a recall to what Cowper regarded as true religion, and *Charity* concerns itself with Christian love. The last two poems, *Conversation* and *Retirement*, the most attractive and competently written of the series, are in a much lighter and livelier vein. They were written in the first flush of Cowper's friendship with the vivacious Lady Austen, who now for a time succeeded Newton as his sounding-board. She had musical talent, interest in literature, and the gift of enthusiasm; and by her influence probably helped Cowper to move on from writing didactic verse, in which he seldom excelled, to the lyrical and descriptive poetry where his true and original genius lay.

The text of all the poems is that of the first edition, 1782.

TABLE TALK

Si te forte meæ gravis uret sarcina chartæ,
Abjicito.[1]—Horace, *Epistles*, I, xiii.

A. You told me, I remember, glory built
On selfish principles, is shame and guilt.
The deeds that men admire as half divine,
Stark naught, because corrupt in their design.
Strange doctrine this! that without scruple tears
The laurel that the very light'ning spares,
Brings down the warrior's trophy to the dust,[2]
And eats into his bloody sword like rust.
　B. I grant, that men continuing what they are,
Fierce, avaricious, proud, there must be war.
And never meant the rule should be applied
To him that fights with justice on his side.
　Let laurels, drench'd in pure Parnassian[3] dews,
Reward his mem'ry, dear to ev'ry muse,
Who, with a courage of unshaken root,
In honour's field advancing his firm foot,
Plants it upon the line that justice draws,
And will prevail or perish in her cause.
'Tis to the virtues of such men, man owes
His portion in the good that heav'n bestows,
And when recording history displays
Feats of renown, though wrought in antient days,
Tells of a few stout hearts that fought and dy'd
Where duty plac'd them, at their country's side,
The man that is not mov'd with what he reads,
That takes not fire at their heroic deeds,
Unworthy of the blessings of the brave,
Is base in kind, and born to be a slave.

---

[1] 'If it be that the heavy burden of my writings chafes you, cast it away.'

[2] The Romans believed laurel to be a protection against lightning.

[3] One of the twin summits of Mount Parnassus was sacred to Apollo and the Muses: it was held that whoever slept on it became either an inspired poet or a madman.

But let eternal infamy pursue
The wretch to nought but his ambition true,
Who, for the sake of filling with one blast
The post horns of all Europe, lays her waste.
Think yourself station'd on a tow'ring rock,
To see a people scatter'd like a flock,
Some royal mastiff panting at their heels,
With all the savage thirst a tyger feels,
Then view him self-proclaim'd in a gazette,
Chief monster that has plagu'd the nations yet,
The globe and sceptre in such hands misplac'd,
Those ensigns of dominion, how disgrac'd!
The glass that bids man mark the fleeting hour,
And death's own scythe, would better speak his pow'r,
Then grace the boney phantom in their stead
With the king's shoulder knot and gay cockade,
Cloath the twin brethren in each other's dress,
The same their occupation and success.
    A. 'Tis your belief the world was made for man,
Kings do but reason on the self-same plan,
Maintaining your's, you cannot their's condemn,
Who think, or seem to think, man made for them.
    B. Seldom, alas! the power of logic reigns
With much sufficiency in royal brains.
Such reas'ning falls like an inverted cone,
Wanting its proper base to stand upon.
Man made for kings! those optics are but dim
That tell you so—say rather, they for him.
That were indeed a king-enobling thought,
Could they, or would they, reason as they ought.
The diadem with mighty projects lin'd,
To catch renown by ruining mankind,
Is worth, with all its gold and glitt'ring store,
Just what the toy will sell for and no more.
   Oh! bright occasions of dispensing good,
How seldom used, how little understood!
To pour in virtue's lap her just reward,
Keep vice restrain'd behind a double guard,
To quell the faction that affronts the throne,

184

By silent magnanimity alone;
To nurse with tender care the thriving arts,
Watch every beam philosophy imparts;
To give religion her unbridl'd scope,
Nor judge by statute[1] a believer's hope;
With close fidelity and love unfeign'd,
To keep the matrimonial bond unstain'd;
Covetous only of a virtuous praise,
His life a lesson to the land he sways;
To touch the sword with conscientious awe,
Nor draw it but when duty bids him draw,
To sheath it in the peace-restoring close
With joy, beyond what victory bestows,
Blest country! where these kingly glories shine,
Blest England! if this happiness be thine.

    A. Guard what you say, the patriotic tribe[2]
Will sneer and charge you with a bribe.—*B.* A bribe?
The worth of his three kingdoms I defy,
To lure me to the baseness of a lie.
And of all lies (be that one poet's boast)
The lie that flatters I abhor the most.
Those arts be their's that hate his gentle reign,
But he that loves him has no need to feign.

    A. Your smooth eulogium to one crown address'd,
Seems to imply a censure on the rest.

    B. Quevedo,[3] as he tells his sober tale,
Ask'd, when in hell, to see the royal jail,
Approv'd their method in all other things,
But where, good Sir, do you confine your kings?
There—said his guide, the group is full in view.
Indeed?—replied the Don—there are but few.
His black interpreter the charge disdain'd—
Few, fellow? There are all that ever reign'd.

---

[1] Probably a reference to the Test Act. See n., p. 249.

[2] *the patriotic tribe:* the party opposed to the political influence of King George III, who is the subject of the foregoing lines.

[3] Francisco Gómez de Quevedo y Villegas (1580–1645). 'The tale does not occur in Quevedo.' (Mrs Russell).

Wit undistinguishing is apt to strike
The guilty and not guilty, both alike.
I grant the sarcasm is too severe,
And we can readily refute it here,
While Alfred's name, the father of his age,
And the Sixth Edward's grace th' historic page.

   A. Kings then at last have but the lot of all,
By their own conduct they must stand or fall.

   B. True. While they live, the courtly laureat pays
His quit-rent ode, his pepper-corn of praise,[1]
And many a dunce whose fingers itch to write,
Adds, as he can, his tributary mite;
A subject's faults, a subject may proclaim,
A monarch's errors are forbidden game.
Thus free from censure, overaw'd by fear,
And prais'd for virtues that they scorn to wear,
The fleeting forms of majesty engage
Respect, while stalking o'er life's narrow stage,
Then leave their crimes for history to scan,
And ask with busy scorn, Was this the man?

   I pity kings whom worship waits upon
Obsequious, from the cradle to the throne,
Before whose infant eyes the flatt'rer bows,
And binds a wreath about their baby brows.
Whom education stiffens into state,
And death awakens from that dream too late.
Oh! if servility with supple knees,
Whose trade it is to smile, to crouch, to please;
If smooth dissimulation, skill'd to grace
A devil's purpose with an angel's face;
If smiling peeresses and simp'ring peers,
Incompassing his throne a few short years;
If the gilt carriage and the pamper'd steed,
That wants no driving and disdains the lead;
If guards, mechanically form'd in ranks,
Playing, at beat of drum, their martial pranks;
Should'ring and standing as if struck to stone,

---

[1] *Quit-rent...peppercorn*: nominal rents.

While condescending majesty looks on;
If monarchy consist in such base things,
Sighing, I say again, I pity kings!
  To be suspected, thwarted, and withstood,
E'en when he labours for his country's good,
To see a band call'd patriot for no cause,
But that they catch at popular applause,
Careless of all th' anxiety he feels,
Hook disappointment on the public wheels,
With all their flippant fluency of tongue,
Most confident, when palpably most wrong,
If this be kingly, then farewell for me
All kingship, and may I be poor and free.
  To be the Table Talk of clubs up stairs,
To which th' unwash'd artificer[1] repairs,
T' indulge his genius after long fatigue,
By diving into cabinet intrigue,
(For what kings deem a toil, as well they may,
To him is relaxation and mere play)
To win no praise when well wrought plans prevail,
But to be rudely censur'd when they fail,
To doubt the love his fav'rites may pretend,
And in reality to find no friend,
If he indulge a cultivated taste,
His gall'ries with the works of art well grac'd,
To hear it call'd extravagance and waste,
If these attendants, and if such as these,
Must follow royalty, then welcome ease;
However humble and confin'd the sphere,
Happy the state that has not these to fear.
  A. Thus men whose thoughts contemplative have dwelt,
On situations that they never felt,
Start up sagacious, cover'd with the dust
Of dreaming study and pedantic rust,
And prate and preach about what others prove,
As if the world and they were hand and glove.

---

[1] Cf. Shakespeare, *King John*, IV, ii, 201: 'another lean unwash'd artificer.'

Leave kingly backs to cope with kingly cares,
They have their weight to carry, subjects their's;
Poets, of all men, ever least regret
Increasing taxes and the nation's debt.
Could you contrive the payment, and rehearse
The mighty plan, oracular, in verse,
No bard, howe'er majestic, old or new,
Should claim my fixt attention more than you.

B. Not Brindley[1] nor Bridgewater[2] would essay
To turn the course of Helicon that way;
Nor would the nine[3] consent, the sacred tide
Should purl amidst the traffic of Cheapside,
Or tinkle in 'Change Alley, to amuse
The leathern ears of stock-jobbers and jews.

A. Vouchsafe, at least, to pitch the key of rhime
To themes more pertinent, if less sublime.
When ministers and ministerial arts,
Patriots who love good places at their hearts,
When admirals extoll'd for standing still,
Or doing nothing with a deal of skill;
Gen'rals who will not conquer when they may,
Firm friends to peace, to pleasure, and good pay,
When freedom wounded almost to despair,
Though discontent alone can find out where,
When themes like these employ the poet's tongue,
I hear as mute as if a syren sung.
Or tell me if you can, what pow'r maintains
A Briton's scorn of arbitrary chains?
That were a theme might animate the dead,
And move the lips of poets cast in lead.

B. The cause, though worth the search, may yet elude
Conjecture and remark, however shrewd.
They take, perhaps, a well-directed aim.
Who seek it in his climate and his frame.

---

[1] James Brindley (1716–72), the engineer of the Manchester Ship Canal and of many others.

[2] The 3rd Duke of Bridgewater (1736–1803), the originator of British inland navigation, Brindley's first patron.

[3] The Nine Muses, to whom Mount Helicon and its springs were sacred.

Lib'ral in all things else, yet nature here
With stern severity deals out the year.
Winter invades the spring, and often pours
A chilling flood on summer's drooping flow'rs,
Unwelcome vapors quench autumnal beams,
Ungenial blasts attending, curl the streams,
The peasants urge their harvest, plie the fork,
With double toil, and shiver at their work,
Thus with a rigor, for his good design'd,
She rears her fav'rite man of all mankind.
His form robust and of elastic tone,
Proportion'd well, half muscle and half bone,
Supplies with warm activity and force
A mind well lodg'd, and masculine of course.
Hence liberty, sweet liberty inspires,
And keeps alive his fierce but noble fires.
Patient of constitutional controul,
He bears it with meek manliness of soul;
But, if authority grow wanton, woe
To him that treads upon his free-born toe,
One step beyond the bound'ry of the laws
Fires him at once in freedom's glorious cause.
Thus proud prerogative, not much rever'd,
Is seldom felt, though sometimes seen and heard;
And in his cage, like parrot fine and gay,
Is kept to strut, look big, and talk away.
    Born in a climate softer far than our's,
Not form'd like us, with such Herculean pow'rs,
The Frenchman, easy, debonair, and brisk,
Give him his lass, his fiddle and his frisk,
Is always happy, reign whoever may,
And laughs the sense of mis'ry far away.
He drinks his simple bev'rage with a gust,
And feasting on an onion and a crust,
We never feel th' alacrity and joy
With which he shouts and carols, *Vive le Roy*,
Fill'd with as much true merriment and glee,
As if he heard his king say—Slave be free.
    Thus happiness depends, as nature shews.

Less on exterior things than most suppose.
Vigilant over all that he has made,
Kind Providence attends with gracious aid,
Bids equity throughout his works prevail,
And weighs the nations in an even scale;
He can encourage slav'ry to a smile,
And fill with discontent a British isle.
    A. Freeman and slave then, if the case be such,
Stand on a level, and you prove too much.
If all men indiscriminately share
His fost'ring pow'r and tutelary care,
As well be yok'd by despotism's hand,
As dwell at large in Britain's charter'd land.
    B. No. Freedom has a thousand charms to show,
That slaves, howe'er contented, never know.
The mind attains beneath her happy reign,
The growth that nature meant she should attain.
The varied fields of science, ever new,
Op'ning and wider op'ning on her view,
She ventures onward with a prosp'rous force,
While no base fear impedes her in her course.
Religion, richest favour of the skies,
Stands most reveal'd before the freeman's eyes;
No shades of superstition blot the day,
Liberty chaces all that gloom away;
The soul, emancipated, unoppress'd,
Free to prove all things and hold fast the best,[1]
Learns much, and to a thousand list'ning minds,
Communicates with joy the good she finds.
Courage, in arms, and ever prompt to show
His manly forehead to the fiercest foe;
Glorious in war, but for the sake of peace,
His spirits rising as his toils increase,
Guards well what arts and industry have won,
And freedom claims him for her first-born son.
Slaves fight for what were better cast away—
The chain that binds them, and a tyrant's sway,

[1] 1 Thessalonians, v, 21.

But they that fight for freedom, undertake
The noblest cause mankind can have at stake,
Religion, virtue, truth, whate'er we call
A blessing, freedom is the pledge of all.
Oh liberty! the pris'ner's pleasing dream,
The poet's muse, his passion and his theme,
Genius is thine, and thou art fancy's nurse,
Lost without thee th' ennobling pow'rs of verse,
Heroic song from thy free touch acquires
Its clearest tone, the rapture it inspires;
Place me where winter breathes his keenest air,
And I will sing if liberty be there;
And I will sing at liberty's dear feet,
In Afric's torrid clime or India's fiercest heat.

 A. Sing where you please, in such a cause I grant
An English poet's privilege to rant,
But is not freedom, at least is not our's
Too apt to play the wanton with her pow'rs,
Grow freakish, and o'erleaping ev'ry mound,
Spread anarchy and terror all around?

 B. Agreed. But would you sell or slay your horse
For bounding and curvetting in his course;
Or if, when ridden with a careless rein,
He break away, and seek the distant plain?
No. His high mettle under good controul,
Gives him Olympic speed, and shoots him to the goal.

 Let discipline employ her wholesome arts,
Let magistrates[1] alert perform their parts,
Not skulk or put on a prudential mask,
As if their duty were a desp'rate task;
Let active laws apply the needful curb
To guard the peace that riot would disturb,
And liberty preserv'd from wild excess,
Shall raise no feuds for armies to suppress.
When tumult lately burst his prison door,
And set plebeian thousands in a roar,

[1] The weakness of the magistrates during the Gordon Riots of 1780 (the subject of this paragraph) angered public opinion. See letters, pp. 587–8, 592.

When he usurp'd authority's just place,
And dar'd to look his master in the face;
When the rude rabble's watch-word was destroy,
And blazing London seem'd a second Troy,
Liberty blush'd and hung her drooping head,
Beheld their progress with the deepest dread,
Blush'd, that effects like these she should produce,
Worse than the deeds of galley-slaves broke loose.
She loses in such storms her very name,
And fierce licentiousness should bear the blame.

Incomparable gem! thy worth untold,
Cheap, though blood-bought; and thrown away when sold;
May no foes ravish thee, and no false friend
Betray thee, while professing to defend;
Prize it ye ministers, ye monarchs spare,
Ye patriots guard it with a miser's care.

A. Patriots, alas! the few that have been found
Where most they flourish, upon English ground,
The country's need have scantily supplied,
And the last left the scene, when Chatham died.

B. Not so—the virtue still adorns our age,
Though the chief actor died upon the stage.[1]
In him, Demosthenes was heard again,
Liberty taught him her Athenian strain;
She cloath'd him with authority and awe,
Spoke from his lips, and in his looks, gave law.
His speech, his form, his action, full of grace,
And all his country beaming in his face,
He stood, as some inimitable hand
Would strive to make a Paul or Tully stand.
No sycophant or slave that dar'd oppose
Her sacred cause, but trembled when he rose;
And ev'ry venal stickler for the yoke,
Felt himself crush'd at the first word he spoke.

Such men are rais'd to station and command,

[1] Chatham was seized with an apoplectic fit in the Lords' debate on the proposal to surrender the American Colonies, April 7, 1778. He died on May 11, but popular opinion, confirmed by poets and painters, identified the seizure with his death.

When providence means mercy to a land.
He speaks, and they appear; to him they owe
Skill to direct, and strength to strike the blow,
To manage with address, to seize with pow'r
The crisis of a dark decisive hour.
So Gideon earn'd a vict'ry not his own,[1]
Subserviency[2] his praise, and that alone.
   Poor England! thou art a devoted deer,
Beset with ev'ry ill but that of fear.
The nations[3] hunt; all mark thee for a prey,
They swarm around thee, and thou stand'st at bay.
Undaunted still, though wearied and perplex'd,
Once Chatham sav'd thee, but who saves thee next?
Alas! the tide of pleasure sweeps along
All that should be the boast of British song.
'Tis not the wreath that once adorn'd thy brow,
The prize of happier times will serve thee now.
Our ancestry, a gallant christian race,
Patterns of ev'ry virtue, ev'ry grace,
Confess'd a God, they kneel'd before they fought,
And prais'd him in the victories he wrought.
Now from the dust of ancient days bring forth
Their sober zeal, integrity and worth;
Courage, ungrac'd by these, affronts the skies,
Is but the fire without the sacrifice.
The stream that feeds the well-spring of the heart
Not more invigorates life's noblest part,
Than virtue quickens with a warmth divine,
The pow'rs that sin has brought to a decline.
   _A._ Th' inestimable estimate of Brown[4]
Rose like a paper-kite, and charm'd the town;
But measures plann'd and executed well,
Shifted the wind that rais'd it, and it fell.

[1] The victory over the Midianites: Judges, vii.

[2] _Subserviency_: obedient service.

[3] See p. 610, n. 1.

[4] The Rev. John Brown's _Estimate of the Principles and Manners of the Times_, 1758, had national decadence as its theme. 1759 was a year of victories: see p. 651, n. 2.

He trod the very self-same ground you tread,
And victory refuted all he said.
   B. And yet his judgment was not fram'd amiss,
Its error, if it err'd, was merely this—
He thought the dying hour already come,
And a complete recov'ry struck him dumb.
   But that effeminacy, folly, lust,
Enervate and enfeeble, and needs must,
And that a nation shamefully debas'd,
Will be despis'd and trampled on at last,
Unless sweet penitence her pow'rs renew,
Is truth, if history itself be true.
There is a time, and justice marks the date,
For long-bearing clemency to wait;
That hour elaps'd, th' incurable revolt
Is punish'd and down comes the thunder-bolt.
If mercy *then* put by the threat'ning blow,
Must she perform the same kind office *now*?
May she! and, if offended heav'n be still
Accessible and pray'r prevail, she will.
'Tis not however insolence and noise,
The tempest of tumultuary joys,
Nor is it yet despondence and dismay,
Will win her visits, or engage her stay;
Pray'r only, and the penitential tear,
Can call her smiling down, and fix her here.
   But, when a country (one that I could name)
In prostitution sinks the sense of shame;
When infamous venality, grown bold,
Writes on his bosom, *to be let or sold*;
When perjury, that heav'n defying vice,
Sells oaths by tale, and at the lowest price,
Stamps God's own name upon a lie just made,
To turn a penny in the way of trade;
When av'rice starves, and never hides his face,
Two or three millions of the human race,
And not a tongue enquires, how, where, or when,
Though conscience will have twinges now and then;
When profanation of the sacred cause

In all its parts, times, ministry, and laws,
Bespeaks a land once christian, fall'n and lost
In all that wars against that title most;
What follows next let cities of great name,
And regions long since desolate proclaim.
Nineveh, Babylon, and ancient Rome,
Speak to the present times and times to come;
They cry aloud, in ev'ry careless ear,
Stop, while ye may, suspend your mad career;
O learn from our example and our fate,
Learn wisdom and repentance ere too late.
   Not only vice disposes and prepares
The mind that slumbers sweetly in her snares,
To stoop to tyranny's usurp'd command,
And bend her polish'd neck beneath his hand,
(A dire effect, by one of nature's laws
Unchangeably connected with its cause)
But providence himself will intervene
To throw his dark displeasure o'er the scene.
All are his instruments; each form of war,
What burns at home, or threatens from afar,
Nature in arms, her elements at strife,
The storms that overset the joys of life,
Are but his rods to scourge a guilty land,
And waste it at the bidding of his hand.
He gives the word, and mutiny soon roars
In all her gates, and shakes her distant shores;
The standards of all nations are unfurl'd,
She has one foe, and that one foe, the world.
And if he doom that people with a frown,
And mark them with the seal of wrath, press'd down,
Obduracy takes place; callous and tough
The reprobated race grows judgment proof:
Earth shakes beneath them, and heav'n roars above,
But nothing scares them from the course they love;
To the lascivious pipe and wanton song
That charm down fear, they frolic it along,
With mad rapidity and unconcern,
Down to the gulph from which is no return.

They trust in navies, and their navies fail,
God's curse can cast away ten thousand sail;
They trust in armies, and their courage dies,
In wisdom, wealth, in fortune, and in lies;
But all they trust in, withers, as it must,
When he commands, in whom they place no trust.
Vengeance at last pours down upon their coast,[1]
A long despis'd, but now victorious host;
Tyranny sends the chain that must abridge
The noble sweep of all their privilege,
Gives liberty the last, the mortal shock,
Slips the slave's collar on, and snaps the lock.

    A. Such lofty strains embellish what you teach,
Mean you to prophesy, or but to preach?

    B. I know the mind that feels indeed the fire
The muse imparts, and can command the lyre,
Acts with a force, and kindles with a zeal,
Whate'er the theme, that others never feel.
If human woes her soft attention claim,
A tender sympathy pervades the frame,
She pours a sensibility divine
Along the nerve of ev'ry feeling line.
But if a deed not tamely to be borne
Fire indignation and a sense of scorn,
The strings are swept with such a pow'r, so loud,
The storm of music shakes th' astonish'd crowd.
So when remote futurity is brought
Before the keen enquiry of her thought,
A terrible sagacity informs
The poet's heart, he looks to distant storms,
He hears the thunder ere the tempest low'rs,
And arm'd with strength surpassing human pow'rs,
Seizes events as yet unknown to man,
And darts his soul into the dawning plan.
Hence, in a Roman mouth, the graceful name
Of prophet and of poet was the same,[2]
Hence British poets too the priesthood shar'd,

[1] See p. 425, n. 2.
[2] *vates.*

And ev'ry hallow'd druid was a bard.
But no prophetic fires to me belong,
I play with syllables, and sport in song.
   A. At Westminster, where little poets strive
To set a distich upon six and five,[1]
Where discipline helps op'ning buds of sense,
And makes his pupils proud with silver pence,[2]
I was a poet too—but modern taste
Is so refin'd and delicate and chaste,
That verse, whatever fire the fancy warms,
Without a creamy smoothness has no charms.
Thus, all success depending on an ear,
And thinking I might purchase it too dear,
If sentiment were sacrific'd to sound,
And truth cut short to make a period round,
I judg'd a man of sense could scarce do worse,
Than caper in the morris-dance of verse.
   B. Thus reputation is a spur to wit,
And some wits flag through fear of losing it.
Give me the line, that plows its stately course
Like a proud swan, conq'ring the stream by force,
That like some cottage beauty strikes the heart,
Quite unindebted to the tricks of art.
When labour and when dullness, club in hand,
Like the two figures at St. Dunstan's[3] stand,
Beating alternately, in measur'd time,
The clockwork tintinabulum of rime,
Exact and regular the sounds will be,
But such mere quarter-strokes are not for me.
   From him who rears a poem lank and long,
To him who strains his all into a song,
Perhaps some bonny Caledonian air,
All birks and braes, though he was never there;
Or having whelp'd a prologue with great pains,
Feels himself spent, and fumbles for his brains;

[1] Hexameters and pentameters.

[2] School prizes.

[3] The clock of St Dunstan-in-the-West, Fleet Street, London.

A prologue interdash'd with many a stroke,
An art contriv'd to advertise a joke,
So that the jest is clearly to be seen,
Not in the words—but in the gap between.
Manner is all in all, whate'er is writ,
The substitute for genius, sense, and wit.

 To dally much with subjects mean and low,
Proves that the mind is weak, or makes it so.
Neglected talents rust into decay,
And ev'ry effort ends in push-pin[1] play,
The man that means success, should soar above
A soldier's feather, or a lady's glove,
Else, summoning the muse to such a theme,
The fruit of all her labour is whipt-cream.
As if an eagle flew aloft, and then—
Stoop'd from his highest pitch to pounce[2] a wren.
As if the poet purposing to wed,
Should carve himself a wife in gingerbread.

 Ages elaps'd ere Homer's lamp appear'd,
And ages ere the Mantuan swan was heard:
To carry nature lengths unknown before,
To give a Milton birth, ask'd ages more.[3]
Thus genius rose and set at order'd times,
And shot a day-spring into distant climes,
Ennobling ev'ry region that he chose;
He sunk in Greece, in Italy he rose,
And tedious years of Gothic darkness pass'd,
Emerg'd all splendor in our isle at last.
Thus lovely Halcyons dive into the main,

---

[1] A child's game.

[2] To seize with the talons.

[3] These lines allude to Dryden's epigram on Milton, which was published under his portrait in the folio edition of 1688:

> 'Three poets, in three distant ages born,
> Greece, Italy and England did adorn.
> The first in loftiness of thought surpass'd,
> The next in majesty, in both the last:
> The force of nature could no farther go:
> To make a third she join'd the other two.'

Then show far off their shining plumes again.

   A. Is genius only found in epic lays?
Prove this, and forfeit all pretence to praise.
Make their heroic pow'rs your own at once,
Or candidly confess yourself a dunce.

   B. These were the chief, each interval of night
Was grac'd with many an undulating light;
In less illustrious bards his beauty shone
A meteor or a star, in these, the sun.

   The nightingale may claim the topmost bough,
While the poor grasshopper must chirp below.
Like him unnotic'd, I, and such as I,
Spread little wings, and rather skip than fly,
Perch'd on the meagre produce of the land,
An ell or two of prospect we command,
But never peep beyond the thorny bound,
Or oaken fence, that hems the paddoc round.

   In Eden ere yet innocence of heart
Had faded, poetry was not an art;
Language above all teaching, or if taught,
Only by gratitude and glowing thought,
Elegant as simplicity, and warm
As exstasy, unmanacled by form,
Not prompted as in our degen'rate days,
By low ambition and the thirst of praise,
Was natural as is the flowing stream,
And yet magnificent, a God the theme.
That theme on earth exhausted, though above
'Tis found as everlasting as his love,
Man lavish'd all his thoughts on human things,
The feats of heroes and the wrath of kings,
But still while virtue kindled his delight,
The song was moral, and so far was right.
'Twas thus till luxury seduc'd the mind,
To joys less innocent, as less refin'd;
Then genius danc'd a bacchanal; he crown'd
The brimming goblet, seiz'd the thyrsus, bound
His brows with ivy, rush'd into the field
Of wild imagination, and there reel'd,

The victim of his own lascivious fires,
And dizzy with delight, profan'd the sacred wires.
Anacreon, Horace, play'd in Greece and Rome
This Bedlam[1] part; and, others nearer home.
When Cromwell fought for pow'r, and while he reign'd
The proud protector of the pow'r he gain'd,
Religion, harsh, intolerant, austere,
Parent of manners like herself severe,
Drew a rough copy of the Christian face
Without the smile, the sweetness, or the grace;
The dark and sullen humour of the time
Judg'd ev'ry effort of the muse a crime;
Verse in the finest mould of fancy cast,
Was lumber in an age so void of taste;
But when the second Charles assum'd the sway,
And arts reviv'd beneath a softer day,
Then like a bow long forc'd into a curve,
The mind, releas'd from too constrain'd a nerve,
Flew to its first position with a spring
That made the vaulted roofs of pleasure ring.
His court, the dissolute and hateful school
Of wantonness, where vice was taught by rule,
Swarm'd with a scribbling herd as deep inlaid
With brutal lust as ever Circe[2] made.
From these a long succession, in the rage
Of rank obscenity debauch'd their age,
Nor ceas'd, 'till ever anxious to redress
Th' abuses of her sacred charge, the press,
The muse instructed a well nurtur'd train
Of abler votaries to cleanse the stain,
And claim the palm for purity of song,
That lewdness had usurp'd and worn so long.
Then decent pleasantry and sterling sense,
That neither gave nor would endure offence,
Whipp'd out of sight with satyr just and keen,
The puppy pack that had defil'd the scene.

[1] See n., p. 371.

[2] In the *Odyssey*, the enchantress Circe transformed the companions of Ulysses into pigs.

In front of these came Addison. In him
Humour in holiday and sightly trim,
Sublimity and Attic taste combin'd
To polish, furnish, and delight the mind:
Then Pope, as harmony itself exact,
In verse well disciplin'd, complete, compact,
Gave virtue and morality a grace
That quite eclipsing pleasure's painted face,
Levied a tax of wonder and applause,
Ev'n on the fools that trampled on their laws.
But he (his musical finesse was such,
So nice his ear, so delicate his touch)
Made poetry a mere mechanic art,
And ev'ry warbler has his tune by heart.
Nature imparting her satyric gift,
Her serious mirth, to Arbuthnot and Swift,
With droll sobriety they rais'd a smile
At Folly's cost, themselves unmov'd the while.
That constellation set, the world in vain
Must hope to look upon their like again.

    A. Are we then left—*B.* Not wholly in the dark,
Wit now and then, struck smartly, shows a spark,
Sufficient to redeem the modern race
From total night and absolute disgrace.
While servile trick and imitative knack
Confine the million in the beaten track,
Perhaps some courser who disdains the road,
Snuffs up the wind and flings himself abroad.

    Contemporaries all surpass'd, see one,
Short his career, indeed, but ably run,
Churchill;[1] himself unconscious of his pow'rs,
In penury consum'd his idle hours,
And like a scatter'd seed at random sown,
Was left to spring by vigor of his own.
Lifted at length by dignity of thought,
And dint of genius to an affluent lot,

---

[1] The satirical poet, Charles Churchill (1731–64), friend of Cowper's youth.

He laid his head in luxury's soft lap,
And took too often there his easy nap.
If brighter beams than all he threw not forth,
'Twas negligence in him, not want of worth.
Surly and slovenly and bold and coarse,
Too proud for art, and trusting in mere force,
Spendthrift alike of money and of wit,
Always at speed and never drawing bit,
He struck the lyre in such a careless mood,
And so disdain'd the rules he understood.
The laurel seem'd to wait on his command,
He snatch'd it rudely from the muses' hand.

    Nature exerting an unwearied pow'r,
Forms, opens, and gives scent to ev'ry flow'r,
Spreads the fresh verdure of the field, and leads
The dancing Naiads through the dewy meads;
She fills profuse ten thousand little throats
With music, modulating all their notes,
And charms the woodland scenes, and wilds unknown,
With artless airs and concerts of her own;
But seldom (as if fearful of expence)
Vouchsafes to man a poet's just pretence:
Fervency, freedom, fluency of thought,
Harmony, strength, words exquisitely sought;
Fancy that from the bow that spans the sky,
Brings colours dipt in heav'n that never die;
A soul exalted above earth, a mind
Skill'd in the characters that form mankind;
And as the sun in rising beauty dress'd,
Looks to the westward from the dappled east,
And marks, whatever clouds may interpose,
Ere yet his race begins, its glorious close;
An eye like his to catch the distant goal,
Or ere the wheels of verse begin to roll,
Like his to shed illuminating rays
On ev'ry scene and subject it surveys:
Thus grac'd the man asserts a poet's name,
And the world chearfully admits the claim.

    Pity! Religion has so seldom found

A skilful guide into poetic ground,
The flow'rs would spring where'er she deign'd to stray,
And ev'ry muse attend her in her way.
Virtue indeed meets many a rhiming friend,
And many a compliment politely penn'd;
But unattir'd in that becoming vest
Religion weaves for her, and half undress'd,
Stands in the desart shiv'ring and forlorn,
A wintry figure, like a wither'd thorn.
The shelves are full, all other themes are sped,
Hackney'd and worn to the last flimsy thread,
Satyr has long since done his best, and curst
And loathsome ribaldry has done his worst;
Fancy has sported all her pow'rs away
In tales, in trifles, and in children's play;
And 'tis the sad complaint, and almost true,
Whate'er we write, we bring forth nothing new.
'Twere new indeed to see a bard all fire,
Touch'd with a coal from heav'n, assume the lyre,[1]
And tell the world, still kindling as he sung,
With more than mortal music on his tongue,
That he who died below, and reigns above,
Inspires the song, and that his name is love.
    For after all, if merely to beguile
By flowing numbers and a flow'ry style,
The tædium that the lazy rich endure,
Which now and then sweet poetry may cure,
Or if to see the name of idol self,
Stamp'd on the well-bound quarto, grace the shelf,
To float a bubble on the breath of fame,
Prompt his endeavour, and engage his aim,
Debas'd to servile purposes of pride,
How are the pow'rs of genius misapplied?
The gift whose office is the giver's praise,
To trace him in his word, his works, his ways,
Then spread the rich discov'ry, and invite
Mankind to share in the divine delight;

[1] Cf. Isaiah, vi, 6, 7.

Distorted from its use and just design,
To make the pitiful possessor shine;
To purchase at the fool-frequented fair
Of vanity, a wreath for self to wear,
Is profanation of the basest kind,
Proof of a trifling and a worthless mind.

    A. Hail Sternhold[1] then and Hopkins[1] hail!—*B*. Amen.
If flatt'ry, folly, lust employ the pen,
If acrimony, slander, and abuse,
Give it a charge to blacken and traduce;
Though Butler's wit, Pope's numbers, Prior's ease,
With all that fancy can invent to please,
Adorn the polish'd periods as they fall,
One Madrigal of their's is worth them all.

    A. 'Twould thin the ranks of the poetic tribe,
To dash the pen through all that you proscribe.

    B. No matter—we could shift when they were not,
And should no doubt if they were all forgot.

THE PROGRESS OF ERROR

Si quid loquar audiendum.[2]—
Horace, *Odes*, IV, ii

SING muse (if such a theme, so dark, so long,
May find a muse to grace it with a song)
By what unseen and unsuspected arts,
The serpent error twines round human hearts;
Tell where she lurks, beneath what flow'ry shades,
That not a glimpse of genuine light pervades;
The pois'nous, black, insinuating worm,
Successfully conceals her loathsome form.

    [1] *The Whole Booke of Psalmes*, translated into English verse by Thomas Sternhold, John Hopkins and others, 1562. Added to the Book of Common Prayer, it was used in churches well into C.'s day. See pp. 144 and 382.

    [2] 'If I utter anything worth listening to.'

Take, if ye can, ye careless and supine!
Counsel and caution from a voice like mine;
Truths that the theorist could never reach,
And observation taught me, I would teach.
 Not all whose eloquence the fancy fills,
Musical as the chime of tinkling rills,
Weak to perform, though mighty to pretend,
Can trace her mazy windings to their end;
Discern the fraud beneath the specious lure,
Prevent the danger, or prescribe the cure.
The clear harangue, and cold as it is clear,
Falls soporific on the listless ear;
Like quicksilver, the rhet'ric they display,
Shines as it runs, but grasp'd at, slips away.
 Plac'd for his trial on this bustling stage,
From thoughtless youth to ruminating age,
Free in his will to chuse or to refuse,
Man may improve the crisis, or abuse;
Else, on the fatalist's unrighteous plan,
Say, to what bar amenable were man?
With nought in charge, he could betray no trust,
And if he fell, would fall because he must;
If love reward him, or if vengeance strike,
His recompence in both, unjust alike.
Divine authority within his breast
Brings every thought, word, action, to the test,
Warns him or prompts, approves him or restrains,
As reason, or as passion, takes the reins.
Heav'n from above, and conscience from within,
Cry in his startled ear, abstain from sin!
The world around solicits his desire,
And kindles in his soul a treach'rous fire,
While all his purposes and steps to guard,
Peace follows virtue as its sure reward;
And pleasure brings as surely in her train
Remorse and sorrow and vindictive pain.
 Man thus endued with an elective voice,
Must be supplied with objects of his choice.
Where'er he turns, enjoyment and delight,

Or present, or in prospect, meet his sight;
These open on the spot their honey'd store,
Those call him loudly to pursuit of more.
His unexhausted mine, the sordid vice
Avarice shows, and virtue is the price.
Here, various motives his ambition raise,
Pow'r, pomp, and splendor, and the thirst of praise;
There beauty woos him with expanded arms,
E'en Bacchanalian madness has its charms.

  Nor these alone, whose pleasures less refin'd
Might well alarm the most unguarded mind,
Seek to supplant his unexperienc'd youth,
Or lead him devious from the path of truth;
Hourly allurements on his passions press,
Safe in themselves, but dang'rous in th' excess.

  Hark! how it floats upon the dewy air,
O what a dying, dying close was there!
'Tis harmony from yon sequester'd bow'r,
Sweet harmony that sooths the midnight hour;
Long ere the charioteer of day had run
His morning course, the enchantment was begun,
And he shall gild yon mountain's height again,
Ere yet the pleasing toil becomes a pain.

  Is this the rugged path, the steep ascent,
That virtue points to? Can a life thus spent
Lead to the bliss she promises the wise,
Detach the soul from earth, and speed her to the skies?
Ye devotees to your ador'd employ,
Enthusiasts, drunk with an unreal joy,
Love makes the music of the blest above,
Heav'n's harmony is universal love;
And earthly sounds, though sweet and well combin'd,
And lenient as soft opiates to the mind,
Leave vice and folly unsubdu'd behind.

  Grey dawn appears, the sportsman and his train
Speckle the bosom of the distant plain,
'Tis he, the Nimrod of the neighb'ring lairs,
Save that his scent is less acute than their's;
For persevering chace, and headlong leaps,

True beagle as the staunchest hound he keeps.
Charg'd with the folly of his life's mad scene,
He takes offence, and wonders what you mean;
The joy, the danger and the toil o'erpays,
'Tis exercise, and health and length of days;
Again impetuous to the field he flies,
Leaps ev'ry fence but one, there falls and dies;
Like a slain deer, the tumbrel brings him home,
Unmiss'd but by his dogs and by his groom.
 Ye clergy, while your orbit is your place,
Lights of the world, and stars of human race;
But if eccentric ye forsake your sphere,
Prodigious, ominous, and view'd with fear;
The comet's[1] baneful influence is a dream,
Your's real and pernicious in th' extreme.
What then—are appetites and lusts laid down,
With the same ease the man puts on his gown?
Will av'rice and concupiscence give place,
Charm'd by the sounds, your rev'rence, or your grace?
No. But his own engagement binds him fast,
Or if it does not, brands him to the last
What atheists call him, a designing knave,
A mere church juggler, hypocrite, and slave.
Oh laugh, or mourn with me, the rueful jest,
A cassock'd huntsman, and a fiddling priest;
He from Italian songsters takes his cue,
Set Paul to music, he shall quote him too.
He takes the field, the master of the pack
Cries, well done Saint— and claps him on the back.
Is this the path of sanctity? Is this
To stand a way-mark in the road to bliss?
Himself a wand'rer from the narrow way,
His silly sheep, what wonder if they stray?
Go, cast your orders at your bishop's feet,
Send your dishonour'd gown to Monmouth-Street,[2]
The sacred function, in your hands is made,

---

[1] Comets were once believed to portend catastrophe.

[2] Monmouth Street was then occupied by dealers in second-hand clothes.

Sad sacrilege! no function but a trade.
  Occiduus is a pastor of renown,
When he has pray'd and preach'd the sabbath down,
With wire and catgut he concludes the day,
Quav'ring and semiquav'ring care away.
The full concerto swells upon your ear;
All elbows shake. Look in, and you would swear
The Babylonian tyrant[1] with a nod
Had summon'd them to serve his golden God.
So well that thought th' employment seems to suit,
Psalt'ry and sackbut, dulcimer, and flute.
Oh fie! 'tis evangelical and pure,
Observe each face, how sober and demure,
Extacy sets her stamp on ev'ry mien,
Chins fall'n, and not an eye-ball to be seen.
Still I insist, though music heretofore
Has charm'd me much, not ev'n Occiduus more,
Love, joy, and peace, make harmony more meet
For sabbath ev'nings, and perhaps as sweet.
  Will not the sickliest sheep of every flock
Resort to this example as a rock,
There stand and justify the foul abuse
Of sabbath hours, with plausible excuse?
If apostolic gravity be free
To play the fool on Sundays, why not we?
If he, the tinkling harpsichord regards
As inoffensive, what offence in cards?
Strike up the fiddles, let us all be gay,
Laymen have leave to dance, if parsons play.
  Oh Italy!—thy sabbaths will be soon
Our sabbaths, clos'd with mumm'ry and buffoon.
Preaching and pranks will share the motley scene,
Our's parcell'd out, as thine have ever been,
God's worship and the mountebank between.
What says the prophet? Let that day be blest
With holiness and consecrated rest.[2]

---

[1] Nebuchadnezzar: Daniel, iii, 1–5.
[2] Isaiah, lvi, 2: lviii, 13, 14.

Pastime and bus'ness both it should exclude,
And bar the door the moment they intrude;
Nobly distinguish'd above all the six,
By deeds in which the world must never mix.
Hear him again. He calls it a delight,
A day of luxury, observ'd aright,
When the glad soul is made heav'n's welcome guest,
Sits banquetting, and God provides the feast.
But triflers are engag'd and cannot come;
Their answer to the call is—*Not at home*.
   Oh the dear pleasures of the velvet plain,
The painted tablets, dealt and dealt again.
Cards with what rapture, and the polish'd die,
The yawning chasm of indolence supply!
Then to the dance, and make the sober moon
Witness the joys that shun the sight of noon.
Blame, cynic, if you can, quadrille or ball,
The snug close party, or the splendid hall,
Where night down-stooping from her ebon throne,
Views constellations brighter than her own.
'Tis innocent, and harmless, and refin'd,
The balm of care, elysium of the mind.
Innocent! Oh if venerable time
Slain at the foot of pleasure, be no crime,
Then with his silver beard and magic wand,
Let Comus[1] rise Archbishop of the land,
Let him your rubric and your feasts prescribe,
Grand metropolitan of all the tribe.
Of manners rough, and coarse athletic cast,
The rank debauch suits Clodio's filthy taste.
Rufillus, exquisitely form'd by rule,
Not of the moral, but the dancing school,
Wonders at Clodio's follies, in a tone
As tragical, as others at his own.
He cannot drink five bottles, bilk the score,
Then kill a constable, and drink five more;
But he can draw a pattern, make a tart,

---

[1] The spirit of revelry.

And has the ladies etiquette[1] by heart.
Go, fool, and arm in arm with Clodio, plead
Your cause before a bar you little dread;
But know, the law that bids the drunkard die,
Is far too just to pass the trifler by.
Both baby-featur'd and of infant size,
View'd from a distance, and with heedless eyes,
Folly and innocence are so alike,
The diff'rence, though essential, fails to strike.
Yet folly ever has a vacant stare,
A simp'ring count'nance, and a trifling air;
But innocence, sedate, serene, erect,
Delights us, by engaging our respect.

   Man, nature's guest by invitation sweet,
Receives from her both appetite and treat,
But if he play the glutton and exceed,
His benefactress blushes at the deed.
For nature, nice, as lib'ral to dispense,
Made nothing but a brute the slave of sense.
Daniel[2] ate pulse by choice, example rare!
Heav'n bless'd the youth, and made him fresh and fair.
Gorgonius sits abdominous and wan,
Like a fat squab upon a Chinese fan:
He snuffs far off th' anticipated joy,
Turtle and ven'son all his thoughts employ,
Prepares for meals, as jockeys take a sweat,
Oh nauseous!—an emetic for a whet—
Will providence o'erlook the wasted good?
Temperance were no virtue if he could.

   That pleasures, therefore, or what such we call,
Are hurtful, is a truth confess'd by all.
And some, that seem to threaten virtue less,
Still hurtful, in th' abuse, or by th' excess.

   Is man then only for his torment plac'd
The centre of delights he may not taste?
Like fabled Tantalus condemn'd to hear
The precious stream still purling in his ear,

   [1] Probably the title of a book.
   [2] Daniel, i, 11–16.

Lip-deep in what he longs for, and yet curst
With prohibition and perpetual thirst?[1]
No, wrangler—destitute of shame and sense,
The precept, that injoins him abstinence,
Forbids him none but the licentious joy,
Whose fruit, though fair, tempts only to destroy.
Remorse, the fatal egg by pleasure laid
In every bosom where her nest is made,
Hatch'd by the beams of truth denies him rest,
And proves a raging scorpion in his breast.
No pleasure? Are domestic comforts dead?
Are all the nameless sweets of friendship fled?
Has time worn out, or fashion put to shame
Good sense, good health, good conscience, and good fame?
All these belong to virtue, and all prove
That virtue has a title to your love.
Have you no touch of pity, that the poor
Stand starv'd at your inhospitable door?
Or if yourself too scantily supplied,
Need help, let honest industry provide.
Earn, if you want; if you abound, impart,
These both are pleasures to the feeling heart.
No pleasure? Has some sickly eastern waste
Sent us a wind to parch us at a blast?
Can British paradise no scenes afford
To please her sated and indiff'rent lord?
Are sweet philosophy's enjoyments run
Quite to the lees? And has religion none?
Brutes capable should tell you 'tis a lie,
And judge you from the kennel and the stye.
Delights like these, ye sensual and profane,
Ye are bid, begg'd, besought to entertain;
Call'd to these crystal streams, do ye turn off,
Obscene, to swill and swallow at a trough?
Envy the beast then, on whom heav'n bestows
Your pleasures, with no curses in the close.

[1] *Odyssey*, Bk. 11.

Pleasure admitted in undue degree,
Enslaves the will, nor leaves the judgment free.
'Tis not alone the grape's enticing juice
Unnerves the moral pow'rs, and mars their use;
Ambition, av'rice, and the lust of fame,
And woman, lovely woman, does the same.
The heart, surrender'd to the ruling pow'r
Of some ungovern'd passion ev'ry hour,
Finds, by degrees, the truths that once bore sway,
And all their deep impression, wear away.
So coin grows smooth, in traffic current pass'd,
Till Cæsar's image is effac'd at last.

The breach, though small at first, soon op'ning wide,
In rushes folly with a full-moon tide.
Then welcome errors of whatever size,
To justify it by a thousand lies.
As creeping ivy clings to wood or stone,
And hides the ruin that it feeds upon,
So sophistry cleaves close to, and protects,
Sin's rotten trunk, concealing its defects.
Mortals whose pleasures are their only care,
First wish to be impos'd on, and then are.
And lest the fulsome artifice should fail,
Themselves will hide its coarseness with a veil.
Not more industrious are the just and true
To give to virtue what is virtue's due,
The praise of wisdom, comeliness, and worth,
And call her charms to public notice forth,
Than vice's mean and disingenuous race
To hide the shocking features of her face.
Her form with dress and lotion they repair,
Then kiss their idol and pronounce her fair.

The sacred implement I now employ
Might prove a mischief or at best a toy;
A trifle if it move but to amuse,
But if to wrong the judgment and abuse,
Worse than a poignard in the basest hand,
It stabs at once the morals of a land.

Ye writers of what none with safety reads,
Footing it in the dance that fancy leads.
Ye novellists who mar what ye would mend,
Sniv'ling and driv'ling folly without end,
Whose corresponding misses fill the ream
With sentimental frippery and dream,
Caught in a delicate soft silken net
By some lewd Earl, or rakehell Baronet:
Ye pimps, who, under virtue's fair pretence,
Steal to the closet of young innocence,
And teach her, unexperienc'd yet and green,
To scribble as you scribble at fifteen;
Who kindling a combustion of desire,
With some cold moral think to quench the fire,
Though all your engineering proves in vain,
The dribbling stream ne'er puts it out again.
Oh that a verse had pow'r, and could command
Far, far away, these flesh-flies of the land,
Who fasten without mercy on the fair,
And suck, and leave a craving maggot there.
Howe'er disguis'd th' inflammatory tale,
And covered with a fine-spun specious veil,
Such writers and such readers owe the gust
And relish of their pleasure all to lust.
   But the muse, eagle-pinion'd, has in view
A quarry more important still than you;
Down down the wind she swims and sails away,
Now stoops upon it and now grasps the prey.
   Petronius![1] all the muses weep for thee,
But ev'ry tear shall scald thy memory.
The graces too, while virtue at their shrine
Lay bleeding under that soft hand of thine,
Felt each a mortal stab in her own breast,
Abhorr'd the sacrifice,[2] and curs'd the priest.

[1] *Petronius*: The 4th Earl of Chesterfield, whose *Letters to his Son*, 1774, are referred to in the lines that follow. The Roman poet Petronius was known as the *arbiter elegantiae*.

[2] *abhorr'd the sacrifice*: Chesterfield, *op. cit.*, letter of March 9, 1748, 'Sacrifice to the Graces'.

Thou polish'd and high-finish'd foe to truth,
Gray-beard corrupter of our list'ning youth,
To purge and skim away the filth of vice,
That so refin'd it might the more entice,
Then pour it on the morals of thy son
To taint *his* heart, was worthy of *thine own*.
Now while the poison all high life pervades,
Write if thou canst, one letter from the shades,
One, and one only, charg'd with deep regret,
That thy worst part, thy principles live yet;
One sad epistle thence, may cure mankind,
Of the plague spread by bundles left behind.

'Tis granted, and no plainer truth appears,
Our most important are our earliest years;
The mind impressible and soft, with ease
Imbibes and copies what she hears and sees,
And through life's labyrinth holds fast the clue
That education gives her, false or true.
Plants rais'd with tenderness are seldom strong,
Man's coltish disposition asks the thong,
And without discipline the fav'rite child,
Like a neglected forester[1] runs wild.
But we, as if good qualities would grow
Spontaneous, take but little pains to sow;
We give some latin and a smatch of greek,
Teach him to fence and figure twice a week,
And having done, we think, the best we can,
Praise his proficiency and dub him man.

From school to Cam or Isis, and thence home,
And thence with all convenient speed to Rome,
With rev'rend tutor clad in habit lay,
To teaze for cash, and quarrel with all day;
With memorandum-book for ev'ry town,
And ev'ry post, and where the chaise broke down;
His stock, a few French phrases got by heart,
With much to learn, but nothing to impart,
The youth, obedient to his sire's commands,

---

[1] *Forester*: a New Forest pony (Mrs Russell's note).

Sets off a wand'rer into foreign lands:
Surpriz'd at all they meet, the gosling pair
With awkward gait, stretch'd neck, and silly stare,
Discover huge cathedrals built with stone,
And steeples tow'ring high much like our own;
But show peculiar light by many a grin
At Popish practices observ'd within.
    Ere long, some bowing, smirking, smart Abbé
Remarks two loit'rers that have lost their way,
And being always prim'd with *politesse*
For men of their appearance and address,
With much compassion undertakes the task,
To tell them more than they have wit to ask;
Points to inscriptions wheresoe'er they tread,
Such as when legible were never read,
But being canker'd now, and half worn out,
Craze antiquarian brains with endless doubt:
Some headless hero, or some Cæsar shows —
Defective only in his Roman nose;
Exhibits elevations, drawings, plans,
Models of Herculanean pots and pans,
And sells them medals, which, if neither rare
Nor ancient, will be so, preserv'd with care.
    Strange the recital! from whatever cause
His great improvement and new lights he draws,
The squire, once bashful, is shame-fac'd no more,
But teems with powers he never felt before:
Whether increas'd momentum, and the force
With which from clime to clime he sped his course,
As axles sometimes kindle as they go,
Chaf'd him and brought dull nature to a glow;
Or whether clearer skies and softer air,
That make Italian flow'rs so sweet and fair,
Fresh'ning his lazy spirits as he ran,
Unfolded genially and spread the man;
Returning he proclaims by many a grace,
By shrugs and strange contortions of his face,
How much a dunce that has been sent to roam,
Excels a dunce that has been kept at home.

Accomplishments have taken virtue's place,
And wisdom falls before exterior grace;
We slight the precious kernel of the stone,
And toil to polish its rough coat alone.
A just deportment, manners grac'd with ease,
Elegant phrase, and figure form'd to please,
Are qualities that seem to comprehend
Whatever parents, guardians, schools, intend;
Hence an unfurnish'd and a listless mind,
Though busy, trifling; empty, though refin'd;
Hence all that interferes, and dares to clash
With indolence and luxury, is trash;
While learning, once the man's exclusive pride,
Seems verging fast towards the female side.

Learning itself, receiv'd into a mind
By nature weak, or viciously inclin'd,
Serves but to lead philosophers astray,
Where children would with ease discern the way.
And of all arts sagacious dupes invent,
To cheat themselves and gain the world's assent,
The worst is scripture warp'd from its intent.

The carriage bowls along and all are pleas'd
If Tom be sober, and the wheels well greas'd,
But if the rogue have gone a cup too far,
Left out his linch-pin, or forgot his tar,[1]
It suffers interruption and delay,
And meets with hindrance in the smoothest way.
When some hypothesis absurd and vain
Has fill'd with all its fumes a critic's brain,
The text that sorts not with his darling whim,
Though plain to others, is obscure to him.
The will made subject to a lawless force,
All is irregular, and out of course;
And judgment drunk, and brib'd to lose his way,
Winks hard, and talks of darkness at noon day.

A critic on the sacred book should be
Candid and learn'd, dispassionate and free;

[1] *tar*: the material with which wheels were greased.

Free from the wayward bias bigots feel,
From fancy's influence, and intemp'rate zeal:
But above all, (or let the wretch refrain,
Nor touch the page he cannot but profane)
Free from the domineering pow'r of lust;
A lewd interpreter is never just.
    How shall I speak thee, or thy pow'r address,
Thou God of our idolatry,[1] the press?
By thee, religion, liberty and laws
Exert their influence, and advance their cause;
By thee, worse plagues than Pharaoh's land befel,
Diffus'd, make earth the vestibule of hell:
Thou fountain, at which drink the good and wise,
Thou ever-bubbling spring of endless lies,
Like Eden's dread probationary tree,
Knowledge of good and evil is from thee.
    No wild enthusiast ever yet could rest,
Till half mankind were like himself possess'd.
Philosophers, who darken and put out
Eternal truth by everlasting doubt,
Church quacks, with passions under no command,
Who fill the world with doctrines contraband,
Discov'rers of they know not what, confin'd
Within no bounds the blind that lead the blind,
To streams of popular opinion drawn,
Deposit in those shallows all their spawn.
The wriggling fry soon fill the creeks around,
Pois'ning the waters where their swarms abound;
Scorn'd by the nobler tenants of the flood,
Minnows and gudgeons gorge th' unwholesome food.
The propagated myriads spread so fast,
E'en Leuwenhoek[2] himself would stand aghast,

---

[1] *Romeo and Juliet*, II, i, 113:

> 'Or, if thou wilt, swear by thy gracious self,
> Which is the god of my idolatry.'

[2] Anthony van Leeuwenhoek (1632–1723). J. C. Bailey has suggested that 'Cowper is probably alluding to his accounts of the infinite number and infinitesimally small size of the spermatic animalcules, which he claimed to have discovered'.

Employ'd to calculate th' enormous sum,
And own his crab-computing pow'rs o'ercome.
Is this Hyperbole? The world well known,
Your sober thoughts will hardly find it one.
  Fresh confidence the speculatist takes
From ev'ry hair-brain'd proselyte he makes,
And therefore prints, himself but half deceiv'd,
Till others have the soothing tale believ'd.
Hence comment after comment, spun as fine
As bloated spiders draw the flimsy line.
Hence the same word that bids our lusts obey,
Is misapplied to sanctify their sway.
If stubborn Greek refuse to be his friend,
Hebrew or Syriac shall be forc'd to bend;
If languages and copies all cry, No—
Somebody prov'd it centuries ago.
Like trout pursued, the critic in despair
Darts to the mud and finds his safety there.
Women, whom custom has forbid to fly
The scholar's pitch (the scholar best knows why)
With all the simpler and unletter'd poor,
Admire his learning, and almost adore.
Whoever errs, the priest can ne'er be wrong,
With such fine words familiar to his tongue.
  Ye ladies! (for, indiff'rent in your cause,
I should deserve to forfeit all applause)
Whatever shocks, or gives the least offence
To virtue, delicacy, truth, or sense,
(Try the criterion, 'tis a faithful guide)
Nor has, nor can have scripture on its side.[1]
  None but an author knows an author's cares,
Or fancy's fondness for the child she bears.
Committed once into the public arms,
The baby seems to smile with added charms.
Like something precious ventur'd far from shore,
'Tis valued for the danger's sake the more.

[1] The passage may be a comment on the Rev. Martin Madan's
Thelyphthora. See n., p. 581.

He views it with complacency supreme,
Solicits kind attention to his dream,
And daily more enamour'd of the cheat,
Kneels, and asks heav'n to bless the dear deceit.
So one, whose story serves at least to show
Men lov'd their own productions long ago,
Woo'd an unfeeling statue for his wife,
Nor rested till the Gods had given it life.[1]
If some mere driv'ler suck the sugar'd fib,
One that still needs his leading string and bib,
And praise his genius, he is soon repaid
In praise applied to the same part, his head.
For 'tis a rule that holds for ever true,
Grant me discernment, and I grant it you.

Patient of contradiction as a child,
Affable, humble, diffident and mild,
Such was Sir Isaac, and such Boyle and Locke,
Your blund'rer is as sturdy as a rock.
The creature is so sure to kick and bite,
A muleteer's the man to set him right.
First appetite enlists him truth's sworn foe,
Then obstinate self-will confirms him so.

Tell him he wanders, that his error leads
To fatal ills, that though the path he treads
Be flow'ry, and he see no cause of fear,
Death and the pains of hell attend him there;
In vain; the slave of arrogance and pride,
He has no hearing on the prudent side.
His still refuted quirks he still repeats,
New rais'd objections with new quibbles meets,
'Till sinking in the quicksand he defends,
He dies disputed, and the contest ends;
But not the mischiefs: they still left behind,
Like thistle-seeds, are sown by ev'ry wind.

Thus men go wrong with an ingenious skill,
Bend the straight rule to their own crooked will,

[1] Pygmalion, who fell in love with his statue, Galatea, and married her after Venus had given it life.

And with a clear and shining lamp supplied,
First put it out, then take it for a guide.
Halting on crutches of unequal size,
One leg by truth supported, one by lies,
They sidle to the goal with awkward pace,
Secure of nothing, but to lose the race.

   Faults in the life breed errors in the brain,
And these, reciprocally, those again.
The mind and conduct mutually imprint
And stamp their image in each other's mint;
Each sire and dam of an infernal race
Begetting and conceiving all that's base.

   None sends his arrow to the mark in view,
Whose hand is feeble, or his aim untrue.
For though e'er yet the shaft is on the wing,
Or when it first forsakes th' elastic string,
It err but little from th' intended line,
It falls at last, far wide of his design,
So he that seeks a mansion in the sky,
Must watch his purpose with a stedfast eye,
That prize belongs to none but the sincere,
The least obliquity is fatal here.

   With caution taste the sweet Circæan cup,
He that sips often, at last drinks it up.
Habits are soon assum'd, but when we strive
To strip them off, 'tis being flay'd alive.
Call'd to the temple of impure delight,
He that abstains, and he alone, does right.
If a wish wander that way, call it home,
He cannot long be safe, whose wishes roam.
But, if you pass the threshold, you are caught,
Die then, if pow'r Almighty save you not:
There hard'ning by degrees, 'till double steel'd,
Take leave of nature's God, and God reveal'd,
Then laugh at all you trembled at before,
And, joining the free-thinkers' brutal roar,
Swallow the two grand nostrums they dispense,
That scripture lies, and blasphemy is sense:
If clemency revolted by abuse

Be damnable, then, damn'd without excuse.
　　Some dream that they can silence when they will
The storm of passion, and say, *Peace, be still*;[1]
But '*Thus far and no farther*,'[2] when address'd
To the wild wave, or wilder human breast,
Implies authority that never can,
That never ought to be the lot of man.
　　But muse forbear, long flights forebode a fall,
Strike on the deep-ton'd chord the sum of all.
　　Hear the just law—the judgment of the skies!
He that hates truth shall be the dupe of lies.
And he that *will* be cheated to the last,
Delusions, strong as hell, shall bind him fast.[3]
But if the wand'rer his mistake discern,
Judge his own ways, and sigh for a return,
Bewilder'd once, must he bewail his loss
For ever and for ever? No—the cross.
There, and there only (though the deist rave,
And atheist, if earth bear so base a slave)
There, and there only, is the pow'r to save.
There no delusive hope invites despair,
No mock'ry meets you, no deception there.
The spells and charms, that blinded you before,
All vanish there, and fascinate no more.
　　I am no preacher, let this hint suffice,
The cross once seen, is death to ev'ry vice:
Else he that hung there, suffer'd all his pain,
Bled, groan'd, and agoniz'd, and died in vain.

[1] Mark, iv, 39.
[2] Job, xxxviii, 11.
[3] 2 Thessalonians, ii, 11.

TRUTH

Pensantur trutina.[1]—
Horace, *Epistles*, II, i

MAN on the dubious waves of error toss'd,
His ship half founder'd, and his compass lost,
Sees far as human optics may command,
A sleeping fog, and fancies it dry land:
Spreads all his canvass, ev'ry sinew plies,
Pants for't, aims at it, enters it, and dies.
Then farewell all self-satisfying schemes,
His well-built systems, philosophic dreams,
Deceitful views of future bliss, farewell!
He reads his sentence at the flames of hell.

Hard lot of man! to toil for the reward
Of virtue, and yet lose it—wherefore hard?
He that would win the race must guide his horse
Obedient to the customs of the course,
Else, though unequall'd to the goal he flies,
A meaner than himself shall gain the prize.
Grace leads the right way, if you chuse the wrong,
Take it and perish, but restrain your tongue;
Charge not, with light sufficient and left free,
Your wilful suicide on God's decree.

Oh how unlike the complex works of man,
Heav'n's easy, artless, unincumber'd plan!
No meretricious graces to beguile,
No clust'ring ornaments to clog the pile,
From ostentation as from weakness free,
It stands like the cærulean arch we see,
Majestic in its own simplicity.
Inscrib'd above the portal, from afar
Conspicuous as the brightness of a star,

[1] 'They are weighed in the balance.'

Legible only by the light they give,
Stand the soul-quick'ning words—BELIEVE, AND LIVE.[1]
Too many, shock'd at what should charm them most,
Despise the plain direction and are lost.
Heav'n on such terms! they cry with proud disdain,
Incredible, impossible, and vain—
Rebel because 'tis easy to obey,
And scorn, for its own sake, the gracious way.
These are the sober, in whose cooler brains
Some thought of immortality remains;
The rest too busy, or too gay, to wait
On the sad theme, their everlasting state,
Sport for a day and perish in a night,
The foam upon the waters not so light.
　　Who judg'd the Pharisee? What odious cause
Expos'd him to the vengeance of the laws?
Had he seduc'd a virgin, wrong'd a friend,
Or stabb'd a man to serve some private end?
Was blasphemy his sin? Or did he stray
From the strict duties of the sacred day?
Sit long and late at the carousing board?
(Such were the sins with which he charg'd his Lord)[2]
No—the man's morals were exact, what then?
'Twas his ambition to be seen of men;[3]
His virtues were his pride; and that one vice
Made all his virtues gewgaws of no price;
He wore them as fine trappings for a show,
A praying, synagogue frequenting beau.
　　The self-applauding bird, the peacock see—
Mark what a sumptuous Pharisee is he!
Meridian sun-beams tempt him to unfold
His radiant glories, azure, green, and gold;
He treads as if some solemn music near,
His measur'd step were govern'd by his ear,

[1] 'And this is the will of Him that sent me, that every one that seeth the Son, and believeth on Him, may have everlasting life; and I will raise him up at the last day.' (John, vi, 40).

[2] Mark, ii, 15–28.

[3] Matthew, vi, 5.

And seems to say, ye meaner fowl, give place,
I am all splendor, dignity, and grace.
   Not so the pheasant on his charms presumes,
Though he too has a glory in his plumes.
He, christian like, retreats with modest mien
To the close copse or far sequester'd green,
And shines without desiring to be seen.
The plea of works, as arrogant and vain,
Heav'n turns from with abhorrence and disdain:
Not more affronted by avow'd neglect,
Than by the mere dissembler's feign'd respect.
What is all righteousness that men devise,
What, but a sordid bargain for the skies?
But Christ as soon would abdicate his own,
As stoop from heav'n to sell the proud a throne.
   His dwelling a recess in some rude rock,
Book, beads, and maple-dish[1] his meagre stock,
In shirt of hair and weeds of canvass dress'd,
Girt with a bell-rope that the Pope has bless'd,
Adust with stripes told out for ev'ry crime,
And sore tormented long before his time,
His pray'r preferr'd to saints that cannot aid,
His praise postpon'd, and never to be paid,
See the sage hermit, by mankind admir'd,
With all that bigotry adopts, inspir'd,
Wearing out life in his religious whim,
'Till his religious whimsy wears out him.
His works, his abstinence, his zeal allow'd,
You think him humble, God accounts him proud;
High in demand, though lowly in pretence,
Of all his conduct, this the genuine sense—
My penitential stripes, my streaming blood
Have purchas'd heav'n, and prove my title good.
   Turn eastward now, and fancy shall apply
To your weak sight here telescopic eye.
The Bramin kindles on his own bare head

[1] Milton, *Comus*, 389–90:

> 'For who would rob a Hermit of his Weeds,
> His few Books, or his Beads, or Maple Dish...?'

The sacred fire, self-torturing his trade;
His voluntary pains, severe and long,
Would give a barb'rous air to British song;
Nor grand inquisitor could worse invent,
Than he contrive to suffer, well content.
   Which is the saintlier worthy of the two?
Past all dispute, yon anchorite say you.
Your sentence and mine differ. What's a name?
I say the Bramin has the fairer claim.
If suff'rings scripture nowhere recommends,
Devis'd by self to answer selfish ends,
Give saintship, than all Europe must agree,
Ten starvling hermits suffer less than he.
   The truth is (if the truth may suit your ear,
And prejudice have left a passage clear)
Pride has attain'd its most luxuriant growth,
And poison'd ev'ry virtue in them both.
Pride may be pamper'd while the flesh grows lean;
Humility may clothe an English Dean;
That grace was Cowper's[1]—his confess'd by all—
Though plac'd in golden Durham's second stall.
Not all the plenty of a Bishop's board,
His palace, and his lacqueys, and, 'My Lord!'
More nourish pride, that condescending vice,
Than abstinence, and beggary and lice.
It thrives in mis'ry, and abundant grows
In mis'ry fools upon themselves impose.
   But why before us, Protestants, produce
An Indian mystic or a French recluse?
Their sin is plain, but what have we to fear,
Reform'd and well instructed? You shall hear.
   Yon ancient prude, whose wither'd features show
She might be young some forty years ago,
Her elbows pinion'd close upon her hips,
Her head erect, her fan upon her lips,
Her eye-brows arch'd, her eyes both gone astray

---

[1] The Rev. and Hon. Spencer Cowper, 1713–74, Dean of Durham, who left C. a legacy.

To watch yon am'rous couple in their play,
With bony and unkerchief'd neck defies
The rude inclemency of wintry skies.
And sails with lappet-head and mincing airs
Duely at clink of bell, to morning pray'rs.
To thrift and parsimony much inclin'd,
She yet allows herself that boy behind;
The shiv'ring urchin, bending as he goes,
With slipshod heels, and dew drop at his nose;
His predecessor's coat advanc'd to wear,
Which future pages are yet doom'd to share,
Carries her bible tuck'd beneath his arm,
And hides his hands to keep his fingers warm.[1]

She, half an angel in her own account,
Doubts not hereafter with the saints to mount,
Though not a grace appears on strictest search,
But that she fasts, and, *item*, goes to church.
Conscious of age she recollects her youth,
And tells, not always with an eye to truth,
Who spann'd her waist, and who, whe'er he came,
Scrawl'd upon glass Miss Bridget's lovely name,
Who stole her slipper, fill'd it with tokay,
And drank the little bumper ev'ry day:
Of temper as invenom'd as an asp,
Censorious, and her ev'ry word a wasp,
In faithful mem'ry she records the crimes
Or real, or fictitious, of the times,
Laughs at the reputations she has torn,
And holds them dangling at arms length in scorn.

Such are the fruits of sanctimonious pride,
Of malice fed while flesh is mortified.
Take, Madam, the reward of all your pray'rs,
Where hermits and where Bramins meet with theirs;
Your portion is with them: nay, never frown,
But, if you please, some fathoms lower down.

Artist attend! your brushes and your paint—
Produce them—take a chair—now draw a Saint.

[1] 'These lines were evidently formed upon Hogarth's print of
Mourning': Southey.

Oh sorrowful and sad! the streaming tears
Channel her cheeks, a Niobe appears.
Is this a Saint? Throw tints and all away,
True piety is cheerful as the day,
Will weep indeed and heave a pitying groan
For others' woes, but smiles upon her own.
 What purpose has the King of Saints in view?
Why falls the gospel like a gracious dew?
To call up plenty from the teeming earth,
Or curse the desart with a tenfold dearth?
Is it that Adam's offspring may be sav'd
From servile fear, or be the more enslav'd?
To loose the links that gall'd mankind before,
Or bind them faster on, and add still more?
The freeborn Christian has no chains to prove,
Or if a chain, the golden one of love;
No fear attends to quench his glowing fires,
What fear he feels his gratitude inspires.
Shall he for such deliv'rance freely wrought,
Recompense ill? He trembles at the thought:
His master's int'rest and his own combin'd,
Prompt ev'ry movement of his heart and mind;
Thought, word, and deed, his liberty evince,
His freedom is the freedom of a Prince.
 Man's obligations infinite, of course
His life should prove that he perceives their force,
His utmost he can render is but small,
The principle and motive all in all.
You have two servants—Tom, an arch, sly rogue,
From top to toe the Geta[1] now in vogue,
Genteel in figure, easy in address,
Moves without noise, and swift as an express,
Reports a message with a pleasing grace,
Expert in all the duties of his place:
Say, on what hinge does his obedience move?
Has he a world of gratitude and love?
No, not a spark—'tis all mere sharper's play;

[1] *Geta*: the name of a servant in Terence's plays *Adelphi* and *Phormio*.

He likes your house, your housemaid, and your pay;
Reduce his wages, or get rid of her,
Tom quits you, with, your most obedient Sir—
   The dinner serv'd, Charles takes his usual stand,
Watches your eye, anticipates command,
Sighs if perhaps your appetite should fail,
And if he but suspects a frown, turns pale;
Consults all day your int'rest and your ease,
Richly rewarded if he can but please;
And proud to make his firm attachment known,
To save your life would nobly risque his own.
   Now, which stands highest in your serious thought?
Charles, without doubt, say you— and so he ought;
One act that from a thankful heart proceeds,
Excels ten thousand mercenary deeds.
   Thus heav'n approves as honest and sincere,
The work of gen'rous love and filial fear,
But with averted eyes th' omniscient judge
Scorns the base hireling and the slavish drudge.
   Where dwell these matchless Saints? Old Curio cries—
Ev'n at your side, Sir, and before your eyes,
The favour'd few, th' enthusiasts you despise.
And pleas'd at heart because on holy ground
Sometimes a canting hypocrite is found,
Reproach a people with his single fall,
And cast his filthy raiment at them all.
Attend— an apt similitude shall show,
Whence springs the conduct that offends you so.
   See where it smokes along the sounding plain,
Blown all aslant, a driving, dashing rain,
Peal upon peal redoubling all around,
Shakes it again and faster to the ground,
Now flashing wide, now glancing as in play,
Swift beyond thought the light'nings dart away;
Ere yet it came the trav'ler urg'd his steed,
And hurried, but with unsuccessful speed,
Now drench'd throughout, and hopeless of his case,
He drops the rein, and leaves him to his pace;
Suppose, unlook'd for in a scene so rude,

Long hid by interposing hill or wood,
Some mansion, neat and elegantly dress'd,
By some kind hospitable heart possess'd,
Offer him warmth, security, and rest;
Think with what pleasure, safe and at his ease,
He hears the tempest howling in the trees,
What glowing thanks his lips and heart employ,
While danger past is turn'd to present joy.
So fares it with the sinner when he feels
A growing dread of vengeance at his heels,
His conscience, like a glassy lake before,
Lash'd into foaming waves begins to roar,
The law grown clamorous, though silent long,
Arraigns him, charges him with ev'ry wrong,
Asserts the rights of his offended Lord,
And death or restitution is the word;
The last impossible, he fears the first,
And having well deserv'd, expects the worst.
Then welcome refuge, and a peaceful home,
Oh for a shelter from the wrath to come!
Crush me ye rocks, ye falling mountains hide,[1]
Or bury me in ocean's angry tide—
The scrutiny of those all-seeing eyes
I dare not—and you need not, God replies;
The remedy you want I freely give,
The book shall teach you, read, believe, and live:
'Tis done—the raging storm is heard no more,
Mercy receives him on her peaceful shore,
And justice, guardian of the dread command,
Drops the red vengeance from his willing hand.
A soul redeem'd demands a life of praise,
Hence the complexion of his future days,
Hence a demeanor holy and unspeck'd,
And the world's hatred as its sure effect.

Some lead a life unblameable and just,
Their own dear virtue, their unshaken trust.
They never sin—or, if (as all offend)

[1] Revelation, vi, 16.

229

Some trivial slips their daily walk attend,
The poor are near at hand, the charge is small,
A slight gratuity atones for all.
For though the Pope has lost his int'rest here,
And pardons are not sold as once they were,
No Papist more desirous to compound,
Than some grave sinners upon English ground:
That plea refuted, other quirks they seek,
Mercy is infinite, and man is weak,
The future shall obliterate the past,
And heav'n no doubt shall be their home at last.

Come then—a still, small whisper in your ear,
He has no hope that never had a fear;
And he that never doubted of his state,
He may perhaps—perhaps he may—too late.

The path to bliss abounds with many a snare,
Learning is one, and wit, however rare:
The Frenchman, first in literary fame,
(Mention him if you please. Voltaire?—the same.)
With spirit, genius, eloquence supplied,
Liv'd long, wrote much, laugh'd heartily, and died;
The scripture was his jest-book,[1] whence he drew
Bon mots to gall the Christian and the Jew:
An infidel in health, but what when sick?
Oh then, a text would touch him at the quick:
View him at Paris in his last career,
Surrounding throngs the demi-god revere,
Exalted on his pedestal of pride,
And fum'd with frankincense on ev'ry side,
He begs their flatt'ry with his latest breath,
And smother'd in't at last, is prais'd to death.

Yon cottager who weaves at her own door,
Pillow and bobbins all her little store,
Content, though mean, and cheerful, if not gay,
Shuffling her threads about the live-long day,
Just earns a scanty pittance, and at night
Lies down secure, her heart and pocket light;

[1] The reference is probably to the *Dictionnaire Philosophique*, 1764.

She, for her humble sphere by nature fit,
Has little understanding, and no wit,
Receives no praise, but (though her lot be such,
Toilsome and indigent) she renders much;
Just knows, and knows no more, her Bible true,
A truth the brilliant Frenchman never knew;
And in that charter reads with sparkling eyes,
Her title to a treasure in the skies.[1]
   Oh happy peasant! Oh unhappy bard!
His the mere tinsel, hers the rich reward;
He prais'd perhaps for ages yet to come,
She never heard of half a mile from home;
He lost in errors his vain heart prefers,
She safe in the simplicity of hers.
   Not many wise, rich, noble, or profound
In science, win one inch of heav'nly ground;
And is it not a mortifying thought
The poor should gain it, and the rich should not?
No—the voluptuaries, who ne'er forget
One pleasure lost, lose heav'n without regret;
Regret would rouse them and give birth to pray'r,
Pray'r would add faith, and faith would fix them there.
   Not that the Former of us all in this,
Or aught he does, is govern'd by caprice,
The supposition is replete with sin,
And bears the brand of blasphemy burnt in.
Not so—the silver trumpet's heav'nly call,
Sounds for the poor, but sounds alike for all;
Kings are invited, and would kings obey,
No slaves on earth more welcome were than they:
But royalty, nobility, and state,
Are such a dead preponderating weight,
That endless bliss (how strange soe'er it seem)
In counterpoise, flies up and kicks the beam.

---

[1] Isaac Watts, *Hymns and Spiritual Songs*, II, 65:

> When I can read my title clear
>   To mansions in the skies,
> I bid farewell to every fear,
>   And wipe my weeping eyes.

'Tis open and ye cannot enter—why?
Because ye will not, Conyers[1] would reply—
And he says much that many may dispute
And cavil at with ease, but none refute.
Oh bless'd effect of penury and want,
The seed sown there, how vig'rous is the plant!
No soil like poverty for growth divine,
As leanest land supplies the richest wine.
Earth gives too little, giving only bread,
To nourish pride or turn the weakest head:
To them the sounding jargon of the schools
Seems what it is, a cap and bells for fools:
The light they walk by, kindled from above,
Shows them the shortest way to life and love:
They, strangers to the controversial field,
Where deists, always foil'd, yet scorn to yield,
And never check'd by what impedes the wise,
Believe, rush forward, and possess the prize.
　　Envy, ye great, the dull unletter'd small,
Ye have much cause for envy—but not all;
We boast some rich ones whom the gospel sways,
And one[2] that wears a coronet and prays;

[1] Dr Richard Conyers, a notable Evangelical divine, vicar of St Paul's, Deptford, from 1775 to his death in 1786. He introduced John Newton to C.

[2] William Legge, 2nd Earl of Dartmouth (1731–1801) was successively Principal Secretary of State for the American Department (Dartmouth College, New Hampshire, is named after him), Lord Privy Seal and Lord Steward. Shortly after their marriage, the Dartmouths met Whitefield and the Wesleys at the house of Selina, Countess of Huntingdon, and soon became noted for their steadfast support of clergymen suspected of 'Methodism'. It was Dartmouth who persuaded a bishop to ordain John Newton, and who appointed him to a curacy at Olney. Katharine, Duchess of Buckingham, on the other hand, wrote to Lady Huntingdon: 'I thank your ladyship for the information concerning the Methodist preachers. Their doctrines are most repulsive, and strongly tinctured with impertinence and disrespect towards their superiors. It is monstrous to be told that you have a heart as sinful as the common wretches that crowd the earth. I cannot but wonder that your ladyship should relish any sentiments so much at variance with high rank and good breeding.'

Like gleanings of an olive-tree they show,
Here and there one upon the topmost bough.[1]
   How readily, upon the gospel plan,
That question has its answer—what is man?
Sinful and weak, in ev'ry sense a wretch,
An instrument whose cords upon the stretch
And strain'd to the last screw that he can bear,
Yield only discord in his Maker's ear:
Once the blest residence of truth divine,
Glorious as Solyma's[2] interior shrine,
Where in his own oracular abode,
Dwelt visibly the light-creating God;
But made long since, like Babylon of old,
A den of mischiefs never to be told:
And she, once mistress of the realms around,
Now scatter'd wide and nowhere to be found,
As soon shall rise and re-ascend the throne,
By native pow'r and energy her own,
As nature at her own peculiar cost
Restore to man the glories he has lost.
Go bid the winter cease to chill the year,
Replace the wand'ring comet in his sphere,
Then boast (but wait for that unhop'd for hour)
The self-restoring arm of human pow'r.
But what is man in his own proud esteem?
Hear him, himself the poet and the theme;
A monarch cloth'd with majesty and awe,
His mind his kingdom and his will his law,
Grace in his mien and glory in his eyes,
Supreme on earth and worthy of the skies,
Strength in his heart, dominion in his nod,
And, thunderbolts excepted, quite a God.
   So sings he, charm'd with his own mind and form,
The song magnificent, the theme a worm:
Himself so much the source of his delight,
His maker has no beauty in his sight:

[1] Cf. Isaiah, xvii, 6.
[2] Jerusalem.

See where he sits, contemplative and fix'd,
Pleasure and wonder in his features mix'd;
His passions tam'd and all at his controul,
How perfect the composure of his soul!
Complacency has breath'd a gentle gale
O'er all his thoughts, and swell'd his easy sail:
His books well trimm'd and in the gayest style,
Like regimented coxcombs rank and file,
Adorn his intellects as well as shelves,
And teach him notions splendid as themselves:
The Bible only stands neglected there,
Though that of all most worthy of his care,
And like an infant, troublesome awake,
Is left to sleep for peace and quiet sake.
  What shall the man deserve of human kind,
Whose happy skill and industry combin'd,
Shall prove (what argument could never yet)
The Bible an imposture and a cheat?
The praises of the libertine profess'd,
The worst of men, and curses of the best.
Where should the living, weeping o'er his woes,
The dying, trembling at the awful close,
Where the betray'd, forsaken and oppress'd,
The thousands whom the world forbids to rest,
Where should they find, (those comforts at an end
The scripture yields) or hope to find a friend?
Sorrow might muse herself to madness then,
And seeking exile from the sight of men,
Bury herself in solitude profound,
Grow frantic with her pangs and bite the ground.
Thus often unbelief, grown sick of life,
Flies to the tempting pool or felon knife,
The jury meet, the coroner is short,
And lunacy the verdict of the court:
Reverse the sentence, let the truth be known,
Such lunacy is ignorance alone;
They knew not, what some bishops may not know,
That scripture is the only cure of woe:
That field of promise, how it flings abroad

Its odour o'er the Christian's thorny road;
The soul, reposing on assur'd relief,
Feels herself happy amidst all her grief,
Forgets her labour as she toils along,
Weeps tears of joy, and bursts into a song.
  But the same word that like the polish'd share
Ploughs up the roots of a believer's care,
Kills too the flow'ry weeds, where'er they grow,
That bind the sinner's Bacchanalian brow.
Oh that unwelcome voice of heav'nly love,
Sad messenger of mercy from above,
How does it grate upon his thankless ear,
Crippling his pleasures with the cramp of fear!
His will and judgment at continual strife,
That civil war imbitters all his life;
In vain he points his pow'rs against the skies,
In vain he closes or averts his eyes,
Truth will intrude—she bids him yet beware—
And shakes the sceptic in the scorner's chair.[1]
  Though various foes against the truth combine,
Pride above all opposes her design;
Pride, of a growth superior to the rest,
The subtlest serpent with the loftiest crest,
Swells at the thought, and kindling into rage,
Would hiss the cherub mercy from the stage.
  And is the soul indeed so lost, she cries,
Fallen from her glory and too weak to rise,
Torpid and dull beneath a frozen zone,
Has she no spark that may be deem'd her own?
Grant her indebted to what zealots call
Grace undeserv'd, yet surely not for all—
Some beams of rectitude she yet displays,
Some love of virtue and some pow'r to praise;
Can lift herself above corporeal things,
And soaring on her own unborrow'd wings,
Possess herself of all that's good or true,
Assert the skies, and vindicate her due.

[1] Psalm i, 1.

Past indiscretion is a venial crime,
And if the youth, unmellow'd yet by time,
Bore on his branch, luxuriant then and rude,
Fruits of a blighted size, austere and crude,
Maturer years shall happier stores produce,
And meliorate the well concocted juice.
Then, conscious of her meritorious zeal,
To justice she may make her bold appeal,
And leave to mercy with a tranquil mind,
The worthless and unfruitful of mankind.
Hear then how mercy, slighted and defied,
Retorts th' affront against the crown of pride.
      Perish the virtue, as it ought, abhorr'd,
And the fool with it that insults his Lord.
Th' atonement a Redeemer's love has wrought
Is not for you—the righteous need it not.
Seest thou yon harlot wooing all she meets,
The worn out nuisance of the public streets,
Herself from morn to night, from night to morn,
Her own abhorrence, and as much your scorn;
The gracious show'r, unlimited and free,
Shall fall on her, when heav'n denies it thee.
Of all that wisdom dictates, this the drift,
That man is dead in sin, and life a gift.[1]
      Is virtue then, unless of christian growth,
Mere fallacy, or foolishness, or both,
Ten thousand sages lost in endless woe,
For ignorance of what they could not know?
That speech betrays at once a bigot's tongue,
Charge not a God with such outrageous wrong.
Truly not I—the partial light men have,
My creed persuades me, well employ'd, may save,
While he that scorns the noon-day beam, perverse,
Shall find the blessing, unimprov'd, a curse.
Let heathen worthies, whose exalted mind
Left sensuality and dross behind,
Possess for me their undisputed lot,

[1] Romans, vi, 20–23.

And take, unenvied, the reward they sought.
But still in virtue of a Saviour's plea,
Not blind by choice, but destin'd not to see.
Their fortitude and wisdom were a flame
Celestial, though they knew not whence it came,
Deriv'd from the same source of light and grace
That guides the christian in his swifter race.
Their judge was conscience, and her rule their law,
That rule pursued with rev'rence and with awe,
Led them, however falt'ring, faint and slow,
From what they knew, to what they wish'd to know;
But let not him that shares a brighter day,
Traduce the splendor of a noon-tide ray,
Prefer the twilight of a darker time,
And deem his base stupidity no crime;
The wretch that slights the bounty of the skies,
And sinks, while favour'd with the means to rise,
Shall find them rated at their full amount,
The good he scorn'd all carried to account.

   Marshalling all his terrors as he came,
Thunder and earthquake and devouring flame,
From Sinai's top Jehovah gave the law,
Life for obedience,[1] death for ev'ry flaw.
When the great sov'reign would his will express,
He gives a perfect rule; what can he less?
And guards it with a sanction as severe
As vengeance can inflict, or sinners fear:
Else his own glorious rights he would disclaim,
And man might safely trifle with his name:
He bids him glow with unremitting love
To all on earth, and to himself above;
Condemns th' injurious deed, the sland'rous tongue,
The thought that meditates a brother's wrong;
Brings not alone, the more conspicuous part,
His conduct to the test, but tries his heart.

   Hark! universal nature shook and groan'd,
'Twas the last trumpet—see the judge enthron'd;

---

[1] Exodus, xix, 1–6.

Rouse all your courage at your utmost need,
Now summon ev'ry virtue, stand and plead.
What, silent? Is your boasting heard no more?
That self-renouncing wisdom, learn'd before,
Had shed immortal glories on your brow,
That all your virtues cannot purchase now.

 All joy to the believer! He can speak—
Trembling yet happy, confident yet meek.

 Since the dear hour that brought me to thy foot,
And cut up all my follies by the root,
I never trusted in an arm but thine,
Nor hop'd, but in thy righteousness divine:
My pray'rs and alms, imperfect and defil'd,
Were but the feeble efforts of a child,
Howe'er perform'd, it was their brightest part,
That they proceeded from a grateful heart:
Cleans'd in thine own all-purifying blood,
Forgive their evil and accept their good;
I cast them at thy feet—my only plea
Is what it was, dependence upon thee;
While struggling in the vale of tears below,
That never fail'd, nor shall it fail me now.

 Angelic gratulations rend the skies,
Pride falls unpitied, never more to rise,
Humility is crown'd, and faith receives the prize.

EXPOSTULATION

Tantane, tam patiens, nullo certamine tolli
Dona sines?[1]—Virgil, *Aeneid* V, 390

WHY weeps the muse for England? What appears
In England's case to move the muse to tears?
From side to side of her delightful isle,
Is she not cloath'd with a perpetual smile?

---

[1] 'Will you be so submissive as to allow such great gifts to be taken away from you without a struggle?'

Can nature add a charm, or art confer
A new-found luxury not seen in her?
Where under heav'n is pleasure more pursued,
Or where does cold reflection less intrude?
Her fields a rich expanse of wavy corn
Pour'd out from plenty's overflowing horn;
Ambrosial gardens in which art supplies
The fervor and the force of Indian skies;
Her peaceful shores, where busy commerce waits
To pour his golden tide through all her gates;
Whom fiery suns that scorch the russet spice
Of eastern groves, and oceans floor'd with ice,
Forbid in vain to push his daring way
To darker climes, or climes of brighter day;
Whom the winds waft where'er the billows roll,
From the world's girdle to the frozen pole;
The chariots bounding in her wheel-worn streets,
Her vaults below where ev'ry vintage meets,
Her theatres, her revels, and her sports,
The scenes to which not youth alone resorts,
But age in spite of weakness and of pain
Still haunts, in hope to dream of youth again,
All speak her happy—let the muse look round
From East to West, no sorrow can be found,
Or only what, in cottages confin'd,
Sighs unregarded to the passing wind;
Then wherefore weep for England, what appears
In England's case to move the muse to tears?

The prophet[1] wept for Israel, wish'd his eyes
Were fountains fed with infinite supplies;
For Israel dealt in robbery and wrong,
There were the scorner's and the sland'rer's tongue;
Oaths, us'd as playthings or convenient tools,
As int'rest bias'd knaves, or fashion fools;
Adult'ry neighing at his neighbour's door,[2]
Oppression labouring hard to grind the poor,

---

[1] Jeremiah, ix, 1.
[2] Cf. Jeremiah, v, 8.

The partial balance and deceitful weight,
The treach'rous smile, a mask for secret hate,
Hypocrisy, formality in pray'r,
And the dull service of the lip were there.
Her women insolent and self-caress'd,
By vanity's unwearied finger dress'd,
Forgot the blush that virgin fears impart
To modest cheeks, and borrow'd one from art;
Were just such trifles, without worth or use,
As silly pride and idleness produce:
Curl'd, scented, furbelow'd and flounc'd around,
With feet too delicate to touch the ground,
They stretch'd the neck, and roll'd the wanton eye,
And sighed for ev'ry fool that flutter'd by.

  He saw his people slaves to ev'ry lust,
Lewd, avaricious, arrogant, unjust,
He heard the wheels of an avenging God
Groan heavily along the distant road;
Saw Babylon set wide her two-leav'd brass[1]
To let the military deluge pass;
Jerusalem a prey, her glory soil'd,
Her princes captive, and her treasures spoil'd;
Wept till all Israel heard his bitter cry,
Stamped with his foot and smote upon his thigh;[2]
But wept, and stamp'd, and smote his thigh in vain,
Pleasure is deaf when told of future pain,
And sounds prophetic are too rough to suit
Ears long accustom'd to the pleasing lute;
They scorn'd his inspiration and his theme,
Pronounc'd him frantic and his fears a dream;
With self-indulgence wing'd the fleeting hours,
Till the foe found them, and down fell the tow'rs.

  Long time Assyria bound them in her chain,
Till penitence had purg'd the public stain,

---

[1] 'At the end of each street a little gate is formed in the wall along the river side...and they are all made of brass.' Herodotus, trans. Cary, p. 78, London 1850. *Bruce.*

[2] Cf. Ezekiel, vi, 11.

And Cyrus, with relenting pity mov'd,
Return'd them happy to the land they lov'd:
There, proof against prosperity, awhile
They stood the test of her ensnaring smile,
And had the grace in scenes of peace to show
The virtue they had learn'd in scenes of woe.
But man is frail and can but ill sustain
A long immunity from grief and pain,
And after all the joys that plenty leads,
With tip-toe step vice silently succeeds.
    When he that rul'd them with a shepherd's rod,
In form a man, in dignity a God,
Came, not expected in that humble guise,
To sift, and search them with unerring eyes,
He found conceal'd beneath a fair outside,
The filth of rottenness and worm of pride;
Their piety a system of deceit,
Scripture employ'd to sanctify the cheat,
The Pharisee the dupe of his own art,
Self-idoliz'd, and yet a knave at heart.
    When nations are to perish in their sins,
'Tis in the church the leprosy begins:
The priest, whose office is with zeal sincere
To watch the fountain, and preserve it clear,
Carelessly nods and sleeps upon the brink,
While others poison what the flock must drink;
Or waking at the call of lust alone,
Infuses lies and errors of his own:
His unsuspecting sheep believe it pure,
And, tainted by the very means of cure,
Catch from each other a contagious spot,
The foul forerunner of a gen'ral rot:
Then truth is hush'd that heresy may preach,
And all is trash that reason cannot reach;
Then God's own image on the soul impress'd,
Becomes a mock'ry and a standing jest;
And faith, the root whence only can arise
The graces of a life that wins the skies,
Loses at once all value and esteem,

Pronounced by graybeards a pernicious dream:
Then ceremony leads her bigots forth,
Prepar'd to fight for shadows of no worth,
While truths on which eternal things depend,
Find not, or hardly find, a single friend:
As soldiers watch the signal of command,
They learn to bow, to kneel, to sit, to stand;
Happy to fill religion's vacant place
With hollow form and gesture and grimace.
   Such, when the teacher of his church was there,
People and priest, the sons of Israel were,
Stiff in the letter, lax in the design
And import, of their oracles divine;
Their learning legendary, false, absurd,
And yet exalted above God's own word,
They drew a curse from an intended good,
Puff'd up with gifts they never understood.
He judg'd them with as terrible a frown
As if, not love, but wrath, had brought him down:
Yet he was gentle as soft summer airs,
Had grace for others' sins, but none for theirs:
Through all he spoke a noble plainness ran,
Rhet'ric is artifice, the work of man,
And tricks and turns that fancy may devise,
Are far too mean for him that rules the skies.
Th' astonish'd vulgar trembled while he tore
The mask from faces never seen before;
He stripp'd th' impostors in the noon-day sun,
Show'd that they follow'd all they seem'd to shun,
Their pray'rs made public, their excess kept
As private as the chambers where they slept;
The temple and its holy rites, profan'd
By mumm'ries he that dwelt in it disdain'd;
Uplifted hands that at convenient times
Could act extortion and the worst of crimes,
Wash'd with a neatness scrupulously nice,[1]
And free from ev'ry taint but that of vice.

---

[1] Mark, vii, 3–4.

Judgment, however tardy, mends her pace
When obstinacy once has conquer'd grace.
They saw distemper heal'd, and life restor'd,
In answer to the fiat of his word;
Confess'd the wonder, and with daring tongue,
Blasphem'd th' authority from which it sprung.
They knew, by sure prognostics seen on high,
The future tone and temper of the sky,[1]
But, grave dissemblers, could not understand
That sin let loose speaks punishment at hand.

Ask now of history's authentic page,
And call up evidence from ev'ry age,
Display with busy and laborious hand
The blessings of the most indebted land,
What nation will you find, whose annals prove
So rich an int'rest in almighty love?
Where dwell they now, where dwelt in ancient day
A people planted, water'd, blest as they?
Let Egypt's plagues, and Canaan's woes proclaim
The favours pour'd upon the Jewish name;
Their freedom purchas'd for them, at the cost
Of all their hard oppressors valued most,
Their title to a country, not their own,
Made sure by prodigies till then unknown;
For them, the state they left made waste and void,
For them, the states to which they went, destroy'd;
A cloud to measure out their march by day,
By night a fire to cheer the gloomy way,
That moving signal summoning, when best
Their host to move, and when it stay'd, to rest.[2]
For them the rocks dissolv'd into a flood,[3]
The dews condens'd into angelic food.
Their very garments sacred, old yet new,[4]
And time forbid to touch them as he flew;

[1] Matthew, xvi, 2-3.
[2] Exodus, xiii, 21.
[3] Numbers, xx, 8-11.
[4] Deuteronomy, viii, 4.

Streams swell'd above the bank, enjoin'd to stand,[1]
While they pass'd through to their appointed land;
Their leader arm'd with meekness, zeal and love,
And grac'd with clear credentials from above,
Themselves secur'd beneath th' Almighty wing;
Their God their captain,[2] lawgiver and king;
Crown'd with a thousand vict'ries, and at last
Lords of the conquer'd soil, there rooted fast,
In peace possessing what they won by war,
Their name far publish'd and rever'd as far;
Where will you find a race like theirs, endow'd
With all that man e'er wish'd, or heav'n bestow'd?
  They and they only amongst all mankind
Receiv'd the transcript of th' eternal mind,
Were trusted with his own engraven laws,
And constituted guardians of his cause;
Theirs were the prophets, theirs the priestly call,
And theirs by birth the Saviour of us all.[3]
In vain the nations that had seen them rise,
With fierce and envious yet admiring eyes,
Had sought to crush them, guarded as they were
By pow'r divine, and skill that could not err;
Had they maintain'd allegiance firm and sure,
And kept the faith immaculate and pure,
Then the proud eagles of all-conqu'ring Rome,
Had found one city not to be o'ercome,
And the twelve standards of the tribes unfurl'd,
Had bid defiance to the warring world.
But grace abus'd brings forth the foulest deeds,
As richest soil the most luxuriant weeds;
Cur'd of the golden calves, their fathers sin,
They set up self, that idol god within,
View'd a Deliv'rer with disdain and hate,
Who left them still a tributary state,
Seiz'd fast his hand, held out to set them free

---

[1] Exodus, xiv, 21: Joshua, iii, 13–16.
[2] Vide Joshua, v, 14 [C].
[3] Cf. Romans, ix, 4, 5.

From a worse yoke, and nail'd it to the tree;
There was the consummation and the crown,
The flow'r of Israel's infamy full blown;
Thence date their sad declension and their fall;
Their woes not yet repealed, thence date them all.
　　Thus fell the best instructed in her day,
And the most favour'd land, look where we may.
Philosophy indeed on Grecian eyes
Had pour'd the day, and clear'd the Roman skies;
In other climes perhaps creative art,
With pow'r surpassing theirs, perform'd her part,
Might give more life to marble, or might fill
The glowing tablets with a juster skill,
Might shine in fable, and grace idle themes
With all th' embroid'ry of poetic dreams;
'Twas theirs alone to dive into the plan
That truth and mercy had reveal'd to man,
And while the world beside, that plan unknown,
Deified useless wood or senseless stone,
They breath'd in faith their well-directed pray'rs,
And the true God, the God of truth, was theirs.
　　Their glory faded, and their race dispers'd,
The last of nations now, though once the first;
They warn and teach the proudest, would they learn,
Keep wisdom or meet vengeance in your turn:
If we escap'd not, if Heav'n spar'd not us,
Peel'd, scatter'd, and exterminated thus;[1]
If vice receiv'd her retribution due
When we were visited, what hope for you?
When God arises with an awful frown,
To punish lust, or pluck presumption down;
When gifts perverted or not duly priz'd,
Pleasure o'ervalued and his grace despis'd,
Provoke the vengeance of his righteous hand
To pour down wrath upon a thankless land,
He will be found impartially severe,
Too just to wink, or speak the guilty clear.

[1] Cf. Isaiah, xviii, 2, 7.

Oh Israel, of all nations most undone!
Thy diadem displac'd, thy sceptre gone;
Thy temple, once thy glory, fall'n and ras'd,
And thou a worshipper e'en where thou may'st;
Thy services once holy without spot,
Mere shadows now, their ancient pomp forgot;
Thy Levites, once a consecrated host,
No longer Levites, and their lineage lost,
And thou thyself o'er ev'ry country sown,
With none on earth that thou canst call thine own;
Cry aloud thou that sittest in the dust,
Cry to the proud, the cruel and unjust,
Knock at the gates of nations, rouse their fears,
Say wrath is coming and the storm appears,
But raise the shrillest cry in British ears.

What ails thee, restless as the waves that roar,
And fling their foam against thy chalky shore?
Mistress, at least while Providence shall please,
And trident-bearing queen of the wide seas—
Why, having kept good faith, and often shown
Friendship and truth to others, findst thou none?
Thou that hast set the persecuted free,
None interposes now to succour thee;
Countries indebted to thy pow'r, that shine
With light deriv'd from thee, would smother thine;
Thy very children[1] watch for thy disgrace,
A lawless brood, and curse thee to thy face:
Thy rulers load thy credit, year by year,[2]
With sums Peruvian mines could never clear,
As if like arches built with skilful hand,
The more 'twere prest the firmer it would stand.

The cry in all thy ships is still the same,
Speed us away to battle and to fame,
Thy mariners explore the wild expanse,
Impatient to descry the flags of France,
But though they fight as thine have ever fought,

[1] The Americans.
[2] The National Debt was doubled as a result of the American War.

246

Return asham'd without the wreaths they sought:
Thy senate is a scene of civil jar,
Chaos of contrarieties at war,
Where sharp and solid, phlegmatic and light,
Discordant atoms meet, ferment and fight,
Where obstinacy takes his sturdy stand,
To disconcert what policy has plann'd,
Where policy is busied all night long
In setting right what faction has set wrong,
Where flails of oratory thresh the floor,
That yields them chaff and dust, and nothing more.
Thy rack'd inhabitants repine, complain,
Tax'd 'till the brow of labour sweats in vain;
War lays a burthen on the reeling state,
And peace does nothing to relieve the weight;
Successive loads succeeding broils impose,
And sighing millions prophesy the close.
   Is adverse providence, when ponder'd well,
So dimly writ or difficult to spell,
Thou canst not read with readiness and ease,
Providence adverse in events like these?
Know then, that heav'nly wisdom on this ball
Creates, gives birth to, guides, consummates all:
That while laborious and quick-thoughted man
Snuffs up the praise of what he seems to plan;
He first conceives, then perfects his design,
As a mere instrument in hands divine:
Blind to the working of that secret pow'r
That balances the wings of ev'ry hour,
The busy trifler dreams himself alone,
Frames many a purpose, and God works his own.
States thrive or wither as moons wax and wane,
Ev'n as his will and his decrees ordain.
While honour, virtue, piety, bear sway,
They flourish, and as these decline, decay.
In just resentment of his injur'd laws,
He pours contempt on them and on their cause,
Strikes the rough thread of error right athwart
The web of ev'ry scheme they have at heart,

Bids rottenness invade and bring to dust
The pillars of support in which they trust,
And do his errand of disgrace and shame
On the chief strength and glory of the frame.
None ever yet impeded what he wrought,
None bars him out from his most secret thought:
Darkness itself before his eye is light[1]
And hell's close mischief naked in his sight.

    Stand now, and judge thyself — hast thou incurr'd
His anger, who can waste thee with a word,
Who poises and proportions sea and land,
Weighing them in the hollow of his hand,[2]
And in whose awful sight all nations seem
As grasshoppers, as dust, a drop, a dream?
Hast thou (a sacrilege his soul abhors)
Claim'd all the glory of thy prosp'rous wars,
Proud of thy fleets and armies, stol'n the gem
Of his just praise to lavish it on them?
Hast thou not learn'd what thou art often told,
A truth still sacred, and believ'd of old,
That no success attends on spears and swords
Unblest, and that the battle is the Lord's?[3]
That courage is his creature, and dismay
The post that at his bidding speeds away,
Ghastly in feature, and his stamm'ring tongue
With doleful rumor and sad presage hung,
To quell the valor of the stoutest heart,
And teach the combatant a woman's part?
That he bids thousands fly when none pursue,[4]
Saves as he will, by many or by few,[5]
And claims for ever as his royal right,
Th' event and sure decision of the fight?

    Hast thou, though suckled at fair freedom's breast,
Exported slav'ry to the conquer'd East,

[1] Cf. Psalm cxxxix, 12.
[2] Cf. Isaiah, xl, 12.
[3] 1 Samuel, xvii, 47.
[4] Cf. Proverbs, xxviii, 1.
[5] Cf. 1 Samuel, xiv, 6.

Pull'd down the tyrants India serv'd with dread,
And rais'd thyself, a greater, in their stead,
Gone thither arm'd and hungry, return'd full,
Fed from the richest veins of the Mogul,
A despot big with pow'r obtain'd by wealth,
And that obtain'd by rapine and by stealth?
With Asiatic vices stor'd thy mind,
But left their virtues and thine own behind,
And having truck'd thy soul, brought home the fee,
To tempt the poor to sell himself to thee?
  Hast thou by statute, shov'd from its design
The Saviour's feast, his own blest bread and wine,
And made the symbols of atoning grace
An office-key, a pick-lock to a place,
That infidels may prove their title good
By an oath dipp'd in sacramental blood?[1]
A blot that will be still a blot, in spite
Of all that grave apologists may write,
And though a Bishop[2] toil to cleanse the stain,
He wipes and scours the silver cup in vain.
And hast thou sworn, on ev'ry slight pretence,
Till perjuries are common as bad pence,
While thousands, careless of the damning sin,
Kiss the book's outside who ne'er look within?
  Hast thou, when heav'n has cloath'd thee with disgrace,
And long provok'd, repaid thee to thy face,
(For thou hast known eclipses, and endur'd
Dimness and anguish, all thy beams obscur'd,
When sin has shed dishonour on thy brow,
And never of a sabler hue than now)
Hast thou, with heart perverse and conscience sear'd,
Despising all rebuke, still persever'd,

[1] The Test Act, passed in 1673, was not repealed until 1828. It required everyone holding office under the Crown to take the oath of supremacy, to abjure the doctrine of transubstantiation, and to receive the sacrament according to the rites of the Church of England.

[2] William Warburton, Bishop of Gloucester, critic and theologian: *Essay on the Alliance between Church and State, and the Necessity and Equity of a Test Law,* 1756.

And having chosen evil, scorn'd the voice
That cried, Repent—and gloried in thy choice?
Thy fastings, when calamity at last
Suggests th' expedient of a yearly fast,
What mean they? Canst thou dream there is a pow'r
In lighter diet at a later hour,
To charm to sleep the threat'ning of the skies,
And hide past folly from all-seeing eyes?
The fast that wins deliv'rance, and suspends
The stroke that a vindictive God intends,
Is to renounce hypocrisy, to draw
Thy life upon the pattern of the law,
To war with pleasure idoliz'd before,
To vanquish lust, and wear its yoke no more.
All fasting else, whate'er be the pretence,
Is wooing mercy by renew'd offence.
  Hast thou within thee sin that in old time
Brought fire[1] from heav'n, the sex-abusing crime,
Whose horrid perpetration stamps disgrace
Baboons are free from, upon human race?
Think on the fruitful and well water'd spot[2]
That fed the flocks and herds of wealthy Lot,
Where Paradise seem'd still vouchsaf'd on earth,
Burning and scorch'd into perpetual dearth,
Or, in his words who damn'd the base desire,
Suff'ring the vengeance of eternal fire:[3]
Then nature injur'd, scandaliz'd, defil'd,
Unveil'd her blushing cheek, look'd on and smil'd,
Beheld with joy the lovely scene defac'd,
And prais'd the wrath that lay'd her beauties waste.
  Far be the thought from any verse of mine,
And farther still the form'd and fix'd design,
To thrust the charge of deeds that I detest
Again an innocent unconscious breast:

[1] 'Then the Lord rained upon Sodom and upon Gomorrah brimstone and fire from the Lord out of heaven': Genesis, xix, 24.

[2] Sodom: Genesis, xiii, 10.

[3] Jude, 7.

The man that dares traduce because he can,
With safety to himself, is not a man:
An individual is a sacred mark,
Not to be pierc'd in play or in the dark,
But public censure speaks a public foe,
Unless a zeal for virtue guide the blow.
    The priestly brotherhood, devout, sincere,
From mean self-int'rest and ambition clear,
Their hope in Heav'n, servility their scorn,
Prompt to persuade, expostulate and warn,
Their wisdom pure, and giv'n them from above,
Their usefulness insur'd by zeal and love,
As meek as the man Moses,[1] and withal
As bold as in Agrippa's presence Paul,[2]
Should fly the world's contaminating touch,
Holy and unpolluted—are thine such?
Except a few with Eli's spirit blest,
Hophni and Phineas may describe the rest.[3]
    Where shall a teacher look in days like these,
For ears and hearts that he can hope to please?
Look to the poor—the simple and the plain
Will hear perhaps thy salutary strain;
Humility is gentle, apt to learn,
Speak but the word, will listen and return:
Alas, not so! the poorest of the flock
Are proud, and set their faces as a rock,
Denied that earthly opulence they chuse,
God's better gift they scoff at and refuse.
The rich, the produce of a nobler stem,
Are more intelligent at least, try them:
Oh vain enquiry! they without remorse
Are altogether gone a devious course;
Where beck'ning pleasure leads them, wildly stray,
Have burst the bands and cast the yoke away.[4]

[1] Numbers, xii, 3.

[2] Acts, xxvi.

[3] 1 Samuel, ii, 12: 'Now the sons of Eli [Hophni and Phinehas] were sons of Belial; they knew not the Lord.'

[4] Psalm ii, 3.

Now borne upon the wings of truth, sublime
Review thy dim original and prime;
This island spot of unreclaim'd rude earth,
The cradle that receiv'd thee at thy birth,
Was rock'd by many a rough Norwegian blast,
And Danish howlings scar'd thee as they pass'd;
For thou wast born amid the din of arms,
And suck'd a breast that panted with alarms.
While yet thou wast a grov'ling puling chit,
Thy bones not fashion'd and thy joints not knit,
The Roman taught thy stubborn knee to bow,
Though twice a Cæsar could not bend thee now:
His victory was that of orient light,
When the sun's shafts disperse the gloom of night:
Thy language at this distant moment shows
How much the country to the conqu'ror owes;[1]
Expressive, energetic and refin'd,
It sparkles with the gems he left behind:
He brought thy land a blessing when he came,
He found thee savage, and he left thee tame,
Taught thee to clothe thy pink'd and painted hide,
And grace thy figure with a soldier's pride,
He sow'd the seeds of order where he went,
Improv'd thee far beyond his own intent,
And while he rul'd thee by the sword alone,
Made thee at last a warrior like his own.
Religion, if in heav'nly truths attir'd,
Needs only to be seen to be admir'd,
But thine as dark as witch'ries of the night,
Was form'd to harden hearts and shock the sight:
Thy Druids strung the well-strung harps they bore
With fingers deeply dy'd in human gore,
And while the victim slowly bled to death,
Upon the tolling chords rung out his dying breath.
Who brought the lamp that with awak'ning beams
Dispell'd thy gloom and broke away thy dreams,

---

[1] 'The absurdity of the belief that the Latin element in our tongue comes from the Roman occupation of Britain needs no comment.' *Benham.*

Tradition, now decrepid and worn out,
Babbler of ancient fables, leaves a doubt:
But still light reach'd thee; and those gods of thine[1]
Woden and Thor, each tott'ring in his shrine,
Fell broken and defac'd at his own door,
As Dagon[2] in Philistia long before.
But Rome with sorceries and magic wand,
Soon rais'd a cloud that darken'd ev'ry land,
And thine was smother'd in the stench and fog
Of Tiber's marshes and the papal bog:
Then priests with bulls and briefs, and shaven crowns,
And griping fists and unrelenting frowns,
Legates and delegates with pow'rs from hell,
Though heavenly in pretension, fleec'd thee well;
And to this hour, to keep it fresh in mind,
Some twigs of that old scourge are left[3] behind.
Thy soldiery, the pope's well manag'd pack,
Were train'd beneath his lash and knew the smack,
And when he laid them on the scent of blood,
Would hunt a Saracen through fire and flood.
Lavish of life to win an empty tomb,
That prov'd a mint of wealth, a mine to Rome,
They left their bones beneath unfriendly skies,
His worthless absolution all the prize.
Thou wast the veriest slave in days of yore,
That ever dragg'd a chain or tugg'd an oar;
Thy monarchs arbitrary, fierce, unjust,
Themselves the slaves of bigotry or lust,
Disdain'd thy counsels, only in distress
Found thee a goodly spunge for pow'r to press.
Thy chiefs, the lords of many a petty fee,

---

[1] *Woden and Thor*: Saxon, not British, deities.

[2] 1 Samuel, v, 3.

[3] Which may be found at Doctors' Commons [C]. This college for the study and practice of the civil law, near St Paul's Cathedral, had four ecclesiastical courts. Their jurisdiction over matters of probate and divorce (from which a right of appeal to the Pope existed until the Reformation) was removed by statute in 1857.

Provok'd and harass'd, in return plagu'd thee,
Call'd thee away from peaceable employ,
Domestic happiness and rural joy,
To waste thy life in arms, or lay it down
In causeless feuds and bick'rings of their own:
Thy parliaments ador'd, on bended knees,
The sov'reignty they were conven'd to please;
Whate'er was ask'd, too timid to resist,
Comply'd with, and were graciously dismiss'd;
And if some Spartan soul a doubt express'd,
And blushing at the tameness of the rest,
Dar'd to suppose the subject had a choice,
He was a traitor by the gen'ral voice.
Oh slave! with pow'rs thou didst not dare exert,
Verse cannot stoop so low as thy desert,
It shakes the sides of splenetic disdain,
Thou self-entitled ruler of the main,
To trace thee to the date when yon fair sea,
That clips thy shores, had no such charms for thee;
When other nations flew from coast to coast,
And thou hadst neither fleet nor flag to boast.
    Kneel now, and lay thy forehead in the dust,
Blush if thou canst, not petrified, thou must:
Act but an honest and a faithful part,
Compare what then thou wast, with what thou art,
And God's disposing providence confess'd,
Obduracy itself must yield the rest—
Then thou art bound to serve him, and to prove
Hour after hour thy gratitude and love.
    Has he not hid thee and thy favour'd land
For ages safe beneath his shelt'ring hand,
Giv'n thee his blessing on the clearest proof,
Bid nations leagu'd against thee stand aloof,
And charg'd hostility and hate to roar
Where else they would, but not upon thy shore?
His pow'r secur'd thee when presumptuous Spain
Baptiz'd her fleet invincible in vain;
Her gloomy monarch, doubtful and resign'd
To ev'ry pang that racks an anxious mind,

Ask'd of the waves that broke upon his coast,
What tidings? and the surge replied—all lost—
And when the Stuart[1] leaning on the Scot,
Then too much fear'd and now too much forgot,
Pierc'd to the very center of the realm,
And hop'd to seize his abdicated helm,
'Twas but to prove how quickly with a frown,
He that had rais'd thee could have pluck'd thee down.
Peculiar is the grace by thee possess'd,
Thy foes implacable, thy land at rest;
Thy thunders travel over earth and seas,
And all at home is pleasure, wealth and ease.
'Tis thus, extending his tempestuous arm,
Thy Maker fills the nations with alarm,
While his own Heav'n surveys the troubled scene,
And feels no change, unshaken and serene.
Freedom, in other lands scarce known to shine,
Pours out a flood of splendour upon thine;
Thou hast as bright an int'rest in her rays,
As ever Roman had in Rome's best days.
True freedom is, where no restraint is known
That scripture, justice, and good sense disown,
Where only vice and injury are tied,
And all from shore to shore is free beside;
Such freedom is—and Windsor's hoary tow'rs
Stood trembling at the boldness of thy pow'rs,
That won a nymph on that immortal plain,
Like her the fabled Phœbus[2] woo'd in vain;
He found the laurel only—happier you
Th' unfading laurel and the virgin[3] too.

Now think, if pleasure have a thought to spare,
If God himself be not beneath her care;
If bus'ness, constant as the wheels of time,
Can pause an hour to read a serious rhime;

[1] The Young Pretender's march to Derby, 1745.

[2] The nymph Daphne, pursued by Apollo, was transformed into a laurel.

[3] Alluding to the grant of Magna Charta, which was extorted from King John by the Barons at Runnymede near Windsor [C].

If the new mail thy merchants now receive,
Or expectation of the next, give leave,
Oh think, if chargeable with deep arrears
For such indulgence, gilding all thy years,
How much, though long neglected, shining yet,
The beams of heav'nly truth have swell'd the debt.
When persecuting zeal made royal sport,
With tortur'd innocence in Mary's court,
And Bonner,[1] blithe as shepherd at a wake,
Enjoy'd the show, and danc'd about the stake;
The sacred book, its value understood,
Receiv'd the seal of martyrdom in blood.
Those holy men, so full of truth and grace,
Seem to reflection, of a diff'rent race,
Meek, modest, venerable, wise, sincere,
In such a cause they could not dare to fear,
They could not purchase earth with such a prize,
Nor spare a life too short to reach the skies.
From them to thee convey'd along the tide,
Their streaming hearts pour'd freely when they died,
Those truths which neither use nor years impair,
Invite thee, woo thee, to the bliss they share.
What dotage will not vanity maintain?
What web too weak to catch a modern brain?
The moles and bats in full assembly find,
On special search, the keen-ey'd eagle blind.
And did they dream, and art thou wiser now?
Prove it—if better, I submit and bow.
Wisdom and goodness are twin-born, one heart
Must hold both sisters, never seen apart.
So then—as darkness overspread the deep,
Ere nature rose from her eternal sleep,
And this delightful earth, and that fair sky,
Leap'd out of nothing, call'd by the Most High;
By such a change thy darkness is made light,
Thy chaos order, and thy weakness, might;
And he whose pow'r mere nullity obeys,

---

[1] Edmund Bonner, Bishop of London: a zealous burner of heretics.

256

Who found thee nothing, form'd thee for his praise.
To praise him is to serve him, and fulfil,
Doing and suff'ring, his unquestion'd will,
'Tis to believe what men inspir'd of old,
Faithful and faithfully inform'd, unfold;
Candid and just, with no false aim in view,
To take for truth what cannot but be true;
To learn in God's own school the Christian part,
And bind the task assign'd thee to thine heart:
Happy the man there seeking and there found,
Happy the nation where such men abound.

How shall a verse impress thee? by what name
Shall I adjure thee not to court thy shame?
By theirs whose bright example unimpeach'd
Directs thee to that eminence they reach'd,
Heroes and worthies of days past, thy sires?
Or his, who touch'd their heart with hallow'd fires?
Their names, alas! in vain reproach an age
Whom all the vanities they scorn'd, engage,
And his that seraphs tremble at, is hung
Disgracefully on ev'ry trifler's tongue,
Or serves the champion in forensic war,
To flourish and parade with at the bar.[1]
Pleasure herself perhaps suggests a plea,
If int'rest move thee, to persuade ev'n thee:
By ev'ry charm that smiles upon her face,
By joys possess'd, and joys still held in chace.
If dear society be worth a thought,
And if the feast of freedom cloy thee not,
Reflect that these and all that seems thine own,
Held by the tenure of his will alone,
Like angels in the service of their Lord,
Remain with thee, or leave thee at his word;
That gratitude and temp'rance in our use
Of what he gives, unsparing and profuse,
Secure the favour and enhance the joy,

[1] Thomas Erskine, whose defence of Lord George Gordon, February 5, 1781, made him famous, was much given to rhetorical invocation of the Deity.

That thankless waste and wild abuse destroy.
    But above all reflect, how cheap soe'er
Those rights that millions envy thee, appear,
And though resolv'd to risk them, and swim down
The tide of pleasure, heedless of his frown,
That blessings truly sacred, and when giv'n
Mark'd with the signature and stamp of Heav'n,
The word of prophesy, those truths divine
Which make that Heav'n, if thou desire it, thine;
(Awful alternative! believ'd, belov'd,
Thy glory, and thy shame if unimprov'd)
Are never long vouchsaf'd, if push'd aside
With cold disgust or philosophic pride,
And that judicially withdrawn, disgrace,
Error and darkness occupy their place.
    A world is up in arms,[1] and thou, a spot
Not quickly found if negligently sought.
Thy soul as ample as thy bounds are small.
Endur'st the brunt, and dar'st defy them all:
And wilt thou join to this bold enterprize
A bolder still, a contest with the skies?
Remember, if he guard thee and secure,
Whoe'er assails thee, thy success is sure;
But if he leave thee, though the skill and pow'r
Of nations sworn to spoil thee and devour,
Were all collected in thy single arm,
And thou could'st laugh away the fear of harm,
That strength would fail, oppos'd against the push
And feeble onset of a pigmy rush.
    Say not (and, if the thought of such defence
Should spring within thy bosom, drive it thence)
What nation amongst all my foes is free
From crimes as base as any charg'd on me?
Their measure fill'd—they too shall pay the debt
Which God, though long forborn, will not forget;
But know, that wrath divine, when most severe,

[1] See p. 610, n. 1.

Makes justice still the guide of his career,
And will not punish in one mingled crowd,
Them without light, and thee without a cloud.
   Muse, hang this harp upon yon aged beech,
Still murm'ring with the solemn truths I teach,
And while, at intervals, a cold blast sings
Through the dry leaves, and pants upon the strings,
My soul shall sigh in secret, and lament
A nation scourg'd, yet tardy to repent.
I know the warning song is sung in vain,
That few will hear, and fewer heed the strain:
But if a sweeter voice, and one design'd
A blessing to my country and mankind,
Reclaim the wand'ring thousands, and bring home
A flock so scatter'd and so wont to roam,
Then place it once again between my knees,
The sound of truth will then be sure to please,
And truth alone, where'er my life be cast,
In scenes of plenty or the pining waste,
Shall be my chosen theme, my glory to the last.

HOPE

Doceas iter, et sacra ostia pandas.[1]—
Virgil, *Aeneid* VI, [109]

Ask what is human life—the sage replies,
With disappointment low'ring in his eyes,
A painful passage o'er a restless flood,
A vain pursuit of fugitive false good,
A scene of fancied bliss and heart-felt care,
Closing at last in darkness and despair—
The poor, inur'd to drudg'ry and distress,

[1] 'Be pleased to teach the way and open the sacred gates.'

Act without aim, think little and feel less,
And nowhere but in feign'd Arcadian scenes,
Taste happiness, or know what pleasure means.
Riches are pass'd away from hand to hand,
As fortune, vice or folly, may command;
As in a dance the pair that take the lead
Turn downward, and the lowest pair succeed,
So shifting and so various is the plan
By which Heav'n rules the mixt affairs of man;
Vicissitude wheels round the motley crowd,
The rich grow poor, the poor become purse-proud:
Bus'ness is labour, and man's weakness such,
Pleasure is labour too, and tires as much,
The very sense of it foregoes its use,
By repetition pall'd, by age obtuse.
Youth lost in dissipation, we deplore,
Through life's sad remnant, what no sighs restore;
Our years, a fruitless race without a prize,
Too many, yet too few to make us wise.

Dangling his cane about, and taking snuff,
Lothario cries, what philosophic stuff.
Oh querulous and weak! whose useless brain
Once thought of nothing, and now thinks in vain;
Whose eye reverted weeps o'er all the past,
Whose prospect shows thee a disheart'ning waste;
Would age in thee resign his wintry reign,
And youth invigorate that frame again,
Renew'd desire would grace with other speech
Joys always priz'd—when plac'd within our reach.

For lift thy palsied head, shake off the gloom
That overhangs the borders of thy tomb,
See nature gay as when she first began,
With smiles alluring her admirer, man;
She spreads the morning over eastern hills,
Earth glitters with the drops the night distils;
The sun obedient, at her call appears
To fling his glories o'er the robe she wears;
Banks cloath'd with flow'rs, groves fill'd with sprightly
        sounds,

The yellow tilth, green meads, rocks, rising grounds,
Streams edg'd with osiers, fatt'ning ev'ry field
Where'er they flow, now seen and now conceal'd;
From the blue rim where skies and mountains meet,
Down to the very turf beneath thy feet,
Ten thousand charms that only fools despise,
Or pride can look at with indiff'rent eyes,
All speak one language, all with one sweet voice
Cry to her universal realm, rejoice.
Man feels the spur of passions and desires,
And she gives largely more than he requires;
Not that his hours devoted all to care,
Hollow-ey'd abstinence and lean despair,
The wretch may pine, while to his smell, taste, sight,
She holds a paradise of rich delight;
But gently to rebuke his awkward fear,
To prove that what she gives, she gives sincere,
To banish hesitation, and proclaim
His happiness, her dear, her only aim.
'Tis grave philosophy's absurdest dream,
That Heav'n's intentions are not what they seem,
That only shadows are dispens'd below,
And earth has no reality but woe.

   Thus things terrestrial wear a diff'rent hue,
As youth or age persuades, and neither true;
So Flora's wreath through colour'd chrystal seen,
The rose or lily appears blue or green,
But still th' imputed tints are those alone
The medium represents, and not their own.

   To rise at noon, sit slipshod and undress'd,
To read the news, or fiddle, as seems best,
'Till half the world comes rattling at his door,
To fill the dull vacuity till four;
And, just when ev'ning turns the blue vault grey,
To spend two hours in dressing for the day;
To make the sun a bauble without use,
Save for the fruits his heav'nly beams produce;
Quite to forget, or deem it worth no thought,
Who bids him shine, or if he shine or not;

Through mere necessity to close his eyes
Just when the larks and when the shepherds rise;
Is such a life, so tediously the same,
So void of all utility or aim,
That poor JONQUIL, with almost ev'ry breath,
Sighs for his exit, vulgarly call'd death:
For he, with all his follies, has a mind
Not yet so blank, or fashionably blind,
But now and then, perhaps, a feeble ray
Of distant wisdom shoots across his way,
By which he reads, that life without a plan,
As useless as the moment it began,
Serves merely as a soil for discontent
To thrive in an incumbrance, ere half spent.
Oh weariness beyond what asses feel,
That tread the circuit of the cistern wheel;
A dull rotation, never at a stay,
Yesterday's face twin image of to-day,
While conversation, an exhausted stock,
Grows drowsy as the clicking of a clock.
No need, he cries, of gravity stuff'd out
With academic dignity devout,
To read wise lectures, vanity the text,
Proclaim the remedy, ye learned, next,
For truth, self-evident, with pomp impress'd,
Is vanity surpassing all the rest.

That remedy, not hid in deeps profound,
Yet seldom sought, where only to be found,
While passion turns aside from its due scope
Th' enquirer's aim, that remedy, is hope.
Life is his gift, from whom what'er life needs,
And ev'ry good and perfect gift proceeds;[1]
Bestow'd on man, like all that we partake,
Royally, freely, for his bounty sake;
Transient indeed, as is the fleeting hour,
And yet the seed of an immortal flow'r,
Design'd in honour of his endless love,

[1] St James, i, 17.

To fill with fragrance his abode above;
No trifle, howsoever short it seem,
And howsoever shadowy, no dream;
Its value, what no thought can ascertain,
Nor all an angel's eloquence explain.
    Men deal with life, as children with their play,
Who first misuse, then cast their toys away;
Live to no sober purpose, and contend
That their Creator had no serious end.
When God and man stand opposite in view,
Man's disappointment must of course ensue.
The just Creator condescends to write,
In beams of inextinguishable light,
His names of wisdom, goodness, pow'r and love,
On all that blooms below or shines above;
To catch the wand'ring notice of mankind,
And teach the world, if not perversely blind,
His gracious attributes, and prove the share
His offspring hold in his paternal care.
If led from earthly things to things divine,
His creature thwart not his august design,
Then praise is heard instead of reas'ning pride,
And captious cavil and complaint subside.
Nature employ'd in her allotted place,
Is hand-maid to the purposes of grace;
By good vouchsaf'd, makes known superior good,
And bliss not seen, by blessings understood:
That bliss, reveal'd in scripture, with a glow
Bright as the covenant-insuring bow,
Fires all his feelings with a noble scorn
Of sensual evil, and thus Hope is born.
    Hope sets the stamp of vanity on all
That men have deem'd substantial since the fall,
Yet has the wond'rous virtue to educe
From emptiness itself, a real use,
And while she takes, as at a father's hand,
What health and sober appetite demand,
From fading good derives, with chymic art,
That lasting happiness, a thankful heart.

Hope, with uplifted foot set free from earth,
Pants for the place of her ethereal birth,
On steady wing sails through th' immense abyss,
Plucks amaranthine joys from bow'rs of bliss,
And crowns the soul, while yet a mourner here,
With wreaths like those triumphant spirits wear.
Hope, as an anchor firm and sure, holds fast
The Christian vessel, and defies the blast;
Hope! nothing else can nourish and secure
His new-born virtues, and preserve him pure;
Hope! let the wretch, once conscious of the joy,
Whom now despairing agonies destroy,
Speak, for he can, and none so well as he,
What treasures centre, what delights in thee.
Had he the gems, the spices, and the land
That boasts the treasure, all at his command,
The fragrant grove, th' inestimable mine,
Were light when weigh'd against one smile of thine.
  Though clasp'd and cradled in his nurse's arms,
He shine with all a cherub's artless charms,
Man is the genuine offspring of revolt,
Stubborn and sturdy, a wild ass's colt;
His passions, like the wat'ry stores that sleep
Beneath the smiling surface of the deep,
Wait but the lashes of a wintry storm,
To frown and roar, and shake his feeble form.
From infancy through childhood's giddy maze,
Froward at school, and fretful in his plays,
The puny tyrant burns to subjugate
The free republic of the whip-gig state.
If one, his equal in athletic frame,
Or more provoking still, of nobler name,
Dare step across his arbitrary views,
An Iliad, only not in verse, ensues.
The little Greeks look trembling at the scales,
Till the best tongue or heaviest hand prevails.
  Now see him launched into the world at large;
If priest, supinely droning o'er his charge,
Their fleece his pillow, and his weekly drawl,

Though short, too long, the price he pays for all;
If lawyer, loud whatever cause he plead,
But proudest of the worst, if that succeed.
Perhaps a grave physician, gath'ring fees,
Punctually paid for length'ning out disease;
No COTTON[1], whose humanity sheds rays
That make superior skill his second praise.
If arms engage him, he devotes to sport
His date of life, so likely to be short;
A soldier may be any thing, if brave;
So may a tradesman, if not quite a knave.
Such stuff the world is made of; and mankind,
To passion, int'rest, pleasure, whim resign'd,
Insist on, as if each were his own pope,
Forgiveness, and the privilege of hope;
But conscience, in some awful silent hour,
When captivating lusts have lost their pow'r,
Perhaps when sickness, or some fearful dream,
Reminds him of religion, hated theme!
Starts from the down on which she lately slept,
And tells of laws despis'd, at least not kept;
Shows, with a pointing finger and no noise,
A pale procession of past sinful joys,
All witnesses of blessings foully scorn'd,
And life abus'd—and not to be suborn'd.
Mark these, she says, these, summon'd from afar,
Begin their march to meet thee at the bar;
There find a Judge, inexorably just,
And perish there, as all presumption must.

Peace be to those (such peace as earth can give)
Who live in pleasure, dead ev'n while they live,[2]
Born capable indeed of heav'nly truth,
But down to latest age, from earliest youth,
Their mind a wilderness through want of care,

---

[1] Dr Nathaniel Cotton (1705–1788), Evangelical poet and physician, at whose *Collegium Insanorum* in St Albans Cowper recovered from his second breakdown.

[2] Cf. 1 Timothy, v, 6.

The plough of wisdom never ent'ring there.
Peace (if insensibility may claim
A right to the meek honours of her name)
To men of pedigree, their noble race,
Emulous always of the nearest place
To any throne, except the throne of grace.
Let cottagers, and unenlighten'd swains,
Revere the laws they dream that heav'n ordains,
Resort on Sundays to the house of pray'r,
And ask, and fancy they find blessings there.
Themselves, perhaps, when weary they retreat
T' enjoy cool nature in a country seat,
T' exchange the centre of a thousand trades,
For clumps and lawns and temples and cascades,
May now and then their velvet cushions take,
And seem to pray, for good example sake;
Judging, in charity, no doubt, the town
Pious enough, and having need of none.
Kind souls! to teach their tenantry to prize
What they themselves, without remorse, despise;
Nor hope have they, nor fear, of aught to come,
As well for them had prophecy been dumb;
They could have held the conduct they pursue,
Had Paul of Tarsus liv'd and died a Jew;
And truth propos'd to reas'ners wise as they,
Is a pearl cast—completely cast away.

They die—Death lends them, pleas'd and as in sport,
All the grim honours of his ghastly court;
Far other paintings grace the chamber now,
Where late we saw the mimic landscape glow;
The busy heralds hang the sable scene,
With mournful 'scutcheons,[1] and dim lamps between;
Proclaim their titles to the crowd around,
But they that wore them, move not at the sound;
The coronet plac'd idly at their head,
Adds nothing now to the degraded dead,

[1] At this time hatchments, displaying the appropriate armorial bearings, were fixed in front of the houses of persons of rank, at their death.

And ev'n the star that glitters on the bier,
Can only say, nobility lies here.
Peace to all such—'twere pity to offend,
By useless censure, whom we cannot mend;
Life without hope can close but in despair,
'Twas there we found them, and must leave them there.

   As, when two pilgrims in a forest stray,
Both may be lost, yet each in his own way,
So fares it with the multitudes beguil'd,
In vain opinion's waste and dang'rous wild;
Ten thousand rove, the brakes and thorns among,
Some eastward, and some westward, and all wrong:
But here, alas! the fatal diff'rence lies,
Each man's belief is right in his own eyes;
And he that blames, what they have blindly chose,
Incurs resentment for the love he shows.

   Say botanist! within whose province fall
The cedar and the hyssop on the wall,[1]
Of all that deck the lanes, the fields, the bow'rs,
What parts the kindred tribes of weeds and flow'rs?
Sweet scent, or lovely form, or both combin'd,
Distinguish ev'ry cultivated kind;
The want of both denotes a meaner breed,
And Chloe from her garland picks the weed.
Thus hopes of ev'ry sort, whatever sect
Esteem them, sow them, rear them and protect;
If wild in nature, and not duly found,
Gethsemane! in thy dear, hallow'd ground,
That cannot bear the blaze of scripture light;
Nor cheer the spirit, nor refresh the sight,
Nor animate the soul to Christian deeds,
Oh cast them from thee! are weeds, arrant weeds.

   Ethelred's house, the centre of six ways,
Diverging each from each, like equal rays,
Himself as bountiful as April rains,
Lord paramount of the surrounding plains,
Would give relief of bed and board to none,

----

[1] 1 Kings, iv, 33.

But guests that sought it in th' appointed ONE.
And they might enter at his open door,
Ev'n till his spacious hall would hold no more.
He sent a servant forth by ev'ry road,
To sound his horn and publish it abroad,
That all might mark—knight, menial, high and low,
An ord'nance it concern'd them much to know.
If after all, some headstrong hardy lout
Would disobey, though sure to be shut out,
Could he with reason murmur at his case,
Himself sole author of his own disgrace?
No! the decree was just and without flaw,
And he that made, had right to make the law;
His sov'reign pow'r and pleasure unrestrain'd,
The wrong was his, who wrongfully complain'd.

Yet half mankind maintain a churlish strife
With him the donor of eternal life,
Because the deed, by which his love confirms
The largess he bestows, prescribes the terms.
Compliance with his will your lot insures,
Accept it only, and the boon is yours;
And sure it is as kind to smile and give,
As with a frown to say, do this, and live.
Love is not pedlars trump'ry bought and sold;
He *will* give freely, or he *will* withhold;
His soul abhors a mercenary thought,
And him as deeply who abhors it not;
He stipulates indeed, but merely this,
That man will freely take an unbought bliss,
Will trust him for a faithful gen'rous part,
Nor set a price upon a willing heart.
Of all the ways that seem to promise fair,
To place you where his saints his presence share,
This only can—for this plain cause, express'd
In terms as plain; himself has shut the rest.
But oh the strife, the bick'ring and debate,
The tidings of unpurchas'd heav'n create!
The flirted fan, the bridle and the toss,
All speakers, yet all language at a loss.

268

From stucco'd walls smart arguments rebound,
And beaus, adepts in ev'ry thing profound,
Die of disdain, or whistle off the sound.
Such is the clamor of rooks, daws, and kites,
Th' explosion of the levell'd tube excites,
Where mould'ring abbey-walls o'erhang the glade,
And oaks coeval spread a mournful shade.
The screaming nations hov'ring in mid air,
Loudly resent the stranger's freedom there,
And seem to warn him never to repeat,
His bold intrusion on their dark retreat.
  Adieu, Vinoso cries, ere yet he sips
The purple bumper trembling at his lips,
Adieu to all morality! if grace
Make works a vain ingredient in the case.
The Christian hope is—waiter, draw the cork—
If I mistake not—blockhead! with a fork!
Without good works, whatever some may boast,
Mere folly and delusion—Sir, your toast.
My firm persuasion is, at least sometimes,
That heav'n will weigh man's virtues and his crimes,
With nice attention, in a righteous scale,
And save or damn as these or those prevail.
I plant my foot upon this ground of trust,
And silence ev'ry fear with—God is just;
But if perchance on some dull drizzling day,
A thought intrude that says or seems to say,
If thus th' important cause is to be tried,
Suppose the beam should dip on the wrong side;
I soon recover from these needless frights,
And God is merciful—sets all to rights.
Thus, between justice, as my prime support,
And mercy, fled to as the last resort,
I glide and steal along with heav'n in view,
And, pardon me, the bottle stands with you.
  I never will believe, the col'nel cries,
The sanguinary schemes that some devise,
Who make the good Creator on their plan,
A being of less equity than man.

If appetite, or what divines call lust,
Which men comply with, e'en because they must,
Be punish'd with perdition, who is pure?
Then theirs, no doubt, as well as mine, is sure.
If sentence of eternal pain belong,
To ev'ry sudden slip and transient wrong,
Then heav'n enjoins the fallible and frail
An hopeless task, and damns them if they fail.
My creed (whatever some creed-makers mean
By Athanasian nonsense or Nicene)
My creed is, he is safe that does his best,
And death's a doom sufficient for the rest.

Right, says an ensign, and for aught I see,
Your faith and mine substantially agree:
The best of ev'ry man's performance here,
Is to discharge the duties of his sphere.
A lawyer's dealing should be just and fair,
Honesty shines with great advantage there;
Fasting and pray'r, sit well upon a priest,
A decent caution and reserve at least.
A soldier's best is courage in the field,
With nothing here that wants to be conceal'd:
Manly deportment, gallant, easy, gay,
An hand as lib'ral as the light of day;
The soldier thus endow'd, who never shrinks,
Nor closets up his thought, whate'er he thinks,
Who scorns to do an injury by stealth,
Must go to heav'n—and I must drink his health.

Sir Smug, he cries (for lowest at the board,
Just made fifth chaplain of his patron lord,
His shoulders witnessing by many a shrug
How much his feelings suffer'd, sat Sir Smug)
Your office is to winnow false from true,
Come, prophet, drink, and tell us, what thinks you.

Sighing and smiling as he takes his glass,
Which they that woo preferment, rarely pass,
Fallible man, the church-bred youth replies,
Is still found fallible, however wise,
And diff'ring judgments serve but to declare,

That truth lies somewhere if we knew but where.
Of all it ever was my lot to read,
Of critics now alive or long since dead,
The book of all the world that charm'd me most
Was, well-a-day, the title page was lost;
The writer well remarks, an heart that knows
To take with gratitude what heav'n bestows,
With prudence always ready at our call,
To guide our use of it, is all in all.
Doubtless it is—to which, of my own store,
I superadd a few essentials more;
But these, excuse the liberty I take,
I waive just now, for conversation sake.—
Spoke like an oracle, they all exclaim,
And add Right Rev'rend to Smug's honour'd name.

  And yet our lot is giv'n us in a land
Where busy arts are never at a stand,
Where science points her telescopic eye,
Familiar with the wonders of the sky,
Where bold enquiry diving out of sight,
Brings many a precious pearl of truth to light,
Where nought eludes the persevering quest,
That fashion, taste, or luxury suggest.

  But above all, in her own light array'd,
See mercy's grand apocalypse display'd!
The sacred book no longer suffers wrong,
Bound in the fetters of an unknown tongue;
But speaks, with plainness art could never mend,
What simplest minds can soonest comprehend.
God gives the word, the preachers throng around,
Live from his lip, and spread the glorious sound:
That sound bespeaks salvation on her way,
The trumpet of a life-restoring day.
'Tis heard where England's eastern glory shines,
And in the gulphs of her Cornubian[1] mines.
And still it spreads. See Germany send forth

---

[1] The preaching of John Wesley had an extraordinary influence among the miners of Cornwall.

Her sons[1] to pour it on the farthest north:
Fir'd with a zeal peculiar, *they* defy
The rage and rigor of a polar sky,
And plant successfully sweet Sharon's rose
On icy plains and in eternal snows.
   Oh blest within th' inclosure of your rocks,
Nor herds have ye to boast, nor bleating flocks,
No fertilizing streams your fields divide,
That show revers'd the villas on their side,
No groves have ye; no cheerful sound of bird,
Or voice of turtle in your land is heard;
Nor grateful eglantine regales the smell,
Of those that walk at ev'ning where ye dwell—
But winter, arm'd with terrors here unknown,
Sits absolute on his unshaken throne;
Piles up his stores amidst the frozen waste,
And bids the mountains he has built, stand fast;
Beckons the legions of his storms away
From happier scenes, to make your land a prey;
Proclaims the soil a conquest he has won,
And scorns to share it with the distant sun.
— Yet truth is yours, remote, unenvied isle,
And peace, and genuine offspring of her smile;
The pride of letter'd ignorance that binds,
In chains or error, our accomplish'd minds,
That decks with all the splendor of the true,
A false religion, is unknown to you.
Nature indeed vouchsafes for our delight,
The sweet vicissitudes of day and night;
Soft airs and genial moisture, feed and cheer,
Field, fruit and flow'r, and ev'ry creature here;
But brighter beams than his who fires the skies,
Have ris'n at length on your admiring eyes,
That shoot into your darkest caves the day,

---

[1] The Moravian missionaries in Greenland. Vide Krantz [C]. The English translation of David Crantz's *History of Greenland*, containing an account of the Moravian mission there, was published in 1767. A translation of Crantz's *History of the Moravian Brethren* appeared in 1780.

From which our nicer optics turn away.
   Here see th' encouragement grace gives to vice,
The dire effect of mercy without price!
What were they?—what some fools are made by art,
They were by nature, atheists, head and heart.
The gross idolatry blind heathens teach
Was too refin'd for them, beyond their reach.
Not ev'n the glorious sun, though men revere
The monarch most that seldom will appear,
And though his beams that quicken where they shine,
May claim some right to be esteem'd divine,
Not ev'n the sun, desirable as rare,
Could bend one knee, engage one vot'ry there;
They were what base credulity believes
True Christians are, dissemblers, drunkards, thieves.
The full-gorg'd savage at his nauseous feast
Spent half the darkness, and snor'd out the rest,
Was one, whom justice on an equal plan,
Denouncing death upon the sins of man,
Might almost have indulg'd with an escape,
Chargeable only with an human shape.
   What are they now?—morality may spare
Her grave concern, her kind suspicions there:
The wretch, who once sang wildly, danc'd and laugh'd,
And suck'd in dizzy madness with his draught,
Has wept a silent flood, revers'd his ways,
Is sober, meek, benevolent, and prays;
Feeds sparingly, communicates his store,
Abhors the craft he boasted of before,
And he that stole has learn'd to steal no more.
Well spake the prophet,[1] let the desart sing,
Where sprang the thorn, the spiry fir shall spring,
And where unsightly and rank thistles grew,
Shall grow the myrtle and luxuriant yew.
Go now, and with important tone demand,
On what foundation virtue is to stand,
If self-exalting claims be turn'd adrift,

---

[1] Isaiah, lv, 12, 13.

And grace be grace indeed, and life a gift;
The poor, reclaim'd inhabitant, his eyes
Glist'ning at once with pity and surprise,
Amaz'd that shadows should obscure the sight,
Of one whose birth was in a land of light,
Shall answer, Hope, sweet Hope, has set me free,
And made all pleasures else, mere dross to me.

    These, amidst scenes as waste as if denied
The common care that waits on all beside,
Wild as if nature there, void of all good,
Play'd only gambols in a frantic mood;
Yet charge not heav'nly skill with having plann'd
A play-thing world, unworthy of his hand,
Can see his love, though secret evil lurks
In all we touch, stamp'd plainly on his works;
Deem life a blessing with its num'rous woes,
Nor spurn away a gift a God bestows.

    Hard task indeed, o'er arctic seas to roam!
Is hope exotic? grows it not at home?
Yes, but an object, bright as orient morn,
May press the eye too closely to be borne,
A distant virtue we can all confess,
It hurts our pride and moves our envy, less.

    Leuconomus[1] (beneath well-sounding Greek
I slur a name a poet must not speak)
Stood pilloried on infamy's high stage,
And bore the pelting scorn of half an age,
The very butt of slander, and the blot
For ev'ry dart that malice ever shot.
The man that mention'd *him*, at once dismiss'd
All mercy from his lips, and sneer'd and hiss'd;
His crimes were such as Sodom never knew,
And perjury stood up to swear all true;
His aim was mischief, and his zeal pretence,
His speech rebellion against common sense;
A knave when tried on honesty's plain rule,

---

[1] A Greek version of the name of George Whitefield (1714–1770), the greatest preacher of the Methodists.

And when by that of reason, a mere fool;[1]
The world's best comfort was, his doom was pass'd,
Die when he might, he must be damn'd at last.

Now truth, perform thine office, waft aside
The curtain drawn by prejudice and pride,
Reveal (the man is dead) to wand'ring eyes
This more than monster in his proper guise.

He lov'd the world that hated him: the tear
That dropp'd upon his Bible was sincere:
Assail'd by scandal and the tongue of strife,
His only answer was, a blameless life,
And he that forged, and he that threw the dart,
Had each a brother's interest in his heart.
Paul's love of Christ, and steadiness unbrib'd,
Were copied close in him, and well transcrib'd;
He followed Paul: his zeal a kindred flame,
His apostolic charity the same,
Like him, cross'd chearfully tempestuous seas,[2]
Forsaking country, kindred, friends, and ease;
Like him he labour'd, and like him, content
To bear it, suffer'd shame where'er he went.

Blush calumny! and write upon his tomb,
If honest eulogy can spare thee room,
Thy deep repentence of thy thousand lies,
Which aim'd at him, have pierc'd th' offended skies,
And say, blot out my sin, confess'd, deplor'd,
Against thine image in thy saint, oh Lord!

No blinder bigot, I maintain it still,
Than he who must have pleasure, come what will;
He laughs, whatever weapon truth may draw,
And deems her sharp artillery mere straw.
Scripture indeed is plain, but God and he,
On scripture-ground, are sure to disagree;
Some wiser rule must teach him how to live,
Than that his Maker has seen fit to give;

[1] Cowper shared Whitefield's views on predestination.

[2] Whitefield undertook seven tours in the American colonies and played a major part in the 'Great Awakening'. He died at Newburyport, Mass.

Supple and flexible as Indian cane,
To take the bend his appetites ordain;
Contriv'd to suit frail nature's crazy case,
And reconcile his lusts with saving grace.
By this, with nice precision of design,
He draws upon life's map a zig-zag line,
That shows how far 'tis safe to follow sin,
And where his danger and God's wrath begin:
By this he forms, as pleas'd he sports along,
His well pois'd estimate of right and wrong,
And finds the modish manners of the day,
Though loose, as harmless as an infant's play.

Build by whatever plan caprice decrees,
With what material, on what ground you please,
Your hope shall stand unblam'd, perhaps admir'd,
If not that hope the scripture has requir'd:
The strange conceits, vain projects and wild dreams,
With which hypocrisy for ever teems,
(Though other follies strike the public eye,
And raise a laugh) pass unmolested by;
But if, unblameable in word and thought,
A *man* arise, a man whom God has taught,
With all Elijah's dignity of tone,
And all the love of the beloved John,
To storm the citadels they build in air,
And smite th' untemper'd wall, 'tis death to spare;[1]
To sweep away all refuges of lies,
And place, instead of quirks themselves devise,
LAMA SABACTHANI, before their eyes;[2]
To prove that without Christ, all gain is loss,
All hope, despair, that stands not on his cross:
Except the few his God may have impress'd,
A tenfold frenzy seizes all the rest.

Throughout mankind, the Christian kind at least,
There dwells a consciousness in ev'ry breast,
That folly ends where genuine hope begins,

[1] Ezekiel, xiii, 10.
[2] Matthew, xxvii, 46.

276

And he that finds his heav'n must lose his sins:
Nature opposes with her utmost force,
This riving stroke, this ultimate divorce,
And while religion seems to be her view,
Hates with a deep sincerity, *the true*:
For this, of all that ever influenc'd man,
Since Abel worshipp'd, or the world began,
This only spares no lust, admits no plea,
But makes him, if at all, completely free,
Sounds forth the signal, as she mounts her car,
Of an eternal, universal war;
Rejects all treaty, penetrates all wiles,
Scorns with the same indiff'rence frowns and smiles;
Drives through the realms of sin, where riot reels,
And grinds his crown beneath her burning wheels!
Hence all that is in man, pride, passion, art,
Pow'rs of the mind, and feelings of the heart,
Insensible of truth's almighty charms,
Starts at her first approach, and sounds to arms!
While bigotry, with well dissembled fears,
His eyes shut fast, his fingers in his ears,
Mighty to parry, and push by God's word
With senseless noise, his argument the sword,
Pretends a zeal for godliness and grace,
And spits abhorrence in the Christian's face.
    Parent of hope, immortal truth! make known
Thy deathless wreaths, and triumphs all thine own:
The silent progress of thy pow'r is such,
Thy means so feeble, and despis'd so much,
That few believe the wonders thou hast wrought,
And none can teach them but whom thou hast taught.
Oh see me sworn to serve thee, and command,
A painter's skill into a poet's hand,
That while I trembling trace a work divine,
Fancy may stand aloof from the design,
And light and shade and ev'ry stroke be thine.
    If ever thou hast felt another's pain,
If ever when he sigh'd, hast sigh'd again,
If ever on thine eye-lid stood the tear

That pity had engender'd, drop one here.
This man was happy—had the world's good word,
And with it ev'ry joy it can afford;
Friendship and love seem'd tenderly at strife,
Which most should sweeten his untroubled life;
Politely learn'd, and of a gentle race,
Good-breeding and good sense gave all a grace,
And whether at the toilette of the fair
He laugh'd and trifled, made him welcome there;
Or, if in masculine debate he shar'd,
Insur'd him mute attention and regard.
Alas how chang'd! expressive of his mind,
His eyes are sunk, arms folded, head reclin'd,
Those awful syllables, hell, death, and sin,
Though whisper'd, plainly tell what works within,
That conscience there performs her proper part,
And writes a doomsday sentence on his heart;
Forsaking, and forsaken of all friends,
He now perceives where earthly pleasure ends;
Hard task! for one who lately knew no care,
And harder still as learnt beneath despair:
His hours no longer pass unmark'd away,
A dark importance saddens every day,
He hears the notice of the clock, perplex'd,
And cries, perhaps eternity strikes next:
Sweet music is no longer music here,
And laughter sounds like madness in his ear:
His grief the world of all her pow'r disarms,
Wine has no taste, and beauty has no charms:
God's holy word, once trivial in his view,
Now by the choice of his experience, true,
Seems, as it is, the fountain whence alone,
Must spring that hope he pants to make his own.
    Now let the bright reverse be known abroad,
Say, man's a worm and pow'r belongs to God.
    As when a felon whom his country's laws
Have justly doom'd for some atrocious cause,
Expects in darkness and heart-chilling fears,
The shameful close of all his mispent years;

If chance, on heavy pinions slowly borne,
A tempest usher in the dreaded morn,
Upon his dungeon walls the lightnings play,
The thunder seems to summon him away,
The warder at the door his key applies,
Shoots back the bolt, and all his courage dies:
If then, just then, all thoughts of mercy lost,
When Hope long ling'ring, at last yields the ghost,
The sound of pardon pierce his startled ear,
He drops at once his fetters and his fear,
A transport glows in all he looks and speaks,
And the first thankful tears bedew his cheeks.
Joy, far superior joy, that much outweighs
The comfort of a few poor added days,
Invades, possesses, and o'erwhelms the soul
Of him whom hope has with a touch made whole:
'Tis heav'n, all heav'n descending on the wings
Of the glad legions of the King of Kings;
'Tis more—'tis God diffus'd through ev'ry part,
'Tis God himself triumphant in his heart.
Oh welcome now, the sun's once hated light,
His noon-day beams were never half so bright,
Not kindred minds alone are call'd t' employ
Their hours, their days, in list'ning to his joy,
Unconscious nature, all that he surveys,
Rocks, groves, and streams, must join him in his praise.
   These are thy glorious works,[1] eternal truth,
The scoff of wither'd age and beardless youth;
These move the censure and illib'ral grin
Of fools that hate thee and delight in sin:
But these shall last when night has quench'd the pole,
And heav'n is all departed as a scroll:[2]
And when, as justice has long since decreed,
This earth shall blaze, and a new world succeed,[3]
Then these thy glorious works, and they that share

[1] An echo from *Paradise Lost*, v, 153.
[2] Revelation, vi, 14.
[3] 2 Peter, iii, 10–13.

That Hope which can alone exclude despair,
Shall live exempt from weakness and decay,
The brightest wonders of an endless day.
  Happy the bard, (if that fair name belong
To him that blends no fable with his song)
Whose lines uniting, by an honest art,
The faithful monitor's and poet's part,
Seek to delight, that they may mend mankind,
And while they captivate, inform the mind:
Still happier, if he till a thankful soil,
And fruit reward his honourable toil:
But happier far who comfort those that wait
To hear plain truth at Judah's hallow'd gate:
Their language simple, as their manners meek,
No shining ornaments have they to seek,
Nor labour they, nor time nor talents waste,
In sorting flow'rs to suit a fickle taste;
But while they speak the wisdom of the skies,
Which art can only darken and disguise,
Th' abundant harvest, recompence divine,
Repays their work—the gleaning only, mine.

CHARITY

Qua nihil majus meliusve terris
Fata donavere, bonique divi;
Nec dabunt, quamvis redeant in aurum
    Tempora priscum.[1]—Horace, *Odes*, IV, ii

FAIREST and foremost of the train that wait,
On man's most dignified and happiest state,
Whether we name thee Charity or love,
Chief grace below, and all in all above,
Prosper (I press thee with a pow'rful plea)
A task I venture on, impell'd by thee:

[1] 'The fates and the kind gods have bestowed no greater or better gift upon earth, nor will they, even though times return to the primæval days of gold.'

Oh never seen but in thy blest effects,
Nor felt but in the soul that heav'n selects;
Who seeks to praise thee, and to make thee known
To other hearts, must have thee in his own.
Come, prompt me with benevolent desires,
Teach me to kindle at thy gentle fires,
And though disgrac'd and slighted, to redeem
A poet's name, by making thee the theme.
    God, working ever on a social plan,
By various ties attaches man to man:
He made at first, though free and unconfin'd,
One man the common father of the kind,
That ev'ry tribe, though plac'd as he sees best,
Where seas or desarts part them from the rest,
Diff'ring in language, manners, or in face,
Might feel themselves allied to all the race.
When Cook[1]—lamented, and with tears as just
As ever mingled with heroic dust,
Steer'd Britain's oak into a world unknown,
And in his country's glory sought his own,
Wherever he found man, to nature true,
The rights of man were sacred in his view:
He sooth'd with gifts and greeted with a smile,
The simple native of the new-found isle,
He spurn'd the wretch that slighted or withstood,
The tender argument of kindred blood,
Nor would endure that any should controul,
His free-born brethren of the southern pole.
    But though some nobler minds a law respect,
That none shall with impunity neglect,
In baser souls unnumber'd evils meet,
To thwart its influence and its end defeat.
While Cook is lov'd for savage lives he sav'd,
See Cortez odious for a world enslav'd!
Where wast thou then, sweet Charity, where then
Thou tutelary friend of helpless men?

[1] Captain James Cook was murdered by natives in Hawaii, 1779. His
death was mourned as a national misfortune.

Wast thou in monkish cells and nunn'ries found,
Or building hospitals on English ground?
No—Mammon makes the world his legatee
Through fear, not love, and heav'n abhors the fee:
Wherever found (and all men need thy care)
Nor age nor infancy could find thee there.
The hand that slew 'till it could slay no more,
Was glu'd to the sword-hilt with Indian gore;
Their prince,[1] as justly seated on his throne,
As vain imperial Philip on his own,
Trick'd out of all his royalty by art,
That stripp'd him bare and broke his honest heart,
Died by the sentence of a shaven priest,
For scorning what they taught him to detest.
How dark the veil that intercepts the blaze
Of heav'ns mysterious purposes and ways:
God stood not, though he seem'd to stand aloof,
And at this hour the conqu'ror feels the proof:
The wreath he won drew down an instant curse,
The fretting plague is in the public purse,
The canker'd spoil corrodes the pining state,
Starved by that indolence their mines create.

Oh could their ancient Incas rise again,
How would they take up Israel's taunting strain![2]
Art thou too fall'n, Iberia, do we see
The robber and the murd'rer weak as we?
Thou that hast wasted earth, and dar'd despise
Alike the wrath and mercy of the skies,
Thy pomp is in the grave, thy glory laid
Low in the pits thine avarice has made.
We come with joy from our eternal rest,

---

[1] 'Every schoolboy knows who imprisoned Montezuma, and who strangled Atahualpa.' Thus Macaulay: but Cowper confused the two. It was Pizarro, not Cortez, who ordered the strangulation of Atahualpa, the last Inca of Peru—after exacting from him an enormous ransom, and arranging his conversion to Christianity by Father Vincent. The event took place in the reign of the Emperor Charles V, and not of his son, King Philip II.

[2] Isaiah, xiv, 10–11.

To see th' oppressor, in his turn oppress'd.
Art thou the god, the thunder of whose hand,
Roll'd over all our desolated land,
Shook principalities and kingdoms down,
And made the mountains tremble at his frown?
The sword shall light upon thy boasted pow'rs,
And waste them, as thy sword has wasted ours.
'Tis thus Omnipotence his law fulfils,
And vengeance executes what justice wills.
    Again—the band of commerce was design'd
T' associate all the branches of mankind,
And if a boundless plenty be the robe,
Trade is the golden girdle of the globe:
Wise to promote whatever end he means,
God opens fruitful nature's various scenes,
Each climate needs what other climes produce,
And offers something to the gen'ral use;
No land but listens to the common call,
And in return receives supply from all;
This genial intercourse and mutual aid,
Cheers what were else an universal shade;
Calls nature from her ivy-mantled den,
And softens human rock-work into men.
Ingenious Art, with her expressive face,
Steps forth to fashion and refine the race,
Not only fills necessity's demand,
But overcharges her capacious hand;
Capricious taste itself can crave no more
Than she supplies from her abounding store;
She strikes out all that luxury can ask,
And gains new vigour at her endless task.
Hers is the spacious arch, the shapely spire,
The painter's pencil and the poet's lyre;
From her the canvass borrows light and shade,
And verse more lasting, hues that never fade.
She guides the finger o'er the dancing keys,
Gives difficulty all the grace of ease,
And pours a torrent of sweet notes around,
Fast as the thirsting ear can drink the sound.

These are the gifts of art, and art thrives most,
Where commerce has enrich'd the busy coast:
He catches all improvements in his flight,
Spreads foreign wonders in his country's sight,
Imports what others have invented well,
And stirs his own to match them, or excel.
'Tis thus reciprocating, each with each,
Alternately the nations learn and teach;
While Providence enjoins to ev'ry soul
An union with the vast terraqueous whole.

Heav'n speed the canvass gallantly unfurl'd
To furnish and accommodate a world;
To give the Pole the produce of the sun,
And knit th' unsocial climates into one.—
Soft airs and gentle heavings of the wave
Impel the fleet whose errand is to save,
To succour wasted regions, and replace
The smile of opulence in sorrow's face.—
Let nothing adverse, nothing unforeseen,
Impede the bark that plows the deep serene,
Charg'd with a freight transcending in its worth
The gems of India, nature's rarest birth,
That flies like Gabriel on his Lord's commands,[1]
An herald of God's love, to pagan lands.—
But ah! what wish can prosper, or what pray'r,
For merchants rich in cargoes of despair,
Who drive a loathsome traffic, gage and span,
And buy the muscles and the bones of man?
The tender ties of father, husband, friend,
All bonds of nature in that moment end,
And each endures while yet he draws his breath,
A stroke as fatal as the scythe of death.
The sable warrior, frantic with regret
Of her he loves, and never can forget,
Loses in tears the far receding shore,
But not the thought that they must meet no more;
Depriv'd of her and freedom at a blow,

[1] Luke, i, 19, 26.

What has he left that he can yet forego?
Yes, to deep sadness sullenly resign'd,
He feels his body's bondage in his mind,
Puts off his gen'rous nature, and to suit
His manners with his fate, puts on the brute.
　Oh most degrading of all ills that wait
On man, a mourner in his best estate!
All other sorrows virtue may endure,
And find submission more than half a cure;
Grief is itself a med'cine, and bestow'd
T' improve the fortitude that bears the load,
To teach the wand'rer, as his woes encrease,
The path of wisdom, all whose paths are peace,[1]
But slav'ry!—virtue dreads it as her grave,
Patience itself is meanness in a slave:
Or if the will and sov'reignty of God
Bid suffer it awhile, and kiss the rod,
Wait for the dawning of a brighter day,
And snap the chain the moment when you may.
Nature imprints upon whate'er we see
That has a heart and life in it, be free;
The beasts are chartered—neither age nor force
Can quell the love of freedom in a horse;
He breaks the cord that held him at the rack,
And conscious of an unincumber'd back,
Snuffs up the morning air, forgets the rein,
Loose fly his forelock and his ample mane:
Responsive to the distant neigh he neighs,
Nor stops, till overleaping all delays,
He finds the pasture where his fellows graze.
　Canst thou, and honor'd with a Christian name,
Buy what is woman-born, and feel no shame?
Trade in the blood of innocence, and plead
Expedience as a warrant for the deed?
So may the wolf, whom famine has made bold
To quit the forest and invade the fold:
So may the ruffian, who with ghostly glide,

[1] Proverbs, iii, 17.

Dagger in hand, steals close to your bed-side;
Not he, but his emergence forc'd the door,
He found it inconvenient to be poor.
Has God then giv'n its sweetness to the cane,
Unless his laws be trampled on—in vain?
Built a brave world, which cannot yet subsist,
Unless his right to rule it be dismiss'd?
Impudent blasphemy! so folly pleads,
And av'rice being judge, with ease succeeds.

But grant the plea, and let it stand for just,
That man make man his prey, because he *must*,
Still there is room for pity to abate
And soothe the sorrows of so sad a state.
A Briton knows, or, if he knows it not,
The Scripture plac'd within his reach, he ought,
That souls have no discriminating hue,
Alike important in their Maker's view;
That none are free from blemish since the fall,
And love divine has paid one price for all.
The wretch that works and weeps without relief
Has one that notices his silent grief,
He from whose hands alone all pow'r proceeds,
Ranks its abuse among the foulest deeds,
Considers *all* injustice with a frown,
But *marks* the man that treads his fellow down.
Begone, the whip and bell in that hard hand
Are hateful ensigns of usurp'd command.
Not Mexico could purchase kings a claim
To scourge him, weariness his only blame.
Remember, heav'n has an avenging rod;
To smite the poor is treason against God.

Trouble is grudgingly and hardly brook'd,
While life's sublimest joys are overlook'd;
We wander o'er a sun-burnt thirsty soil,
Murm'ring and weary of our daily toil,
Forget t' enjoy the palm-tree's offer'd shade,
Or taste the fountain in the neighb'ring glade:
Else who would lose, that had the pow'r t' improve,
Th' occasion of transmuting fear to love?

Oh 'tis a godlike privilege to save,
And he that scorns it is himself a slave.—
Inform his mind, one flash of heav'nly day
Would heal his heart and melt his chains away;
'Beauty for ashes'[1] is a gift indeed,
And slaves, by truth enlarg'd, are doubly freed:
Then would he say, submissive at thy feet,
While gratitude and love made service sweet,
My dear deliv'rer out of hopeless night,
Whose bounty bought me but to give me light,
I was a bondman on my native plain,
Sin forg'd, and ignorance made fast, the chain;
Thy lips have shed instruction as the dew,
Taught me what path to shun, and what pursue;
Farewell my former joys! I sigh no more
For Africa's once lov'd, benighted shore;
Serving a benefactor I am free,
At my best home if not exil'd from thee.
　　Some men make gain a fountain, whence proceeds
A stream of lib'ral and heroic deeds;
The swell of pity, not to be confin'd
Within the scanty limits of the mind,
Disdains the bank, and throws the golden sands,
A rich deposit, on the bord'ring lands:
These have an ear for *his* paternal call,
Who makes some rich for the supply of all,
God's gift with pleasure in his praise employ,
And THORNTON[2] is familiar with the joy.

---

[1] Isaiah, lxi, 3: 'To appoint unto them that mourn in Zion, to give unto them beauty for ashes, the oil of joy for mourning, the garment of praise for the spirit of heaviness,' etc.

[2] John Thornton (1720–90) of Clapham. He inherited a fortune from his father, a governor of the Bank of England, and increased it in the Russian trade. He gave much of his income away for the furtherance of the Evangelical movement, distributed thousands of Bibles and religious books throughout the world, and bought up livings to bestow upon 'truly religious ministers'. *Olney Hymns* was published at his expense. He made Newton an allowance of £200 p.a., and doubled it when Cowper was an inmate of his house.

Oh could I worship aught beneath the skies,
That earth hath seen or fancy can devise,
Thine altar, sacred liberty, should stand,
Built by no mercenary vulgar hand,
With fragrant turf and flow'rs as wild and fair
As ever dress'd a bank or scented summer air.
Duly as ever on the mountain's height
The peep of morning shed a dawning light;
Again, when ev'ning in her sober vest
Drew the grey curtain of the fading west,
My soul should yield thee willing thanks and praise
For the chief blessings of my fairest days:
But that were sacrilege—praise is not thine,
But his who gave thee and preserves thee mine:
Else I would say, and as I spake, bid fly
A captive bird into the boundless sky,
This triple realm adores thee—thou art come
From Sparta hither, and art here at home.
We feel thy force still active, at this hour
Enjoy immunity from priestly pow'r,
While conscience, happier than in ancient years,
Owns no superior but the God she fears.
Propitious spirit! yet expunge a wrong[1]
Thy rights have suffer'd, and our land, too long,
Teach mercy on ten thousand hearts that share
The fears and hopes of a commercial care;
Prisons expect the wicked, and were built
To bind the lawless and to punish guilt,
But shipwreck, earthquake, battle, fire and flood,
Are mighty mischiefs, not to be withstood,
And honest merit stands on slipp'ry ground,
Where covert guile and artifice abound;
Let just restraint, for public peace design'd,
Chain up the wolves and tigers of mankind,
The foe of virtue has no claim to thee,
But let insolvent innocence go free.

    Patron of else the most despis'd of men,

---

[1] The state of debtors' prisons.

Accept the tribute of a stranger's pen;
Verse, like the laurel, its immortal meed,
Should be the guerdon of a noble deed;
I may alarm thee, but I fear the shame
(Charity chosen as my theme and aim)
I must incur, forgetting HOWARD's[1] name.
Blest with all wealth can give thee, to resign
Joys doubly sweet to feelings quick as thine,
To quit the bliss thy rural scenes bestow,
To seek a nobler amidst scenes of woe,
To traverse seas, range kingdoms, and bring home,
Not the proud monuments of Greece or Rome,
But knowledge such as only dungeons teach,
And only sympathy like thine could reach;
That grief, sequester'd from the public stage,
Might smooth her feathers and enjoy her cage,
Speaks a divine ambition, and a zeal,
The boldest patriot might be proud to feel.
Oh that the voice of clamor and debate,
That pleads for peace 'till it disturbs the state,
Were hush'd in favour of thy gen'rous plea,
The poor thy clients, and heav'n's smile thy fee.
    Philosophy, that does not dream or stray,
Walks arm in arm with nature all his way,
Compasses earth, dives into it, ascends
Whatever steep enquiry recommends,
Sees planetary wonders smoothly roll
Round other systems under her control,
Drinks wisdom as the milky stream of light
That cheers the silent journey of the night,
And brings at his return a bosom charg'd
With rich instruction, and a soul enlarg'd.
The treasur'd sweets of the capacious plan
That heav'n spreads wide before the view of man,
All prompt his pleas'd pursuit, and to pursue
Still prompt him, with a pleasure always new;
He too has a connecting pow'r, and draws

[1] John Howard, the prison reformer. See letter, pp. 921–2.

Man to the centre of the common cause,
Aiding a dubious and deficient sight,
With a new medium and a purer light.
All truth is precious, if not all divine,
And what dilates the pow'rs must needs refine.
He reads the skies, and watching ev'ry change,
Provides the faculties an ampler range,
And wins mankind, as his attempts prevail,
A prouder station on the gen'ral scale.
But reason still, unless divinely taught,
Whate'er she learns, learns nothing as she ought;
The lamp of revelation only, shows,
What human wisdom cannot but oppose,
That man in nature's richest mantle clad,
And grac'd with all philosophy can add,
Though fair without, and luminous within,
Is still the progeny and heir of sin.
Thus taught, down falls the plumage of his pride,
He feels his need of an unerring guide,
And knows that falling he shall rise no more,
Unless the pow'r that bade him stand, restore.
This is indeed philosophy; this known,
Makes wisdom, worthy of the name, his own;
And without this, whatever he discuss,
Whether the space between the stars and us,
Whether he measure earth, compute the sea,
Weigh sun-beams, carve a fly, or spit a flea—,
The solemn trifler with his boasted skill
Toils much, and is a solemn trifler still;
Blind was he born, and, his misguided eyes
Grown dim in trifling studies, blind he dies.
Self-knowledge truly learn'd, of course implies
The rich possession of a nobler prize,
For self to self, and God to man reveal'd,
(Two themes to nature's eye for ever seal'd)
Are taught by rays that fly with equal pace
From the same center of enlight'ning grace.
Here stay thy foot, how copious and how clear,
Th' o'erflowing well of Charity springs here!

Hark! 'tis the music of a thousand rills,
Some through the groves, some down the sloping hills,
Winding a secret or an open course,
And all supplied from an eternal source.
The ties of nature do but feebly bind,
And commerce partially reclaims, mankind;
Philosophy, without his heav'nly guide,
May blow up self-conceit and nourish pride,
But while his province is the reas'ning part,
Has still a veil of midnight on his heart:
'Tis truth divine, exhibited on earth,
Gives Charity her being and her birth.

Suppose (when thought is warm, and fancy flows,
What will not argument sometimes suppose?)
An isle possess'd by creatures of our kind,
Endu'd with reason, yet by nature blind.
Let supposition lend her aid once more,
And land some grave optician on the shore,
He claps his lens, if haply they may see,
Close to the part where vision ought to be,
But finds that though his tubes assist the sight,
They cannot give it, or make darkness light.
He reads wise lectures, and describes aloud
A sense they know not, to the wond'ring crowd,
He talks of light and the prismatic hues,
As men of depth in erudition use,
But all he gains for his harangue is — Well —
What monstrous lies some travellers will tell.

The soul whose sight all-quick'ning grace renews,
Takes the resemblance of the good she views,
As di'monds stript of their opaque disguise,
Reflect the noon-day glory of the skies.
She speaks of him, her author, guardian, friend,
Whose love knew no beginning, knows no end,
In language warm as all that love inspires,
And in the glow of her intense desires,
Pants to communicate her noble fires.
She sees a world stark blind to what employs
Her eager thought, and feeds her flowing joys.

Though wisdom hail them, heedless of her call,
Flies to save some, and feels a pang for all:
Herself as weak as her support is strong,
She feels that frailty she denied so long,
And, from a knowledge of her own disease,
Learns to compassionate the sick she sees.
Here see, acquitted of all vain pretence,
The reign of genuine Charity commence;
Though scorn repay her sympathetic tears,
She still is kind, and still she perseveres;
The truth she loves, a sightless world blaspheme,
'Tis childish dotage, a delirious dream,
The danger they discern not, they deny,
Laugh at their only remedy, and die:
But still a soul thus touch'd, can never cease,
Whoever threatens war, to speak of peace;
Pure in her aim and in her temper mild,
Her wisdom seems the weakness of a child;
She makes excuses where she might condemn,
Reviled by those that hate her, prays for them;
Suspicion lurks not in her artless breast,
The worst suggested, she believes the best;
Not soon provok'd, however stung and teaz'd,
And if perhaps made angry, soon appeas'd,
She rather waives than will dispute her right,
And injur'd, makes forgiveness her delight.

    Such was the portrait an apostle drew,[1]
The bright original was one he knew,
Heav'n held his hand, the likeness must be true.

    When one that holds communion with the skies,
Has fill'd his urn where these pure waters rise,
And once more mingles with us meaner things,
'Tis ev'n as if an angel shook his wings;
Immortal fragrance fills the circuit wide,[2]

[1] 1 Corinthians, xiii.
  Paradise Lost, v, 285–7:

> Like Maia's son he stood,
> And shook his Plumes, that Heavenly fragrance fill'd
> The circuit wide.

That tells us whence his treasures are supplied.
So when a ship well freighted with the stores
The sun matures on India's spicy shores,
Has dropt her anchor and her canvas furl'd,
In some safe haven of our western world,
'Twere vain enquiry to what port she went,
The gale informs us, laden with the scent.
　　Some seek, when queasy conscience has its qualms,
To lull the painful malady with alms;
But charity not feign'd, intends alone
Another's good—theirs centres in their own;
And too short liv'd to reach the realms of peace,
Must cease for ever when the poor shall cease.
Flavia, most tender of her own good name,
Is rather careless of a sister's fame,
Her superfluity the poor supplies,
But if she touch a character, it dies.
The seeming virtue weigh'd against the vice,
She deems all safe, for she has paid the price;
No charity but alms aught values she,
Except in porcelain on her mantle-tree.
How many deeds with which the world has rung,
From pride, in league with ignorance, have sprung?
But God o'errules all human follies still,
And bends the tough materials to his will.
A conflagration or a wintry flood,
Has left some hundreds without home or food,
Extravagance and av'rice shall subscribe,
While fame and self-complacence are the bribe.
The brief[1] proclaim'd, it visits ev'ry pew,
But first the Squire's, a compliment but due:
With slow deliberation he unties
His glitt'ring purse, that envy of all eyes,
And while the clerk just puzzles out the psalm,
Slides guinea behind guinea in his palm,
'Till finding what he might have found before,

---

[1] *Brief:* A 'licence and protection' issued under the Great Seal to the clergy, authorizing them to collect alms for a particular cause.

A smaller piece amidst the precious store,
Pinch'd close between his finger and his thumb,
He half exhibits, and then drops the sum;
Gold to be sure!—throughout the town 'tis told
How the good Squire gives never less than gold.
From motives such as his, though not the best,
Springs in due time supply for the distress'd,
Not less effectual than what love bestows,
Except that office clips it as it goes.

But lest I seem to sin against a friend,
And wound the grace I mean to recommend,
(Though vice derided with a just design
Implies no trespass against love divine)
Once more I would adopt the graver style,
A teacher should be sparing of his smile.

Unless a love of virtue light the flame,
Satyr is more than those he brands, to blame;
He hides behind a magisterial air
His own offences, and strips others bare;
Affects indeed a most humane concern,
That men if gently tutor'd will not learn,
That mulish folly not to be reclaim'd
By softer methods, must be made asham'd,
But (I might instance in St Patrick's dean)[1]
Too often rails to gratify his spleen.
Most sat'rists are indeed a public scourge,
Their mildest physic is a farrier's purge,
Their acrid temper turns, as soon as stirr'd,
The milk of their good purpose all to curd,
Their zeal begotten, as their works rehearse,
By lean despair upon an empty purse;
The wild assassins start into the street,
Prepar'd to poignard whomsoe'er they meet;
No skill in swordmanship, however just,
Can be secure against a madman's thrust,
And even virtue so unfairly match'd,
Although immortal, may be prick'd or scratch'd.

[1] Jonathan Swift.

When scandal has new minted an old lie,
Or tax'd invention for a fresh supply,
'Tis call'd a satyr, and the world appears
Gath'ring around it with erected ears;
A thousand names are toss'd into the crowd,
Some whisper'd softly, and some twang'd aloud,
Just as the sapience of an author's brain
Suggests it safe or dang'rous to be plain.
Strange! how the frequent interjected dash,
Quickens a market and helps off the trash,
Th' important letters that include the rest,
Serve as a key to those that are suppress'd,
Conjecture gripes the victims in his paw,
The world is charm'd, and Scrib.¹ escapes the law.
So, when the cold damp shades of night prevail,
Worms may be caught by either head or tail,
Forcibly drawn from many a close recess,
They meet with little pity, no redress;
Plung'd in the stream they lodge upon the mud,
Food for the famish'd rovers of the flood.
   All zeal for a reform that gives offence
To peace and charity, is mere pretence:
A bold remark, but which, if well applied,
Would humble many a tow'ring poet's pride:
Perhaps, the man was in a sportive fit,
And had no other play-place for his wit;
Perhaps enchanted with the love of fame,
He sought the jewel in his neighbour's shame;
Perhaps—whatever end he might pursue,
The cause of virtue could not be his view.
At ev'ry stroke wit flashes in our eyes,
The turns are quick, the polish'd points surprise,
But shine with cruel and tremendous charms,
That while they please possess us with alarms:
So have I seen, (and hasten'd to the sight
On all the wings of holiday delight)

¹ *Scrib*: a satirist, perhaps abbreviated from the Scriblerus Club, whose members included Pope, Swift, Gay and Arbuthnot, and their satirical production, *Memoirs of Martinus Scriblerus*.

Where stands that monument of ancient pow'r,
Nam'd with emphatic dignity, the tow'r,[1]
Guns, halberts, swords and pistols, great and small,
In starry forms dispos'd upon the wall;
We wonder, as we gazing stand below,
That brass and steel should make so fine a show;
But though we praise th' exact designer's skill,
Account them implements of mischief still.

No works shall find acceptance in that day
When all disguises shall be rent away,
That square not truly with the Scripture plan,
Nor spring from love to God, or love to man.
As he ordains things sordid in their birth
To be resolv'd into their parent earth,
And though the soul shall seek superior orbs,
Whate'er this world produces, it absorbs;
So self starts nothing but what tends apace
Home to the goal where it began the race.
Such as our motive is, our aim must be,
If this be servile, that can ne'er be free;
If self employ us, whatsoe'er is wrought,
We glorify that self, not him we ought:
Such virtues had need prove their own reward,
The judge of all men owes them no regard.
True Charity, a plant divinely nurs'd,
Fed by the love from which it rose at first,
Thrives against hope and in the rudest scene,
Storms but enliven its unfading green;
Exub'rant is the shadow it supplies,
Its fruit on earth, its growth above the skies.
To look at him who form'd us and redeem'd,
So glorious now, though once so disesteem'd,
To see a God stretch forth his human hand,
T' uphold the boundless scenes of his command,
To recollect that in a form like ours,
He bruis'd beneath his feet th' infernal pow'rs,
Captivity led captive, rose to claim

[1] The Tower of London.

The wreath he won so dearly, in our name;
That, thron'd above all height,[1] he condescends
To call the few that trust in him his friends;[2]
That in the heav'n of heav'ns, that space he deems
Too scanty for th' exertion of his beams,
And shines as if impatient to bestow
Life and a kingdom upon worms below;
That sight imparts a never-dying flame,
Though feeble in degree, in kind the same.
Like him, the soul thus kindled from above,
Spreads wide her arms of universal love,
And still enlarg'd as she receives the grace,
Includes creation in her close embrace.
Behold a Christian — and without the fires
The founder of that name alone inspires,
Though all accomplishments, all knowledge meet,
To make the shining prodigy complete,
Whoever boasts that name — behold a cheat.

    Were love, in these the world's last doting years,
As frequent as the want of it appears,
The churches warm'd, they would no longer hold
Such frozen figures, stiff as they are cold;
Relenting forms would lose their pow'r or cease,
And ev'n the dipt and sprinkled, live in peace;[3]
Each heart would quit its prison in the breast,
And flow in free communion with the rest.
The statesman, skill'd in projects dark and deep
Might burn his useless Machiavel, and sleep;
His budget often fill'd, yet always poor,
Might swing at ease behind his study door,
No longer prey upon our annual rents,
Nor scare the nation with its big contents:
Disbanded legions freely might depart,
And slaying man would cease to be an art.
No learned disputants would take the field,
Sure not to conquer, and sure not to yield,

[1] *Paradise Lost*, iii, 58.
[2] Cf. St John, xv, 14–15.
[3] *dipt*: Baptists: *sprinkled*, other Christians.

Both sides deceiv'd, if rightly understood,
Pelting each other for the public good.
Did Charity prevail, the press would prove
A vehicle of virtue, truth and love,
And I might spare myself the pains to show
What few can learn, and all suppose they know.
　　Thus have I sought to grace a serious lay
With many a wild indeed, but flow'ry spray,
In hopes to gain what else I must have lost,
Th' attention pleasure has so much engross'd.
But if unhappily deceiv'd I dream,
And prove too weak for so divine a theme,
Let Charity forgive me a mistake
That zeal, not vanity, has chanc'd to make,
And spare the poet for his subject sake.

CONVERSATION

Nam neque me tantum venientis sibilus austri,
Nec percussa juvant fluctu tam litora, nec quæ
Saxosas inter decurrunt flumina valles.[1]
　　　　　　　　Virgil, *Eclogues*, v, [82–84]

THOUGH nature weigh our talents, and dispense
To ev'ry man his modicum of sense,
And Conversation in its better part
May be esteem'd a gift and not an art,
Yet much depends, as in the tiller's toil,
On culture, and the sowing of the soil.
Words learn'd by rote, a parrot may rehearse,
But talking is not always to converse,
Not more distinct from harmony divine
The constant creaking of a country sign.

---

[1] 'For I am not so much delighted by the whistling onset of the south wind, or by the dash of the waves upon the shore, or by the streams that flow down through the rocky glens.'

As alphabets in ivory employ
Hour after hour the yet unletter'd boy,
Sorting and puzzling with a deal of glee
Those seeds of science call'd his A B C;
So language in the mouths of the adult,
Witness its insignificant result,
Too often proves an implement of play,
A toy to sport with, and pass time away.
Collect at ev'ning what the day brought forth,
Compress the sum into its solid worth,
And if it weigh th' importance of a fly,
The scales are false, or Algebra a lie.
Sacred interpreter of human thought,
How few respect or use thee as they ought!
But all shall give account of ev'ry wrong,[1]
Who dare dishonour or defile the tongue,
Who prostitute it in the cause of vice,
Or sell their glory at a market-price,
Who vote for hire, or point it with lampoon,
The dear-bought placeman, and the cheap buffoon.
　　There is a prurience in the speech of some,
Wrath stays him, or else God would strike them dumb;
His wise forbearance has their end in view;
They fill their measure and receive their due.
The heathen law-givers of ancient days,
Names almost worthy of a Christian praise,
Would drive them forth from the resort of men,
And shut up ev'ry satyr in his den.
Oh come not ye near innocence and truth,
Ye worms that eat into the bud of youth!
Infectious as impure, your blighting pow'r
Taints in its rudiments the promis'd flow'r,
Its odour perish'd and its charming hue,
Thenceforth 'tis hateful for it smells of you.
Not ev'n the vigorous and headlong rage
Of adolescence or a firmer age,
Affords a plea allowable or just,

[1] Cf. Matthew, xii, 36–37.

For making speech the pamperer of lust;
But when the breath of age commits the fault,
'Tis nauseous as the vapor of a vault.
So wither'd stumps disgrace the sylvan scene,
No longer fruitful and no longer green,
The sapless wood, divested of the bark,
Grows fungous and takes fire at ev'ry spark.

    Oaths terminate, as Paul observes, all strife[1]—
Some men have surely then a peaceful life;
Whatever subject occupy discourse,
The feats of Vestris[2] or the naval force,
Asseveration blust'ring in your face
Makes contradiction such an hopeless case;
In ev'ry tale they tell, or false or true,
Well known, or such as no man ever knew,
They fix attention, heedless of your pain,
With oaths like rivets forc'd into the brain;
And ev'n when sober truth prevails throughout,
They swear it, 'till affirmance breeds a doubt.
A Persian, humble servant of the sun,
Who though devout yet bigotry had none,
Hearing a lawyer, grave in his address,
With adjurations ev'ry word impress,
Suppos'd the man a bishop, or at least,
God's name so much upon his lips, a priest;
Bow'd at the close with all his graceful airs,
And begg'd an int'rest in his frequent pray'rs.

    Go quit the rank to which ye stood preferr'd,
Henceforth associate in one common herd;
Religion, virtue, reason, common sense,
Pronounce your human form a false pretence,
A mere disguise in which a devil lurks,
Who yet betrays his secret by his works.

    Ye pow'rs who rule the tongue, if such there are,
And make colloquial happiness your care,
Preserve me from the thing I dread and hate,

---

[1] Hebrews, vi, 16.
[2] Gaetano Vestris, Italian dancer; he retired in 1781.

A duel in the form of a debate;
The clash of arguments and jar of words,
Worse than the mortal brunt of rival swords,
Decide no question with their tedious length,
For opposition gives opinion strength,
Divert the champions, prodigal of breath,
And put the peaceably-disposed to death.
Oh thwart me not, Sir Soph., at ev'ry turn,
Nor carp at ev'ry flaw you may discern,
Though syllogisms hang not on my tongue,
I am not surely always in the wrong;
'Tis hard if all is false that I advance,
A fool must now and then be right, by chance.
Not that all freedom of dissent I blame,
No—there I grant the privilege I claim.
A disputable point is no man's ground,
Rove where you please, 'tis common all around,
Discourse may want an animated—No—
To brush the surface and to make it flow;
But still remember, if you mean to please,
To press your point with modesty and ease.
The mark at which my juster aim I take,
Is contradiction for its own dear sake;
Set your opinion at whatever pitch,
Knots and impediments make something hitch;
Adopt his own, 'tis equally in vain,
Your thread of argument is snapt again;
The wrangler, rather than accord with you,
Will judge *himself* deceiv'd, and prove it too.
Vociferated logic kills me quite,
A noisy man is always in the right,
I twirl my thumbs, fall back into my chair,
Fix on the wainscot a distressful stare,
And, when I hope his blunders are all out,
Reply discreetly—to be sure—no doubt.

  DUBIUS is such a scrupulous good man—
Yes—you may catch him tripping if you can.
He would not, with a peremptory tone,
Assert the nose upon his face his own;

With hesitation admirably slow,
He humbly hopes—presumes it may be so.
His evidence, if he were call'd by law
To swear to some enormity he saw,
For want of prominence and just relief,
Would hang an honest man and save a thief.
Through constant dread of giving truth offence,
He ties up all his hearers in suspense;
Knows what he knows as if he knew it not,
What he remembers, seems to have forgot;
His sole opinion, whatsoe'er befall,
Cent'ring at last in having none at all.
Yet though he teaze and baulk your list'ning ear,
He makes one useful point exceeding clear;
Howe'er ingenious on his darling theme,
A sceptic in philosophy may seem,
Reduc'd to practice, his beloved rule
Would only prove him a consummate fool;
Useless in him alike both brain and speech,
Fate having plac'd all truth above his reach,
His ambiguities his total sum,
He might as well be blind and deaf and dumb.
   Where men of judgment creep and feel their way,
The positive pronounce without dismay,
Their want of light and intellect supplied,
By sparks absurdity strikes out of pride:
Without the means of knowing right from wrong,
They always are decisive, clear and strong;
Where others toil with philosophic force,
Their nimble nonsense takes a shorter course,
Flings at your head conviction in the lump,
And gains remote conclusions at a jump:
Their own defect invisible to them,
Seen in another they at once condemn,
And though self-idoliz'd in ev'ry case,
Hate their own likeness in a brother's face.
The cause is plain and not to be denied,
The proud are always most provok'd by pride,
Few competitions but engender spite

And those the most, where neither has a right.
    The point of honour has been deem'd of use,
To teach good manners and to curb abuse,
Admit it true, the consequence is clear,
Our polish'd manners are a mask we wear,
And at the bottom, barb'rous still and rude,
We are restrain'd indeed, but not subdued;
The very remedy, however sure,
Springs from the mischief it intends to cure,
And savage in its principle appears,
Tried, as it should be, by the fruit it bears.
'Tis hard indeed if nothing will defend
Mankind from quarrels but their fatal end,
That now and then an hero must decease,
That the surviving world may live in peace.
Perhaps at last, close scrutiny may show
The practice dastardly and mean and low,
That men engage in it, compell'd by force,
And fear, not courage, is its proper source,
The fear of tyrant custom, and the fear
Lest fops should censure us, and fools should sneer;
At least to trample on our Maker's laws,
And hazard life, for any or no cause,
To rush into a fixt eternal state,
Out of the very flames of rage and hate,
Or send another shiv'ring to the bar
With all the guilt of such unnat'ral war,
Whatever use may urge or honor plead,
On reason's verdict is a madman's deed.
Am I to set my life upon a throw
Because a bear is rude and surly? No—
A moral, sensible and well-bred man
Will not affront me, and no other can.
Were I empow'r'd to regulate the lists,
They should encounter with well-loaded fists,
A Trojan combat would be something new,
Let DARES beat ENTELLUS[1] black and blue;

[1] *Aeneid* v, 362–472.

Then each might show, to his admiring friends,
In honourable bumps his rich amends,
And carry, in contusions of his scull,
A satisfactory receipt in full.
   A story in which native humour reigns
Is often useful, always entertains.
A graver fact enlisted on your side,
May furnish illustration, well applied;
But sedentary weavers of long tales
Give me the fidgets and my patience fails.
'Tis the most asinine employ on earth
To hear them tell of parentage and birth,
And echo conversations, dull and dry,
Embellish'd with, *he said*, and *so said I*.
At ev'ry interview their route the same,
The repetition makes attention lame,
We bustle up with unsuccessful speed,
And in the saddest part cry — Droll indeed!
The path of narrative with care pursue,
Still making probability your clue,
On all the vestiges of truth attend,
And let *them* guide you to a decent end;
Of all ambitions man may entertain,
The worst that can invade a sickly brain
Is that which angles hourly for surprize,
And baits its hook with prodigies and lies.
Credulous infancy, or age as weak,
Are fittest auditors for such to seek,
Who to please others will themselves disgrace,
Yet please not, but affront you to your face.
A great retailer of this curious ware,
Having unloaded and made many stare,
Can this be true? an arch observer cries —
Yes, rather mov'd, I saw it with these eyes.
Sir! I believe it on that ground alone,
I could not, had I seen it with my own.
   A tale should be judicious, clear, succinct,
The language plain, and incidents well link'd,
Tell not as new, what ev'ry body knows,

And new or old, still hasten to a close,
There cent'ring in a focus, round and neat,
Let all your rays of information meet:
What neither yields us profit or delight,
Is like a nurse's lullaby at night,
Guy Earl of Warwick[1] and fair Eleanore,
Or giant-killing Jack would please me more.
   The pipe, with solemn interposing puff,
Makes half a sentence at a time enough;
The dozing sages drop the drowsy strain,
Then pause, and puff—and speak, and pause again.
Such often, like the tube they so admire,
Important triflers! have more smoke than fire.
Pernicious weed! whose scent the fair annoys,
Unfriendly to society's chief joys,
Thy worst effect is banishing for hours
The sex whose presence civilizes ours:
Thou art indeed the drug a gard'ner wants,
To poison vermin that infest his plants:
But are we so to wit and beauty blind,
As to despise the glory of our kind,
And show the softest minds and fairest forms
As little mercy, as he, grubs and worms?
They dare not wait the riotous abuse,
Thy thirst-creating streams at length produce,
When wine has giv'n indecent language birth,
And forc'd the flood-gates of licentious mirth;
For sea-born Venus her attachment shows
Still to that element from which she rose,
And with a quiet which no fumes disturb,
Sips meek infusions of a milder herb.
   Th' emphatic speaker dearly loves t' oppose
In contact inconvenient, nose to nose,
As if the gnomon on his neighbour's phiz,
Touch'd with a magnet had attracted his.

[1] Sir Guy of Warwick, hero of a popular mediæval romance, was a slayer of dragons who saved England by his victory over the Danish giant Colbrand.

His whisper'd theme, dilated and at large,
Proves after all a wind-gun's airy charge,
An extract of his diary—no more,
A tasteless journal of the day before.
He walk'd abroad, o'ertaken in the rain
Called on a friend, drank tea, stept home again,
Resum'd his purpose, had a world of talk
With one he stumbled on, and lost his walk.
I interrupt him with a sudden bow,
Adieu, dear Sir! lest you should lose it now.

 I cannot talk with civet in the room,
A fine puss-gentleman that's all perfume;
The sight's enough—no need to smell a beau—
Who thrusts his nose into a raree-show?
His odoriferous attempts to please,
Perhaps might prosper with a swarm of bees,
But we that make no honey, though we sting,
Poets, are sometimes apt to maul the thing.
'Tis wrong to bring into a mixt resort
What makes some sick, and others *a-la-mort*,
An argument of cogence, we may say,
Why such an one should keep *himself* away.

 A graver coxcomb we may sometimes see,
Quite as absurd, though not so light as he:
A shallow brain behind a serious mask,
An oracle within an empty cask,
The solemn fop; significant and budge;[1]
A fool with judges, amongst fools a judge.
He says but little, and that little said
Owes all its weight, like loaded dice, to lead.
His wit invites you by his looks to come,
But when you knock it never is at home:
'Tis like a parcel sent you by the stage,
Some handsome present, as your hopes presage,
'Tis heavy, bulky, and bids fair to prove
An absent friend's fidelity and love,

---

[1] *Budge*: i.e., wearing a fur robe: hence, pompous in demeanour.
Cf. *Comus*, 707.

But when unpack'd your disappointment groans,
To find it stuff'd with brickbats, earth and stones.
  Some men employ their health, an ugly trick,
In making known how oft they have been sick,
And give us in recitals of disease
A doctor's trouble, but without the fees:
Relate how many weeks they kept their bed,
How an emetic or cathartic sped,
Nothing is slightly touch'd, much less forgot,
Nose, ears, and eyes seem present on the spot.
Now the distemper, spite of draught or pill,
Victorious seem'd, and now the doctor's skill;
And now—alas for unforeseen mishaps!
They put on a damp night-cap and relapse;
They thought they must have died they were so bad,
Their peevish hearers almost wish they had.
  Some fretful tempers wince at ev'ry touch,
You always do too little or too much:
You speak with life, in hopes to entertain,
Your elevated voice goes through the brain;
You fall at once into a lower key,
That's worse—the drone-pipe of an humble bee.
The southern sash admits too strong a light,
You rise and drop the curtain—now it's night.
He shakes with cold—you stir the fire and strive
To make a blaze—that's roasting him alive.
Serve him with ven'son and he chuses fish,
With soal—that's just the sort he would not wish,
He takes what he at first profess'd to loath,
And in due time feeds heartily on both;
Yet still, o'erclouded with a constant frown,
He does not swallow, but he gulps it down.
Your hope to please him, vain on ev'ry plan,
Himself should work that wonder if he can—
Alas! his efforts double his distress,
He likes yours little, and his own still less.
Thus always teazing others, always teaz'd,
His only pleasure is—to be displeas'd.
  I pity bashful men, who feel the pain

Of fancied scorn and undeserv'd disdain,
And bear the marks upon a blushing face
Of needless shame and self-impos'd disgrace.
Our sensibilities are so acute,
The fear of being silent makes us mute.
We sometimes think we could a speech produce,
Much to the purpose, if our tongues were loose,
But being tied, it dies upon the lip,
Faint as a chicken's note that has the pip:
Our wasted oil unprofitably burns,
Like hidden lamps in old sepulchral urns.[1]
Few Frenchmen of this evil have complain'd,
It seems as if we Britons were ordain'd,
By way of wholesome curb upon our pride,
To fear each other, fearing none beside.
The cause perhaps enquiry may descry,
Self-searching with an introverted eye,
Conceal'd within an unsuspected part,
The vainest corner of our own vain heart:
For ever aiming at the world's esteem,
Our self-importance ruins its own scheme;
In other eyes our talents rarely shown,
Become at length so splendid in our own,
We dare not risque them into public view,
Lest they miscarry of what seems their due.
True modesty is a discerning grace,
And only blushes in the proper place,
But counterfeit is blind, and skulks through fear,
Where 'tis a shame to be asham'd t' appear;
Humility the parent of the first,
The last by vanity produc'd and nurst,
The circle form'd we sit in silent state,
Like figures drawn upon a dial-plate;
Yes ma'am, and no ma'am, utter'd softly, show

---

[1] It was at one time believed that the ancients possessed the power of constructing lamps which, once lighted, would burn, some said, for a thousand years, others for ever, and that the lamps found in sepulchres were of that character. *Bruce.*

Ev'ry five minutes how the minutes go;
Each individual suffering a constraint
Poetry may, but colours cannot paint;
As if in close committtee on the sky,
Reports it hot or cold, or wet or dry;
And finds a changing clime, an happy source
Of wise reflection and well-tim'd discourse.
We next enquire, but softly and by stealth,
Like conservators of the public health,
Of epidemic throats, if such there are,
And coughs and rheums and phtisic and catarrh.
That theme exhausted, a wide chasm ensues,
Fill'd up at last with interesting news,
Who danc'd with whom, and who are like to wed,
And who is hang'd, and who is brought to bed,
But fear to call a more important cause,
As if 'twere treason against English laws.
The visit paid, with extasy we come,
As from a seven years transportation, home,
And there resume an unembarrass'd brow,
Recov'ring what we lost we know not how,
The faculties that seem'd reduc'd to nought,
Expression and the privilege of thought.
　The reeking, roaring hero of the chace,
I give him over as a desp'rate case.
Physicians write in hopes to work a cure,
Never, if honest ones, when death is sure;
And though the fox he follows may be tam'd,
A mere fox-follower never is reclaim'd.
Some farrier should prescribe his proper course,
Whose only fit companion is his horse,
Or if, deserving of a better doom,
The noble beast judge otherwise, his groom.
Yet ev'n the rogue that serves him, though he stand
To take his honour's orders, cap in hand,
Prefers his fellow-grooms, with much good sense,
Their skill a truth, his master's a pretence.
If neither horse nor groom affect the squire,
Where can at last his jockeyship retire?

Oh to the club, the scene of savage joys,
The school of coarse good fellowship and noise;
There in the sweet society of those
Whose friendship from his boyish years he chose,
Let him improve his talent if he can,
Till none but beasts acknowledge him a man.
   Man's heart had been impenetrably seal'd,
Like theirs that cleave the flood or graze the field,
Had not his Maker's all-bestowing hand
Giv'n him a soul and bade him understand.
The reas'ning pow'r vouchsaf'd of course inferr'd
The pow'r to cloath that reason with his word,
For all is perfect that God works on earth,
And he that gives conception, adds the birth.
If this be plain, 'tis plainly understood,
What uses of his boon the Giver would.
The mind, dispatch'd upon her busy toil,
Should range where Providence has blest the soil,
Visiting ev'ry flow'r with labour meet,
And gathering all her treasures sweet by sweet,
She should imbue the tongue with what she sips,
And shed the balmy blessing on the lips,
That good diffus'd may more abundant grow,
And speech may praise the power that bids it flow.
Will the sweet warbler of the live-long night,
That fills the list'ning lover with delight,
Forget his harmony, with rapture heard,
To learn the twitt'ring of a meaner bird,
Or make the parrot's mimickry his choice,
That odious libel on an human voice?
No—nature unsophisticate by man,
Starts not aside from her Creator's plan;
The melody that was at first design'd
To chear the rude forefathers of mankind,
Is note for note deliver'd in our ears,
In the last scene of her six thousand years:
Yet fashion, leader of a chatt'ring train,
Whom man for his own hurt permits to reign,
Who shifts and changes all things but his shape,

And would degrade her vot'ry to an ape,
The fruitful parent of abuse and wrong,
Holds an usurp'd dominion o'er his tongue;
There sits and prompts him with his own disgrace,
Prescribes the theme, the tone and the grimace,
And when accomplish'd in her wayward school,
Calls gentleman whom she has made a fool.
'Tis an unalterable fix'd decree
That none could frame or ratify but she,
That heav'n and hell and righteousness and sin,
Snares in his path and foes that lurk within,
God and his attributes (a field of day
Where 'tis an angel's happiness to stray),
Fruits of his love and wonders of his might,
Be never nam'd in ears esteem'd polite.
That he who dares, when she forbids, be grave,
Shall stand proscrib'd, a madman or a knave,
A close designer not to be believ'd,
Or if excus'd that charge, at least deceiv'd.
Oh folly worthy of the nurse's lap,
Give it the breast or stop its mouth with pap!
Is it incredible or can it seem
A dream to any except those that dream,
That man should love his Maker, and *that* fire,
Warming his heart should at his lips transpire?
Know then, and modestly let fall your eyes,
And vail your daring crest that braves the skies,
That air of insolence affronts your God,
You need his pardon, and provoke his rod:
Now, in a posture that becomes you more
Than that heroic strut assum'd before,
Know, your arrears with ev'ry hour accrue,
For mercy shown, while wrath is justly due.
The time is short, and there are souls on earth,
Though future pain may serve for present mirth,
Acquainted with the woes that fear or shame,
By fashion taught, forbade them once to name,
And having felt the pangs you deem a jest,
Have prov'd them truths too big to be express'd:

311

Go seek on revelation's hallow'd ground,
Sure to succeed, the remedy they found;
Touch'd by that pow'r that you have dar'd to mock,
That makes seas stable and dissolves the rock,
Your heart shall yield a life-renewing stream,
That fools, as you have done, shall call a dream.

   It happen'd on a solemn even-tide,
Soon after He that was our surety died,
Two bosom-friends,[1] each pensively inclin'd,
The scene of all those sorrows left behind,
Sought their own village, busied as they went,
In musings worthy of the great event:
They spake of him they lov'd, of him whose life,
Though blameless, had incurr'd perpetual strife,
Whose deeds had left, in spite of hostile arts,
A deep memorial graven on their hearts;
The recollection, like a vein of ore,
The farther trac'd enrich'd them still the more,
They thought him, and they justly thought him one,
Sent to do more than he appear'd t' have done;
T' exalt a people, and to place them high
Above all else, and wonder'd he should die.
Ere yet they brought their journey to an end,
A stranger join'd them, courteous as a friend,
And asked them, with a kind engaging air,
What their affliction was, and begg'd a share.
Inform'd, he gather'd up the broken thread,
And truth and wisdom gracing all he said,
Explain'd, illustrated, and search'd so well
The tender theme on which they chose to dwell,
That reaching home, the night, they said, is near,
We must not now be parted, sojourn here—
The new acquaintance soon became a guest,
And made so welcome at their simple feast,
He bless'd the bread, but vanish'd at the word,
And left them both exclaiming, 'twas the Lord!

[1] The two disciples to whom Christ appeared on the way to Emmaus:
Luke, xxiv, 13–31.

Did not our hearts feel all he deign'd to say,
Did they not burn within us by the way?
    Now theirs was converse such as it behoves
Man to maintain, and such as God approves;
Their views indeed were indistinct and dim,
But yet successful, being aim'd at him.
Christ and his character their only scope,
Their object and their subject and their hope,
They felt what it became them much to feel,
And wanting him to loose the sacred seal,
Found him as prompt as their desire was true,
To spread the new-born glories in their view.
Well—what are ages and the lapse of time
Match'd against truths as lasting as sublime?
Can length of years on God himself exact,
Or make that fiction which was once a fact?
No—marble and recording brass decay,
And like the graver's mem'ry pass away:
The works of man inherit, as is just,
Their author's frailty and return to dust;
But truth divine for ever stands secure,
Its head as guarded as its base is sure,
Fix'd in the rolling flood of endless years,
The pillar of th' eternal plan appears,
The raving storm and dashing wave defies,
Built by that architect who built the skies.
Hearts may be found that harbour at this hour
That love of Christ in all its quick'ning power,
And lips unstain'd by folly or by strife,
Whose wisdom, drawn from the deep well of life,
Tastes of its healthful origin, and flows
A Jordan for th' ablution of our woes.
Oh days of heav'n and nights of equal praise,
Serene and peaceful as those heav'nly days,
When souls drawn upward in communion sweet,
Enjoy the stillness of some close retreat,
Discourse as if releas'd and safe at home,
Of dangers past and wonders yet to come,
And spread the sacred treasures of the breast

313

Upon the lap of covenanted rest.
　What, always dreaming over heav'nly things,
Like angel-heads in stone with pigeon-wings?
Canting and whining out all day the word,
And half the night? fanatic and absurd!
Mine be the friend less frequent in his pray'rs,
Who makes no bustle with his soul's affairs,
Whose wit can brighten up a wintry day,
And chase the splenetic dull hours away,
Content on earth in earthly things to shine,
Who waits for heav'n ere he becomes divine,
Leaves saints t' enjoy those altitudes they teach,
And plucks the fruit plac'd more within his reach.
　Well spoken, Advocate of sin and shame,
Known by thy bleating, Ignorance thy name.
Is sparkling wit the world's exclusive right,
The fixt fee-simple[1] of the vain and light?
Can hopes of heav'n, bright prospects of an hour,
That come to waft us out of sorrow's pow'r,
Obscure or quench a faculty that finds
Its happiest soil in the serenest minds?
Religion curbs indeed its wanton play,
And brings the trifler under rig'rous sway,
But gives it usefulness unknown before,
And, purifying, makes it shine the more.
A Christian's wit is inoffensive light,
A beam that aids but never grieves the sight;
Vig'rous in age as in the flush of youth,
'Tis always active on the side of truth;
Temp'rance and peace insure its healthful state,
And make it brightest at its latest date.
Oh I have seen (nor hope perhaps in vain,
Ere life go down to see such sights again)
A vet'ran warrior in the Christian field,
Who never saw the sword he could not wield;
Grave without dullness, learned without pride,
Exact yet not precise, though meek, keen-ey'd;

---

[1] *fee-simple:* absolute legal possession.

A man that would have foiled at their own play,
A dozen would-be's of the modern day:
Who when occasion justified its use,
Had wit as bright as ready, to produce,
Could fetch from records of an earlier age,
Or from philosophy's enlighten'd page,
His rich materials, and regale your ear
With strains it was a privilege to hear;
Yet above all, his luxury supreme,
And his chief glory, was the gospel theme;
There he was copious as old Greece or Rome,
His happy eloquence seem'd there at home,
Ambitious, not to shine or to excel,
But to treat justly what he lov'd so well.
    It moves me more perhaps than folly ought,
When some green heads, as void of wit as thought,
Suppose *themselves* monopolists of sense,
And wiser men's ability, pretence.
Though time will wear us, and we must grow old,
Such men are not forgot as soon as cold,
Their fragrant mem'ry will outlast their tomb,
Embalm'd for ever in its own perfume:
And to say truth, though in its early prime,
And when unstain'd with any grosser crime,
Youth has a sprightliness and fire to boast,
That in the valley of decline are lost,
And virtue with peculiar charms appears,
Crown'd with the garland of life's blooming years;
Yet age by long experience well inform'd,
Well read, well temper'd, with religion warm'd,
That fire abated which impells rash youth,
Proud of his speed, to overshoot the truth,
As time improves the grape's authentic juice,
Mellows and makes the speech more fit for use,
And claims a rev'rence in its short'ning day,
That 'tis an honour and a joy to pay.
The fruits of age, less fair, are yet more sound
Than those a brighter season pours around.
And like the stores autumnal suns mature,

Through wintry rigours unimpair'd endure.
　What is fanatic frenzy, scorn'd so much,
And dreaded more than a contagious touch?
I grant it dang'rous, and approve your fear,
That fire is catching if you draw too near,
But sage observers oft mistake the flame,
And give true piety that odious name.
To tremble (as the creature of an hour
Ought at the view of an almighty power)
Before his presence, at whose awful throne
All tremble in all worlds, except our own,
To supplicate his mercy, love his ways,
And prize them above pleasure, wealth or praise,
Though common sense allow'd a casting voice,
And free from bias, must approve the choice,
Convicts a man fanatic in th' extreme,
And wild as madness in the world's esteem.
But that disease, when soberly defin'd,
Is the false fire of an o'erheated mind,
It views the truth with a distorted eye,
And either warps or lays it useless by;
'Tis narrow, selfish, arrogant, and draws
Its sordid nourishment from man's applause;
And while at heart sin unrelinquish'd lies,
Presumes itself chief fav'rite of the skies.
'Tis such a light as putrefaction breeds
In fly-blown flesh whereon the maggot feeds,
Shines in the dark, but usher'd into day,
The stench remains, the lustre dies away.
　True bliss, if man may reach it, is compos'd
Of hearts in union mutually disclos'd:
And, farewell else all hope of pure delight,
Those hearts should be reclaim'd, renew'd, upright.
Bad men, profaning friendship's hallow'd name,
Form, in its stead, a covenant of shame,
A dark confed'racy against the laws
Of virtue, and religion's glorious cause:
They build each other up with dreadful skill,
As bastions set point blank against God's will,

Enlarge and fortify the dread redoubt,
Deeply resolv'd to shut a Saviour out;
Call legions up from hell to back the deed;
And curst with conquest, finally succeed:
But souls that carry on a blest exchange
Of joys they meet with in their heav'nly range,
And with a fearless confidence make known,
The sorrows sympathy esteems its own,
Daily derive encreasing light and force
From such communion in their pleasant course;
Feel less the journey's roughness and its length,
Meet their opposers with united strength,
And one in heart, in int'rest and design,
Gird up each other to the race divine.

But Conversation, chuse what theme we may,
And chiefly when religion leads the way,
Should flow, like waters after summer show'rs,
Not as if rais'd by mere mechanic pow'rs.
The Christian in whose soul, though now distress'd,
Lives the dear thought of joys he once possess'd,
When all his glowing language issued forth
With God's deep stamp upon its current worth,
Will speak without disguise, and must impart,
Sad as it is, his undissembling heart;
Abhors constraint, and dares not feign a zeal,
Or seem to boast a fire he does not feel.
The song of Sion is a tasteless thing
Unless, when rising on a joyful wing,
The soul can mix with the celestial bands,
And give the strain the compass it demands.

Strange tidings these to tell a world who treat
All but their own experience as deceit!
Will they believe, though credulous enough
To swallow much upon much weaker proof,
That there are blest inhabitants of earth,
Partakers of a new æthereal birth,
Their hopes, desires and purposes estrang'd
From things terrestrial, and divinely chang'd,
Their very language of a kind that speaks

The soul's sure int'rest in the good she seeks,
Who deal with scripture, its importance felt,
As Tully with philosophy once dealt,
And in the silent watches of the night,
And through the scenes of toil-renewing light,
The social walk, or solitary ride,
Keep still the dear companion at their side?
No—shame upon a self-disgracing age,
God's work may serve an ape upon a stage,
With such a jest as fill'd with hellish glee
Certain invisibles as shrewd as he,
But veneration or respect finds none,
Save from the subjects of that work alone.
The world grown old, her deep discernment shows,
Claps spectacles on her sagacious nose,
Peruses closely the true Christian's face,
And finds it a mere mask of sly grimace,
Usurps God's office, lays his bosom bare,
And finds hypocrisy close-lurking there,
And serving God herself through mere constraint,
Concludes his unfeign'd love of him, a feint.
And yet God knows, look human nature through,
(And in due time the world shall know it too)
That since the flow'rs of Eden felt the blast,
That after man's defection laid all waste,
Sincerity towards th' heart-searching God
Has made the new-born creature her abode,
Nor shall be found in unregen'rate souls,
Till the last fire burn all between the poles.
Sincerity! Why 'tis his only pride,
Weak and imperfect in all grace beside,
He knows that God demands his heart entire,
And gives him all his just demands require.
Without it, his pretensions were as vain,
As having it, he deems the world's disdain;
That great defect would cost him not alone
Man's favourable judgment, but his own,
His birthright shaken, and no longer clear,
Than while his conduct proves his heart sincere:

Retort the charge, and let the world be told
She boasts a confidence she does not hold,
That conscious of her crimes, she feels instead,
A cold misgiving, and a killing dread,
That while in health, the ground of her support
Is madly to forget that life is short;
That sick, she trembles, knowing she must die,
Her hope presumption, and her faith a lie.
That while she doats, and dreams that she believes,
She mocks her Maker, and herself deceives,
Her utmost reach, historical assent,
The doctrines warpt to what they never meant.
That truth itself is in her head as dull
And useless as a candle in a scull,
And all her love of God a groundless claim,
A trick upon the canvass, painted flame.
Tell her again, the sneer upon her face,
And all her censures of the work of grace,
Are insincere, meant only to conceal
A dread she would not, yet is forc'd to feel,
That in her heart the Christian she reveres,
And while she seems to scorn him, only fears.

  A poet does not work by square or line,
As smiths and joiners perfect a design,
At least we moderns, our attention less,
Beyond th' example of our sires, digress,
And claim a right to scamper and run wide,
Wherever chance, caprice, or fancy guide.
The world and I fortuitously met;
I ow'd a trifle and have paid the debt,
She did me wrong, I recompens'd the deed,
And having struck the balance, now proceed.
Perhaps, however, as some years have pass'd,
Since she and I convers'd together last,
And I have liv'd recluse in rural shades,
Which seldom a distinct report pervades,
Great changes and new manners have occurr'd,
And blest reforms that I have never heard,
And she may now be as discreet and wise,

As once absurd in all discerning eyes.
Sobriety, perhaps may now be found,
Where once intoxication press'd the ground.
The subtle and injurious may be just,
And he grown chaste that was the slave of lust;
Arts once esteem'd may be with shame dismiss'd,
Charity may relax the miser's fist,
The gamester may have cast his cards away,
Forgot to curse and only kneel to pray.
It has indeed been told me (with what weight,
How credibly, 'tis hard for me to state)
That fables old that seem'd for ever mute,
Reviv'd, are hast'ning into fresh repute,
And gods and goddesses discarded long,
Like useless lumber or a stroller's song,
Are bringing into vogue their heathen train,
And Jupiter bids fair to rule again.
That certain feasts[1] are instituted now,
Where Venus hears the lover's tender vow,
That all Olympus through the country roves,
To consecrate our few remaining groves,
And echo learns politely to repeat
The praise of names for ages obsolete,
That having prov'd the weakness, it should seem,
Of revelation's ineffectual beam,
To bring the passions under sober sway,
And give the moral springs their proper play,
They mean to try what may at last be done
By stout substantial gods of wood and stone,
And whether Roman rites may not produce
The virtues of old Rome for English use.
May much success attend the pious plan,
May Mercury once more embellish man,
Grace him again with long forgotten arts,
Reclaim his taste and brighten up his parts,
Make him athletic as in days of old,

[1] The Medmenham revels of Sir Francis Dashwood and his friends.

Learn'd at the bar, in the palæstra bold,
Divest the rougher sex of female airs,
And teach the softer not to copy theirs:
The change shall please, nor shall it matter aught
Who works the wonder if it be but wrought.
'Tis time, however, if the case stand thus,
For us plain folks, and all who side with us,
To build our altar, confident and bold,
And say as stern Elijah said of old,[1]
The strife now stands upon a fair award,
If Israel's Lord be God, then serve the Lord—
If he be silent, faith is all a whim,
Then Baal is the God, and worship him.
　　Digression is so much in modern use,
Thought is so rare, and fancy so profuse,
Some never seem so wide of their intent,
As when returning to the theme they meant;
As mendicants, whose business is to roam,
Make ev'ry parish, but their own, their home.
Though such continual zigzags in a book,
Such drunken reelings, have an aukward look,
And I had rather creep to what is true,
Than rove and stagger with no mark in view;
Yet to consult a little, seem'd no crime,
The freakish humour of the present time.
But now, to gather up what seems dispers'd,
And touch the subject I design'd at first,
May prove, though much beside the rules of art,
Best for the public, and my wisest part.
And first, let no man charge me that I mean
To cloath in sables every social scene,
And give good company a face severe,
As if they met around a father's bier;
For tell some men that pleasure all their bent,
And laughter all their work, is life mispent,
Their wisdom bursts into this sage reply,
Then mirth is sin, and we should always cry.

[1] 1 Kings, xviii, 21.

To find the medium asks some share of wit,
And therefore 'tis a mark fools never hit.
But though life's valley be a vale of tears,
A brighter scene beyond that vale appears,
Whose glory with a light that never fades,
Shoots between scatter'd rocks and op'ning shades,
And while it shows the land the soul desires,
The language of the land she seeks, inspires.
Thus touch'd, the tongue receives a sacred cure,
Of all that was absurd, profane, impure;
Held within modest bounds, the tide of speech
Pursues the course that truth and nature teach;
No longer labours merely to produce
The pomp of sound, or tinkle without use:
Where'er it winds, the salutary stream,
Sprightly and fresh, enriches ev'ry theme,
While all the happy man possess'd before,
The gift of nature or the classic store,
Is made subservient to the grand design
For which heav'n form'd the faculty divine.
So should an ideot, while at large he strays,
Find the sweet lyre on which an artist plays,
With rash and aukward force the chords he shakes,
And grins with wonder at the jar he makes;
But let the wise and well-instructed hand,
Once take the shell beneath his just command,
In gentle sounds it seems as it complain'd
Of the rude injuries it late sustain'd;
'Till tun'd at length, to some immortal song,
It sounds Jehovah's name, and pours his praise along.

RETIREMENT

—— studiis florens ignobilis oti.[1]— Virgil, *Georgics*, iv, [564]

HACKNEY'D in business, wearied at that oar
Which thousands once fast chain'd to, quit no more,
But which when life at ebb runs weak and low,
All wish, or seem to wish they could forego,
The statesman, lawyer, merchant, man of trade,
Pants for the refuge of some rural shade,
Where all his long anxieties forgot
Amid the charms of a sequester'd spot,
Or recollected only to gild o'er
And add a smile to what was sweet before,
He may possess the joys he thinks he sees,
Lay his old age upon the lap of ease,
Improve the remnant of his wasted span,
And having liv'd a trifler, die a man.
Thus conscience pleads her cause within the breast,
Though long rebell'd against, not yet suppress'd,
And calls a creature form'd for God alone,
For heav'ns high purposes and not his own,
Calls him away from selfish ends and aims,
From what debilitates and what inflames,
From cities humming with a restless crowd,
Sordid as active, ignorant as loud,
Whose highest praise is that they live in vain
The dupes of pleasure, or the slaves of gain,
Where works of man are cluster'd close around,
And works of God are hardly to be found,
To regions where in spite of sin and woe,
Traces of Eden are still seen below,
Where mountain, river, forest, field and grove,
Remind him of his Maker's power and love.
'Tis well if look'd for at so late a day,
In the last scene of such a senseless play,

[1] 'Flourishing in the employments of ignoble ease.'

True wisdom will attend his feeble call,
And grace his action ere the curtain fall.
Souls that have long despised their heav'nly birth,
Their wishes all impregnated with earth,
For threescore years employed with ceaseless care,
In catching smoke and feeding upon air,
Conversant only with the ways of men,
Rarely redeem the short remaining ten.
Invet'rate habits choak th' unfruitful heart,
Their fibres penetrate its tend'rest part,
And draining its nutritious pow'rs to feed
Their noxious growth, starve ev'ry better seed.
  Happy if full of days—but happier far
If ere we yet discern life's evening star,
Sick of the service of a world that feeds
Its patient drudges with dry chaff and weeds,
We can escape from custom's ideot sway,
To serve the sov'reign we were born t' obey.
Then sweet to muse upon his skill display'd
(Infinite skill) in all that he has made!
To trace in nature's most minute design
The signature and stamp of pow'r divine,
Contrivance intricate, express'd with ease,
Where unassisted sight no beauty sees,
The shapely limb and lubricated joint,
Within the small dimensions of a point,
Muscle and nerve miraculously spun,
His mighty work who speaks and it is done,
Th' invisible in things scarce seen reveal'd,
To whom an atom is an ample field.
To wonder at a thousand insect forms,
These hatch'd, and those resuscitated worms,
New life ordain'd and brighter scenes to share,
Once prone to earth, now buoyant upon air,
Whose shape would make them, had they bulk and size,
More hideous foes than fancy can devise,
With helmed heads and dragon scales adorn'd,
The mighty myriads, now securely scorn'd,
Would mock the majesty of man's high birth,

Despise his bulwarks and unpeople earth.
Then with a glance of fancy to survey,
Far as the faculty can stretch away,
Ten thousand rivers poured at his command
From urns that never fail through every land,
These like a deluge with impetuous force,
Those winding modestly a silent course;
The cloud-surmounting alps, the fruitful vales,
Seas on which ev'ry nation spreads her sails,
The sun, a world whence other worlds drink light,
The crescent moon, the diadem of night,
Stars countless, each in his appointed place,
Fast-anchor'd in the deep abyss of space—
At such a light to catch the poet's flame,
And with a rapture like his own exclaim,
These are thy glorious works,[1] thou source of good,
How dimly seen, how faintly understood!—
Thine, and upheld by thy paternal care,
This universal frame, thus wondrous fair;
Thy pow'r divine and bounty beyond thought,
Ador'd and prais'd in all that thou hast wrought.
Absorbed in that immensity I see,
I shrink abased, and yet aspire to thee;
Instruct me, guide me to that heav'nly day
Thy words, more clearly than thy works, display.
That, while my truths my grosser thoughts refine,
I may resemble thee and call thee mine.

   Oh blest proficiency! surpassing all
That men erroneously their glory call
The recompence that arts or arms can yield,
The bar, the senate or the tented field.
Compar'd with this sublimest life below,
Ye kings and rulers what have courts to show?
Thus studied, used and consecrated thus,
Whatever *is*, seems form'd indeed for us,
Not as the plaything of a froward child,
Fretful unless diverted and beguiled,

[1] *Paradise Lost*, v, 153, already echoed in *Hope*, p. 279.

Much less to feed and fan the fatal fires
Of pride, ambition or impure desires,
But as a scale by which the soul ascends
From mighty means to more important ends,
Securely, though by steps but rarely trod,
Mounts from inferior beings up to God,
And sees by no fallacious light or dim,
Earth made for man, and man himself for him.
   Not that I mean t' approve, or would inforce,
A superstitious and monastic course:
Truth is not local, God alike pervades
And fills the world of traffic and the shades,
And may be fear'd amidst the busiest scenes,
Or scorn'd where business never intervenes.
But 'tis not easy with a mind like ours,
Conscious of weakness in its noblest pow'rs,
And in a world where (other ills apart)
The roving eye misleads the careless heart,
To limit thought, by nature prone to stray
Wherever freakish fancy points the way;
To bid the pleadings of self-love be still,
Resign our own and seek our Maker's will;
To spread the page of scripture, and compare
Our conduct with the laws engraven there,
To measure all that passes in the breast,
Faithfully, fairly, by that sacred test,
To dive into the secret deeps within,
To spare no passion and no fav'rite sin,
And search the themes, important above all,
Ourselves and our recov'ry from our fall.
But leisure, silence, and a mind releas'd
From anxious thoughts how wealth may be encreas'd,
How to secure in some propitious hour
The point of int'rest or the post of pow'r,
A soul serene, and equally retired
From objects too much dreaded or desired,
Safe from the clamours of perverse dispute,
At least are friendly to the great pursuit.
   Op'ning the map of God's extensive plan,

We find a little isle, this life of man,
Eternity's unknown expanse appears
Circling around and limiting his years;
The busy race examine and explore
Each creek and cavern of the dang'rous shore,
With care collect what in their eyes excells,
Some, shining pebbles, and some, weeds and shells,
Thus laden dream that they are rich and great,
And happiest he that groans beneath his weight;
The waves o'ertake them in their serious play,
And ev'ry hour sweeps multitudes away,
They shriek and sink, survivors start and weep,
Pursue their sport, and follow to the deep;
A few forsake the throng, with lifted eyes
Ask wealth of heav'n, and gain a real prize,
Truth, wisdom, grace, and peace like that above,
Seal'd with his signet whom they serve and love;
Scorn'd by the rest, with patient hope they wait
A kind release from their imperfect state,
And unregretted are soon snatch'd away
From scenes of sorrow into glorious day.
   Nor these alone prefer a life recluse,
Who seek retirement for its proper use,
The love of change that lives in ev'ry breast,
Genius, and temper, and desire of rest,
Discordant motives in one center meet,
And each inclines its vot'ry to retreat.
Some minds by nature are averse to noise,
And hate the tumult half the world enjoys,
The law of av'rice, or the pompous prize
That courts display before ambitious eyes,
The fruits that hang on pleasure's flow'ry stem,
Whate'er enchants them are no snares to them.
To them the deep recess of dusky groves,
Or forest where the deer securely roves,
The fall of waters and the song of birds,
And hills that echo to the distant herds,
Are luxuries excelling all the glare
The world can boast, and her chief fav'rites share.

With eager step and carelessly array'd,
For such a cause the poet seeks the shade,
From all he sees he catches new delight,
Pleas'd fancy claps her pinions at the sight,
The rising or the setting orb of day,
The clouds that flit, or slowly float away,
Nature in all the various shapes she wears,
Frowning in storms, or breathing gentle airs,
The snowy robe her wintry state assumes,
Her summer heats, her fruits, and her perfumes,
All, all alike transport the glowing bard,
Success in rhime his glory and reward.
Oh nature! whose Elysian scenes disclose
His bright perfections at whose word they rose,
Next to that pow'r who form'd thee and sustains,
Be thou the great inspirer of my strains.
Still as I touch the lyre, do thou expand
Thy genuine charms, and guide an artless hand,
That I may catch a fire but rarely known,
Give useful light though I should miss renown,
And poring on thy page, whose ev'ry line
Bears proof of an intelligence divine,
May feel an heart enrich'd by what it pays,
That builds its glory on its Maker's praise.
Woe to the man whose wit disclaims its use,
Glitt'ring in vain, or only to seduce,
Who studies nature with a wanton eye,
Admires the work, but slips the lesson by,
His hours of leisure and recess employs
In drawing pictures of forbidden joys,
Retires to blazon his own worthless name,
Or shoot the careless with a surer aim.

The lover too shuns business and alarms,
Tender idolater of absent charms.
Saints offer nothing in their warmest pray'rs,
That he devotes not with a zeal like theirs;
'Tis consecration of his heart, soul, time,
And ev'ry thought that wanders is a crime.
In sighs he worships his supremely fair,

And weeps a sad libation in despair,
Adores a creature, and devout in vain,
Wins in return an answer of disdain.
As woodbine weds the plant within her reach,
Rough elm, or smooth-grain'd ash, or glossy beech,
In spiral rings ascends the trunk, and lays
Her golden tassels on the leafy sprays,
But does a mischief while she lends a grace,
Strait'ning its growth by such a strict embrace,
So love that clings around the noblest minds,
Forbids th' advancement of the soul he binds,
The suitor's air indeed he soon improves,
And forms it to the taste of her he loves,
Teaches his eyes a language, and no less
Refines his speech and fashions his address;
But farewell promises of happier fruits,
Manly designs, and learning's grave pursuits,
Girt with a chain he cannot wish to break,
His only bliss is sorrow for her sake;
Who will, may pant for glory and excell,
Her smile his aim, all higher aims farewell!
Thyrsis, Alexis, or whatever name[1]
May least offend against so pure a flame,
Though sage advice of friends the most sincere,
Sounds harshly in so delicate an ear,
And lovers of all creatures, tame or wild,
Can least brook management, however mild,
Yet let a poet (poetry disarms
The fiercest animals with magic charms)
Risque an intrusion on thy pensive mood,
And woo and win thee to thy proper good.
Pastoral images and still retreats,
Umbrageous walks and solitary seats,
Sweet birds in concert with harmonious streams,
Soft airs, nocturnal vigils, and day-dreams,
Are all enchantments in a case like thine,
Conspire against thy peace with one design,

[1] Shepherds in Virgil's *Eclogues*, vii and ii.

329

Sooth thee to make thee but a surer prey,
And feed the fire that wastes thy pow'rs away.
Up—God has formed thee with a wiser view,
Not to be led in chains, but to subdue,
Calls thee to cope with enemies, and first
Points out a conflict with thyself, the worst.
Woman indeed, a gift he would bestow
When he design'd a paradise below,
The richest earthly boon his hands afford,
Deserves to be belov'd, but not ador'd.
Post away swiftly to more active scenes,
Collect the scatter'd truths that study gleans,
Mix with the world, but with its wiser part,
No longer give an image all thine heart,
Its empire is not hers, nor is it thine,
'Tis God's just claim, prerogative divine.

Virtuous and faithful HEBERDEN![1] whose skill
Attempts no task it cannot well fulfill,
Gives melancholy up to nature's care,
And sends the patient into purer air,
Look where he comes—in this embow'r'd alcove,
Stand close conceal'd, and see a statue move:
Lips busy, and eyes fixt, foot falling slow,
Arms hanging idly down, hands clasp'd below,
Interpret to the marking eye, distress,
Such as its symptoms can alone express.
That tongue is silent now, that silent tongue
Could argue once, could jest or join the song,
Could give advice, could censure or commend,
Or charm the sorrows of a drooping friend.
Renounced alike its office and its sport,
Its brisker and its graver strains fall short,
Both fail beneath a fever's secret sway,
And like a summer-brook are past away.

[1] Dr William Heberden, 1710–1801, the friend and physician of many celebrated persons, had attended C. in London. His contributions to the science of medicine survive in the terms 'Heberden's Disease' (angina pectoris and arthritis deformans) and 'Heberden's nodes' (deformity of the fingers in arthritis).

This is a sight for pity to peruse
'Till she resemble faintly what she views,
'Till sympathy contract a kindred pain,
Pierced with the woes that she laments in vain.
This of all maladies that man infest,
Claims most compassion, and receives the least,
Job felt it when he groan'd beneath the rod
And the barbed arrows of a frowning God,
And such emollients as his friends could spare,
Friends such as his, for modern Jobs prepare.
Blest, (rather curst) with hearts that never feel,
Kept snug in caskets of close-hammer'd steel,
With mouths made only to grin wide and eat,
And minds that deem derided pain a treat,
With limbs of British oak and nerves of wire,
And wit that puppet-prompters might inspire,
Their sov'reign nostrum is a clumsy joke,
On pangs inforc'd with God's severest stroke.
But with a soul that ever felt the sting
Of sorrow, sorrow is a sacred thing;
Not to molest, or irritate, or raise
A laugh at its expence, is slender praise;
He that has not usurp'd the name of man
Does all, and deems too little, all he can,
T' assuage the throbbings of the fester'd part,
And staunch the bleedings of a broken heart;
'Tis not as heads that never ach suppose,
Forg'ry of fancy and a dream of woes,
Man is an harp whose chords elude the sight,
Each yielding harmony, dispos'd aright,
The screws revers'd (a task which if he please
God in a moment executes with ease),
Ten thousand thousand strings at once go loose,
Lost, 'till he tune them, all their pow'r and use.
Then neither heathy wilds, nor scenes as fair
As ever recompensed the peasant's care,
Nor soft declivities with tufted hills,
Nor view of waters turning busy mills,
Parks in which art preceptress nature weds,

Nor gardens interspers'd with flow'ry beds,
Nor gales that catch the scent of blooming groves,
And waft it to the mourner as he roves,
Can call up life into his faded eye,
That passes all he sees unheeded by:
No wounds like those a wounded spirit feels,
No cure for such, 'till God who makes them, heals.
And thou sad suff'rer under nameless ill,
That yields not to the touch of human skill,
Improve the kind occasion, understand
A father's frown, and kiss his chast'ning hand:
To thee the day-spring and the blaze of noon,
The purple ev'ning and resplendent moon,
The stars that sprinkled o'er the vault of night,
Seem drops descending in a show'r of light,
Shine not, or undesired and hated shine,
Seen through the medium of a cloud like thine:
Yet seek him, in his favour life is found,
All bliss beside, a shadow or a sound:
Then heav'n eclipsed so long, and this dull earth
Shall seem to start into a second birth,
Nature assuming a more lovely face,
Borrowing a beauty from the works of grace,
Shall be despised and overlook'd no more,
Shall fill thee with delights unfelt before,
Impart to things inanimate a voice,
And bid her mountains and her hills rejoice,
The sound shall run along the winding vales,
And thou enjoy an Eden ere it fails.

Ye groves (the statesman[1] at his desk exclaims
Sick of a thousand disappointed aims)
My patrimonial treasure and my pride,
Beneath your shades your gray possessor hide,
Receive me languishing for that repose
The servant of the public never knows.
Ye saw me once (ah those regretted days

---

[1] These lines have been taken to refer to Fox: Sir G. Trevelyan, *Early Life of C. J. Fox*, vii, 299.

When boyish innocence was all my praise)
Hour after hour delightfully allot
To studies then familiar, since forgot,
And cultivate a taste for antient song,
Catching its ardour as I mus'd along;
Nor seldom, as propitious heav'n might send,
What once I valued and could boast, a friend,
Were witnesses how cordially I press'd
His undissembling virtue to my breast;
Receive me now, not uncorrupt as then,
Nor guiltless of corrupting other men,
But vers'd in arts that while they seem to stay
A falling empire, hasten its decay.
To the fair haven of my native home,
The wreck of what I was, fatigued I come;
For once I can approve the patriot's voice,
And make the course he recommends my choice,
We meet at last in one sincere desire,
His wish and mine both prompt me to retire.
'Tis done—he steps into the welcome chaise,
Lolls at his ease behind four handsome bays
That whirl away from business and debate
The disincumber'd Atlas of the state.
Ask not the boy, who when the breeze of morn
First shakes the glitt'ring drops from every thorn,
Unfolds his flock, then under bank or bush
Sits linking cherry stones or platting rush,
How fair is freedom?—he was always free.
To carve his rustic name upon a tree,
To snare the mole, or with ill-fashion'd hook
To draw th' incautious minnow from the brook,
Are life's prime pleasures in his simple view,
His flock the chief concern he ever knew:
She shines but little in his heedless eyes,
The good we never miss, we rarely prize.
But ask the noble drudge in state-affairs,
Escap'd from office and its constant cares,
What charms he sees in freedom's smile express'd,
In freedom lost so long, now repossess'd,

The tongue whose strains were cogent as commands,
Revered at home, and felt in foreign lands,
Shall own itself a stamm'rer in that cause,
Or plead its silence as its best applause.
He knows indeed that whether dress'd or rude,
Wild without art, or artfully subdued,
Nature in ev'ry form inspires delight,
But never mark'd her with so just a sight.
Her hedge-row shrubs, a variegated store,
With woodbine and wild roses mantled o'er,
Green baulks[1] and furrow'd lands, the stream that spreads
Its cooling vapour o'er the dewy meads,
Downs that almost escape th' enquiring eye,
That melt and fade into the distant skie,
Beauties he lately slighted as he pass'd,
Seem all created since he travell'd last.
Master of all th' enjoyments he design'd,
No rough annoyance rankling in his mind,
What early philosophic hours he keeps,
How regular his meals, how sound he sleeps!
Not sounder he that on the mainmast head,
While morning kindles with a windy red,
Begins a long look-out for distant land,
Nor quits till ev'ning-watch his giddy stand,
Then swift descending with a seaman's haste,
Slips to his hammock, and forgets the blast.
He chooses company, but not the squire's,
Whose wit is rudeness, whose good breeding tires;
Nor yet the parson's, who would gladly come,
Obsequious when abroad, though proud at home,
Nor can he much affect the neighb'ring peer,
Whose toe of emulation treads too near,
But wisely seeks a more convenient friend,
With whom, dismissing forms, he may unbend,
A man whom marks of condescending grace
Teach, while they flatter him, his proper place,

[1] *Baulks:* the unploughed ridges between the furrows, at the ends of the fields. *Benham.*

Who comes when call'd, and at a word withdraws,
Speaks with reserve, and listens with applause;
Some plain mechanic, who without pretence
To birth or wit, nor gives nor takes offence,
On whom he rests well pleas'd his weary pow'rs,
And talks and laughs away his vacant hours.
The tide of life, swift always in its course,
May run in cities with a brisker force,
But nowhere with a current so serene,
Or half so clear as in the rural scene.
Yet how fallacious is all earthly bliss,
What obvious truths the wisest heads may miss;
Some pleasures live a month, and some a year,
But short the date of all we gather here,
Nor happiness is felt, except the true,
That does not charm the more for being new.
This observation, as it chanced, not made,
Or if the thought occurr'd, not duely weigh'd,
He sighs—for after all, by slow degrees,
The spot he loved has lost the pow'r to please;
To cross his ambling poney day by day,
Seems at the best, but dreaming life away,
The prospect, such as might enchant despair,
He views it not, or sees no beauty there,
With aching heart and discontented looks,
Returns at noon, to billiards or to books,
But feels while grasping at his faded joys,
A secret thirst of his renounced employs.
He chides the tardiness of ev'ry post,
Pants to be told of battles won or lost,
Blames his own indolence, observes, though late,
'Tis criminal to leave a sinking state,
Flies to the levee, and receiv'd with grace,
Kneels, kisses hands, and shines again in place.
  Suburban villas, highway-side retreats,
That dread th' encroachment of our growing streets,
Tight boxes, neatly sash'd, and in a blaze
With all a July sun's collected rays,
Delight the citizen, who gasping there

Breathes clouds of dust and calls it country air.
Oh sweet retirement, who would baulk the thought,
That could afford retirement, or could not?
'Tis such an easy walk, so smooth and strait,
The second milestone fronts the garden gate,
A step if fair, and if a shower approach,
You find safe shelter in the next stage-coach.
There prison'd in a parlour snug and small,
Like bottled wasps upon a southern wall,
The man of bus'ness and his friends compress'd,
Forget their labours, and yet find no rest;
But still 'tis rural—trees are to be seen
From ev'ry window, and the fields are green,
Ducks paddle in the pond before the door,
And what could a remoter scene show more?
A sense of elegance we rarely find
The portion of a mean or vulgar mind,
And ignorance of better things, makes man
Who cannot much, rejoice in what he can;
And he that deems his leisure well bestow'd
In contemplation of a turnpike road,
Is occupied as well, employs his hours
As wisely, and as much improves his pow'rs,
As he that slumbers in pavilions grac'd
With all the charms of an accomplish'd taste.
Yet hence alas! Insolvencies, and hence
The unpitied victim of ill-judg'd expence,
From all his wearisome engagements freed,
Shakes hands with bus'ness, and retires indeed.

    Your prudent grandmammas, ye modern belles,
Content with Bristol, Bath, and Tunbridge-wells,
When health requir'd it would consent to roam,
Else more attach'd to pleasures found at home.
But now alike, gay widow, virgin, wife,
Ingenious to diversify dull life,
In coaches, chaises, caravans and hoys,
Fly to the coast for daily, nightly joys,
And all impatient of dry land, agree
With one consent, to rush into the sea.—

Ocean exhibits, fathomless and broad,
Much of the pow'r and majesty of God.
He swathes about the swelling of the deep,
That shines and rests, as infants smile and sleep,
Vast as it is, it answers as it flows
The breathing of the lightest air that blows,
Curling and whit'ning over all the waste,
The rising waves obey th' increasing blast,
Abrupt and horrid as the tempest roars,
Thunder and flash upon the stedfast shores,
'Till he that rides the whirlwind, checks the rein,
Then, all the world of waters sleeps again. —
Nereids or Dryads, as the fashion leads,
Now in the floods, now panting in the meads,
Vot'ries of pleasure still, where'er she dwells,
Near barren rocks, in palaces or cells,
Oh grant a poet leave to recommend
(A poet fond of nature and your friend)
Her slighted works to your admiring view,
Her works must needs excel, who fashion'd you.
Would ye, when rambling in your morning ride,
With some unmeaning coxcomb at your side,
Condemn the prattler for his idle pains,
To waste unheard the music of his strains,
And deaf to all impertinence of tongue,
That while it courts, affronts and does you wrong,
Mark well the finish'd plan without a fault,
The seas globose and huge, th' o'erarching vault,
Earth's millions daily fed, a world employ'd
In gath'ring plenty yet to be enjoy'd,
Till gratitude grew vocal in the praise
Of God, beneficent in all his ways,
Grac'd with such wisdom how would beauty shine?
Ye want but that to seem indeed divine.

Anticipated rents and bills unpaid,
Force many a shining youth into the shade,
Not to redeem his time but his estate,
And play the fool, but at a cheaper rate.
There hid in loath'd obscurity, remov'd

From pleasures left, but never more belov'd,
He just endures, and with a sickly spleen
Sighs o'er the beauties of the charming scene.
Nature indeed looks prettily in rhime,
Streams twinkle sweetly in poetic chime,
The warblings of the black-bird, clear and strong,
Are musical enough in Thomson's song,[1]
And Cobham's groves[2] and Windsor's green retreats,[3]
When Pope describes them, have a thousand sweets,
He likes the country, but in truth must own,
Most likes it, when he studies it in town.
  Poor Jack—no matter who—for when I blame
I pity, and must therefore sink the name,
Liv'd in his saddle, lov'd the chace, the course,
And always, ere he mounted, kiss'd his horse.
Th' estate his sires had own'd in antient years
Was quickly distanc'd, match'd against a peer's.
Jack vanish'd, was regretted and forgot,
'Tis wild good-nature's never-failing lot.
At length, when all had long suppos'd him dead,
By cold submersion, razor, rope or lead,
My lord alighting at his usual place,
The Crown, took notice of an ostler's face.
Jack knew his friend, but hope'd that in that disguise
He might escape the most observing eyes,
And whistling as if unconcern'd and gay,
Curried his nag and look'd another way.
Convinc'd at last upon a nearer view,
'Twas he, the same, the very Jack he knew,
O'erwhelm'd at once with wonder, grief and joy,
He press'd him much to quit his base employ,
His countenance, his purse, his heart, his hand,
Infl'ence, and pow'r, were all at his command.
Peers are not always gen'rous as well-bred,

[1] *The Seasons: Spring,* 708–9.

[2] Stowe, the Buckinghamshire seat of Richard Temple, 1st Viscount Cobham, described in Pope's *Moral Essays,* iv, 69.

[3] Described in *Windsor Forest.*

But Granby was, meant truly what he said.
Jack bow'd and was oblig'd—confess'd 'twas strange
That so retir'd he should not wish a change,
But knew no medium between guzzling beer
And his old stint, three thousand pounds a year.
Thus some retire to nourish hopeless woe,
Some seeking happiness not found below,
Some to comply with humour, and a mind
To social scenes by nature disinclin'd,
Some sway'd by fashion, some by deep disgust,
Some self-impoverish'd, and because they must,
But few that court Retirement, are aware
Of half the toils they must encounter there.
  Lucrative offices are seldom lost
For want of pow'rs proportion'd to the post:
Give ev'n a dunce th' employment he desires,
And soon he finds the talents it requires;
A business with an income at its heels
Furnishes always oil for its own wheels.
But in his arduous enterprize to close
His active years with indolent repose,
He finds the labours of that state exceed
His utmost faculties, severe indeed.
'Tis easy to resign a toilsome place,
But not to manage leisure with a grace,
Absence of occupation is not rest,
A mind quite vacant is a mind distress'd.
The vet'ran steed excused his task at length,
In kind compassion of his failing strength,
And turn'd into the park or mead to graze,
Exempt from future service all his days,
There feels a pleasure perfect in its kind,
Ranges at liberty, and snuffs the wind.
But when his lord would quit the busy road
To taste a joy like that he has bestow'd,
He proves, less happy than his favour'd brute,
A life of ease a difficult pursuit.
Thought, to the man that never thinks, may seem
As natural, as when asleep, to dream,

But reveries (for human minds will act)
Specious in show, impossible in fact,
Those flimsy webs that break as soon as wrought,
Attain not to the dignity of thought.
Nor yet the swarms that occupy the brain
Where dreams of dress, intrigue, and pleasure reign,
Nor such as useless conversation breeds,
Or lust engenders, and indulgence feeds.
Whence, and what are we? to what end ordain'd?
What means the drama by the world sustain'd?
Business or vain amusement, care or mirth,
Divide the frail inhabitants of earth.
Is duty a mere sport, or an employ?
Life an entrusted talent, or a toy?
Is there, as reason, conscience, scripture say,
Cause to provide for a great future day,
When earth's assign'd duration at an end,
Man shall be summon'd and the dead attend?
The trumpet— will it sound? the curtain rise?
And show th' august tribunal of the skies,
Where no prevarication shall avail,
Where eloquence and artifice shall fail,
The pride of arrogant distinctions fall,
And conscience and our conduct judge us all?
Pardon me, ye that give the midnight oil
To learned cares of philosophic toil,
Though I revere your honourable names,
Your useful labors and important aims,
And hold the world indebted to your aid,
Enrich'd with the discoveries ye have made,
Yet let me stand excused, if I esteem
A mind employ'd on so sublime a theme,
Pushing her bold enquiry to the date
And outline of the present transient state,
And after poising her advent'rous wings,
Settling at last upon eternal things,
Far more intelligent, and better taught
The strenuous use of profitable thought,
Than ye when happiest, and enlighten'd most,

340

And highest in renown, can justly boast.
   A mind unnerv'd, or indispos'd to bear
The weight of subjects worthiest of her care,
Whatever hopes a change of scene inspires,
Must change her nature, or in vain retires.
An idler is a watch that wants both hands,
As useless if it goes as when it stands.
Books therefore, not the scandal of the shelves,
In which lewd sensualists print out themselves,
Nor those in which the stage gives vice a blow,
With what success, let modern manners show,
Nor his[1] who, for the bane of thousands born,
Built God a church and laugh'd his word to scorn,
Skilful alike to seem devout and just,
And stab religion with a sly side-thrust:
Nor those of learn'd philologists,[2] who chase
A panting syllable through time and space;
Start it at home, and hunt it in the dark,
To Gaul, to Greece, and into Noah's ark;
But such as learning without false pretence,
The friend of truth, th' associate of sound sense,
And such as in the zeal of good design,
Strong judgment lab'ring in the scripture mine,
All such as manly and great souls produce,
Worthy to live, and of eternal use;
Behold in these what leisure hours demand,
Amusement and true knowledge hand in hand.
Luxury gives the mind a childish cast,
And while she polishes, perverts the taste;
Habits of close attention, thinking heads,
Become more rare as dissipation spreads,
Till authors hear at length, one gen'ral cry,
Tickle and entertain us, or we die.
The loud demand from year to year the same,
Beggars invention and makes fancy lame,
Till farce itself most mournfully jejune,

[1] Voltaire, who built a chapel at Ferney.
[2] John Horne Tooke: *A Letter to John Dunning, Esq.*, 1778.

Calls for the kind assistance of a tune;
And novels (witness ev'ry month's review)
Belie their name, and offer nothing new.
The mind relaxing into needful sport,
Should turn to writers of an abler sort,
Whose wit well manag'd, and whose classic style,
Give truth a lustre, and make wisdom smile.

Friends (for I cannot stint as some have done,
Too rigid in my view, that name to one,
Though one, I grant it in the gen'rous breast
Will stand advanc'd a step above the rest,
Flow'rs by that name promiscuously we call,
But one, the rose, the regent of them all)
Friends, not adopted with a school-boy's haste,
But chosen with a nice discerning taste,
Well-born, well-disciplin'd, who plac'd apart
From vulgar minds, have honour much at heart,
And, tho' the world may think th' ingredients odd,
The love of virtue, and the fear of God!
Such friends prevent what else would soon succeed,
A temper rustic as the life we lead,
And keep the polish of the manners clean,
As their's who bustle in the busiest scene.
For solitude, however some may rave,
Seeming a sanctuary, proves a grave,
A sepulchre in which the living lie,
Where all good qualities grow sick and die.
I praise the Frenchman,[1] his remark was shrewd—
How sweet, how passing sweet, is solitude!
But grant me still a friend in my retreat,
Whom I may whisper, solitude is sweet.
Yet neither these delights, nor aught beside

---

[1] Identified as 'Bruyere' in C.'s footnote, *1782*; but the allusion remained a puzzle until Mr H. G. Wright, in the *Modern Language Review*, XL, 1945, pp. 129–30, traced it to the *Entretiens*, 1657, of J.-L. Guez de Balzac. In the first of these, which deals with 'Les plaisirs de la vie retirée', a passage reads: 'La solitude est certainement vne belle chose; mais il y a plaisir d'avoir quelqu'vn qui sçache respondre, à qui on puisse dire de temps en temps que c'est vne belle chose.'

That appetite can ask, or wealth provide,
Can save us always from a tedious day,
Or shine the dullness of still life away;
Divine communion carefully enjoy'd,
Or sought with energy, must fill the void.
Oh sacred art, to which alone life owes
Its happiest seasons, and a peaceful close,
Scorn'd in a world, indebted to that scorn
For evils daily felt and hardly borne,
Not knowing thee, we reap with bleeding hands,
Flow'rs of rank odor upon thorny lands,
And while experience cautions us in vain,
Grasp seeming happiness, and find it pain.
Despondence, self-deserted in her grief,
Lost by abandoning her own relief,
Murmuring and ungrateful discontent,
That scorns afflictions mercifully meant,
Those humours tart as wines upon the fret,
Which idleness and weariness beget,
These and a thousand plagues that haunt the breast
Fond of the phantom of an earthly rest,
Divine communion chases, as the day
Drives to their dens th' obedient beasts of prey.
See Judah's promis'd king,[1] bereft of all,
Driv'n out an exile from the face of Saul,
To distant caves the lonely wand'rer flies,
To seek that peace a tyrant's frown denies.
Hear the sweet accents of his tuneful voice,
Hear him o'erwhelm'd with sorrow, yet rejoice,
No womanish or wailing grief has part,
No, not a moment, in his royal heart,
'Tis manly music, such as martyrs make,
Suff'ring with gladness for a Saviour's sake;
His soul exults, hope animates his lays,
The sense of mercy kindles into praise,
And wilds familiar with the lion's roar,
Ring with extatic sounds unheard before;

[1] David's flight to the cave of Adullam: 1 Samuel, xxii, i.

'Tis love like his that can alone defeat
The foes of man, or make a desart sweet.
   Religion does not censure or exclude
Unnumber'd pleasures harmlessly pursu'd.
To study culture, and with artful toil
To meliorate and tame the stubborn soil,
To give dissimilar yet fruitful lands
The grain or herb or plant that each demands,
To cherish virtue in an humble state,
And share the joys your bounty may create,
To mark the matchless workings of the pow'r
That shuts within its seed the future flow'r,
Bids these in elegance of form excell,
In colour these, and those delight the smell,
Sends nature forth the daughter of the skies,
To dance on earth, and charm all human eyes;
To teach the canvass innocent deceit,
Or lay the landscape on the snowy sheet,
These, these are arts pursu'd without a crime,
That leave no stain upon the wing of time.
   Me poetry (or rather, notes that aim
Feebly and vainly at poetic fame)
Enploys, shut out from more important views,
Fast by the banks of the slow-winding Ouse;
Content, if thus sequester'd I may raise
A monitor's though not a poet's praise,
And while I teach an art too little known,
To close life wisely, may not waste my own.

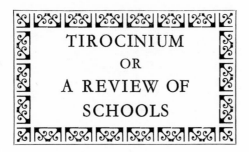

TIROCINIUM
OR
A REVIEW OF
SCHOOLS

IN 1776, two years after his recovery from a severe depression, Cowper was casting around for something to keep his mind occupied, and conceived a plan which would have the further advantage of supplementing his slender income. 'As you have an extensive acquaintance,' he wrote to Joseph Hill on July 6, 'you may possibly be able to serve me in a design I have lately formed of taking two, three or four boys under my tuition, to instruct them in the Greek and Latin languages. I should pursue, with some few exceptions, the Westminster method of instruction, being that which I am best acquainted with myself, and the best upon the whole that I have had an opportunity of observing. They would lodge and board under our roof, and be in all respects accommodated and attended in a manner that would well warrant the demand of a hundred guineas per annum. You have often wished me an employment, and I know none but this for which I am qualified...'

Nothing came of this project, but Cowper continued to ruminate on the advantages of private tuition, preferably by a country clergyman. He was delighted when Unwin decided to educate his two sons himself, and set out his views in several letters, two of which are included in this edition.[1] Cowper's objections to the boarding school system were all of a piece with his Evangelical outlook. He held that the segregation of adolescent boys deprived them of the influence of a Christian home and of intercourse with decent society. He believed, too, that discipline had been so far relaxed that boys were 'debauched in general the moment they were capable of being so'. A suppressed passage of the letter to Newton of November 27, 1784, reveals the spur of moral indignation which drove him to resume *Tirocinium*: 'I just add by way of note...that at Westminster a surgeon is kept, with the privity and under the connivance of the Master, whose chief business is to attend the boys, *peste venerea contaminatos*; an anecdote which I learned last summer from unquestionable authority, and which indeed determined me to the subject.' His informant was probably the Rev. Henry Venn, who had visited

[1] Sept. 7 and Oct. 5, 1780: pp. 597–8 and 602–04.

347

Olney at the end of August. Cowper wrote to Unwin on October 20 that he had 'lately resumed' work on a long poem, begun 'two years since' and soon abandoned. He added on November 1: 'I am proceeding with my work (which at present I feel myself inclined to call *Tirocinium*) as fast as the Muses permit.' The dedication dates its completion.

Cowper was at pains to avoid giving the impression that his strictures were aimed at Westminster School, where he had formed warm friendships, 'excelled at cricket and football,' and had left as head of his house and third in the sixth form.[1] So, in the Advertisement printed at the beginning of his volume of 1785, he wrote:

'In the poem on the subject of education he would be very sorry to stand suspected of having aimed his censure at any particular school. His objections are such as naturally apply themselves to schools in general. If there were not, as for the most part there is, wilful neglect in those who manage them, and an omission even of such discipline as they are susceptible of, the objects are yet too numerous for minute attention; and the aching hearts of ten thousand parents mourning under the bitterest of all disappointments, attest the truth of the allegation. His quarrel therefore is with the mischief at large, and not with any particular instance of it.'

Almost a century and a half later, Dr G. M. Trevelyan wrote in his *English Social History*: 'How much reason careful and pious parents had to dread the influence on their sons of the public school before the period of "Arnold" reforms and the growth of organized games, can be read in Cowper's *Tirocinium*... The whole poem is worth the attention of the student of social history.'

A brief explanation of the title may not be misplaced. *Tirocinium* was a course of basic preparation for military service attended by Roman boys of the equestrian order between the ages of fourteen and seventeen. The *Shorter Oxford Dictionary* defines the word as 'first experience of or training in anything: apprenticeship, pupilage, novitiate'.

The text is that of 1785.

---

[1] Lawrence E. Tanner: *Westminster School*, 1934, p. 27.

TIROCINIUM

OR

A REVIEW OF SCHOOLS

Κεφαλαιον δη παιδειας ὀρθη τροφη.[1]   Plato.
'Αρχη πολιτειας ἁπασης, νεων τροφα.[2]   Diogenes Laertes

TO THE

REV. WILLIAM CAWTHORNE UNWIN,
RECTOR OF STOCK IN ESSEX,

THE TUTOUR OF HIS TWO SONS,

THE FOLLOWING POEM, RECOMMENDING PRIVATE TUITION
IN PREFERENCE TO AN EDUCATION AT SCHOOL, IS
INSCRIBED, BY HIS AFFECTIONATE FRIEND,

WILLIAM COWPER

Olney, Nov. 6, 1784.

[1] 'The principal part of education is right nurture.'
[2] 'The foundation of every society lies in the upbringing of the young.'
Both mottoes were supplied by the Rev. William Bull.

349

It is not from his form in which we trace
Strength joined with beauty, dignity with grace,
That man, the master of this globe, derives
His right to empire over all that lives.
That form indeed, th' associate of a mind
Vast in its pow'rs, ethereal in its kind,
That form, the labour of almighty skill,
Framed for the service of a free-born will,
Asserts precedence, and bespeaks controul,
But borrows all its grandeur from the soul.
Hers is the state, the splendour and the throne,
An intellectual kingdom, all her own.
For her, the mem'ry fills her ample page
With truths pour'd down from ev'ry distant age,
For her amasses an unbounded store,
The wisdom of great nations, now no more,
Though laden, not incumber'd with her spoil,
Laborious, yet unconscious of her toil,
When copiously supplied, then most enlarged,
Still to be fed, and not to be surcharged.
For her, the fancy roving unconfined,
The present muse of ev'ry pensive mind,
Works magic wonders, adds a brighter hue
To nature's scenes, than nature ever knew,
At her command, winds rise and waters roar,
Again she lays them slumb'ring on the shore,
With flow'r and fruit the wilderness supplies,
Or bids the rocks in ruder pomp arise.
For her, the judgment, umpire in the strife,
That grace and nature have to wage through life,
Quick-sighted arbiter of good and ill,
Appointed sage preceptor to the will,
Condemns, approves, and with a faithful voice
Guides the decision of a doubtful choice.
   Why did the fiat of a God give birth
To yon fair sun and his attendant earth,

And when descending he resigns the skies,
Why takes the gentler moon her turn to rise,
Whom ocean feels through all his countless waves,
And owns her pow'r on ev'ry shore he laves?
Why do the seasons still enrich the year,
Fruitful and young as in their first career?
Spring hangs her infant blossoms on the trees,
Rock'd in the cradle of the western breeze,
Summer in haste the thriving charge receives
Beneath the shade of her expanded leaves,
'Till autumn's fiercer heats and plenteous dews
Dye them at last in all their glowing hues—
'Twere wild profusion all, and bootless waste,
Pow'r misemployed, munificence misplaced,
Had not its author dignified the plan,
And crowned it with the majesty of man.
Thus form'd, thus placed, intelligent, and taught,
Look where he will, the wonders God has wrought,
The wildest scorner of his Maker's laws
Finds in a sober moment time to pause,
To press th' important question on his heart,
'Why form'd at all, and wherefore as thou art?'
If man be what he seems, this hour a slave,
The next mere dust and ashes in the grave,
Endued with reason only to descry
His crimes and follies with an aching eye,
With passions, just that he may prove with pain
The force he spends against their fury, vain,
And if, soon after having burnt by turns
With ev'ry lust with which frail nature burns,
His being end where death dissolves the bond,
The tomb take all, and all be blank beyond,
Then he, of all that nature has brought forth
Stands self-impeach'd the creature of least worth,
And, useless while he lives, and when he dies,
Brings into doubt the wisdom of the skies.
   Truths that the learn'd pursue with eager thought,
Are not important always as dear-bought,
Proving at last, though told in pompous strains,

A childish waste of philosophic pains;
But truths on which depends our main concern,
That 'tis our shame and mis'ry not to learn,
Shine by the side of ev'ry path we tread
With such a lustre, he that runs may read.
'Tis true, that if to trifle life away
Down to the sun-set of their latest day,
Then perish on futurity's wide shore
Like fleeting exhalations, found no more,
Were all that heav'n required of human kind,
And all the plan their destiny designed,
What none could rev'rence all might justly blame,
And man would breathe but for his Maker's shame.
But reason heard, and nature well perused,
At once the dreaming mind is disabused.
If all we find possessing earth, sea, air,
Reflect his attributes who plac'd them there,
Fulfill the purpose, and appear design'd
Proofs of the wisdom of th' all-seeing mind,
'Tis plain, the creature whom he chose t' invest
With kingship and dominion o'er the rest,
Received his nobler nature, and was made
Fit for the power in which he stands array'd,
That first or last, hereafter if not here,
He too might make his author's wisdom clear,
Praise him on earth, or obstinately dumb
Suffer his justice in a world to come.
This once believed, 'twere logic misapplied
To prove a consequence by none denied,
That we were bound to cast the minds of youth
Betimes into the mould of heav'nly truth,
That taught of God they may indeed be wise,
Nor ignorantly wand'ring miss the skies.

In early days the conscience has in most
A quickness, which in later life is lost,
Preserved from guilt by salutary fears,
Or, guilty, soon relenting into tears.
Too careless often as our years proceed,
What friends we sort with, or what books we read,

Our parents yet exert a prudent care
To feed our infant minds with proper fare,
And wisely store the nurs'ry by degrees
With wholesome learning, yet acquired with ease.
Neatly secured from being soiled or torn
Beneath a pane of thin translucent horn,
A book (to please us at a tender age
'Tis call'd a book, though but a single page)
Presents the pray'r the Saviour deign'd to teach,[1]
Which children use, and parsons—when they preach.
Lisping our syllables, we scramble next,
Through moral narrative, or sacred text,
And learn with wonder how this world began,
Who made, who marr'd, and who has ransom'd man.
Points, which unless the Scripture made them plain,
The wisest heads might agitate in vain.
Oh thou, whom borne on fancy's eager wing
Back to the season of life's happy spring,
I pleased remember, and while mem'ry yet
Holds fast her office here, can ne'er forget,
Ingenious dreamer,[2] in whose well-told tale
Sweet fiction and sweet truth alike prevail,
Whose hum'rous vein, strong sense, and simple stile,
May teach the gayest, make the gravest smile,
Witty, and well-employed, and like thy Lord,
Speaking in parables his slighted word,
I name thee not, lest so despised a name
Should move a sneer at thy deserved fame;
Yet ev'n in transitory life's late day,
That mingles all my brown with sober gray,
Revere the man, whose *Pilgrim* marks the road,
And guides the *Progress* of the soul to God.
'Twere well with most, if books that could engage

[1] Until the eighteenth century most children learned the alphabet from the horn-book. It usually contained the Lord's Prayer and sometimes numerals.

[2] Bunyan: *The Pilgrim's Progress from this World to that which is to come, delivered under the similitude of a dream.* C. was almost alone among 18th century writers in admiring it.

Their childhood, pleased them at a riper age;
The man, approving what had charm'd the boy,
Would die at last in comfort, peace, and joy,
And not with curses on his art who stole
The gem of truth from his unguarded soul.
The stamp of artless piety impressed
By kind tuition on his yielding breast,
The youth now bearded, and yet pert and raw,
Regards with scorn, though once received with awe,
And warp'd into the labyrinth of lies
That babblers, called philosophers, devise,
Blasphemes his creed as founded on a plan
Replete with dreams, unworthy of a man.
Touch but his nature in its ailing part,
Assert the native evil of his heart,
His pride resents the charge, although the proof[1]
Rise in his forehead, and seem rank enough;
Point to the cure, describe a Saviour's cross
As God's expedient to retrieve his loss,
The young apostate sickens at the view,
And hates it with the malice of a Jew.

How weak the barrier of mere nature proves
Oppos'd against the pleasures nature loves!
While self-betray'd, and wilfully undone,
She longs to yield, no sooner wooed than won.
Try now the merits of this blest exchange
Of modest truth for wit's eccentric range.
'Time was, he closed as he began the day
With decent duty, not ashamed to pray.
The practice was a bond upon his heart,
A pledge he gave for a consistent part,
Nor could he dare presumptuously displease
A pow'r confess'd so lately on his knees.
But now, farewell all legendary tales,
The shadows fly, philosophy prevails,
Pray'r to the winds and caution to the waves,
Religion makes the free by nature slaves,

[1] See 2 Chron. ch. xxvi, verse 19. [C].

Priests have invented, and the world admired
What knavish priests promulgate as inspired,
'Till reason, now no longer overawed,
Resumes her pow'rs, and spurns the clumsy fraud,
And common sense diffusing real day,
The meteor of the gospel dies away.
Such rhapsodies our shrewd discerning youth
Learn from expert enquirers after truth,
Whose only care, might truth presume to speak,
Is not to find what they profess to seek.
And thus well-tutor'd only while we share
A mother's lectures and a nurse's care,
And taught at schools much mythologic stuff,[1]
But sound religion sparingly enough;
Our early notices of truth disgraced,
Soon lose their credit, and are all effaced.

　Would you your son should be a sot or dunce,
Lascivious, headstrong, or all these at once,
That in good time, the stripling's finish'd taste
For loose expence and fashionable waste,
Should prove your ruin, and his own at last,
Train him in public with a mob of boys,
Childish in mischief only and in noise,
Else of a mannish growth, and five in ten
In infidelity and lewdness, men.
There shall he learn, ere sixteen winters old,
That authors are most useful, pawn'd or sold,
That pedantry is all that schools impart,
But taverns teach the knowledge of the heart,
There waiter Dick with Bacchanalian lays,
Shall win his heart and have his drunken praise,
His counsellor and bosom-friend shall prove,
And some street-pacing harlot his first love.

[1] The author begs leave to explain, sensible that without such knowledge, neither the ancient poets nor historians can be tasted or indeed
understood, he does not mean to censure the pains that are taken to
instruct a school-boy in the religion of the heathen, but merely that
neglect of christian culture which leaves him shamefully ignorant of his
own [C].

Schools, unless discipline were doubly strong,
Detain their adolescent charge too long;
The management of tiros of eighteen
Is difficult, their punishment obscene,
The stout tall Captain, whose superior size
The minor heroes view with envious eyes,
Becomes their pattern, upon whom they fix
Their whole attention, and ape all his tricks,
His pride, that scorns t' obey or to submit,
With them is courage, his effont'ry wit.
His wild excursions, window-breaking feats,
Robb'ry of gardens, quarrels in the streets,
His hair-breadth 'scapes, and all his daring schemes,
Transport them, and are made their fav'rite themes.
In little bosoms such atchievements strike
A kindred spark, they burn to do the like.
Thus half-accomplish'd, ere he yet begin
To show the peeping down upon his chin,
And as maturity of years comes on
Made just th' adept that you design'd your son;
T' insure the perseverance of his course,
And give your monstrous project all its force,
Send him to college. If he there be tamed,
Or in one article of vice reclaimed,
Where no regard of ord'nances is shown
Or look'd for now, the fault must be his own.
Some sneaking virtue lurks in him no doubt,
Where neither strumpets' charms nor drinking-bout,
Nor gambling practices can find it out.
Such youths of spirit, and that spirit too,
Ye nurs'ries of our boys, we owe to you.
Though from ourselves the mischief more proceeds,
For public schools 'tis public folly feeds.
The slaves of custom and establish'd mode,
With pack-horse constancy we keep the road,
Crooked or straight, through quags or thorny dells,
True to the jingling of our leader's bells.
To follow foolish precedents, and wink
With both our eyes, is easier than to think,

And such an age as ours baulks no expence,
Except of caution and of common-sense,
Else sure, notorious fact and proof so plain
Would turn our steps into a wiser train.
I blame not those who with what care they can
O'erwatch the num'rous and unruly clan,
Or if I blame, 'tis only that they dare
Promise a work of which they must despair.
Have ye, ye sage intendants of the whole,
An ubiquarian presence and controul,
Elisha's eye that, when Gehazi stray'd
Went with him, and saw all the game he play'd?[1]
Yes—ye are conscious; and on all the shelves
Your pupils strike upon, have struck yourselves.
Or if, by nature sober, ye had then
Boys as ye were, the gravity of men,
Ye knew at least, by constant proofs address'd
To ears and eyes, the vices of the rest.
But ye connive at what ye cannot cure,
And evils not to be endured, endure,
Lest pow'r exerted, but without success,
Should make the little ye retain still less.
Ye once were justly famed for bringing forth
Undoubted scholarship and genuine worth,
And in the firmament of fame still shines
A glory bright as that of all the signs
Of poets raised by you, and statesmen and divines.
Peace to them all, those brilliant times are fled,
And no such lights are kindling in their stead.
Our striplings shine indeed, but with such rays
As set the midnight riot in a blaze,
And seem, if judged by their expressive looks,
Deeper in none than in their surgeons' books.
　　Say muse (for education made the song,
No muse can hesitate or linger long)
What causes move us, knowing as we must
That these *Menageries* all fail their trust,

[1] 2 Kings, v, 21–27.

357

To send our sons to scout and scamper there,
While colts and puppies cost us so much care?
  Be it a weakness, it deserves some praise,
We love the play-place of our early days.
The scene is touching, and the heart is stone
That feels not at that sight, and feels at none.
The wall on which we tried our graving skill,
The very name we carved subsisting still,
The bench on which we sat while deep employ'd,
Though mangled, hack'd and hew'd, not yet destroy'd,
The little ones unbutton'd, glowing hot,
Playing our games, and on the very spot,
As happy as we once, to kneel and draw
The chalky ring, and knuckle down at taw,
To pitch the ball into the grounded hat,
Or drive it devious with a dext'rous pat;
The pleasing spectacle at once excites
Such recollection of our own delights,
That viewing it, we seem almost t' obtain
Our innocent sweet simple years again.
This fond attachment to the well-known place
Whence first we started into life's long race,
Maintains its hold with such unfailing sway,
We feel it ev'n in age, and at our latest day.
Hark! how the sire of chits whose future share
Of classic food begins to be his care,
With his own likeness placed on either knee,
Indulges all a father's heart-felt glee,
And tells them, as he strokes their silver locks,
That they must soon learn Latin, and to box;
Then turning, he regales his list'ning wife
With all th' adventures of his early life,
His skill in coachmanship or driving chaise,
In bilking tavern bills and spouting plays,
What shifts he used detected in a scrape,
How he was flogg'd, or had the luck t' escape,
What sums he lost at play, and how he sold
Watch, seals, and all, till all his pranks are told.
Retracing thus his *frolics* ('tis a name

That palliates deeds of folly and of shame)
He gives the local biass all its sway,
Resolves that where he play'd his sons shall play,
And destines their bright genius to be shown
Just in the scene where he display'd his own.
The meek and bashful boy will soon be taught
To be as bold and forward as he ought,
The rude will scuffle through with ease enough,
Great schools suit best the sturdy and the rough.
Ah happy designation, prudent choice,
Th' event is sure, expect it and rejoice!
Soon see your wish fulfilled in either child,
The pert made perter, and the tame made wild.
The great indeed, by titles, riches, birth,
Excus'd th' incumbrance of more solid worth,
Are best disposed of, where with most success
They may acquire that confident address,
Those habits of profuse and lewd expence,
That scorn of all delights but those of sense,
Which though in plain plebeians we condemn,
With so much reason all expect from them.
But families of less illustrious fame.
Whose chief distinction is their spotless name,
Whose heirs, their honors none, their income small,
Must shine by true desert, or not at all,
What dream they of, that with so little care
They risk their hopes, their dearest treasure there?
They dream of little Charles or William graced
With wig prolix,[1] down-flowing to his waist,
They see th' attentive crowds his talents draw,
They hear him speak—the oracle of law.
The father who designs his babe a priest,
Dreams him episcopally such at least,
And while the playful jockey scow'rs the room
Briskly, astride upon the parlour broom,
In fancy sees him more superbly ride
In coach with purple lined, and mitres on its side.

[1] *prolix*: long and loose.

359

Events improbable and strange as these,
Which only a parental eye foresees,
A public school shall bring to pass with ease.
But how? resides such virtue in that air
As must create an appetite for pray'r?
And will it breathe into him all the zeal
That candidates for such a prize should feel,
To take the lead and be the foremost still
In all true worth and literary skill?
   "Ah blind to bright futurity, untaught
"The knowledge of the world, and dull of thought!
"Church-ladders are not always mounted best
"By learned Clerks and Latinists profess'd.
"Th' exalted prize demands an upward look,
"Not to be found by poring on a book.
"Small skill in Latin, and still less in Greek,
"Is more than adequate to all I seek,
"Let erudition grace him or not grace,
"I give the bawble but the second place,
"His wealth, fame, honors, all that I intend,
"Subsist and center in one point—a friend.
"A friend, whate'er he studies or neglects,
"Shall give him consequence, heal all defects,
"His intercourse with peers, and sons of peers—
"There dawns the splendour of his future years,
"In that bright quarter his propitious skies
"Shall blush betimes, and there his glory rise.
"*Your Lordship, and Your Grace*, what school can teach
"A rhetoric equal to those parts of speech?
"What need of Homer's verse or Tully's prose,
"Sweet interjections! if he learn but those?
"Let rev'rend churls his ignorance rebuke,
"Who starve upon a dogs-eared Pentateuch,
"The parson knows enough who knows a Duke."—
Egregious purpose! worthily begun
In barb'rous prostitution of your son,
Press'd on *his* part by means that would disgrace
A scriv'ners clerk or footman out of place,
And ending, if at last its end be gained,

In sacrilege, in God's own house profaned.
It may succeed; and if his sins should call
For more than common punishment, it shall
The wretch shall rise, and be the thing on earth
Least qualified in honour, learning, worth,
To occupy a sacred, awful post,
In which the best and worthiest tremble most.
The *royal letters* are a thing of course,
A king that would, might recommend his horse,
And Deans no doubt and Chapters, with one voice,
As bound in duty, would confirm the choice.
Behold your Bishop! well he plays his part,
Christian in name, and Infidel in heart,
Ghostly in office, earthly in his plan,
A slave at court, elsewhere a lady's man,
Dumb as a senator, and as a priest,
A piece of mere church-furniture at best;
To live estranged from God his total scope,
And his end sure, without one glimpse of hope.
But fair although and feasible it seem,
Depend not much upon your golden dream;
For Providence that seems concern'd t' exempt
The hallow'd bench from absolute contempt,
In spite of all the wrigglers into place,
Still keeps a seat or two for worth and grace,
And therefore 'tis, that, though the sight be rare,
We sometimes see a Lowth[1] or Bagot[2] there.
Besides, school-friendships are not always found,
Though fair in promise, permanent and sound.
The most disint'rested and virtuous minds
In early years connected, time unbinds.
New situations give a diff'rent cast
Of habit, inclination, temper, taste,
And he that seem'd our counterpart at first,

[1] Robert Lowth, Bishop of London, author of *Lectures on Hebrew Poetry*, 1753 and of a *Short Introduction to English Grammar*, 1762.

[2] Lewis Bagot (1710–1802) successively Bishop of Bristol, Norwich (1783) and St Asaph (1710). He was a brother of Cowper's friends and schoolfellows Walter Bagot and Charles Chester.

Soon shows the strong similitude revers'd.
Young heads are giddy, and young hearts are warm,
And make mistakes for manhood to reform.
Boys are at best but pretty buds unblown,
Whose scent and hues are rather guess'd than known.
Each dreams that each is just what he appears,
But learns his error in maturer years,
When dispositions like a sail unfurl'd
Shows all its rents and patches to the world.
If therefore, ev'n when honest in design,
A boyish friendship may so soon decline,
'Twere wiser sure t' inspire a little heart
With just abhorrence of so mean a part,
Than set your son to work at a vile trade
For wages so unlikely to be paid.

  Our public hives of puerile resort,
That are of chief and most approved report,
To such base hopes in many a sordid soul
Owe their repute in part, but not the whole.
A principle, whose proud pretensions pass
Unquestioned, though the jewel be but glass,
That with a world not often over-nice
Ranks as a virtue, and is yet a vice,
Or rather a gross compound, justly tried,
Of envy, hatred, jealousy, and pride,
Contributes most perhaps t' enhance their fame,
And Emulation is its specious name.
Boys once on fire with that contentious zeal,
Feel all the rage that female rivals feel,
The prize of beauty in a woman's eyes
Not brighter than in theirs the scholar's prize.
The spirit of that competition burns
With all varieties of ill by turns,
Each vainly magnifies his own success,
Resents his fellow's, wishes it were less,
Exults in his miscarriage if he fail,
Deems his reward too great if he prevail,
And labors to surpass him day and night,
Less for improvement, than to tickle spite.

The spur is powerful, and I grant its force,
It pricks the genius forward in its course,
Allows short time for play, and none for sloth,
And felt alike by each, advances both,
But judge where so much evil intervenes,
The end, though plausible, not worth the means.
Weigh, for a moment, classical desert
Against an heart depraved and temper hurt,
Hurt too perhaps for life, for early wrong
Done to the nobler part, affects it long,
And you are staunch indeed in learning's cause,
If you can crown a discipline that draws
Such mischiefs after it, with much applause.
    Connection form'd for int'rest, and endeared
By selfish views, thus censured and cashier'd,
And emulation, as engend'ring hate,
Doom'd to a no less ignominious fate,
The props of such proud seminaries fall,
The JACHIN and the BOAZ[1] of them all.
Great schools rejected then, as those that swell
Beyond a size that can be managed well,
Shall royal institutions miss the bays,
And small academies win all the praise?
Force not my drift beyond its just intent,
I praise a school as Pope a government;
So take my judgment in his language dress'd,
"Whate'er is best administer'd is best."[2]
Few boys are born with talents that excel,
But all are capable of living well.
Then ask not, whether limited or large,
But, watch they strictly, or neglect their charge?
If anxious only that their boys may *learn*,
While *Morals* languish, a despised concern,
The great and small deserve one common blame,
Diff'rent in size, but in effect the same.
Much zeal in virtue's cause all teachers boast,

[1] Names given by Solomon to the pillars supporting the porch of his Temple: 1 Kings, vii, 21
[2] *An Essay on Man*, Epistle iii, 304.

Though motives of mere lucre sway the most.
Therefore in towns and cities they abound,
For there, the game they seek is easiest found,
Though there, in spite of all that care can do.
Traps to catch youth are most abundant too.
If shrewd, and of a well-constructed brain,
Keen in pursuit, and vig'rous to retain,
Your son come forth a prodigy of skill,
As wheresoever taught, so form'd, he will,
The pædagogue, with self-complacent air,
Claims more than half the praise as his due share;
But if with all his genius he betray,
Not more intelligent, than loose and gay,
Such vicious habits as disgrace his name,
Threaten his health, his fortune, and his fame,
Though want of due restraint alone have bred
The symptoms that you see with so much dread,
Unenvied there, he may sustain alone
The whole reproach, the fault was all his own.

Oh 'tis a sight to be with joy perused
By all whom sentiment has not abused,
New-fangled sentiment, the boasted grace
Of those who never feel in the right place,
A sight surpassed by none that we can show,
Though Vestris[1] on one leg still shine below,
A father blest with an ingenuous son,
Father and friend and tutour all in one.
How? turn again to tales long since forgot,
Æsop and Phædrus,[2] and the rest?—why not?
He will not blush that has a father's heart,
To take in childish plays a childish part,
But bends his sturdy back to any toy
That youth takes pleasure in, to please his boy;
Then why resign into a stranger's hand
A task as much within your own command,
That God and nature and your int'rest too

[1] See *n.*, p. 262.
[2] Roman fabulist.

Seem with one voice to delegate to you?
Why hire a lodging in a house unknown
For one whose tend'rest thoughts all hover round your
This second weaning, needless as it is,   [own?
How does it lacerate both your heart and his!
Th' indented stick that loses day by day
Notch after notch, 'till all are smooth'd away,
Bears witness, long ere his dismission come,
With what intense desire he wants his home.
But though the joys he hopes beneath your roof
Bid fair enough to answer in the proof
Harmless and safe and nat'ral as they are,
A disappointment waits him even there:
Arrived, he feels an unexpected change,
He blushes, hangs his head, is shy and strange,
No longer takes, as once, with fearless ease,
His fav'rite stand between his father's knees,
But seeks the corner of some distant seat,
And eyes the door, and watches a retreat,
And least familiar where he should be most,
Feels all his happiest privileges lost.
Alas poor boy!—the natural effect
Of love by absence chilled into respect.
Say, what accomplishments, at school acquired,
Brings he to sweeten fruits so undesired?
Thou well deserv'st an alienated son,
Unless thy conscious heart acknowledge—none.
None that in thy domestic snug recess,
He had not made his own with more address,
Though some perhaps that shock thy feeling mind,
And better never learn'd, or left behind.
Add too, that thus estranged, thou can'st obtain
By no kind arts his confidence again,
That here begins with most that long complaint
Of filial frankness lost, and love grown faint,
Which, oft neglected in life's waning years,
A parent pours into regardless ears.
   Like caterpillars dangling under trees
By slender threads, and swinging in the breeze,

Which filthily bewray and sore disgrace
The boughs in which are bred th' unseemly race,
While ev'ry worm industriously weaves
And winds his web about the rivell'd leaves;
So numerous are the follies that annoy
The mind and heart of every sprightly boy,
Imaginations noxious and perverse,
Which admonition can alone disperse.
Th' encroaching nuisance asks a faithful hand,
Patient, affectionate, of high command,
To check the procreation of a breed
Sure to exhaust the plant on which they feed.
'Tis not enough that Greek or Roman page
At stated hours his freakish thoughts engage,
Ev'n in his pastimes he requires a friend
To warn, and teach him safely to unbend,
O'er all his pleasures gently to preside,
Watch his emotions, and controul their tide,
And levying thus, and with an easy sway,
A tax of profit from his very play,
T' impress a value not to be eras'd
On moments squander'd else, and running all to waste.
And seems it nothing in a father's eye
That unimproved those many moments fly?
And is he well content, his son should find
No nourishment to feed his growing mind
But conjugated verbs and nouns declined?
For such is all the mental food purvey'd
By public hacknies in the schooling trade,
Who feed a pupil's intellect with store
Of syntax truely, but with little more,
Dismiss their cares when they dismiss their flock,
Machines themselves, and govern'd by a clock.
Perhaps a father blest with any brains
Would deem it no abuse or waste of pains,
T' improve this diet, at no great expence,
With sav'ry truth and wholesome common sense.
To lead his son for prospects of delight
To some not steep, though philosophic height,

Thence to exhibit to his wondering eyes
Yon circling worlds, their distance, and their size,
The moons of Jove, and Saturn's belted ball,
And the harmonious order of them all;
To show him in an insect or a flow'r,
Such microscopic proofs of skill and pow'r,
As hid from ages past, God now displays
To combat Atheists with in modern days:
To spread the earth before him, and commend
With designation of the finger's end,
Its various parts to his attentive note,
Thus bringing home to him the most remote;
To teach his heart to glow with gen'rous flame,
Caught from the deeds of men of ancient fame,
And more than all, with commendation due
To set some living worthy in his view,
Whose fair example may at once inspire
A wish to copy what he must admire.
Such knowledge gained betimes, and which appears
Though solid, not too weighty for his years,
Sweet in itself, and not forbidding sport,
When health demands it, of athletic sort,
Would make him what some lovely boys have been,
And more than one perhaps that I have seen,
An evidence and reprehension both
Of the mere school-boy's lean and tardy growth.
  Art thou a man professionally tied,
With all thy faculties elsewhere applied,
Too busy to intend a meaner care
Than how t' enrich thyself, and next, thine heir;
Or art thou (as though rich, perhaps thou art)
But poor in knowledge, having none to impart—
Behold that figure, neat, though plainly clad,
His sprightly mingled with a shade of sad,
Not of a nimble tongue, though now and then
Heard to articulate like other men,
No jester, and yet lively in discourse,
His phrase well chosen, clear and full of force,
And his address, if not quite French in ease,

Not English stiff, but frank and formed to please,
Low in the world because he scorns its arts,
A man of letters, manners, morals, parts,
Unpatronized, and therefore little known,
Wise for himself and his few friends alone,
In him, thy well-appointed proxy see,
Armed for a work too difficult for thee,
Prepared by taste, by learning, and true worth,
To form thy son, to strike his genius forth,
Beneath thy roof, beneath thine eye to prove
The force of discipline when back'd by love,
To double all thy pleasure in thy child,
His mind informed, his morals undefiled.
Safe under such a wing, the boy shall show
No spots contracted among grooms below,
Nor taint his speech with meannesses design'd
By footman Tom for witty and refin'd.
There—in his commerce with the liveried herd
Lurks the contagion chiefly to be fear'd.
For since (so fashion dictates) all who claim
An higher than a mere plebeian fame,
Find it expedient, come what mischief may,
To entertain a thief or two in pay,
And they that can afford th' expence of more,
Some half a dozen, and some half a score,
Great cause occurs to save him from a band
So sure to spoil him, and so near at hand,
A point secured, if once he be supplied
With some such Mentor[1] always at his side.
Are such men rare? perhaps they would abound
Were occupation easier to be found,
Were education, else so sure to fail,
Conducted on a manageable scale,
And schools that have outlived all just esteem,
Exchanged for the secure domestic scheme.
But having found him, be thou duke or earl,
Show thou hast sense enough to prize the pearl,

---

[1] The friend of Ulysses and tutor of his son Telemachus.

And as thou wouldst th' advancement of thine heir
In all good faculties beneath his care,
Respect, as is but rational and just,
A man deem'd worthy of so dear a trust.
Despised by thee, what more can he expect
From youthful folly, than the same neglect?
A flat and fatal negative obtains
That instant, upon all his future pains;
His lessons tire, his mild rebukes offend,
And all th' instructions of thy son's best friend
Are a stream choak'd, or trickling to no end.
Doom him not then to solitary meals,
But recollect that he has sense, and feels.
And, that possessor of a soul refin'd,
An upright heart and cultivated mind,
His post not mean, his talents not unknown,
He deems it hard to vegetate alone.
And if admitted at thy board he sit,
Account him no just mark for idle wit,
Offend not him whom modesty restrains
From repartee, with jokes that he disdains,
Much less transfix his feelings with an oath,
Nor frown, unless he vanish with the cloth. —
And trust me, his utility may reach
To more than he is hir'd or bound to teach,
Much trash unutter'd, and some ills undone,
Through rev'rence of the censor of thy son.
  But if thy table be indeed unclean,
Foul with excess, and with discourse obscene,
And thou a wretch, whom, following her old plan
The world accounts an honourable man,
Because forsooth thy courage has been tried
And stood the test, perhaps on the wrong side,
Though thou hadst never grace enough to prove
That any thing but vice could win thy love;
Or hast thou a polite, card-playing wife,
Chained to the routs that she frequents, for life,
Who, just when industry begins to snore,
Flies, wing'd with joy, to some coach-crouded door,

369

And thrice in ev'ry winter throngs thine own
With half the chariots and sedans in town,
Thyself meanwhile e'en shifting as thou may'st,
Not very sober though, nor very chaste;
Or is thine house, though less superb thy rank,
If not a scene of pleasure, a mere blank,
And thou at best, and in thy sob'rest mood,
A trifler, vain, and empty of all good?
Though mercy for thyself thou canst have none,
Hear nature plead, show mercy to thy son.
Saved from his home, where ev'ry day brings forth
Some mischief fatal to his future worth,
Find him a better in a distant spot,
Within some pious pastor's humble cot,
Where vile example (yours chiefly mean,
The most seducing and the oft'nest seen)
May never more be stamp'd upon his breast
Not yet perhaps incurably impress'd.
Where early rest makes early rising sure,
Disease or comes not or finds easy cure,
Prevented much by diet neat and plain,
Or if it enter, soon starved out again.
Where all th' attention of his faithful host
Discreetly limited to two at most,
May raise such fruits as shall reward his care,
And not at last evaporate in air.
Where stillness aiding study, and his mind
Serene, and to his duties much inclined,
Not occupied in day-dreams, as at home,
Of pleasures past or follies yet to come,
His virtuous toil may terminate at last
In settled habit and decided taste.
But whom do I advise? the fashion-led,
Th' incorrigibly wrong, the deaf, the dead,
Whom care and cool deliberation suit
Not better much, than spectacles a brute,
Who if their sons some slight tuition share,
Deem it of no great moment, whose, or where,
Too proud t' adopt the thoughts of one unknown,

And much too gay t' have any of their own.
But courage, man! methought the muse replied,
Mankind are various, and the world is wide;
The ostrich, silliest of the feather'd kind,
And form'd of God without a parent's mind,
Commits her eggs, incautious, to the dust,
Forgetful that the foot may crush the trust;
And while on public nurs'ries they rely,
Not knowing, and too oft not caring why,
Irrational in what they thus prefer,
No few, that would seem wise, resemble her.
But all are not alike. Thy warning voice
May here and there prevent erroneous choice,
And some perhaps, who, busy as they are,
Yet make their progeny their dearest care,
Whose hearts will ache once told what ills may reach
Their offspring left upon so wild a beach,
Will need no stress of argument t' inforce
Th' expedience of a less advent'rous course.
The rest will slight thy counsel, or condemn.
But *they* have human feelings. Turn to *them*.

To you then, tenants of life's middle state,
Securely placed between the small and great,
Whose character, yet undebauch'd, retains
Two thirds of all the virtue that remains,
Who wise yourselves, desire your sons should learn
Your wisdom and your ways—to you I turn.
Look round you on a world perversely blind,
See what contempt is fall'n on human kind
See wealth abused, and dignities misplac'd,
Great titles, offices, and trusts disgrac'd,
Long lines of ancestry renowned of old,
Their noble qualities all quench'd and cold,
See Bedlam's[1] closetted and hand-cuffed charge
Surpass'd in frenzy by the mad at large,

---

[1] Staring at the lunatics in Bedlam (the New Bethlehem Hospital for the
insane, in Moorfields) was a favourite pastime of 18th century Londoners.

See great commanders making war a trade,
Great lawyers, lawyers without study made,
Churchmen, in whose esteem their blest employ
Is odious, and their wages all their joy,
Who far enough from furnishing their shelves
With gospel lore, turn infidels themselves,
See womanhood despised, and manhood shamed
With infamy too nauseous to be named,
Fops at all corners, lady-like in mien,
Civetted fellows, smelt ere they are seen,
Else coarse and rude in manners, and their tongue
On fire with curses and with nonsense hung,
Now flush'd with drunkeness, now with whoredom pale,
Their breath a sample of last night's regale,
See volunteers in all the vilest arts
Men well endowed, of honourable parts,
Design'd by nature wise, but self-made fools;
All these, and more like these, were bred at schools.
And if it chance, as sometimes chance it will,
That though school bred, the boy be virtuous still,
Such rare exceptions shining in the dark,
Prove rather than impeach the just remark,
As here and there a twinkling star descried
Serves but to show how black is all beside.
Now look on him whose very voice in tone
Just echoes thine, whose features are thine own,
And stroke his polish'd cheek of purest red,
And lay thine hand upon his flaxen head,
And say, my boy, th' unwelcome hour is come,
When thou, transplanted from thy genial home
Must find a colder soil and bleaker air,
And trust for safety to a stranger's care;
What character, what turn, thou wilt assume
From constant converse with I know not whom,
Who there will court thy friendship, with what views,
And artless as thou art, whom thou wilt chuse,
Though much depends on what thy choice shall be,
Is all chance-medley, and unknown to me.
Canst thou, the tear just trembling on thy lids,

And while the dreadful risque foreseen, forbids,
Free too, and under no constraining force,
Unless the sway of custom warp thy course,
Lay such a stake upon the losing side,
Merely to gratify so blind a guide?
Thou canst not: Nature pulling at thine heart
Condemns th' unfatherly, th' imprudent part.
Thou wouldst not, deaf to Nature's tend'rest plea,
Turn him adrift upon a rolling sea,
Nor say, *go thither*, conscious that there lay
A brood of asps, or quicksands in his way,
Then only govern'd by the self-same rule
Of nat'ral pity, send him not to school.
No— Guard him better: Is he not thine own,
Thyself in miniature, thy flesh, thy bone?
And hopest thou not ('tis ev'ry father's hope)
That since thy strength must with thy years elope,
And thou wilt need some comfort, to assuage
Health's last farewell, a staff of thine old age,
That then, in recompense of all thy cares,
Thy child shall show respect to thy grey hairs,
Befriend thee of all other friends bereft,
And give thy life its only cordial left?
Aware then how much danger intervenes,
To compass that good end, forecast the means.
His heart, now passive, yields to thy command;
Secure it thine. Its key is in thine hand.
If thou desert thy charge and throw it wide,
Nor heed what guests there enter and abide,
Complain not if attachments lewd and base
Supplant thee in it, and usurp thy place.
But if thou guard its sacred chambers sure
From vicious inmates and delights impure,
Either his gratitude shall hold him fast,
And keep him warm and filial to the last,
Or if he prove unkind, as who can say
But being man, and therefore frail, he may,
One comfort yet shall cheer thine aged heart,
Howe'er he slight thee, thou hast done thy part.

Oh barb'rous! would'st thou with a Gothic hand
Pull down the schools—what!—all the schools i' th' land?
Or throw them up to liv'ry-nags and grooms,
Or turn them into shops and auction rooms?
A captious question, sir, and yours is one,
Deserves an answer similar, or none.
Wouldst thou, possessor of a flock, employ
(Apprized that he is such) a careless boy,
And feed him well and give him handsome pay,
Merely to sleep, and let them run astray?
Survey our schools and colleges, and see
A sight not much unlike my simile.
From education, as the leading cause,
The public character its colour draws,
Thence the prevailing manners take their cast,
Extravagant or sober, loose or chaste.
And though I would not advertize them yet,
Nor write on each— *This Building to be Let*,
Unless the world were all prepared t' embrace
A plan well worthy to supply their place,
Yet backward as they are, and long have been,
To cultivate and keep the MORALS clean,
(Forgive the crime) I wish them, I confess,
Or better managed, or encouraged less.

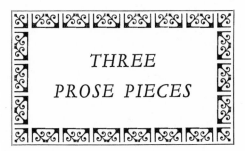

*THREE
PROSE PIECES*

THE PRESENT STATE OF
COUNTRY CHURCHES

COWPER, as a young man, was a close friend of the editors of *The Connoisseur*, Bonnell Thornton and George Colman the elder. All three were members of the Nonsense Club, a group of seven former contemporaries at Westminster School who dined together on Thursdays. *The Connoisseur* also appeared each Thursday, and ran from January 31, 1754 until September 30, 1756. It set out to satisfy the demand for the light-hearted periodical essay. Boswell mentioned it at one of his earliest meetings with Johnson (July 1, 1763): 'He said it wanted matter. — No doubt (Boswell comments) it has not the deep thinking of Johnson's writings. But surely it has just views of the surface of life, and a very sprightly manner.'

Five numbers have been attributed to Cowper. The authority is as follows. First, there are some hints on the identity of contributors in the final number of *The Connoisseur*, including this: 'From a friend, a Gentleman of the Temple, we received Nos. 111, 115 and 119.' Numbers 134 and 138 are not mentioned; but they, with No. 119 are claimed for Cowper by Hayley in his *Life and Letters of William Cowper, Esq.*, vol. IV: 'During Cowper's visit to Eartham he kindly pointed out to me three of his papers in the last volume of the Connoisseur. I inscribed them with his name at the time, and imagine that the readers of his life may be gratified in seeing them inserted here. I find other numbers of that work ascribed to him, but the three following I print as his, on his own explicit authority. Number 119, Thursday, May 6, 1756 — Number 134, Thursday, August 19, 1756 — Number 138, Thursday, September 16, 1756.' Finally, in the letter to Unwin of April 6, 1780, Cowper remarks, 'I once wrote a Connoisseur upon the subject of secret-keeping.' (Number 119).

The text followed here is that of the first edition of the bound volumes of the *Connoisseur*, 1755–57, where the title is first published.

THE HISTORY OF MY THREE HARES

Cowper's essay about his tame hares was first published in the *Gentleman's Magazine* for June, 1784, in the form of a letter to the publisher, 'Sylvanus Urban, Gent.' In the number for December of the same year, Cowper's *Epitaph on a Hare* (p. 86) was printed under the following note:

'In June Mag. p. 412, you published the history of my three hares; an epitaph, therefore, upon one of them, as a suitable sequel to that narrative, you may possibly think not unworthy a place among the poetical compositions in your magazine. W. C.'

Thus the title given to the essay in this edition, although not originally placed over it by Cowper, is at any rate the description that he applied to it.

The piece was first collected in the 1800 edition of the *Poems*. 1808 and later editions introduced it with the words: 'The following Account of the Treatment of his Hares was inserted by Mr Cowper in the Gentleman's Magazine, whence it is transcribed.' It had not, however, been transcribed in full. The first paragraph and parts of sentences in other paragraphs were omitted. Cowper's editors, with one exception, have followed the text of 1800. I have followed Bruce in preferring the original version of 1784.

EPITAPHIUM ALTERUM

This Latin epitaph on Puss was first printed in the editions of 1800, the text of which is reproduced here, together with a 'memorandum found among Mr. Cowper's papers'. It reads: 'Tuesday ,March 9, 1786. This day died poor Puss, aged eleven years eleven months. She [*sic*] died between twelve and one at noon, of mere old age, and apparently without pain.' *Epitaphium Alterum* may have received that title simply because it was placed, in the 1800 editions, immediately after the English epitaph, mentioned above, on another hare, Tiney.

The lines on Tiney, written in March, 1783, end by anticipating the death of Puss, whose epitaph must have been written at about the same time, since it gives his age as nine years.

A LETTER FROM MR. VILLAGE, GIVING AN ACCOUNT OF THE PRESENT STATE OF COUNTRY CHURCHES, THEIR CLERGY, AND THEIR CONGREGATIONS.

(*The Connoisseur*, No. 134, August 19, 1756)

MR. VILLAGE TO MR. TOWN

Dear Cousin,

The country at present, no less than the metropolis, abounding with politicians of every kind, I begin to despair of picking up any intelligence, that might possibly be entertaining to your readers. However, I have made a tour to some of the most distant parts of the kingdom with a clergyman of my acquaintance; and shall not trouble you with an account of the improvements that have been made in the seats we saw according to the modern taste, but proceed to give you some reflections, which occurred to us on observing several country churches, and the behaviour of their congregations.

The ruinous condition of some of these churches gave me great offence; and I could not help wishing, that the honest vicar, instead of indulging his genius for improvements, by inclosing his gooseberry bushes with a *Chinese* rail,[1] and converting half an acre of his glebe-land into a bowling-green, would have applied part of his income to the more laudable purpose of sheltering his parishioners from the weather during their attendance on divine service. It is no uncommon thing to see the parsonag[e]-house well thatched, and in exceeding

---

[1] Chinoiserie was becoming fashionable in architecture and landscape gardening (Sir William Chambers) and in the design of furniture (Chippendale). At a guess, it is conceivable that a 'Chinese rail' resembled the fence illustrated in willow-pattern plates, although that design was not introduced until 1780.

good repair, while the church perhaps has no better roof than the ivy that grows over it. The noise of owls, bats and magpies makes a principal part of the church musick in many of these ancient edifices; and the walls, like a large map, seem to be portioned out into capes, seas, and promontories by the various colours with which the damps have stained them. Sometimes it has happened, that the foundation being too weak to support the steeple any longer, it has been found expedient to pull down that part of the building, and to hang the bells under a wooden shed on the ground beside it. This is the case in a parish in *Norfolk*, through which I lately passed, and where the clerk and the sexton, like the two figures at St. *Dunstan's*,[1] serve the bells in capacity of clappers, by striking them alternately with a hammer. In other churches I have observed, that nothing unseemly or ruinous is to be found, except in the clergyman, and in the appendages of his person. The squire of the parish, or his ancestors perhaps, to testify their devotion, and leave a lasting monument of their magnificence, have adorned the altar-piece with the richest crimson velvet, embroidered with vine-leaves and ears of wheat,and have dressed up the pulpit with the same splendour and expence; while the gentleman who fills it is exalted in the midst of all this finery with a surplice as dirty as a farmer's frock, and a periwig that seems to have transferred its faculty of curling to the band, that appears in full-buckle[2] beneath it.

But if I was concerned to see many of our country churches in a tottering condition, I was more offended with the indecency of worship in others. I could wish that the pastors would inform their hearers, that there is no occasion to scream themselves hoarse in making the responses, that the town-cryer is not the only person qualified to pray with due devotion, and that he who bawls the loudest may nevertheless be the wickedest fellow in the parish. The old women too in the ayle might be told that their time would be better employed in attending to the sermon than in fumbling over their tattered testaments till they have found the text, by which time the discourse is near drawing to a conclusion; while a

[1] See n. 3, p. 159.
[2] *Full-buckle*: in curling apparatus.

word or two of instruction might not be thrown away upon the younger part of the congregation to teach them, that making posies in summertime, and cracking nuts in autumn, is no part of the religious ceremony.

The good old practice of psalm-singing is, indeed, wonderfully improved in many country churches since the days of *Sternhold* and *Hopkins*; and there is scarce a parish-clerk, who has so little taste as not to pick his staves out of the New Version.[1] This has occasioned great complaints in some places, where the clerk has been forced to bawl by himself, because the rest of the congregation cannot find the psalm at the end of their prayer-books; while others are highly disgusted at the innovation, and stick as obstinately to the Old Version as to the Old Stile.[2] The tunes themselves have also been new-set to jiggish measures; and the sober drawl, which used to accompany the two first staves of the hundredth psalm with the *gloria patri*, is now split into as many quavers as an *Italian* air. For this purpose there is in every county an itinerant band of vocal musicians, who make it their business to go round to all the churches in their turns, and, after a prelude with the pitch-pipe, astonish the audience with hymns set to the new *Winchester* measure[3] and anthems of their own composing. As these new-fashioned psalmodists are necessarily made up of young men and maids, we may naturally suppose, that there is a perfect concord and sympathy between them: and, indeed, I have known it happen, that these sweet singers have been brought more than once into disgrace, by too close an unison between the thorough-bass and the treble.

It is a difficult matter to decide, which is looked upon to be

[1] See introduction to Selections from Olney Hymns, p. 143 and *n.*, p. 204.

[2] *Old Stile*: the Julian calendar. The Gregorian method of compilation was not officially adopted in Great Britain until September 1752.

[3] *New Winchester measure*: The tune taken over by Wesley from the Moravians, and called by him 'the swift German tune', was known as 'Winchester' by 1750. But as that name was already applied to the tune associated with the hymn 'While shepherds watch their flocks by night', the two tunes came to be styled 'New' and 'Old' Winchester respectively.

the greatest man in a country church, the parson or his clerk.
The latter is most certainly held in higher veneration, where
the former happens to be only a poor curate, who rides post[1]
every sabbath from village to village, and mounts and dis-
mounts at the church-door. The clerk's office is not only to
tag the prayers with an *Amen*, or usher in the sermon with a
stave; but he is also the universal father to give away the
brides, and the standing god-father to all the new-born brats.
But in many places there is still a greater man belonging to
the church, than either the parson or the clerk himself. The
person I mean is the squire; who, like the King, may be
stiled Head of the Church in his own parish. If the benefice
be in his own gift, the vicar is his creature, and of consequence
entirely at his devotion: or, if the care of the church is left
to a curate, the Sunday fees of roast beef and plumb pudding,
and a liberty to shoot in the manor, will bring him as much
under the squire's command as his dogs and horses. For this
reason the bell is often kept tolling, and the people waiting
in the church-yard, an hour longer than the usual time; nor
must the service begin, till the squire has strutted up the ayle,
and seated himself in the great pew in the chancel. The length
of the sermon is also measured by the will of the squire, as
formerly by the hour-glass: and I know one parish where
the preacher has always the complaisance to break off to a
conclusion, the minute that the squire gives the signal by
rising up after his nap.

In a village church, the squire's lady or the vicar's wife are
perhaps the only females that are stared at for their finery: but
in the larger cities and towns, where the newest fashions are
brought down weekly by the stage-coach or waggon, all the
wives and daughters of the most topping[2] tradesmen vie with
each other every Sunday in the elegance of their apparel. I
could even trace the gradations in their dress according to the
opulence, the extent, and the distance of the place from
London. I was at church in a populous city in the north, where
the mace-bearer cleared the way for Mrs Mayoress, who

[1] *ride post*: to ride with all possible speed.
[2] *topping*: proud.

came sidling after him in an enormous fan-hoop, of a pattern which had never been seen before in those parts. At another church in a corporation-town, I saw several Negligées,[1] with furbelow'd[2] aprons, which had long disputed the prize of superiority; but these were most woefully eclipsed by a burgess's daughter just come from *London*, who appeared in a Trollopée or Slammerkin,[1] with treble ruffles to the cuffs, pinked and gymped,[3] and the sides of the petticoat drawn up in festoons. In some lesser borough towns the contest, I found, lay between three or four black and green bibs and aprons: at one a grocer's wife attracted our eyes by a new-fashioned cap called a Joan; and at another they were wholly taken up by a mercer's daughter in a Nun's Hood.

I need not say any thing of the behaviour of the congregations in these more polite places of religious resort; as the same genteel ceremonies are practised there as at the most fashionable churches at the court end of the town. The ladies immediately on their entrance breathe a pious ejaculation through their fan-sticks, and the beaus very gravely address themselves to the Haberdashers' Bills glewed upon the linings of their hats. This pious duty is no sooner performed, than the exercise of bowing and curtsying succeeds; the locking and unlocking of the pews drowns the reader's voice at the beginning of the service; and the rustling of silks, added to the whispering and tittering of so much good company, renders him totally unintelligible to the very end of it.

I am, dear Cousin, yours, &c.

---

[1] *Negligée, Trollopée, Slammerkin*: loosely worn, informal dresses.

[2] *furbelow'd*: flounced.

[3] *pinked*: ornamented with perforations; *gymped*, trimmed with fine cord.

THE HISTORY OF MY THREE HARES

(The *Gentleman's Magazine*, June 1784)

May 28

MR URBAN,

Convinced that you despise no communications that may gratify curiosity, amuse rationally, or add, though but a little, to the stock of public knowledge, I send you a circumstantial account of an animal, which, though its general properties are pretty well known, is for the most part such a stranger to man, that we are but little aware of its peculiarities. We know indeed that the hare is good to hunt and good to eat, but in all other respects poor Puss is a neglected subject.

In the year 1774, being much indisposed both in mind and body, incapable of diverting myself either with company or books, and yet in a condition that made some diversion necessary, I was glad of any thing that would engage my attention without fatiguing it. The children of a neighbour of mine had a leveret given them for a plaything; it was at that time about three months old. Understanding better how to tease the poor creature than to feed it, and soon becoming weary of their charge, they readily consented that their father, who saw it pining and growing leaner every day, should offer it to my acceptance. I was willing enough to take the prisoner under my protection, perceiving that in the management of such an animal, and in the attempt to tame it, I should find just that sort of employment which my case required. It was soon known among the neighbours that I was pleased with the present; and the consequence was, that in a short time I had as many leverets offered to me as would have stocked a paddock. I undertook the care of three, which it is necessary that I should here distinguish by the names I gave them, Puss, Tiney, and Bess. Notwithstanding the two feminine appellatives, I must inform you that they were all males. Immediately commencing carpenter, I built them houses to sleep in; each had a separate apartment so contrived that their ordure would pass thro' the bottom of it; an earthen pan placed under each received whatsoever fell, which being duly emptied and washed, they were thus kept perfectly sweet and clean. In the daytime they had the range of a hall, and at night retired each to his own bed, never intruding into that of another.

Puss grew presently familiar, would leap into my lap, raise himself upon his hinder feet, and bite the hair from my temples. He would suffer me to take him up and to carry him about in my arms, and has more than once fallen fast asleep upon my knee. He was ill three days, during which time I nursed him, kept him apart from his fellows that they might not molest him (for, like many other wild animals, they persecute one of their own species that is sick), and by constant care and trying him with a variety of herbs, restored him to perfect health. No creature could be more grateful than my patient after his recovery; a sentiment which he most significantly expressed, by licking my hand, first the back of it, then the palm, then every finger separately, then between all the fingers, as if anxious to leave no part of it unsaluted; a ceremony which he never performed but once again upon a similar occasion. Finding him extremely tractable, I made it my custom to carry him always after breakfast into the garden, where he hid himself generally under the leaves of a cucumber vine, sleeping or chewing the cud till evening; in the leaves also of that vine he found a favourite repast. I had not long habituated him to this taste of liberty, before he began to be impatient for the return of the time when he might enjoy it. He would invite me to the garden by drumming upon my knee, and by a look of such expression as it was not possible to misinterpret. If this rhetoric did not immediately succeed, he would take the skirt of my coat between his teeth, and pull at it with all his force. Thus Puss might be said to be perfectly tamed, the shyness of his nature was done away, and on the whole it was visible, by many symptoms which I have not room to enumerate, that he was happier in human society than when shut up with his natural companions.

Not so Tiney. Upon him the kindest treatment had not the least effect. He too was sick, and in his sickness had an equal share of my attention; but if, after his recovery, I took the liberty to stroke him, he would grunt, strike with his fore feet, spring forward and bite. He was, however, very entertaining in his way, even his surliness was matter of mirth, and in his play he preserved such an air of gravity, and performed his feats with such a solemnity of manner, that in him too I had an agreeable companion.

Bess, who died soon after he was full grown, and whose death was occasioned by his being turned into his box which had been washed, while it was yet damp, was a hare of great humour and drollery. Puss was tamed by gentle usage; Tiney was not to be tamed at all; and Bess had a courage and confidence that made him tame from the beginning. I always admitted them into the parlour after supper, when the carpet affording their feet a firm hold, they would frisk and bound and play a thousand gambols, in which, Bess, being remarkably strong and fearless, was always superior to the rest, and proved himself the Vestris of the party. One evening the cat being in the room had the hardiness to pat Bess upon the cheek, an indignity which he resented by drumming upon her back, with such violence, that the cat was happy to escape from under his paws and hide herself.

You observe, Sir, that I describe these animals as having each a character of his own. Such they were in fact, and their countenances were so expressive of that character, that, when I looked only on the face of either, I immediately knew which it was. It is said, that a shepherd, however numerous his flock, soon becomes so familiar with their features, that he can by that indication only distinguish each from all the rest, and yet to a common observer the difference is hardly perceptible. I doubt not that the same discrimination in the cast of countenances would be discoverable in hares, and am persuaded that among a thousand of them no two could be found exactly similar; a circumstance little suspected by those who have not had opportunity to observe it. These creatures have a singular sagacity in discovering the minutest alteration that is made in the place to which they are accustomed, and instantly apply their nose to the examination of a new object. A small hole being burnt in the carpet, it was mended with a patch, and that patch in a moment underwent the strictest scrutiny. They

seem too to be very much directed by the smell in the choice of
their favourites; to some persons, though they saw them daily,
they could never be reconciled, and would even scream when
they attempted to touch them; but a miller coming in, engaged
their affections at once; his powdered coat had charms that
were irresistible. You will not wonder, Sir, that my intimate
acquaintance with these specimens of the kind has taught me
to hold the sportsman's amusement in abhorrence; he little
knows what amiable creatures he persecutes, of what gratitude
they are capable, how cheerful they are in their spirits, what
enjoyment they have of life, and that, impressed as they seem
with a peculiar dread of man, it is only because man gives
them peculiar cause for it.

That I may not be tedious, I will just give you a short
summary of those articles of diet that suit them best, and then
retire to make room for some more important correspondent.

I take it to be a general opinion that they graze, but it is an
erroneous one, at least grass is not their staple; they seem
rather to use it medicinally, soon quitting it for leaves of
almost any kind. Sowthistle, dent-de-lion, and lettuce are their
favourite vegetables, especially the last. I discovered by accident that fine white sand is in great estimation with them; I
suppose as a digestive. It happened that I was cleaning a bird-
cage while the hares were with me; I placed a pot filled with
such sand upon the floor, to which being at once directed by
a strong instinct, they devoured it voraciously; since that time
I have generally taken care to see them well supplied with it.
They account green corn a delicacy, both blade and stalk, but
the ear they seldom eat; straw of any kind, especially wheat-
straw, is another of their dainties; they will feed greedily upon
oats, but if furnished with clean straw never want them; it
serves them also for a bed, and, if shaken up daily, will be kept
sweet and dry for a considerable time. They do not indeed
require aromatic herbs, but will eat a small quantity of them
with great relish, and are particularly fond of the plant called
musk; they seem to resemble sheep in this, that, if their pas-
tures be too succulent, they are very subject to the rot; to
prevent which, I always made bread their principal nourishment, and, filling a pan with it cut into small squares, placed

it every evening in their chambers, for they feed only at evening and in the night; during the winter, when vegetables are not to be got, I mingled this mess of bread with shreds of carrot, adding to it the rind of apples cut extremely thin; for tho' they are fond of the paring, the apple itself disgusts them. These, however, not being a sufficient substitute for the juice of summer herbs, they must at this time be supplied with water; but so placed, that they cannot overset it into their beds. I must not omit that occasionally they are much pleased with twigs of hawthorn and of the common briar, eating even the very wood when it is of considerable thickness.

Bess, I have said, died young; Tiney lived to be nine years old, and died at last, I have reason to think, of some hurt in his loins by a fall. Puss is still living, and has just completed his tenth year, discovering no signs of decay nor even of age, except that he is grown more discreet and less frolicksome than he was. I cannot conclude, Sir, without informing you that I have lately introduced a dog to his acquaintance, a spaniel that had never seen a hare to a hare that had never seen a spaniel. I did it with great caution, but there was no real need of it. Puss discovered no token of fear, nor Marquis the least symptom of hostility. There is therefore, it should seem, no natural antipathy between dog and hare, but the pursuit of the one occasions the flight of the other, and the dog pursues because he is trained to it; they eat bread at the same time out of the same hand, and are in all respects sociable and friendly.

Yours, &c., W.C.

P.S. I should not do complete justice to my subject, did I not add, that they have no ill scent belonging to them, that they are indefatigably nice in keeping themselves clean, for which purpose nature has furnished them with a brush under each foot; and that they are never infested by any vermin.

EPITAPHIUM ALTERUM

Hic etiam jacet
Qui totum novennium vixit
Puss.
Siste paulisper
Qui præteriturus es,
Et tecum sic reputa—
Hunc neque canis venaticus
Nec plumbum missile
Nec laqueus
Nec imbres nimii
Confecere
Tamen mortuus est—
Et moriar ego.[1]

[1783]

---

[1] 'Here Puss still rests, after nine whole years of life. Stay awhile, you who would pass by, and thus reflect: no huntsman's hound, no leaden ball, no snare, no drenching downpour, brought about his end—yet he is dead, and I too shall die.'

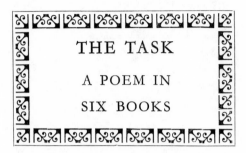

THE TASK

A POEM IN

SIX BOOKS

THE TASK was written in 1783 and 1784, when Cowper's creative powers were responding to the stimulus of Lady Austen's companionship. In Hayley's words:

'This lady happened, as an admirer of Milton, to be partial to blank verse, and often solicited her poetical friend to try his powers in that species of composition. After repeated solicitations, he promised her, if she would furnish the subject, to comply with her request. "Oh!" she replied, "you can never be in want of a subject—you can write upon any—write upon this sofa!"' [1]

The Sofa, as the poem was first called, began as a *jeu d'esprit* (hence the mock-heroic opening lines) and soon turned into something else. As the author explained in the introductory 'Advertisement', he accepted the suggestion of writing about a sofa, 'and having much leisure, connected another subject with it; and pursuing the train of thought to which his situation and turn of mind led him, brought forth at length, instead of the trifle which he at first intended, a serious affair—a Volume.'

The Task expresses Cowper's ideas about man's situation in the world, and how he should live. The unifying theme is that the whole duty of man is to put himself into right relations with God, without which happiness is sought in vain. Or, as Cowper put it obliquely in a letter to William Unwin: 'The whole has one tendency: to discountenance the modern enthusiasm after a London life, and to recommend rural ease and leisure as friendly to piety and virtue.'

So the title of *The Task*, though it may also refer to the task which Lady Austen set the author, embraces the Christian's task in this world. Milton, who was never far from Cowper's mind—witness the numberless Miltonic echoes in this poem—

[1] See also the letter to Lady Hesketh, pp. 768–75.

may possibly have supplied the title; Cowper, too, longed for 'inward ripeness':

> 'Yet be it less or more, or soon or slow,
> It shall be still in strictest measure ev'n,
> To that same lot, however mean or high,
> Toward which Time leads me, and the will of Heav'n;
> All is, if I have grace to use it so,
> As ever in my great task Master's eye.'

Once the unity of the theme is recognised, the apparent ragbag inconsequence of the writing, which is no small part of its charm, falls into shape. The vignettes of landscape, observed with photographic clarity of detail, are illustrations of the wholesome joys of the simple life; the comments on contemporary events are related to Cowper's view of the world; the diversions, such as the instructions for raising cucumbers, turn out to be parables. The link is the originality and cohesiveness of the poet's vision and the transparent sincerity of his style.

Throughout the poem, and especially in Book VI, Cowper addressed the world. He did not address it in vain. *The Task*, recognised by the critics as a masterpiece, raised him out of obscurity and made him the most famous poet in England. It was of incalculable importance to the Evangelicals in their work of bringing about a revolution in the field of morals. According to G. R. Balleine, the historian of the movement:

'This poem carried its message into quarters which the movement had not yet touched. Men who would have scorned the preaching of Grimshaw or the pages of Venn could not help reading the masterpiece of the first poet of the day, and the world of culture awoke to the fact that Evangelicalism was not a vulgar delusion, but a philosophy of life which could appeal effectively to educated opinion.'

The text is that of the first edition of 1785.

THE TASK

BOOK I

THE SOFA

ARGUMENT OF THE FIRST BOOK.—*Historical
deduction of seats, from the stool to the Sofa— A School-
boy's ramble— A walk in the country— The scene
described— Rural sounds as well as sights delightful—
Another walk— Mistake concerning the charms of solitude, corrected— Colonnades commended— Alcove and
the view from it— The Wilderness— The Grove— The
Thresher— The necessity and the benefits of exercise—
The works of nature superior to and in some instances
inimitable by art— The wearisomeness of what is commonly called a life of pleasure— Change of scene
sometimes expedient— A common described, and the
character of crazy Kate introduced upon it— Gipsies—
The blessings of civilized life— That state most favourable
to virtue— The South Sea Islanders compassionated, but
chiefly Omai— His present state of mind supposed—
Civilized life friendly to virtue, but not great cities—
Great cities, and London in particular, allowed their due
praise, but censured— Fete Champetre— The book
concludes with a reflection on the fatal effects of dissipation and effeminacy upon our public measures.*

I SING the SOFA. I who lately sang
Truth, Hope, and Charity, and touch'd with awe
The solemn chords, and with a trembling hand,
Escap'd with pain from that advent'rous flight,
Now seek repose upon an humbler theme;
The theme though humble, yet august and proud
Th' occasion—for the Fair commands the song.[1]

[1] Lady Austen.

Time was, when cloathing sumptuous or for use,
Save their own painted skins, our sires had none.
As yet[1] black breeches were not; sattin smooth,
Or velvet soft, or plush with shaggy pile:
The hardy chief upon the rugged rock
Wash'd by the sea, or on the grav'ly bank
Thrown up by wintry torrents roaring loud,
Fearless of wrong, repos'd his weary strength.
Those barb'rous ages past, succeeded next
The birth-day of invention, weak at first,
Dull in design, and clumsy to perform.
Joint-stools were then created; on three legs
Upborne they stood. Three legs upholding firm
A massy slab, in fashion square or round.
On such a stool immortal Alfred sat,
And sway'd the sceptre of his infant realms;
And such in ancient halls and mansions drear
May still be seen, but perforated sore
And drill'd in holes the solid oak is found,
By worms voracious eating through and through.

  At length a generation more refined
Improv'd the simple plan, made three legs four,
Gave them a twisted form vermicular,
And o'er the seat with plenteous wadding stuff'd
Induced a splendid cover green and blue,
Yellow and red, of tap'stry richly wrought
And woven close, or needle-work sublime.
There might ye see the pioney spread wide,
The full-blown rose, the shepherd and his lass,
Lap-dog and lambkin with black staring eyes,
And parrots with twin cherries in their beak.

  Now came the cane from India, smooth and bright
With Nature's varnish; sever'd into stripes
That interlaced each other, these supplied
Of texture firm a lattice work, that braced
The new machine, and it became a chair.
But restless was the chair; the back erect

---

[1] 'As yet this world was not:' *Paradise Lost*, V, 577.

Distress'd the weary loins that felt no ease;
The slipp'ry seat betray'd the sliding part
That press'd it, and the feet hung dangling down,
Anxious in vain to find the distant floor.
These for the rich: the rest, whom fate had placed
In modest mediocrity, content
With base materials, sat on well tann'd hides
Obdurate and unyielding, glassy smooth,
With here and there a tuft of crimson yarn,
Or scarlet crewel[1] in the cushion fixt:
If cushion might be call'd, what harder seem'd
Than the firm oak of which the frame was form'd.
No want of timber then was felt or fear'd
In Albion's happy isle. The lumber[2] stood
Pond'rous and fixt by its own massy weight.
But elbows still were wanting; these, some say,
An Alderman of Cripplegate contrived,
And some ascribe th' invention to a priest
Burly and big and studious of his ease.
But rude at first, and not with easy slope
Receding wide, they press'd against the ribs,
And bruised the side, and elevated high,
Taught the rais'd shoulders to invade the ears.
Long time elapsed or e'er our rugged sires
Complain'd, though incommodiously pent in,
And ill at ease behind. The Ladies first
'Gan murmur, as became the softer sex.
Ingenious fancy, never better pleas'd
Than when employ'd t' accommodate the fair,
Heard the sweet moan with pity, and devised
The soft settee; one elbow at each end,
And in the midst an elbow, it receiv'd
United yet divided, twain at once.
So sit two Kings of Brentford[3] on one throne;

[1] *crewel*: fine worsted.

[2] *umber 1785*: *lumber* first *1800*.

[3] Characters in *The Rehearsal*, a play by John Sheffield, Duke of Buckingham. 'They were represented as entering upon the stage hand in hand, and sitting upon one throne.' — *Bruce*.

And so two citizens who take the air,
Close pack'd and smiling in a chaise and one.
But relaxation of the languid frame
By soft recumbency of outstretched limbs,
Was bliss reserved for happier days. So slow
The growth of what is excellent, so hard
T' attain perfection in this nether world.
Thus first necessity invented stools,
Convenience next suggested elbow chairs,
And luxury th' accomplish'd Sofa last.

  The nurse sleeps sweetly, hired to watch the sick,
Whom snoring she disturbs. As sweetly he
Who quits the coach-box at the midnight hour
To sleep within the carriage more secure,
His legs depending at the open door.
Sweet sleep enjoys the Curate in his desk,
The tedious Rector drawling o'er his head[1]
And sweet the Clerk below: but neither sleep
Of lazy Nurse, who snores the sick man dead,
Nor his who quits the box at midnight hour
To slumber in the carriage more secure,
Nor sleep enjoy'd by Curate in his desk,
Nor yet the dozings of the Clerk are sweet,
Compared with the repose the Sofa yields.

  Oh may I live exempted (while I live
Guiltless of pamper'd appetite obscene)
From pangs arthritic that infest the toe
Of libertine excess. The Sofa suits
The gouty limb, 'tis true; but gouty limb,
Though on a Sofa, may I never feel:
For I have loved the rural walk through lanes
Of grassy swarth close cropt by nibbling sheep,
And skirted thick with intertexture firm
Of thorny boughs: have loved the rural walk
O'er hills, through valleys, and by rivers' brink,
E'er since a truant boy I pass'd my bounds
T' enjoy a ramble on the banks of Thames.

---

[1] i.e., preaching from a three-decker pulpit.

And still remember, nor without regret
Of hours that sorrow since has much endear'd,
How oft, my slice of pocket store consumed,
Still hung'ring pennyless and far from home,
I fed on scarlet hips and stoney haws,
Or blushing crabs, or berries, that imboss
The bramble, black as jet, or sloes austere.
Hard fare! but such as boyish appetite
Disdains not, nor the palate undepraved
By culinary arts, unsav'ry deems.
No Sofa then awaited my return,
Nor Sofa then I needed. Youth repairs
His wasted spirits quickly, by long toil
Incurring short fatigue; and though our years
As life declines, speed rapidly away,
And not a year but pilfers as he goes[1]
Some youthful grace that age would gladly keep,
A tooth or auburn lock, and by degrees
Their length and color from the locks they spare;
Th' elastic spring of an unwearied foot
That mounts the stile with ease, or leaps the fence,
That play of lungs inhaling and again
Respiring freely the fresh air, that makes
Swift pace or steep ascent no toil to me,
Mine have not pilfer'd yet; nor yet impair'd
My relish of fair prospect; scenes that sooth'd
Or charm'd me young, no longer young, I find
Still soothing and of power to charm me still.
And witness, dear companion[2] of my walks,
Whose arm this twentieth winter I perceive
Fast lock'd in mine, with pleasure such as love
Confirm'd by long experience of thy worth
And well-tried virtues could alone inspire—
Witness a joy that thou hast doubled long.
Thou know'st my praise of nature most sincere,
And that my raptures are not conjured up

---

[1] cf. Horace, *Epistles*, II, ii, 45: *singula de nobis anni prædantur euntes.*
[2] Mrs Unwin.

To serve occasions of poetic pomp,
But genuine, and art partner of them all.
How oft upon yon eminence, our pace
Has slacken'd to a pause, and we have borne
The ruffling wind scarce conscious that it blew,
While admiration feeding at the eye,
And still unsated, dwelt upon the scene.
Thence with what pleasure have we just discern'd
The distant plough slow-moving, and beside
His lab'ring team that swerv'd not from the track,
The sturdy swain diminish'd to a boy!
Here Ouse, slow winding through a level plain
Of spacious meads with cattle sprinkled o'er,
Conducts the eye along his sinuous course
Delighted. There, fast rooted in his bank
Stand, never overlook'd, our fav'rite elms,
That screen the herdsman's solitary hut;
While far beyond and overthwart the stream
That as with molten glass inlays the vale,
The sloping land recedes into the clouds;
Displaying on its varied side, the grace
Of hedge-row beauties numberless, square tow'r,[1]
Tall spire,[2] from which the sound of chearful bells
Just undulates upon the list'ning ear;
Groves, heaths, and smoking villages remote.[3]
Scenes must be beautiful which daily view'd
Please daily, and whose novelty survives
Long knowledge and the scrutiny of years.
Praise justly due to those that I describe.

Nor rural sights alone, but rural sounds
Exhilarate the spirit, and restore
The tone of languid Nature. Mighty winds
That sweep the skirt of some far-spreading wood
Of ancient growth, make music not unlike
The dash of ocean on his winding shore,
And lull the spirit while they fill the mind,

[1] *Square tower*: Clifton.
[2] *Tall spire*: Olney.
[3] *Villages remote*: Emberton, Steventon.

Unnumber'd branches waving in the blast,
And all their leaves fast flutt'ring, all at once.
Nor less composure waits upon the roar
Of distant floods, or on the softer voice
Of neighb'ring fountain, or of rills that slip
Through the cleft rock, and chiming as they fall
Upon loose pebbles, lose themselves at length
In matted grass, that with a livelier green
Betrays the secret of their silent course.
Nature inanimate employs sweet sounds,
But animated Nature sweeter still,
To sooth and satisfy the human ear.
Ten thousand warblers chear the day, and one
The live-long night: nor these alone whose notes
Nice-finger'd art must emulate in vain,
But cawing rooks, and kites that swim sublime
In still repeated circles, screaming loud,
The jay, the pie, and ev'n the boding owl
That hails the rising moon, have charms for me.
Sounds inharmonious in themselves and harsh,
Yet heard in scenes where peace for ever reigns,
And only there, please highly for their sake.

　　Peace to the artist, whose ingenious thought
Devised the weather-house, that useful toy!
Fearless of humid air and gathering rains
Forth steps the man, an emblem of myself,
More delicate, his tim'rous mate retires.
When Winter soaks the fields, and female feet
Too weak to struggle with tenacious clay,
Or ford the rivulets, are best at home,
The task of new discov'ries falls on me.
At such a season and with such a charge
Once went I forth, and found, till then unknown,
A cottage, whither oft we since repair:
'Tis perch'd upon the green-hill top, but close
Inviron'd with a ring of branching elms
That overhang the thatch, itself unseen,
Peeps at the vale below; so thick beset
With foliage of such dark redundant growth,

I call'd the low-roof'd lodge the *peasant's nest*.
And hidden as it is, and far remote
From such unpleasing sounds as haunt the ear
In village or in town, the bay of curs
Incessant, clinking hammers, grinding wheels,
And infants clam'rous whether pleas'd or pain'd,
Oft have I wish'd the peaceful covert mine.
Here, I have said, at least I should possess
The poet's treasure, silence, and indulge
The dreams of fancy, tranquil and secure.
Vain thought! the dweller in that still retreat
Dearly obtains the refuge it affords.
Its elevated site forbids the wretch
To drink sweet waters of the chrystal well;
He dips his bowl into the weedy ditch,
And heavy laden, brings his bev'rage home
Far-fetch'd and little worth; nor seldom waits,
Dependent on the baker's punctual call,
To hear his creaking panniers at the door,
Angry and sad and his last crust consumed.
So farewel envy of the *peasant's nest*.
If solitude make scant the means of life,
Society for me! thou seeming sweet,
Be still a pleasing object in my view,
My visit still, but never mine abode.
Not distant far, a length of colonade
Invites us. Monument of ancient taste,
Now scorn'd, but worthy of a better fate.
Our fathers knew the value of a screen
From sultry suns, and in their shaded walks
And long-protracted bow'rs, enjoy'd at noon
The gloom and coolness of declining day.
We bear our shades about us; self depriv'd
Of other screen, the thin umbrella spread,
And range an Indian waste without a tree.
Thanks to Benevolus[1]—he spares me yet
These chesnuts ranged in corresponding lines,

[1] John Courtney Throckmorton, Esq., of Weston Underwood [C].

And though himself so polish'd, still reprieves
The obsolete prolixity of shade.

    Descending now (but cautious, lest too fast)
A sudden steep, upon a rustic bridge
We pass a gulph in which the willows dip
Their pendent boughs, stooping as if to drink.
Hence ancle deep in moss and flow'ry thyme
We mount again, and feel at ev'ry step
Our foot half sunk in hillocks green and soft,
Rais'd by the mole, the miner of the soil.
He not unlike the great ones of mankind,[1]
Disfigures earth, and plotting in the dark
Toils much to earn a monumental pile,
That may record the mischiefs he has done.

    The summit gain'd, behold the proud alcove
That crowns it! yet not all its pride secures
The grand retreat from injuries impress'd
By rural carvers, who with knives deface
The pannels, leaving an obscure rude name,
In characters uncouth, and spelt amiss.
So strong the zeal t' immortalize himself
Beats in the breast of man, that ev'n a few
Few transient years won from th' abyss abhorr'd
Of blank oblivion, seem a glorious prize,
And even to a clown. Now roves the eye,
And posted on this speculative height,
Exults in its command. The sheep-fold here
Pours out its fleecy tenants o'er the glebe.
At first, progressive as a stream, they seek
The middle field; but scatter'd by degrees
Each to his choice, soon whiten all the land.
There from the sun-burnt hay-field homeward creeps
The loaded wain, while lighten'd of its charge,
The wain that meets it, passes swiftly by,
The boorish driver leaning o'er his team

---

[1] In England, contrary to the general practice on the Continent, coal
was held to be the property of the owner of the land under which it lay.
Consequently many great noblemen owned collieries.

Vocif'rous, and impatient of delay.
Nor less attractive is the woodland scene,
Diversified with trees of ev'ry growth
Alike yet various. Here the grey smooth trunks
Of ash or lime, or beech, distinctly shine,
Within the twilight of their distant shades;
There lost behind a rising ground, the wood
Seems sunk, and shorten'd to its topmost boughs.
No tree in all the grove but has its charms,
Though each its hue peculiar; paler some,
And of a wannish grey; the willow such
And poplar, that with silver lines his leaf,
And ash far-stretching his umbrageous arm.
Of deeper green the elm; and deeper still,
Lord of the woods, the long-surviving oak.
Some glossy-leav'd and shining in the sun,
The maple, and the beech of oily nuts
Prolific, and the lime at dewy eve
Diffusing odors: nor unnoted pass
The sycamore, capricious in attire,
Now green, now tawny, and ere autumn yet
Have changed the woods, in scarlet honors bright.
O'er these, but far beyond, (a spacious map
Of hill and valley interpos'd between)
The Ouse, dividing the well water'd land,
Now glitters in the sun, and now retires,
As bashful, yet impatient to be seen.

Hence the declivity is sharp and short,
And such the re-ascent; between them weeps
A little Naiad her impov'rish'd urn
All summer long, which winter fills again.
The folded gates would bar my progress now,
But that the Lord[1] of this inclosed demesne,
Communicative of the good he owns,
Admits me to a share: the guiltless eye
Commits no wrong, nor wastes what it enjoys.
Refreshing change! where now the blazing sun?

[1] See the foregoing note [C].

By short transition we have lost his glare
And stepp'd at once into a cooler clime.
Ye fallen avenues! once more I mourn
Your fate unmerited, once more rejoice
That yet a remnant of your race survives.
How airy and how light the graceful arch,
Yet awful as the consecrated roof
Re-echoing pious anthems! while beneath
The chequer'd earth seems restless as a flood
Brush'd by the wind. So sportive is the light
Shot through the boughs, it dances as they dance,
Shadow and sunshine intermingling quick,
And darkning and enlightning, as the leaves
Play wanton, ev'ry moment, ev'ry spot.

   And now with nerves new-brac'd and spirits chear'd
We tread the wilderness, whose well-roll'd walks
With curvature of slow and easy sweep,
Deception innocent—give ample space
To narrow bounds. The grove receives us next;
Between the upright shafts of whose tall elms
We may discern the thresher at his task.
Thump after thump, resounds the constant flail,
That seems to swing uncertain, and yet falls
Full on the destin'd ear. Wide flies the chaff,
The rustling straw sends up a frequent mist
Of atoms, sparkling in the noon-day beam.
Come hither, ye that press your beds of down
And sleep not: see him sweating o'er his bread
Before he eats it.—'Tis the primal curse,
But soften'd into mercy; made the pledge
Of chearful days, and nights without a groan.

   By ceaseless action, all that is, subsists.
Constant rotation of th' unwearied wheel
That nature rides upon, maintains her health,
Her beauty, her fertility. She dreads
An instant's pause, and lives but while she moves.
Its own revolvency upholds the world.
Winds from all quarters agitate the air,
And fit the limpid element for use,

Else noxious: oceans, rivers, lakes, and streams,
All feel the fresh'ning impulse, and are cleansed
By restless undulation; ev'n the oak
Thrives by the rude concussion of the storm;
He seems indeed indignant, and to feel
Th' impression of the blast with proud disdain,
Frowning as if in his unconscious arm
He held the thunder. But the monarch owes
His firm stability to what he scorns,
More fixt below, the more disturb'd above.
The law by which all creatures else are bound,
Binds man the lord of all. Himself derives
No mean advantage from a kindred cause,
From strenuous toil his hours of sweetest ease.
The sedentary stretch their lazy length
When custom bids, but no refreshment find,
For none they need: the languid eye, the cheek
Deserted of its bloom, the flaccid, shrunk,
And wither'd muscle, and the vapid soul,
Reproach their owner with that love of rest
To which he forfeits ev'n the rest he loves.
Not such th' alert and active. Measure life
By its true worth, the comforts it affords,
And theirs alone seems worthy of the name.
Good health and, its associate in the most,
Good temper; spirits prompt to undertake,
And not soon spent, though in an arduous task;
The pow'rs of fancy and strong thought are theirs;
Ev'n age itself seems privileged in them
With clear exemption from its own defects.
A sparkling eye beneath a wrinkled front
The vet'ran shows, and gracing a grey beard
With youthful smiles, descends toward the grave
Sprightly, and old almost without decay.
    Like a coy maiden, ease, when courted most,
Farthest retires — an idol, at whose shrine
Who oft'nest sacrifice are favor'd least.
The love of Nature, and the scenes she draws,
Is Nature's dictate. Strange! there should be found

Who self-imprison'd in their proud saloons,
Renounce the odors of the open field
For the unscented fictions of the loom.
Who satisfied with only pencil'd scenes,
Prefer to the performance of a God
Th' inferior wonders of an artist's hand.
Lovely indeed the mimic works of art,
But Nature's works far lovelier. I admire—
None more admires the painter's magic skill,
Who shews me that which I shall never see,
Conveys a distant country into mine,
And throws Italian light on English walls.
But imitative strokes can do no more
Than please the eye, sweet Nature ev'ry sense.
The air salubrious of her lofty hills,
The chearing fragrance of her dewy vales
And music of her woods—no works of man
May rival these; these all bespeak a power
Peculiar, and exclusively her own.
Beneath the open sky she spreads the feast;
'Tis free to all—'tis ev'ry day renew'd,
Who scorns it, starves deservedly at home.
He does not scorn it, who imprison'd long
In some unwholesome dungeon, and a prey
To sallow sickness, which the vapors dank
And clammy of his dark abode have bred,
Escapes at last to liberty and light.
His cheek recovers soon its healthful hue,
His eye relumines its extinguish'd fires,
He walks, he leaps, he runs—is wing'd with joy,
And riots in the sweets of ev'ry breeze.
He does not scorn it, who has long endur'd
A fever's agonies, and fed on drugs.
Nor yet the mariner, his blood inflamed
With acrid salts; his very heart athirst
To gaze at Nature in her green array.
Upon the ship's tall side he stands, possess'd
With visions prompted by intense desire;
Fair fields appear below, such as he left,

Far distant, such as he would die to find—
He seeks them headlong, and is seen no more.
  The spleen is seldom felt where Flora reigns;
The low'ring eye, the petulance, the frown,
And sullen sadness that o'ershade, distort,
And mar the face of beauty, when no cause
For such immeasurable woe appears,
These Flora banishes, and gives the fair
Sweet smiles and bloom less transient than her own.
It is the constant revolution stale
And tasteless, of the same repeated joys,
That palls and satiates, and makes languid life
A pedlar's pack, that bows the bearer down.
Health suffers, and the spirits ebb; the heart
Recoils from its own choice—at the full feast
Is famish'd—finds no music in the song,
No smartness in the jest, and wonders why.
Yet thousands still desire to journey on,
Though halt and weary of the path they tread.
The paralitic who can hold her cards
But cannot play them, borrows a friend's hand
To deal and shuffle, to divide and sort
Her mingled suits and sequences, and sits,
Spectatress both and spectacle, a sad
And silent cypher, while her proxy plays.
Others are dragg'd into the crowded room
Between supporters; and once seated, sit
Through downright inability to rise,
'Till the stout bearers lift the corpse again.
These speak a loud memento. Yet ev'n these
Themselves love life, and cling to it, as he
That overhangs a torrent, to a twig.
They love it, and yet loath it; fear to die,
Yet scorn the purposes for which they live.
Then wherefore not renounce them? No—the dread,
The slavish dread of solitude, that breeds
Reflection and remorse, the fear of shame,
And their invet'rate habits, all forbid.
  Whom call we gay? That honor has been long

The boast of mere pretenders to the name.
The innocent are gay—the lark is gay
That dries his feathers saturate with dew
Beneath the rosy cloud, while yet the beams
Of day-spring overshoot his humble nest.
The peasant too, a witness of his song,
Himself a songster, is as gay as he.
But save me from the gaiety of those
Whose head-aches nail them to a noon-day bed;
And save me too from theirs whose haggard eyes
Flash desperation, and betray their pangs
For property stripp'd off by cruel chance;
From gaiety that fills the bones with pain,
The mouth with blasphemy, the heart with woe.
　　The earth was made so various, that the mind
Of desultory man, studious of change,
And pleas'd with novelty, might be indulged.
Prospects however lovely may be seen
'Till half their beauties fade; the weary sight,
Too well acquainted with their smiles, slides off,
Fastidious, seeking less familiar scenes.
Then snug inclosures in the shelter'd vale,
Where frequent hedges intercept the eye,
Delight us, happy to renounce awhile,
Not senseless of its charms, what still we love,
That such short absence may endear it more.
Then forests, or the savage rock may please,
That hides the sea-mew in his hollow clefts
Above the reach of man: his hoary head,
Conspicuous many a league, the mariner
Bound homeward, and in hope already there,
Greets with three cheers exulting. At his waist
A girdle of half-wither'd shrubs he shows,
And at his feet the baffled billows die.
The common overgrown with fern, and rough
With prickly goss,[1] that, shapeless and deform,[2]

[1] *goss: gorse* first *1787*. *Goss* was the word used in local dialect: cf.
A. E. Baker, *Glossary of Northamptonshire Words and Phrases*, 1854.
[2] *deform : deform'd* first *1787*.

And dang'rous to the touch, has yet its bloom,
And decks itself with ornaments of gold,
Yields no unpleasing ramble; there the turf
Smells fresh, and rich in odorif'rous herbs
And fungous fruits of earth, regales the sense
With luxury of unexpected sweets.

 There often wanders one, whom better days
Saw better clad, in cloak of sattin trimm'd
With lace, and hat with splendid ribband bound.
A serving maid was she, and fell in love
With one who left her, went to sea, and died.
Her fancy followed him through foaming waves
To distant shores, and she would sit and weep
At what a sailor suffers; fancy too,
Delusive most where warmest wishes are,
Would oft anticipate his glad return,
And dream of transports she was not to know.
She heard the doleful tidings of his death,
And never smil'd again. And now she roams
The dreary waste; there spends the livelong day,
And there, unless when charity forbids,
The livelong night. A tatter'd apron hides,
Worn as a cloak, and hardly hides a gown
More tatter'd still; and both but ill conceal
A bosom heaved with never-ceasing sighs.
She begs an idle pin of all she meets,
And hoards them in her sleeve; but needful food,
Though press'd with hunger oft, or comelier cloaths,
Though pinch'd with cold, asks never. — Kate is craz'd.

 I see a column of slow-rising smoke
O'ertop the lofty wood that skirts the wild.
A vagabond and useless tribe there eat
Their miserable meal. A kettle slung
Between two poles upon a stick transverse,
Receives the morsel; flesh obscene of dog,
Or vermin, or at best, of cock purloin'd
From his accustom'd perch. Hard-faring race!
They pick their fuel out of ev'ry hedge,
Which kindled with dry leaves, just saves unquench'd

The spark of life. The sportive wind blows wide
Their flutt'ring rags, and shows a tawny skin,
The vellum of the pedigree they claim.[1]
Great skill have they in palmistry, and more
To conjure clean away the gold they touch,
Conveying worthless dross into its place.
Loud when they beg, dumb only when they steal.
Strange! that a creature rational, and cast
In human mould, should brutalize by choice
His nature, and though capable of arts
By which the world might profit and himself,
Self-banish'd from society, prefer
Such squalid sloth to honourable toil.
Yet even these, though feigning sickness oft,
They swathe the forehead, drag the limping limb
And vex their flesh with artificial sores,
Can change their whine into a mirthful note
When safe occasion offers, and with dance
And music of the bladder and the bag,
Beguile their woes and make the woods resound.
Such health and gaiety of heart enjoy
The houseless rovers of the sylvan world;
And breathing wholesome air, and wand'ring much,
Need other physic none to heal th' effects
Of loathsome diet, penury, and cold.
   Blest he, though undistinguish'd from the crowd
By wealth or dignity, who dwells secure
Where man, by nature fierce, has laid aside
His fierceness, having learnt, though slow to learn,
The manners and the arts of civil life.
His wants, indeed, are many; but supply
Is obvious, placed within the easy reach
Of temp'rate wishes and industrious hands.
Here virtue thrives as in her proper soil;
Not rude and surly, and beset with thorns
And terrible to sight, as when she springs,
(If e'er she spring spontaneous) in remote

[1] The supposed Egyptian origin of the Gypsies.

411

And barb'rous climes, where violence prevails,
And strength is lord of all; but gentle, kind,
By culture tam'd, by liberty refresh'd,
And all her fruits by radiant truth matur'd.
War and the chace engross the savage whole.
War follow'd for revenge, or to supplant
The envied tenants of some happier spot,
The chace for sustenance, precarious trust!
His hard condition with severe constraint
Binds all his faculties, forbids all growth
Of wisdom, proves a school in which he learns
Sly circumvention, unrelenting hate,
Mean self-attachment, and scarce aught beside.
Thus fare the shiv'ring natives of the north,
And thus the rangers of the western world
Where it advances far into the deep,
Towards th' Antarctic. Ev'n the favor'd isles[1]
So lately found, although the constant sun
Cheer all their seasons with a grateful smile,
Can boast but little virtue; and inert
Through plenty, lose in morals, what they gain
In manners, victims of luxurious ease.
These therefore I can pity, placed remote
From all that science traces, art invents,
Or inspiration teaches; and inclosed
In boundless oceans never to be pass'd
By navigators uninformed as they,
Or plough'd perhaps by British bark again.
But far beyond the rest, and with most cause,
Thee, gentle savage![2] whom no love of thee
Or thine, but curiosity perhaps,
Or else vain glory, prompted us to draw
Forth from thy native bow'rs, to show thee here

[1] The Society Islands (Tahiti) and the Friendly Islands (Tonga).

[2] Omia [C]. Omai, a native of Tahiti, was brought to England by Captain Furneaux in 1774, and became the lion of London society (see Boswell's *Life of Johnson*, April 3, 1776). Cook took him back on his last voyage of 1776–79; it was said afterwards that he pleaded to go back to England.

With what superior skill we can abuse
The gifts of providence, and squander life.
The dream is past. And thou hast found again
Thy cocoas and bananas, palms and yams,
And homestall thatch'd with leaves. But hast thou found
Their former charms? And having seen our state,
Our palaces, our ladies, and our pomp
Of equipage, our gardens,[1] and our sports,
And heard our music; are thy simple friends,
Thy simple fare, and all thy plain delights,
As dear to thee as once? And have thy joys
Lost nothing by comparison with ours?
Rude as thou art (for we return'd thee rude
And ignorant, except of outward show)
I cannot think thee yet so dull of heart
And spiritless, as never to regret
Sweets tasted here, and left as soon as known.
Methinks I see thee straying on the beach,
And asking of the surge that bathes thy foot
If ever it has wash'd our distant shore.
I see thee weep, and thine are honest tears,
A patriot's for his country. Thou art sad
At thought of her forlorn and abject state,
From which no power of thine can raise her up.
Thus fancy paints thee, and though apt to err,
Perhaps errs little, when she paints thee thus.
She tells me too that duly ev'ry morn
Thou climb'st the mountain top, with eager eye
Exploring far and wide the wat'ry waste
For sight of ship from England. Ev'ry speck
Seen in the dim horizon, turns thee pale
With conflict of contending hopes and fears.
But comes at last the dull and dusky eve,
And sends thee to thy cabbin, well-prepar'd
To dream all night of what the day denied.
Alas! expect it not. We found no bait
To tempt us in thy country. Doing good,

[1] Public pleasure gardens, such as Marylebone, Vauxhall and Ranelagh

413

Disinterested good, is not our trade.
We travel far 'tis true, but not for nought;
And must be brib'd to compass earth again,
By other hopes and richer fruits than yours.
　　But though true worth and virtue, in the mild
And genial soil of cultivated life
Thrive most, and may perhaps thrive only there,
Yet not in cities oft. In proud and gay
And gain-devoted cities; thither flow,
As to a common and most noisome sew'r,
The dregs and fæculence of ev'ry land.
In cities foul example on most minds
Begets its likeness. Rank abundance breeds
In gross and pamper'd cities sloth and lust,
And wantonness and gluttonous excess.
In cities, vice is hidden with most ease,
Or seen with least reproach; and virtue taught
By frequent lapse, can hope no triumph there
Beyond th' atchievement of successful flight.
I do confess them nurs'ries of the arts,
In which they flourish most. Where in the beams
Of warm encouragement, and in the eye
Of public note they reach their perfect size.
Such London is, by taste and wealth proclaim'd
The fairest capital of all the world,
By riot and incontinence the worst.
There, touch'd by Reynolds, a dull blank becomes
A lucid mirror, in which nature sees
All her reflected features. Bacon[1] there
Gives more than female beauty to a stone,
And Chatham's eloquence to marble lips.
Nor does the chissel occupy alone
The pow'rs of sculpture, but the style as much;
Each province of her art her equal care.
With nice incision of her guided steel

---

[1] John Bacon, sculptor, and a prominent Evangelical layman, had admired C.'s *Poems* and sent him an engraving of his monument to Chatham in Westminster Abbey.

She ploughs a brazen field, and clothes a soil
So sterile with what charms soe'er she will,
The richest scen'ry and the loveliest forms.
Where finds philosophy[1] her eagle eye
With which she gazes at yon burning disk
Undazzled, and detects and counts his spots?
In London; where her implements exact
With which she calculates, computes and scans
All distance, motion, magnitude, and now
Measures an atom, and now girds a world?
In London; where has commerce such a mart,
So rich, so throng'd, so drain'd, and so supplied,
As London—opulent, enlarged, and still
Increasing London? Babylon of old
Not more the glory of the earth, than she,
A more accomplish'd world's chief glory now.

   She has her praise. Now mark a spot or two
That so much beauty would do well to purge;
And show this queen of cities, that so fair
May yet be foul, so witty, yet not wise.
It is not seemly, nor of good report,
That she is slack in discipline. More prompt
T' avenge than to prevent the breach of law.
That she is rigid in denouncing death
On petty robbers, and indulges life
And liberty, and oft-times honor too
To peculators of the public gold.
That thieves at home must hang; but[2] he that puts
Into his overgorged and bloated purse
The wealth of Indian provinces, escapes.
Nor is it well, nor can it come to good,[3]
That through profane and infidel contempt
Of holy writ, she has presum'd t' annul
And abrogate, as roundly as she may,
The total ordonance and will of God;

---

[1] *Philosophy*: natural science.
[2] See p. 707 and *n*.
[3] Cf. *Hamlet*, I, ii, 158: 'It is not, nor it cannot come to, good.'

Advancing fashion to the post of truth,
And cent'ring all authority in modes
And customs of her own, till sabbath rites
Have dwindled into unrespected forms,
And knees and hassocks are well-nigh divorced.
    God made the country, and man made the town.
What wonder then, that health and virtue, gifts
That can alone make sweet the bitter draught
That life holds out to all, should most abound
And least be threatened in the fields and groves?
Possess ye therefore, ye who borne about
In chariots and sedans, know no fatigue
But that of idleness, and taste no scenes
But such as art contrives, possess ye still
Your element; there only ye can shine,
There only minds like yours can do no harm.
Our groves were planted to console at noon
The pensive wand'rer in their shades. At eve
The moon-beam sliding softly in between
The sleeping leaves, is all the light they wish,
Birds warbling all the music. We can spare
The splendor of your lamps, they but eclipse
Our softer satellite. Your songs confound
Our more harmonious notes. The thrush departs
Scared, and th' offended nightingale is mute.
There is a public mischief in your mirth,
It plagues your country. Folly such as yours,
Graced with a sword, and worthier of a fan,
Has made, which enemies could ne'er have done,
Our arch of empire, stedfast but for you,
A mutilated structure, soon to fall.

BOOK II

THE TIME-PIECE[1]

ARGUMENT OF THE SECOND BOOK.—*Which opens with reflections suggested by the conclusion of the former—Peace among the nations recommended on the ground of their common fellowship in sorrow—Prodigies enumerated—Sicilian earthquakes—Man rendered obnoxious to these calamities by sin—God the agent in them—The philosophy that stops at secondary causes, reproved—Our own late miscarriages accounted for—Satyrical notice taken of our trips to Fontainbleau—But the pulpit, not satire, the proper engine of reformation—The Reverend Advertiser of engraved sermons—Petit maitre parson—The good preacher—Picture of a theatrical clerical coxcomb—Story-tellers and jesters in the pulpit reproved—Apostrophe to popular applause—Retailers of ancient philosophy expostulated with—Sum of the whole matter—Effects of sacerdotal mismanagement on the laity—Their folly and extravagance—The mischiefs of profusion—Profusion itself, with all its consequent evils, ascribed as to its principal cause, to the want of discipline in the Universities.*

OH for a lodge in some vast wilderness,[2]
Some boundless contiguity of shade,
Where rumour of oppression and deceit,
Of unsuccessful or successful war
Might never reach me more. My ear is pain'd,

[1] The title is explained in a letter to Newton, dated Dec. 13, 1784: 'The book to which it belongs is intended to strike the hour that gives notice of approaching judgment.'

[2] Jeremiah, ix, 2: 'Oh that I had in the wilderness a lodging place.'

My soul is sick with ev'ry day's report
Of wrong and outrage with which earth is fill'd.
There is no flesh in man's obdurate heart,
It does not feel for man. The nat'ral bond
Of brotherhood is sever'd as the flax
That falls asunder at the touch of fire.
He finds his fellow guilty of a skin
Not colour'd like his own, and having pow'r
T' inforce the wrong, for such a worthy cause
Dooms and devotes him as his lawful prey.
Lands intersected by a narrow frith
Abhor each other. Mountains interposed
Make enemies of nations who had else
Like kindred drops been mingled into one.
Thus man devotes his brother, and destroys;
And worse than all, and most to be deplored
As human nature's broadest, foulest blot,
Chains him, and tasks him, and exacts his sweat
With stripes, that mercy with a bleeding heart
Weeps when she sees inflicted on a beast.
Then what is man? And what man seeing this,
And having human feelings, does not blush
And hang his head, to think himself a man?
I would not have a slave to till my ground,
To carry me, to fan me while I sleep,
And tremble when I wake, for all the wealth
That sinews bought and sold have ever earn'd.
No: dear as freedom is, and in my heart's
Just estimation priz'd above all price,
I had much rather be myself the slave
And wear the bonds, than fasten them on him.
We have no slaves at home. — Then why abroad?
And they themselves once ferried o'er the wave
That parts us, are emancipate and loos'd.
Slaves cannot breathe in England;[1] if their lungs
Receive our air, that moment they are free,

[1] In the Somerset case of 1772 a negro slave brought to England by his master claimed his freedom under English law. Lord Mansfield, the Lord Chief Justice, decided that the institution of slavery did not exist in

They touch our country and their shackles fall.
That's noble, and bespeaks a nation proud
And jealous of the blessing. Spread it then,
And let it circulate through ev'ry vein
Of all your empire. That where Britain's power
Is felt, mankind may feel her mercy too.
  Sure there is need of social intercourse,
Benevolence and peace and mutual aid
Between the nations, in a world that seems
To toll the death-bell of its own decease,
And by the voice of all its elements
To preach the gen'ral doom.[1] When were the winds
Let slip with such a warrant to destroy,
When did the waves so haughtily o'erleap
Their ancient barriers, deluging the dry?
Fires from beneath, and meteors[2] from above
Portentous, unexampled, unexplained,
Have kindled beacons in the skies and th' old
And crazy earth has had her shaking fits
More frequent, and forgone her usual rest.
Is it a time to wrangle, when the props
And pillars of our planet seem to fail,
And Nature[3] with a dim and sickly eye
To wait the close of all? But grant her end
More distant, and that prophecy demands

England: 'the air of England has long been too pure for a slave and every man is free that breathes it. Every man who comes into England is entitled to the protection of English law, whatever oppression he may heretofore have suffered, and whatsoever may be the colour of his skin... let the negro be discharged.'

[1] Alluding to the late calamities at Jamaica [C]. The island was devastated by a succession of hurricanes in the years 1780-86. See pp. 607-08.

[2] August 18, 1783 [C]. Described in the *Annual Register*, 1783, p. 214. 'Many of the facts stated seem to indicate an unusually bright display of the Northern Lights.' — *Bruce*.

[3] Alluding to the fog that covered both Europe and Asia during the whole summer of 1783 [C]. It was popularly believed that the fog portended an earthquake or the Day of Judgment.

A longer respite, unaccomplished yet;
Still they are frowning signals, and bespeak
Displeasure in his breast who smites the earth
Or heals it, makes it languish or rejoice.
And 'tis but seemly, that where all deserve
And stand exposed by common peccancy
To what no few have felt, there should be peace,
And brethren in calamity should love.

    Alas for Sicily![1] rude fragments now
Lie scatter'd where the shapely column stood.
Her palaces are dust. In all her streets
The voice of singing and the sprightly chord
Are silent. Revelry and dance and show
Suffer a syncope and solemn pause,
While God performs upon the trembling stage
Of his own works, his dreadful part alone.
How does the earth receive him? — With what signs
Of gratulation and delight, her king?
Pours she not all her choicest fruits abroad,
Her sweetest flow'rs, her aromatic gums,
Disclosing paradise where'er he treads?
She quakes at his approach. Her hollow womb
Conceiving thunders, through a thousand deeps
And fiery caverns roars beneath his foot.
The hills move lightly[2] and the mountains smoke,
For he has touch'd them. From th' extremest point
Of elevation down into th' abyss,
His wrath is busy and his frown is felt.
The rocks fall headlong and the vallies rise,
The rivers die into offensive pools,
And charged with putrid verdure, breathe a gross
And mortal nuisance into all the air.
What solid was, by transformation strange,
Grows fluid, and the fixt and rooted earth
Tormented into billows heaves and swells,

[1] In 1783 a succession of earthquakes devastated Calabria and destroyed towns in Sicily, causing the loss of 20,000 lives.
[2] Jeremiah, iv, 24: Psalm cxliv, 5.

Or with vortiginous and hideous whirl
Sucks down its prey insatiable. Immense
The tumult and the overthrow, the pangs
And agonies of human and of brute
Multitudes, fugitive on ev'ry side,
And fugitive in vain. The sylvan scene
Migrates uplifted, and with all its soil
Alighting in far distant fields, finds out
A new possessor, and survives the change.
Ocean has caught the frenzy, and upwrought
To an enormous and o'erbearing height,
Not by a mighty wind, but by that voice[1]
Which winds and waves obey, invades the shore
Resistless. Never such a sudden flood,
Upridg'd so high, and sent on such a charge,
Possess'd an inland scene. Where now the throng
That press'd the beach and hasty to depart,
Look'd to the sea for safety? They are gone,
Gone with the refluent wave into the deep,
A prince with half his people.[2] Ancient tow'rs,
And roofs embattled high, the gloomy scenes
Where beauty oft and letter'd worth consume
Life in the unproductive shades of death,
Fall prone; the pale inhabitants come forth,
And happy in their unforeseen release
From all the rigors of restraint, enjoy
The terrors of the day that sets them free.
Who then that has thee, would not hold thee fast,
Freedom! whom they that lose thee, so regret,
That ev'n a judgment making way for thee,
Seems in their eyes, a mercy, for thy sake.
    Such evil sin hath wrought; and such a flame
Kindled in heaven, that it burns down to earth,
And in the furious inquest that it makes
On God's behalf, lays waste his fairest works.
The very elements, though each be meant

[1] Matthew, viii, 27.
[2] This incident took place at Messina.

The minister of man, to serve his wants,
Conspire against him. With his breath, he draws
A plague into his blood. And cannot use
Life's necessary means, but he must die.
Storms rise t' o'erwhelm him: or if stormy winds
Rise not, the waters of the deep shall rise,
And needing none assistance of the storm,
Shall roll themselves ashore, and reach him there.
The earth shall shake him out of all his holds,
Or make his house his grave. Nor so content,
Shall counterfeit the motions of the flood,
And drown him in her dry and dusty gulphs.
What then— were they the wicked above all,[1]
And we the righteous, whose fast-anchor'd isle
Moved not, while their's was rock'd like a light skiff,
The sport of ev'ry wave? No: none are clear,
And none than we more guilty. But where all
Stand chargeable with guilt, and to the shafts
Of wrath obnoxious, God may chuse his mark.
May punish, if he please, the less, to warn
The more malignant. If he spar'd not them,
Tremble and be amaz'd at thine escape,
Far guiltier England, lest he spare not thee.
   Happy the man who sees a God employed
In all the good and ill that checquer life!
Resolving all events, with their effects
And manifold results, into the will
And arbitration wise of the Supreme.
Did not his eye rule all things, and intend
The least of our concerns (since from the least
The greatest oft originate) could chance
Find place in his dominion, or dispose
One lawless particle to thwart his plan,
Then God might be surpriz'd, and unforeseen
Contingence might alarm him, and disturb
The smooth and equal course of his affairs.
This truth, philosophy, though eagle-ey'd

[1] Cf. Luke, xiii, 2–5.

In nature's tendencies, oft overlooks,
And having found his instrument, forgets
Or disregards, or more presumptuous still
Denies the pow'r that wields it. God proclaims
His hot displeasure against foolish men
That live an atheist life. Involves the heav'n
In tempests, quits his grasp upon the winds
And gives them all their fury. Bids a plague
Kindle a fiery boil upon the skin,
And putrify the breath of blooming health.
He calls for famine, and the meagre fiend
Blows mildew from between his shrivel'd lips,
And taints the golden ear. He springs his mines,
And desolates a nation at a blast.
Forth steps the spruce philosopher, and tells
Of homogeneal and discordant springs
And principles; of causes how they work
By necessary laws their sure effects,
Of action and re-action. He has found
The source of the disease that nature feels,
And bids the world take heart and banish fear.
Thou fool! will thy discovery of the cause
Suspend th' effect or heal it? Has not God
Still wrought by means since first he made the world,
And did he not of old employ his means
To drown it? What is his creation less
Than a capacious reservoir of means
Form'd for his use, and ready at his will?
Go, dress thine eyes with eye-salve, ask of him,
Or ask of whomsoever he has taught,
And learn, though late, the genuine cause of all.
  England, with all thy faults, I love thee still,[1]
My country! and while yet a nook is left
Where English minds and manners may be found,
Shall be constrain'd to love thee. Though thy clime

---

[1] Cf. Charles Churchill, *The Farewell*, 27:
           Be England what she will,
       With all her faults, she is my country still.

Be fickle, and thy year, most part, deform'd
With dripping rains, or wither'd by a frost,
I would not yet exchange thy sullen skies
And fields without a flow'r, for warmer France
With all her vines; nor for Ausonia's groves
Of golden fruitage and her myrtle bow'rs.
To shake thy senate, and from heights sublime
Of patriot eloquence to flash down fire
Upon thy foes, was never meant my task;
But I can feel thy fortunes, and partake
Thy joys and sorrows with as true a heart
As any thund'rer there. And I can feel
Thy follies too, and with a just disdain
Frown at effeminates, whose very looks
Reflect dishonor on the land I love.
How, in the name of soldiership and sense,
Should England prosper, when such things, as smooth
And tender as a girl, all essenc'd o'er
With odors, and as profligate as sweet,
Who sell their laurel for a myrtle wreath,
And love when they should fight; when such as these
Presume to lay their hand upon the ark
Of her magnificent and awful cause?
Time was when it was praise and boast enough
In ev'ry clime, and travel where we might,
That we were born her children. Praise enough
To fill th' ambition of a private man,
That Chatham's language was his mother tongue,
And Wolfe's great name compatriot with his own.
Farewell those honors, and farewell with them
The hope of such hereafter. They have fall'n
Each in his field of glory: one in arms,
And one in council. — Wolfe upon the lap
Of smiling victory that moment won,[1]
And Chatham, heart-sick of his country's shame.[2]
They made us many soldiers. Chatham still

[1] The Battle of the Heights of Abraham, 1759.
[2] See p. 192, note.

424

Consulting England's happiness at home,
Secured it by an unforgiving frown,
If any wrong'd her. Wolfe, where'er he fought,
Put so much of his heart into his act,
That his example had a magnet's force,
And all were swift to follow whom all loved.
Those suns are set. Oh rise some other such!
Or all that we have left, is empty talk
Of old atchievements, and despair of new.
    Now hoist the sail, and let the streamers float
Upon the wanton breezes. Strew the deck
With lavender, and sprinkle liquid sweets,
That no rude savour maritime invade
The nose of nice nobility. Breathe soft
Ye clarionets, and softer still ye flutes,
That winds and waters lull'd by magic sounds
May bear us smoothly to the Gallic shore.
True, we have lost an empire—let it pass.
True, we may thank the perfidy of France,
That pick'd the jewel[1] out of England's crown,
With all the cunning of an envious shrew.
And let that pass—'twas but a trick of state.
A brave man knows no malice, but at once
Forgets in peace, the injuries of war,
And gives his direst foe a friend's embrace.
And shamed as we have been, to th' very beard
Braved and defied, and in our own sea[2] proved
Too weak for those decisive blows that once
Insured us mast'ry there, we yet retain
Some small pre-eminence, we justly boast
At least superior jockeyship, and claim
The honors of the turf as all our own.
Go then, well worthy of the praise ye seek,
And show the shame ye might conceal at home,
In foreign eyes!—be grooms, and win the plate

[1] The reference is to the treaties of peace which ended the War of American Independence. See pp. 680–81.

[2] In 1779 the joint fleets of France and Spain were masters of the English Channel and even threatened a descent upon the British coast.

Where once your nobler fathers won a crown!—
'Tis gen'rous to communicate your skill
To those that need it. Folly is soon learn'd.
And under such preceptors, who can fail?
　　There is a pleasure in poetic pains
Which only poets know. The shifts and turns,
Th' expedients and inventions multiform
To which the mind resorts, in chace of terms
Though apt, yet coy, and difficult to win—
T' arrest the fleeting images that fill
The mirror of the mind, and hold them fast,
And force them sit, 'till he has pencil'd off
A faithful likeness of the forms he views;
Then to dispose his copies with such art
That each may find its most propitious light,
And shine by situation, hardly less,
Than by the labor and the skill it cost,
Are occupations of the poet's mind
So pleasing, and that steal away the thought
With such address, from themes of sad import,
That lost in his own musings, happy man!
He feels th' anxieties of life, denied
Their wonted entertainment, all retire.
Such joys has he that sings. But ah! not such,
Or seldom such, the hearers of his song.
Fastidious, or else listless, or perhaps
Aware of nothing arduous in a task
They never undertook, they little note
His dangers or escapes, and haply find
There least amusement where he found the most.
But is amusement all? studious of song,
And yet ambitious not to sing in vain,
I would not trifle merely, though the world
Be loudest in their praise who do no more.
Yet what can satire, whether grave or gay?
It may correct a foible, may chastise
The freaks of fashion, regulate the dress,
Retrench a sword-blade, or displace a patch;
But where are its sublimer trophies found?

What vice has it subdued? whose heart reclaim'd
By rigour, or whom laugh'd into reform?
Alas! Leviathan[1] is not so tamed
Laugh'd at, he laughs again; and stricken hard,
Turns to the stroke his adamantine scales,
That fear no discipline of human hands,
   The pulpit therefore (and I name it, fill'd
With solemn awe, that bids me well beware
With what intent I touch that holy thing)
The pulpit (when the sat'rist has at last,
Strutting and vap'ring in an empty school,
Spent all his force and made no proselyte)
I say the pulpit (in the sober use
Of its legitimate, peculiar pow'rs)
Must stand acknowledg'd, while the world shall stand,
The most important and effectual guard,
Support and ornament of virtue's cause.
There stands the messenger of truth. There stands
The legate of the skies.[2] His theme divine,
His office sacred, his credentials clear.
By him, the violated law speaks out
Its thunders, and by him, in strains as sweet
As angels use, the gospel whispers peace.
He stablishes the strong, restores the weak,
Reclaims the wand'rer, binds the broken heart,
And arm'd himself in panoply complete
Of heav'nly temper, furnishes with arms,
Bright as his own, and trains by ev'ry rule
Of holy discipline, to glorious war,
The sacramental host of God's elect.
Are all such teachers? would to heav'n all were!
But hark—the Doctor's[3] voice—fast wedg'd between

[1] Job, xli.

[2] 'Ambassadors for Christ': 2 Corinthians, v, 20.

[3] *the doctor's voice*: Dr Trusler, d. 1820, a publicist who gained wealth and renown by potting standard works. 'One of his most successful projects was that alluded to by Cowper at the close of this paragraph—abridging the sermons of eminent divines, and printing the abridgements in a manuscript character for the use of clergymen in the pulpit.'—*Bruce.*

Two empirics he stands, and with swoln cheeks
Inspires the news, his trumpet. Keener far
Than all invective is his bold harangue,
While through that public organ of report
He hails the clergy; and defying shame,
Announces to the world his own and theirs.
He teaches those to read, whom schools dismiss'd,
And colleges untaught; sells accent, tone,
And emphasis in score, and gives to pray'r
Th' *adagio* and *andante* it demands.
He grinds divinity of other days
Down into modern use; transforms old print
To zig-zag manuscript, and cheats the eyes
Of gall'ry critics by a thousand arts.
Are there who purchase of the Doctor's ware?
Oh name it not in Gath![1]— it cannot be,
That grave and learned Clerks should need such aid.
He doubtless is in sport, and does but droll,
Assuming thus a rank unknown before,
Grand caterer and dry-nurse of the church.
   I venerate the man, whose heart is warm,
Whose hands are pure, whose doctrine and whose life
Coincident, exhibit lucid proof
That he is honest in the sacred cause.
To such I render more than mere respect,
Whose actions say that they respect themselves.
But loose in morals, and in manners vain,
In conversation frivolous, in dress
Extreme, at once rapacious and profuse,
Frequent in park, with lady at his side,
Ambling and prattling scandal as he goes,
But rare at home, and never at his books,
Or with his pen, save when he scrawls a card;
Constant at routs, familiar with a round
Of ladyships, a stranger to the poor;
Ambitious of preferment for its gold,
And well-prepar'd by ignorance and sloth,

[1] 2 Samuel, i, 20.

By infidelity and love o' th' world,
To make God's work a sinecure; a slave
To his own pleasures and his patron's pride.
From such apostles, Oh ye mitred heads
Preserve the church! and lay not careless hands
On sculls that cannot teach, and will not learn.
    Would I describe a preacher, such as Paul
Were he on earth, would hear, approve, and own,
Paul should himself direct me. I would trace
His master-strokes, and draw from his design.
I would express him simple, grave, sincere;
In doctrine uncorrupt; in language plain;
And plain in manner. Decent, solemn, chaste,
And natural in gesture. Much impress'd
Himself, as conscious of his awful charge,
And anxious mainly that the flock he feeds
May feel it too. Affectionate in look,
And tender in address, as well becomes
A messenger of grace to guilty men.
Behold the picture!—Is it like?—Like whom?
The things that mount the rostrum with a skip,
And then skip down again; pronounce a text,
Cry, hem; and reading, what they never wrote,
Just fifteen minutes, huddle up their work,
And with a well bred whisper close the scene.
    In man or woman, but far most in man,
And most of all in man that ministers
And serves the altar, in my soul I loath
All affectation. 'Tis my perfect scorn;
Object of my implacable disgust.
What!—will a man play tricks, will he indulge
A silly fond conceit of his fair form
And just proportion, fashionable mien,
And pretty face in presence of his God?
Or will he seek to dazzle me with tropes,
As with the di'mond on his lily hand,
And play his brilliant parts before my eyes
When I am hungry for the bread of life?
He mocks his Maker, prostitutes and shames

429

His noble office, and instead of truth,
Displaying his own beauty, starves his flock.
Therefore, avaunt! all attitude and stare,
And start theatric, practised at the glass.
I seek divine simplicity in him
Who handles things divine; and all beside,
Though learn'd with labor, and much admir'd
By curious eyes and judgments ill-inform'd,
To me is odious as the nasal twang
At conventicle heard, where worthy men,
Misled by custom, strain celestial themes
Through the prest nostril, spectacle-bestrid.
Some, decent in demeanor while they preach,
That task perform'd, relapse into themselves,
And having spoken wisely, at the close
Grow wanton, and give proof to ev'ry eye—
Whoe'er was edified, themselves were not.
Forth comes the pocket mirror. First we stroke
An eye-brow; next, compose a straggling lock;
Then with an air, most gracefully perform'd,
Fall back into our seat; extend an arm
And lay it at its ease with gentle care,
With handkerchief in hand, depending low.
The better hand more busy, gives the nose
Its bergamot, or aids th' indebted eye
With op'ra glass to watch the moving scene,
And recognize the slow-retiring fair.
Now this is fulsome; and offends me more
Than in a churchman slovenly neglect
And rustic coarseness would. An heav'nly mind
May be indiff'rent to her house of clay,[1]
And slight the hovel as beneath her care;
But how a body so fantastic, trim,
And quaint, in its deportment and attire,
Can lodge an heav'nly mind—demands a doubt.
  He that negotiates between God and man,
As God's ambassador, the grand concerns

---

[1] Cf. Job, iv, 19.

Of judgment and of mercy, should beware
Of lightness in his speech. 'Tis pitiful
To court a grin, when you should woo a soul;
To break a jest, when pity would inspire
Pathetic exhortation; and t' address
The skittish fancy with facetious tales,
When sent with God's commission to the heart.
So did not Paul. Direct me to a quip
Or merry turn in all he ever wrote,
And I consent you take it for your text,
Your only one, till sides and benches fail.
No: he was serious in a serious cause,
And understood too well the weighty terms
That he had ta'en in charge. He would not stoop
To conquer those by jocular exploits,
Whom truth and soberness assail'd in vain.[1]

Oh, popular applause! what heart of man
Is proof against thy sweet seducing charms?
The wisest and the best feel urgent need
Of all their caution in thy gentlest gales;
But swell'd into a gust—who then, alas!
With all his canvass set, and inexpert,
And therefore heedless, can withstand thy power?
Praise from the rival'd lips of toothless, bald
Decrepitude; and in the looks of lean
And craving poverty; and in the bow
Respectful of the smutch'd artificer
Is oft too welcome, and may much disturb
The bias of the purpose. How much more
Pour'd forth by beauty splendid and polite,
In language soft as adoration breathes?
Ah spare your idol! think him human still.
Charms he may have, but he has frailties too.
Doat not too much, nor spoil what ye admire.

All truth is from the sempiternal source
Of light divine. But Egypt, Greece, and Rome
Drew from the stream below. More favor'd we

---

[1] Acts, xxvi, 25.

Drink, when we choose it, at the fountain head.
To them it flow'd much mingled and defiled
With hurtful error, prejudice, and dreams
Illusive of philosophy, so call'd,
But falsely. Sages after sages strove
In vain to filter off a chrystal draught
Pure from the lees, which often more enhanc'd
The thirst than slak'd it, and not seldom bred
Intoxication and delirium wild.
In vain they push'd enquiry to the birth
And spring-time of the world, ask'd, whence is man?
Why form'd at all? And wherefore as he is?
Where must he find his Maker? With what rites
Adore him? Will he hear, accept, and bless?
Or does he sit regardless of his works?
Has man within him an immortal seed?
Or does the tomb take all? If he survive
His ashes, where? and in what weal or woe?
Knots worthy of solution, which alone
A Deity could solve. Their answers vague,
And all at random, fabulous and dark,
Left them as dark themselves. Their rules of life
Defective and unsanction'd, proved too weak
To bind the roving appetite, and lead
Blind nature to a God not yet reveal'd.
'Tis Revelation satisfies all doubts,
Explains all mysteries, except her own,
And so illuminates the path of life,
That fools discover it, and stray no more.
Now tell me, dignified and sapient sir,
My man of morals, nurtur'd in the shades
Of Academus, is this false or true?
Is Christ the abler teacher, or the schools?
If Christ, then why resort to ev'ry turn
To Athens or to Rome, for wisdom short
Of man's occasions, when in him reside
Grace, knowledge, comfort, an unfathom'd store?
How oft, when Paul has serv'd us with a text,
Has Epictetus, Plato, Tully, preach'd!

Men that, if now alive, would sit content
And humble learners of a Saviour's worth,
Preach it who might. Such was their love of truth,
Their thirst of knowledge, and their candour too.
    And thus it is. The pastor, either vain
By nature, or by flatt'ry made so, taught
To gaze at his own splendor, and t' exalt
Absurdly, not his office, but himself;
Or unenlighten'd, and too proud to learn,
Or vicious, and not therefore apt to teach,
Perverting often by the stress of lewd
And loose example, whom he should instruct,
Exposes and holds up to broad disgrace
The noblest function, and discredits much
The brightest truths that man has ever seen.
For ghostly counsel, if it either fall
Below the exigence, or be not back'd
With show of love, at least with hopeful proof
Of some sincerity on th' giver's part;
Or be dishonor'd in th' exterior form
And mode of its conveyance, by such tricks
As move derision, or by foppish airs
And historic mumm'ry, that let down
The pulpit to the level of the stage,
Drops from the lips a disregarded thing.
The weak perhaps are moved, but are not taught,
While prejudice in men of stronger minds
Takes deeper root, confirm'd by what they see.
A relaxation of religion's hold
Upon the roving and untutor'd heart
Soon follows, and, the curb of conscience snapt,
The laity run wild.—But do they now?
Note their extravagance, and be convinced.
    As nations ignorant of God, contrive
A wooden one, so we, no longer taught
By monitors that mother church supplies,
Now make our own. Posterity will ask
(If e'er posterity see verse of mine)
Some fifty or an hundred lustrums hence,

433

What was a monitor in George's days?
My very gentle reader, yet unborn,
Of whom I needs must augur better things,
Since heav'n would sure grow weary of a world
Productive only of a race like us,
A monitor is wood. Plank shaven thin.
We wear it at our backs. There closely braced
And neatly fitted, it compresses hard
The prominent and most unsightly bones,
And binds the shoulders flat. We prove its use
Sov'reign and most effectual to secure
A form not now gymnastic as of yore,
From rickets and distortion, else our lot.
But thus admonish'd we can walk erect,
One proof at least of manhood; while the friend
Sticks close, a Mentor worthy of his charge.
Our habits costlier than Lucullus wore,
And by caprice as multiplied as his,
Just please us while the fashion is at full,
But change with ev'ry moon. The sycophant
That waits to dress us, arbitrates their date,
Surveys his fair reversion with keen eye;
Finds one ill made, another obsolete,
This fits not nicely, that is ill conceived,
And making prize of all that he condemns,
With our expenditure defrays his own.
Variety's the very spice of life
That gives it all its flavor. We have run
Through ev'ry change that fancy at the loom
Exhausted, has had genius to supply,
And studious of mutation still, discard
A real elegance a little used,
For monstrous novelty and strange disguise.
We sacrifice to dress, till houshold joys
And comforts cease. Dress drains our cellar dry,
And keeps our larder lean. Puts out our fires,
And introduces hunger, frost, and woe,
Where peace and hospitality might reign.
What man that lives and that knows how to live,

Would fail t' exhibit at the public shows
A form as splendid as the proudest there,
Though appetite raise outcries at the cost?
A man o' th' town dines late, but soon enough
With reasonable forecast and dispatch,
T' insure a side-box station at half price.[1]
You think, perhaps, so delicate his dress,
His daily fare as delicate. Alas!
He picks clean teeth, and busy as he seems
With an old tavern quill, is hungry yet.
The rout is folly's circle, which she draws
With magic wand. So potent is the spell,
That none decoy'd into that fatal ring,
Unless by heav'n's peculiar grace, escape.
There we grow early grey, and never wise,
There form connexions, but acquire no friend.
Solicit pleasure hopeless of success;
Waste youth in occupations only fit
For second childhood, and devote old age
To sports which only childhood could excuse.
There they are happiest who dissemble best
Their weariness; and they the most polite
Who squander time and treasure with a smile
Though at their own destruction. She that asks
Her dear five hundred friends, contemns them all,
And hates their coming. They, what can they less?
Make just reprisals, and with cringe and shrug,
And bow obsequious, hide their hate of her.
All catch the frenzy, downward from her Grace,
Whose flambeaux flash against the morning skies,
And gild our chamber cielings as they pass,
To her who frugal only that her thrift
May feed excesses she can ill afford,
Is hackney'd home unlacquey'd. Who in haste
Alighting, turns the key in her own door,
And at the watchman's lantern borrowing light,

---

[1] At the theatre, men sat in the side-boxes and women in the front box,
corresponding to the dress circle.

Finds a cold bed her only comfort left.
Wives beggar husbands, husbands starve their wives,
On fortune's velvet altar off'ring up
Their last poor pittance. Fortune, most severe
Of goddesses yet known, and costlier far
Than all that held their routs in heathen heav'n[1]—
So fare we in this prison-house the world.
And 'tis a fearful spectacle to see
So many maniacs dancing in their chains.
They gaze upon the links that hold them fast
With eyes of anguish, execrate their lot,
Then shake them in despair, and dance again.
  Now basket up the family of plagues
That waste our vitals. Peculation, sale
Of honor, perjury, corruption, frauds
By forgery, by subterfuge of law,
By tricks and lies as num'rous and as keen
As the necessities their authors feel;
Then cast them closely bundled, ev'ry brat
At the right door. Profusion is its sire.
Profusion unrestrain'd, with all that's base
In character, has litter'd all the land,
And bred within the mum'ry of no few,
A priesthood such as Baal's was of old,
A people such as never was 'till now.
It is a hungry vice:—it eats up all
That gives society its beauty, strength,
Convenience, and security, and use.
Makes men mere vermin, worthy to be trapp'd
And gibbetted as fast as catchpole claws
Can seize the slipp'ry prey. Unties the knot
Of union, and converts the sacred band
That holds mankind together, to a scourge.
Profusion deluging a state with lusts
Of grossest nature and of worst effects,
Prepares it for its ruin. Hardens, blinds,
And warps the consciences of public men,

---

[1] *heathen heav'n*: *Juno's heav'n* first *1787*.

Till they can laugh at virtue; mock the fools
That trust them; and in th' end, disclose a face
That would have shock'd credulity herself
Unmask'd, vouchsafing this their sole excuse,
Since all alike are selfish—why not they?
This does Profusion, and th' accursed cause
Of such deep mischief, has itself a cause.

In colleges and halls, in ancient days,
When learning, virtue, piety and truth,
Were precious, and inculculated with care,
There dwelt a sage call'd Discipline. His head
Not yet by time completely silver'd o'er,
Bespoke him past the bounds of freakish youth,
But strong for service still, and unimpair'd.
His eye was meek and gentle, and a smile
Play'd on his lips, and in his speech was heard
Paternal sweetness, dignity, and love.
The occupation dearest to his heart
Was to encourage goodness. He would stroke
The head of modest and ingenuous worth,
That blush'd at its own praise, and press the youth
Close to his side that pleas'd him. Learning grew
Beneath his care, a thriving, vig'rous plant;
The mind was well inform'd, the passions held
Subordinate, and diligence was choice.
If e'er it chanc'd, as sometimes chance it must,
That one among so many overleap'd
The limits of controul, his gentle eye
Grew stern, and darted a severe rebuke;
His frown was full of terror, and his voice
Shook the delinquent with such fits of awe
As left him not, till penitence had won
Lost favor back again, and clos'd the breach.
But Discipline, a faithful servant long,
Declined at length into the vale of years;
A palsy struck his arm, his sparkling eye
Was quench'd in rheums of age, his voice unstrung
Grew tremulous, and mov'd derision more
Than rev'rence, in perverse rebellious youth.

So colleges and halls neglected much
Their good old friend, and Discipline at length,
O'erlook'd and unemploy'd, fell sick and died.
Then study languish'd, emulation slept,
And virtue fled. The schools became a scene
Of solemn farce, where ignorance in stilts,
His cap well lined with logic not his own,
With parrot tongue perform'd the scholar's part,
Proceeding soon a graduated dunce.
Then compromise had place, and scrutiny
Became stone-blind, precedence went in truck,
And he was competent whose purse was so.
A dissolution of all bonds ensued,
The curbs invented for the muleish mouth
Of head-strong youth were broken; bars and bolts
Grew rusty by disuse, and massy gates
Forgot their office, op'ning with a touch;
'Till gowns at length are found mere masquerade;
The tassell'd cap and the spruce band a jest,
A mock'ry of the world. What need of these
For gamesters, jockies, brothellers impure,
Spendthrifts and booted sportsmen, oft'ner seen
With belted waist and pointers at their heels
Than in the bounds of duty? What was learn'd,
If aught was learn'd in childhood, is forgot,
And such expence as pinches parents blue,
And mortifies the lib'ral hand of love,
Is squander'd in pursuit of idle sports
And vicious pleasures. Buys the boy a name,
That sits a stigma on his father's house,
And cleaves through life inseparably close
To him that wears it. What can after-games
Of riper joys, and commerce with the world,
The lewd vain world that must receive him soon,
Add to such erudition thus acquir'd,
Where science and where virtue are profess'd?
They may confirm his habits, rivet fast
His folly, but to spoil him is a task
That bids defiance to th' united pow'rs

Of fashion, dissipation, taverns, stews.
Now, blame we most the nurslings or the nurse?
The children crook'd and twisted and deform'd,
Through want of care, or her whose winking eye
And slumb'ring oscitancy marrs the brood?
The nurse no doubt. Regardless of her charge
She needs herself correction. Needs to learn
That it is dang'rous sporting with the world,
With things so sacred as a nation's trust,
The nurture of her youth, her dearest pledge.
　All are not such. I had a brother once.—
Peace to the mem'ry of a man of worth,
A man of letters, and of manners too.
Of manners sweet as virtue always wears,
When gay good-nature dresses her in smiles.
He graced a college,[1] in which order yet
Was sacred, and was honor'd, lov'd and wept,
By more than one, themselves conspicuous there.
Some minds are temper'd happily, and mixt
With such ingredients of good sense and taste
Of what is excellent in man, they thirst
With such a zeal to be what they approve,
That no restraints can circumscribe them more,
Than they themselves by choice, for wisdom's sake.
Nor can example hurt them. What they see
Of vice in others but enhancing more
The charms of virtue in their just esteem.
If such escape contagion, and emerge
Pure, from so foul a pool, to shine abroad,
And give the world their talents and themselves,
Small thanks to those whose negligence or sloth
Exposed their inexperience to the snare,
And left them to an undirected choice.
　See then the quiver broken and decay'd,
In which are kept our arrows.[2] Rusting there

---

[1] Ben'et Coll. Cambridge [C]: i.e. Corpus Christi. The Rev. John C.,
1737–70, became a Fellow in 1763 and Bursar in 1767.
[2] Psalm cxxvii, 4, 5.

In wild disorder, and unfit for use,
What wonder, if discharged into the world,
They shame their shooters with a random flight,
Their points obtuse, and feathers drunk with wine.
Well may the church wage unsuccessful war,
With such artill'ry arm'd. Vice parries wide
Th' undreaded volley with a sword of straw,
And stands an impudent and fearless mark.

Have we not track'd the felon home, and found
His birth-place and his dam? the country mourns,
Mourns, because ev'ry plague that can infest
Society, and that saps and worms the base
Of th' edifice that policy has rais'd,
Swarms in all quarters; meets the eye, the ear,
And suffocates the breath at ev'ry turn.
Profusion breeds them. And the cause itself
Of that calamitous mischief has been found.
Found too where most offensive, in the skirts
Of the rob'd pædagogue. Else, let the arraign'd
Stand up unconscious, and refute the charge.
So when the Jewish Leader[1] stretched his arm
And waved his rod divine, a race obscene
Spawn'd in the muddy beds of Nile, came forth,
Polluting Ægypt. Gardens, fields, and plains
Were cover'd with the pest. The streets were fill'd;
The croaking nuisance lurk'd in ev'ry nook,
Nor palaces nor even chambers 'scap'd,
And the land stank, so num'rous was the fry.

[1] Aaron: Exodus, viii, 1-14.

BOOK III

THE GARDEN

ARGUMENT OF THE THIRD BOOK. —*Self-recollection and reproof— Address to domestic happiness —Some account of myself— The vanity of many of their pursuits who are reputed wise— Justification of my censures— Divine illumination necessary to the most expert philosopher— The question, What is truth? answered by other questions— Domestic happiness addressed again— Few lovers of the country— My tame hare— Occupations of a retired gentleman in his garden— Pruning— Framing — Greenhouse— Sowing of flower-seeds— The country preferable to the town even in winter— Reasons why it is deserted at that season— Ruinous effects of gaming and of expensive improvement— Book concludes with an apostrophé to the metropolis.*

As one who long in thickets and in brakes
Entangled, winds now this way and now that
His devious course uncertain, seeking home;
Or having long in miry ways been foil'd
And sore discomfited, from slough to slough
Plunging, and half despairing of escape,
If chance at length he find a green-sward smooth
And faithful to the foot, his spirits rise,
He chirrups brisk his ear-erecting steed,
And winds his way with pleasure and with ease;
So I, designing other themes, and call'd
T' adorn the Sofa with eulogium due,
To tell its slumbers and to paint its dreams,
Have rambled wide. In country, city, seat
Of academic fame (howe'er deserved)

Long held, and scarcely disengag'd at last.
But now with pleasant pace, a cleanlier road
I mean to tread. I feel myself at large,
Courageous, and refresh'd for future toil,
If toil await me, or if dangers new.

    Since Pulpits fail, and sounding-boards reflect
Most part an empty ineffectual sound,
What chance that I, to fame so little known,
Nor conversant with men or manners much,
Should speak to purpose, or with better hope
Crack the satyric thong? 'twere wiser far
For me, enamour'd of sequester'd scenes,
And charm'd with rural beauty, to repose
Where chance may throw me, beneath elm or vine,
My languid limbs when summer sears the plains,
Or when rough winter rages, on the soft
And shelter'd Sofa, while the nitrous air[1]
Feeds a blue flame and makes a chearful hearth;
There undisturb'd by folly, and appriz'd
How great the danger of disturbing her,
To muse in silence, or at least confine
Remarks that gall so many, to the few
My partners in retreat. Disgust conceal'd
Is oft-times proof of wisdom, when the fault
Is obstinate, and cure beyond our reach.

    Domestic happiness, thou only bliss
Of Paradise that has survived the fall!
Though few now taste thee unimpair'd and pure,
Or tasting, long enjoy thee, too infirm
Or too incautious, to preserve thy sweets
Unmixt with drops of bitter, which neglect
Or temper sheds into thy chrystal cup.
Thou art the nurse of virtue. In thine arms
She smiles, appearing, as in truth she is,
Heav'n-born, and destin'd to the skies again.
Thou art not known where pleasure is ador'd,

---

    [1] *nitrous air*: It was believed that the air was charged with particles of nitre, the ingredient which assists the combustion of gunpowder.

That reeling goddess with the zoneless waist[1]
And wand'ring eyes, still leaning on the arm
Of novelty, her fickle frail support;
For thou art meek and constant, hating change,
And finding in the calm of truth-tied love[2]
Joys that her stormy raptures never yield.
Forsaking thee, what shipwreck have we made
Of honor, dignity, and fair renown;
'Till prostitution elbows us aside
In all our crowded streets, and senates seem
Convened for purposes of empire less,
Than to release th' adultress from her bond.
Th' adultress! what a theme for angry verse,
What provocation to th' indignant heart
That feels for injur'd love! but I disdain
The nauseous task to paint her as she is,
Cruel, abandon'd, glorying in her shame.
No—Let her pass, and chariotted along
In guilty splendor, shake the public ways;
The frequency of crimes has wash'd them white.
And verse of mine shall never brand the wretch,
Whom matrons now of character unsmirch'd,
And chaste themselves, are not asham'd to own.
Virtue and vice had bound'ries in old time
Not to be pass'd. And she that had renounced
Her sex's honor, was renounc'd herself
By all that priz'd it; not for prud'ry's sake,
But dignity's, resentful of the wrong.
'Twas hard perhaps on here and there a waif,
Desirous to return and not received,
But was an wholesome rigor in the main,
And taught th' unblemish'd to preserve with care
That purity, whose loss was loss of all.
Men too were nice in honor in those days,
And judg'd offenders well. And he that sharp'd,
And pocketted a prize by fraud obtain'd

[2] *zoneless*: ungirt.
[1] *truth-tied*: *truth-tried* first *1788*.

Was mark'd and shunn'd as odious. He that sold
His country, or was slack when she requir'd
His ev'ry nerve in action and at stretch,
Paid with the blood that he had basely spared
The price of his default. But now, yes, now,
We are become so candid and so fair,
So lib'ral in construction, and so rich
In christian charity, a good-natur'd age!
That they are safe, sinners of either sex,
Transgress what laws they may. Well dress'd, well bred,
Well equipag'd, is ticket good enough
To pass us readily through ev'ry door.
Hypocrisy, detest her as we may,
(And no man's hatred ever wrong'd her yet)
May claim this merit still, that she admits
The worth of what she mimics with such care,
And thus gives virtue indirect applause;
But she has burnt her mask not needed here,
Where vice has such allowance, that her shifts
And specious semblances have lost their use.
    I was a stricken deer[1] that left the herd
Long since; with many an arrow deep infixt
My panting side was charged when I withdrew
To seek a tranquil death in distant shades.
There was I found by one who had himself
Been hurt by th' archers.[2] In his side he bore
And in his hands and feet the cruel scars.
With gentle force soliciting the darts
He drew them forth, and heal'd and bade me live.
Since then, with few associates, in remote
And silent woods I wander, far from those
My former partners of the peopled scene,
With few associates, and not wishing more.
Here much I ruminate, as much I may,
With other views of men and manners now
Than once, and others of a life to come.
I see that all are wand'rers, gone astray

---

[1] *Hamlet*, III, ii, 271.   [2] Genesis, xlix, 23.

Each in his own delusions; they are lost
In chace of fancied happiness, still woo'd
And never won. Dream after dream ensues,
And still they dream that they shall still succeed,
And still are disappointed; rings the world
With the vain stir. I sum up half mankind,
And add two thirds of the remainder half,
And find the total of their hopes and fears
Dreams, empty dreams. The million flit as gay
As if created only like the fly,
That spreads his motley wings in th' eye of noon,
To sport their season, and be seen no more.
The rest are sober dreamers, grave and wise,
And pregnant with discov'ries new and rare.
Some write a narrative of wars and feats
Of heroes little known, and call the rant
An history. Describe the man, of whom
His own coevals took but little note,
And paint his person, character and views,
As they had known him from his mother's womb.
They disentangle from the puzzled skein
In which obscurity has wrapp'd them up,
The threads of politic and shrewd design,
That ran through all his purposes, and charge
His mind with meanings that he never had,
Or having, kept conceal'd. Some drill and bore
The solid earth, and from the strata there
Extract a register, by which we learn
That he who made it and reveal'd its date[1]
To Moses, was mistaken in its age.
Some more acute and more industrious still
Contrive creation. Travel nature up
To the sharp peak of her sublimest height,
And tell us whence the stars. Why some are fixt,
And planetary some. What gave them first
Rotation, from what fountain flow'd their light.

[1] The chronology inserted in the Authorized Version was taken from Archbp. Ussher's *Annals of the World*, 1658.

Great contest follows, and much learned dust
Involves the combatants, each claiming truth,
And truth disclaiming both. And thus they spend
The little wick of life's poor shallow lamp,
In playing tricks with nature, giving laws
To distant worlds and trifling in their own.
Is't not a pity now that tickling rheums
Should ever teaze the lungs and blear the sight
Of oracles like these? Great pity too,
That having wielded th' elements, and built
A thousand systems, each in his own way,
They should go out in fume and be forgot?
Ah! what is life thus spent? and what are they
But frantic who thus spend it? all for smoke—
Eternity for bubbles, proves at last
A senseless bargain. When I see such games
Play'd by the creatures of a pow'r who swears
That he will judge the earth, and call the fool
To a sharp reck'ning that has liv'd in vain,
And when I weigh this seeming wisdom well,
And prove it in th' infallible result
So hollow and so false—I feel my heart
Dissolve in pity, and account the learn'd,
If this be learning, most of all deceived.
Great crimes alarm the conscience, but she sleeps
While thoughtful man is plausibly amused.
Defend me therefore common sense, say I,
From reveries so airy, from the toil
Of dropping buckets into empty wells,
And growing old in drawing nothing up!
    'Twere well, says one sage erudite, profound,
Terribly arch'd and aquiline his nose,
And overbuilt with most impending brows,
'Twere well could you permit the world to live
As the world pleases. What's the world to you?
Much. I was born of woman, and drew milk
As sweet as charity from human breasts.
I think, articulate, I laugh and weep
And exercise all functions of a man.

How then should I and any man that lives
Be strangers to each other?[1] pierce my vein,
Take of the crimson stream meandring there,
And catechise it well. Apply your glass,
Search it, and prove now if it be not blood
Congenial with thine own. And if it be,
What edge of subtlety canst thou suppose
Keen enough, wise and skilful as thou art,
To cut the link of brotherhood, by which
One common Maker bound me to the kind.
True; I am no proficient, I confess,
In arts like yours. I cannot call the swift
And perilous lightnings from the angry clouds,
And bid them hide themselves in th' earth beneath,
I cannot analyse the air, nor catch
The parallax of yonder luminous point
That seems half quench'd in the immense abyss;
Such pow'rs I boast not—neither can I rest
A silent witness of the headlong rage
Or heedless folly by which thousands die,
Bone of my bone, and kindred souls to mine.
  God never meant that man should scale the heav'ns
By strides of human wisdom. In his works,
Though wondrous, he commands us in his word
To seek him rather, where his mercy shines.
The mind indeed enlighten'd from above,
Views him in all. Ascribes to the grand cause
The grand effect. Acknowledges with joy
His manner, and with rapture tastes his style.
But never yet did philosophic tube[2]
That brings the planets home into the eye
Of observation, and discovers, else
Not visible, his family of worlds,
Discover him that rules them; such a veil
Hangs over mortal eyes, blind from the birth

---

[1] Cf. Terence, *Heauton Timoreumenos*, I, i, 25: Homo sum: humani nil a me alienum puto.

[2] *philosophic tube*: telescope.

And dark in things divine. Full often too,
Our wayward intellect, the more we learn
Of nature, overlooks her author more,
From instrumental causes proud to draw
Conclusions retrograde and mad mistake.
But if his word once teach us, shoot a ray
Through all the heart's dark chambers, and reveal
Truths undiscern'd but by that holy light,
Then all is plain. Philosophy baptized
In the pure fountain of eternal love
Has eyes indeed; and viewing all she sees
As meant to indicate a God to man,
Gives *him* his praise, and forfeits not her own.
Learning has borne such fruit in other days
On all her branches. Piety has found
Friends in the friends of science, and true pray'r
Has flow'd from lips wet with Castalian[1] dews.
Such was thy wisdom, Newton, childlike sage!
Sagacious reader of the works of God,
And in his word sagacious. Such too thine,
Milton, whose genius had angelic wings,
And fed on manna. And such thine, in whom
Our British Themis[2] gloried with just cause,
Immortal Hale![3] for deep discernment prais'd,
And sound integrity, not more than famed
For sanctity of manners undefiled.

All flesh is grass,[4] and all its glory fades
Like the fair flow'r dishevell'd in the wind;
Riches have wings,[5] and grandeur is a dream;
The man we celebrate must find a tomb,
And we that worship him, ignoble graves.
Nothing is proof against the gen'ral curse
Of vanity, that seizes all below.
The only amaranthine flow'r on earth

[1] *Castalia*: a spring, sacred to the Muses, at the foot of Parnassus.
[2] *Themis*: Greek goddess of justice; hence, law and justice personified.
[3] Sir Matthew Hale, jurist.
[4] Isaiah, xl, 6.
[5] Proverbs, xxiii, 5.

448

Is virtue, th' only lasting treasure, truth.
But what is truth? 'twas Pilate's question[1] put
To truth itself, that deign'd him no reply.
And wherefore? will not God impart his light
To them that ask it?—Freely—'tis his joy,
His glory, and his nature to impart.
But to the proud, uncandid, insincere
Or negligent enquirer, not a spark.
What's that which brings contempt upon a book,
And him that writes it, though the stile be neat,
The method clear, and argument exact?
That makes a minister in holy things
The joy of many and the dread of more,
His name a theme for praise and for reproach?—
That while it gives us worth in God's account,
Depreciates and undoes us in our own?
What pearl is it that rich men cannot buy,
That learning is too proud to gather up,
But which the poor, and the despised of all
Seek and obtain, and often find unsought?
Tell me, and I will tell thee, what is truth.

Oh friendly to the best pursuits of man,
Friendly to thought, to virtue, and to peace,
Domestic life in rural leisure pass'd!
Few know thy value, and few taste thy sweets,
Though many boast thy favours, and affect
To understand and chuse thee for their own.
But foolish man foregoes his proper bliss,
Ev'n as his first progenitor, and quits,
Though placed in paradise (for earth has still
Some traces of her youthful beauty left)
Substantial happiness for transient joy.
Scenes form'd for contemplation, and to nurse
The growing seeds of wisdom; that suggest,
By ev'ry pleasing image they present,
Reflections such as meliorate the heart,
Compose the passions, and exalt the mind;

---

[1] John, xviii, 38

Scenes such as these, 'tis his supreme delight
To fill with riot and defile with blood.
Should some contagion kind to the poor brutes
We persecute, annihilate the tribes
That drew the sportsman over hill and dale
Fearless, and rapt away from all his cares;
Should never game-fowl hatch her eggs again,
Nor baited hook deceive the fish's eye;
Could pageantry and dance and feast and song
Be quell'd in all our summer-month retreats;
How many self-deluded nymphs and swains
Who dream they have a taste for fields and groves,
Would find them hideous nurs'ries of the spleen,
And crowd the roads, impatient for the town!
They love the country, and none else, who seek
For their own sake its silence and its shade.
Delights which who would leave, that has a heart
Susceptible of pity, or a mind
Cultured and capable of sober thought,
For all the savage din of the swift pack,
And clamours of the field? Detested sport,
That owes its pleasures to another's pain,
That feeds upon the sobs and dying shrieks
Of harmless nature, dumb, but yet endu'd
With eloquence that agonies inspire
Of silent tears and heart-distending sighs!
Vain tears alas! and sighs that never find
A corresponding tone in jovial souls.
Well—one at least is safe. One shelter'd hare[1]
Has never heard the sanguinary yell
Of cruel man, exulting in her woes.
Innocent partner of my peaceful home,
Whom ten long years experience of my care
Has made at last familiar, she has lost
Much of her vigilant instinctive dread,
Not needful here, beneath a roof like mine.
Yes—thou may'st eat thy bread, and lick the hand

---

[1] Puss: see *The History of My Three Hares*, p. 385.

That feeds thee; thou may'st frolic on the floor
At evening, and at night retire secure
To thy straw-couch, and slumber unalarm'd.
For I have gain'd thy confidence, have pledg'd
All that is human in me, to protect
Thine unsuspecting gratitude and love.
If I survive thee I will dig thy grave,
And when I place thee in it, sighing say,
I knew at least one hare that had a friend.[1]
  How various his employments, whom the world
Calls idle, and who justly in return
Esteems that busy world an idler too!
Friends, books, a garden, and perhaps his pen,
Delightful industry enjoy'd at home.
And nature in her cultivated trim
Dressed to his taste, inviting him abroad—
Can he want occupation who has these?
Will he be idle who has much t' enjoy?
Me therefore, studious of laborious ease,
Not slothful; happy to deceive the time
Not waste it; and aware that human life
Is but a loan to be repaid with use,[2]
When he shall call his debtors to account,
From whom are all our blessings, bus'ness finds
Ev'n here. While sedulous I seek t' improve,
At least neglect not, or leave unemploy'd,
The mind he gave me; driving it, though slack
Too oft, and much impeded in its work
By causes not to be divulg'd in vain,
To its just point, the service of mankind.
He that attends to his interior self,
That has a heart and keeps it; has a mind
That hungers and supplies it; and who seeks
A social, not a dissipated life,
Has business. Feels himself engag'd t' atchieve
No unimportant, though a silent task.

[1] An allusion to *The Hare and Many Friends*, one of John Gay's *Fables*, 1727.
  [2] *use*: interest.

A life all turbulence and noise, may seem
To him that leads it, wise and to be prais'd;
But wisdom is a pearl with most success
Sought in still water, and beneath clear skies.
He that is ever occupied in storms,
Or dives not for it, or brings up instead,
Vainly industrious, a disgraceful prize.

The morning finds the self-sequester'd man
Fresh for his task, intend what task he may.
Whether inclement seasons recommend
His warm but simple home, where he enjoys
With her who shares his pleasures and his heart,
Sweet converse, sipping calm the fragrant lymph
Which neatly she prepares; then to his book
Well chosen, and not sullenly perused
In selfish silence, but imparted oft
As ought occurs that she may smile to hear,
Or turn to nourishment digested well.
Or if the garden with its many cares,
All well repay'd, demand him, he attends
The welcome call, conscious how much the hand
Of lubbard[1] labor needs his watchful eye,
Oft loit'ring lazily if not o'erseen,
Or misapplying his unskilful strength.
Nor does he govern only or direct,
But much performs himself. No works indeed
That ask robust tough sinews bred to toil,
Servile employ—but such as may amuse,
Not tire, demanding rather skill than force.
Proud of his well-spread walls, he views his trees
That meet (no barren interval between)
With pleasure more than ev'n their fruits afford,
Which, save himself who trains them, none can feel:
These therefore are his own peculiar charge,
No meaner hand may discipline the shoots,
None but his steel approach them. What is weak,
Distemper'd, or has lost prolific pow'rs,

[1] *lubbard*: sluggish.

452

Impair'd by age, his unrelenting hand
Dooms to the knife! Nor does he spare the soft
And succulent that feeds its giant growth
But barren, at th' expence of neighb'ring twigs
Less ostentatious, and yet studded thick
With hopeful gems. The rest, no portion left
That may disgrace his art, or disappoint
Large expectation, he disposes neat
At measur'd distances, that air and sun
Admitted freely may afford their aid,
And ventilate and warm the swelling buds.
Hence summer has her riches, autumn hence,
And hence ev'n winter fills his wither'd hand
With blushing fruits, and plenty not his own[1]
Fair recompense of labour well bestow'd
And wise precaution, which a clime so rude
Makes needful still, whose spring is but the child
Of churlish winter, in her froward moods
Discov'ring much the temper of her sire.
For oft, as if in her the stream of mild
Maternal nature had revers'd its course,
She brings her infants forth with many smiles,
But once deliver'd, kills them with a frown.
He therefore, timely warn'd, himself supplies
Her want of care, screening and keeping warm
The plenteous bloom, that no rough blast may sweep
His garlands from the boughs. Again, as oft
As the sun peeps and vernal airs breathe mild,
The fence withdrawn, he gives them ev'ry beam,
And spreads his hopes before the blaze of day.
    To raise the prickly and green-coated gourd
So grateful to the palate, and when rare
So coveted, else base and disesteem'd—
Food for the vulgar merely—is an art
That toiling ages have but just matured,

---

[1] Miraturque novos fructus et non sua poma. VIRG. [C]. *Georgios*, II, 82. *Novos fructus* should read *novas frondes*. 'And marvels at fresh leaves and fruits not of its own.'

And at this moment unassay'd in song.
Yet gnats have had, and frogs and mice[1] long since,
Their eulogy; those sang the Mantuan bard,
And these the Grecian in ennobling strains,
And in thy numbers, Phillips,[2] shines for ay
The solitary shilling. Pardon them
Ye sage dispensers of poetic fame!
Th' ambition of one meaner far, whose pow'rs
Presuming an attempt not less sublime,
Pant for the praise of dressing to the taste
Of critic appetite, no sordid fare,
A cucumber, while costly yet and scarce.

 The stable yields a stercorarious[3] heap,
Impregnated with quick fermenting salts,
And potent to resist the freezing blast:
For ere the beech and elm have cast their leaf
Deciduous, and when now November dark
Checks vegetation in the torpid plant
Exposed to his cold breath, the task begins.
Warily therefore, and with prudent heed,
He seeks a favor'd spot. That where he builds
Th' agglomerated pile, his frame may front
The sun's meridian dusk, and at the back
Enjoy close shelter, wall, or reeds, or hedge
Impervious to the wind. First he bids spread
Dry fern or litter'd hay, that may imbibe
Th' ascending damps; then leisurely impose,
And lightly, shaking it with agile hand
From the full fork, the saturated straw.
What longest binds the closest, forms secure
The shapely side, that as it rises takes
By just degrees an overhanging breadth,
Shelt'ring the base with its projected eaves.
Th' uplifted frame compact at ev'ry joint,

---

 [1] Allusions to the *Culex* (gnat) and the *Batrachomyomachia* (the battle of the frogs and mice), poems once attributed to Virgil and Homer.

 [2] John Philips, *The Splendid Shilling*, a burlesque of Milton, much admired by Cowper.

 [3] Latin *stercorarius*: relating to dung.

And overlaid with clear translucent glass
He settles next upon the sloping mount,
Whose sharp declivity shoots off secure
From the dash'd pane the deluge as it falls.
He shuts it close, and the first labor ends.
Thrice must the voluble[1] and restless earth
Spin round upon her axle, ere the warmth,
Slow gathering in the midst, through the square mass
Diffused, attain the surface. When behold!
A pestilent and most corrosive steam,
Like a gross fog Bœotian, rising fast,
And fast condensed upon the dewy sash,
Asks egress; which obtained, the overcharged
And drench'd conservatory breathes abroad,
In volumes wheeling slow, the vapor dank,
And purified, rejoices to have lost
Its foul inhabitant. But to assuage
Th' impatient fervor which it first conceives
Within its reeking bosom threat'ning death
To his young hopes, requires discreet delay.
Experience, slow preceptress, teaching oft
The way to glory by miscarriage foul,
Must prompt him, and admonish how to catch
Th' auspicious moment, when the temper'd heat,
Friendly to vital motion, may afford
Soft fermentation, and invite the seed.
The seed, selected wisely, plump and smooth
And glossy, he commits to pots of size
Diminutive, well fill'd with well-prepar'd
And fruitful soil, that has been treasur'd long,
And drunk no moisture from the dripping clouds.
These, on the warm and genial earth that hides
The smoking manure and o'erspreads it all,
He places lightly, and as time subdues
The rage of fermentation, plunges deep
In the soft medium, 'till they stand immers'd.
Then rise the tender germs upstarting quick

[1] *voluble*: rotating.

And spreading wide their spongy lobes, at first
Pale, wan, and livid, but assuming soon,
If fann'd by balmy and nutritious air,
Strain'd through the friendly mats, a vivid green.
Two leaves produced, two rough indented leaves,
Cautious, he pinches from the second stalk
A pimple, that portends a future sprout,
And interdicts its growth. Thence straight succeed
The branches, sturdy to his utmost wish,
Prolific all, and harbingers of more.
The crowded roots demand enlargement now
And transplantation in an ampler space.
Indulged in what they wish, they soon supply
Large foliage, overshadowing golden flowers,
Blown on the summit of th' apparent fruit.
These have their sexes, and when summer shines
The bee transports the fertilizing meal
From flow'r to flow'r, and ev'n the breathing air
Wafts the rich prize to its appointed use.
Not so when winter scowls. Assistant art
Then acts in nature's office, brings to pass
The glad espousals and insures the crop.

   Grudge not, ye rich, (since luxury must have
His dainties, and the world's more num'rous half
Lives by contriving delicates for you)
Grudge not the cost. Ye little know the cares,
The vigilance, the labor and the skill
That day and night are exercis'd, and hang
Upon the ticklish balance of suspense,
That ye may garnish your profuse regales
With summer fruits brought forth by wintry suns.
Ten thousand dangers lie in wait to thwart
The process. Heat and cold, and wind and steam,
Moisture and drought, mice, worms, and swarming flies,
Minute as dust and numberless, oft work
Dire disappointment that admits no cure,
And which no care can obviate. It were long,
Too long, to tell th' expedients and the shifts
Which he that fights a season so severe

Devises, while he guards his tender trust,
And oft, at last, in vain. The learn'd and wise
Sarcastic would exclaim, and judge the song
Cold as its theme, and like its theme, the fruit
Of too much labor, worthless when produced.
    Who loves a garden, loves a green-house too.
Unconscious of a less propitious clime
There blooms exotic beauty, warm and snug,
While the winds whistle and the snows descend.
The spiry myrtle with unwith'ring leaf
Shines there and flourishes. The golden boast
Of Portugal and western India there,
The ruddier orange and the paler lime,
Peep through their polish'd foliage at the storm,
And seem to smile at what they need not fear.
Th' amomum[1] there with intermingling flow'rs
And cherries hangs her twigs. Geranium boasts
Her crimson honors, and the spangled beau
Ficoides,[2] glitters bright the winter long.
All plants of ev'ry leaf that can endure
The winter's frown if screen'd from his shrewd bite,
Live there and prosper. Those Ausonia claims,
Levantine regions these; th' Azores send
Their jessamine, her jessamine remote
Caffraia;[3] foreigners from many lands,
They form one social shade, as if conveyed
By magic summons of th' Orphean lyre.
Yet just arrangement, rarely brought to pass
But by a master's hand, disposing well
The gay diversities of leaf and flow'r,
Must lend its aid t' illustrate all their charms,
And dress the regular yet various scene.
Plant behind plant aspiring, in the van
The dwarfish, in the rear retired, but still
Sublime above the rest, the statelier stand.

[1] *Bruce* suggests that this may be the Jamaica Pepper, *myrtus pimenta*.
[2] The Ice-plant: *mesembryanthemum crystallinum: Bruce.*
[3] The S.E. part of Cape Province, S. Africa.

So once were ranged the sons of ancient Rome,
A noble show! while Roscius trod the stage;
And so, while Garrick, as renown'd as he,
The sons of Albion; fearing each to lose
Some note of Nature's music from his lips,
And covetous of Shakespeare's beauty seen
In ev'ry flash of his far-beaming eye.
Nor taste alone and well contrived display
Suffice to give the marshall'd ranks the grace
Of their complete effect. Much yet remains
Unsung, and many cares are yet behind
And more laborious. Cares on which depend
Their vigor, injur'd soon, not soon restored.
The soil must be renew'd, which often wash'd,
Loses its treasure of salubrious salts,
And disappoints the roots; the slender roots
Close interwoven where they meet the vase
Must smooth be shorn away; the sapless branch
Must fly before the knife; the wither'd leaf
Must be detach'd, and where it strews the floor
Swept with a woman's neatness, breeding else
Contagion, and disseminating death.
Discharge but these kind offices, (and who
Would spare, that loves them, offices like these?)
Well they reward the toil. The sight is pleased,
The scent regaled, each odorif'rous leaf,
Each opening blossom freely breathes abroad
Its gratitude, and thanks him with its sweets.
   So manifold, all pleasing in their kind,
All healthful, are th' employs of rural life,
Reiterated as the wheel of time
Runs round, still ending, and beginning still.
Nor are these all. To deck the shapely knoll,
That softly swell'd and gaily dress'd, appears
A flow'ry island from the dark green lawn
Emerging, must be deemed a labor due
To no mean hand, and asks the touch of taste.
Here also grateful mixture of well match'd
And sorted hues, (each giving each relief,

And by contrasted beauty shining more)
Is needful. Strength may wield the pond'rous spade,
May turn the clod, and wheel the compost home,
But elegance, chief grace the garden shows,
And most attractive, is the fair result
Of thought, the creature of a polish'd mind.
Without it, all is Gothic as the scene[1]
To which th' insipid citizen resorts
Near yonder heath; where industry mispent,
But proud of his uncouth ill-chosen task,
Has made a heav'n on earth; with suns and moons
Of close-ramm'd stones has charg'd th' encumber'd soil,
And fairly laid the Zodiac in the dust.
He therefore who would see his flow'rs dispos'd
Sightly and in just order, ere he gives
The beds the trusted treasure of their seeds,
Forecasts the future whole; that when the scene
Shall break into its preconceiv'd display,
Each for itself, and all as with one voice
Conspiring, may attest his bright design.
Nor even then, dismissing as perform'd
His pleasant work, may he suppose it done.
Few self-supported flow'rs endure the wind
Uninjur'd, but expect th' upholding aid
Of the smooth-shaven prop, and neatly tied,
Are wedded thus like beauty to old age,
For int'rest sake, the living to the dead.
Some cloath the soil that feeds them, far diffus'd
And lowly creeping, modest and yet fair,
Like virtue, thriving most where little seen.
Some, more aspiring, catch the neighbour shrub
With clasping tendrils, and invest his branch,
Else unadorn'd, with many a gay festoon
And fragrant chaplet, recompensing well

[1] In the 18th century the Spaniard's Inn, near Hampstead Heath, had a 'very curious garden', in which the lawns and alleys were adorned with designs in coloured pebbles. The designs included 'the sun in his glory' and 'the twelve signs of the Zodiac'. See Wroth, *London Pleasure Gardens of the 18th Century*, 1896.

The strength they borrow with the grace they lend.
All hate the rank society of weeds,
Noisome, and ever greedy to exhaust
Th' impov'rish'd earth; an overbearing race,
That like the multitude, made faction-mad,
Disturb good order, and degrade true worth.
  Oh blest seclusion from a jarring world,
Which he, thus occupied, enjoys! Retreat
Cannot indeed to guilty man restore
Lost innocence, or cancel follies past,
But it has peace, and much secures the mind
From all assaults of evil, proving still
A faithful barrier, not o'erleap'd with ease
By vicious custom, raging uncontroul'd
Abroad, and desolating public life.
When fierce temptation, seconded within
By traitor appetite, and arm'd with darts
Temper'd in hell, invades the throbbing breast,
To combat may be glorious, and success
Perhaps may crown us, but to fly is safe.
Had I the choice of sublunary good,
What could I wish, that I possess not here?
Health, leisure, means t' improve it, friendship, peace,
No loose or wanton, though a wand'ring muse,
And constant occupation without care.
Thus blest, I draw a picture of that bliss;
Hopeless indeed that dissipated minds,
And profligate abusers of a world
Created fair so much in vain for them,
Should seek the guiltless joys that I describe,
Allur'd by my report: but sure no less,
That, self-condemn'd, they must neglect the prize,
And what they will not taste, must yet approve.
What we admire we praise; and when we praise,
Advance it into notice, that its worth
Acknowledg'd, others may admire it too.
I therefore recommend, though at the risk
Of popular disgust, yet boldly still,
The cause of piety and sacred truth,

And virtue, and those scenes which God ordain'd
Should best secure them and promote them most;
Scenes that I love, and with regret perceive
Forsak'n, or through folly not enjoy'd.
Pure is the nymph, though lib'ral of her smiles,
And chaste, though unconfin'd, whom I extol.
Not as the prince in Shushan,[1] when he call'd,
Vain-glorious of her charms, his Vashti forth
To grace the full pavilion. His design
Was but to boast his own peculiar good,
Which all might view with envy, none partake.
My charmer is not mine alone; my sweets,
And she that sweetens all my bitters too,
Nature, enchanting Nature, in whose form
And lineaments divine I trace a hand
That errs not, and find raptures still renew'd,
Is free to all men, universal prize.
Strange that so fair a creature should yet want
Admirers, and be destin'd to divide
With meaner objects, ev'n the few she finds!
Stripp'd of her ornaments, her leaves and flow'rs,
She loses all her influence. Cities then
Attract us, and neglected Nature pines,
Abandon'd, as unworthy of our love.
But are not wholesome airs, though unperfum'd
By roses; and clear suns, though scarcely felt,
And groves, if unharmonious, yet secure
From clamour, and whose very silence charms,
To be preferr'd to smoke, to the eclipse
That Metropolitan volcanos make,
Whose Stygian throats breathe darkness all day long,
And to the stir of commerce, driving slow,
And thund'ring loud, with his ten thousand wheels?
They would be, were not madness in the head,
And folly in the heart; were England now
What England was, plain, hospitable, kind,
And undebauch'd. But we have bid farewel

[1] Ahasuerus: Esther, i, 10-11.

To all the virtues of those better days,
And all their honest pleasures. Mansions once
Knew their own masters, and laborious hinds
That had surviv'd the father, serv'd the son.
Now the legitimate and rightful Lord
Is but a transient guest, newly arriv'd,
And soon to be supplanted. He that saw
His patrimonial timber cast its leaf,
Sells the last scantling, and transfers the price
To some shrewd sharper, ere it buds again.
Estates are landscapes, gaz'd upon a while,
Then advertis'd, and auctioneer'd away.
The country starves, and they that feed th' o'ercharg'd
And surfeited lewd town with her fair dues,
By a just judgment strip and starve themselves.
The wings that waft our riches out of sight
Grow on the gamester's elbows, and th' alert
And nimble motion of those restless joints,
That never tire, soon fans them all away.
Improvement too, the idol of the age,
Is fed with many a victim. Lo! he comes—
Th' omnipotent magician, Brown,[1] appears.
Down falls the venerable pile, th' abode
Of our forefathers, a grave whisker'd race,
But tasteless. Springs a palace in its stead,
But in a distant spot; where more expos'd,
It may enjoy th' advantage of the north
And aguish east, till time shall have transform'd
Those naked acres to a shelt'ring grove.
He speaks. The lake in front becomes a lawn,
Woods vanish, hills subside, and vallies rise,
And streams, as if created for his use,
Pursue the track of his directing wand,
Sinuous or straight, now rapid and now slow,
Now murm'ring soft, now roaring in cascades,
Ev'n as he bids. Th' enraptur'd owner smiles.
'Tis finish'd; and yet, finish'd as it seems,

[1] Lancelot ('Capability') Brown, the landscape gardener.

Still wants a grace, the loveliest it could show,
A mine to satisfy th' enormous cost.
Drain'd to the last poor item of his wealth,
He sighs, departs, and leaves th' accomplish'd plan
That he has touch'd, retouch'd, many a long day
Labor'd, and many a night pursu'd in dreams,
Just when it meets his hopes, and proves the heav'n
He wanted, for a wealthier to enjoy.
And now perhaps the glorious hour is come,
When, having no stake left, no pledge t' endear
Her int'rests, or that gives her sacred cause
A moment's operation on his love,
He burns with most intense and flagrant zeal
To serve his country. Ministerial grace
Deals him out money from the public chest,
Or, if that mine be shut, some private purse
Supplies his need with an usurious loan,
To be refunded duly, when his vote,
Well-manag'd, shall have earn'd its worthy price.
Oh innocent, compar'd with arts like these,
Crape[1] and cock'd pistol, and the whistling ball
Sent through the trav'ller's temples! He that finds
One drop of heav'n's sweet mercy in his cup,
Can dig, beg, rot, and perish well content,
So he may wrap himself in honest rags
At his last gasp; but could not for a world
Fish up his dirty and dependent bread
From pools and ditches of the commonwealth,
Sordid and sick'ning at his own success.
    Ambition, av'rice, penury incurr'd
By endless riot; vanity, the lust
Of pleasure and variety, dispatch,
As duly as the swallows disappear,
The world of wand'ring knights and squires to town.
London ingulphs them all. The shark is there,
And the shark's prey; the spendthrift, and the leech
That sucks him. There the sycophant, and he

---

[1] *Crape:* the mask used by highwaymen.

That, with bare-headed and obsequious bows,
Begs a warm office, doom'd to a cold jail,
And groat per diem, if his patron frown.
The levee swarms, as if, in golden pomp,
Were character'd on ev'ry statesman's door,
'BATTER'D AND BANKRUPT FORTUNES MENDED HERE.'
These are the charms that sully and eclipse
The charms of nature. 'Tis the cruel gripe
That lean hard-handed poverty inflicts,
The hope of better things, the chance to win,
The wish to shine, the thirst to be amus'd,
That at the sound of Winter's hoary wing
Unpeople all our counties, of such herds
Of flutt'ring, loit'ring, cringing, begging, loose
And wanton vagrants, as make London, vast
And boundless as it is, a crowded coop.

Oh thou, resort and mart of all the earth,
Chequer'd with all complexions of mankind,
And spotted with all crimes; in whom I see
Much that I love, and more that I admire,[1]
And all that I abhor; thou freckled fair,
That pleases and yet shocks me, I can laugh
And I can weep, can hope, and can despond,
Feel wrath and pity, when I think on thee!
Ten righteous would have sav'd a city once,
And thou hast many righteous. — Well for thee —
That salt preserves thee; more corrupted else,
And therefore more obnoxious at this hour,
Than Sodom in her day had pow'r to be,
For whom God heard his Abr'am plead in vain.[2]

[1] *admire:* wonder at.
[2] Genesis, xviii, 23–32.

BOOK IV

THE WINTER EVENING

ARGUMENT OF THE FOURTH BOOK.—*The post comes in—The newspaper is read—The world contemplated at a distance—Address to Winter—The amusements of a rural winter evening compared with the fashionable ones—Address to evening—A brown study—Fall of snow in the evening—The waggoner—A poor family piece—The rural thief—Public houses—The multitude of them censured—The farmer's daughter, what she was—What she is—The simplicity of country manners almost lost—Causes of the change—Deser- of the country by the rich—Neglect of magistrates—The militia principally in fault—The new recruit and his trans- formation—Reflection on bodies corporate—The love of rural objects natural to all, and never to be totally extinguished.*

HARK! 'tis the twanging horn! O'er yonder bridge,[1]
That with its wearisome but needful length
Bestrides the wintry flood, in which the moon
Sees her unwrinkled face reflected bright,
He comes, the herald of a noisy world,
With spatter'd boots, strapp'd waist, and frozen locks,
News from all nations lumb'ring at his back.
True to his charge the close-pack'd load behind,
Yet careless what he brings, his one concern
Is to conduct it to the destin'd inn,
And having dropp'd th' expected bag—pass on.
He whistles as he goes, light-hearted wretch,
Cold and yet cheerful: messenger of grief
Perhaps to thousands, and of joy to some,
To him indiff'rent whether grief or joy.
Houses in ashes, and the fall of stocks,

---

[1] The 'Long Bridge' over the Ouse at Olney, rebuilt in 1832.

Births, deaths, and marriages, epistles wet
With tears, that trickled down the writer's cheeks
Fast as the periods from his fluent quill,
Or charg'd with am'rous sighs of absent swains,
Or nymphs responsive, equally affect
His horse and him, unconscious of them all.
But oh th' important budget! usher'd in
With such heart-shaking music, who can say
What are its tidings? have our troops awaked?
Or do they still, as if with opium drugg'd,
Snore to the murmurs of th' Atlantic wave?[1]
Is India[2] free? and does she wear her plumed
And jewelled turban with a smile of peace,
Or do we grind her still? The grand debate,
The popular harrangue, the tart reply,
The logic and the wisdom and the wit
And the loud laugh—I long to know them all;
I burn to set th' imprison'd wranglers free,
And give them voice and utt'rance once again.
    Now stir the fire, and close the shutters fast,
Let fall the curtains, wheel the sofa round,
And while the bubbling and loud-hissing urn
Throws up a steamy column, and the cups,
That cheer but not inebriate, wait on each,
So let us welcome peaceful evening in.
Not such his evening, who with shining face
Sweats in the crowded theatre, and squeezed
And bored with elbow-points through both his sides,
Out-scolds the ranting actor on the stage.
Nor his, who patient stands 'till his feet throb,
And his head thumps, to feed upon the breath
Of patriots bursting with heroic rage,
Or placemen, all tranquility and smiles.
This folio of four pages, happy work!
Which not ev'n critics criticise, that holds

[1] Cowper thought that the British generals in America did not wage
war as energetically as they might have done.

[2] Fox's East India Bill, 1783 (see pp. 704–07) was followed by Pitt's
in 1784.

Inquisitive attention while I read,
Fast bound in chains of silence, which the fair,
Though eloquent themselves, yet fear to break,
What is it, but a map of busy life,
Its fluctuations and its vast concerns?
Here runs the mountainous and craggy ridge
That tempts ambition. On the summit, see,
The seals of office glitter in his eyes;
He climbs, he pants, he grasps them. At his heels,
Close at his heels a demagogue ascends,
And with a dext'rous jerk soon twists him down
And wins them, but to lose them in his turn.
Here rills of oily eloquence in soft
Mæanders lubricate the course they take;
The modest speaker is ashamed and grieved
T' engross a moment's notice, and yet begs,
Begs a propitious ear for his poor thoughts,
However trivial all that he conceives.
Sweet bashfulness! it claims, at last, this praise;
The dearth of information and good sense
That it foretells us, always comes to pass.
Cataracts of declamation thunder here,
There forests of no-meaning spread the page
In which all comprehension wanders lost;
While fields of pleasantry amuse us there,
With merry descants on a nation's woes.
The rest appears a wilderness of strange
But gay confusion; roses for the cheeks,
And lilies for the brows of faded age,
Teeth for the toothless, ringlets for the bald,
Heav'n, earth, and ocean plunder'd of their sweets,
Nectareous essences, Olympian dews,
Sermons and city feasts and fav'rite airs,
Ætherial journies,[1] submarine exploits,

[1] *Aetherial journies:* balloon ascents. See nn., pp. 695, 700. *Submarine exploits:* the allusion may be to Spalding, who although 'professionally ingenious in the art of constructing and managing the diving bell', perished when viewing a wreck off the Kish bank in Ireland, June 1783. See *Annual Register* for 1783, p. 206.

And Katterfelto[1] with his hair on end
At his own wonders, wond'ring for his bread.
    'Tis pleasant through the loop-holes of retreat
To peep at such a world. To see the stir
Of the great Babel and not feel the crowd.
To hear the roar she sends through all her gates,
At a safe distance, where the dying sound
Falls a soft murmur on th' uninjured ear.
Thus sitting and surveying thus at ease
The globe and its concerns, I seem advanced
To some secure and more than mortal height,
That lib'rates and exempts me from them all.
It turns submitted to my view, turns round
With all its generations; I behold
The tumult and am still. The sound of war
Has lost its terrors ere it reaches me;
Grieves but alarms me not. I mourn the pride
And av'rice that make man a wolf to man,[2]
Hear the faint echo of those brazen throats
By which he speaks the language of his heart,
And sigh, but never tremble at the sound.
He travels and expatiates, as the bee
From flow'r to flow'r, so he from land to land;
The manners, customs, policy of all
Pay contribution to the store he gleans,
He sucks intelligence in ev'ry clime,
And spreads the honey of his deep research
At his return, a rich repast for me.
He travels and I too. I tread his deck,
Ascend his topmast, through his peering eyes
Discover countries, with a kindred heart
Suffer his woes, and share in his escapes,
While fancy, like the finger of a clock,
Runs the great circuit, and is still at home.

    [1] Katerfelto, a well-known London quack, habitually announced forth-
coming appearances in advertisements headed 'Wonders! Wonders!'
    [2] *Lupus est homo homini:* a felicitous misquotation by Robert Burton,
Anatomy of Melancholy, I, i, 1621, from Plautus, *Asinaria,* line 495: *Lupus
est homo, non homo.* (Man is not a man, but a wolf).

Oh Winter! ruler of th' inverted year,
Thy scatter'd hair with sleet like ashes fill'd,
Thy breath congeal'd upon thy lips, thy cheeks
Fring'd with a beard made white with other snows
Than those of age; thy forehead wrapt in clouds,
A leafless branch thy sceptre, and thy throne
A sliding car indebted to no wheels,
But urged by storms along its slipp'ry way;
I love thee, all unlovely as thou seem'st,
And dreaded as thou art. Thou hold'st the sun
A pris'ner in the yet undawning East,
Short'ning his journey between morn and noon,
And hurrying him impatient of his stay
Down to the rosy West. But kindly still
Compensating his loss with added hours
Of social converse and instructive ease,
And gathering at short notice in one group
The family dispers'd, and fixing thought,
Not less dispersed by day-light and its cares.
I crown thee King of intimate delights,
Fireside enjoyments, home-born happiness,
And all the comforts that the lowly roof
Of undisturb'd retirement, and the hours
Of long uninterrupted evening, know.
No ratt'ling wheels stop short before these gates.
No powder'd pert proficient in the art
Of sounding an alarm, assaults these doors
'Till the street rings. No stationary steeds
Cough their own knell, while heedless of the sound
The silent circle fan themselves, and quake.
But here the needle plies its busy task,
The pattern grows, the well-depicted flow'r
Wrought patiently into the snowy lawn
Unfolds its bosom, buds and leaves and sprigs
And curling tendrils, gracefully disposed,
Follow the nimble finger of the fair,
A wreath that cannot fade, of flow'rs that blow
With most success when all besides decay.
The poet's or historian's page, by one

Made vocal for th' amusement of the rest;
The sprightly lyre, whose treasure of sweet sounds
The touch from many a trembling chord shakes out;
And the clear voice symphonious, yet distinct,
And in the charming strife triumphant still,[1]
Beguile the night, and set a keener edge
On female industry; the threaded steel
Flies swiftly, and unfelt the task proceeds.
The volume closed, the customary rites
Of the last meal commence. A Roman meal,
Such as the mistress of the world once found
Delicious, when her patriots of high note,
Perhaps by moonlight, at their humble doors,
And under an old oak's domestic shade,
Enjoy'd, spare feast! a radish and an egg.
Discourse ensues, not trivial, yet not dull,
Nor such as with a frown forbids the play
Of fancy, or proscribes the sound of mirth.
Nor do we madly, like an impious world,
Who deem religion frenzy, and the God
That made them an intruder on their joys,
Start at his awful name, or deem his praise
A jarring note. Themes of a graver tone
Exciting oft our gratitude and love,
While we retrace with mem'ry's pointing wand
That calls the past to our exact review,
The dangers we have 'scaped, the broken snare,
The disappointed foe, deliv'rance found
Unlook'd for, life preserved and peace restored,
Fruits of omnipotent eternal love.
Oh ev'nings worthy of the Gods! exclaim'd
The Sabine bard.[2] Oh evenings, I reply,
More to be prized and coveted than yours,
As more illumin'd and with nobler truths,
That I and mine and those we love, enjoy.
   Is winter hideous in a garb like this?

---

[1] Cf. Horace, *concordia discors* (*Epistles*, I, xii, 19).
[2] Horace, *Satires*, II, vi, 65: *O noctes cenaeque deum!*

Needs he the tragic fur, the smoke of lamps,
The pent-up breath of an unsav'ry throng,
To thaw him into feeling, or the smart
And snappish dialogue that flippant wits
Call comedy, to prompt him with a smile?
The self-complacent actor when he views
(Stealing a side long glance at a full house)
The slope of faces, from the floor to th' roof,
(As if one master-spring controul'd them all)
Relax'd into an universal grin,
Sees not a count'nance there that speaks a joy
Half so refin'd or so sincere as ours.
Cards were superfluous here, with all the tricks
That idleness has ever yet contrived
To fill the void of an unfurnish'd brain,
To palliate dullness and give time a shove.
Time as he passes us, has a dove's wing,
Unsoiled and swift and of a silken sound.
But the world's time, is time in masquerade.
Theirs, should I paint him, has his pinions fledg'd
With motley plumes and where the peacock shows
His azure eyes, is tinctured black and red
With spots quadrangular of di'mond form,
Ensanguin'd hearts, clubs typical of strife,
And spades, the emblem of untimely graves.
What should be, and what was an hour-glass once,
Becomes a dice-box, and a billiard mace[1]
Well does the work of his destructive scythe.
Thus deck'd he charms a world whom fashion blinds
To his true worth, most pleas'd when idle most,
Whose only happy are their wasted hours.
Ev'n misses, at whose age their mothers wore
The back-string and the bib, assume the dress
Of womanhood, sit pupils in the school
Of card-devoted time, and, night by night,
Plac'd at some vacant corner of the board,
Learn ev'ry trick, and soon play all the game.

[1] *mace: mast 1875.*

But truce with censure. Roving as I rove,
Where shall I find an end, or how proceed?
As he that travels far, oft turns aside
To view some rugged rock or mould'ring tow'r,
Which seen delights him not; then coming home,
Describes and prints it, that the world may know
How far he went for what was nothing worth;
So I with brush in hand and pallet spread
With colours mixt for a far diff'rent use,
Paint cards and dolls, and ev'ry idle thing
That fancy finds in her excursive flights.

    Come evening once again, season of peace,[1]
Return sweet evening, and continue long!
Methinks I see thee in the streaky west,
With matron-step slow-moving, while the night
Treads on thy sweeping train; one hand employ'd
In letting fall the curtain of repose
On bird and beast, the other charged for man
With sweet oblivion of the cares of day;
Not sumptuously adorn'd, nor needing aid
Like homely featur'd night, of clust'ring gems;
A star or two just twinkling on thy brow
Suffices thee; save that the moon is thine
No less than hers, not worn indeed on high
With ostentatious pageantry, but set
With modest grandeur in thy purple zone,
Resplendent less, but of an ampler round.
Come then and thou shalt find thy vot'ry calm,
Or make me so. Composure is thy gift.
And whether I devote thy gentle hours
To books, to music, or the poet's toil,
To weaving nets for bird-alluring fruit;
Or twining silken threads round iv'ry reels
When they command whom man was born to please;
I slight thee not, but make thee welcome still.

    Just when our drawing-rooms begin to blaze
With lights by clear reflection multiplied

[1] Cf. *Paradise Lost*, IV, 598–609.

From many a mirrour, in which he of **Gath,**
Goliah, might have seen his giant bulk
Whole without stooping, tow'ring crest and **all,**
My pleasures too begin. But me perhaps
The glowing hearth may satisfy awhile
With faint illumination that uplifts
The shadow to the cieling, there by fits
Dancing uncouthly to the quiv'ring flame
Not undelightful is an hour to me
So spent in parlour twilight; such a gloom
Suits well the thoughtful or unthinking mind,
The mind contemplative, with some new theme
Pregnant, or indisposed alike to all.
Laugh ye, who boast your more mercurial **pow'rs**
That never feel a stupor, know no pause,
Nor need one. I am conscious, and confess,
Fearless, a soul that does not always think.
Me oft has fancy ludicrous and wild,
Sooth'd with a waking dream of houses, tow'rs,
Trees, churches, and strange visages express'd
In the red cinders, while with poring eye
I gazed, myself creating what I saw.
Nor less amused have I quiescent watch'd
The sooty films that play upon the bars
Pendulous and foreboding in the view
Of superstition prophesying still
Though still deceiv'd, some stranger's near approach.
'Tis thus the understanding takes repose
In indolent vacuity of thought,
And sleeps and is refresh'd. Meanwhile the face
Conceals the mood lethargic with a mask
Of deep deliberation, as the man
Were task'd to his full strength, absorb'd and lost.
Thus oft reclin'd at ease, I lose an hour
At evening, till at length the freezing blast
That sweeps the bolted shutter, summons home
The recollected powers, and snapping short
The glassy threads with which the fancy weaves
Her brittle toys, restores me to myself.

How calm is my recess, and how the frost,
Raging abroad, and the rough wind, endear
The silence and the warmth enjoy'd within.
I saw the woods and fields at close of day,
A variegated show; the meadows green,
Though faded; and the lands where lately waved
The golden harvest, of a mellow brown,
Upturn'd so lately by the forceful share.
I saw far off the weedy fallows smile
With verdure not unprofitable, grazed
By flocks fast feeding and selecting each
His fav'rite herb; while all the leafless groves
That skirt th' horizon wore a sable hue,
Scarce noticed in the kindred dusk of eve.
To-morrow brings a change, a total change!
Which even now, though silently perform'd
And slowly, and by most unfelt, the face
Of universal nature undergoes.
Fast falls a fleecy show'r. The downy flakes,
Descending and with never-ceasing lapse,
Softly alighting upon all below,
Assimilate all objects. Earth receives
Gladly the thick'ning mantle, and the green
And tender blade that fear'd the chilling blast,
Escapes unhurt beneath so warm a veil.
    In such a world, so thorny, and where none
Finds happiness unblighted, or, if found,
Without some thistly sorrow at its side,
It seems the part of wisdom, and no sin
Against the law of love, to measure lots
With less distinguish'd than ourselves, that thus
We may with patience bear our mod'rate ills,
And sympathize with others, suffering more.
Ill fares the trav'ller now, and he that stalks
In pond'rous boots beside his reeking team.
The wain goes heavily, impeded sore
By congregated loads adhering close
To the clogg'd wheels; and in its sluggish pace
Noiseless, appears a moving hill of snow.

The toiling steeds expand the nostril wide,
While ev'ry breath by respiration strong
Forc'd downward, is consolidated soon
Upon their jutting chests. He, form'd to bear
The pelting brunt of the tempestuous night,
With half-shut eyes and pucker'd cheeks, and teeth
Presented bare against the storm, plods on.
One hand secures his hat, save when with both
He brandishes his pliant length of whip,
Resounding oft, and never heard in vain.
Oh happy! and, in my account, denied
That sensibility of pain with which
Refinement is endued, thrice happy thou.
Thy frame robust and hardy, feels indeed
The piercing cold, but feels it unimpair'd.
The learned finger never need explore
Thy vig'rous pulse, and the unhealthful East,
That breathes the spleen, and searches ev'ry bone
Of the infirm, is wholesome air to thee.
Thy days roll on exempt from household care,
Thy waggon is thy wife; and the poor beasts
That drag the dull companion to and fro,
Thine helpless charge, dependent on thy care.
Ah treat them kindly! rude as thou appear'st,
Yet show that thou hast mercy, which the great
With needless hurry whirl'd from place to place,
Humane as they would seem, not always show.
  Poor, yet industrious, modest, quiet, neat,
Such claim compassion in a night like this,
And have a friend in ev'ry feeling heart.
Warm'd, while it lasts, by labor, all day long
They brave the season, and yet find at eve
Ill clad and fed but sparely time to cool.
The frugal housewife trembles when she lights
Her scanty stock of brush-wood, blazing clear
But dying soon, like all terrestrial joys.
The few small embers left she nurses well,
And while her infant race, with outspread hands
And crowded knees sit cow'ring o'er the sparks,

Retires, content to quake, so they be warm'd.
The man feels least, as more inur'd than she
To winter, and the current in his veins
More briskly moved by his severer toil;
Yet he too finds his own distress in theirs.
The taper soon extinguished, which I saw
Dangled along at the cold finger's end
Just when the day declined, and the brown loaf
Lodged on the shelf, half-eaten without sauce
Of sav'ry cheese, or butter costlier still,
Sleep seems their only refuge. For alas!
Where penury is felt the thought is chain'd,
And sweet colloquial pleasures are but few.
With all this thrift they thrive not. All the care
Ingenious parsimony takes, but just
Saves the small inventory, bed and stool,
Skillet[1] and old carved chest from public sale.
They live, and live without extorted alms
From grudging hands, but other boast have none
To sooth their honest pride, that scorns to beg;
Nor comfort else, but in their mutual love.
I praise you much, ye meek and patient pair,
For ye are worthy; chusing rather far
A dry but independent crust, hard-earn'd,
And eaten with a sigh, than to endure
The rugged frowns and insolent rebuffs
Of knaves in office, partial in the work
Of distribution; lib'ral of their aid
To clam'rous importunity in rags,
But oft-times deaf to suppliants who would blush
To wear a tatter'd garb however coarse,
Whom famine cannot reconcile to filth;
These ask with painful shyness, and refused
Because deserving, silently retire.
But be ye of good courage. Time itself
Shall much befriend you. Time shall give increase,
And all your num'rous progeny well train'd

[1] Cooking-pot.

But helpless, in few years shall find their hands,
And labor too. Meanwhile ye shall not want
What, conscious of your virtues, we can spare,
Nor what a wealthier than ourselves may send.
I mean the man,[1] who, when the distant poor
Need help, denies them nothing but his name.
  But poverty with most who whimper forth
Their long complaints, is self inflicted woe,
Th' effect of laziness or sottish waste.
Now goes the nightly thief prowling abroad
For plunder; much solicitous how best
He may compensate for a day of sloth,
By works of darkness and nocturnal wrong.
Woe to the gard'ner's pale, the farmer's hedge,
Plash'd neatly, and secured with driven stakes
Deep in the loamy bank. Uptorn by strength
Resistless in so bad a cause, but lame
To better deeds, he bundles up the spoil,
An ass's burthen, and when laden most
And heaviest, light of foot steals fast away.
Nor does the boarded hovel better guard
The well stack'd pile of riven logs and roots
From his pernicious force. Nor will he leave
Unwrench'd the door, however well secured,
Where chanticleer amidst his haram sleeps
In unsuspecting pomp. Twitched from the perch
He gives the princely bird with all his wives
To his voracious bag, struggling in vain,
And loudly wond'ring at the sudden change
Nor this to feed his own. 'Twere some excuse
Did pity of their sufferings warp aside
His principle, and tempt him into sin
For their support, so destitute. But they
Neglected pine at home, themselves, as more
Exposed than others, with less scruple made
His victims, robb'd of their defenceless all.

[1] Robert Smith, (1752–38), banker and M.P. for Nottingham 1779–97, created baron Carrington, 1797. He gave Cowper money for distribution to the poor of Olney (pp. 676–7).

Cruel is all he does. 'Tis quenchless thirst
Of ruinous ebriety that prompts
His ev'ry action and imbrutes the man.
Oh for a law to noose the villain's neck
Who starves his own. Who persecutes the blood
He gave them, in his children's veins, and hates
And wrongs the woman he had sworn to love.

   Pass where we may, through city or through town,
Village or hamlet of this merry land
Though lean and beggar'd, ev'ry twentieth pace
Conducts th' unguarded nose to such a whiff
Of stale debauch forth-issuing from the styes
That law has licensed, as makes temp'rance reel.
There sit involved and lost in curling clouds
Of Indian fume, and guzzling deep, the boor,
The lacquey and the groom. The craftsman there
Takes a Lethæan leave of all his toil;
Smith, cobler, joiner, he that plies the sheers,
And he that kneads the dough; all loud alike,
All learned, and all drunk. The fiddle screams
Plaintive and piteous, as it wept and wailed
Its wasted tones and harmony unheard:
Fierce the dispute whate'er the theme. While she,
Fell Discord, arbitress of such debate,
Perch'd on the sign-post, holds with even hand
Her undecisive scales. In this she lays
A weight of ignorance, in that, of pride,
And smiles delighted with th' eternal poise.
Dire is the frequent curse and its twin sound
The cheek-distending oath, not to be praised
As ornamental, musical, polite,
Like those which modern senators employ,
Whose oath is rhet'ric, and who swear for fame.
Behold the schools in which plebeian minds,
Once simple, are initiated in arts,
Which some may practise with politer grace,
But none with readier skill! 'tis here they learn
The road that leads, from competence and peace
To indigence and rapine; till at last

Society grown weary of the load,
Shakes her incumber'd lap, and casts them out.
But censure profits little. Vain th' attempt
To advertize in verse a public pest,
That, like the filth with which the peasant feeds
His hungry acres, stinks, and is of use.
Th' excise is fatten'd with the rich result
Of all this riot. And ten thousand casks
For ever dribbling out their base contents,
Touched by the Midas finger of the state,
Bleed gold for Ministers to sport away.
Drink, and be mad then. 'Tis your country bids.
Gloriously drunk obey th' important call,
Her cause demands th' assistance of your throats,
Ye all can swallow, and she asks no more.

Would I had fall'n upon those happier days
That poets celebrate. Those golden times
And those Arcadian scenes that Maro sings,[1]
And Sydney,[2] warbler of poetic prose.
Nymphs were Dianas then, and swains had hearts
That felt their virtues. Innocence it seems,
From courts dismiss'd, found shelter in the groves.
The footsteps of simplicity impress'd
Upon the yielding herbage (so they sing)
Then were not all effaced. Then, speech profane
And manners profligate were rarely found,
Observed as prodigies, and soon reclaim'd.
Vain wish! those days were never. Airy dreams
Sat for the picture. And the poet's hand,
Imparting substance to an empty shade,
Imposed a gay delirium for a truth.
Grant it—I still must envy them an age
That favor'd such a dream, in days like these
Impossible, when virtue is so scarce
That to suppose a scene where she presides,
Is tramontane, and stumbles all belief.

[1] Virgil's *Eclogues*.
[2] Sir Philip Sidney: *The Countess of Pembroke's Arcadia*, 1590.

No. We are polish'd now. The rural lass,
Whom once her virgin modesty and grace,
Her artless manners and her neat attire
So dignified, that she was hardly less
Than the fair shepherdess of old romance,
Is seen no more. The character is lost.
Her head adorn'd with lappets pinn'd aloft
And ribbands streaming gay, superbly raised,
And magnified beyond all human size,
Indebted to some smart wig-weaver's hand
For more than half the tresses it sustains;
Her elbows ruffled, and her tott'ring form
Ill propp'd upon French heels, she might be deemed
(But that the basket dangling on her arm
Interprets her more truely) of a rank
Too proud for dairy-work or sale of eggs.
Expect her soon with foot-boy at her heels,
No longer blushing for her awkward load,
Her train and her umbrella all her care.
    The town has tinged the country. And the stain
Appears a spot upon a vestal's robe,
The worse for what it soils. The fashion runs
Down into scenes still rural, but alas!
Scenes rarely graced with rural manners now.
Time was when in the pastoral retreat
Th' unguarded door was safe. Men did not watch
T' invade another's right, or guard their own.
Then sleep was undisturb'd by fear, unscar'd
By drunken howlings; and the chilling tale
Of midnight murther was a wonder heard
With doubtful credit, told to frighten babes.
But farewell now to unsuspicious nights,
And slumbers unalarm'd. Now, 'ere you sleep,
See that your polish'd arms be prim'd with care,
And drop the night-bolt. Ruffians are abroad,
And the first larum of the cock's shrill throat
May prove a trumpet, summoning your ear
To horrid sounds of hostile feet within.
Ev'n day-light has its dangers. And the walk

Through pathless wastes and woods, unconscious once
Of other tenants than melodious birds
Or harmless flocks, is hazardous and bold.
Lamented change! to which full many a cause
Invet'rate, hopeless of a cure, conspires.
The course of human things from good to ill,
From ill to worse, is fatal, never fails.
Increase of pow'r begets increase of wealth,
Wealth luxury, and luxury excess;
Excess, the scrophulous and itchy plague
That seizes first the opulent, descends
To the next rank contagious, and in time
Taints downward all the graduated scale
Of order, from the chariot to the plough.
The rich, and they that have an arm to check
The license of the lowest in degree,
Desert their office; and themselves intent
On pleasure, haunt the capital, and thus,
To all the violence of lawless hands
Resign the scenes their presence might protect.
Authority herself not seldom sleeps,
Though resident, and witness of the wrong.
The plump convivial parson often bears
The magisterial sword in vain, and lays
His rev'rence and his worship both to rest
On the same cushion of habitual sloth.
Perhaps timidity restrains his arm,
When he should strike he trembles, and sets free,
Himself enslaved by terror of the band,
Th' audacious convict, whom he dares not bind.
Perhaps, though by profession ghostly pure,
He too may have his vice, and sometimes prove
Less dainty than becomes his grave outside,
In lucrative concerns. Examine well
His milk-white hand. The palm is hardly clean—
But here and there an ugly smutch appears.
Foh! 'twas a bribe that left it. He has touched
Corruption. Whoso seeks an audit here
Propitious, pays his tribute, game or fish,

Wild-fowl or ven'son, and his errand speeds.
   But faster far and more than all the rest,
A noble cause, which none who bears a spark
Of public virtue, ever wish'd removed,
Works the deplor'd and mischievous effect.
'Tis universal soldiership[1] has stabb'd
The heart of merit in the meaner class.
Arms through the vanity and brainless rage
Of those that bear them in whatever cause,
Seem most at variance with all moral good,
And incompatible with serious thought.
The clown, the child of nature, without guile,
Blest with an infant's ignorance of all
But his own simple pleasures, now and then
A wrestling-match, a foot-race, or a fair,
Is ballotted, and trembles at the news:
Sheepish he doffs his hat, and mumbling swears
A Bible-oath to be whate'er they please,
To do he knows not what. The task perform'd,
That instant he becomes the serjeant's care,
His pupil, and his torment, and his jest.
His aukward gait, his introverted toes,
Bent knees, round shoulders, and dejected looks,
Procure him many a curse. By slow degrees,
Unapt to learn, and formed of stubborn stuff,
He yet by slow degrees puts off himself,
Grows conscious of a change, and likes it well.
He stands erect, his slouch becomes a walk,
He steps right onward, martial in his air,
His form and movement; is as smart above
As meal and larded locks can make him; wears
His hat or his plumed helmet with a grace,
And his three years of heroship expired,
Returns indignant to the slighted plough.
He hates the field in which no fife or drum

[1] In 1757 the elder Pitt, to meet the needs of the Seven Years' War, greatly increased the size of the regular army and of the militia. The militiamen were enrolled by ballot for a term of three years' service in Britain only.

Attends him, drives his cattle to a march,
And sighs for the smart comrades he has left.
'Twere well if his exterior change were all—
But with his clumsy port the wretch has lost
His ignorance and harmless manners too.
To swear, to game, to drink; to shew at home
By lewdness, idleness, and sabbath-breach,
The great proficiency he made abroad,
T' astonish and to grieve his gazing friends,
To break some maiden's and his mother's heart,
To be a pest where he was useful once,
Are his sole aim, and all his glory now.

   Man in society is like a flow'r
Blown in its native bed. 'Tis there alone
His faculties expanded in full bloom
Shine out, there only reach their proper use.
But man associated and leagued with man
By regal warrant, or self-joined by bond
For interest-sake, or swarming into clans
Beneath one head for purposes of war,
Like flow'rs selected from the rest, and bound
And bundled close to fill some crowded vase,
Fades rapidly, and by compression marred,
Contracts defilement not to be endured.
Hence charter'd boroughs are such public plagues,
And burghers, men immaculate perhaps
In all their private functions, once combined,
Become a loathsome body, only fit
For dissolution, hurtful to the main.
Hence merchants, unimpeachable of sin
Against the charities of domestic life,
Incorporated, seem at once to lose
Their nature, and disclaiming all regard
For mercy and the common rights of man,
Build factories with blood, conducting trade
At the sword's point, and dyeing the white robe
Of innocent commercial justice red.[1]

[1] The reference is to the East India Company: see pp. 706–07.

Hence too the field of glory, as the world
Misdeems it, dazzled by its bright array,
With all the majesty of its thund'ring pomp,
Enchanting music and immortal wreaths,
Is but a school where thoughtlessness is taught
On principle, where foppery atones
For folly, gallantry for ev'ry vice.
   But slighted as it is, and by the great
Abandon'd, and, which still I more regret,
Infected with the manners and the modes
It knew not once, the country wins me still.
I never fram'd a wish, or form'd a plan,
That flatter'd me with hopes of earthly bliss.
But there I laid the scene. There early stray'd
My fancy, 'ere yet liberty of choice
Had found me, or the hope of being free.
My very dreams were rural, rural too
The first-born efforts of my youthful muse
Sportive, and jingling her poetic bells
'Ere yet her ear was mistress of their pow'rs.
No bard could please me but whose lyre was tuned
To Nature's praises. Heroes and their feats
Fatigued me, never weary of the pipe
Of Tityrus, assembling as he sang
The rustic throng beneath his fav'rite beech.[1]
Then Milton had indeed a poet's charms.
New to my taste, his Paradise surpass'd
The struggling efforts of my boyish tongue
To speak its excellence; I danced for joy.
I marvel'd much that at so ripe an age
As twice sev'n years, her beauties had then first
Engag'd my wonder, and admiring still,
And still admiring, with regret supposed
The joy half lost because not sooner found.
Thee too enamour'd of the life I loved,
Pathetic in its praise, in its pursuit
Determined, and possessing it at last

[1] Virgil: *Eclogues*, i, 1-2.

With transports such as favor'd lovers feel,
I studied, prized, and wished that I had known
Ingenious Cowley! and though now reclaimed
By modern lights from an erroneous taste,
I cannot but lament thy splendid wit
Entangled in the cobwebs of the schools;
I still revere thee, courtly though retired,
Though stretch'd at ease in Chertsey's silent bow'rs,
Not unemploy'd, and finding rich amends
For a lost world in solitude and verse.
'Tis born with all. The love of Nature's works
Is an ingredient in the compound, man,
Infus'd at the creation of the kind.
And though th' Almighty Maker has throughout
Discriminated each from each, by strokes
And touches of his hand with so much art
Diversified, that two were never found
Twins at all points—yet this obtains in all,
That all discern a beauty in his works
And all can taste them. Minds that have been form'd
And tutor'd, with a relish more exact,
But none without some relish, none unmoved.
It is a flame that dies not even there
Where nothing feeds it. Neither business, crowds,
Nor habits of luxurious city-life,
Whatever else they smother of true worth
In human bosoms, quench it or abate.
The villas with which London stands begirt
Like a swarth Indian with his belt of beads,
Prove it. A breath of unadult'rate air,
The glimpse of a green pasture, how they cheer
The citizen, and brace his languid frame!
Ev'n in the stifling bosom of the town,
A garden, in which nothing thrives, has charms
That soothe the rich possessor; much consoled,
That here and there some sprigs of mournful mint,
Of nightshade or valerian grace the well
He cultivates. These serve him with a hint
That Nature lives, that sight-refreshing green

Is still the liv'ry she delights to wear,
Though sickly samples of th' exub'rant whole.
What are the casements lin'd with creeping herbs,
The prouder sashes fronted with a range
Of orange, myrtle, of the fragrant weed,
The Frenchman's darling?[1] are they not all proofs
That man immured in cities, still retains
His inborn inextinguishable thirst
Of rural scenes, compensating his loss
By supplemental shifts, the best he may?
The most unfurnished with the means of life,
And they that never pass their brick-wall bounds
To range the fields and treat their lungs with air,
Yet feel the burning instinct: over-head
Suspend their crazy boxes planted thick
And water'd duely. There the pitcher stands
A fragment, and the spoutless tea-pot there;
Sad witnesses how close-pent man regrets
The country, with what ardour he contrives
A peep at nature, when he can no more.

Hail therefore patroness of health and ease
And contemplation, heart-consoling joys
And harmless pleasures in the throng'd abode
Of multitudes unknown! hail rural life!
Address himself who will to the pursuit
Of honors or emolument or fame,
I shall not add myself to such a chace,
Thwart his attempts, or envy his success.
Some must be great. Great offices will have
Great talents. And God gives to ev'ry man
The virtue, temper, understanding, taste,
That lifts him into life, and lets him fall
Just in the niche he was ordain'd to fill.
To the deliv'rer of an injured land
He gives a tongue t' enlarge upon, an heart
To feel, and courage to redress her wrongs;
To monarchs dignity, to judges sense,

[1] Mignonette [C.].

To artists ingenuity and skill;
To me an unambitious mind, content
In the low vale of life, that early felt
A wish for ease and leisure, and 'ere long
Found here that leisure and that ease I wish'd.

BOOK V

ARGUMENT OF THE FIFTH BOOK.—*A frosty morning— The foddering of cattle— The woodman and his dog— The poultry— Whimsical effects of frost at a waterfall— The Empress of Russia's palace of ice— Amusements of monarchs— War one of them— Wars, whence— And whence monarchy— The evils of it— English and French loyalty contrasted— The Bastile and a prisoner there— Liberty the chief recommendation of this country— Modern patriotism questionable, and why— The perishable nature of the best human institutions— Spiritual liberty not perishable— The slavish state of man by nature— Deliver him Deist if you can— Grace must do it— The respective merits of patriots and martyrs stated— Their different treatment— Happy freedom of the man whom grace makes free— His relish of the works of God— Address to the Creator.*

'TIS morning; and the sun with ruddy orb
Ascending fires the horizon; while the clouds
That crowd away before the driving wind,
More ardent as the disk emerges more,
Resemble most some city in a blaze,
Seen through the leafless wood. His slanting ray
Slides ineffectual down the snowy vale,
And tinging all with his own rosy hue,
From ev'ry herb and ev'ry spiry blade
Stretches a length of shadow o'er the field.
Mine, spindling into longitude immense,
In spite of gravity and sage remark
That I myself am but a fleeting shade,
Provokes me to a smile. With eye askance
I view the muscular proportioned limb
Transformed to a lean shank. The shapeless pair

488

As they designed to mock me, at my side
Take step for step, and as I near approach
The cottage, walk along the plaister'd wall,
Prepost'rous sight! the legs without the man.
The verdure of the plain lies buried deep
Beneath the dazzling deluge, and the bents
And coarser grass upspearing o'er the rest,
Of late unsightly and unseen, now shine
Conspicuous, and in bright apparel clad
And fledged with icy feathers, nod superb.
The cattle mourn in corners where the fence
Screens them, and seem half petrified to sleep
In unrecumbent sadness. There they wait
Their wonted fodder, not like hung'ring man
Fretfull if unsupplied, but silent, meek,
And patient of the slow-paced swain's delay.
He from the stack carves out th' accustomed load,
Deep-plunging and again deep plunging oft
His broad keen knife into the solid mass.
Smooth as a wall the upright remnant stands,
With such undeviating and even force
He severs it away. No needless care,
Lest storms should overset the leaning pile
Deciduous, or its own unbalanced weight.
Forth goes the woodman leaving unconcerned
The cheerful haunts of man, to wield the axe
And drive the wedge in yonder forest drear,
From morn to eve his solitary task.
Shaggy, and lean, and shrew'd, with pointed ears
And tail cropp'd short, half lurcher and half cur
His dog attends him. Close behind his heel
Now creeps he slow, and now with many a frisk
Wide-scampering, snatches up the drifted snow
With iv'ry teeth, or ploughs it with his snout;
Then shakes his powder'd coat and barks for joy.
Heedless of all his pranks the sturdy churl
Moves right toward the mark. Nor stops for aught,
But now and then with pressure of his thumb
T' adjust the fragment charge of a short tube

That fumes beneath his nose. The trailing cloud
Streams far behind him, scenting all the air.
Now from the roost or from the neighb'ring pale,
Where diligent to catch the first faint gleam
Of smiling day, they gossip'd side by side,
Come trooping at the housewife's well-known call
The feather'd tribes domestic. Half on wing
And half on foot, they brush the fleecy flood
Conscious, and fearful of too deep a plunge.
The sparrows peep, and quit the shelt'ring eaves
To seize the fair occasion. Well they eye
The scatter'd grain, and thievishly resolved
T' escape th' impending famine, often scared
As oft return, a pert voracious kind.
Clean riddance quickly made, one only care
Remains to each, the search of sunny nook,
Or shed impervious to the blast. Resign'd
To sad necessity—the cock foregoes
His wonted strut, and wading at their head
With well-consider'd steps, seems to resent
His alter'd gait and stateliness retrenched.
How find the myriads that in summer cheer
The hills and vallies with their ceaseless songs
Due sustenance, or where subsist they now?
Earth yields them nought: the imprison'd worm is safe
Beneath the frozen cold; all seeds of herbs
Lie covered close, and berry-bearing thorns
That feed the thrush (whatever some suppose)
Afford the smaller minstrels no supply.
The long protracted rigor of the year
Thins all their num'rous flocks. In chinks and holes
Ten thousand seek an unmolested end
As instinct prompts, self buried 'ere they die.
The very rooks and daws forsake the fields,
Where neither grub nor root nor earth-nut now
Repays their labor more; and perch'd aloft
By the way-side, or stalking in the path,
Lean pensioners upon the trav'ller's track,
Pick up their nauseous dole, though sweet to them,

Of voided pulse or half digested grain.
The streams are lost amid the splendid blank
O'erwhelming all distinction. On the flood
Indurated and fixt the snowy weight
Lies undissolved; while silently beneath,
And unperceived, the current steals away.
Not so, where scornful of a check it leaps
The mill-dam, dashes on the restless wheel,
And wantons in the pebbly gulph below.
No frost can bind it there. Its utmost force
Can but arrest the light and smokey mist
That in its fall the liquid sheet throws wide.
And see where it has hung th' embroider'd banks
With forms so various, that no pow'rs of art,
The pencil or the pen, may trace the scene!
Here glitt'ring turrets rise, upbearing high
(Fantastic misarrangement) on the roof
Large growth of what may seem the sparkling trees
And shrubs of fairy land. The chrystal drops
That trickle down the branches, fast congeal'd
Shoot into pillars of pellucid length,
And prop the pile they but adorned before.
Here grotto within grotto safe defies
The sun-beam. There imboss'd and fretted wild,
The growing wonder takes a thousand shapes
Capricious, in which fancy seeks in vain
The likeness of some object seen before.
Thus nature works as if to mock at art,
And in defiance of her rival pow'rs;
By these fortuitous and random strokes
Performing such inimitable feats
As she with all her rules can never reach.
Less worthy of applause, though more admired,
Because a novelty, the work of man,
Imperial mistress of the fur-clad Russ!
Thy most magnificent and mighty freak,
The wonder of the North.[1] No forest fell

[1] The palace of ice built by the Tsarina Anna at St Petersburg in the winter of 1740.

When thou wouldst build: no quarry sent its stores
T' enrich thy walls. But thou didst hew the floods,
And make thy marble of the glassy wave.
In such a palace Aristæus[1] found
Cyrene, when he bore the plaintive tale
Of his lost bees to her maternal ear.
In such a palace poetry might place
The armoury of winter, where his troops,
The gloomy clouds find weapons, arrowy sleet,
Skin-piercing volley, blossom-bruising hail,
And snow that often blinds the trav'ller's course,
And wraps him in an unexpected tomb.
Silently as a dream the fabric rose.
No sound of hammer or of saw was there.[2]
Ice upon ice, the well-adjusted parts
Were soon conjoined, nor other cement ask'd
Than water interfused to make them one.
Lamps gracefully disposed and of all hues
Illumined ev'ry side. A wat'ry light
Gleamed through the clear transparency, that seemed
Another moon new risen, or meteor fall'n
From heav'n to earth, of lambent flame serene.
So stood the brittle prodigy, though smooth
And slipp'ry the materials, yet frost-bound
Firm as a rock. Nor wanted aught within
That royal residence might well befit,
For grandeur or for use. Long wavy wreaths
Of flow'rs that feared no enemy but warmth,
Blushed on the pannels. Mirrour needed none
Where all was vitreous, but in order due
Convivial table and commodious seat
(What seemed at least commodious seat) were there,
Sofa and couch and high-built throne august.
The same lubricity was found in all,
And all was moist to the warm touch, a scene

---

[1] Aristaeus, son of Apollo and Cyrene, was deprived of his bees for his involuntary part in the death of Eurydice. The 'plaintive tale' is given in Virgil: *Georgics*, iv, 317.

[2] 1 Kings, vi, 7.

Of evanescent glory, once a stream,
And soon to slide into a stream again.
Alas! 'twas but a mortifying stroke
Of undesigned severity, that glanced
(Made by a monarch) on her own estate,
On human grandeur and the courts of kings.
'Twas transient in its nature, as in show
'Twas durable. As worthless as it seemed
Intrinsically precious. To the foot
Treach'rous and false, it smiled and it was cold.
    Great princes have great playthings. Some have played
At hewing mountains into men, and some
At building human wonders mountain-high.[1]
Some have amused the dull, sad years of life,
Life spent in indolence, and therefore sad,
With schemes of monumental fame, and sought
By pyramids and mausolæan pomp,
Short-lived themselves, t' immortalize their bones.
Some seek diversion in the tented field,
And make the sorrows of mankind their sport.
But war's a game, which were their subjects wise,
Kings should not play at. Nations would do well
T' extort their truncheons from the puny hands
Of heroes, whose infirm and baby minds
Are gratified with mischief, and who spoil
Because men suffer it, their toy the world.
    When Babel was confounded,[2] and the great
Confed'racy of projectors wild and vain
Was split into diversity of tongues.
Then, as a shepherd separates his flock,
These to the upland, to the valley those,
God drave asunder and assigned their lot
To all the nations. Ample was the boon
He gave them, in its distribution fair
And equal, and he bade them dwell in peace.

---

[1] The allusion is probably to the story that the sculptor Dinocrates offered to cut Mount Athos into a figure of Alexander the Great.
[2] Genesis, xi, 3–9.

Peace was awhile their care. They plough'd and sow'd,
And reap'd their plenty without grudge or strife.
But violence can never longer sleep
Than human passions please. In ev'ry heart
Are sown the sparks that kindle fiery war,
Occasion needs but fan them, and they blaze.
Cain had already shed a brother's blood,
The deluge wash'd it out; but left unquenched
The seeds of murther in the breast of man.
Soon, by a righteous judgment, in the line
Of his descending progeny was found
The first artificer of death;[1] the shrew'd
Contriver who first sweated at the forge,
And forced the blunt and yet unblooded steel
To a keen edge, and made it bright for war.
Him Tubal named, the Vulcan of old times,
The sword and faulchion their inventor claim,
And the first smith was the first murd'rer's son.
His art survived the waters; and 'ere long,
When man was multiplied and spread abroad
In tribes and clans, and had begun to call
These meadows and that range of hills his own,
The tasted sweets of property begat
Desire of more; and industry in some
To improve and cultivate their just demesne,
Made others covet what they saw so fair.
Thus wars began on earth. These fought for spoil,
And those in self-defence. Savage at first
The onset, and irregular. At length
One eminent above the rest, for strength,
For stratagem or courage, or for all,
Was chosen leader. Him they served in war,
And him in peace for sake of warlike deeds
Rev'renced no less. Who could with him compare?
Or who so worthy to controul themselves
As he whose prowess had subdued their foes?
Thus war affording field for the display

[1] Tubal Cain: Genesis, iv, 22.

Of virtue, made one chief, whom times of peace,
Which have their exigencies too, and call
For skill in government, at length made king.
King was a name too proud for man to wear
With modesty and meekness, and the crown,
So dazzling in their eyes who set it on,
Was sure t' intoxicate the brows it bound.
It is the abject property of most,
That being parcel of the common mass,
And destitute of means to raise themselves,
They sink and settle lower than they need.
They know not what it is to feel within
A comprehensive faculty that grasps
Great purposes with ease, that turns and wields
Almost without an effort, plans too vast
For their conception, which they cannot move.
Conscious of impotence they soon grow drunk
With gazing, when they see an able man
Step forth to notice; and besotted thus
Build him a pedestal and say, stand there,
And be our admiration and our praise.
They roll themselves before him in the dust,
Then most deserving in their own account
When most extravagant in his applause,
As if exalting him they raised themselves.
Thus by degrees self-cheated of their sound
And sober judgment that he is but man,
They demi-deify and fume him so,
That in due season he forgets it too.
Inflated and astrut with self-conceit
He gulps the windy diet, and 'ere long,
Adopting their mistake, profoundly thinks
The world was made in vain if not for him.
Thenceforth they are his cattle. Drudges born
To bear his burthens, drawing in his gears[1]
And sweating in his service. His caprice
Becomes the soul that animates them all.

[1] *gears:* harness.

He deems a thousand or ten thousand lives
Spent in the purchase of renown for him
An easy reck'ning, and they think the same.
Thus kings were first invented, and thus kings
Were burnished into heroes, and became
The arbiters of this terraqueous swamp,
Storks among frogs, that have but croak'd and died.
Strange that such folly as lifts bloated man
To eminence fit only for a God,
Should ever drivel out of human lips
Ev'n in the cradled weakness of the world!
Still stranger much, that when at length mankind
Had reached the sinewy firmness of their youth,
And could discriminate and argue well
On subjects more mysterious, they were yet
Babes in the cause of freedom, and should fear
And quake before the Gods themselves had made.
But above measure strange, that neither proof
Of sad experience, nor examples set
By some whose patriot virtue has prevailed,
Can even now, when they are grown mature
In wisdom, and with philosophic deeps
Familiar, serve t' emancipate the rest!
Such dupes are men to custom, and so prone
To rev'rence what is ancient and can plead
A course of long observance for its use,
That even servitude the worst of ills,
Because deliver'd down from sire to son,
Is kept and guarded as a sacred thing.
But is it fit, or can it bear the shock
Of rational discussion, that a man
Compounded and made up like other men
Of elements tumultuous, in whom lust
And folly in as ample measure meet
As in the bosoms of the slaves he rules,
Should be a despot absolute, and boast
Himself the only freeman of his land?
Should when he pleases, and on whom he will
Wage war, with any or with no pretence

Of provocation giv'n or wrong sustained,
And force the beggarly last doit, by means
That his own humour dictates, from the clutch
Of poverty, that thus he may procure
His thousands weary of penurious life,
A splendid opportunity to die?
Say ye, who (with less prudence than of old
Jotham[1] ascribed to his assembled trees
In politic convention) put your trust
I' th' shadow of a bramble, and reclined
In fancied peace beneath his dang'rous branch,
Rejoice in him and celebrate his sway,
Where find ye passive fortitude? Whence springs
Your self-denying zeal that holds it good
To stroke the prickly grievance, and to hang
His thorns with streamers of continual praise?
We too are friends to loyalty. We love
The king who loves the law, respects his bounds
And reigns content within them. Him we serve
Freely and with delight, who leaves us free.
But recollecting still that he is man,
We trust him not too far. King, though he be,
And king in England too, he may be weak
And vain enough to be ambitious still,
May exercise amiss his proper pow'rs,
Or covet more than freemen chuse to grant:
Beyond that mark is treason. He is ours,
T' administer, to guard, t' adorn the state,
But not to warp or change it. We are his,
To serve him nobly in the common cause
True to the death, but not to be his slaves.[2]
Mark now the diff'rence, ye that boast your love
Of kings, between your loyalty and ours.
We love the man. The paultry pageant you.
We the chief patron of the Commonwealth;
You the regardless author of its woes.

---

[1] Judges, ix, 7–15.
[2] Cowper may have had Charles I in mind. See p. 587.

We for the sake of liberty, a king;
You chains and bondage for a tyrant's sake.
Our love is principle, and has its root
In reason, is judicious, manly, free.
Yours, a blind instinct, crouches to the rod,
And licks the foot that treads it in the dust.
Were king-ship as true treasure as it seems,
Sterling, and worthy of a wise man's wish,
I would not be a king to be beloved
Causeless, and daubed with undiscerning praise,
Where love is mere attachment to the throne,
Not to the man who fills it as he ought.

   Whose freedom is by suff'rance, and at will
Of a superior, he is never free.
Who lives and is not weary of a life
Exposed to manacles, deserves them well.
The state that strives for liberty, though foiled,
And forced t' abandon what she bravely sought,
Deserves at least applause for her attempt,
And pity for her loss. But that's a cause
Not often unsuccessful; pow'r usurp'd
Is weakness when oppos'd; conscious of wrong
'Tis pusillanimous and prone to flight.
But slaves that once conceive the glowing thought
Of freedom, in that hope itself possess
All that the contest calls for; spirit, strength,
The scorn of danger, and united hearts
The surest presage of the good they seek.[1]

   Then shame to manhood, and opprobrious more
To France, than all her losses and defeats
Old or of later date, by sea or land,
Her house of bondage worse than that of old
Which God avenged on Pharaoh—the Bastile.
Ye horrid tow'rs, th' abode of broken hearts,

[1] The author hopes that he shall not be censured for unnecessary warmth upon so interesting a subject. He is aware that it is become almost fashionable to stigmatize such sentiments as no better than empty declamation; but it is an ill symptom, and peculiar to modern times [C].

Ye dungeons and ye cages of despair,
That monarchs have supplied from age to age
With music such as suits their sov'reign ears,
The sighs and groans of miserable men!
There's not an English heart that would not leap
To hear that ye were fall'n at last, to know
That ev'n our enemies, so oft employed
In forging chains for us, themselves were free.
For he that values liberty confines
His zeal for her predominance within
No narrow bounds; her cause engages him
Wherever pleaded. 'Tis the cause of man.
There dwell the most forlorn of human kind,
Immured though unaccused, condemn'd untried,
Cruelly spared, and hopeless of escape.
There like the visionary emblem seen
By him[1] of Babylon, life stands a stump,
And filletted about with hoops of brass,
Still lives, though all its pleasant boughs are gone.
To count the hour-bell and expect no change;
And ever as the sullen sound is heard,
Still to reflect that though a joyless note
To him whose moments all have one dull pace,
Ten thousand rovers in the world at large
Account it music; that it summons some
To theatre or jocund feast or ball;
The wearied hireling finds it a release
From labor, and the lover that has chid
Its long delay, feels ev'ry welcome stroke
Upon his heart-strings trembling with delight—
To fly for refuge from distracting thought
To such amusements as ingenious woe
Contrives, hard-shifting and without her tools—
To read engraven on the mouldy walls
In stagg'ring types, his predecessor's tale,
A sad memorial, and subjoin his own—
To turn purveyor to an overgorged

---

[1] Nebuchadnezzar's dream: Daniel, iv, 10–18.

And bloated spider, till the pamper'd pest
Is made familiar, watches his approach,
Comes at his call, and serves him for a friend—
To wear out time in numb'ring to and fro
The studs that thick emboss his iron door,
Then downward and then upward, then aslant
And then alternate, with a sickly hope
By dint of change to give his tasteless task
Some relish, till the sum exactly found
In all directions, he begins again—
Oh comfortless existence! hemm'd around
With woes, which who that suffers, would not kneel
And beg for exile, or the pangs of death?
That man should thus encroach on fellow man,
Abridge him of his just and native rights,
Eradicate him, tear him from his hold
Upon th' endearments of domestic life
And social, nip his fruitfulness and use,
And doom him for perhaps an heedless word
To barrenness and solitude and tears,
Moves indignation. Makes the name of king,
(Of king whom such prerogative can please)
As dreadful as the Manichean god,
Adored through fear, strong only to destroy.
    'Tis liberty alone that gives the flow'r
Of fleeting life its lustre and perfume,
And we are weeds without it. All constraint,
Except what wisdom lays on evil men,
Is evil; hurts the faculties, impedes
Their progress in the road of science; blinds
The eyesight of discov'ry, and begets,
In those that suffer it, a sordid mind
Bestial, a meagre intellect, unfit
To be the tenant of man's noble form.
Thee therefore still, blame-worthy as thou art,
With all thy loss of empire, and though squeezed
By public exigence 'till annual food
Fails for the craving hunger of the state,
Thee I account still happy, and the chief

Among the nations, seeing thou art free!
My native nook of earth! Thy clime is rude,
Replete with vapours, and disposes much
All hearts to sadness, and none more than mine;
Thine unadult'rate manners are less soft
And plausible than social life requires,
And thou hast need of discipline and art
To give thee what politer France receives
From Nature's bounty—that humane address
And sweetness, without which no pleasure is
In converse, either starved by cold reserve,
Or flush'd with fierce dispute, a senseless brawl;
Yet being free, I love thee. For the sake
Of that one feature, can be well content,
Disgraced as thou hast been, poor as thou art,
To seek no sublunary rest beside.
But once enslaved, farewell! I could endure
Chains nowhere patiently, and chains at home
Where I am free by birthright, not at all.
Then what were left of roughness in the grain
Of British natures, wanting its excuse
That it belongs to freemen, would disgust
And shock me. I should then with double pain
Feel all the rigor of thy fickle clime,
And if I must bewail the blessing lost,
For which our Hampdens[1] and our Sidneys bled,
I would at least bewail it under skies
Milder, among a people less austere,
In scenes which having never known me free,
Would not reproach me with the loss I felt.
Do I forebode impossible events,
And tremble at vain dreams? Heav'n grant I may!
But th' age of virtuous politics is past,

[1] The allusion may be to the great John Hampden (1594–1643), who inspired resistance to the arbitary rule of Charles I or to John Hampden the younger (c. 1656–96), or to both. It is logical to couple the latter with Algernon Sidney (1620–96); both were leaders of the opposition to Charles II, and were arrested for alleged complicity in the 'Rye House plot' to assassinate the king and his brother. Sidney was executed.

And we are deep in that of cold pretence.
Patriots are grown too shrewd to be sincere,
And we too wise to trust them. He that takes
Deep in his soft credulity the stamp
Designed by loud declaimers on the part
Of liberty, themselves the slaves of lust,
Incurs derision for his easy faith
And lack of knowledge, and with cause enough.
For when was public virtue to be found
Where private was not? can he love the whole
Who loves no part? He be a nation's friend,
Who is, in truth, the friend of no man there?
Can he be strenuous in his country's cause
Who slights the charities for whose dear sake
That country, if at all, must be beloved?
   'Tis therefore, sober and good men are sad
For England's glory, seeing it wax pale
And sickly, while her champions wear their hearts
So loose to private duty, that no brain
Healthful and undisturbed by factious fumes,
Can dream them trusty to the gen'ral weal.
Such were not they of old, whose temper'd blades
Dispersed the shackles of usurp'd controul,
And hew'd them link from link. Then Albion's sons
Were sons indeed. They felt a filial heart
Beat high within them at a mother's wrongs,
And shining each in his domestic sphere,
Shone brighter still once call'd to public view.
'Tis therefore, many whose sequester'd lot
Forbids their interference, looking on
Anticipate perforce some dire event;
And seeing the old castle of the state,
That promised once more firmness, so assail'd
That all its tempest-beaten turrets shake,
Stand motionless expectants of its fall.
All has its date below. The fatal hour
Was register'd in heav'n 'ere time began.
We turn to dust, and all our mightiest works
Die too. The deep foundations that we lay,

Time ploughs them up, and not a trace remains.
We build with what we deem eternal rock,
A distant age asks where the fabric stood,
And in the dust sifted and search'd in vain,
The undiscoverable secret sleeps.
　　But there is yet a liberty unsung
By poets, and by senators unpraised,
Which monarchs cannot grant, nor all the powers
Of earth and hell confed'rate take away
A liberty, which persecution, fraud,
Oppression, prisons, have no power to bind,
Which whoso tastes can be enslaved no more.
'Tis liberty of heart, derived from heav'n,
Bought with HIS blood who gave it to mankind,
And seal'd with the same token. It is held
By charter, and that charter sanction'd sure
By th' unimpeachable and awful oath
And promise of a God. His other gifts
All bear the royal stamp that speaks them his,
And are august, but this transcends them all.
His other works, this visible display
Of all-creating energy and might,
Are grand no doubt, and worthy of the word
That, finding an interminable space
Unoccupied, has filled the void so well,
And made so sparkling what was dark before.[1]
But these are not his glory. Man, 'tis true,
Smit with the beauty of so fair a scene,
Might well suppose th' artificer divine
Meant it eternal, had he not himself
Pronounced it transient, glorious as it is,
And still designing a more glorious far,
Doom'd it, as insufficient for his praise.[2]
These therefore are occasional and pass.
Form'd for the confrontation of the fool
Whose lying heart disputes against a God,

[1] John, i, 1-5.
[2] Cf. 2 Peter, iii, 10-13.

That office served, they must be swept away.
Not so the labours of his love. They shine
In other heav'ns than these that we behold,
And fade not. There is paradise that fears
No forfeiture, and of its fruits he sends
Large prelibation off to saints below.
Of these the first in order, and the pledge
And confident assurance of the rest,
Is liberty. A flight into his arms
'Ere yet mortality's fine threads give way,
A clear escape from tyrannizing lust,
And full immunity from penal woe.

   Chains are the portion of revolted man,
Stripes and a dungeon; and his body serves
The triple purpose. In that sickly, foul,
Opprobrious residence, he finds them all.
Propense his heart to idols, he is held
In silly dotage on created things
Careless of their Creator. And that low
And sordid gravitation of his pow'rs
To a vile clod, so draws him, with such force
Resistless from the center he should seek,
That he at last forgets it. All his hopes
Tend downward, his ambition is to sink,
To reach a depth profounder still, and still
Profounder, in the fathomless abyss
Of folly, plunging in pursuit of death.
But 'ere he gain the comfortless repose
He seeks, an acquiescence of his soul
In heav'n-renouncing exile, he endures—
What does he not? from lusts oppos'd in vain,
And self-reproaching conscience. He foresees
The fatal issue to his health, fame, peace,
Fortune and dignity; the loss of all
That can ennoble man, and make frail life
Short as it is, supportable. Still worse,
Far worse than all the plagues with which his sins
Infect his happiest moments, he forebodes
Ages of hopeless misery. Future death,

And death still future. Not an hasty stroke
Like that which sends him to the dusty grave,
But unrepealable enduring death.
Scripture is still a trumpet to his fears;
What none can prove a forg'ry, may be true,
What none but bad men wish exploded, must.
That scruple checks him. Riot is not loud
Nor drunk enough to drown it. In the midst
Of laughter his compunctions are sincere,
And he abhors the jest by which he shines.
Remorse begets reform. His master-lust
Falls first before his resolute rebuke,
And seems dethroned and vanquish'd. Peace ensues,
But spurious and short-liv'd, the puny child
Of self-congratulating pride, begot
On fancied Innocence. Again he falls,
And fights again; but finds his best essay
A presage ominous, portending still
Its own dishonor by a worse relapse.
Till Nature, unavailing Nature foiled
So oft, and wearied in the vain attempt,
Scoffs at her own performance. Reason now
Takes part with appetite, and pleads the cause,
Perversely, which of late she so condemn'd;
With shallow shifts and old devices, worn
And tatter'd in the service of debauch,
Cov'ring his shame from his offended sight.
    'Hath God indeed giv'n appetites to man,
'And stored the earth so plenteously with means
'To gratify the hunger of his wish,
'And doth he reprobate and will he damn
'The use of his own bounty? making first
'So frail a kind, and then enacting laws
'So strict, that less than perfect must despair?
'Falsehood! which whoso but suspects of truth,
'Dishonors God, and makes a slave of man.
'Do they themselves, who undertake for hire
'The teacher's office, and dispense at large
'Their weekly dole of edifying strains

'Attend to their own music? have they faith
'In what with such solemnity of tone
'And gesture they propound to our belief?
'Nay—conduct hath the loudest tongue. The voice
'Is but an instrument on which the priest
'May play what tune he pleases. In the deed,
'The unequivocal authentic deed,
'We find sound argument, we read the heart.'
   Such reas'nings (if that name must needs belong
T' excuses in which reason has no part)
Serve to compose a spirit well inclined
To live on terms of amity with vice,
And sin without disturbance. Often urged
(As often as libidinous discourse
Exhausted, he resorts to solemn themes
Of theological and grave import)
They gain at last his unreserved assent.
Till harden'd his heart's temper in the forge
Of lust, and on the anvil of despair,
He slights the strokes of conscience. Nothing moves,
Or nothing much, his constancy in ill,
Vain tamp'ring has but foster'd his disease,
'Tis desp'rate, and he sleeps the sleep of death.
Haste now, philosopher, and set him free.
Charm the deaf serpent[1] wisely. Make him hear
Of rectitude and fitness; moral truth
How lovely, and the moral sense how sure,
Consulted and obey'd, to guide his steps
Directly to the FIRST AND ONLY FAIR.[2]
Spare not in such a cause. Spend all the pow'rs

---

[1] 'The wicked ... go astray as soon as they be born, speaking lies. Their poison is like the poison of a serpent; they are like the deaf adder that stoppeth her ear, which will not hearken to the voice of charmers, charming never so wisely'. Psalm lviii, 3–5.

[2] Cf. Pope, *Essay on Man*, Epistle ii, 23 :

      'Go, soar with Plato to the empyreal sphere,
       To the first Good, first Perfect, and first Fair.'

i.e., to God, according to C., or to Plato's archetypal Ideas, according to Pope.

Of rant and rhapsody in virtue's praise,
Be most sublimely good, verbosely grand,
And with poetic trappings grace thy prose,
Till it out-mantle all the pride of verse. —
Ah, tinkling cymbal and high sounding brass,[1]
Smitten in vain! such music cannot charm
Th' eclipse that intercepts truth's heav'nly beam,
And chills and darkens a wide-wand'ring soul.
The *still small voice*[2] is wanted. He must speak
Whose word leaps forth at once to its effect,
Who calls for things that are not, and they come.
    Grace makes the slave a freeman. 'Tis a change
That turns to ridicule the turgid speech
And stately tone of moralists, who boast,
As if like him, of fabulous renown
They had indeed ability to smooth
The shag of savage nature, and were each
An Orpheus and omnipotent in song.
But transformation of apostate man
From fool to wise, from earthly to divine,
Is work for Him that made him. He alone,
And he by means in philosophic eyes
Trivial and worthy of disdain, atchieves
The wonder; humanizing what is brute
In the lost kind, extracting from the lips
Of asps their venom, overpow'ring strength
By weakness, and hostility by love.
    Patriots have toiled, and in their country's cause
Bled nobly, and their deeds, as they deserve,
Receive proud recompense. We give in charge
Their names to the sweet lyre. Th' historic muse,
Proud of the treasure, marches with it down
To latest times; and sculpture in her turn,
Gives bond in stone and ever-during brass
To guard them, and t' immortalize her trust.
But fairer wreaths are due, though never paid,
To those who, posted at the shrine of truth,

[1] 1 Corinthians, xiii, 1.
[2] 1 Kings, xix, 12.

Have fall'n in her defence. A patriot's blood,
Well spent in such a strife may earn indeed
And for a time insure to his loved land
The sweets of liberty and equal laws;
But martyrs struggle for a brighter prize,
And win it with more pain. Their blood is shed
In confirmation of the noblest claim,
Our claim to feed upon immortal truth,
To walk with God, to be divinely free,
To soar, and to anticipate the skies.
Yet few remember them. They lived unknown
Till persecution dragg'd them into fame
And chased them up to heav'n. Their ashes flew
—No marble tells us whither. With their names
No bard embalms and sanctifies his song,
And History, so warm on meaner themes,
Is cold on this. She execrates indeed
The tyranny that doom'd them to the fire,
But gives the glorious suff'rers little praise.[1]

He is a freeman whom the truth makes free,[2]
And all are slaves beside. There's not a chain
That hellish foes, confed'rate for his harm
Can wind around him, but he casts it off
With as much ease as Samson his green wyths.[3]
He looks abroad into the varied field
Of Nature, and though poor perhaps, compared
With those whose mansions glitter in his sight,
Calls the delightful scen'ry all his own.
His are the mountains, and the vallies his,
And the resplendent rivers. His t' enjoy
With a propriety that none can feel,[4]
But who with filial confidence inspired,
Can lift to heaven an unpresumptuous eye,
And smiling say—my father made them all.

[1] See Hume [C]. *History of Great Britain*, ch. xxxvii: 'The glory of martyrdom stimulates all the more furious zealots . . .'

[2] Cf. John, viii, 32.

[3] Judges, xvi, 7-9.

[4] *propriety*: sense of absolute possession.

Are they not his by a peculiar right,
And by an emphasis of int'rest his,
Whose eye they fill with tears of holy joy,
Whose heart with praise, and whose exalted mind
With worthy thoughts of that unwearied love
That plann'd, and built, and still upholds a world
So cloath'd with beauty, for rebellious man?
Yes—ye may fill your garners, ye that reap
The loaded soil, and ye may waste much good
In senseless riot; but ye will not find
In feast or in the chace, in song or dance
A liberty like his, who unimpeach'd
Of usurpation and to no man's wrong,
Appropriates nature as his father's work,
And has a richer use of yours, than you.
He is indeed a freeman. Free by birth
Of no mean city,[1] plann'd or 'ere the hills
Were built, the fountains open'd, or the sea
With all his roaring multitude of waves.[2]
His freedom is the same in ev'ry state,
And no condition of this changeful life,
So manifold in cares, whose ev'ry day
Brings its own evil with it, makes it less.
For he has wings that neither sickness, pain,
Nor penury, can cripple or confine.
No nook so narrow but he spreads them there
With ease, and is at large. Th' oppressor holds
His body bound, but knows not what a range
His spirit takes, unconscious of a chain;
And that to bind him is a vain attempt
Whom God delights in, and in whom he dwells.
   Acquaint thyself with God if thou would'st taste
His works. Admitted once to his embrace,
Thou shalt perceive that thou wast blind before:
Thine eye shalt be instructed, and thine heart
Made pure, shall relish, with divine delight
'Till then unfelt, what hands divine have wrought.

[1] Acts, xxi, 39.
[2] Proverbs, viii, 23-9.

Brutes graze the mountain-top with faces prone
And eyes intent upon the scanty herb
It yields them, or recumbent on its brow,
Ruminate heedless of the scene outspread
Beneath, beyond, and stretching far away
From inland regions to the distant main.
Man views it and admires, but rests content
With what he views. The landscape has his praise,
But not its author. Unconcern'd who form'd
The paradise he sees, he finds it such,
And such well-pleased to find it, asks no more.
Not so the mind that has been touch'd from heav'n,
And in the school of sacred wisdom taught
To read his wonders, in whose thought the world,
Fair as it is, existed ere it was.
Not for its own sake merely, but for his
Much more who fashioned it, he gives it praise;
Praise that from earth resulting as it ought,
To earth's acknowledg'd sov'reign, finds at once
Its only just proprietor in Him.
The soul that sees him, or receives sublimed
New faculties, or learns at least t' employ
More worthily the pow'rs she own'd before;
Discerns in all things, what with stupid gaze
Of ignorance, till then she overlook'd,
A ray of heav'nly light gilding all forms
Terrestrial, in the vast and the minute
The unambiguous footsteps of the God
Who gives its lustre to an insect's wing,
And wheels his throne upon the rolling worlds.
Much conversant with heav'n, she often holds
With those fair ministers of light to man,
That fill the skies nightly with silent pomp,
Sweet conference. Enquires what strains were they
With which heav'n rang, when ev'ry star, in haste
To gratulate the new-created earth,
Sent forth a voice, and all the sons of God[1]

[1] Job, xxxviii, 7.

Shouted for joy.— 'Tell me, ye shining hosts
'That navigate a sea that knows no storms,
'Beneath a vault unsullied with a cloud,
'If from your elevation, whence ye view
'Distinctly scenes invisible to man,
'And systems of whose birth no tidings yet
'Have reach'd this nether world, ye spy a race
'Favor'd as our's, transgressors from the womb
'And hasting to a grave, yet doom'd to rise,
'And to possess a brighter heav'n than yours?
'As one who long detain'd on foreign shores
'Pants to return, and when he sees afar
'His country's weather-bleach'd and batter'd rocks,
'From the green wave emerging, darts an eye
'Radiant with joy towards the happy land;
'So I with animated hopes behold,
'And many an aching wish, your beamy fires,
'That shew like beacons in the blue abyss
'Ordain'd to guide th' embodied spirit home
'From toilsome life to never-ending rest.
'Love kindles as I gaze. I feel desires
'That give assurance of their own success,
'And that infus'd from heav'n must thither tend.'
So reads he nature whom the lamp of truth
Illuminates. Thy lamp, mysterious word![1]
Which whoso sees, no longer wanders lost,
With intellects bemaz'd in endless doubt,[2]
But runs the road of wisdom. Thou hast built,
With means that were not 'till by thee employ'd,
Worlds that had never been had'st thou in strength
Been less, or less benevolent than strong.
They are thy witnesses, who speak thy pow'r
And goodness infinite, but speak in ears
That hear not, or receive not their report.
In vain thy creatures testify of thee

[1] Psalm cxix, 105.
[2] *Paradise Lost*, II, 555–61: '... And found no end, in wand'ring mazes lost.'

'Till thou proclaim thyself. Their's is indeed
A teaching voice; but 'tis the praise of thine
That whom it teaches it makes prompt to learn,
And with the boon gives talents for its use.
'Till thou art heard, imaginations vain
Possess the heart, and fables false as hell;
Yet deemed oracular, lure down to death
The uninform'd and heedless souls of men.
We give to chance, blind chance, ourselves as blind,
The glory of thy work, which yet appears
Perfect and unimpeachable of blame,
Challenging human scrutiny, and proved
Then skilful most when most severely judged.
But chance is not; or is not where thou reign'st:
Thy providence forbids that fickle pow'r
(If power she be that works but to confound)
To mix her wild vagaries with thy laws.
Yet thus we doat, refusing while we can
Instruction, and inventing to ourselves
Gods such as guilt makes welcome, Gods that sleep
Or disregard our follies, or that sit
Amused spectators of this bustling stage.
Thee we reject, unable to abide
Thy purity, 'till pure as thou art pure,
Made such by thee, we love thee for that cause
For which we shunn'd and hated thee before.
Then we are free. Then liberty like day,
Breaks on the soul, and by a flash from heav'n
Fires all the faculties with glorious joy.
A voice is heard that mortal ears hear not
Till thou hast touch'd them; 'tis the voice of song,
A loud Hosanna sent from all thy works,
Which he that hears it with a shout repeats,
And adds his rapture to the gen'ral praise.
In that blest moment, nature throwing wide
Her veil opaque, discloses with a smile
The author of her beauties, who retired
Behind his own creation, works unseen
By the impure, and hears his power denied.

Thou art the source and centre of all minds,
Their only point of rest, eternal word!
From thee departing, they are lost and rove
At random, without honor, hope, or peace.
From thee is all that sooths the life of man,
His high endeavour, and his glad success,
His strength to suffer and his will to serve.
But oh thou bounteous giver of all good,
Thou art of all thy gifts thyself the crown!
Give what thou can'st, without thee we are poor,
And with thee rich, take what thou wilt away.

BOOK VI

THE WINTER WALK AT NOON

Argument of the Sixth Book.—*Bells at a distance—Their effect—A fine noon in winter—A sheltered walk—Meditation better than books—Our familiarity with the course of nature makes it appear less wonderful than it is—The transformation that spring effects in a shrubbery described—A mistake concerning the course of nature corrected—God maintains it by an unremitted act—The amusements fashionable at this hour of the day reproved—Animals happy, a delightful sight—Origin of cruelty to animals—That it is a great crime proved from scripture—That proof illustrated by a tale—A line drawn between the lawful and unlawful destruction of them—Their good and useful properties insisted on—Apology for the encomiums bestowed by the author upon animals—Instances of man's extravagant praise of man—The groans of the creation shall have an end—A view taken of the restoration of all things—An Invocation and an Invitation of him who shall bring it to pass—The retired man vindicated from the charge of uselessness—Conclusion.*

There is in souls a sympathy with sounds,
And as the mind is pitch'd the ear is pleas'd
With melting airs or martial, brisk or grave.
Some chord in unison with what we hear
Is touched within us, and the heart replies.
How soft the music of those village bells
Falling at intervals upon the ear
In cadence sweet! now dying all away,
Now pealing loud again and louder still,

Clear and sonorous as the gale comes on.
With easy force it opens all the cells
Where mem'ry slept. Wherever I have heard
A kindred melody, the scene recurs,
And with it all its pleasures and its pains.
Such comprehensive views the spirit takes,
That in a few short moments I retrace
(As in a map the voyager his course)
The windings of my way through many years.
Short as in retrospect the journey seems,
It seem'd not always short; the rugged path
And prospect oft so dreary and forlorn,
Moved many a sigh at its disheart'ning length.
Yet feeling present evils, while the past
Faintly impress the mind, or not at all,
How readily we wish time spent revoked,
That we might try the ground again, where once
(Through inexperience as we now perceive)
We miss'd that happiness we might have found.
Some friend is gone, perhaps his son's best friend
A father, whose authority, in show
When most severe, and must'ring all its force,
Was but the graver countenance of love.
Whose favour, like the clouds of spring, might low'r,
And utter now and then an awful voice,
But had a blessing in its darkest frown,
Threat'ning at once and nourishing the plant.
We loved, but not enough, the gentle hand
That reared us. At a thoughtless age allured
By ev'ry gilded folly, we renounced
His shelt'ring side, and wilfully forewent
That converse which we now in vain regret.
How gladly would the man recall to life
The boy's neglected sire! a mother too,
That softer friend, perhaps more gladly still,
Might he demand them at the gates of death.
Sorrow has since they went subdued and tamed
The playful humour; he could now endure,
(Himself grown sober in the vale of tears)

And feel a parent's presence no restraint.
But not to understand a treasure's worth
'Till time has stol'n away the slighted good,
Is cause of half the poverty we feel,
And makes the world the wilderness it is.
The few that pray at all pray oft amiss,
And seeking grace t' improve the prize they hold,
Would urge a wiser suit than asking more.
   The night was winter in his roughest mood,
The morning sharp and clear. But now at noon
Upon the southern side of the slant hills,
And where the woods fence off the northern blast,
The season smiles resigning all its rage
And has the warmth of May. The vault is blue
Without a cloud, and white without a speck
The dazzling splendour of the scene below.
Again the harmony comes o'er the vale,
And through the trees I view th' embattled tow'r[1]
Whence all the music. I again perceive
The soothing influence of the wafted strains,
And settle in soft musings as I tread
The walk still verdant under oaks and elms
Whose outspread branches overarch the glade.
The roof though moveable through all its length
As the wind sways it, has yet well sufficed,
And intercepting in their silent fall
The frequent flakes, has kept a path for me.
No noise is here, or none that hinders thought.
The red-breast warbles still, but is content
With slender notes and more than half suppress'd.
Pleased with his solitude, and flitting light
From spray to spray, where'er he rests he shakes
From many a twig the pendent drops of ice,
That twinkle in the wither'd leaves below.
Stillness accompanied with sounds so soft
Charms more than silence. Meditation here
May think down hours to moments. Here the heart

[1] Emberton church.

May give an useful lesson to the head,
And learning wiser grow without his books.
Knowledge and wisdom, far from being one,
Have oft times no connexion. Knowledge dwells
In heads replete with thoughts of other men,
Wisdom in minds attentive to their own.
Knowledge, a rude unprofitable mass,
The mere materials with which wisdom builds,
'Till smooth'd and squared and fitted to its place
Does but incumber whom it seems t' enrich.
Knowledge is proud that he has learn'd so much,
Wisdom is humble that he knows no more.
Books are not seldom talismans and spells
By which the magic art of shrewder wits
Holds an unthinkable multitude enthrall'd.
Some to the fascination of a name
Surrender judgment hood-wink'd. Some the stile
Infatuates, and through labyrinths and wilds
Of error, leads them by a tune entranced.
While sloth seduces more, too weak to bear
The insupportable fatigue of thought,
And swallowing therefore without pause or choice
The total grist unsifted, husks and all.
But trees, and rivulets whose rapid course
Defies the check of winter, haunts of deer,
And sheep-walks populous with bleating lambs,
And lanes in which the primrose 'ere her time
Peeps through the moss that cloaths the hawthorn root,
Deceive no student. Wisdom there, and truth,
Not shy as in the world, and to be won
By slow solicitation, seize at once
The roving thought, and fix it on themselves.
    What prodigies can pow'r divine perform
More grand, than it produces year by year,
And all in sight of inattentive man?
Familiar with th' effect we slight the cause,
And in the constancy of nature's course,
The regular return of genial months,
And renovation of a faded world,

See nought to wonder at. Should God again,
As once in Gibeon,[1] interrupt the race
Of the undeviating and punctual sun,
How would the world admire! but speaks it less
An agency divine, to make him know
His moment when to sink and when to rise
Age after age, than to arrest his course?
All we behold is miracle, but seen
So duly, all is miracle in vain.
Where now the vital energy that moved,
While summer was, the pure and subtle lymph
Through th' imperceptible mæand'ring veins
Of leaf and flow'r? It sleeps; and the icy touch
Of unprolific winter has impress'd
A cold stagnation on th' intestine tide.
But let the months go round, a few short months,
And all shall be restored. These naked shoots
Barren as lances, among which the wind
Makes wintry music, sighing as it goes,
Shall put their graceful foliage on again,
And more aspiring and with ampler spread,
Shall boast new charms, and more than they have lost.
Then, each in its peculiar honors clad,
Shall publish even to the distant eye
Its family and tribe. Laburnum rich
In streaming gold; syringa iv'ry-pure;
The scented and the scentless rose; this red
And of an humbler growth, the other tall,[2]
And throwing up into the darkest gloom
Of neighb'ring cypress or more sable yew
Her silver globes, light as the foamy surf
That the wind severs from the broken wave.
The lilac various in array, now white,
Now sanguine, and her beauteous head now set
With purple spikes pyramidal, as if
Studious of ornament, yet unresolved

[1] Joshua, x, 12–13.
[2] The Guelder-rose [C].

Which hue she most approved, she chose them all.
Copious of flow'rs the woodbine, pale and wan,
But well compensating their sickly looks
With never-cloying odours, early and late.
Hypericum[1] all bloom, so thick a swarm
Of flow'rs like flies cloathing her slender rods
That scarce a leaf appears. Mezerion[2] too
Though leafless well attired, and thick beset
With blushing wreaths investing ev'ry spray.
Althæa[3] with the purple eye, the broom,
Yellow and bright, as bullion unalloy'd
Her blossoms, and luxuriant above all
The jasmine, throwing wide her elegant sweets,
The deep dark green of whose unvarnish'd leaf
Makes more conspicuous, and illumines more
The bright profusion of her scatter'd stars.—
These have been, and these shall be in their day.
And all this uniform uncoloured scene
Shall be dismantled of its fleecy load,
And flush into variety again.
From dearth to plenty, and from death to life,
Is Nature's progress when she lectures man
In heav'nly truth; evincing as she makes
The grand transition, that there lives and works
A soul in all things, and that soul is God.
The beauties of the wilderness are his,
That make so gay the solitary place
Where no eye sees them. And the fairer forms
That cultivation glories in, are his.
He sets the bright procession on its way,
And marshals all the order of the year.
He marks the bounds which winter may not pass,
And blunts his pointed fury. In its case
Russet and rude, folds up the tender germ
Uninjured, with inimitable art,

[1] *Hypericum perforatum*, the common St John's wort. *Bruce.*
[2] Spurge laurel. *Benham.*
[3] The marsh-mallow. *Benham.*

And, ere one flow'ry season fades and dies
Designs the blooming wonders of the next.
  Some say that in the origin of things
When all creation started into birth,
The infant elements received a law
From which they swerve not since. That under force
Of that controuling ordinance they move,
And need not his immediate hand, who first
Prescribed their course, to regulate it now.
Thus dream they, and contrive to save a God
The incumbrance of his own concerns, and spare
The great Artificer of all that moves
The stress of a continual act, the pain
Of unremitted vigilance and care,
As too laborious and severe a task.
So man the moth is not afraid, it seems,
To span Omnipotence, and measure might
That knows no measure, by the scanty rule
And standard of his own, that is today,
And is not, ere to-morrow's sun go down.
But how should matter occupy a charge
Dull as it is, and satisfy a law
So vast in its demands, unless impell'd
To ceaseless service by a ceaseless force,
And under pressure of some conscious cause?
The Lord of all, himself through all diffused,
Sustains and is the life of all that lives.
Nature is but a name for an effect
Whose cause is God. He feeds the secret fire
By which the mighty process is maintain'd,
Who sleeps not, is not weary; in whose sight
Slow-circling ages are as transient days;[1]
Whose work is without labor, whose designs
No flaw deforms, no difficulty thwarts,
And whose beneficence no charge exhausts.

---

[1] Cf. Isaac Watts: *O God, our help in ages past:*
          'A thousand ages in thy sight
          Are like an Evening gone.'

Him blind antiquity profaned, not serv'd,
With self-taught rites and under various names
Female and male, Pomona,[1] Pales,[1] Pan
And Flora and Vertumnus,[1] peopling earth
With tutelary goddesses and gods
That were not, and commending as they would
To each some province, garden, field, or grove.
But all are under one. One spirit—His
Who wore the platted thorns with bleeding brows,
Rules universal nature. Not a flow'r
But shows some touch in freckle, streak or stain,
Of his unrivall'd pencil. He inspires
Their balmy odors and imparts their hues,
And bathes their eyes with nectar, and includes
In grains as countless as the sea-side sands,
The forms with which he sprinkles all the earth.
Happy who walks with him! whom what he finds
Of flavour or of scent in fruit or flow'r,
Or what he views of beautiful or grand
In Nature, from the broad majestic oak
To the green blade that twinkles in the sun,
Prompts with remembrance of a present God.
His presence, who made all so fair, perceived,
Makes all still fairer. As with him no scene
Is dreary, so with him all seasons please.[2]
Though winter had been none, had man been true,
And earth be punished for its tenant's sake,
Yet not in vengeance; as this smiling sky,
So soon succeeding such an angry night,
And these dissolving snows, and this clear stream
Recov'ring fast its liquid music, prove.

Who then that has a mind well strung and tuned
To contemplation, and within his reach
A scene so friendly to his fav'rite task,

---

[1] *Pomona:* the goddess of fruits and gardens.
Pales: the goddess of flocks and shepherds.
Vertumnus: god of the seasons.
[2] *Paradise Lost*, iv, 637.

Would waste attention at the chequer'd board,
His host of wooden warriors to and fro
Marching and counter-marching, with an eye
As fixt as marble, with a forehead ridged
And furrow'd into storms, and with a hand
Trembling, as if eternity were hung
In balance on his conduct of a pin?
Nor envies he aught more their idle sport
Who pant with application misapplied
To trivial toys, and pushing iv'ry balls
Across a velvet level, feel a joy
Akin to rapture, when the bawble finds
Its destin'd goal of difficult access.
Nor deems he wiser him, who gives his noon
To Miss, the Mercer's plague, from shop to shop
Wand'ring, and litt'ring with unfolded silks
The polished counter, and approving none,
Or promising with smiles to call again.
Nor him, who by his vanity seduced,
And sooth'd into a dream that he discerns
The difference of a Guido from a daub,
Frequents the crowded auction. Station'd there
As duly as the Langford[1] of the show,
With glass at eye, and catalogue in hand,
And tongue accomplish'd in the fulsome cant
And pedantry that coxcombs learn with ease,
Oft as the price-deciding hammer falls
He notes it in his book, then raps his box
Swears 'tis a bargain, rails at his hard fate
That he has let it pass — but never bids.

　Here unmolested, through whatever sign
The sun proceeds, I wander. Neither mist,
Nor freezing sky, nor sultry, checking me,
Nor stranger intermeddling with my joy.[2]
Ev'n in the spring and play-time of the year,

[1] Abraham Langford of Covent Garden, the most famous auctioneer of the age.
[2] Proverbs, xiv, 10.

That calls the unwonted villager abroad
With all her little ones, a sportive train,
To gather king-cups in the yellow mead,
And prink their hair with daisies, or to pick
A cheap but wholesome sallad from the brook,
These shades are all my own. The tim'rous hare,
Grown so familiar with her frequent guest,
Scarce shuns me; and the stock-dove unalarm'd,
Sits cooing in the pine-tree, nor suspends
His long love-ditty for my near approach.
Drawn from his refuge in some lonely elm
That age or injury has hollow'd deep,
Where on his bed of wool and matted leaves
He has outslept the winter, ventures forth
To frisk awhile, and bask in the warm sun,
The squirrel, flippant, pert, and full of play.
He sees me, and at once, swift as a bird
Ascends the neighb'ring beech; there whisks his brush
And perks his ears, and stamps and scolds aloud,
With all the prettiness of feign'd alarm,
And anger insignificantly fierce.
    The heart is hard in nature, and unfit
For human fellowship, as being void
Of sympathy, and therefore dead alike
To love and friendship both, that is not pleased
With sight of animals enjoying life,
Nor feels their happiness augment his own.
The bounding fawn that darts across the glade
When none pursues, through mere delight of heart,
And spirits buoyant with excess of glee;
The horse, as wanton and almost as fleet,
That skims the spacious meadow at full speed,
Then stops and snorts, and throwing high his heels
Starts to the voluntary race again;
The very kine that gambol at high noon,
The total herd receiving first from one
That leads the dance, a summons to be gay,
Though wild their strange vagaries, and uncouth
Their efforts, yet resolved with one consent

To give such act and utt'rance as they may
To extasy too big to be suppress'd—
These, and a thousand images of bliss,
With which kind nature graces ev'ry scene
Where cruel man defeats not her design,
Impart to the benevolent, who wish
All that are capable of pleasure, pleased,
A far superior happiness to theirs,
The comfort of a reasonable joy.
   Man scarce had ris'n, obedient to his call
Who form'd him, from the dust his future grave,
When he was crown'd as never king was since.
God set the diadem upon his head,
And angel choirs attended. Wond'ring stood
The new-made monarch, while before him pass'd,
All happy, and all perfect in their kind
The creatures, summon'd from their various haunts
To see their sov'reign, and confess his sway.
Vast was his empire, absolute his pow'r,
Or bounded only by a law whose force
'Twas his sublimest privilege to feel
And own: the law of universal love.
He rul'd with meekness, they obey'd with joy.
No cruel purpose lurk'd within his heart,
And no distrust of his intent in theirs.
So Eden was a scene of harmless sport,
Where kindness on his part who ruled the whole
Begat a tranquil confidence in all,
And fear as yet was not, nor cause for fear.
But sin marr'd all. And the revolt of man,
That source of evils not exhausted yet.
Was punish'd with revolt of his from him.
Garden of God, how terrible the change
Thy groves and lawns then witness'd! ev'ry heart,
Each animal of ev'ry name, conceived
A jealousy and an instinctive fear,
And conscious of some danger, either fled
Precipitate the loath'd abode of man,
Or growl'd defiance in such angry sort,

As taught him too to tremble in his turn.
Thus harmony and family accord
Were driv'n from Paradise; and in that hour
The seeds of cruelty that since have swell'd
To such gigantic and enormous growth,
Were sown in human nature's fruitful soil.
Hence date the persecution and the pain
That man inflicts on all inferior kinds,
Regardless of the plaints. To make him sport,
To gratify the frenzy of his wrath,
Or his base gluttony, are causes good
And just in his account, why bird and beast
Should suffer torture, and the streams be dyed
With blood of their inhabitants impaled.
Earth groans beneath the burthen of a war
Waged with defenceless innocence, while he,
Not satisfied to prey on all around,
Adds tenfold bitterness to death, by pangs
Needless, and first torments ere he devours.
Now happiest they that occupy the scenes
The most remote from his abhorr'd resort,
Whom once as delegate of God on earth,
They fear'd, and as his perfect image loved.
The wilderness is theirs with all its caves,
Its hollow glenns, its thickets, and its plains
Unvisited by man. There they are free,
And howl and roar as likes them, uncontroul'd,
Nor ask his leave to slumber or to play.
Woe to the tyrant if he dare intrude
Within the confines of their wild domain;
The lion tells him—I am monarch here—
And if he spare him, spares him on the terms
Of royal mercy, and through gen'rous scorn
To rend a victim trembling at his foot.
In measure as by force of instinct drawn,
Or by necessity constrain'd, they live
Dependent upon man, those in his fields,
These at his crib, and some beneath his roof.
They prove too often at how dear a rate

He sells protection. Witness, at his foot
The spaniel dying for some venial fault,
Under dissection of the knotted scourge.
Witness, the patient ox, with stripes and yells
Driv'n to the slaughter, goaded as he runs
To madness, while the savage at his heels
Laughs at the frantic suff'rer's fury spent
Upon the guiltless passenger o'erthrown.
He too is witness, noblest of the train
That wait on man, the flight-performing horse.
With unsuspecting readiness he takes
His murth'rer on his back, and push'd all day
With bleeding sides and flanks that heave for life
To the far-distant goal, arrives and dies.
So little mercy shows who needs so much!
Does law, so jealous in the cause of man,
Denounce no doom on the delinquent? None.
He lives, and o'er his brimming beaker boasts
(As if barbarity were high desert)
Th' inglorious feat, and clamorous in praise
Of the poor brute, seems wisely to suppose
The honors of his matchless horse his own.
But many a crime deem'd innocent on earth,
Is register'd in heav'n, and these no doubt,
Have each their record, with a curse annext.
Man may dismiss compassion from his heart,
But God will never. When he charged the Jew[1]
T' assist his foe's down-fallen beast to rise,
And when the bush-exploring boy that seized
The young, to let the parent bird go free,[2]
Proved he not plainly that his meaner works
Are yet his care, and have an int'rest all,
All, in the universal father's love?
On Noah, and in him on all mankind,
The charter[3] was conferr'd by which we hold

[1] Exodus, xxiii, 5.
[2] Deuteronomy, xxii, 4, 6, 7.
[3] Genesis, ix, 1–3.

The flesh of animals in fee, and claim
O'er all we feed on, pow'r of life and death.
But read the instrument, and mark it well.
Th' oppression of a tyrannous coutroul
Can find no warrant there. Feed then, and yield
Thanks for thy food. Carnivorous through sin
Feed on the slain, but spare the living brute.

The Governor of all, himself to all
So bountiful, in whose attentive ear
The unfledged raven and the lion's whelp[1]
Plead not in vain for pity on the pangs
Of hunger unassuaged, has interposed,
Not seldom, his avenging arm, to smite
Th' injurious trampler upon nature's law
That claims forbearance even for a brute.
He hates the hardness of a Balaam's heart;[2]
And prophet as he was, he might not strike
The blameless animal, without rebuke,
On which he rode. Her opportune offence
Saved him, or th' unrelenting seer had died.
He sees that human equity is slack
To interfere, though in so just a cause,
And makes the task his own. Inspiring dumb
And helpless victims with a sense so keen
Of injury, with such knowledge of their strength,
And such sagacity to take revenge,
That oft the beast has seemed to judge the man.
An ancient, not a legendary tale,
By one of sound intelligence rehears'd
(If such, who plead for Providence, may seem
In modern eyes) shall make the doctrine clear.

Where England stretch'd towards the setting sun
Narrow and long, o'erlooks the western wave,
Dwelt young Misagathus.[3] A scorner he
Of God and goodness, atheist in ostent,[4]

---

[1] Psalms, cxlvii, 9: civ, 21.

[2] Numbers, xxii, 21–24.

[3] Greek = 'hater of good'.

[4] *atheist in ostent:* a professed atheist.

Vicious in act, in temper savage-fierce.
He journey'd, and his chance was as he went,
To join a trav'ller of far diff'rent note
Evander,[1] famed for piety, for years
Deserving honor, but for wisdom more.
Fame had not left the venerable man
A stranger to the manners of the youth,
Whose face too was familiar to his view.
Their way was on the margin of the land,
O'er the green summit of the rocks whose base
Beats back the roaring surge, scarce heard so high.
The charity that warm'd his heart was moved
At sight of the man-monster. With a smile
Gentle, and affable, and full of grace,
As fearful of offending whom he wish'd
Much to persuade, he plied his ear with truths
Not harshly thunder'd forth or rudely press'd,
But like his purpose, gracious, kind, and sweet.
And dost thou dream, th' impenetrable man
Exclaim'd, that me, the lullabies of age
And fantasies of dotards such as thou
Can cheat, or move a moment's fear in me?
Mark now the proof I give thee, that the brave
Need no such aids as superstition lends
To steel their hearts against the dread of death.
He spoke, and to the precipice at hand
Push'd with a madman's fury. Fancy shrinks,
And the blood thrills and curdles, at the thought
Of such a gulph as he design'd his grave.
But though the felon on his back could dare
The dreadful leap, more rational his steed
Declined the death, and wheeling swiftly round
Or e'er his hoof had press'd the crumbling verge,
Baffled his rider, sav'd against his will.
The frenzy of the brain may be redress'd
By med'cine well applied, but without grace
The heart's insanity admits no cure.

[1] Greek = 'good man'.

Enraged the more by what might have reform'd
His horrible intent, again he sought
Destruction, with a zeal to be destroyed,
With sounding whip and rowels dyed in blood.
But still in vain. The providence that meant
A longer date to the far nobler beast,
Spar'd yet again th' ignobler for his sake.
And now, his prowess proved, and his sincere
Incurable obduracy evinced,
His rage grew cool; and pleased perhaps t' have earn'd
So cheaply the renown of that attempt,
With looks of some complacence he resumed
His road, deriding much the blank amaze
Of good Evander, still where he was left
Fixt motionless, and petrified with dread.
So on they fared; discourse on other themes
Ensuing, seem'd to obliterate the past,
And tamer far for so much fury shown,
(As is the course of rash and fiery men)
The rude companion smiled as if transform'd.
But 'twas a transient calm. A storm was near,
An unsuspected storm. His hour was come.
The impious challenger of pow'r divine
Was now to learn, that heav'n though slow to wrath,
Is never with impunity defied.
His horse, as he had caught his master's mood,
Snorting, and starting into sudden rage,
Unbidden, and not now to be controul'd,
Rush'd to the cliff, and, having reach'd it, stood.
At once the shock unseated him. He flew
Sheer o'er the craggy barrier, and immersed
Deep in the flood, found, when he sought it not,
The death he had deserved and died alone.
So God wrought double justice; made the fool
The victim of his own tremendous choice
And taught a brute the way to safe revenge.
     I would not enter on my list of friends
(Tho' grac'd with polish'd manners and fine sense
Yet wanting sensibility) the man

Who needlessly sets foot upon a worm.
An inadvertent step may crush the snail
That crawls at evening in the public path,
But he that has humanity, forewarned,
Will tread aside, and let the reptile live.
The creeping vermin, loathsome to the sight,
And charged perhaps with venom, that intrudes
A visitor unwelcome into scenes
Sacred to neatness and repose, th' alcove,
The chamber, or refectory, may die.
A necessary act incurs no blame.
Not so when held within their proper bounds,
And guiltless of offence, they range the air,
Or take their pastime in the spacious field.
There they are privileged. And he that hunts
Or harms them there, is guilty of a wrong,
Disturbs th' œconomy of nature's realm,
Who when she form'd, designed them an abode.
The sum is this: if man's convenience, health,
Or safety interfere, his rights and claims
Are paramount, and must extinguish theirs.
Else they are all— the meanest things that are,
As free to live, and to enjoy that life,
As God was free to form them at the first,
Who in his sov'reign wisdom made them all.
Ye therefore who love mercy, teach your sons
To love it too. The spring-time of our years
Is soon dishonour'd and defiled in most
By budding ills, that ask a prudent hand
To check them. But alas! none sooner shoots,
If unrestrain'd, into luxuriant growth,
Than cruelty, most dev'lish of them all.
Mercy to him that shows it, is the rule
And righteous limitation of its act
By which heav'n moves in pard'ning guilty man;
And he that shows none, being ripe in years,
And conscious of the outrage he commits,
Shall seek it, and not find it in his turn.
  Distinguish'd much by reason, and still more

By our capacity of grace divine,
From creatures that exist but for our sake,
Which having served us, perish, we are held
Accountable, and God, some future day,
Will reckon with us roundly for th' abuse
Of what he deems no mean or trivial trust.
Superior as we are, they yet depend
Not more on human help than we on theirs.
Their strength, or speed, or vigilance, were giv'n
In aid of our defects. In some are found
Such teachable and apprehensive parts,
That man's attainments in his own concerns
Match'd with th' expertness of the brutes in theirs,
Are oft-times vanquish'd and thrown far behind.
Some show that nice sagacity of smell,
And read with such discernment, in the port
And figure of the man, his secret aim,
That oft we owe our safety to a skill
We could not teach, and must despair to learn.
But learn we might, if not too proud to stoop
To quadrupede instructors, many a good
And useful quality, and virtue too,
Rarely exemplified among ourselves.
Attachment never to be wean'd, or changed
By any change of fortune, proof alike
Against unkindness, absence, and neglect;
Fidelity, that neither bribe nor threat
Can move or warp, and gratitude for small
And trivial favors, lasting as the life,
And glist'ning even in the dying eye.

    Man praises man. Desert in arts or arms
Wins public honor; and ten thousand sit
Patiently present at a sacred song,
Commemoration-mad; content to hear
(Oh wonderful effect of music's pow'r!)
Messiah's eulogy, for Handel's sake.
But less, methinks, than sacrilege might serve—
(For was it less? what heathen would have dared
To strip Jove's statue of his oaken wreath,

And hang it up in honor of a man?)
Much less might serve, when all that we design
Is but to gratify an itching ear,
And give the day to a musician's praise.[1]
Remember Handel? who that was not born
Deaf as the dead to harmony, forgets,
Or can, the more than Homer of his age?
Yes—we remember him. And while we praise
A talent so divine, remember too
That His most holy book from whom it came
Was never meant, was never used before,
To buckram out the mem'ry of a man.
But hush!—the muse perhaps is too severe,
And with a gravity beyond the size
And measure of th' offence, rebukes a deed
Less impious than absurd, and owing more
To want of judgment than to wrong design.
So in the chapel of old Ely House,[2]
When wand'ring Charles, who meant to be the third,
Had fled from William,[3] and the news was fresh,[4]
The simple clerk, but loyal, did announce,
And eke did rear right merrily, two staves,
Sung to the praise and glory of King George.
—Man praises man, and Garrick's mem'ry next,
When time hath somewhat mellow'd it, and made
The idol of our worship while he lived
The god of our idolatry once more,
Shall have its altar; and the world shall go

[1] The Handel Commemoration of June 1784 was the first of five held at Westminster Abbey. Dr Burney considered it to be the greatest aggregation of vocal and instrumental performers ever assembled: C. thought it a profanation of a sacred building and of sacred music.

[2] The inn or hostel of the Bishop of Ely in Holborn, demolished in 1775. The chapel survives as St Etheldreda's.

[3] William, Duke of Cumberland, (1721–65).

[4] The news of the battle of Culloden reached London on a Sunday morning. The clerk of Ely Chapel, his head full of the news, is said to have given out the Psalm with the formula 'Let us sing to the praise and glory of King George'.

In pilgrimage to bow before his shrine.
The theatre too small, shall suffocate
Its squeezed contents, and more than it admits
Shall sigh at their exclusion, and return
Ungratified. For there some noble lord
Shall stuff his shoulders with King Richard's bunch,
Or wrap himself in Hamlet's inky cloak,
And strut, and storm and straddle, stamp and stare,
To show the world how Garrick did not act.
For Garrick was a worshipper himself;
He drew the Liturgy, and framed the rites
And solemn ceremonial of the day,
And call'd the world to worship on the banks
Of Avon fam'd in song.[1] Ah pleasant proof
That piety has still in human hearts
Some place, a spark or two not yet extinct.
The mulb'ry-tree[2] was hung with blooming wreaths,
The mulb'ry-tree stood center of the dance,
The mulb'ry-tree was hymn'd with dulcet airs,
And from his touchwood trunk, the mulb'ry-tree
Supplied such relics as devotion holds
Still sacred, and preserves with pious care.
So 'twas an hallow'd time. Decorum reign'd,
And mirth without offence. No few return'd,
Doubtless much edified, and all refreshed.
—Man praises man. The rabble all alive,
From tippling benches, cellars, stalls, and styes,
Swarm in the streets. The statesman of the day,
A pompous and slow-moving pageant, comes.
Some shout him, and some hang upon his car
To gaze in's eyes and bless him. Maidens wave
Their 'kerchiefs, and old women weep for joy.
While others not so satisfied unhorse

[1] Garrick's Shakespeare Commemoration, held at Stratford in September 1769.

[2] The mulberry tree planted by Shakespeare in the garden of New Place was cut down by the Rev. Francis Gastrell, who demolished the house in 1759. Snuff boxes and other relics made from the tree were offered for sale at the Commemoration.

The gilded equipage, and turning loose
His steeds, usurp a place they well deserve.
Why? what has charm'd them? Hath he saved the state?
No. Doth he purpose its salvation? No.
Inchanting novelty, that moon at full,
That finds out ev'ry crevice of the head
That is not sound and perfect, hath in theirs
Wrought this disturbance. But the wane is near,
And his own cattle must suffice him soon.
Thus idly do we waste the breath of praise,
And dedicate a tribute, in its use
And just direction, sacred, to a thing
Doomed to the dust, or lodged already there.
Encomium in old time was poet's work.
But poets having lavishly long since
Exhausted all materials of the art,
The task now falls into the public hand.
And I, contented with an humble theme,
Have poured my stream of panegyric down
The vale of nature, where it creeps and winds
Among her lovely works, with a secure
And unambitious course, reflecting clear,
If not the virtues yet the worth of brutes.
And I am recompensed, and deem the toils
Of poetry not lost, if verse of mine
May stand between an animal and woe,
And teach one tyrant pity for his drudge.

  The groans of nature in this nether world
Which heav'n has heard for ages, have an end.
Foretold by prophets, and by poets sung
Whose fire was kindled at the prophet's lamp,
The time of rest, the promised sabbath comes.
Six thousand years of sorrow have well-nigh
Fulfilled their tardy and disastrous course
Over a sinful world. And what remains
Of this tempestuous state of human things,
Is merely as the working of a sea
Before a calm, that rocks itself to rest.
For he whose car the winds are, and the clouds

The dust that waits upon his sultry march,
When sin hath moved him, and his wrath is hot,
Shall visit earth in mercy; shall descend
Propitious, in his chariot paved with love,
And what his storms have blasted and defaced
For man's revolt, shall with a smile repair.

    Sweet is the harp of prophecy. Too sweet
Not to be wrong'd by a mere mortal touch;
Nor can the wonders it records be sung
To meaner music, and not suffer loss.
But when a poet, or when one like me,
Happy to rove among poetic flow'rs,
Though poor in skill to rear them, lights at last
On some fair theme, some theme divinely fair,
Such is the impulse and the spur he feels
To give it praise proportioned to its worth,
That not t' attempt it, arduous as he deems
The labor, were a task more arduous still.

    Oh scenes surpassing fable, and yet true,
Scenes of accomplish'd bliss! which who can see,
Though but in distant prospect, and not feel
His soul refresh'd with foretaste of the joy?
Rivers of gladness water all the earth,
And clothe all climes with beauty; the reproach
Of barrenness is past. The fruitful field
Laughs with abundance, and the land once lean,[1]
Or fertile only in its own disgrace,
Exults to see its thistly curse repealed.[2]
The various seasons woven into one,
And that one season an eternal spring,
The garden fears no blight, and needs no fence
For there is none to covet, all are full.
The lion and the libbard[3] and the bear
Graze with the fearless flocks. All bask at noon
Together, or all gambol in the shade

[1] Psalm lxv, 14 (Prayer-book version).
[2] Cf. Genesis, iii, 17–18.
[3] Leopard.

Of the same grove, and drink one common stream.
Antipathies are none.[1] No foe to man
Lurks in the serpent now. The mother sees
And smiles to see her infant's playful hand
Stretch'd forth to dally with the crested worm,
To stroak his azure neck, or to receive
The lambent homage of his arrowy tongue.[2]
All creatures worship man, and all mankind
One Lord, one Father. Error has no place;
That creeping pestilence is driv'n away;
The breath of heav'n has chased it. In the heart
No passion touches a discordant string,
But all is harmony and love. Disease
Is not. The pure and uncontaminate blood
Holds its due course, nor fears the frost of age.
One song employs all nations, and all cry,
'Worthy the Lamb, for he was slain for us'.[3]
The dwellers in the vales and on the rocks
Shout to each other, and the mountain tops
From distant mountains catch the flying joy,
'Till nation after nation taught the strain,
Earth rolls the rapturous Hosanna round.
Behold the measure of the promise filled;
See Salem built,[4] the labour of a God!
Bright as a sun the sacred city shines;
All kingdoms and all princes of the earth
Flock to that light; the glory of all lands
Flows into her; unbounded is her joy,
And endless her encrease. Thy rams are there
Nebaioth,[5] and the flocks of Kedar there;
The looms of Ormus, and the mines of Ind,

[1] Isaiah, xi, 6–7.

[2] Isaiah, xi, 8.

[3] The line is from Isaac Watts's hymn, 'Come, let us join our cheerful songs' and is based on Revelation, v, 12–13.

[4] Jerusalem: Revelation, xxi, 2.

[5] Nebaioth and Kedar, the sons of Ishmael, and progenitors of the Arabs, in the prophetic scripture here alluded to, may be reasonably considered as representatives of the Gentiles at large [C]. Cf. Isaiah, lx, 6–7.

And Saba's spicey groves pay tribute there.
Praise is in all her gates. Upon her walls,
And in her streets, and in her spacious courts,
Is heard salvation.[1] Eastern Java there
Kneels with the native of the fairest West,
And Æthiopia spreads abroad the hand
And worships. Her report has travell'd forth
Into all lands. From ev'ry clime they come
To see thy beauty and to share thy joy
O Sion! an assembly such as earth
Saw never, such as Heav'n stoops down to see.
 Thus heav'n-ward all things tend. For all were once
Perfect, and all must be at length restored.
So God has greatly purpos'd; who would else
In his dishonoured works himself endure
Dishonor, and be wrong'd without redress.
Haste then, and wheel away a shatter'd world
Ye slow-revolving seasons! we would see
(A sight to which our eyes are strangers yet)
A world that does not dread and hate his laws,
And suffer for its crime. Would learn how fair
The creature is that God pronounces good,
How pleasant in itself what pleases him.
Here ev'ry drop of honey hides a sting,
Worms wind themselves into our sweetest flow'rs,
And ev'n the joy that haply some poor heart
Derives from heav'n, pure as the fountain is,
Is sullied in the stream; taking a taint
From touch of human lips, at best impure.
Oh for a world in principle as chaste
As this is gross and selfish! over which
Custom and prejudice shall bear no sway
That govern all things here, should'ring aside
The meek and modest truth, and forcing her
To seek a refuge from the tongue of strife
In nooks obscure, far from the ways of men.
Where violence shall never lift the sword,

[1] Isaiah, lx, 18.

Nor cunning justify the proud man's wrong,
Leaving the poor no remedy but tears.
Where he that fills an office, shall esteem
Th' occasion it presents of doing good
More than the perquisite. Where law shall speak
Seldom, and never but as wisdom prompts
And equity; not jealous more to guard
A worthless form, than to decide aright.
Where fashion shall not sanctify abuse,
Nor smooth good-breeding (supplemental grace)
With lean performance ape the work of love.

  Come then, and added to thy many crowns
Receive yet one, the crown of all the earth,
Thou who alone art worthy! It was thine
By antient covenant 'ere nature's birth,
And thou hast made it thine by purchase since,
And overpaid its value with thy blood.
Thy saints proclaim thee king; and in their hearts
Thy title is engraven with a pen
Dipt in the fountain of eternal love.
Thy saints proclaim thee king; and thy delay
Gives courage to their foes, who, could they see
The dawn of thy last advent long-desired,
Would creep into the bowels of the hills,
And flee for safety to the falling rocks.[1]
The very spirit of the world is tired
Of its own taunting question ask'd so long,
'Where is the promise of your Lord's approach?'[2]
The infidel has shot his bolts away,
'Till his exhausted quiver yielded none,
He gleans the blunted shafts that have recoiled,
And aims them at the shield of truth again.
The veil is rent, rent too by priestly hands,
That hides divinity from mortal eyes,
And all the mysteries to faith proposed,
Insulted and traduced, are cast aside

[1] Revelation, vi, 15-17.
[2] 2 Peter, iii, 4.

As useless, to the moles and to the bats.
They now are deem'd the faithful and are praised
Who, constant only in rejecting thee,
Deny thy Godhead with a martyr's zeal,
And quit their office for their error's sake.[1]
Blind and in love with darkness! yet ev'n these
Worthy, compared with sycophants who knee
Thy name, adoring, and then preach thee man.
So fares thy church. But how thy church may fare
The world takes little thought; who will may preach,
And what they will. All pastors are alike
To wand'ring sheep, resolved to follow none.
Two gods divide them all, pleasure and gain.
For these they live, they sacrifice to these,
And in their service wage perpetual war
With conscience and with thee. Lust in their hearts,
And mischief in their hands, they roam the earth
To prey upon each other; stubborn, fierce,
High-minded, foaming out their own disgrace.
Thy prophets speak of such; and noting down
The features of the last degen'rate times,
Exhibit ev'ry lineament of these.
Come then, and added to thy many crowns
Receive yet one, as radiant as the rest,
Due to thy last and most effectual work,
Thy word fulfilled, the conquest of a world.

    He is the happy man, whose life ev'n now
Shows somewhat of that happier life to come.
Who doomed to an obscure but tranquil state
Is pleas'd with it, and were he free to chuse,
Would make his fate his choice. Whom peace, the fruit
Of virtue, and whom virtue, fruit of faith,
Prepare for happiness; bespeak him one
Content indeed to sojourn while he must
Below the skies, but having there his home.

---

[1] An association was formed in 1771 for the relief of clergy from subscription to the 39 Articles of the Church of England. It failed to achieve
its object; and a number of clergy resigned to become Unitarian ministers.

The world o'erlooks him in her busy search
Of objects more illustrious in her view;
And occupied as earnestly as she
Though more sublimely, he o'erlooks the world.
She scorns his pleasures, for she knows them not;
He seeks not hers, for he has proved them vain.
He cannot skim the ground like summer birds
Pursuing gilded flies, and such he deems
Her honors, her emoluments, her joys.
Therefore in contemplation is his bliss,
Whose pow'r is such, that whom she lifts from earth
She makes familiar with a heav'n unseen,
And shows him glories yet to be revealed.
Not slothful he, though seeming unemployed,
And censured oft as useless. Stillest streams
Oft water fairest meadows, and the bird
That flutters least, is longest on the wing.
Ask him indeed, what trophies he has raised,
Or what atchievements of immortal fame
He purposes, and he shall answer—none.
His warfare is within. There unfatigued
His fervent spirit labors. There he fights,
And there obtains fresh triumphs o'er himself,
And never with'ring wreaths, compar'd with which
The laurels that a Cæsar reaps are weeds.
Perhaps the self-approving haughty world
That as she sweeps him with her whistling silks
Scarce deigns to notice him, or if she see
Deems him a cypher in the works of God,
Receives advantage from his noiseless hours,
Of which she little dreams. Perhaps she owes
Her sunshine and her rain, her blooming spring
And plenteous harvest, to the pray'r he makes,
When Isaac-like, the solitary saint
Walks forth to meditate at even tide,[1]
And think on her, who thinks not for herself.
Forgive him then, thou bustler in concerns

[1] Genesis, xxiv, 63.

Of little worth, and idler in the best,
If author of no mischief and some good,
He seeks his proper happiness by means
That may advance, but cannot hinder thine.
Nor though he tread the secret path of life,
Engage no notice, and enjoy much ease,
Account him an incumbrance on the state,
Receiving benefits, and rend'ring none.
His sphere though humble, if that humble sphere
Shine with his fair example, and though small
His influence, if that influence all be spent
In soothing sorrow and in quenching strife,
In aiding helpless indigence, in works
From which at least a grateful few derive
Some taste of comfort in a world of woe,
Then let the supercilious great confess
He serves his country; recompenses well
The state beneath the shadow of whose vine
He sits secure, and in the scale of life
Holds no ignoble, though a slighted place.
The man whose virtues are more felt than seen,
Must drop indeed the hope of public praise,
But he may boast what few that win it can,
That if his country stand not by his skill,
At least his follies have not wrought her fall.
Polite refinement offers him in vain
Her golden tube, through which a sensual world
Draws gross impurity, and likes it well,
The neat conveyance hiding all th' offence.[1]
Not that he peevishly rejects a mode
Because that world adopts it. If it bear
The stamp and clear impression of good sense,
And be not costly more than of true worth,
He puts it on, and for decorum sake

---

[1] No editor, I think, has commented on this puzzling passage. I conjecture that *golden tube* means a tobacco pipe (cf. 'The Winter Morning Walk', line 55); *golden*, because it is a meerschaum pipe with an amber stem—a type coming into use among persons of *polite refinement*. The *gross impurity* is smoke; C. detested it. See p. 636.

Can wear it e'en as gracefully as she.
She judges of refinement by the eye,
He by the test of conscience, and a heart
Not soon deceived; aware that what is base
No polish can make sterling, and that vice,
Though well perfumed and elegantly dress'd,
Like an unburied carcase trick'd with flow'rs,
Is but a garnish'd nuisance, fitter far
For cleanly riddance than for fair attire.
So life glides smoothly and by stealth away,
More golden than that age of fabled gold
Renown'd in ancient song; not vex'd with care
Or stained with guilt, beneficent, approved
Of God and man, and peaceful in its end.
So glide my life away! and so at last
My share of duties decently fulfilled,
May some disease, not tardy to perform
Its destin'd office, yet with gentle stroke,
Dismiss me weary to a safe retreat
Beneath the turf that I have often trod.
It shall not grieve me, then, that once when called
To dress a Sofa with the flow'rs of verse,
I play'd awhile, obedient to the fair
With that light task, but soon to please her more
Whom flow'rs alone I knew would little please,
Let fall th' unfinish'd wreath, and roved for fruit;
Roved far, and gather'd much. Some harsh, 'tis true,
Pick'd from the thorns and briars of reproof,
But wholesome, well-digested. Grateful some
To palates that can taste immortal truth,
Insipid else, and sure to be despised.
But all is in his hand whose praise I seek.
In vain the poet sings, and the world hears,
If he regard not, though divine the theme.
'Tis not in artful measures, in the chime
And idle tinkling of a minstrel's lyre
To charm his ear, whose eye is on the heart;
Whose frown can disappoint the proudest strain,
Whose approbation—prosper even mine.

SELECTED
LETTERS

IF COWPER'S WISHES had been followed in the form that he expressed to Mrs Unwin's son-in-law, none of his letters would have survived. 'I keep no letters', he told the Rev. Matthew Powley, 'except such as are recommended for preservation by the importance of their contents...By *important contents*, I mean what is commonly called *business* of some sort or other. In the destruction of all other epistles I consult the good of my friends; for I account it a point of delicacy not to leave behind me, when I die, such bundles of their communications as I otherwise should, for the inspection of I know not whom; and as I deal with theirs, for the very same reason, I most heartily wish them all to deal with mine. In fact, there seems to be no more reason for perpetuating or preserving what passes the pen in the course of a common correspondence, than what passes the lips in every day's conversation. A thousand folios of the latter are forgotten without any regret; and octavos, at least, of the former are frequently treasured till death, for no use whatever either to ourselves or others. They then, perhaps, go to the grocer's, and serve to amuse such of his customers as can read *written hand*, as they call it; or now and then, which is fifty times worse they find their way to the press; a misfortune which never, at least seldom, fails to happen, if the deceased has been so unfortunate as to leave behind him a friend more affectionate to his memory than discreet in his choice of means to honour it...'[1]

Lady Hesketh probably never knew of this letter, and fortunately so, for as the administratrix of Cowper's estate, she was loyal to a fault and a stubborn fighter until disarmed

[1] Letter dated 'about 1786' by Southey and Wright. Internal evidence points to a date between September 8 and 24, 1793.

by failing physical powers. She already had, in his letter of
July 5, 1788 (page 899 of this edition) 'free permission' to
publish his letters 'but not till I am dead. No, not even then,
till you have given them a complete revisal, erasing all that
the critics in such matters might condemn...' These conditions
were possibly Cowper's way of saying 'Yes' when he really
meant 'No'. Passages in Lady Hesketh's own letters indicate
that she did her best to enforce them; but she was not alone
in considering herself the guardian of his memory. Within a
month of his death in April 1800, she was dealing out heavy
rebuffs to 'the quill-drivers of the age' who wanted to write
his life. Thomas Park, the antiquary, was given to understand
that he could put 'all ideas of the biographical kind quite out
of his head'. 'I can only say,' she wrote to John Johnson,
'that I, who certainly know more of this dear creature's life
than anybody, have never furnished any materials upon the
subject, on the contrary have uniformly discouraged all
attempts of the kind.'[1] The silencing of Cowper's closer
friends, particularly clergymen with a doctrinal axe to grind,
proved more difficult. At Olney, in May, Samuel Greatheed
preached a memorial sermon in which he went out of his way
to point out that Cowper's malady had not been provoked
by his 'conversion', since he had had two breakdowns before
it, and had attempted suicide. Its publication in September,
dedicated to Lady Hesketh, but ignoring her express wish that
this matter should not be mentioned, gave deep offence.
Newton preached a sermon on similar lines in London. Worse
still, he announced his intention of writing Cowper's life,
'convinced that it is for the glory of God that every painful
circumstance we wish to keep secret, should be revealed.'
She came to the conclusion that Cowper's memory, if it was
to be recorded in the form she thought suitable, would be
best served by appointing Hayley, subject to stringent conditions of censorship, as the authorized biographer. 'What I
most fear,' she told him, 'is misrepresentations of his religious
sentiments and opinions...as I know the sectarists of all

---

[1] *Letters of Lady Hesketh to the Rev. John Johnson*, ed. C. Bodham Johnson,
1901. Letter of May 28, 1800.

denominations are anxious to claim him for their own.'[1] Hayley was a tepid sectarist, to say the least. 'In your hands, Sir, I know he will be safe.'

She made it clear from the start that she, not the biographer, would decide which subjects and materials were suitable for publication. To begin with, there was to be no mention of Cowper's early love for her sister Theadora, 'and indeed as he is not to be the hero of a novel, circumstances of this kind would be perfectly unnecessary.'[2] When Hayley asked whether she had kept letters written to herself, he got the bleak answer that she had indeed 'a large collection...but none that can I apprehend be useful in the work you have so kindly undertaken, the less, as most of them relate to sentiments and events with which the world can have nothing to do.'[3] As to letters addressed to Hayley himself, she must make it her 'particular regard that nothing that may relate to family affairs, or to events that (Cowper) might wish concealed from the public' should be included. At this time she wrote to John Johnson, asking him to despatch to her three bound volumes of unpublished MSS, so that these too might be kept within her control.[4]

At the end of 1800, Hayley gave her a fright by announcing that he had tracked down Lady Austen, who had given him 'some valuable MSS.' Lady Hesketh instantly conjured him 'not to suffer any productions of my dear cousin's to see the light that bear any mention of that cruel malady with which it pleased Heaven so frequently to afflict him'.[5] She then offered a qualified concession; having 'picked out several of my beloved cousin's sweet letters' to herself, she put it to Hayley that he should publish only such parts as were 'likely to meet with a favourable reception', and 'nothing which can in the slightest degree affect any living characters'. Further, 'every

[1] BM. Add. MSS 38,887 (Correspondence of Lady Hesketh and William Hayley). Letter of July 5, 1800.

[2] *Ibid.*, August 14, 1800.

[3] *Ibid.*, August 26, 1800.

[4] *Letters of Lady Hesketh*, September 3, 1800.

[5] BM. MSS *cit.*, December 6, 1800.

remark in favour of Royalty or Government' must be included, and 'any hints of a contrary nature' were to be buried in oblivion.[1] Cowper, she reminded Hayley on a later occasion, had described her as 'Loyalty Personified' and 'I suffer so much when I hear our dear friend accused of democratic principles'. In her opinion, she added, his beliefs, religious or political, were 'perfectly orthodox'. All the same, 'experience has taught me that one cannot be too guarded on these occasions.'[2] To John Johnson she expressed some relief that she had been unable to trace Cowper's letters to Mrs Unwin, which she would 'by no means' wish to publish, since their style 'though quite filial is yet too Enthusiastic — and it is my wish that while this dear Being is by Mr Hayley's charming pen consigned to latest posterity as the truly Christian Poet, nothing should be brought forward that should cause him to be considered as a Visionary! an Enthusiast! or a Calvinist! for I am very sure that he was neither in reality.'[3] She was therefore much upset, on reading Hayley's *Life*, to find that he had included, without consulting her, early letters to Maria Cowper which confirmed, only too strongly, 'the idea which I have taken unwearied pains to eradicate.'[4]

Nothing less than Lady Hesketh's 'earnest and repeated request' would have induced Joseph Hill[5] 'to search among the rubbish of forty years for letters from Mr Cowper... Whatever he wrote was neat and correct, and in a style peculiar to himself, but I cannot consider such letters...as interesting to the public...It has long been my opinion that no posthumous letters should be published but those which relate to subjects of literature, or of a public or general nature. Private letters likewise are apt to mention persons and characters with whom an editor has no right to meddle...' Hill went on to express his confidence that Hayley's judgment

[1] *Ibid.*, December 19 and 29, 1800.
[2] *Ibid.*, November 9, 1802.
[3] *Letters of Lady Hesketh*, January 3, 1802.
[4] BM. MSS *cit.*, January 10, 1803.
[5] Letter to Hayley, February 19, 1802, in Cowper Johnson MSS.

would 'not exceed the bounds I have mentioned'. Just to make sure, he added: 'I must request that no passage from those letters that I have drawn a pen through may be published or extracted'. This point of view differed little from Hayley's. He told Lady Hesketh that it would be 'highly unbecoming' for the letters between Cowper and himself 'though to our mutual credit' to be published in his lifetime. Those he did publish he mutilated characteristically. A fair example of the damage he did may be seen by comparing the superb description of a fox-hunt in the letter to Lady Hesketh of March 3, 1788, as printed from the Panshanger MSS. in the present volume, with the version in any of the collected editions.

Altogether Hayley printed 479 extracts from Cowper's letters. Another 221 were added by John Johnson in his *Private Correspondence*, 1824, most of which were printed from the originals lent by Newton's niece and the widows of Bull, Hill and Unwin. Among them are many to Newton, and a few to Bull, on religious subjects, which Hayley had 'utterly excluded' (Johnson asserts in his preface) 'out of tenderness to the feelings of the reader...and for the gloominess they attach to the writer's mind'. The omission of these letters, he added, had obscured Cowper's image; because people read Hayley's edition with *The Task* in mind, or vice versa, and were perplexed. 'They look for the Cowper of each, in the other, and find him not. The correspondency is destroyed. Hence the character of Cowper is undetermined; mystery hangs over it; and the opinions formed of him are as various as the minds of the enquirers.' The balance of Johnson's collection was made up with letters 'of a lively description' which Hayley had 'probably rejected as comparatively trifling' but which illustrated his 'playful humour' or 'some characteristic turn of thought or expression'. The second object of Johnson's edition was 'to exculpate the religious opinions of Cowper from the charge of originating his mental distress'. This alone led to a number of silent omissions. In deference to 'good taste', Johnson also left out uncomplimentary allusions to persons still living, or whose near relatives survived, many requests or expressions of thanks for gin and other types of alcoholic liquor, references to pregnancy, childbirth, breast-feeding, remedies for constipation and other physical ailments, expressions such as 'a kick on the breech', and comments on marriage-making or the desirability of exemplary punishments for crimes of violence:[1] anything, in fact, which revealed Cowper in rather too worldly a light.

Southey's *Life and Works*, 1835–37, brought the total of the collected letters to 753, and added fragments from 128 others. He was hindered by a dispute with the Rev. T. S. Grimshawe, Mrs Johnson's brother-in-law, who was bringing out a rival edition of the letters. Grimshawe's publishers were the successors of the firm which had paid Johnson £700 for the editorship and the copyright of the *Private Correspondence*; and Southey believed at first that he had no right to use these letters, except in the form of extracts threaded into his biographical narrative. It then came out that Johnson had never obtained an assignment of the copyright from Cowper's heirs, represented by the venerable Mrs Bodham, who publicly supported Southey. Grimshawe's edition proved to be nothing but 'a clumsy re-handling of Hayley's, inspired by a ludicrous zeal for the interests of religion and morality'.[2] Southey, by contrast, went to a good deal of trouble to obtain access to the originals of Cowper's letters. He wrote to his publisher that he was surprised 'to find out how much both Dr Johnson and Hayley have left out in the letters to Mr Unwin, which is quite as characteristic and quite as interesting as what they have printed'. A second letter described his working methods: 'Every evening I read a portion of them aloud, which one of my daughters compares with the printed copy; and if there arose no other advantage from this than the correction of the text, by restoring Cowper's own English, it would be worth the cost of time. But I have found a great

---

[1] e.g. an unpublished passage in the letter of April 30, 1790 to Lady Hesketh reads: '...I long to have a woman-wounder caught and hanged, hanged in chains, hanged with his heels uppermost, hanged every way by which it is possible to hang a thing in human form. What a theme for music. Oh rare Astley...' (Panshanger MSS).

[2] K. Povey: 'The Text of Cowper's Letters , *Modern Language Review*, xxi, 1927, pp. 22–27.

deal of good matter to insert.' And to another correspondent: 'My business has been to collate the printed copies with the originals; to fill up omissions, many of which were of the most curious kind...and to rejoin heads, tails, and *between-ities*, which Hayley had severed, and then pieced according to his own fancy, and which were sometimes scattered between his volume and Dr J. Johnson's.'[1] Often, lacking the originals, Southey reprinted Hayley's distorted versions.

Thomas Wright, the Olney schoolmaster who edited the *Correspondence of William Cowper*, in four volumes, 1904, printed 1041 letters, according to his summary, of which 105 were unpublished and 132 had been published in part. Wright claimed to have seen the originals of over 400, and to have printed them complete, but neglected to state which these were. John Bailey's edition of the *Poems* added 35 new or partly new letters in 1905; Wright printed 31 *Unpublished and Uncollected Letters* by Cowper in 1925, and Dr Ryskamp a few more in his biography of 1959. Many others have been published in periodicals, or await resurrection from private archives in this country or the U.S.A.

Forty years later, there is little to add to the late Kenneth Povey's judgment that 'the text of Cowper's letters is in such an incomplete, corrupt and muddled state that anyone who has occasion to go beyond a popular selection, whether for pleasure or for purposes of study, must soon find how little any of the four collected editions is to be trusted.'[2] Happily it seems only a matter of time before much of the damage will be repaired. An advertisement inserted by the late Professor Neilson C. Hannay of Belmont, Massachusetts, in *The Times Literary Supplement* for August 14, 1953, stated: 'For many years I been engaged upon a comprehensive and, I hope, definitive edition of the letters by and to the poet William Cowper...collated with all known originals. This work is now in a far advanced stage...' Hannay was an ordained minister who had presented a doctor's dissertation

---

[1] *Selections from the letters of R. Southey* ed. J. W. Warter, 1856, IV, 402, 448–49.

[2] *Lit. cit.*

on 'The Religious Element in the Life and Character of William Cowper' in 1919. For the next forty years, much of his leisure was devoted to tracing, acquiring or copying manuscript letters and associated items. He published only a few notices or reviews; and when he died at the age of over eighty in 1961, the edition had not progressed beyond the preparation of thousands of notes. His rich and comprehensive collection, which includes four hundred letters by Cowper, about a hundred addressed to him by Newton, and Newton's diary from 1773 to 1805, was acquired by Princeton University,[1] where the long-delayed definitive edition of the letters is now being prepared by a member of the Department of English, Professor Charles Ryskamp. My own effort to supply a complete text of some of the letters is therefore of a strictly limited and provisional nature.

The source of each letter is indicated separately in the text. Two asterisks after the source reference mean that the letter, so far as I have been able to discover, has not previously been published. A single asterisk means (again with the same qualification) that a substantial proportion of the letter has apparently not been printed before. The sign † means that the MS. originates from a family collection, but is not in Cowper's autograph and may not be complete. The Barham Johnson MSS. includes original MS. letters, copies of or extracts from original MSS. made by John Johnson for the opinion of clerical friends, and notebooks supplying the suppressed passages. I have collated these with the help of Miss Mary Barham Johnson.

---

[1] C. Ryskamp, 'William Cowper and His Circle: a Study of the Hannay Collection': *The Princeton University Library Chronicle*, XXIV, No. 1.

TO LADY HESKETH[1]

The Temple, August 9, 1763

My dear cousin,

Having promised to write to you, I make haste to be as good as my word. I have a pleasure in writing to you at any time, but especially at the present, when my days are spent in reading the Journals,[2] and my nights in dreaming of them—an employment not very agreeable to a head that has long been habituated to the luxury of choosing its subject, and has been as little employed upon business, as if it had grown upon the shoulders of a much wealthier gentleman. But the numskull pays for it now, and will not presently forget the discipline it has undergone lately. If I succeed in this doubtful piece of promotion, I shall have at least this satisfaction to reflect upon, that the volumes I write will be treasured up with the utmost care for ages, and will last as long as the English constitution—a duration which ought to satisfy the vanity of any author who has a spark of love for his country. Oh, my good cousin! if I was to open my heart to you, I could show you strange sights; nothing, I flatter myself, that would shock you, but a great deal that would make you wonder. I am of a very singular temper, and very unlike all the men that I have ever conversed with. Certainly I am not an absolute fool; but I have more weakness than the greatest of all the fools I can recollect at present. In short, if I was

[1] Harriot Lady Hesketh (1733–1807), daughter of Ashley Cowper, was the poet's first cousin and sister to the Theadora Cowper whom he wished to marry. She was the wife of Thomas Hesketh of Rufford Hall in Lancashire, who was created a baronet in 1761 and died in 1778, leaving Cowper a small legacy. The Heskeths went to Italy after Cowper moved to Olney and lost touch with him; but when *The Task* made him famous, she resumed correspondence and henceforth devoted much of her energy to his welfare.

[2] Cowper was at this time the nominated candidate for the clerkship of the Journals of the House of Lords.

as fit for the next world as I am unfit for this, and God forbid I should speak it in vanity, I would not change conditions with any saint in Christendom.

My destination is settled at last, and I have obtained a furlough. Margate is the word, and what do you think will ensue, cousin? I know what you expect, but ever since I was born I have been good at disappointing the most natural expectations. Many years ago, cousin, there was a possibliity that I might prove a very different thing from what I am at present. My character is now fixed, and riveted fast upon me, and, between friends, is not a very splendid one, or likely to be guilty of much fascination.

Adieu, my dear cousin! So much as I love you, I wonder how the deuce it has happened I was never in love with you. Thank Heaven that I never was, for at this time I have had a pleasure in writing to you, which in that case I should have forfeited. Let me hear from you, or I shall reap but half the reward that is due to my noble indifference.

Yours ever, and evermore,   W.C.

TEXT: *Southey*

TO JOSEPH HILL[1]

Huntingdon, June 24, 1765

Dear Joe,

The only recompense I can make you for your friendly attention to my affairs during my illness, is to tell you that by the mercy of God I am restored to perfect health both of mind and body. This I believe will give you pleasure; and I would gladly do anything from which you may receive it.

I left St. Albans on the 17th, arrived that day at Cambridge, spent some time there with my brother, and came hither on

[1] Joseph Hill (1733–1811), a solicitor, attorney and one of the 'Sixty Sworn Clerks' in the Lord Chancellor's department, was C.'s lifelong friend and the manager of his financial affairs from 1764 onwards. See p. 570, n.

the 22nd. I have a lodging that puts me continually in mind of our summer excursions; we have had many worse, and except the size of it, which however is sufficient for a single man, but few better. I am not quite alone, having brought a servant[2] with me from St Albans, who is the very mirror of fidelity and affection for his master, and whereas the Turkish Spy[3] says he kept no servant because he would not have an enemy in his house, I hired mine because I would have a friend. Men do not usually bestow these encomiums upon their lackeys, nor do they usually deserve them; but I have had experience of mine both in sickness and in health and never saw his fellow.

The river Ouse, I forget how they spell it, is the most agreeable circumstance in this part of the world. At this town it is I believe as wide as the Thames at Windsor; nor does the silver Thames better deserve that epithet, nor has it more flowers upon its banks, these being attributes which in strict truth belong to neither. Fluellin would say they are as like as my fingers to my fingers, and there is salmon in both.[4] It is a noble stream to bathe in, and I shall make that use of it three times a week, having introduced myself to it for the first time this morning.

I beg you will remember me to all my friends, which is a task it will cost you no great pains to execute. Particularly remember me to those of your own house, and believe me

Your very affectionate,

Wm Cowper

Direct to me at Mr Martin's, grocer, at Huntingdon.

TEXT: *Cowper Johnson MSS.*

[2] Sam Roberts remained in C.'s service until 1796.

[3] *Eight Volumes of Letters written by a Turkish Spy*: 1734. The anonymous author of this pseudo-Oriental romance was G. P. Marana.

[4] *King Henry V*, IV, vii, 28–33.

TO JOSEPH HILL

Huntingdon, July 3, '65

Dear Joe,

Whatever you may think of the matter, it is no such easy thing to keep house for two people. A man cannot always live upon sheeps' heads and liver and lights like the lions in the Tower, and a joint of meat in so small a family is an endless encumbrance. My butcher's bill for last week amounted to four shillings and ten-pence. — I set off with a leg of lamb, and was forced to give part of it away to my washer-woman; then I made an experiment upon a sheep's heart, and that was too little; next I put three pounds of beef into a pie, and this had like to have been too much, for it lasted three days, though my landlord was admitted to a share in it. Then as to small beer, I am puzzled to pieces about it. I have bought as much for a shilling as will serve us at least a month, and it is grown sour already. In short I never knew how to pity poor house-keepers before, but now I cease to wonder at that politic cast which their occupation usually gives to their countenance, for it is really a matter full of perplexity.

I have received but one visit since here I came—I don't mean that I have refused any, but that only one has been offered. This was from my woollen-draper, a very healthy, wealthy, sensible, sponsible man, and extremely civil. He has a cold bath, and has promised me a key of it, which I shall probably make use of in the winter. He has undertaken too to get me the *St James's Chronicle* 3 times a week, and to show me Hinchinbrook House, and to do every service for me in his power; so that I did not exceed the truth you see when I spoke of his civility.

Here is a card assembly, and a dancing assembly, and a horse-race, and a club and a bowling-green, so that I am well off you perceive in point of diversions; especially as I shall go to 'em just as much as I should if I lived a thousand miles off. But no matter for that; the spectator at a play is more entertained than the actor, and in real life it's much the same. You will say perhaps that if I never frequent these places, I shall not come within the description of a spectator; and you will say right; I have made a blunder which shall be corrected in the next edition.

You are [an] old dog at a bad tenant; witness all my uncle's and your mother's geese and gridirons. There is something so extremely impertinent in entering upon a man's premises, and using them without paying for 'em, that I could easily resent it if I would, but I rather choose to entertain myself with thinking how you will scour the man about, and worry him to death if once you begin with him. Poor toad! I leave him entirely to your mercy.

My dear Joe, you desire me to write long letters—I have neither matter enough nor perseverance enough for the purpose. However if you can but contrive to be tired of reading as soon as I am tired of writing, we shall find that short ones answer just as well; and in my opinion this is a very practicable measure.

My friend Colman[1] has had good fortune. I wish him [better] fortune still; which is that he may make a right use of it. The tragedies of Lloyd and Bensley[2] are both very deep. If they are not of use to the surviving part of the Society,[3] it is their own fault.

I was debtor to Bensley seven pounds or nine I forget which, the remaining part of a hundred I had borrowed of him. If you can find out his brother, you will do me a great favour if you will pay him for me. But do it at your leisure.

Yrs and theirs*

Wm Cowper

[1] George Colman the elder (1732–94), dramatist and theatrical manager. In 1764 he inherited an income of 900 guineas and in 1765 published a successful translation of Terence's comedies.

[2] Robert Lloyd (1733–64), minor poet and editor of the unsuccessful *St James's Magazine*, had died in a debtor's prison. James Bensley (c. 1731–65), a barrister, had been killed by a fall from his horse.

[3] Colman, Bensley, Lloyd and C. had all been friends at Westminster School, and afterwards (with Hill) as members of the Nonsense Club.

*The author is supposed to mean Mrs Hill & her 2 daughters. The word *theirs* cannot so well refer to the last antecedents, the persons who stand in that relation with it being both dead at the time he wrote, as is evident from the context.

Lipsius

TEXT: *Cowper Johnson MSS.*

TO JOSEPH HILL

Huntingdon, August 14, 1765

Dear Joe,

Both Lady Hesketh and my brother had apprized me of your intention to give me a call, and herein I find they were not mistaken; but they both informed me likewise that you was already set out for Warwickshire; in consequence of which latter intelligence I have lived in continual expectation of seeing you any time this fortnight. Now how these two ingenious personages (for such they are both) should mistake an expedition to French Flanders for a journey to Warwickshire, is more than I with all my ingenuity can imagine. I am glad however that I have still a chance for seeing you, and shall treasure it up amongst my agreeable expectations. In the mean time, you are welcome to the British shore, as the song has it, and I thank you for your epitome of your travels. You don't tell me how you escaped the vigilance of the custom-house officers, though I dare say you was knuckle-deep in contrabands, and had your boots stuffed with all and all manner of unlawful wares and merchandizes.

You know, Joe, I am very deep in debt to my little physician at St Albans, and that the handsomest thing I can do will be to pay him *le plutôt qu'il sera possible* (that is vile French, I believe, but you can now correct it). My brother informs me that you have such a quantity of cash in your hands on my account, that I may venture to send him £40 immediately. This therefore I shall be glad if you will manage for me;

and when you receive the £100 which my brother likewise brags you are shortly to receive, I shall be glad if you will discharge the remainder of that debt, without waiting for any further advice from your humble servant.

I am become a professed horseman, and do hereby assume to myself the style and title of the Knight of the Bloody Spur. It has cost me as much ass's skin as would make a reasonable pocket book to bring this point to bear, but I think I have at last accomplished it.

The snuff arrived safe.

My love to all your family—

Yrs ever,

Wm Cowper

If you see Lady Hesketh, give my love to her, and thank her much for the little book which I received after having given it over.

TEXT: *Cowper Johnson MSS.*

TO LADY HESKETH

Huntingdon, Oct. 18, 1765

I wish you joy, my dear cousin, of being safely arrived in port from the storms of Southampton. For my own part, who am but as a Thames wherry, in a world full of tempest and commotion, I know so well the value of the creek I have put into, and the snugness it affords me, that I have a sensible sympathy with you in the pleasure you find in being once more blown to Droxford.[1] I know enough of Miss Morley to send her my compliments; to which, if I had never seen her, her affection for you would sufficiently entitle her. If I neglected to do it sooner, it is only because I am naturally apt to neglect what I ought to do; and if I was as genteel as I am negligent, I should be the most delightful creature in the universe.

[1] Near Southampton.

I am glad you think so favourably of my Huntingdon acquaintance;[2] they are indeed a nice set of folks, and suit me exactly. I should have been more particular in my account of Miss Unwin, if I had had materials for a minute description. She is about eighteen years of age, rather handsome and genteel. In her mother's company she says little; not because her mother requires it of her, but because she seems glad of that excuse for not talking, being somewhat inclined to bashfulness. There is the most remarkable cordiality between all the parts of the family; and the mother and daughter seem to dote upon each other. The first time I went to the house I was introduced to the daughter alone; and sat with her near half an hour, before her brother came in, who had appointed me to call upon him. Talking is necessary in a *tête-à-tête*, to distinguish the persons of the drama from the chairs they sit on: accordingly she talked a great deal, and extremely well; and, like the rest of the family, behaved with as much ease of address as if we had been old acquaintance. She resembles her mother in her great piety, who is one of the most remarkable instances of it I have ever seen. They are altogether the cheerfulest and most engaging family-piece it is possible to conceive.

Since I wrote the above, I met Mrs Unwin in the street, and went home with her. She and I walked together near two hours in the garden, and had a conversation which did me more good than I should have received from an audience of the first prince in Europe. That woman is a blessing to me, and I never see her without being the better for her company. I am treated in the family as if I was a near relation, and have been repeatedly invited to call upon them at all times. You know what a shy fellow I am; I cannot prevail with myself to make so much use of this privilege as I am sure they intend I should; but perhaps this awkwardness will wear off hereafter. It was my earnest request before I left St Albans, that wherever it might please Providence to dispose of me, I might

[2] They were the Rev. Morley Unwin (1724–67); his wife Mary Cawthorne (1724–96); their son, later the Rev. William Unwin (1744–86); and their daughter Susanna, 1746–1835, who married the Rev. Matthew Powley in 1774.

meet with such an acquaintance as I find in Mrs Unwin. How happy it is to believe, with a steadfast assurance, that our petitions are heard even while we are making them; and how delightful to meet with a proof of it in the effectual and actual grant of them! Surely it is a gracious finishing given to those means, which the Almighty has been pleased to make use of for my conversion. After having been deservedly rendered unfit for any society, to be again qualified for it, and admitted at once into the fellowship of those whom God regards as the excellent of the earth, and whom, in the emphatical language of Scripture,[3] he preserves as the apple of his eye, is a blessing which carries with it the stamp and visible superscription of divine bounty,—a grace unlimited as undeserved; and like its glorious Author, free in its course, and blessed in its operation!

My dear cousin! health and happiness, and above all, the favour of our great and gracious Lord, attend you! While we seek it in spirit and in truth, we are infinitely more secure of it than of the next breath we expect to draw. Heaven and earth have their destined periods; ten thousand worlds will vanish at the consummation of all things; but the word of God standeth fast; and they who trust in him shall never be confounded. My love to all who inquire after me.

Yours affectionately,

W.C.

TEXT: *Southey*

TO JOSEPH HILL

Oct. 25, 1765

Dear Joe,

I am afraid the month of October has proved rather unfavourable to the *belle assemblée* at Southampton; high winds and continual rains being bitter enemies to that

[3] Deuteronomy, xxxii, 10.

agreeable lounge which you and I are equally fond of.[1] I have very cordially betaken myself to my book and my fireside, and seldom leave them unless merely for exercise. I have added another family to the number of those I was acquainted with when you was here. Their name is Unwin—the most agreeable people imaginable; quite sociable, and as free from the ceremonious civility of country gentlefolks as any I ever met with. They treat me more like a near relation than a stranger, and their house is always open to me. The old gentleman carries me to Cambridge in his chaise; he is a man of learning and good sense, and as simple as Parson Adams.[2] His wife, who is young compared with her husband, has a very uncommon understanding, has read much to excellent purpose, and is more polite than a duchess. The son, who belongs to Cambridge, is a most amiable young man, and the daughter quite of a piece with the rest of the family. They see but little company which suits me exactly; go when I will, I find a house full of peace and cordiality in all its parts, and am sure to hear no scandal, but such discourse instead of it as we are all the better for. You remember Rousseau's description of an English morning;[3] such are the mornings I spend with these good people; and the evenings differ from them in nothing, except that they are still more snug and quieter. Now I know them, I wonder that I liked Huntingdon so well before I knew them, and am apt to think I should find every place disagreeable that had not an Unwin belonging to it.

This incident convinces me of the truth of an observation I have often made, that when we circumscribe our estimate of all that is clever within the limits of our own acquaintance (which I at least have been always apt to do), we are guilty of a very uncharitable censure upon the rest of the world, and of

[1] Southampton became a fashionable resort in the 1760's. Assemblies for dancing and cards were held at the Long Rooms on West Quay in the summer, and at the Dolphin Hotel in the winter.

[2] A character in Fielding's *Joseph Andrews*.

[3] *La Nouvelle Héloïse*, V, letter III: '...Nous avons passé aujourd'hui une matinée à l'angloise, réunis et dans le silence, goûtant à la fois le plaisir d'être ensemble et la douceur du recueillement. Que les délices de cet état sont connues de peu de gens!'

a narrowness of thinking disgraceful to ourselves.[4] Wapping and Redriff may contain some of the most amiable persons living, and such as one would go even to Wapping and Redriff to make acquaintance with. You remember Mr Gray's stanza—

> Full many a gem of purest ray serene
> The deep unfathom'd caves of ocean bear,
> Full many a rose is born to blush unseen,
> And waste its fragrance on the desert air.'[5]

I have wrote to Eamonson, and as I expected, have received no answer. My letter went the day after you left Cambridge. I am afraid the ten pounds you spoke of will grow mouldy if they lie at Child's any longer; shall be obliged therefore if you will remit them to Huntingdon.

My love to all your family,

Yrs dear Joe,

Wm Cowper

TEXT: *Cowper Johnson MSS.*

TO JOSEPH HILL

Huntingdon, Nov. 5, 1765

Dear Joe,

I wrote to you about 10 days ago,

> Soliciting a quick return of gold
> To purchase certain horse that likes me well.

Either my letter or your answer to it I fear has miscarried: the former I hope; because a miscarriage of the latter might be attended with bad consequences. I shall want more cash however than I wrote for at that time, having totally changed my scheme of operations. Upon taking a deliberate view of

[4] Redriffe: Rotherhithe. Both districts were notorious for robberies, especially of visiting sailors.

[5] Slightly misquoted from the 'Elegy written in a Country Church-Yard'.

my outgoings and incomings, I find it impossible to proceed any longer in my present course without danger of bankruptcy. I have therefore entered into an agreement with the Revd. Mr Unwin to lodge and board with him, by which means I shall save some 50 or 60 pounds per annum. The family are the most agreeable in the world. They live in a special good house, and in a very genteel way. I know nobody so like Mrs Unwin as my aunt Madan.[1] I don't mean in person for she is a much younger woman, but in character. They are all exactly what I should wish them to be, and I know I shall be as happy with them as I can be on this side of the sun. You may remember perhaps that as we walked on the morning of your arrival here towards the bridge end of the town, we heard a harpsichord from a parlour window on the right hand; that is the house. I was not acquainted with them at that time, nor did I dream of this matter till about 5 days ago. But now the whole is settled.

I shall transfer myself thither as soon as I have satisfied all demands upon me here, for which purpose I shall want thirty pounds instead of ten which I wrote for before, being engaged here you know for a year certain, and having a few odd bills to pay besides.

My love to your mother and sisters

Yrs ever

Wm Cowper

If the ten pounds should arrive in the interim, you will be pleased to add 20 in a twinkling.

TEXT: *Cowper Johnson MSS.* *

[1] Judith Cowper (1702–81): a noted beauty, the friend and correspondent of Pope, had married Colonel Martin Madan, M.P., Equerry to Frederick Prince of Wales. She had been 'converted' by John Wesley's preaching. She was the mother of C.'s correspondent Maria Cowper, and of the Rev. Martin Madan and Spencer Madan, Bishop of Peterborough.

TO MARIA COWPER[1]

Huntingdon, Oct. 20, 1766

My dear cousin,

I am sorry for poor George's[2] illness, and hope you will soon have cause to thank God for his complete recovery. We have an epidemical fever in this country likewise, which leaves behind it a continual sighing almost to suffocation; not that I have seen any instance of it, for blessed be God, our family have hitherto escaped it, but such was the account I heard of it this morning.

I am obliged to you for the interest you take in my welfare, and for your inquiring so particularly after the manner in which my time passes here. As to amusements, I mean what the world calls such, we have none: the place indeed swarms with them, and cards and dancing are the professed business of almost all the *gentle* inhabitants of Huntingdon. We refuse to take part in them, or to be accessories to this way of murdering our time, and by so doing have acquired the name of Methodists. Having told you how we *do not* spend our time, I will next say how we *do*. We breakfast commonly between 8 and 9; till 11, we read either the Scripture, or the sermons of some faithful preacher of those holy mysteries; at 11 we attend divine service which is performed here twice every day, and from 12 to 3 we separate and amuse ourselves as we please. During that interval I either read in my own apartment, or walk or ride, or work in the garden. We seldom sit an hour after dinner, but if the weather permits adjourn to the garden, where with Mrs Unwin and her son I have generally the pleasure of religious conversation till tea-time; if it rains or is too windy for walking, we either converse within doors,

---

[1] Maria Cowper (1726–97) was the daughter of Colonel Madan, M.P., and Judith Cowper, the poet's aunt, and had married her cousin and his, Major William Cowper of the Park House, Hertingfordbury. She was a fervent Evangelical. Her *Original Poems on Various Occasions*, revised by C., was published anonymously in 1792.

[2] A note, not in C.'s hand, reads, 'he meant Charles.'

or sing some hymns of Martin's Collection,[3] and by the help of Mrs Unwin's harpsichord make up a tolerable concert, in which however our hearts I hope are the best and most musical performers. After tea we sally forth to walk in good earnest. Mrs Unwin is a good walker, and we have generally travelled about 4 miles before we see home again. When the days are short we make this excursion in the former part of the day, between church-time and dinner. At night we read and converse as before till supper, and commonly finish the evening either with hymns or a sermon, and last of all the family are called in to prayers. I need not tell *you* that such a life as this is consistent with the utmost cheerfulness; accordingly we are all happy, and dwell together in unity as brethren. Mrs Unwin has almost a maternal affection for me, and I have something very like a filial one for her, and her son and I are brothers. Blessed be the God of our salvation for such companions, and for such a life; [above] all, for a heart to like it.

I have had many anxious thoughts about taking orders; and I believe every new convert is apt to think himself called upon for that purpose; but it has pleased God, by means which there is no need to particularize, to give me full satisfaction as to the propriety of declining it. Indeed, they who have the least idea of what I have suffered from the dread of public exhibitions, will readily excuse my never attempting them hereafter. In the meantime, if it please the Almighty, I may be an instrument of turning many to the truth, in a private way, and hope that my endeavours in this way have not been entirely unsuccessful. Had I the zeal of Moses, I should want an Aaron to be my spokesman,

Yours ever, my dear cousin,

Wm Cowper

I beg you will give my affectionate respects to Mrs Maitland when you write to her, & to my Aunt Madan, whom now I *cannot* see her, I know how to value.

TEXT: *Panshanger MSS.*

[3] The *Collection of Psalms and Hymns* published by the Rev. Martin Madan in 1760. He was Maria Cowper's brother.

TO MARIA COWPER

July 13, 1767

My dear cousin,

The newspaper has told you the truth. Poor Mr Unwin being flung from his horse as he was going to his cure on Sunday morning, received a dreadful fracture on the back part of his skull, under which he languished till Thursday evening and then died. This awful dispensation has left an impression upon our spirits which will not presently be worn off. He died in a poor cottage to which he was carried immediately after his fall, about a mile from home, and his body could not be brought to his house till the spirit was gone to Him who gave it. May it be a lesson to us to watch, since we know not the day nor the hour when our Lord cometh.[1]

The effect of it upon my circumstances will only be a change of the place of my abode, for I shall still, by God's leave, continue with Mrs Unwin, whose behaviour to me has always been that of a mother to a son. By this afflictive Providence, it has pleased God, who always drops comfort into the bitterest cup, to open a door for us out of an unevangelical pasture, such as this is, into some better ministry where we may hear the glad tidings of Salvation, and be nourished by the sincere milk of the Word. We know not yet where we shall settle, but we trust that the Lord whom we seek, will go before us, and prepare a rest for us. We have employed our friend Haweis,[2] Dr Conyers[3] of Helmsley in Yorkshire, and Mr Newton[4] of Olney to look out for us, but

[1] Matthew, xxiv, 42.

[2] The Rev. Thomas Haweis (1734–1820) had been assistant chaplain at the Lock Hospital, London, under Martin Madan, and was now rector of Aldwinkle, Northants.

[3] Conyers (see n., p. 232) when taking a doctorate of divinity at Cambridge, had met William Unwin, whom he introduced to Newton.

[4] The Rev. John Newton (1725–1807), co-author with C. of *Olney Hymns*, had been curate of Olney since 1764. His autobiography, *An Authentic Narrative*, tells the story of his life as the master of a slave-ship, and of his conversion.

at present are entirely ignorant under which of the three we shall settle, or whether under either. I have wrote too to my Aunt Madan, to desire Martin to assist us with his inquiries. It is probable we shall stay here till Michaelmas.

I beg my affectionate respects to Mr Cowper & all your family, & am, my dear cousin,

Yr affectionate friend & servant,

Wm Cowper

TEXT: *BM. Add. MSS.* 39,673

TO JOSEPH HILL

[? 1769]

Dear Joe,

I received the notes for thirty pounds.

Sir Thomas[1] crosses the Alps, and Sir Cowper (for that is his title at Olney) prefers his home to any other spot of earth in the world. Horace, observing this difference of temper in different persons, cried out a good many years ago, in the true spirit of poetry, How much one man differs from another![2] This does not seem a very sublime exclamation in English, but I remember at Westminster we were taught to admire it in the original.

My dear friend, I am obliged to you for your kind invitation: but being long accustomed to retirement, which I was always fond of, I am now more than ever unwilling to revisit those noisy & crowded scenes which I never loved & which I now abhor. I remember you with all the friendship I ever

[1] The Heskeths had settled in Italy.

[2] The allusion may be to the *Epistles*, I, xiv, 10–11: '*Rure ego viventem tu dicis in urbe, beatum: cui placet alterius, sua nimirum est odio sors.*' (I call a country life happy, you life in the town; and no doubt he who likes another man's life must dislike his own.)

professed, which is as much as I ever entertained for any man. But the strange and uncommon incidents of my life have given an entire new turn to my whole character and conduct, and rendered me incapable of receiving pleasure from the same employments and amusements of which I could readily partake in former days.

I love you and yours; I thank you for your continued remembrance of me, and shall not cease to be their and your affectionate friend and servant,

Wm Cowper

I am glad to hear of my uncle's recovery.

TEXT: *Cowper Johnson MSS.*

TO JOSEPH HILL

Nov. 12, '76

Dear friend,

The very agreeable contents of your last came safe to hand in the shape of two notes for £30. — I am to thank you likewise for a barrel of very good oysters received about a fortnight ago.

One to whom fish is so welcome as it is to me can have no great occasion to distinguish the sorts; in general therefore whatever fish are likely to think a jaunt into the country agreeable, will be sure to find me ready to receive them: butts, plaice, flounder, or any other. If herrings are yet to be had, as they cannot be bought at Olney till they are good for nothing, they will be welcome too. We have seen none this year except a parcel that Mrs Unwin sent for, and the fishmonger sent stale ones. A trick they are apt to put upon their customers at a distance.

Having suffered so much by nervous fevers myself I know

how to congratulate Ashley[1] upon his recovery. Other distempers only batter the walls, but they creep silently into the citadel and put the garrison to the sword.

You perceive I have not made a squeamish use of your obliging offer. The remembrance of past years, and of the sentiments formerly exchanged in our evening walks convinces me still that an unreserved acceptance of what is generously offered is the handsomest way of dealing with one of your character.

Believe me Yrs

Wm Cowper

The Wellingborough diligence passes our door every Tuesday, Thursday and Saturday, and inns at the Cross Keys, St John Street, Smithfield.

As to the frequency which you leave to my choice too, you have no need to exceed the number of your former remittances.

TEXT: *Cowper Johnson MSS.*

---

[1] Ashley Cowper (1701–88), C.'s uncle. He held the sinecure of Chafe-Wax in Chancery, and for forty years until his death, that of Clerk of the Parliaments, bought in perpetuity by his father, with the right of appointing the clerks on the staff of the House of Lords. Difficulties arising from C.'s nomination to one of these clerkships brought on his breakdown of 1763. (See *Ryskamp*, pp. 148–49). C. spent most of his time in 1750–53 at his uncle's house in Southampton Row, where he first met Hill. 'I always lived in great intimacy with...Mr. Ashley Cowper and his family', Hill wrote to Hayley on February 19, 1802 (Cowper Johnson MSS.) 'and soon after William Cowper came from Westminster School, our friendship commenced and never ceased, and for many years the two Mr. Cowpers went to one or other of the bathing places all round the coast—the year 1763 was the last of these excursions that William Cowper was with us.'

TO JOSEPH HILL

April—I fancy the 20th [?1777]

My dear friend,

Thank for a turbot, a lobster and Capt. Brydone;[1] a gentleman who relates his travels so agreeably that he deserves always to travel with an agreeable companion. I have been reading Gray's works,[2] and think him the only poet since Shakspear entitled to the character of sublime. Perhaps you will remember that I once had a different opinion of him: I was prejudiced: he did not belong to our Thursday Society[3] and was an Eton man, which lowered him prodigiously in our esteem. I once thought Swift's letters the best that could be written, but I like Gray's better; his humour or his wit, or whatever it is to be called, is never ill-natured or offensive, and yet I think equally poignant with the Dean's.

> I am yrs affectionately,
>
> Wm Cowper

TEXT: *Cowper Johnson MSS.*

TO JOSEPH HILL

Mar. 8, 1778

My dear friend,

The last paper made mention of the death of Sir Thomas Hesketh. I cannot upon occasion of so interesting an event be contented to receive no other account than what that uncertain vehicle conveyed to me. As he was said to have died at his house in Berkeley Square, and I never heard of his

---

[1] Patrick Brydone: *A Tour through Sicily and Malta,* 1773.

[2] Mason's *Memoirs of the Life and Writings of Gray, with his Poems,* 1775.

[3] The Nonsense Club: see pp. 377, 557.

removal from Grosvenor Street, a hope is left that it may be a false report. You will oblige me by a speedy answer, as on several accounts I cannot but be anxious for further information.

I am yrs affectionately

Wm Cowper

Many thanks to Mrs Hill for the seeds — and many for the fish and the books.

TEXT: *Cowper Johnson MSS.* **

TO JOSEPH HILL

Received of Mr Hill by draft on Child the sum of twenty pounds: £20.0.0. Wm Cowper

April 11, 1778

My dear friend,

I am obliged to you for the contents of your last. Money is sure to be acceptable, come when it will, and I had not small pleasure in the packet of seeds Mrs Hill was so kind as to sent me. I shall begin the cultivation of them immediately. Pray don't forget to inform her that I have raised 4 plants of the flower fence which are now 4 inches high and in a most flourishing state.

Poor Sir Thomas![1] I knew that I had a place in his affections, and from his own information many years ago, a place in his will; but little thought that after the lapse of so many years without intercourse, I should retain it. His remembrance of

[1] Sir Thomas Hesketh died on March 4, 1778, aged 51, according to the inscription on the memorial tablet erected by his widow in Rufford parish church, Lancashire. It includes a verse which may well have been composed for the occasion by Cowper, who had a legacy of £100:

> His frailer part, his sinful flesh,
> To dust lies here resigned;
> Thy mercy, Lord, his soul implores:
> Oh, may it mercy find.

me after so long a season of separation has done me much honour, and leaves me the more reason to regret his decease. I depend upon your kindness to inform me more particularly upon this subject when you are at liberty to do it.

I am reading the Abbé[2] with great satisfaction, and think him the most intelligent writer upon so extensive a subject I ever met with; in every respect superior to the Abbé in Scotland.

Yours affectionately,

Wm Cowper

P.S. Many thanks for the intended fish.

Sun. morn.

Which is just come, and should have been here last night. We shall bumble my landlady at Newport.

TEXT: *Cowper Johnson MSS.* *

TO THE REV. WILLIAM UNWIN[1]

[Postmarked February 8,] 1779[2]

My dear friend,

The fish happening to swim uppermost in my mind, I give it the precedence, and begin with returning our thanks for it,

[2] The Abbé Raynal: see *n.*, p. 706.

[1] William Unwin (1744–86) had been educated at Charterhouse and at Christ's College, Cambridge. He took his degree, and was awarded the Chancellor's Classical Medal, in 1764; was ordained deacon in 1767 and priest in 1769. When he became curate at Comberton, Cambs., his Evangelical admirers followed him there, including his cook, so that Paley thought him 'unduly favoured, since [I] never got such suppers elsewhere.' He was instituted rector of Stock, Essex, in 1778, and had married Anne Shuttleworth, by whom he had three children, of whom John and William are mentioned in C.'s letters.

[2] This undated letter is placed by Southey and later editors among the letters of 1786. The evidence for the date given above was supplied py Mr Kenneth Povey: *Review of English Studies*, April 1929.

not forgetting the circumstance of free carriage. Upon the whole, I think this a handsomer way of acknowledging a present than to tuck it into a postcript.

I find the *Register*[3] in all respects an entertaining medley, but especially in this, that it has brought to my view some long forgotten pieces of my own production, I mean by the way 2 or 3. These I have marked with my own initials, and you may be sure I found them peculiarly agreeable, as they had not only the grace of being mine but that of novelty likewise to recommend them; it is at least 20 years since I saw them.—You, I think, was never a dabbler in rhyme; I have been one ever since I was 14 years of age, when I began with translating an elegy of Tibullus. I have no more right to the name of a poet than a maker of mousetraps has to that of an engineer, but my little exploits in this way have at times amused me so much that I have often wished myself a good one. Such a talent in verse as mine is like a child's rattle, very entertaining to the trifler that uses it, and very disagreeable to all beside. But it has served to rid me of some melancholy moments, for I only take it up as a gentleman performer does his fiddle. I have this peculiarity belonging to me as a rhymist, that though I am charmed to a great degree with my own work while it is on the anvil, I can seldom bear to look at it when it is once finished. The more I contemplate it, the more it loses of its value, till I am at last quite disgusted with it. I then throw it by, take it up again perhaps ten years after, and am as much delighted with it as at first.

Few people have the art of being agreeable when they talk of themselves. If you are not weary therefore by this time you pay me a high compliment.

I dare say Miss Shuttleworth[4] was much diverted with the conjecture of her friends. The true key to the pleasure she found at Olney was plain enough to be seen, but they chose to overlook it. She brought with her a disposition to be pleased, which whoever does, is sure to find a visit agreeable, because they make it so.

[3] The *Annual Register*.
[4] Unwin's sister-in-law and ward.

Your mother joins me in affectionate remembrances to all your family.

Yours W.C.

We are obliged to little John for his P.S. We think his observation very just, but are a little doubtful about the exactness of his calculation.

TEXT: *BM. Add. MSS.* 24,155

TO THE REV. WILLIAM UNWIN

[? July, '79]

My dear friend,

If you please you may give my service to Mr James Martin, glazier, and tell him that I have furnished myself with glass from Bedford for just half the money.

When I was at Margate it was an excursion of pleasure to go to see Ramsgate. The pier, I remember, was accounted a most excellent piece of stonework, and such I found it. By this time, I suppose, it is finished, and surely it is no small advantage that you have an opportunity of observing how nicely those great stones are put together, as often as you please, without either trouble or expense. But you think Margate more lively. — So is a Cheshire cheese full of mites more lively than a sound one, but that very liveliness only proves its rottenness. I remember too that Margate, though full of company, was generally filled with such company, as people who were nice in the choice of their company were rather fearful of keeping company with. The hoy went to London every week, loaded with mackerel and herrings, and returned loaded with company. The cheapness of the conveyance made it equally commodious for dead fish and lively company. So perhaps your solitude at Ramsgate may turn out another advantage; at least I should think it one.

There was not, at that time, much to be seen in the Isle of Thanet besides the beauty of the country and the fine prospects of the sea, which are nowhere surpassed except in the Isle of Wight and upon some parts of the coast of Hampshire. One sight however I remember engaged my curiosity and I went to see it: a fine piece of ruins[1] built by the late Lord Holland at a great expense, which the day after I saw it tumbled down for nothing. Perhaps therefore it is still a ruin, and if it is I would advise you by all means to visit it, as it must have been much improved by this fortunate incident. It is hardly possible to put stones together with that air of wild and magnificent disorder which they are sure to acquire by falling of their own accord.

We heartily wish that Mrs Unwin may receive the utmost benefit of bathing. At the same time we caution you against the use of it, however the heat of the weather may seem to recommend it. It is not safe for thin habits, hectically inclined.

I remember (the fourth and last thing I mean to remember upon this occasion) that Sam: Cox, the counsel, walking by the sea side as if absorbed in deep contemplation, was questioned about what he was musing on. He replied, 'I was wondering that such an almost infinitive and unwieldy element should produce a sprat.'—Our love attends the whole party.

Yours affectionately

Wm Cowper

You are desired to purchase 3 pounds of sixpenny white worsted at a shop well recommended for that commodity. The Isle of Thanet is famous for it beyond any other place in the kingdom.

TEXT: *BM. Add. MSS.* 24,154

---

[1] Kingsgate House, near the North Foreland, was built by Stephen Fox, first Lord Holland. It was intended 'to represent Tully's Formian villa'.

TO THE REV. WILLIAM UNWIN

Sept. 21, 1779

Amico mio!

Be pleased to buy me a glazier's diamond pencil. I have glazed the two frames designed to receive my pine plants, but I cannot mend the kitchen windows till by the help of that implement I can reduce the glass to its proper dimensions. If I were a plumber I should be a complete glazier, and possibly the happy time may come when I shall be seen trudging away to the neighbouring towns with a shelf of glass hanging at my back. If government should impose another tax upon that commodity,[1] I hardly know a business in which a gentleman might more successfully employ himself. A Chinese of ten times my fortune would avail himself of such an opportunity without scruple, and why should not I, who want money as much as any mandarin in China? Rousseau would have been charmed to have seen me so occupied, and would have exclaimed with rapture that he had found the Emilius who he supposed had subsisted only in his own idea.[2] I would recommend it to you to follow my example. You will presently qualify yourself for the task, and may not only amuse yourself at home but may even exercise your skill in mending the church windows, which as it would save money to the parish, would conduce, together with your other ministerial accomplishments, to make you extremely popular in the place.

I have 8 pair of tame pigeons. When I first enter the garden in a morning, I find them perched upon the wall, waiting for their breakfast, for I feed them always upon the gravel walk. If your wish should be accomplished and you should find yourself furnished with the wings of a dove, I

[1] The window tax was increased in 1778.

[2] In *Emile, ou de l'éducation*, 1762, (translated into English as *Emilius*), Rousseau's imaginary pupil was set to learn a trade.

shall undoubtedly find you amongst them. Only be so good, if that should be the case, as to announce yourself by some means or other, for I imagine your crop will require something better than tares to fill it.

Your Mother and I last week made a trip in a post chaise to Gayhurst, the seat of Mr Wrighte,[3] about 4 miles off. He understood that I did not much affect strange faces and sent over his servant on purpose to inform me that he was going into Leicestershire, and that if I chose to see the gardens, I might gratify myself without danger of seeing the proprietor. I accepted the invitation and was delighted with all I found there; the situation is happy, the gardens elegantly disposed, the hot house in the most flourishing state, and the orange trees the most captivating creatures of the kind I ever saw. A man, in short, had need have the talents of Cox or Langford,[4] the auctioneers, to do the whole scene justice. Our love attends you all.

Yours,

Wm Cowper

The snuff shop is Arnold's in Newgate Street.

TEXT: *BM. Add. MSS.* 24,154

TO THE REV. WILLIAM UNWIN

Oct. 31, 1779

My dear friend,

I wrote my last letter merely to inform you that I had nothing to say; in answer to which you have said nothing. I admire the propriety of your conduct though I am a loser by it. I will endeavour to say something now, and shall hope for something in return.

---

[3] George Wrighte came into the Gayhurst estate in 1766, and died in 1804.

[4] See *n.*, p. 522.

I have been well entertained with Johnson's biography,[1] for which I thank you: with one exception, and that a swingeing one, I think he has acquitted himself with his usual good sense and sufficiency. His treatment of Milton is unmerciful to the last degree. A pensioner is not likely to spare a republican; and the Doctor, in order, I suppose, to convince his royal patron of the sincerity of his monarchial principles, has belaboured that great poet's character with the most industrious cruelty. As a man, he has hardly left him the shadow of one good quality. Churlishness in his private life, and a rancorous hatred of everything royal in his public, are the two colours with which he has smeared all the canvas. If he had any virtues, they are not to be found in the Doctor's picture of him; and it is well for Milton, that some sourness in his temper is the only vice with which his memory has been charged; it is evident enough that if his biographer could have discovered more, he would not have spared him. As a poet, he has treated him with severity enough, and has plucked one or two of the most beautiful feathers out of his Muse's wing, and trampled them under his great foot. He has passed sentence of condemnation upon *Lycidas*, and has taken occasion, from that charming poem, to expose to ridicule, (what is indeed ridiculous enough,) the childish prattlement of pastoral compositions, as if *Lycidas* was the prototype and pattern of them all. The liveliness of the description, the sweetness of the numbers, the classical spirit of antiquity that prevails in it, go for nothing. I am convinced by the way, that he has no ear for poetical numbers, or that it was stopped by prejudice against the harmony of Milton's. Was there ever any thing so delightful as the music of the *Paradise Lost*? It is like that of a fine organ; has the fullest and the deepest tones of majesty, with all the softness and elegance of the Dorian flute. Variety without end and never equalled, unless perhaps by Virgil. Yet the Doctor has little or nothing to say upon this copious theme, but talks something about

[1] Dr Johnson's *Lives of the Poets* appeared, from 1779 to 1781, as *Prefaces Biographical and Critical, to the Works of the English Poets*. Johnson had described Milton as 'an acrimonious and surly republican'.

the unfitness of the English language for blank verse, and how apt it is, in the mouth of some readers, to degenerate into declamation. Oh! I could thresh his old jacket, till I made his pension jingle in his pocket.

I could talk a good while longer, but I have no room; our love attends you.

Yours affectionately,

W.C.

TEXT: *Southey*

TO THE REV. WILLIAM UNWIN

Feb. 27, '80

My dear friend,

As you are pleased to desire my letters, I am the more pleased with writing them, though at the same time I must needs testify my surprise that you should think them worth receiving, as I seldom send one that I think favourably of myself. This is not to be understood as an imputation upon your taste or judgment, but as an encomium upon my own modesty and humility, which I desire you to remark well. It is a just observation of Sir Joshua Reynolds that though men of ordinary talents may be highly satisfied with their own productions, men of true genius never are. Whatever be their subject, they always seem to themselves to fall short of it, even when they seem to others most to excel, and for this reason,—because they have a certain sublime sense of perfection, which other men are strangers to, and which they themselves in their performances are not able to exemplify.— Your servant, Sir Joshua, I little thought of seeing you when I began, but as you have popped in you are welcome.

When I wrote last, I was a little inclined to send you a copy of verses entitled 'The Modern Patriot',[1] but was not quite pleased with a line or two, which I found it difficult to mend, therefore did not. At night I read Mr Burke's speech in the

[1] Page 60.

newspaper, and was so well pleased with his proposals for a reformation,[2] and with the temper in which he made them, that I began to think better of his cause and burnt my verses. Such is the lot of the man who writes upon the subject of the day; the aspect of affairs changes in an hour or two, and his opinion with it. What was just and well deserved satire in the morning, in the evening becomes a libel, the author commences his own judge, and while he condemns with unrelenting severity what he so lately approved, is sorry to find that he has laid his leaf gold upon touchwood which crumbled away under his fingers. Alas! what can I do with my wit? I have not enough to do great things with, and these little things are so fugitive, that while a man catches at the subject, he is only filling his hand with smoke. I must do with it as I do with my linnet. I keep him for the most part in a cage, but now and then set open the door, that he may whisk about the room a little, and then shut him up again. My whisking wit has produced the following,[3] the subject of which is more important than the manner in which I have treated it seems to imply, but a fable may speak the truth, and all truth is sterling. I only premise that in a philosophical tract in the *Register*, I found it asserted that the glowworm is the nightingale's proper food.

Have you heard? who has not? for a recommendatory advertisement of it is already published, that a certain kinsman of your humble servant's has written a tract, now in the press, to prove a polygamy a divine institution![4] A plurality

---

[2] Burke proposed 'a plan for the...Economical Reformation of the Civil Service and other Establishments' on February 11.

[3] This letter contained the fable of the Nightingale and Glow-worm.— Southey. (p. 61.)

[4] *Thelyphthora: or, a Treatise on Female Ruin*, written by the Rev. Martin Madan (1725–90), a leading if erratic Evangelical light, and C.'s first cousin. The book advocated polygamy as a means of solving the problems of prostitution, with which Madan was familiar as honorary chaplain to the Lock Hospital, where patients were treated for venereal disease. Madan's arguments were all the more scandalizing because they were based on passages in the Old Testament, interpreted literally. The Greek words in the title mean 'corruption of women'.

of wives is intended, but not of husbands. The end proposed by the author is to remedy the prevailing practice of adultery, by making the female delinquent *ipso facto* the lawful wife of the male. — An officer of a regiment, part of which is quartered here, gave one of the soldiers leave to be drunk six weeks, in hopes of curing him by satiety. He *was* drunk six weeks, and is so still, as often as he can find an opportunity. One vice may swallow up another but no coroner in the state of ethics ever brought in his verdict, when a vice died, that it was *felo de se*.

They who value the man are sorry for his book. The rest say, *Solvuntur risu tabulae, tu missus abibis.*[5]

Thanks for all you have done, and all you intend; the biography will be particularly welcome.

My truly affectionate respects attend you all

Yours Wm Cowper

When you feel postage a burden send me some franks.

TEXT: *BM. Add. MSS.* 24,154

TO THE REV. JOHN NEWTON

May 3, 1780

Dear Sir,

You indulge me in such a variety of subjects, and allow me such a latitude of excursion in this scribbling employment, that I have no excuse for silence. I am much obliged to you for swallowing such boluses as I send you, for the sake of my gilding, and verily believe that I am the only man alive, from whom they would be welcome to a palate like yours. I wish I could make them more splendid than they are, more alluring to the eye, at least, if not more pleasing to the taste; but my leaf gold is tarnished, and has received such a tinge from the

[5] Horace, *Satires*, II, i, 86: 'The court breaks up in laughter, and you will be discharged.'

vapours that are ever brooding over my mind, that I think it no small proof of your partiality to me, that you will read my letters. I am not fond of longwinded metaphors; I have always observed, that they halt at the latter end of their progress, and so do mine. I deal much in ink indeed, but not such ink as is employed by poets, and writers of essays. Mine is a harmless fluid, and guilty of no deceptions but such as may prevail without the least injury to the person imposed on. I draw mountains, valleys, woods, and streams, and ducks, and dab-chicks. I admire them myself, and Mrs Unwin admires them; and her praise, and my praise put together, are fame enough for me. The man that expects hereafter to be imprisoned in a dungeon where nothing but misery and deformity are to be found, has a peculiar pleasure in contemplating the beauties of Nature and sees a thousand charms in meadows and the flowers that adorn them, in blue skies and skies overhung with tempests, in trees and rocks, and in every circumstance of rural life that are lost upon a mind in security, & are invisible to him that has a peaceful conscience. Oh! I could spend whole days and moonlight nights in feeding upon a lovely prospect! My eye drinks the rivers as they flow, and I say to myself, how sadly I shall thirst hereafter. If every human being upon earth could think for one quarter of an hour, as I have done for many years, there might perhaps be many unconverted miserable men among them, but not an unawakened one would be found from the Arctic to the Antarctic circle. At present the difference between them and me is greatly to their advantage. I delight in baubles, and know them to be so; for rested in and viewed without a reference to their Author, what is the earth, what are the planets, what is the sun itself but a bauble? Better for man never to have seen them, or to see them with the eyes of a brute, stupid and unconscious of what he beholds, than not to be able to say, 'The Maker of all these wonders is my friend!' I cannot say this, neither can they; but their eyes have never been opened to see that they are trifles in themselves, & mine have been, are, and will be till they are closed for ever. They think a fine estate, a large conservatory, a hothouse rich as a West Indian garden, things of consequence; visit them with pleasure, and muse upon them with ten times more. I am pleased with a frame of four lights, doubtful whether the few pines it contains will ever be worth a farthing; amuse myself with a greenhouse which Lord Bute's gardener[1] could take upon his back, and walk away with; and when I have paid it the accustomed visit, and watered it, and given it air, I say to myself—'This is not mine, 'tis a plaything lent me for the present; I must leave it soon', & with it perhaps the very idea of vegetable nature, or if I retain the picture, it will only be that I may regret the loss of the original. Happy they that sleep, in comparison with those who wake to no purpose. Both are in reality miserable, but he is most emphatically so, who knows and feels his misery.

I have written as above while Mrs U. and Hannah[2] are gone to sleep together; if they come down before I have finished I must conclude; for Caesar himself, who could dictate to so many, would have been obliged to wait till another post, if Hannah's tongue had been within his hearing. I have heard that curiosity in a child is a prognostic of future wisdom; if that be true she is likely to be wise indeed, for she asks more questions in one hour than could be discreetly answered in two.

Olney is, as usual, newsless,[3] for it is hardly worth while to tell you that Tom Freeman is returned from the Army, & turned baker, that he makes very light English rolls, & still lighter French ones, that all the world is astonished at his indefatigable industry, & foresee & foretell, that if he perseveres in it, he will be a great man. This to a man who seldom sees the newspapers, may be perhaps worth knowing, possibly it may be as important as the most of what he would find there if he saw them all.

Yrs dr Sir very affectionately,

W.C.

TEXT: *Private Correspondence* and *Barham Johnson MSS.*†*

[1] The third Earl of Bute, Prime Minister, created a celebrated botanical garden at Luton Hoo, Beds.

[2] see *n.*, p. 630.

[3] Newton had left Olney in December 1779 on his presentation to the living of St Mary Woolnoth in the City.

TO THE REV. WILLIAM UNWIN

May 8, '80

My dear friend,

I would advise you by all means to deal frankly with your competitor, if he should pay you the visit you expect. It will infallibly obviate all possibility of misconstruction, and is the only course you can take that will do so. You have a very good story to tell and nothing to be ashamed of; and as for the awkwardness of the occasion, that will be no longer felt than just while you are making your exordium. Your behaviour will please him if he has a taste for propriety, and he cannot but forgive you the crime of having an uncle that loves you too well to overlook or neglect so fair an opportunity to promote your interest.

My scribbling humour has of late been entirely absorbed in the passion of landscape drawing. It is a most amusing art, and like every other art, requires much practice and attention:

> *Nil sine multo*
> *Vita labore dedit mortalibus.*[1]

Excellence is providentially placed beyond the reach of indolence, that success may be the reward of industry, and that idleness may be punished with obscurity and disgrace. So long as I am pleased with an employment, I am capable of unwearied application, because my feelings are all of the intense kind. I never received a *little* pleasure from anything in my life; if I am delighted, it is in the extreme. The unhappy consequence of this temperature is that my attachment to any occupation seldom outlives the novelty of it. That nerve of my imagination that feels the touch of any particular amusement, twangs under the energy of the pressure with so much vehemence, that it soon becomes sensible of weariness and

[1] Horace, *Satires*, I, ix, 59: 'Life grants nothing to man, except through much labour'.

fatigue. Hence I draw an unfavourable prognostic, and expect that I shall shortly be constrained to look out for something else. Then perhaps I may string the lyre again, and be able to comply with your demand.

Now for the visit you propose to pay us, and propose *not* to pay us; the hope of which plays about upon your paper, like a jack-o'-lantern upon the ceiling. This is no mean simile, for Virgil,[2] you remember, uses it. 'Tis here, 'tis there, it vanishes, it returns, it dazzles you, a cloud interposes, and it is gone. However just the comparison, I hope you will contrive to spoil it, and that your final determination will be to come. As to the masons you expect, bring them with you—bring brick, bring mortar, bring everything that would oppose itself to your journey—all shall be welcome. I have a greenhouse that is too small, come and enlarge it; build me a pinery; repair the garden wall that has great need of your assistance; do anything; you cannot do too much; so far from thinking you and your train troublesome, we shall rejoice to see you upon these or upon any terms you can propose. But to be serious— you will do well to consider that a long summer is before you; that the party will not have such another opportunity to meet this great while; that you may finish your masonry long enough before winter, though you should not begin this month, but that you cannot always find your brother and sister Powley at Olney. These, and some other considerations, such as the desire we have to see you, and the pleasure we expect from seeing you all together, may, and, I think, ought to overcome your scruples. We are only sorry Miss Shuttle-worth cannot come with you, which seems to be set down as a postulation not to be disputed.

From a general recollection of Lord Clarendon's *History of the Rebellion*, I thought (and remember I told you so) that there was a striking resemblance between that period and the present. But I am now reading, and have read three volumes of Hume's *History*,[3] one of which is engrossed entirely by that

[2] The flame of good omen which played on the head of Aeneas's son Iulus: *Aeneid* II, 681–4.

[3] *History of Great Britain*, by David Hume (1711–76). It appeared between 1754 and 1761.

subject. There I see reason to alter my opinion, and the seeming resemblance has disappeared upon a more particular information. Charles succeeded to a long train of arbitrary princes, whose subjects had tamely acquiesced in the despotism of their masters, till their privileges were all forgot. He did but tread in their steps, and exemplify the principles in which he had been brought up, when he oppressed his people. But just at that time, unhappily for the monarch, the subject began to see, and to see that he had a right to property and freedom. This marks a sufficient difference between the disputes of that day and the present. But there was another main cause of that rebellion, which at this time does not operate at all. The king was devoted to the hierarchy; his subjects were puritans and would not bear it. Every circumstance of ecclesiastical order and discipline was an abomination to them, and in his esteem an indispensable duty. And though at last he was obliged to give up many things, he would not abolish episcopacy; and till that were done his concessions could have no conciliating effect. These two concurring causes were indeed sufficient to set three kingdoms in a flame. But they subsist not now, nor any other, I hope, notwithstanding the bustle made by the patriots, equal to the production of such terrible events.

Yours, my dear friend,

Wm Cowper

TEXT: *BM. Add. MSS.* 24,154

TO JOSEPH HILL

July 8, 1780

Mon ami!

By this time I suppose you have ventured to take your fingers out of your ears, being delivered from the deafening shouts of the most zealous mob that ever strained their lungs in the cause of religion.[1] I congratulate you upon a gentle

---

[1] The 'No Popery' riots, led by Lord George Gordon.

relapse into the customary sounds of a great city, which, though we rustics abhor them as noisy and dissonant, are a musical and sweet murmur compared with what you have lately heard. The tinkling of a runnel may be distinguished now, where the roaring of a cascade would have been sunk and lost. I never suspected till the newspaper informed me of it a few days since, that the barbarous uproar had reached Great Queen Street. I hope Mrs Hill was in the country—you, I know, are more apt to be angry than terrified but had more prudence, I trust, than to oppose your little person to such a furious torrent. I shall rejoice to hear you are in health, and that as I am sure you did not take up the Protestant cudgels upon this hare-brained occasion, so you have not been pulled in pieces as a Papist.

If you ever take the tip of the Chancellor's ear between your finger and thumb, you can hardly improve the opportunity to better purpose than if you should whisper into it the voice of compassion and lenity to the lace-makers. I am an eye-witness of their poverty, and do know that hundreds in this little town are upon the point of starving, and that the most unremitting industry is but barely sufficient to keep them from it. I know that the bill by which they would have been so fatally affected is thrown out, but Lord Stormont threatens them with another; and if another like it should pass, they are undone. We lately sent a petition from hence to Lord Dartmouth. I signed it, and am sure the contents are true. The purport of it was to inform him that there are very near 1200 lace-makers in this beggarly town, the most of whom had reason enough, while the bill was in agitation, to look upon every loaf they bought as the last they should ever be able to earn.—I can never think it good policy to incur the certain inconvenience of ruining 300,000 in order to prevent a remote and possible damage, though to a much greater number.[2] The measure is like a scythe, and the poor

---

[2] There was a parliamentary debate on Irish affairs in April 1780. The Irish wanted free trade and were arming themselves. The threat of a removal of tariffs on Irish goods must have been what was worrying the lace-makers of Olney. (Information from Mr W. T. O'Dea.)

lace-makers are the sickly crop that trembles before the edge of it. The prospect of peace with America is like the streak of dawn in their horizon, but this bill is like a black cloud behind it, that threatens their hope of a comfortable day with utter extinction. I did not perceive till this moment that I had tacked two similies together; a practice which, though warranted by the example of Homer, and allowable in an epic poem, is rather luxuriant and licentious in a letter: lest I should add a third, I conclude myself, with my best respects to Mrs Hill,

Yr affectionate,

Wm Cowper

TEXT: *Cowper Johnson MSS.* The second part of this letter was the first to be published, by Hayley: the first paragraph followed later in the *Private Correspondence*, and the collected editions print the fragments as two separate letters.

TO THE REV. JOHN NEWTON

July 12, 1780

My dear friend,

Such nights as I frequently spend are but a miserable prelude to the succeeding day, and indispose me, above all things, to the business of writing. Yet with a pen in my hand, if I am able to write at all, I find myself gradually relieved; and as I am glad of any employment that may serve to engage my attention, so especially I am pleased with an opportunity of conversing with you, though it be but upon paper. This occupation above all others assists me in that self-deception to which I am indebted for all the little comfort I enjoy; things seem to be as they were, and I almost forget that they never can be so again.

We are both obliged to you for a sight of Mr Madan's letter. The friendly and obliging manner of it will much enhance the difficulty of answering it. I think I can see plainly that though he does not hope for your applause, he would gladly escape your censure. He seems to approach you smoothly and softly, and to take you gently by the hand, as if he bespoke your lenity, and entreated you at least to spare him. You have such skill in the management of your pen, that I doubt you will be able to send him a balmy reproof that shall give him no reason to complain of a broken head. — How delusive is the wildest speculation when pursued with eagerness, and nourished with such arguments as the perverted ingenuity of such a mind as his can easily furnish! — Judgement falls asleep upon the bench, while Imagination, like a smug, pert counsellor, stands chattering at the bar, and with a deal of fine-spun, enchanting sophistry, carries all before him.

If I had strength of mind, I have not strength of body for the task which, you say, some would impose upon me.[1] I cannot bear much thinking. The meshes of that fine network, the brain, are composed of such mere spinners' threads in me, that when a long thought finds its way into them, it buzzes, and twangs, and bustles about at such a rate as seems to threaten the whole contexture. — No — I must needs refer it again to you.

My enigma will probably find you out, and you will find out my enigma at some future time. I am not in a humour to transcribe it now. Indeed I wonder that a sportive thought should ever knock at the door of my intellects, and still more that it should gain admittance. It is as if harlequin should intrude himself into the gloomy chamber where a corpse is deposited in state. His antic gesticulations would be unseasonable at any rate, but more especially so if they should distort the features of the mournful attendants into laughter. But the mind long wearied with the sameness of a dull, dreary prospect, will gladly fix its eyes on anything that may make a little variety in its contemplations, though it were but a kitten playing with her tail.

You would believe, though I did not say it at the end of

---

[1] *the task*: of writing a refutation of Madan's *Thelyphthora* (*n.*, p. 581) which had appeared on May 31. C.'s first riposte was 'The Doves' (p. 63), originally called 'Anti-Thelyphthora'. The longer poem of that name was probably not begun until October and was printed in December.

every letter, that we remember you and Mrs Newton with the same affection as ever; but I would not therefore excuse myself from writing what it gives you pleasure to read. I have often wished indeed, when writing to an ordinary correspondent, for the revival of the Roman custom—*salutem* at top, and *vale* at bottom. But as the French have taught all Europe to enter a room and to leave it with a most ceremonious bow, so they have taught us to begin and conclude our letters in the same manner. However I can say to you, *sans cérémonie,*

Adieu, mon ami,

Wm Cowper

TEXT: *Wright*

TO MARIA COWPER

July 20, 1780

My dear cousin,

Mr Newton having desired me to be of the party,[1] I am come to meet him. You see me sixteen years older at the least than when I saw you last; but the effects of time seem to have taken place rather on the outside of my head than within it. What was brown is become gray, but what was foolish remains foolish still. Green fruit must rot before it ripens, if the season is such as to afford it nothing but cold winds and dark clouds that intercept every ray of sunshine. My days steal away silently and march on (as poor mad King Lear would have made his soldiers march)[2] as if they were shod with felt. Not so silently but that I hear them: yet were it not that I am always listening to their flight, having no infirmity that I had not when I was much younger, I should deceive myself with an imagination that I am still young.

I am fond of writing, as an amusement, but I do not always

---

[1] Mrs Cowper was a member of Newton's congregation at St Mary Woolnoth.

[2] *King Lear,* IV, vi, 186–7.

find it one. Being rather scantily furnished with subjects that are good for anything, and corresponding only with those who have no relish for such as are good for nothing, I often find myself reduced to the necessity, the disagreeable necessity, of writing about myself. This does not mend the matter much, for though in a description of my own condition, I discover abundant materials to employ my pen upon, yet as the task is not very agreeable to *me*, so I am sufficiently aware that it is likely to prove irksome to others. A painter who should confine himself in the exercise of his art to the drawing of his own picture must be a wonderful coxcomb if he did not soon grow sick of his occupation, and be peculiarly fortunate if he did not make others as sick as himself.

Remote as your dwelling is from the late scene of riot and confusion, I hope that though you could not but hear the report of it, you heard no more, and that the roarings of the mad multitude did not reach you. That was a day of terror to the innocent, and the present is a day of still greater terror to the guilty. The law was for a few moments like an arrow in the quiver, seemed to be of no use, and did no execution; now it is an arrow upon the string, and many who despised it lately are trembling as they stand before the point of it.

I have talked more already than I have formerly done in three visits—you remember my taciturnity, never to be forgotten by those who knew me. Not to depart entirely from what might be for aught I know the most shining part of my character, I here shut my mouth, make my bow, and return to Olney.

My love attends your family. Mrs Unwin presents her affectionate respects, and desires me to add for the satisfaction of Mr and Mrs Newton, who have heard she was indisposed, that she is better.

Yrs my dear cousin,

Wm Cowper

TEXT: *Panshanger MSS.*

TO JOSEPH HILL

Aug. 10, 1780

My dear sir,

I greet you at your Castle of Buen Retiro,[1] and wish you could enjoy the unmixed pleasures of the country there, but it seems you are obliged to dash the cup with a portion of those bitters you are always swallowing in town. Well—you are honourably and usefully employed, and ten times more beneficially to society than if you were piping to a few sheep under a spreading beech, or listening to a tinkling rill. Besides, by the effect of long custom and habitual practice, you are not only enabled to endure your occupation, but even find it agreeable. I remember the time when it would not have suited you so well to have devoted so large a part of your vacation to the objects of your profession; and you, I dare say, have not forgot what a seasonable relaxation you found when, lying at full stretch upon the ruins of an old wall by the seaside, you amused yourself with Tasso's *Jerusalem* and the *Pastor Fido*. I recollect that we both pitied Mr de Grey[2] when we called at his cottage at Taplow, and found, not the master indeed, but his desk with his white-leaved folio upon it, which bespoke him as much a man of business in his retirement as in Westminster Hall. But by these steps he ascended the Bench, and by such steps as these I doubt not but you will rise (perhaps you are already risen) tho' not to the Bench, yet to a rank equally respectable in that part of the profession you have chosen. In time perhaps you may do as he has done; he has retired, and so may you—now he may

[1] The letter was addressed to Hill's country house, Wargrave Hill, Berks. Buen Retiro was the name of a castle of the Kings of Spain, in the present public park of El Retiro, Madrid.

[2] William de Grey, 1719–80, married C.'s cousin Mary Cowper. He had been appointed Lord Chief Justice of the Common Pleas in 1777, but resigned for reasons of ill-health in June 1780. In October he was created Baron Walsingham.

read what he pleases, and ride where he will if the gout will give him leave; and you, who have no gout, and probably never will, when your hour of dismission comes, will, for that reason, if for no other, be a happier man than he.

I am sorry the melons proved no better. I believe they were come too soon, a fault our gardener is very apt to fall into. Else I have found in general that the Old Rock and the Crimson Canteloupe are not only good sorts, but the best that are to be met with, but they require a deal of ripening.

My respects attend Mrs Hill with many thanks for her obliging intentions. I have the plants of several seeds with which she has favoured me in our own garden, and our neighbour at Gayhurst has several more which would not prosper with me for want of those advantages which he could give them. Everything exotic or rare is welcome, and is sure to turn to account in my hands, either as an ornament of our garden or in the way of barter with him.

I am, my dear friend,

Affectionately yours,

Wm Cowper

The author of *Thelyphthora* has not thought proper to favour me with his book, and having no interest in the subject, I have not thought proper to purchase it. Indeed I have no curiosity to read what I am sure must be erroneous before I read it. Truth is worth everything that can be given for it, but a mere display of ingenuity, calculated only to mislead, is worth nothing. —

TEXT: *Cowper Johnson MSS.* *

TO THE REV. JOHN NEWTON

Augt. 21, 1780

My dear sir,

I am willing to try if writing to you will charm the tooth-ache, which has hitherto defied every other remedy. I should

not have been so formal as to wait for your answer to my last
[? had not] other hindrances prevented my [? writing, for]
as often as a cloudy sky will [? permit us,] we walk both morning and [? evening] to the Wilderness but more fr[equently to
the] Spinney, and this exercise [? engrosses the] hours that are
favourable to [? epistolary] employment.

The following occurrence ought not to be passed over in
silence, in a place where so few notable ones are to be met
with. Last Wednesday night while we were at supper, between the hours of 8 and 9, I heard an unusual noise in the
back parlour, as if one of the hares was entangled, & endeavouring to disengage herself. I was just going to rise from the
table, when it ceased. In about 5 minutes, a voice on the
outside of the parlour door enquired if one of my hares had
got away. I immediately rushed into the next room, and found
that my poor favourite Puss had made her escape. She had
gnawed in sunder the strings of a lattice work with which
I thought I had sufficiently secured the window, and which I
preferred to any other sort of blind, because it admitted plenty
of air.

[From t]hence I hastened to the kitchen, where I [saw the]
redoubtable Tom Freeman, who told [me that] having seen
her just after she had [dropped] into the street, he attempted
to cover [her with] his hat, but she screamed out, and [leaped]
directly over his head. I then desired him [to pur]sue as fast as
possible, & added Richard Coleman to the chase, as being
nimbler & carrying less *belly* than Tom; not expecting to see
her again, but desirous if possible to learn what became of
her. In somewhat less than an hour, Richard returned, almost
breathless, with the following account. That soon after he
began to run he left Tom behind him, and came in sight of a
most numerous hunt consisting of men, women, children, and
dogs; that he did his best to keep back the dogs, and presently
outstripped the crowd, so that the race was at last disputed
between himself and Puss. She ran right through the town,
and down the lane that leads to Dropshort. A little before she
came to the house, he got the start and turned her. She
pushed for the town again, and soon after she entered it,
sought Shelter in Mr Wagstaff's tanyard, adjoining to old Mr

Drake's. Sturges's harvest men were at supper and saw her from the opposite side of the way. There she encountered the tanpits full of water & while she was strug[gling out] of one pit & plunging into another, [and almost] drowned, one of the men drew her [out by the ears] and secured her. She was then [well washed in a] bucket, to get the lime out of her [coat, and] brought home in a sack at 10 o'clock. This frolic cost us four shillings but you may suppose we did not grudge a farthing of it. The poor creature received only a little hurt in one of her claws, and in one of her ears, and is now almost as well as ever.

Your book[1] was cried at the Sunday evening meeting but is not yet to be heard of.

Mrs Unwin has had a return of her old spasmodic complaint, which makes writing hurtful to her. She has no atrophy with it, & is better.

I do not call this an answer to your letter, but such as it is I send it, presuming upon that interest I know you take in my minutest concerns, which I cannot express better than in the words of Terence a little varied— *Nihil mei a te alienum putas.*

Our love attends you both with Miss Catlett,[2] & our affectionate remembrances all your household.

Yrs. my dear friend,

Wm C.

Mrs Whitney was here yesterday. She came to ask my sage advice in her disturbed and troublesome affairs. She spoke of you with great affection & of Mrs Newton. Regretted the loss of that instruction she should have received from you had you been at Olney, and expressed the most earnest longings for a letter.

TEXT: *MSS. Cowper Museum, Olney.* * Part of the MS. has been eaten by a mouse. The words enclosed within square brackets in the (unpublished) first paragraph have been supplied by the

---

[1] *Cardiphonia.*
[2] Mrs Newton's niece, and Newton's adopted daughter.

present editor and represent a conjectural restoration of the sense. The words so inserted in the third paragraph have been taken from Hayley's edition.

TO THE REV. WILLIAM UNWIN

Sept. 7, 1780

My dear friend,

As many gentlemen as there are in the world who have children, and heads capable of reflecting on the important subject of their education, so many opinions there are about it; many of them just and sensible, though almost all differing from each other. With respect to the education of boys, I think they are generally made to draw in Latin and Greek trammels too soon. It is pleasing no doubt to a parent to see his child already in some sort a proficient in those languages at an age when most others are entirely ignorant of them; but hence it often happens that a boy who could construe a fable in Aesop at 6 or 7 years of age, having exhausted his little stock of attention and diligence in making that notable acquisition, grows weary of his task, conceives a dislike of study, and perhaps makes but a very indifferent progress afterwards. The mind and the body have in this respect a striking resemblance of each other. In childhood they are both nimble, but not strong; they can skip and frisk about with wonderful agility, but hard labour spoils them both. In maturer years they become less active, but more vigorous, more capable of a fixed application, and can make themselves sport with that which a little earlier would have affected them with intolerable fatigue. I should recommend it to you therefore (but after all you must judge for yourself) to allot the two next years of little John's scholarship to writing and arithmetic, together with which, for variety's sake, and because it is capable of being formed into an amusement, I would mingle geography, a science which, if not attended to betimes, is seldom made an object of much consideration: essentially necessary to the accomplishment of a gentleman, yet (as I know by sad experience) imperfectly, if at all, inculcated in the schools. Lord Spencer's son, when he was four years of age, knew the situation of every kingdom, country, city, river, and remarkable mountain in the world. For this attainment, which I suppose his father had never made, he was indebted to a plaything; having been accustomed to amuse himself with those maps which cut into several compartments, so as to be thrown into a heap of confusion, that they may be put together again with an exact coincidence of all their angles and bearings, so as to form a perfect whole.

If he begins Latin and Greek at eight, or even at 9 years of age, it is surely soon enough. Seven years, the usual allowance for those acquisitions, are more than sufficient for the purpose, especially with his readiness in learning; for you would hardly wish to have him qualified for the university before 15, a period, in my mind, much too early for it, and when he could hardly be trusted there without the utmost danger to his morals. Upon the whole, you will perceive that in my judgement the difficulty as well as the wisdom consists more in bridling in and keeping back a boy of his parts, than in pushing him forward. If, therefore, at the end of the two next years, instead of putting a grammar into his hand, you should allow him to amuse himself with some agreeable writers upon the subjects of natural philosophy for another year, I think it would answer well. There is a book called *Cosmotheoria Puerilis*,[1] there are Derham's[2] *Physico—*, and *Astro-theology*, together with several others, in the same manner, very intelligible even to a child, and full of useful instruction.

Plums and pears in my next.

Your Mother's love and mine attend you all

Yours affectionately

Wm Cowper

TEXT: *BM. Add. MSS.* 24,154

[1] Possibly *Matho: or, the Cosmotheoria puerilis: a dialogue, in which the first principles of philosophy and astronomy are accommodated to the capacity of young persons.* (By Andrew Baxter) 2 vols. London, 1740. 3rd ed., 1765. I owe this reference to Mr F. Norman.

[2] William Derham, (1657–1735): *Physico-Theology*, 1713, *Astro-Theology*, 1715.

TO THE REV. JOHN NEWTON[1]

September 24th, 1780

My dear sir,

I should have acknowledged your letter sooner, and have acknowledged Mrs Newton's favour by an earlier opportunity if it had been in my power. But having dismissed our gardener for manifold good causes and reasons us thereunto moving, a great deal of additional employment has consequently fallen into my hands, and I am sometimes so weary before my morning business is finished, that I am not capable of writing.

If I was not disqualified for the society of good men, there are few of that description who would be more welcome to me than Mr Bull.[2] His eminent spirituality would recommend him to any man desirous of an edifying companion. But my condition renders me incapable of receiving or imparting a real benefit.

The short remainder of my life, the beginning of which was spent in sin, and the latter part of which has been poisoned with despair, must be trifled away in amusements which I despise too much to be entertained with; or sacrificed at the foot of a regret which can know neither end nor abatement. I am conversible upon any topic but the only one which he would wish to converse upon, and being condemned to a state which I in vain endeavour to describe, because it is incredible, I am out of the reach of consolation, and am indeed a fit companion for nobody. If Mrs Unwin attempts to encourage me, and tells me there is hope, I can bear it with some degree of patience, but I can do no more. From her however I can endure it, either because I have been long accustomed to

---

[1] This letter was first printed in Kenneth Povey's article 'New Cowper Letters' in *The Times* for April 28, 1930, and is reproduced by permission of *The Times*. The letters were not in C.'s hand.

[2] The Rev. William Bull (1738–1814), Independent minister of Newport Pagnell. See also p. 740, *n*.

such language from her lips, or because it is impossible for anything that she speaks to give me pain. But I should be otherwise affected by the same things spoken by Mr Bull; and all that he would gain by conversing with me would be summed up in the single word, astonishment. He would wonder that a man whose views of the Scripture are just like his own, who is a Calvinist from experience, and knows his election, should be furnished with a shield of despair impenetrable to every argument by which he might attempt to comfort him. But so it is, and in the end it will be accounted for.

We beg Mrs Newton to accept our thanks for the fish; they were exceedingly good, and came perfectly sweet. Mrs Unwin sends her love; she is better, but not well. It is strange that the ladies, who are said to love talking, are generally glad to shuffle off the business of writing upon the men. She promises fair, however, and is very apt to be as good as her word.

Yours my dear Sir,

Wm Cowper

With two curious five-toed fowls from Lord Northampton's menagerie, fed by 'Squire' Cowper, and two Persian melons. (added by dear Mrs Unwin).

TO MRS NEWTON[1]

Oct. 5, 1780

Dear Madam,

When a lady speaks, it is not civil to make her wait a week for an answer. — I received your letter within this hour, and, foreseeing that the garden will engross much of my time for some days to come, have seized the present opportunity to

---

[1] The greater part of this letter was first printed in the late Kenneth Povey's article, 'New Cowper Letters', in *The Times* for April 28, 1930, and is reproduced here by permission of *The Times*. The remainder is from Southey.

acknowledge it. I congratulate you on Mr Newton's safe arrival at Ramsgate, making no doubt but that he reached the place without difficulty or danger, the road thither from Canterbury being so good as to afford room for neither. He has now a view of the element, with which he was once so familiar, but which I think he has not seen for many years. The sight of his old acquaintance will revive in his mind a pleasing recollection of past deliverances, and when he looks at him from the beach, he may say—'You have formerly given me trouble enough, but I have cast anchor now where your billows can never reach me.'—It is happy for him that he can say so.[2] There are some for whom it would be better to be swallowed up in the deeps of the Ocean, than to sit scribbling quietly and at their ease as I do. Yet it is so natural to shrink back from the thoughts of Eternity, that tho' I know my days are prolonged not in mercy but in judgment, I cannot help preferring the calmness of my present situation to a storm that would endanger my life, though a life that can bring forth nothing but evil to myself, whatever others may think of it. I did not mean to say one word of all this when I began, but it sprang up suddenly in my mind, and what does so, is almost sure to be transferred to the paper, when I am writing to you or Mr Newton.

Dear Madam, we both love fish, are obliged to you for what you have sent, and for what you had a design to send, but when we think of the expense you are at in doing it, we really grudge ourselves the treat with which you have favoured us. The oysters came safe, and were remarkably good. Some people here are likely to pay dear for loving fish, Mr Pell, Mr Lucy, and Johnston of the George, are all under prosecution for poaching in Ravenstone water.

Mrs Unwin returns you many thanks for your anxiety on her account. Her health is considerably mended upon the whole, so as to afford us a hope that it will be established.

Our love attends you.

Yours, dear Madam,

W.C.

[2] Cf. *To Mr Newton, on his return from Ramsgate*, p. 66.

TO THE REV. WILLIAM UNWIN

Oct. 5th, 1780

My dear friend,

Now for the sequel. — You have anticipated one of my arguments in favour of a private education, therefore I need say but little about it. The folly of supposing that the mother-tongue, in some respects the most difficult of all tongues, may be acquired without a teacher, is predominant in all the public schools that I have ever heard of. To pronounce it well, to speak and to write it with fluency and elegance, are no easy attainments; not one in fifty of those who pass through Westminster and Eton arrive at any remarkable proficiency in these accomplishments; and they that do are more indebted to their own study and application for it, than to any instruction received there. In general, there is nothing so pedantic as the style of a schoolboy, if he aims at any style at all; and if he does not, he is of course inelegant, and perhaps ungrammatical. A defect, no doubt, in great measure owing to the want of cultivation; for the same lad that is often commended for his Latin, frequently would deserve to be whipped for his English, if the fault were not more his master's than his own. I know not where this evil is so likely to be prevented as at home, supposing always nevertheless (which is the case in your instance) that the boy's parents, and their acquaintance, are persons of elegance and taste themselves. For to converse with those who converse with propriety, and to be directed to such authors as have refined and improved the language by their productions, are advantages which he cannot elsewhere enjoy in an equal degree. And though it requires some time to regulate the taste and fix the judgement, and these effects must be gradually wrought even upon the best understanding, yet I suppose much less time will be necessary for the purpose than could at first be imagined, because the opportunities of improvement are continual.

I promised to say little on this topic, and I have said so

much, that if I had not a frank I must burn my letter and begin again.

A public education is often recommended as the most effectual remedy for that bashful and awkward constraint so epidemical among the youth of our country. But I verily believe that instead of being a cure, it is often the cause of it. For 7 or 8 years of his life the boy has hardly seen or conversed with a man, or a woman, except the maids at his boarding house. A gentleman or a lady are consequently such novelties to him, that he is perfectly at a loss to know what sort of behaviour he should preserve before them. He plays with his buttons, or the strings of his hat, he blows his nose, and hangs down his head, is conscious of his own deficiency to a degree that makes him quite unhappy, and trembles lest any one should speak to him, because that would quite overwhelm him. Is not all this miserable shyness evidently the effect of his education? To me it appears to be so. If he saw good company every day, he would never be terrified at the sight of it, and a room full of ladies and gentlemen would alarm him no more than the chairs they sit on. Such is the effect of custom.

I need add nothing further on this subject, because I believe little John is as likely to be exempted from this weakness as most young gentlemen we shall meet with. He seems to have his father's spirit in this respect, in whom I could never discern the least trace of bashfulness, though I have often heard him complain of it. Under your management and the influence of your example, I think he can hardly fail to escape it. If he does, he escapes that which makes many a man uncomfortable for life, and has ruined not a few, by forcing them into mean and dishonourable company, where only they could be free and cheerful.

Connexions formed at school are said to be lasting, and often beneficial. There are two or three stories of this kind upon record, which would not be so constantly cited as they are whenever this subject happens to be mentioned, if the chronicle that preserves their remembrance had many beside to boast of. For my own part I found such friendships, though warm enough in their commencement, surprisingly liable to extinction; and of seven or eight, whom I had selected for intimates out of above 300, in ten years' time not one was left me. The truth is, that there may be, and often is, an attachment of one boy to another, that looks very like a friendship, and while they are in circumstances that enable them mutually to oblige and to assist each other, promises well and bids fair to be lasting. But they are no sooner separated from each other by entering into the world at large, than other connexions and new employments, in which they no longer share together, efface the remembrance of what passed in earlier days, and they become strangers to each other for ever. Add to this, that the man frequently differs so much from the boy; his principles, manners, temper and conduct undergo so great an alteration, that we no longer recognize in him our old playfellow, but find him utterly unworthy and unfit for the place he once held in our affections.

To close this article as I did the last, by applying myself immediately to the present concern, little John is happily placed above all occasion for dependence upon such precarious hopes, and need not be sent to school in quest of some great man in embryo who may possibly make his fortune.

I have just left myself room to return Miss Shuttleworth our very sincere thanks for our respective purses, and to assure her that we shall value as we ought her obliging presents and wear them to the last thread. Your Mother sends her love and hopes you will remember the franks. Mine with hers to all at Stock.

Yrs my dear friend

Wm Cowper

TEXT: *BM. Add. MSS.* 24,154

TO JOSEPH JOHNSON[1]

[January, 1781]

I did not write the line, that has been tampered with, hastily, or without due attention to the construction of it; and what appeared to me its only merit is in its present state entirely annihilated.

I know that the ears of modern verse-writers are delicate to an excess, and their readers are troubled with the same squeamishness as themselves. So that if a line do not run as smooth as quicksilver they are offended. A critic of the present day serves a poem as a cook serves a dead turkey, when she fastens the legs of it to a post and draws out all the sinews. For this we may thank Pope; but unless we could imitate him in the closeness and compactness of his expression, as well as in the smoothness of his numbers, we had better drop the imitation, which serves no other purpose than to emasculate and weaken all we write. Give me a manly,

[1] C.'s publisher. This extract is placed by Hayley immediately after a letter dated January 4, 1791, with the comment: 'This letter is, in fact, entitled to a much earlier place in the collection; but having a common subject with the last paragraph of the preceding letter, it seemed to call for insertion immediately after it.' Southey and Wright followed suit. I have supplied the date of January, 1781. First, because I believe this letter is the one referred to in Newton's letter (BM. L. Egerton MSS. 3662) to C. of January 22, 1781: 'My dear friend, I delivered your reproof to Mr Johnson; he said he would show it to Mr. Alterfortheworse the next time he saw him. I believe you will not be so served hereafter. I left with him *The Progress of Error*...' The doctored line would therefore be from *Anti-Thelyphthora*, which was noticed in the *Critical Review* for January, 1781. It was not until April 8 that C. sent Newton 'my works complete' for transmission to the printer. Second, C.'s letter to Unwin of May 23, 1781 (this ed., p. 616) indicates that he had not yet seen the proofs of his first volume of *Poems*, and that by correcting them himself he was confident of being able to thwart any 'presumptuous intermeddler (in a printing-house) who will fancy himself a poet too...'

rough line, with a deal of meaning in it, rather than a whole poem full of musical periods that have nothing but their oily smoothness to recommend them!

I have said thus much, as I hinted in the beginning, because I have just finished a much longer poem than the last, which our common friend[2] will receive by the same messenger that has the charge of this letter. In that poem there are many lines, which an ear so nice as the gentleman's who made the above mentioned alteration, would undoubtedly condemn; and yet (if I may be permitted to say it) they cannot be made smoother without being the worse for it. There is a roughness on a plum, which nobody that understands fruit would rub off, though the plum would be much more polished without it. But lest I tire you, I will only add, that I wish you to guard me from all such meddling; assuring you, that I always write as smoothly as I can; but that I never did, never will, sacrifice the spirit or sense of a passage to the sound of it.

TEXT: *Southey*

TO JOSEPH HILL

Olney Feb. 15, 1781

Received of Mr Hill the sum of twenty pounds by draft on Child & Co.

£20. 0. 0.   Wm Cowper

Feb. 15, 1781

My dear friend,

I am glad you was pleased with my report of so extraordinary a case.[1] If the thought of versifying the decisions of our courts of justice had struck me while I had the honour to attend them, it would perhaps have been no difficult matter

[2] A much longer poem: *The Progress of Error*. Our common friend: Newton.

[1] The verses entitled 'Report of an Adjudged Case.'

to have compiled a volume of such amusing and interesting precedents, which if they wanted the eloquence of the Greek or Roman oratory, would have amply compensated that deficiency by the harmony of rhyme and metre.

Your account of my uncle and your mother gave me great pleasure. I have long been afraid to enquire after some in whose welfare I always feel myself interested, lest the question should produce a painful answer. Longevity is the lot of so few, and is so seldom rendered comfortable by the associations of good health and good spirits, that I could not very reasonably suppose either your relation or mine so happy in those respects as it seems they are. May they continue to enjoy those blessings as long as the date of life shall last. I do not think that in these costermonger days, as I have a notion Falstaff calls them,[2] an antediluvian age is at all a desirable thing; but to live comfortably while we live is a great matter, and comprehends in it everything that can be wished for on this side the curtain that hangs between Time and Eternity.

It is possible that Mrs Hill may not be herself a sufferer by the late terrible catastrophe in the Islands,[3] but I should suppose by her correspondence wth those parts, she may be connected with some that are. In either case I condole with her. For it is reasonable to imagine that since the first tour that Columbus made into the Western World, it never before experienced such a convulsion, perhaps never since the foundation of the globe. You say the state grows old, and discovers many symptoms of decline. A writer, possessed of a genius for hypothesis like that of Burnet, might construct a plausible argument to prove that the world itself is in a state of superannuation, if there be such a word; if not, there must be such a one as superannuity. When that just equilibrium that has hitherto supported all things seems to fail, when the elements burst the chain that has bound them, the wind sweeping away the works of man and man himself together with his works, and the ocean seeming to overleap the command, 'Hitherto shalt thou come and no farther, and here

[2] 2 *King Henry IV*, I, ii.

[3] The West Indies suffered heavy damage from hurricanes in 1780 and 1781.

shall thy proud waves be stayed,'[4] these irregular and prodigious vagaries seem to bespeak a decay, and forebode perhaps not a very distant dissolution. This thought has so run away with my attention that I have left myself no room for the little politics that have only Great Britain for their object. Who knows but that while a thousand and ten thousand tongues are employed in adjusting the scale of our national concerns, in complaining of new taxes, and funds loaded with a debt of accumulating millions, the consummation of all things may discharge it in a moment, and the scene of all this bustle disappear as if it had never been? Charles Fox would say perhaps he thought it very unlikely; I question if he could prove even that. I am sure however he could not prove it to be impossible.

My best respects attend Mrs Hill, with many thanks for her intended favour. — I beg to be remembered to your mother, and to your sisters, and if you [word erased by seal] to think of me when you see my uncle, do not forget to tell him [word erased] much I rejoice in his well-being.

Farewell my better friend than any I have to boast of either among the Lords or gentlemen of the House of Commons.

Yours ever,

Wm Cowper

TEXT: *Cowper Johnson MSS.* The first and second paragraphs were printed by Hayley, and the rest appeared in the *Private Correspondence*; the extracts are published as two separate letters in the collected editions. The MSS. lacks the last sentence and signature.

TO THE REV. JOHN NEWTON

March 5, 1781

My dear friend,

Since writing is become one of my principal amusements, and I have already produced so many verses on subjects that

[4] Job, xxxviii, 11.

entitle them to a hope that they may possibly be useful, I should be sorry to suppress them entirely, or to publish them to no purpose, for want of that cheap ingredient, the name of the author. If my name therefore will serve them in any degree as a passport into the public notice, they are welcome to it; but in that case I must desire to have *The Progress of Error* returned to me that I may cancel the passage relating to *Thelyphthora*, for though in that passage I have neither belied my own judgment, nor slandered the author, yet on account of relationship, and for reasons I need not suggest to you, I should not choose to make a public attack upon his performance. I will entreat you to give it once more an attentive perusal, and if you think that the removal of that passage will clear it from all danger of a personal application to Mr Madan, be so kind as to tell me so. Your opinion in the affirmative will make me easy upon the subject, and I shall set my name to it without fear. It is certain that I had him pretty much in view not there only, but in other parts of the production likewise. But it seems to me, upon present recollection, that the rest are of such a kind as to stand fairly acquitted of the charge of personality. When I have cancelled the offensive portion of it, I will endeavour to supply the hiatus with something that may make amends for the loss, either in the same place, or in some other part of the poem.

If you are of my mind, I think *Table Talk* will be the best to begin with, as the subjects of it are perhaps more popular; and one would wish at first setting out to catch the public by the ear, and hold them by it as fast as possible, that they may be willing to hear one on a second and a third occasion.

The passage you object to I inserted merely by way of catch, and think that it is not unlikely to answer the purpose. My design was to say as many serious things as I could, and yet to be as lively as was compatible with such a purpose. Do not imagine that I mean to stickle for it as a pretty creature of my own that I am loth to part with—but I am apprehensive that without the sprightliness of that passage to introduce it, the following paragraph would not show to advantage. If the world had been filled with men like yourself, I should never have written it; but thinking myself in a measure obliged to tickle, if I meant to please, I therefore affected a jocularity I did not feel. As to the rest, wherever there is war, there is misery and outrage; notwithstanding which it is not only lawful to wish, but even a duty to pray for the success of one's country. And as to the neutralities,[1] I really think the Russian virago[2] an impertinent puss for meddling with us, and engaging half a score kittens of her acquaintance to scratch the poor old lion, who, if he has been insolent in his day, has probably acted no otherwise than they themselves would have acted in his circumstances, and with his power to embolden them.

You will be so good as to insist upon it as from me that when Mr Johnson is in possession of my name he shall not on any account whatever prefix it to Sir Airy[3] or by any means direct or indirect, either now or hereafter, assert or even insinuate that I wrote it.—I believe I have drawn up this precaution with all the precision of a lawyer without intending it. I mean however no more than to desire you to impress him with an idea of the seriousness with which I make this stipulation.

Mr Johnson[4] will therefore, if he pleases, announce me to the world by the style and title of

WILLIAM COWPER, ESQ.
Of the Inner Temple.

I am glad that the myrtles reached you safe, but am persuaded from past experience that no management will keep them long alive in London, especially in the city. Our English

---

[1] The Armed Neutrality, 1780: an alliance between Russia, Sweden and Denmark, joined later by Prussia and Holland.

[2] Catherine the Great.

[3] *Anti-Thelyphthora*, in which Martin Madan was satirized as Sir Airy del Castro.

[4] Newton, whom C. had consulted at every stage of the preparation of *Poems*, 1782, also found the publisher. Joseph Johnson (1738–1809) had been one of the booksellers concerned with the distribution of *Olney Hymns*. He was a man of advanced opinions and had published important works on surgery and medicine. His authors included Joseph Priestley, Erasmus Darwin, Horne Tooke, Mary Wollstonecraft and Tom Paine.

sorts, the natives of the country, are for the most part too delicate to thrive there, much more the nice Italian. To give them, however, the best chance they can have, the lady must keep them well watered, giving them a moderate quantity in summer time every other day, and in winter about twice a week; not spring-water, for that would kill them. At Michaelmas, as much of the mould as can be taken out without disturbing the roots must be evacuated, and its place supplied with fresh, the lighter the better. And once in two years the plants must be drawn out of their pots with the entire ball of earth about them, and the matted roots pared off with a sharp knife, when they must be planted again with an addition of rich light earth as before. Thus dealt with, they will grow luxuriantly in a green-house, where they can have plenty of sweet air, which is absolutely necessary to their health. I used to purchase them at Covent Garden almost every year, when I lived in the Temple; but even in that airy situation they were sure to lose their leaf in winter, and seldom recovered it again in spring. I wish them a better fate at Hoxton.[5]

Olney has seen this day what it never saw before, and what will serve it to talk of, I suppose, for years to come. At eleven o'clock this morning a party of soldiers entered the town, driving before them another party, who, after obstinately defending the bridge for some time, were obliged to quit it and run. They ran in very good order, frequently faced about and fired, but were at last obliged to surrender prisoners of war. There has been much drumming and shouting, much scampering about in the dirt, but not an inch of lace made in the town, at least at the Silver End of it.

It is our joint request that you will not again leave us unwritten to for a fortnight. We are so like yourselves in this particular, that we cannot help ascribing so long a silence to the worst cause. The longer your letters the better, but a short one is better than none.

If the King was to make it his request to us, we could not furnish him with a plate of greens from our garden. It was one of our reasons for dismissing Dartin, that under his

[5] Where Newton then lived.

management, or no management at all, it produced us nothing.

Mrs Unwin is pretty well, and adds the greetings of her love to mine.

Yours, my dear friend,

Wm Cowper

TEXT: *Private Correspondence and Barham Johnson MSS.* *†

TO THE REV. WILLIAM UNWIN

May 1, 1781

My dear friend,

Your Mother says I *must* write, and *must* admits of no apology; I might otherwise plead that I have nothing to say, that I am weary, that I am dull, that it would be more convenient therefore for you as well as for myself that I should let it alone, but all these pleas and whatever pleas besides either disinclination, indolence, or necessity might suggest, are overruled, as they ought to be the moment a lady adduces her irrefragable argument, You Must. You have still however one comfort left, that what I must write, you may, or may read, just as it shall please you, unless Lady Anne[1] at your elbow should say you must read it, and then like a true knight you will obey without looking out for a remedy.

I do not love to harp upon strings that to say the least are not so musical as one would wish. But you I know have many a time sacrificed your own feelings to those of others, and where an act of charity leads you, are not easily put out of your way. This consideration encourages me just to insinuate that your silence on the subject of a certain nomination is distressful to more than you would wish, in particular to the little boy whose clothes are outgrown and worn out; and to his mother, who is unwilling to furnish him with a new suit,

[1] Mrs William Unwin.

having reason to suppose that the long blue petticoat would soon supersede it, if she should.[2]

In the press and speedily will be published, in one volume octavo, price three shillings, *Poems by William Cowper, of the Inner Temple, Esq.* You may suppose by the size of the publication that the greatest part of them have been long kept secret, because you yourself have never seen them, but the truth is, that they are most of them except what you have in your possession, the produce of the last winter. Two thirds of the compilation will be occupied by four pieces, the first of which sprung up in the month of December, and the last of them in the month of March; they contain I suppose in all about 2500 lines, are known or are to be known in due time, by the names of:

Table Talk	Truth
The Progress of Error	Expostulation

Mr Newton writes a preface[3] and Johnson is the printer. The principal, I may say the only reason why I never mentioned to you till now an affair which I am just going to make known to all the world, if *that* Mr All the World should think it worth his knowing, has been this; that till within these few days I had not the honour to know it myself. This may seem strange, but it is true, for not knowing where to find underwriters who would choose to insure them, and not finding it convenient to a purse like mine to run any hazard even upon the credit of my own ingenuity, I was very much in doubt for some weeks whether any bookseller would be willing to subject himself to an ambiguity that might prove very expensive in case of a bad market. But Johnson has heroically set all peradventures at defiance, and takes the whole charge upon himself—so out I come.

      Yours, my dear friend with your Mother's love

                       Wm Cowper

---

[2] Unwin, at C.'s request, was trying to obtain a nomination to Christ's Hospital for a relative of Newton.

[3] Newton's preface was omitted from the first edition: see p. 656.

I shall be glad of my translations from V. Bourne[4] in your next frank. My Muse will lay herself at your feet immediately on her first public appearance.

TEXT: *BM. Add. MSS.* 24,154

TO JOSEPH HILL

Received of Mr Hill the sum of thirty guineas by draft upon Child & Co.

£31. 10. 0.   Wm Cowper

May 9, 1781

My dear Sir,

I am in the press, and it is in vain to deny it. But how mysterious is the conveyance of intelligence from one end to the other of your great city! Not many days since, except one man, and he but little taller than yourself, all London was ignorant of it; for I do not suppose that the public prints have yet announced the most agreeable tidings, the title-page, which is the basis of the advertisement, having so lately reached the publisher: and now it is known to you, who live at least two miles distant from my confidant upon the occasion.

My labours are principally the production of the last winter —all indeed, except a few of the minor pieces. When I can find no other occupation, I think; and when I think, I am very apt to do it in rhyme. Hence it comes to pass that the season of the year which generally pinches off the flowers of poetry, unfolds mine, such as they are, and crowns me with a winter garland. In this respect therefore, I and my cotemporary bards are by no means upon a par. They write when the delightful influences of fine weather, fine prospects, and a brisk motion of the animal spirits, make poetry almost the language of nature; and I, when icicles depend from all the

[4] See p. 163.

leaves of the Parnassian laurel, and when a reasonable man would as little expect to succeed in verse, as to hear a blackbird whistle. — This must be my apology to you for whatsoever want of fire and animation you may observe in what you will shortly have the perusal of. As to the public, if they like me not, there is no remedy. A friend will weigh and consider all disadvantages, and make as large allowances as an author can wish, and larger perhaps than he has any right to expect; but not so the world at large; what they do not like, they will not by any apology be persuaded to forgive, and it would be in vain to tell *them* that I wrote my verses in January, for they would immediately reply, Why did not you write them in May? A question that might puzzle a wiser head than we poets are generally blessed with.

If I had the courage to stand the chance of the market, and printed at my own expense, I should circulate the copy among my friends with the greatest pleasure, and find a peculiar one in laying a volume of my writing upon your desk, but the bookseller is the adventurer, and has the boldness to risk more upon the success of what I have written than I dare to hazard upon it myself.

Your mackerel were excellent. Many thanks to Mrs Hill for the seeds. Mr Wrighte loves a garden dearly, but hates the expense of furnishing it, which makes my gratuitous contributions singularly welcome.

Yours my dear friend as ever

Wm Cowper

Will you be so good as to order for me half a ream of the best post paper. The stationer will be paid by the bookkeeper at the Windmill, St John Street.

TEXT: *Cowper Johnson MSS.* *

TO THE REV. WILLIAM UNWIN

May 23, 1781

My dear friend,

If a writer's friends have need of patience, how much more the writer! Your desire to see my Muse in public, and mine to gratify you, must both suffer the mortification of delay. I expected that my trumpeter would have informed the world by this time of all that is needful for them to know upon such an occasion, and that an advertising blast blown through every newspaper would have said 'The Poet is coming!' But man, especially man that writes verse, is born to disappointments, as surely as printers and booksellers are born to be the most dilatory and tedious of all creatures. — The plain English of this magnificent preamble is, that the season for publication is just elapsed, that the town is going into the country every day, and that my book cannot appear till they return, that is to say, not till next winter.

This misfortune however comes not without its attendant advantage. I shall now have, what I should not otherwise have had, an opportunity to correct the press myself; no small advantage upon any occasion, but especially important where poetry is concerned. A single erratum may knock out the brains of a whole passage, and that perhaps which of all others the unfortunate poet is the most proud of. Add to this, that now and then there is to be found in a printing-house a presumptuous intermeddler, who will fancy himself a poet too, and what is still worse, a better than he that employs him. The consequence is, that with cobbling and tinkering and patching on here and there a shred of his own, he makes such a difference between the original and the copy, that an author cannot know his own work again. Now as I choose to be responsible for nobody's dullness but my own, I am a little comforted when I reflect that it will be in my power to prevent all such impertinence, and yet not without your assistance. It will be quite necessary that the correspondence between me and Johnson should be carried on without the expense of postage, because proof sheets would make double or treble letters, which expense, as in every instance it must occur twice, first when the packet is sent, and again when it is returned, would be rather inconvenient to me, who you perceive am forced to live by my wits, and to him who hopes to get a little matter no doubt by the same means. Half a dozen franks therefore to me, and *totidem* to him, will be singularly acceptable if you can without feeling it in any respect a trouble, procure them for me. — Johnson, bookseller, St Paul's Churchyard—

My neckcloths being all worn out, I intend to wear stocks, but not unless they are more fashionable than the former. In that case I shall be obliged to you if you will buy me a handsome stock-buckle for a very little money; for 20 or 25 shillings perhaps, a second-hand affair may be purchased that will make a figure at Olney.

I am much obliged to you for your offer to support me in a translation of Bourne. It is but seldom however, and never except for my amusement, that I translate, because I find it disagreeable to work by another man's pattern; I should at least be sure to find it so, in a business of any length. Again— *that* is epigrammatic and witty in Latin, which would be perfectly insipid in English; and a translator of Bourne would frequently find himself obliged to supply what is called the turn, which is in fact the most difficult and the most expensive part of the whole composition, and could not perhaps, in many instances, be done with any tolerable success. If a Latin poem is neat, elegant, and musical, it is enough, but English readers are not so easily satisfied— To quote myself, you will find, on comparing the 'Jackdaw' with the original, that I was obliged to sharpen a point which though smart enough in the Latin, would in English have appeared as plain & as blunt as the tag of a lace. I love the memory of Vinny Bourne. I think him a better Latin poet than Tibullus, Propertius, Ausonius, or any of the writers in *his* way, except Ovid, and not at all inferior to *him*. I love him too with a love of partiality, because he was usher of the 5th form at Westminster when I passed through it. He was so good-natured and so indolent, that I lost more than I got by him, for he made me as idle as himself. He was such a sloven, as if he had trusted to his genius as a cloak for everything that could disgust you in his person; and indeed in his writings he has almost made amends for all. His humour is entirely original; he can speak of a magpie or a cat in terms so exquisitely appropriated to the character he draws, that one would suppose him animated by the spirit of the creature he describes. And with all this drollery there is a mixture of rational and even religious reflection at times, and always an air of pleasantry, good-nature and humanity, that makes him in my mind one of the most amiable writers in the world. It is not common to meet with an author who can make you smile, and yet at nobody's expense, who is always entertaining, and yet always harmless, and who though always elegant and classical to a degree not always found even in the classics themselves, charms more by the simplicity & playfulness of his ideas than by the neatness & purity of his verse. Yet such was poor Vinny. I remember seeing the Duke of Richmond set fire to his greasy locks, & box his ears to put it out again.

I am delighted with your project, but not with the view I have of its success. If the world would form its opinion of the clerical character at large, from yours in particular, I have no doubt but the event would be as prosperous as you could wish. But I suppose there is not a Member of either House who does not see within the circle of his own acquaintance a minister, perhaps many ministers, whose integrity would contribute but little to the effect of such a Bill. Here are 7 or 8 in the neighbourhood of Olney who have shaken hands with sobriety, and who would rather suppress the Church, were it not for the emoluments annexed, than discourage the sale of strong beer in a single instance. Were I myself in Parliament, I am not sure that I could favour your scheme; are there not to be found within 5 miles of almost every neighbourhood parsons who would purchase well-accustomed public houses, because they could secure them a licence, and patronise them when they had done? I think no penalty would prevent the abuse, on account of the difficulty of proof, and that no ingenuity could guard against all the possible abuses. To sum up all in a few words, the generality of the clergy, especially within these last 20 or 30 years, have worn their circingles so loose, that I verily believe no measure that proposed an accession of privilege to an order which the laity retain but little respect for, would meet with the countenance of the legislature.— You will do me the justice to suppose that I do not say these things to gratify a splenetic humour or a censorious turn of mind—far from it—it may add perhaps to the severity of the foregoing observations to assert, but if it does, I cannot help asserting, that I verily believe them to be founded upon fact, and that I am sure, partly from my own knowledge, and partly from the report of those whose veracity I can depend upon, that in this part of the world at least, many of the most profligate characters are the very men to whom the morals and even the souls of others are entrusted. And I cannot suppose that the Diocese of Lincoln, or this part of it in particular, is more unfortunate in that respect than the rest of the kingdom.

Since I have begun to write long poems, I seem to turn up my nose at the idea of a short one. I have lately entered upon one, which if ever finished, cannot easily be comprised in much less than a thousand lines. But this must make part of a second publication, and be accompanied in due time by others not yet thought of. For it seems (which I did not know till the bookseller had occasion to tell me so) that single pieces stand no chance, and that nothing less than a volume will go down. You yourself afford me a proof of the certainty of this intelligence by sending me franks which nothing less than a volume can fill. I have accordingly sent you one, but am obliged to add that had the wind been in any other point of the compass, or blowing as it does from the east, had it been less boisterous, you must have been contented with a much shorter letter. But the abridgment of every other occupation is very favourable to that of writing.

Our love attends all the family at Stock. I am glad I did not expect to hear from you by this post, for the boy has lost the bag in which your letter must have been enclosed. Another reason for my prolixity.

Yours affectionately,

Wm Cowper

TEXT: *BM. Add. MSS.* 24,154

TO THE REV. WILLIAM UNWIN

May 28, 1781

My dear friend,

I believe I never give trouble without feeling more than I give; so much by way of preface and apology.

Thus stands the case. Johnson has begun to print, and Mr Newton has already corrected the first sheet. This unexpected dispatch makes it necessary for me to furnish myself with the means of communication, viz. the franks, as soon as may be. There are reasons (I believe I mentioned them in my last) why I choose to revise the proof myself. Nevertheless, if your delicacy must suffer the puncture of a pin's point in procuring the franks for me, I release you entirely from the task: you are as free as if I had never mentioned them. But you will oblige me by a speedy answer upon this subject, because it is expedient that the printer should know to whom he is to send his copy; and when the press is once set, those humble servants of the poets are rather impatient of any delay, because the types are wanted for the works of other authors who are equally in haste to be born.

This fine weather I suppose sets you on horseback and allures the ladies into the garden. If I was at Stock, I should be of their party, and while they sat knotting or netting in the shade should comfort myself with the thought that I had not a beast under me, whose walk would seem tedious, whose trot would jumble me, and whose gallop might throw me into a ditch. What Nature expressly designed me for, I have never been able to conjecture; I seem to myself so universally disqualified for the common and customary occupations and amusements of mankind. When I was a boy, I excelled at cricket and football, but the fame I acquired by achievements in that way is long since forgotten, and I do not know that I have made a figure in anything since. I am sure however that she did not design me for a horseman, and that if all men were of my mind, there would be an end of all jockeyship for ever. I am rather straitened in time, and not very rich in materials; therefore, with our joint love to you all, conclude myself,

Yours ever,

Wm C.

TEXT: *BM. Add. MSS.* 24,154

TO THE REV. JOHN NEWTON

July 12, 1781

My very dear friend,

I am going to send, what when you have read, you may scratch your head, and say, I suppose, there's nobody knows, whether what I have got, be verse or not: by the tune and the time, it ought to be rhyme; but if it be, did you ever see, of late or of yore, such a ditty before? The thought did occur, to me and to her, as Madam[1] and I, did walk not fly, over hills and dales, with spreading sails, before it was dark to Weston Park.

The news at *Oney*[2] is little or noney, but such as it is, I send it — viz. Poor Mr Peace cannot yet cease, addling his head with what you said, and has left parish-church quite in the lurch, having almost swore to go there no more.

Page[3] and his wife, that made such a strife, we met them twain in Dag Lane, we gave them the wall, and that was all. For Mr Scott,[4] we have seen him not, except as he pass'd, in

---

[1] Mrs Unwin's title at Olney.

[2] The local pronunciation.

[3] Newton's successor as curate of Olney.

[4] The Rev. Thomas Scott (1747–1821), curate of Weston, and later of Olney. He was the author of an immense commentary on the Bible (1788–92) and of a remarkable spiritual autobiography, *The Force of Truth*, 1779, which Cowper revised 'as to the style and externals'. Newman wrote in his *Apologia* that Scott was the man 'to whom (humanly speaking) I almost owe my soul.'

wonderful haste, to see a friend in Silver End. Mrs Jones[5] proposes, ere July closes, that she and her sister, and her Jones Mister, and we that are here, our course shall steer, to dine in the Spinney, but for a guinea, if the weather should hold, so hot and so cold, we had better by far stay where we are. For the grass there grows, while nobody mows, (which is very wrong,) so rank and long that so to speak, 'tis at least a week, if it happens to rain, ere it dries again.

I have writ *Charity*, not for popularity, but as well as I could, in hopes to do good; and if the Reviewer[6] should say 'to be sure, the gentleman's Muse, wears Methodist shoes; you may know by her pace, and talk about grace, that she and her bard have little regard, for the tastes and fashions, and ruling passions, and hoidening play, of the modern day; and though she assume a borrowed plume, and now and then wear a tittering air, 'tis only her plan, to catch if she can, the giddy and gay, as they go that way, by a production, on a new construction, and has baited her trap in hopes to snap all that may come, with a sugar-plum.' His opinion in this, will not be amiss; 'tis what I intend, my principal end: and if I succeed, and folks should read, till a few are brought to a serious thought, I shall think I am paid, for all I have said, and all I have done, though I have run, many a time, after a ryhme, as far as from hence, to the end of my sense, and by hook or crook, write another book, if I live and am here, another year.

I have heard before, of a room with a floor, laid upon springs, and such like things, with so much art, in every part, that when you went in, you was forced to begin a minuet pace, with an air and a grace, swimming about, now in and now out, with a deal of state, in a figure of eight, without pipe or string, or any such thing; and now I have writ, in a rhyming fit, what will make you dance, and as you advance, will keep you still, though against your will, dancing away,

[5] The wife of the Rev. Thomas Jones, curate of Clifton Reynes, and sister of Lady Austen. He was one of the six Evangelical undergraduates expelled from Oxford University in 1768.

[6] *The Monthly Review.*

alert and gay, till you come to an end of what I have penn'd,
which that you may do, ere Madam and you are quite worn
out with jigging about, I take my leave, and here you receive
a bow profound, down to the ground, from your humble
me—

W.C.

P.S. When I concluded, doubtless you did, think me right,
as well as you might, in saying what I said of Scott, and then
it was true, but now it is due, to him to note, that since I
wrote, himself and he has visited we.

TEXT: *Southey* and *Barham Johnson MSS.*†

TO THE REV. WILLIAM UNWIN

July 29, 1781

My dear friend,

Having given the case you laid before me in your last all
due consideration, I proceed to answer it; and in order to
clear my way, shall in the first place set down my sense of
those passages in scripture which on an hasty perusal seem
to clash with the opinion I am going to give. If a man smite
one cheek, turn the other—if he take thy cloak, let him take
thy coat also.[1] That is, I suppose, rather than on a vindictive
principle, avail yourself of that remedy the law allows you in
the way of retaliation, for that was the subject immediately
under the discussion of the speaker. Nothing is so contrary
to the genius of the gospel as the gratification of resentment
and revenge, but I cannot easily persuade myself to think that
the author of that dispensation could possibly advise his
followers to consult their own peace at the expense of the
peace of society, or inculcate an universal abstinence from the
use of lawful remedies to the encouragement of injury and
oppression.

St Paul again seems to condemn the practice of going to

---

[1] Matthew, v, 39–40.

law,— Why do ye not rather suffer wrong? etc.[2] but if we look again we shall find that a litigious temper had obtained and was prevalent among the professors of the day. This he condemned, and with good reason. It was unseemly to the last degree that the disciples of the prince of peace should worry and vex each other with injurious treatment and unnecessary disputes, to the scandal of their religion in the eyes of the heathen. But surely he did not mean, any more than his Master in the place above alluded to, that the most harmless members of society should receive no advantage of its laws, or should be the only persons in the world who should derive no benefit from those institutions without which society cannot subsist. Neither of them could mean to throw down the pale of property, and to lay the Christian part of the world open throughout all ages to the incursions of unlimited violence and wrong.

By this time you are sufficiently aware that I think you have an indisputable right to recover at law what is so dishonestly withheld from you. The fellow I suppose has discernment enough to see a difference between you and the generality of the clergy, and cunning enough to conceive the purpose of turning your meekness and forbearance to a good account, and of coining them into hard cash which he means to put in his pocket. But I would disappoint the rascal and show him that though a Christian is not to be quarrelsome, he is not to be crushed, and that though he is but a worm before God, he is not such a worm as every selfish unprincipled wretch may tread upon at his pleasure. You will find otherwise that he will soon cease to be singular in his villainy, and that here and there another will take the liberty to follow his example, till at last your living will be worth no more than your parishioners out of their great goodness will be pleased to allow you.

I lately heard a story from a lady[3] who has spent many

[2] 1 Corinthians, vi, 7.

[3] Lady Austen (c. 1738–1802), formerly Anne Richards, the widow of Sir Robert Austen, baronet (1708–72). She lived for some years at Sancerre, near Bourges. In 1796 she married Count Claude Tardiffe du Granger, a French royalist emigré, and followed him to Paris.

years of her life in France, somewhat to the present purpose. An Abbé universally esteemed for his piety, and especially for the meekness of his manners, had yet undesignedly given some offence to a shabby fellow in his parish. The man, concluding he might do as he pleased with so forgiving and gentle character, struck him on one cheek, and bade him turn the other. The good man did so, and when he had received the two slaps which he thought himself obliged to submit to, turned again and beat him soundly. I do not wish to see you follow the French gentleman's example; but I believe nobody that has heard the story condemns him much for the spirit he showed upon the occasion.

I had the relation from Lady Austen, sister to Mrs Jones the wife of the minister at Clifton. She is a most agreeable woman, and has fallen in love with your mother and me, insomuch that I do not know but she may settle at Olney. Yesterday se'nnight we all dined together in the Spinney, a most delightful retirement belonging to Mrs Throgmorton[4] of Weston. Lady Austen's lackey, and a lad that waits on me in the garden, drove a wheelbarrow full of eatables and drinkables to the scene of our *fête champêtre*. A board laid over the top of the barrow served us for a table, our diningroom was a roothouse lined with moss and ivy. At six o'clock the servants, who had dined under a great elm upon the ground at a little distance, boiled the kettle, and the said wheelbarrow served us again for a tea-table. We then took a walk from thence to the Wilderness, about half a mile off, and were at home again soon after eight, having spent the day together from noon till evening without one cross occurrence, or the least weariness of each other. An happiness few parties of pleasure can boast of.

Yours with our joint love to your family

Wm Cowper

The lace is making, and the parties concerned are desired to take notice that it costs but threepence three farthings per yard.

---

[4] Anna Maria Throckmorton of Weston Hall, the mother of Cowper's friends John and George Throckmorton.

Mr Smith, with the same obliging readiness as before, has furnished me with the franks I wanted. When I publish, my book shall wait on him in acknowledgment of his kindness.

TEXT: *BM. Add. MSS.* 24,154

TO THE REV. JOHN NEWTON

Aug. 16. 1781

My dear friend,

I might date my letter from the greenhouse, which we have converted into a summer parlour. The walls hung with garden mats, and the floor covered with a carpet, the sun too in a great measure excluded by an awning of mats which forbids him to shine any where except upon the carpet, it affords us by far the pleasantest retreat in Olney. We eat, drink, and sleep, where we always did; but here we spend all the rest of our time, and find that the sound of the wind in the trees, and the singing of birds, are much more agreeable to our ears than the incessant barking of dogs and screaming of children, not to mention the exchange of a sweet-smelling garden for the putrid exhalations of Silver End. It is an observation that naturally occurs upon the occasion, and which many other occasions furnish an opportunity to make, that people long for what they have not, and overlook the good in their possession. This is so true in the present instance, that for years past I should have thought myself happy to enjoy a retirement even less flattering to my natural taste than this in which I am now writing; and have often looked wistfully at a snug cottage, which on account of its situation at a distance from noise and disagreeable objects, seemed to promise me all I could wish or expect, so far as happiness may be said to be local; never once adverting to this comfortable nook, which affords me all that could be found in the most sequestered hermitage, with the advantage of having all those accommodations near at hand which no hermitage could possibly afford me. People imagine they should be happy in circumstances which they would find insupportably burthensome in less than a week. A man that has been clothed in fine linen, and fared sumptuously every day, envies the peasant under a thatched hovel; who, in return, envies him as much his palace and his pleasure-ground. Could they change situations, the fine gentleman would find his ceilings were too low, and that his casements admitted too much wind; that he had no cellar for his wine, and no wine to put in his cellar. These, with a thousand other mortifying deficiencies, would shatter his romantic project into innumerable fragments in a moment. The clown, at the same time, would find the accession of so much unwieldy treasure an incumbrance quite incompatible with an hour's ease. His choice would be puzzled by variety. He would drink to excess, because he would foresee no end of his abundance; and he would eat himself sick for the same reason. He would have no idea of any other happiness than sensual gratification; would make himself a beast, and die of his good fortune. The rich gentleman had, perhaps, or might have had if he pleased, at the shortest notice, just such a recess as this; but if he had it, he overlooked it, or, if he had it not, forgot that he might command it whenever he would. The rustic too was actually in possession of some blessings, which he was a fool to relinquish, but which he could neither see nor feel, because he had the daily and constant use of them; such as good health, bodily strength, a head and a heart that never ached, and temperance, to the practice of which he was bound by necessity, that, humanly speaking, was a pledge and a security for the continuance of them all.

Thus I have sent you a schoolboy's theme. When I write to you, I do not write without thinking, but always without premeditation: the consequence is that such thoughts as pass through my head when I am not writing make the subject of my letters to you.

Johnson sent me lately a sort of apology for his printer's negligence, with his promise of greater diligence for the future. There was need enough of both. I have received but one sheet since you left us. Still indeed I see that there is time before us; but I see likewise that no length of time can be sufficient for the accomplishment of a work that does not go forward. I know not yet whether he will add *Conversation* to those poems already in his hands, nor do I care much. No man ever wrote such quantities of verse as I have written this last year, with so much indifference about the event, or rather with so little ambition of public praise. My pieces are such as may possibly be made useful. The more they are approved, the more likely they are to spread, and consequently the more likely to attain the end of usefulness; which, as I said once before, except my present amusement, is the only end I propose. And even in the pursuit of this purpose, commendable as it is in itself, I have not the spur I should once have had; my labour must go unrewarded, and as Mr Raban once said, I am raising a scaffold before a house that others are to live in, and not I.

Mr Symonds's letters certainly are not here. Our servants never touch a paper without leave, and are so observant of our injunction, in this particular , that unless I burn the covers of the News, they accumulate till they make a litter in the parlour. They cannot therefore have been destroyed through carelessness, and consequently if they were with us, we should be able to find them.

Our love to you both,
Yours, my dear Sir,

Wm Cowper

TEXT: *Barham Johnson MSS.*†

TO THE REV. JOHN NEWTON

Aug. 21, 1781

My dear friend,

Natt is very happy in having his loans so well secured, and so advantageously disposed of. The eighteen pence shall be accounted for by some future opportunity. If Mr Crawford will be so kind as to receive the interest for him, he is well content to let it stand in his name.

You wish you could employ your time to better purpose, yet are never idle. In all that you say or do, whether you are alone, or pay visits, or receive them, whether you think or write, or walk or sit still, the state of your mind is such as discovers even to yourself, in spite of all its wanderings, that there is a principle at bottom whose determined tendency is toward the best things. I do not at all doubt what you say, when you complain of that crowd of trifling thoughts that pesters you without ceasing, but then you always have a serious thought standing at the door of your imagination, like a justice of peace with the Riot Act in his hand, ready to read it, and disperse the mob. Here lies the difference between you and me. My thoughts are clad in a sober livery, for the most part, as grave as that of a bishop's servant; they turn too upon spiritual subjects, but the tallest fellow and the loudest amongst them all, is he who is continually crying with a loud voice, *Actum est de te, periisti* ('Tis all over, you must perish.)[1] You wish for more attention, I for less. Dissipation itself would be welcome to me, so it were not a vicious one; but however earnestly invited, is coy, and keeps at a distance. Yet with all this distressing gloom upon my mind, I experience, as you do, the slipperiness of the present hour, and the rapidity with which time escapes me. Every thing around us, and every thing which befalls us, constitutes a variety which, whether agreeable or otherwise, has still a thievish propensity, and steals from us days, months and years with such unparalleled address, that even while we say they are here, they are gone. From infancy to manhood is rather a tedious period, chiefly I suppose because at that time we act under the control of others, and are not suffered to have a will of our own; but thence downward into the vale of years is such a declivity that we have just an opportunity to reflect upon the steepness of it, and then find ourselves at the bottom.

Here is a new scene opening, which, whether it perform what it promises or not, will add fresh plumes to the wings of

---

[1] In the course of his third severe depression, early in 1773, C. had the fateful dream 'before the recollection of which all consolation vanishes, and it seems to me, must always vanish.' In this dream, C. believed, God had revealed to him by 'a Word' that he was shut off for ever from His mercy. T. Wright, in his *Life* of C., 2nd ed., p. 111, suggested that the Latin phrase above was the 'word'. It was spoken, however, by a low character in Terence's play, *Eunuchus*, which C. must have known.

time; at least while it continues to be a subject of contemplation. If the project take effect, a thousand varieties will attend the change it will make in our situation at Olney. If not, it will serve, however, to speculate and converse upon, and steal away many hours, by engaging our attention, before it be entirely dropped. Lady Austen, very desirous of retirement, especially of a retirement near her sister, an admirer of Mr Scott as a preacher, and of your two humble servants now in the greenhouse, as the most agreeable creatures in the world, is at present determined to settle here. That part of our great building which is at present occupied by Dick Coleman,[2] his wife, child, and a thousand rats, is the corner of the world she chooses, above all others, as the place of her future residence. Next spring twelvemonth she begins to repair and beautify, and the following winter (by which time the lease of her house in town will determine) she intends to take possession. I am highly pleased with the plan, upon Mrs Unwin's account who since Mrs Newton's departure is destitute of all female connexion, and has not in any emergency a woman to speak to. Mrs Scott is indeed in the neighbourhood, and an excellent person, but always engaged by a close attention to her family, and no more than ourselves a lover of visiting. But these things are all at present in the clouds. Two years must intervene, and in two years not only this project but all the projects in Europe may be disconcerted.

> Cocoa-nut naught,
> Fish too dear,
> None must be bought
> For us that are here.
>
> No lobster on earth
> That ever I saw,
> To me would be worth
> Sixpence a claw.

---

[2] C. had adopted Coleman at St Albans as a boy of seven. He turned out to be 'utterly good for nothing'. He married Pattie Willson, an illegitimate daughter of Mrs Unwin's father. Hannah Willson, her child by a previous marriage, was another protégée who disappointed expectation.

So, dear Madam, wait
Till fish can be got
At a reas'nable rate,
Whether lobster or not;

Till the French and the Dutch
Have acquitted the seas,
And then send as much
And as oft as you please.

Mr Andrews took charge of a couple of fowls and a duck, and promised to convey them to our friends at Hoxton. Not being mentioned in your last, Mrs Unwin fears they miscarried.

Yours, my dear Sir,

Wm Cowper

TEXT: *Barham Johnson MSS.*†

TO THE REV. WILLIAM UNWIN

August 25, 1781

My dear friend,

We rejoice with you sincerely in the birth of another son, and in the prospect you have of Mrs Unwin's perfect recovery. May your three children, and the next three, when they shall make their appearance, prove so many blessings to their parents, and make you wish that you had twice the number. — But what made you expect daily that you should hear from me? Letter for letter is the law of all correspondence whatsoever, and because I wrote the last, I have indulged myself for some time in expectations of a sheet from you. Not that I govern myself entirely by the punctilio of reciprocation, but having been pretty much occupied of late, I was not sorry to find myself at liberty to exercise my discretion, and furnished with a good excuse if I chose to be silent.

I expected, as you remember, to have been published last

spring, and was disappointed. The delay has afforded me an opportunity to increase the quantity of my publication by about a third; and if my Muse has not forsaken me, which I rather suspect to be the case, may possibly yet add to it. I have a subject in hand which promises me a great abundance of poetical matter, but which, for want of something I am not able to describe, I cannot at present proceed with. The name of it is *Retirement*, and my purpose, to recommend the proper improvement of it, to set forth the requisites for that end, and to enlarge upon the happiness of that state of life when managed as it ought to be. In the course of my journey through this ample theme, I should wish to touch upon the characters, the deficiencies, and the mistakes of thousands who enter on a scene of retirement, unqualified for it in every respect, and with such designs as have no tendency to promote either their own happiness or that of others. But as I have told you before, there are times when I am no more a poet than I am a mathematician; and when such a time occurs, I always think it better to give up the point than to labour it in vain. I shall yet again be obliged to trouble you for franks; the addition of three thousand lines, or near that number, having occasioned a demand which I did not always foresee. But your obliging friend and your obliging self, having allowed me free liberty of application, I make it without apology.

The solitude, or rather the duality of our condition at Olney, seems drawing to a conclusion. You have not forgot perhaps that the building we inhabit consists of two mansions. And because you have only seen the inside of that part of it which is in our occupation, I therefore inform you that the other end of it is by far the most superb as well as the most commodious. Lady Austen has seen it, has set her heart upon it, is going to fit it up and furnish it, and if she can get rid of the remaining two years of the lease of her London house, will probably enter upon it in a twelvemonth. You will be pleased with this intelligence, because I have already told you that she is a woman perfectly well bred, sensible, and in every respect agreeable; and above all because she loves your mother dearly. It has in my eyes (and I doubt not it will have the same in yours) strong marks of a providential interposition. A

female friend, and one who bids fair to prove herself worthy of
the appellation, comes recommended by a variety of considerations to such a place as Olney. Since Mr Newton went, and
till this lady came, there was not in the kingdom a retirement
more absolutely such than ours. We did not want company,
but when it came, we found it agreeable; a person that has
seen much of the world and understands it well, has high
spirits, a lively fancy, and great readiness of conversation,
introduces a sprightliness into such a scene as this, which if
it was peaceful before, is not the worse for being a little
enlivened. In case of illness too, to which all are liable, it was
rather a gloomy prospect if we allowed ourselves to advert to
it, that there was hardly a woman in the place from whom it
would have been reasonable to have expected either comfort
or assistance. The present curate's wife is a valuable person,
but has a family of her own, and though a neighbour, not a
very near one. But if this plan is effected, we shall be in a
manner one family, and I suppose never pass a day without
some intercourse with each other.

Your mother sends her warm affections, and congratula-
tions, and welcomes into the world the new-born William. —
Yours, my dear friend,

Wm Cowper

TEXT: *BM. Add. MSS.* 24,154

TO MRS NEWTON

Sept. 16, 1781

A NOBLE theme demands a noble verse,
In such I thank you for your fine oy*sters*.
The barrel was magnificently large,
But being sent to Olney at free charge,
Was not inserted in the driver's list,
And therefore overlook'd, forgot, or miss'd;
For when the messenger whom we dispatch'd
Enquired for oysters, Hob his noddle scratch'd;

Denying that his waggon or his wain
Did any such commodity contain.
In consequence of which, your welcome boon
Did not arrive till yesterday at noon;
In consequence of which some chanced to die,
And some, though very sweet, were very dry.
Now Madam says, (and what she says must still
Deserve attention, say she what she will,)
That what we call the Diligence, be-case
It goes to London with a swifter pace,
Would better suit the carriage of your gift,
Returning downward with a pace as swift;
And therefore recommends it with this aim—
To save at least three days,—the price the same;
For though it will not carry or convey
For less than twelve pence, send what'er you may
For oysters bred upon the salt sea shore,
Pack'd in a barrel, they will charge no more.

   News have I none that I can deign to write,
Save that it rain'd prodigiously last night;
And that ourselves were, at the seventh hour,
Caught in the first beginning of the show'r;
But walking, running, and with much ado,
Got home—just time enough to be wet through.
Yet both are well, and, wond'rous to be told,
Soused as we were, we yet have caught no cold;
And wishing just the same good hap to you,
We say, good Madam, and good Sir, Adieu!

TEXT: *The Private Correspondence*

TO THE REV. JOHN NEWTON

The Greenhouse, Sept. 18, 1781

My dear friend,
   I return your preface, with many thanks for so affectionate
an introduction to the public. I have observed nothing that

in my judgment required alteration, except a single sentence in the first paragraph, which I have not obliterated, that you may restore it if you please, by obliterating my interlineation. My reason for proposing an amendment of it was that your meaning did not immediately strike me, which therefore I have endeavoured to make more obvious. The rest is what I would wish it to be. You say indeed more in my commendation than I can modestly say of myself: but something will be allowed to the partiality of friendship on so interesting an occasion.

I have no objection in the world to your conveying a copy to Dr Johnson; though I well know that one of his pointed sarcasms, if he should happen to be displeased, would soon find its way into all companies, and spoil the sale. He writes indeed like a man that thinks a great deal, and that sometimes thinks religiously: but report informs me that he has been severe enough in his animadversions upon Dr Watts,[1] who was nevertheless, if I am in any degree a judge of verse, a man of true poetical ability; careless indeed for the most part, and inattentive too often to those niceties which constitute elegance of expression, but frequently sublime in his conceptions and masterly in his execution. Pope, I have heard, had placed him once in the *Dunciad*;[2] but on being advised to read before he judged him, was convinced that he deserved other treatment, and thrust somebody's blockhead into the gap, whose name consisting of a monosyllable happened to fit it. Whatever faults however I may be chargeable with as a poet, I cannot accuse myself of negligence—I never suffer a line to pass till I have made it as good as I can; and though my doctrines may offend this king of critics, he will not, I flatter myself, be disgusted by slovenly inaccuracy either in the numbers, rhymes, or language. Let the rest take its chance.

---

[1] Isaac Watts. 'His devotional poetry is, like that of others, unsatisfactory. The paucity of its topicks enforces perpetual repetition, and the sanctity of the matter rejects the ornaments of figurative diction. It is sufficient for Watts to have done better than others what no man has done well.' For the sequel to Newton's offer, see n., p. 664.

[2] 1st edition, Bk. I, 145–6:
'A Gothic Library! of Greece and Rome
Well purg'd, and worthy W[es]ley, W[att]s and B[roo]me'.

It is possible he may be pleased, and if he should, I shall have engaged on my side one of the best trumpeters in the kingdom. Let him only speak as favourably of me as he has spoken of Sir Richard Blackmore, who, though he shines in his poem called *Creation*, has written more absurdities in verse than any writer of our country, and my success will be secured.

I have often promised myself a laugh with you about your pipe, but have always forgotten it when I have been writing, and at present I am not much in a laughing humour. You will observe however for your comfort and the honour of that same pipe, that it hardly falls within the line of my censure. You never fumigate the ladies, or force them out of company; not do you use it as an incentive to hard drinking. Your friends indeed have reason to complain that it frequently deprives them of the pleasure of your own conversation while it leads you either into your study or your garden; but in all other respects it is as innocent a pipe as can be. Smoke away therefore; and remember that if one poet[3] has condemned the practice, a better than he (the witty and elegant Hawkins Browne[4]) has been warm in the praise of it.

We are sorry for poor Peggy, and for your sakes as well her own shall be glad to hear of her recovery. You will be so kind as to give our love to her, and to Sally, and to Miss Catlett, if at home.

Retirement grows, but more slowly than any of its predecessors. Time was when I could with ease produce fifty or sixty, or seventy lines in a morning: now I generally fall short of thirty, and am sometimes forced to be content with a dozen. It consists at present I suppose of between six and seven hundred; so that there are hopes of an end, and I dare say Johnson will give me time enough to finish it.

> I nothing add but this—that *still I am*
> Your most affectionate and humble *William*

Our joint love attends Mrs Newton.

TEXT: *Barham Johnson MSS.*†

[3] Himself, in *Conversation*, p. 305.
[4] In *A Pipe of Tobacco*, printed in Dodsley's Collection.

TO THE REV. WILLIAM UNWIN

Sept. 26, 1781

My dear friend,

I may, I suppose, congratulate you on your safe arrival at Brighthelmstone; and am better pleased with your design to close the summer there, because I am acquainted with the place and, by the assistance of fancy, can without much difficulty join myself to the party, and partake with you in your amusements and excursions. It happened singularly enough, that just before I received your last, in which you apprize me of your intended journey, I had been writing upon the subject, having found occasion towards the close of my last poem,[1] called *Retirement*, to take some notice of the modern passion for sea-side entertainments, and to direct to the means by which they might be made useful as well as agreeable. I think with you, that the most magnificent object under Heaven is the great deep; and cannot but feel an unpolite species of astonishment, when I consider the multitudes that view it without emotion, and even without reflection. In all its various forms it is an object of all others the most suited to affect us with lasting impressions of the awful power that created and controls it. I am the less inclined to think this negligence excusable, because at a time of life when I gave as little attention to religious subjects as almost any man, I yet remember that the waves would preach to me, and that in the midst of dissipation I had an ear to hear them. One of Shakespear's characters says,[2]—I am never merry when I hear sweet music. The same effect that harmony seems to have had upon him, I have experienced from the sight and sound of the ocean, which have often composed my thoughts into a melancholy not unpleasing, nor without its use. So much for *Signor Nettuno*.

[1] Lines 519–58.
[2] Jessica, in *The Merchant of Venice*, V, i, 69.

Lady Austen goes to London this day se'nnight. We have told her that you shall visit her,—which is an enterprise you may engage in with the more alacrity, because as she loves every thing that has any connexion with your mother, she is sure to feel a sufficient partiality for her son. Add to this, that your own personal recommendations are by no means small, or such as a woman of her fine taste and discernment can possibly overlook. She has many features in her character which you will admire, but one in particular, on account of the rarity of it, will engage your attention and esteem. She has a degree of gratitude in her composition, so quick a sense of obligation, as is hardly to be found in any rank of life, and if report say true, is scarce indeed in the superior. Discover but a wish to please her, and she never forgets it; not only thanks you, but the tears will start into her eyes at the recollection of the smallest service. With these fine feelings she has the most, and the most harmless vivacity you can imagine, in short, she is—what you will find her to be upon half an hour's conversation with her,—and when I hear you have a journey to town in contemplation, I will send you her address.

Your mother is well, and joins with me in wishing that you may spend your time agreeably upon the coast of Sussex. I beg you will trouble Mr Smith with my respectful compliments, not because I have any right to intrude them upon him, but because he has done me favours of which I am sensible, and wish to appear so.

Yrs,

Wm C.

TEXT: *BM. Add. MSS.* 24,154

TO THE REV. WILLIAM UNWIN

October 6, 1781

My dear friend,

What a world are you daily conversant with, which I have not seen these twenty years and shall never see again! The arts of dissipation I suppose are nowhere practised with more refinement or success than at the place of your present residence; by your account of it, it seems to be just what it was when I visited it, a scene of idleness and luxury, music, dancing, cards, walking, riding, bathing, eating, drinking, coffee, tea, scandal, dressing, yawning, sleeping, the rooms perhaps more magnificent, because the proprietors are grown richer, but the manners and occupations of the company just the same. Though my life has long been like that of a recluse, I have not the temper of one, nor am I in the least an enemy to cheerfulness and good humour; but I cannot envy you your situation; I even feel myself constrained to prefer the silence of this nook, and the snug fire-side in our diminutive parlour to all the splendour and gaiety of Brighthelmstone.

You ask me how I feel on the occasion of my approaching publication—perfectly at my ease; if I had not been pretty well assured beforehand that my tranquillity would be but little endangered by such a measure, I would never have engaged in it, for I cannot bear disturbance. I have had in view two principal objects: first, to amuse myself; and secondly to compass that point in such a manner as that others might possibly be the better for my amusement. If I have succeeded, it will give me pleasure; but if I have failed, I shall not be mortified to the degree that might perhaps be expected. I remember an old adage (though not where it is to be found,) *bene vixit, qui bene latuit*[1]—and if I had recollected it at the right time, it should have been the motto to my book. By the way, it will make an excellent one for *Retirement*, if you can but tell me whom to quote for it. The critics cannot deprive me of the pleasure I have in reflecting that so far as my leisure has been employed in writing for the public, it has been conscientiously employed, and with a view to their advantage. There is nothing agreeable to be sure in being chronicled for a dunce, but I believe there lives not a man upon earth who would be less affected by it than myself. With all this indifference to fame, which you know me too well to suppose me

---

[1] Ovid, *Tristia*, III, iv, 25:
'*Crede mihi, bene qui latuit, bene vixit*'. (Believe me, he has led the best life, who lived in the greatest obscurity).

capable of affecting, I have taken the utmost pains to deserve it. This may appear a mystery or a paradox in practice, but it is true. I considered that the taste of the day is refined and delicate to excess, and that to disgust that delicacy of taste by a slovenly inattention to it, would be to forfeit at once all hope of being useful; and for this reason, though I have written more verse this last year than perhaps any man in England, have finished and polished and touched and retouched with the utmost care. If after all I should be converted into waste paper, it may be my misfortune, but it will not be my fault and I shall bear it with the most perfect serenity.

I do not mean to give Quarme a copy; he is a good-natured little man, and crows exactly like a cock, but knows no more of verse than the cock he imitates.

Whoever supposes that Lady Austen's fortune is precarious, is mistaken. I can assure you upon the ground of the most circumstantial and authentic information, that it is both genteel and perfectly safe.

Your mother adds her love, mine accompanies hers, and our united wishes for your prosperity in every respect desire to be of the party.

Yours,

Wm Cowper

TEXT: *BM. Add. MSS.* 24,154

TO THE REV. WILLIAM UNWIN

Nov. 24, 1781

My dear friend,

News is always acceptable, especially from another world. I cannot tell you what has been done in the Chesapeake,[1] but I can tell you what has passed at West Wycombe, in this

[1] The British fleet which attempted to relieve Lord Cornwallis's beleaguered forces at York Town was defeated by the French in Chesapeake Bay on September 8.

county. Do you feel yourself disposed to give credit to a story of an apparition? No, say you.—I am of your mind.—I do not believe more than one in a hundred of those tales with which old women frighten children, and teach children to frighten each other. But you are not such a philosopher, I suppose, as to have persuaded yourself that an apparition is an impossible thing. You can attend to a story of that sort, if well authenticated? Yes.—Then I can tell you one.

You have heard no doubt of the romantic friendship that subsisted once between Paul Whitehead,[2] and Lord le Despencer, the late Sir Francis Dashwood.[2] When Paul died, he left his lordship a legacy. It was his heart, which was taken out of his body, and sent as directed. His friend having built a church,[3] and at that time just finished it, used it as a mausoleum upon this occasion; and having (as I think the newspapers told us at the time) erected an elegant pillar in the centre of it, on the summit of this pillar, enclosed in a golden urn, he placed the heart in question. But not as a lady places a china figure upon her mantel-tree, or on the top of her cabinet, but with much respectful ceremony and all the forms of funeral solemnity. He hired the best singers and the best performers. He composed an anthem for the purpose, he invited all the nobility and gentry in the country to assist at the celebration of these obsequies, and having formed them all into an august procession, marched to the place appointed at their head, and consigned the posthumous treasure with his own hands to its state of honourable elevation. Having thus, as he thought, and as he might well think (for it seems they were both renowned for their infidelity, and if they had any religion at all were pagans) appeased the manes of the deceased, he rested satisfied with what he had done, and supposed his friend would rest. But not so—about a week since I received a letter from a person who cannot have been misinformed, telling me that Paul has appeared so frequently of late to his Lordship, who labours under a complication of

[2] Sir Francis Dashwood, founder, and Paul Whitehead, secretary, of the Hell Fire Club, the 'Monks of Medmenham'.
[3] The church of St Laurence, West Wycombe.

distempers, that it is supposed the shock he has suffered from such unexpected visits will make his recovery, which was before improbable, impossible. Nor is this all; to ascertain the fact, and to put it out of the power of scepticism to argue away the reality of it, there are few if any of his numerous household who have not likewise seen him, sometimes in the park, sometimes in the garden, as well as in the house, by day and by night indifferently. I make no reflections upon this incident, having other things to write about and but little room.

I am much indebted to Mr Smith for more franks, and still more obliged by the handsome note with which he accompanied them. He has furnished me sufficiently for the present occasion, and by his readiness and obliging manner of doing it, encouraged me to have recourse to him in case another exigence of the same kind should offer. A French author[4] I was reading last night says—he that has written, will write again. If the critics do not set their foot upon this first egg that I have laid, and crush it, I shall probably verify his observation; and when I feel my spirits rise, and that I am armed with industry sufficient for the purpose, undertake the production of another volume. At present however I do not feel myself so disposed; and indeed he that would write should read, not that he may retail the observations of other men, but that being thus refreshed and replenished, he may find himself in a condition to make and to produce his own. I reckon it among my principal advantages as a composer of verses, that I have not read an English poet these thirteen years, and but one these twenty years. Imitation even of the best models is my aversion; it is servile and mechanical, a trick that has enabled many to usurp the name of author, who could not have written at all, if they had not written upon the pattern of somebody indeed original. But when the ear and the taste have been much accustomed to the manner of others, it is almost impossible to avoid it; and we imitate

[4] Louis-Antoine, marquis de Caraccioli, *Jouissance de soi-même*, Paris, 1761: a book concerned with Christian morals. A quotation from it appeared on the title-page of *The Task*.

in spite of ourselves, just in proportion as we admire—but enough of this.

Your mother, who is as well as the season of the year will permit, desires me to add her love and in particular, her enquiries after Mrs Unwin, who she hopes does not find her health injured or her strength greatly impaired by her continual remittances to her new-born William. You will be pleased to mention us affectionately to her and to Miss Shuttleworth.—The salmon you sent us arrived safe and was remarkably fresh. What a comfort it is to have a friend who knows that we love salmon, and who cannot pass by a fishmonger's shop without finding his desire to send us some a temptation too strong to be resisted!

Yours, my dear friend,

Wm Cowper

TEXT: *BM. Add. MSS.* 24,154

TO THE REV. WILLIAM UNWIN

Nov. 26, 1781

My dear friend,

I wrote to you by the last post, supposing you at Stock. But lest that letter should not follow you to Leytonstone, and you should suspect me of unreasonable delay, and lest the frank you have sent me should degenerate into waste paper, and perish upon my hands, I write again. The former letter however containing all my present stock of intelligence, it is more than possible that this may prove a blank, or but little worthy of your acceptance. You will do me the justice to suppose that if I could be very entertaining, I would be so, because by giving me credit for such a willingness to please, you only allow me a share of that universal vanity, which inclines every man upon all occasions to exhibit himself to the best advantage. To say the truth however, when I write as I do to you, not about business nor on any subject that approaches to that description, I mean much less my correspondent's amusement, which my modesty will not always permit me to hope for, than my own. There is a pleasure annexed to the communication of one's ideas, whether by word of mouth or by letter, which nothing earthly can supply the place of, and it is the delight we find in this mutual intercourse, that not only proves us to be creatures intended for social life, but more than any thing else perhaps fits us for it. I have no patience with philosophers—they one and all suppose (at least I understand it to be a prevailing opinion among them) that man's weakness, his necessities, his inability to stand alone, have furnished the prevailing motive under the influence of which he renounced at first a life of solitude, and became a gregarious creature. It seems to me more reasonable, as well as more honourable to my species, to suppose that generosity of soul, and a brotherly attachment to our own kind, drew us as it were to one common centre, taught us to build cities and inhabit them, and welcome every stranger that would cast in his lot amongst us, that we might enjoy fellowship with each other, and the luxury of reciprocal endearments, without which a paradise could afford no comfort. There are indeed all sorts of characters in the world; there are some whose understandings are so sluggish, and whose hearts are such mere clods, that they live in society without either contributing to the sweets of it, or having any relish for them. A man of this stamp passes by our window continually. He draws patterns for the lace-makers. I never saw him conversing with a neighbour but once in my life, though I have known him by sight these twelve years. He is of a very sturdy make, has a round belly, extremely protuberant, which he evidently considers as his best friend because it is his only companion, and it is the labour of his life to fill it. I can easily conceive that it is merely the love of good eating and drinking, and now and then the want of a new pair of shoes, that attaches this man so much to the neighbourhood of his fellow mortals. For suppose these exigencies and others of a like kind to subsist no longer, and what is there that could possibly give society the preference in his esteem? He might strut about with his two thumbs upon his hips in a wilderness: he could hardly be more silent than he is at Olney, and for any advantages, or comforts of friendship or brotherly affection, he could not be more destitute of such blessings there than in his present situation. But other men have something more than guts to satisfy; there are the yearnings of the heart, which let philosophers say what they will, are more importunate than all the necessities of the body, that will not suffer a creature worthy to be called human to be content with an insulated life, or to look for his friends among the beasts of the forest. Yourself for instance. It is not because there are no tailors or pastry-cooks to be found upon Salisbury Plain that you do not choose it for your abode, but because you are a philanthropist, because you are susceptible of social impressions, and have a pleasure in doing a kindness when you can. Witness the salmon you sent, and the salmon you still mean to send, to which your mother wishes you to add an handful of prawns, not only because she likes them, but because they agree with her so well that she even finds them medicinal.

Now upon the word of a poor creature, I have said all that I have said, without the least intention to say one word of it when I began. But thus it is with my thoughts. When you shake a crab-tree, the fruit falls; good for nothing indeed when you have got it, but still the best that is to be expected from a crab-tree. You are welcome to them such as they are, and if you approve my sentiments, tell the philosophers of the day that I have outshot them all, and have discovered the true origin of society when I least looked for it.

Except a pain in her face, violent at times, your Mother is tolerably well, and sends her love,

Yours ever,

Wm Cowper

We should be glad to receive this fresh proof of your regard, viz. the additional piece of salmon, at any time before Xmas.

TEXT: *BM. Add. MSS.* 24,154

TO JOSEPH HILL

Dec. 9, 1781

My dear friend,

Having returned you many thanks for the fine cod and oysters you favoured me with, though it is now morning I will suppose it afternoon, that you and I dined together, are comfortably situated by a good fire, and just entering on a sociable conversation. — You speak first, because I am a man of few words.

Well, Cowper—what do you think of this American war?

I. To say the truth I am not very fond of thinking about it; when I do, I think of it unpleasantly enough. I think it bids fair to be the ruin of this country.

You. That's very unpleasant indeed — if that should be the consequence, it will be the fault of those who might put a stop to it if they would.

I. But do you really think that practicable?

You. Why not? If people leave off fighting,[1] peace follows of course. I wish they would withdraw the forces and put an end to the squabble.

Now I am going to make a long speech.

I. You know the complexion of my sentiments upon some subjects well enough, and that I do not look upon public events either as fortuitous, or absolutely derivable either from the wisdom or folly of man. These indeed operate as second causes, but we must look for the cause of the decline or the prosperity of an empire elsewhere. I have long since done with complaining of men and measures; having learned to consider them merely as the instruments of a higher power, by which he either bestows wealth, peace and dignity upon a nation when he favours it, or by which he strips it of all those

[1] On October 19 Cornwallis had surrendered York Town to General Washington, so practically ending the war in America.

honours, when public enormities long persisted in provoke him to inflict a public punishment. The counsels of great men become as foolish and preposterous when he is pleased to make them so, as those of two frantic creatures in Bedlam[2] when they lay their distracted heads together to consider of the state of the nation. But I go still farther. — The wisdom or the want of wisdom that we observe or think we observe in those that rule us, entirely out of the question, I cannot look upon the circumstances of this country, without being persuaded that I discern in them an embranglement and perplexity that I have never met with in the history of any other, which I think preternatural, if I may use the word on such a subject, prodigious in its kind, and such as human sagacity can never remedy. I have a good opinion of the understanding and integrity of some in power, yet I see plainly that they are unequal to the task. — I think as favourably of some that are not in power — yet I am sure they have never yet in any of their speeches recommended the plan that would effect the salutary purpose. If we pursue the war, it is because we are desperate; it is plunging and sinking year after year into still greater depths of calamity; if we relinquish it, the remedy is equally desperate, and would prove, I believe, in the end no remedy at all. Either way we are undone — perseverance will only enfeeble us more; we cannot recover the colonies by arms. If we discontinue the attempt, in that case we fling away voluntarily what in the other we strive ineffectually to regain; and whether we adopt the one measure or the other, are equally undone: for I consider the loss of America as the ruin of England; were we less encumbered than we are, at home, we could but ill afford it; but being crushed as we are under an enormous debt that the public credit can at no rate carry much longer, the consequence is sure. Thus it appears to me that we are squeezed to death between the two sides of that sort of alternative which is commonly called a cleft stick, the most threatening and portentous condition in which the interests of any country can possibly be found. — I think I have done pretty well for a man of few words, and have contrived

[2] See p. 371.

contrived to have all the talk to myself.—I thank you for not interrupting me.

Yours, my dear friend,

Wm Cowper

TEXT: *Cowper Johnson MSS.*

TO THE REV. WILLIAM UNWIN

Jan. 5, 1782

My dear friend,

Did I allow myself to plead the common excuse of idle correspondents, and esteem it a sufficient reason for not writing, that I have nothing to write about, I certainly should not write now. But I have so often found on similar occasions, when a great penury of matter has seemed to threaten me with an utter impossibility of hatching a letter, that nothing is necessary but to put pen to paper and go on, in order to conquer all difficulties, that availing myself of past experience, I now begin with a most assured persuasion that sooner or later, one idea naturally suggesting another, I shall come to a most prosperous conclusion.

In the last *Review*,[1] I mean in the last but one, I saw Johnson's critique upon Prior and Pope. I am bound to acquiesce in his opinion of the latter, because it has always been my own. I could never agree with those who preferred him to Dryden, nor with others (I have known such and persons of taste and discernment too) who could not allow him to be a poet at all. He was certainly a mechanical maker of verses, and in every line he ever wrote we see indubitable marks of the most indefatigable industry and labour. Writers who find it necessary to make such strenuous and painful exertions, are generally as phlegmatic as they are correct; but Pope was in this respect exempted from the common lot of authors of that class. With the unwearied application of a plodding Flemish

[1] The *Monthly Review*.

painter who draws a shrimp with the most minute exactness, he had all the genius of one of the first masters. Never, I believe, were such talents and such drudgery united. But I admire Dryden most, who has succeeded by mere dint of genius, and in spite of a laziness and a carelessness almost peculiar to himself. His faults are numberless, but so are his beauties. His faults are those of a great man, and his beauties are such, at least sometimes, as Pope with all his touching and retouching could never equal. So far therefore I have no quarrel with Johnson. But I cannot subscribe to what he says of Prior. In the first place, though my memory may fail me, I do not recollect that he takes any notice of his *Solomon*,[2] in my mind the best poem, whether we consider the subject of it or the execution, that he ever wrote. In the next place he condemns him for introducing Venus and Cupid into his love-verses, and concludes it impossible his passion could be sincere, because when he would express it he has recourse to fables. But when Prior wrote, those deities were not so obsolete as now; his cotemporary writers and some that succeeded him did not think them beneath their notice. Tibullus in reality disbelieved their existence as much as we do; yet Tibullus is allowed to be the prince of all poetical inamoratos, though he mentions them in almost every page. There is a fashion in these things, which the Doctor seems to have forgot. But what shall we say of his old fusty-rusty remarks upon *Henry and Emma*? I agree with him that morally considered both the knight and his lady are bad characters, and that each exhibits an example which ought not to be followed. The man dissembles in a way that would have justified the woman had she renounced him, and the woman resolves to follow him at the expense of delicacy, propriety, and even modesty itself. But when the critic calls it a dull dialogue, who but a critic will believe him? There are few readers of poetry of either sex in this country who cannot remember how that enchanting piece has bewitched them, who do not know that instead of finding it tedious, they have been so delighted with the romantic turn of it, as to have overlooked all its defects,

[2] *Solomon on the Vanity of the World*, 1718. Johnson does deal with it.

and to have given it a consecrated place in their memories, without ever feeling it a burthen. I wonder almost that, as the Bacchanals served Orpheus, the boys and girls do not tear this husky, dry commentator limb from limb, in resentment of such an injury done to their darling poet. I admire Johnson as a man of great erudition and sense; but when he sets himself up for a judge of writers upon the subject of love, a passion which I suppose he never felt in his life, he might as well think himself qualified to pronounce upon a treatise on Horsemanship or the Art of Fortification.

Mrs Powley having given us reason when she was here to expect her this next spring, your mother has already sent her an invitation, which we suppose she will accept.

We are glad that you are John's tutor. You never I suppose had so teachable a pupil. He certainly could never have found so proper a master. May he prove hereafter by becoming all that you can wish him to be, that neither you nor I were mistaken when we gave the preference to a private education.

Mr Smith having sent me with a parcel of franks a note in which he most obligingly invited me to draw upon him for that commodity, I soon after used the liberty he gave me and received as obliging an answer. The next packet I receive from Johnson will bring me, I imagine, the last proof sheet of my volume, which will consist of about 350 pages, honestly printed. My public *entrée* therefore is not far distant.

Your mother joins me in love to yourself and all at Stock.

Yours, mon Ami,

Wm Cowper

Had we known that the last cheeses were naught, we would not have sent you these. Your mother has however enquired for and found a better dairy, which she means shall furnish you with cheeses another year.

TEXT: *BM. Add. MSS.* 24,155

TO JOSEPH HILL

Jan. 31, 1782

My dear friend,

Having thanked you for a barrel of very fine oysters, I should have nothing more to say, if I did not determine to say every thing that may happen to occur. The political world affords us no very agreeable subjects at present, nor am I sufficiently conversant with it to do justice to so magnificent a theme if it did. A man that lives as I do, whose chief occupation at this season of the year, is to walk ten times in a day from the fireside to his cucumber frame and back again, cannot show his wisdom more, if he has any wisdom to show, than by leaving the mysteries of government to the management of persons in point of situation and information much better qualified for the business. Suppose not however that I am perfectly an unconcerned spectator, or that I take no interest at all in the affairs of my country. Far from it—I read the news—I see that things go wrong in every quarter.[1] I meet now and then with an account of some disaster that seems to be the indisputable progeny of treachery, cowardice, or a spirit of faction. I recollect that in those happier days when you and I could spend our evening in enumerating victories and acquisitions that seemed to follow each other almost in a continued series, there was some pleasure in being a politician, and a man might talk away upon so entertaining a subject, without danger of becoming tiresome to others, or incurring weariness himself. When poor Bob White brought me the news of Boscawen's[2] success off the coast of Portugal, how did I leap for joy! When Hawke demolished Conflans, I was

[1] At this time, Britain was at war with the insurgent Americans, with Hyder Ali in India, and with France, Spain and Holland. She had lost nearly all the American colonies, much of the West Indies, and Minorca.

[2] 1759 was the year of British victories: Admiral Boscawen's at Lagos Bay, Lord Hawke's at Quiberon Bay, the Battle of the Heights of Abraham at Quebec, and the battle of Minden.

still more transported. But nothing could express my rapture when Wolfe made the conquest of Quebec. I am not therefore I suppose destitute of true patriotism, but the course of public events has of late afforded me no opportunity to exert it. I cannot rejoice, because I see no reason, and I will not murmur, because for that, I can find no good one. And let me add, he that has seen both sides of 50, has lived to little purpose, if he has not other views of the world than he had when he was much younger. He finds, if he reflects at all, that it will be to the end what it has been from the beginning, a shifting, uncertain, fluctuating scene; that nations as well as individuals have their seasons of infancy, youth, and age, and if he be an Englishman, he will observe that ours in particular is affected with every symptom of decay, and is already sunk into a state of decrepitude. I am reading Mrs Macaulay's *History*.[3] I am not quite such a superannuated simpleton as to suppose that mankind were wiser or much better when I was young than they are now. But I may venture to assert without exposing myself to the charge of dotage, that the men whose integrity, courage and wisdom broke the bands of tyranny, established our constitution upon its true basis, and gave a people overwhelmed with the scorn of all countries an opportunity to emerge into a state of the highest respect and estimation, make a better figure in history than any of the present day are likely to do, when their pretty harangues are forgotten, and nothing shall survive but the remembrance of the views and motives with which they made them.

My dear friend, I have written at random in every sense, neither knowing what sentiments I should broach when I began, nor whether they would accord with yours. Excuse a rustic if he errs on such a subject, and believe me sincerely yours,

Wm Cowper

My best respects attend Mrs Hill.

TEXT: *Cowper Johnson MSS.*

[3] Catharine Macaulay: *History of England from the Accession of James I to that of the Brunswick Line.*

TO THE REV. WILLIAM UNWIN

Feb. 9. 1782

My dear friend,

I thank you for Mr Lowth's[1] verses. They are so good that had I been present when he spoke them, I should have trembled for the *boy*, lest the *man* shd. disappoint the hopes such early genius had given birth to. It is not common to see so lively a fancy so correctly managed and so free from irregular exuberances at so unexperienced an age; fruitful yet not wanton, and gay without being tawdry. When schoolboys write verse, if they have any fire at all, it generally spends itself in flashes and transient sparks, which may indeed suggest an expectation of something better hereafter, but deserve not to be much commended for any real merit of their own. Their wit is generally forced and false, and their sublimity (if they affect any) bombast. I remember well when it was thus with me, and when a turgid noisy unmeaning speech in a tragedy, which I should now laugh at, afforded me raptures and filled me with wonder. It is not in general till reading and observation have settled the taste, that we can give the prize to the best writing in preference to the worst, much less are we able to execute what is good ourselves. But Lowth seems to have stepped into excellence at once, and to have gained by intuition, what we little folks are happy if we can learn at last, after much labour of our own and instruction of others. The compliments he pays to the memory of King Charles he would probably now retract, though he be a bishop, and his Majesty's zeal for Episcopacy was one of the causes of his ruin. An age or two must pass before some characters can be properly understood. The spirit of party employs itself in veiling their faults and ascribing to them virtues which they never possessed; see Charles's face drawn by Clarendon,[2] and it is an handsome portrait; see it more justly exhibited by Mrs

[1] See p. 361.

[2] Lord Clarendon's *History of the Rebellion and Civil Wars in England*, 1702–4, Bk. XI: 'He was the worthiest gentleman, the best master, the best friend, the best husband, the best father, and the best Christian, that the age in which he lived produced.'

Macaulay, and it is deformed to a degree that shocks us. Every feature expresses cunning employing itself in the attainment of tyranny, and dissimulation pretending itself an advocate for truth.

I have a piece of secret history to communicate which I would have imparted sooner, but that I thought it possible there might be no occasion to mention it at all. When persons for whom I have felt a friendship disappoint and mortify me by their conduct, or act unjustly towards me, though I no longer esteem them friends, I still feel that tenderness for their character that I would conceal the blemish if I could. But in making known the following anecdote to you, I run no risk of a publication, assured that when I have once enjoined you secrecy, you will observe it.

My letters have already apprized you of that close and intimate connection that took place between the lady you visited in Queen Anne Street[3] and us. Nothing could be more promising in its appearance though sudden in its commencement. She treated us with as much unreservedness of communication as if we had been born in the same house and educated together. At her departure she herself proposed a correspondence, and because writing does not agree with your mother, proposed a correspondence with me. This sort of intercourse had not been long maintained, before I discovered by some slight intimations of it, that she had conceived displeasure at somewhat I had written, though I cannot now recollect it. Conscious of none but the most upright and inoffensive intentions, I yet apologized for the passage in question, and the flaw was healed again. Our correspondence after this proceeded smoothly for a considerable time, but at length having had repeated occasion to observe that she expressed a sort of romantic idea of our merits, and built such expectations of felicity upon our friendship, as we were sure that nothing human could possibly answer, I wrote to remind her that we were mortal, to recommend it to her not to think more highly of us than the subject would warrant, and intimating that when we

[3] Lady Austen.

embellish a creature with colours taken from our own fancy, and so adorned, admire and praise it beyond its real merits, we make it an idol, and have nothing to expect in the end but that it will deceive our hopes, and that we shall derive nothing from it but a painful conviction of our error. Your mother heard me read the letter, she read it herself, and honoured it with her warm approbation. But it gave mortal offence. It received indeed an answer, but such an one as I could by no means reply to; and there ended (for it was impossible it should ever be renewed) a friendship that bid fair to be lasting; being formed with a woman whose seeming stability of temper, whose knowledge of the world and great experience of its folly, but above all, whose sense of religion, and seriousness of mind (for with all that gaiety she is a great thinker) induced us both in spite of that cautious reserve that marks our characters, to trust her, to love and value her, and to open our hearts for her reception. It may be necessary to add that by her own desire I wrote to her under the assumed relation of a brother, and she to me as my sister...*Ceu fumus in auras.*[4]

I thank you for the search you have made after my intended motto,[5] but I no longer need it. I have left myself no room for politics, that subject therefore must be postponed to a future letter. Our love is always with yourself and family. — We have recovered from the concern we suffered on account of the fracas abovementioned, though for some days it made us unhappy. Not knowing but that she might possibly become sensible in a few days that she had acted hastily and unreasonably, and renew the correspondence herself, I could not in justice apprize you of this quarrel sooner, but some weeks having passed without any proposals of accommodation, I am now persuaded that none are intended, and in justice to you am obliged to caution you against a repetition of your visit.

Yours my dear friend,

Wm Cowper

TEXT: *BM. Add. MSS.* 24,155

[4] Virgil, *Aeneid* V, 740: '*dixerat et tenuis fugit ceu fumus in auras.*' (He spoke and passed like smoke into thin air.)

[5] See *n.*, p. 639.

TO THE REV. WILLIAM UNWIN

Feb. 24, 1782

My dear friend,

If I should receive a letter from you to-morrow, you must still remember that I am not in your debt, having paid you by anticipation. Knowing that you take an interest in my publication, and that you have waited for it with some impatience, I write to inform you that if it is possible for a printer to be punctual, I shall come forth on the 1st of March. I have ordered 2 copies to Stock—one for Mr Jno Unwin. It is possible after all that my book may come forth without a preface. Mr Newton has written (he could indeed write no other) a very sensible as well as a very friendly one, and it is printed. But the bookseller, who knows him well, and esteems him highly, is anxious to have it cancelled, and with my consent first obtained, has offered to negotiate that matter with the author. He judges that though it would serve to recommend the volume to the religious, it would disgust the profane, and that there is in reality no need of any preface at all. I have found Johnson a very judicious man on other occasions, and am therefore willing that he should determine for me upon this.

Having imparted to you an account of the fracas between us and Lady Ann, it is necessary that you should be made acquainted with every event that bears any relation to that incident. The day before yesterday she sent me, by her brother-in-law Mr Jones, three pair of worked ruffles, with advice that I should soon receive a fourth. I knew they were begun before we quarrelled. I begged Mr Jones to tell her when he wrote next how much I thought myself obliged, and gave him to understand that I should make her a very inadequate, though the only return in my power, by laying my volume at her feet. This likewise she had previous reason given her to expect. Thus stands the affair at present; whether anything in the shape of a reconciliation is to take place hereafter, I know not; but this I know, that when an amicable freedom of intercourse, and that unreserved confidence which belongs only to true friendship, has been once un-rooted, plant it again with what care you may, it is very difficult if not impossible to make it grow. The fear of giving offence to a temper too apt to take it, is unfavourable to that comfort we propose to ourselves even in our ordinary connexions, but absolutely incompatible with the pleasures of real friendship. She is to spend the summer in our neighbour-hood, Lady Peterborough and Miss Mordaunt are to be of the party; the former a dissipated woman of fashion, and the latter a haughty beauty. Retirement is our passion and our delight; it is in still life alone we look for that measure of happiness we can rationally expect below. What have we to do therefore with characters like these? Shall we go to the dancing school again? Shall we cast off the simplicity of our plain and artless demeanour, to learn, and not in a youthful day neither, the manners of those whose manners at the best are their only recommendation, and yet can in reality recommend them to none, but to people like themselves? This would be folly which nothing but necessity could excuse, and in our case no such necessity can possibly obtain. We will not go into the world, and if the world would come to us, we must give it the French answer—*Monsieur et Madame ne sont pas visibles.*

There are but few persons to whom I present my book. The Lord Chancellor is one. I enclose in a packet I send by this post to Johnson a letter to his Lordship which will accompany the volume; and to you I enclose a copy of it, because I know you will have a friendly curiosity to see it. An author is an important character; whatever his merits may be, the mere circumstance of authorship warrants his approach to persons, whom otherwise perhaps he could hardly address without being deemed impertinent. He can do me no good—if I should happen to do him a little, I shall be a greater man than he.—I have ordered a copy likewise to Mr Robert Smith.

Lord Sandwich[1] has been hard run, but I consider the push

[1] John Montagu, 4th Earl of Sandwich, served as First Lord of the Admiralty from 1771 to 1782. 'He rendered the business of the Admiralty subservient to the interests of his party and employed the vast patronage of the office as an engine for bribery and political jobbery.' (DNB.)

that has been made to displace him, as the effort of a faction, rather than as the struggle of true patriotism convinced of his delinquency, and desirous to sacrifice him to the interests of the country. Without public virtue public prosperity cannot be long lived, and where must we look for it? It seems indeed to have a share in the motives that animate one or two of the popular party, but grant them sincere, which is a very charitable concession, the rest are evidently naught, and the quantity of salt is too small to season the mass.

I hope John continues to be pleased and to give pleasure. If he loves instruction he has a tutor who can give him plentifully what he loves, and with his natural abilities his progress must be such as you would wish.

Our love to all the family
Yrs. affectionately

Wm Cowper

TEXT: *BM. Add. MSS.* 24,155

TO THE REV. WILLIAM UNWIN

March 7, 1782

My dear friend,

We have great pleasure in the contemplation of your Northern journey, as it promises us a sight of you and yours by the way, and are only sorry that Miss Shuttleworth cannot be of the party. A line to ascertain the hour when we may expect you, by the next preceding post, will be welcome.

We are far from wishing a renewal of the connexion we have lately talked about. We did indeed find it in a certain way an agreeable one while that lady continued in the country, yet not altogether compatible with out favourite plan, with that silent retirement in which we have spent so many years, and in which we wish to spend what are yet before us. She is exceedingly sensible, has great quickness of parts, and an uncommon fluency of expression, but her vivacity was sometimes too much for us; occasionally perhaps it might refresh and revive us, but it more frequently exhausted us, neither your mother nor I being in that respect at all a match for her. But after all, it does not entirely depend upon us, whether our former intimacy shall take place again or not, or rather whether we shall attempt to cultivate it, or give it over, as we are more inclined to do, in despair. I suspect a little by her sending the ruffles, and by the terms in which she spoke of us to you, that some overtures on her part are to be looked for. Should this happen, however we may wish to be reserved, we must not be rude; but I can answer for us both that we shall enter into the connexion again with great reluctance, not hoping for any better fruit of it than it has already produced. If you thought she fell short of the description I gave her, I still think however that it was not a partial one, and that it did not make too favourable a representation of her character. You *must* have seen her to a disadvantage; a consciousness of a quarrel so recent, and in which she had expressed herself with a warmth that she knew must have affronted and shocked us both, must unavoidably have produced its effect upon her behaviour, which though it could not be awkward, must have been in some degree unnatural, her attention being pretty much engrossed by a recollection of what had passed between us. I would by no means have hazarded you into her company, if I had not been sure that she would treat you with politeness, and almost persuaded that she would soon see the unreasonableness of her conduct, and make a suitable apology.

It is not so much for my advantage that the printer delays so long to gratify your expectation. It is a state of mind that is apt to tire and disconcert us; and there are but few pleasures that make us amends for the pain of repeated disappointment. I take it for granted you have not received the volume, not having received it myself, nor indeed heard from Johnson since he fixed the first of the month for its publication.

What a medley are our public prints. Half the page filled with the ruin of the country, and the other half filled with the vices and pleasures of it! Here an island taken, and there a new comedy, here an empire lost, and there an Italian opera, or the Duke of Gloucester's rout on a Sunday!

May it please your royal Highness—I am an Englishman and must stand or fall with the Nation. Religion, its true

Palladium, has been stolen away, and it is crumbling into dust. Sin ruins us, the sins of the great especially, and of their sins, especially the violation of the Sabbath, because it is naturally productive of all the rest. Is it fit that a Prince should make the Sabbath a day of dissipation, and that not content with his own personal profanation of it, he should invite all whose rank entitles them to the honour of such distinction, to partake with him in his guilt? Are examples operative in proportion to the dignity of those who set them? Whose then more pernicious than your own in this flagrant instance of impiety? For shame, Sir!—if you wish well to your brother's arms, and would be glad to see the kingdom emerging again from her ruins, pay more respect to an ordinance that deserves the deepest. I do not say, pardon this short remonstrance. The concern I feel for my country, and the interest I have in its prosperity, give me a right to make it.—I am, &c.

Thus one might write to his Highness, and I suppose might be as profitably employed in whistling the tune of an old ballad. Lord Plymouth had a rout too on the same day.—Is he the son of that Plymouth who bought Punch for an hundred pounds, and having kept him a week, tore him limb from limb because he was sullen and would not speak?— probably he is.

I have no copy of the preface, nor do I know at present how Johnson & Mr N. have settled it. In the matter of it there was nothing offensively peculiar, but it was thought too pious.

Yours, my dear friend,

Wm Cowper

TEXT: *BM. Add. MSS.* 24,155

TO THE REV. WILLIAM UNWIN

May 27, 1782

My dear friend,

Rather ashamed of having been at all dejected by the censure of the Critical Reviewers, who certainly could not read without prejudice a book complete replete with opinions and doctrines to which they cannot subscribe,[1] I have at present no little occasion to keep a strict guard upon my vanity lest it should be too much flattered by the following eulogium. I send it you for the reasons I gave when I imparted to you some other anecdotes of a similar kind while we were together. Our interests in the success of this same volume are so closely united, that you *must* share with me in the praise or blame that attends it; and sympathizing with me under the burthen of injurious treatment, have a right to enjoy with me the cordials I now and then receive as I happen to meet with more favourable and candid judges.

A merchant, a friend of ours (you will soon guess him) sent my *Poems* to one of the first philosophers, one of the most eminent literary characters, as well as one of the most important in the political world, that the present age can boast of. Now perhaps your conjecturing faculties are puzzled, and you begin to ask, 'who, where, and what is he? speak out, for I am all impatience.' I will not say a word more, the letter in which he returned his thanks for the present shall speak for him.

Passy, May 8, 1782

Sir,

I received the letter you did me the honour of writing to me, and am much obliged by your kind present of a book. The relish for reading of poetry had long since left me, but there is something so new in the manner, so easy, and yet so correct in the language, so clear in the expression, yet concise, and so just in the sentiments, that I have read the whole with great pleasure, and some of the pieces more than once. I beg you to accept my thankful acknowledgements, and to present my respects to the author.

I shall take care to forward the letters to America, and shall be glad of any other opportunity of doing what may be agreeable to you, being with great respect for your character,—
Your most obedient humble servant,

B. Franklin

---

[1] The *Critical Review* found C.'s *Poems* 'coarse, vulgar and unpoetical'.

We may now treat the critics as the Archbishop of Toledo treated Gil Blas, when he found fault with one of his sermons. His grace gave him a kick on the breech and said, 'Begone for a jackanapes, and furnish yourself with a better taste if you know where to find it.'

We are glad that you are safe at home again. Could we see at one glance of the eye what is passing every day upon all the roads in the kingdom, how many are terrified, and hurt, how many plundered and abused, we should indeed find reason enough to be thankful for journeys performed in safety, and for deliverance from dangers we are not perhaps even permitted to see. When in some of the high southern latitudes, and in a dark tempestuous night, a flash of lightning discovered to Captain Cook a vessel, which glanced along close by his side, and which but for the lightning he must have run foul of, both the danger and the transient light that showed it, were undoubtedly designed to convey to him this wholesome instruction, that a particular Providence attended him, and that he was not only preserved from evils of which he had notice, but from many more of which he had no information or even the least suspicion. What unlikely contingencies may nevertheless take place! How improbable that two ships should dash against each other in the midst of the vast Pacific Ocean, and that steering contrary courses from parts of the world so immensely distant from each other, they should yet move so exactly in a line as to clash, fill, and go to the bottom, in a sea where all the ships in the world might be so dispersed as that none should see another! Yet this must have happened but for the remarkable interference which he has recorded. The same Providence indeed might as easily have conducted them so wide of each other that they should never have met at all; but then this lesson would have been lost; at least the heroic voyager would have encompassed the globe without having had occasion to relate an incident that so naturally suggests it.

I am no more delighted with the season than you are. The absence of the sun, which has graced the spring with much less of his presence than he vouchsafed to the winter, has a very uncomfortable effect upon my frame. I feel an invincible aversion to employment, which I am yet constrained to fly to as my only remedy against something worse. If I do nothing, I am dejected; if I do anything, I am weary; and that weariness is best described by the word lassitude, which is of all weariness in the world the most oppressive. But enough of myself and the weather.

The blow we have struck in the West Indies[1] will, I suppose, be decisive at least for the present year, and so far as that part of our possessions is concerned in the present conflict. But the news-writers and their correspondents disgust me and make me sick. One victory after such a long series of adverse occurrences has filled them with self-conceit and impertinent boasting; and while Rodney is almost accounted a Methodist for ascribing his success to Providence, men who have renounced all dependence upon such a friend, without whose assistance nothing can be done, threaten to drive the French out of the sea, laugh at the Spaniards, sneer at the Dutch, and are to carry the world before them. Our enemies are apt to brag, and we deride them for it; but we can sing as loud as they can in the same key, and no doubt wherever our papers go shall be derided in our turn. An Englishman's true glory should be to do his business well and say little about it; but he disgraces himself when he puffs his prowess as if he had finished his task, when he has just begun it.

We expect your sister in a day or two. We are both tolerably well, and our love attends you.

Yours,

Wm Cowper

TEXT: *BM. Add. MSS.* 24,155

TO THE REV. WILLIAM UNWIN

Aug. 3, 1782

My dear friend,

Entertaining some hope that Mr Newton's next letter

[2] Admiral Rodney defeated the French under Count de Grasse, April 12, 1782.

would furnish me with the means of satisfying your enquiry
on the subject of Dr Johnson's opinion,[1] I have till now
delayed my answer to your last; but the information is not yet
come, Mr Newton having intermitted a week more than usual
since his last writing. When I receive it, favourable or not, it
shall be communicated to you; but I am not very sanguine in
my expectations from that quarter; very learned and very
critical heads are hard to please. He may perhaps treat me with
lenity for the sake of my subject and design, but the composition I think will hardly escape his censure. But though all
doctors may not be of the same mind, there is one doctor at
least whom I have lately discovered my professed admirer. He
too like Johnson was with difficulty persuaded to read, having
an aversion to all poetry except the *Night Thoughts*, which on a
certain occasion, when being confined on board a ship he had
no other employment, he got by heart. He was however
prevailed upon, and read me several times over; so that if my
volume had sailed with him instead of Dr Young's, I might
perhaps have occupied that shelf in his memory which he
then allotted to the Doctor. His name is Renny and he lives
at Newport Pagnel.

It is a sort of paradox, but it is true — we are never more in
danger than we think ourselves most secure, nor in reality more
secure than when we seem perhaps to be most in danger. Both
sides of this apparent contradiction were lately verified in my
experience. Passing from the greenhouse to the barn I saw
three kittens (for we have so many in our retinue) looking
with a fixed attention at something which lay on the thresh-
hold of a door nailed up. I took but little notice of them at
first, but a loud hiss engaged me to attend more closely, when
behold! a viper, the largest I remember to have seen, rearing
itself, darting its forked tongue, and ejaculating the afore-
mentioned hiss at the nose of a kitten almost in contact with
his lips. I ran into the hall for a hoe with a long handle with
which I intended to assail him, and returning in a few seconds,
missed him. He was gone, and I feared had escaped me. Still

---

[1] Newton undertook to pass a copy of the *Poems* of 1782 to Dr Johnson.
Johnson nowhere mentions Cowper; but Cowper was given to understand that his opinion was favourable.

however the kittens sat watching immovably upon the same spot. I concluded therefore that sliding between the door and the threshold he had found his way out of the garden into the yard. I went round immediately, and there found him in close conversation with the old cat, whose curiosity being excited by so novel an appearance, inclined her to pat his head repeatedly with her forefoot, with her claws however sheathed, and not in anger, but in the way of philosophical enquiry and examination. To prevent her falling a victim to so laudible an exercise of her talents, I interposed in a moment with the hoe, and performed upon him an act of decapitation which, though not immediately mortal, proved so in the end.[2] Had he slid into the passages, where it is dark, or had he when in the yard met with no interruption from the cat, and secreted himself in any of the outhouses, it is hardly possible but that some of the family must have been bitten. He might have been trodden upon without being perceived and have slipped away before the sufferer could have well distinguished what foe had wounded him. Three years ago we discovered one in the same place, which the barber slew with a trowel.

Our proposed removal to Mr Small's[3] was, as you suppose, a jest, or rather a joco-serious matter. We never looked upon it as entirely feasible, yet we saw in it something so like practicability, that we did not esteem it altogether unworthy of our attention. It was one of those projects which people of lively imagination play with and admire for a few days, and then break in pieces. Lady Austen returned on Thursday from London, where she spent the last fortnight, and whither she was called by an unexpected opportunity to dispose of the remainder of her lease. She has now therefore no longer any connexion with the great city, she has none on earth whom she calls friends but us, and no home but Olney. Her abode is to be at the Vicarage where she has hired as much room as she wants, which she will embellish with her own furniture,

[2] This incident inspired *The Colubriad*, p. 74.

[3] Lady Austen returned to Clifton Reynes in June 1782 and 'seized the first opportunity to embrace' Mrs Unwin. A reconciliation followed. Afterwards she suggested all three should jointly rent Mr Small's house, Clifton Hall.

and which she will occupy as soon as Mrs Scott has produced another child, which is expected to make its entry in October.

Mr Bull, a dissenting minister of Newport, a learned, ingenious, good-natured, pious friend of ours, who sometimes visits us, and whom we visited last week, has put into my hands three volumes of French poetry composed by Madame Guion[4]— a Quietist say you and a fanatic, I will have nothing to do with her. 'Tis very well, you are welcome to have nothing to do with her, but in the meantime her verse is the only French verse I ever read that I found agreeable. There is a neatness in it equal to that which we applaud with so much reason in the compositions of Prior. I have translated several of them, and shall proceed in my translations till I have filled a Lilliputian paper-book I happen to have by me, which when filled I shall present to Mr Bull. He is her passionate admirer, rode 20 miles to see her picture in the house of a stranger, which stranger politely insisted on his acceptance of it, and it now hangs over his parlour chimney. It is a striking portrait, too characteristic not to be a strong resemblance, and were it encompassed with a glory instead of being dressed in a nun's hood, might pass for the face of an angel.

Our meadows are covered with a winter flood in August. The rushes with which our bottomless chairs were to have been bottomed, and much hay which was not carried, are gone down the river on a voyage to Ely, and it is even uncertain whether they will ever return. *Sic transit gloria mundi*! I am glad you have found a curate; may he answer! am happy in Mrs Bouverie's[5] continued approbation; it is worth while to write for such a reader.

Yours with our united love
to all at Stock

(unsigned)

Next time you write shall be glad of a frank to your sister.

TEXT: *BM. Add. MSS.* 24,155

[4] See pp. 163–4.

[5] Elizabeth Bouverie of Barham Court, Teston, Kent, a friend of Hannah More and of the Bluestockings.

TO THE REV. WILLIAM UNWIN

Aug. 27, 1782

The last four days have been days of adventure, teeming with incidents in which the opposite ingredients of pain and pleasure have been plentifully mingled, and of the most interesting kind. Lady Austen's behaviour to us ever since her return to Clifton has been such as to engage our affections to her more than ever. A flood indeed has sometimes parted us for many days, but though it has often been impossible for us who never ride to visit *her*, as soon as the water has become fordable by an ass, she has mounted one & visited *us*. On Thursday last, in the evening, she came down with her sister to the evening lecture. She had not been long seated in her pew, before she was attacked by the most excruciating pains of a bilious colic. Having much resolution however, and being determined not to alarm her sister, the congregation, or the minister, she bore it without discovering much of what she felt even to Mrs Jones till the service was over. — It is a disorder to which she has lately been very subject. — We were just sitting down to supper when a hasty rap alarmed us. I ran to the hall window, for the hares being loose it was impossible to open the door. The evening had been a dismal one, raining almost continually, but just at that time it held up. I entreated Mrs Jones to go round to the gate, and understanding by her tremulous voice that something distressful was at hand, made haste to meet her. I had no sooner reached the yard door and opened it, than Lady Austen appeared leaning on Mr Scott. She could not speak, but thrusting her other arm under mine, with much difficulty made shift to attain the great chair by the fireside in the parlour. There she suffered unutterable anguish for a considerable time, till at length by your mother's application and assistance being a little relieved she contrived to climb the staircase, and after about 3 hours' agony was put to bed. At eleven at night we sent off a messenger to Northampton who returned at 7 the next morning and brought a physician with him. He prescribed and she was better. Friday night she slept tolerably, rose cheerful, and entertained us all Saturday with much agreeable conversation as usual; but her spirits being too great for her strength, the consequence was a frightful hysteric fit which seized her just as she was going to bed. She was alone, for her sister had been obliged to go home, and thinking there was no need of such a precaution, she would have nobody else to sleep with her. The appointed signal was that she should knock if she wanted anything. She did so. Your mother hastened to the chamber, and I after her to know if I could be of any use. She had not begun to undress, so I was admitted, and soon after her disorder became quite convulsive, accompanied with most of the symptoms of the most violent fits of that sort I have ever seen. In about an hour she grew better, rested tolerably, was in good spirits on Sunday, and last night, well enough to return to Clifton upon the ass. Today we dine there.

Are you curious to know her sentiments of *you*? The question has no doubt excited your curiosity if you had none before; suppose however I postpone the gratification of it and make it part of my next letter, finishing this with something more important? No—you must be satisfied this moment; no man that merits the good opinion of others, can be indifferent to it—You shall then.

She would have known you for your mother's son the moment she saw you had you not been announced by name. This is some praise, let me tell you, especially from her, who thinks that mother the best of women, and loves her at least as much as if she were her own. Your figure the most elegant she ever saw—no longer complain of calveless legs and a belly with nothing in it. Your countenance quite handsome—no longer be ashamed of a nose you have sometimes thought too long.—Every motion of your limbs, your action, your attitude bespeak the gentleman. Added to all this, your vivacity and your good sense, together with an amiable disposition which she is sure you possess though she has but an hour's knowledge of you, have placed you so high in her esteem, that had you an opportunity to cultivate an interest there you would soon be without a rival. 14 years ago I would not have made you this relation. Such a stripling as you was at that time would have been spoiled by so much praise, and through the mere hunger after more would have lost what he had acquired already. But being the father of a family and the minister of three parishes, I am not afraid to trust you with it. I beg Mrs Unwin will add a short postcript to your next, just to inform me whether when you perused this picture of yourself, you blushed and how often. I had almost forgot what she desired me to insert, that she wishes as much for a Mr Unwin here, as you can possibly for a Lady Austen at Stock.

Notwithstanding the uncommon rigour of the season, much of our wheat is carried and in good condition. It does not appear that the murmurings of the farmers were with any reason. The corn has suffered much less by the mildew than was reported, and if it is at all injured (in this part of the world at least) it must be ascribed to their foolish impatience, who *would* cut it down too soon. It is so cold this 27th of Augt. that I shake in the greenhouse where I am writing.

Our united love attends you.—Your letter is gone to Dewsbury.[1]

Yours, my dear William,

Wm C.

TEXT: *BM. Add. MSS.* 24,155

TO THE REV. WILLIAM UNWIN

[probably September, 1782][1]

My dear William,

The modest terms in which you express yourself on the

[1] Where Matthew Powley, his sister's husband, was now vicar.

[1] This undated letter is placed by *Wright* between the letters of 17 and 31 January 1782: "it must have been written before the first breach with Lady Austen.' But Lady Austen was in London from October 1781 until June 1782. This letter was written when she was living in C.'s house. The internal evidence shows that the letter was C.'s answer to Unwin's reply to the letter of 27th August 1782.

subject of Lady Austen's commendation embolden me to add my suffrage to hers, and to confirm it by assuring you that I think her just and well-founded in her opinion of you. The compliment indeed glances at myself, for were you less than she accounts you, I ought not to afford you that place in my esteem which you have held so long. My own sagacity therefore and discernment are not a little concerned upon the occasion, for either you resemble the picture, or I have strangely mistaken my man and formed an erroneous judgment of his character. With respect to your face and figure indeed, there I leave the ladies to determine, as being naturally best qualified to decide the point; but whether you are perfectly the man of sense and the gentleman, is a question in which I am as much interested as they, and which, you being my friend, I am of course prepared to settle in your favour.

That lady, whom when you know her as well, you will love as much as we do, is and has been during the last fortnight a part of our family. Before she was perfectly restored to health, she returned to Clifton. Soon after her return Mr Jones had occasion to go to London. No sooner was he gone, than the *château*,[2] being left without a garrison, was besieged as regularly as the night came on. Villains were both heard and seen in the garden and at the doors and windows. The kitchen window in particular was attempted, from which they took a complete pane of glass exactly opposite to the iron by which it was fastened, but providentially the window had been nailed to the woodwork in order to keep it close and that the air might be excluded. Thus they were disappointed and, being discovered by the maid, withdrew. The ladies being worn out with continual watching and repeated alarms, were at last prevailed upon to take refuge with us. Men furnished with firearms were put into the house, and the rascals having intelligence of this circumstance, beat a retreat. Mr Jones returned; Mrs Jones and Miss Green, her daughter, left us, but Lady Austen's spirits having been too much disturbed to be capable of repose in a place where she had been so much

---

[2] Clifton Reynes rectory.

terrified, she was left behind. She remains with us till her lodgings at the Vicarage can be made ready for her reception, which cannot be till Mrs Scott's delivery, who is in daily expectation of her puerperium. I have now sent you what has occurred of most moment in our history, since my last.

I say Amen with all my heart to your observation on religious characters. Men who profess themselves adepts in mathematical knowledge, in astronomy or jurisprudence, are generally as well qualified as they would appear. The reason may be, that they are always liable to detection, should they attempt to impose upon mankind, and therefore take care to be what they pretend. In religion alone, a profession is often slightly taken up and slovenly carried on, because forsooth candour and charity require us to hope the best and to judge favourably of our neighbour, and because it is easy to deceive the ignorant who are a great majority upon this subject. Let a man attach himself to a particular party, contend furiously for what are properly called evangelical doctrines, and enlist himself under the banner of some popular preacher, and the business is done. Behold a Christian, a Saint, a Phoenix! In the meantime perhaps his heart and his temper, and even his conduct are unsanctified, possibly less exemplary than thoes of some avowed infidels. No matter—he can talk—he has the Shibboleth of the true church,—the Bible in his pocket and a head well stored with notions. But the quiet, humble, modest and peaceable person, who is in his practice what the other is only in his profession, who hates a noise and therefore makes none, who knowing the snares that are in the world, keeps himself as much out of it as he can, never enters it but when duty calls, and even then with fear and trembling, is the Christian that will always stand highest in the estimation of those, who bring all characters to the test of true wisdom, and judge of the tree by its fruit.

You are desirous of visiting the prisoners, you wish to administer to their necessities, and to give them instruction. This task you will undertake, though you expect to encounter many things in the performance of it that will give you pain. Now *this* I can understand—you will not listen to the sensibilities that distress yourself, but to the distresses of others.

Therefore when I meet with one of the specious praters abovementioned, I will send him to Stock, that by your diffidence he may be taught a lesson of modesty, by your generosity, a little feeling for others, and by your general conduct in short, to chatter less and to do more.

We pity Mrs Unwin under her sufferings from the tooth-ache. Our best love to her and to her sister. Your little ones with John the great at their head have always an affectionate share of our remembrances.

Yrs. my dear friend,

Wm C.

TEXT: *BM. Add. MSS.* 24,155

TO THE REV. WILLIAM BULL

Oct. 27, 1782

Mon aimable et très cher ami. It is not in the power of chaises or chariots to carry you where my affections will not follow you; if I heard that you were gone to finish your days in the Moon, I should not love you the less; but should contemplate the place of your abode, as often as it appeared in the heavens, and say—Farewell, my friend, for ever! Lost, but not forgotten! Live happy in thy lantern, and smoke the remainder of thy pipes in peace! Thou art rid of Earth, at least of all its cares, and so far can I rejoice in thy removal; and as to the cares that are to be found in the Moon, I am resolved to suppose them lighter than those below; heavier they can hardly be.

I have never since I saw you failed to inquire of all the few that were likely to inform me, whether you were sick or abroad, for I have long wondered at your long silence and your long absence. I believe it was Mr Jones who told me that you were gone from home. I suppose therefore that you have been at Ramsgate, and upon that condition I excuse you;

672

but you should have remembered, my friend, that people do not go to the seaside to bring back with them pains in the bowels and such weakness and lassitude as you complain of. You ought to have returned ten years younger, with your nerves well braced and your spirits at the top of the weather glass. Come to us, however, and Mrs Unwin shall add her attentions and her skill to those of Mrs Bull; and we will give you broth to heal your bowels, and toasted rhubarb to strengthen them, and send you back as brisk and as cheerful as we wish you to be always.

Both your advice and your manner of giving it are gentle and friendly, and like yourself. I thank you for them, and do not refuse your counsel because it is not good, or because I dislike it, but because it is not for me; there is not a man upon earth that might not be the better for it, myself only excepted. Prove to me that I have a right to pray, and I will pray without ceasing; yes, and praise too, even in the belly of this hell,[1] compared with which Jonah's was a palace, a temple of the living God. But let me add, there is no encouragement in the Scriptures so comprehensive as to include my case, nor any consolation so effectual as to reach it. I do not relate it to you, because you could not believe it; you would agree with me if you could. And yet the sin by which I am excluded from the privileges I once enjoyed, you would account no sin, you would even tell me that it was a duty. This is strange; — you will think me mad, — but I am not mad, most noble Festus,[2] I am only in despair, and those powers of mind which I possess are only permitted to me for my amusement at some times, and to acuminate and enhance my misery at others. I have not even asked a blessing upon my food these ten years, nor do I expect that I shall ever ask it again. Yet I love you, and such as you, and determine to enjoy your friendship while I can: — it will not be long, we must soon part for ever.

Madame Guyon is finished, but not quite transcribed. Mrs

[1] Jonah, ii, 2.
[2] Acts, xxvi, 25: 'But he [St Paul] said, I am not mad, most noble Festus but speak fort h the words of truth and soberness.'

Unwin, who has lately been much indisposed, unites her love to you with mine, and we both wish you to be affectionately remembered to Mrs Bull and the young gentleman.

Yours, my friend,

Wm Cowper

TEXT: *Southey*

TO JOSEPH HILL

Nov. 11, 1782

My dear friend,

Your shocking scrawl as you term it was however a very welcome one. The character indeed has not quite the neatness and beauty of an engraving, but if it cost me some pains to decypher it, they were well rewarded by the minute information it conveyed. I am glad your health is such that you have nothing more to complain of than may be expected on the downhill side of life. If mine is better than yours it is to be attributed I suppose principally to the constant enjoyment of country air and retirement; the most perfect regularity in matters of eating, drinking and sleeping, and a happy emancipation from everything that wears the face of business. I lead the life I always wished for, and, the single circumstance of dependence excepted (which between ourselves is very contrary to my predominant humour and disposition) have no want left broad enough for another wish to stand upon.

You may not perhaps live to see your trees attain to the dignity of timber — I nevertheless approve of your planting and the disinterested spirit that prompts you to it. Few people plant when they are young; a thousand other less profitable amusements divert their attention; and most people when the date of youth is once expired, think it too late to begin. I can tell you however for your comfort and encouragement that when a grove which Major Cowper had planted was of 18 years growth, it was no small ornament to his grounds, and afforded as complete a shade as could be desired. Were I as

674

old as your mother, in whose longevity I rejoice and the more, because I consider it as in some sort a pledge and assurance of yours, and should come to the possession of land worth planting, I would begin to-morrow, and even without previously insisting upon a bond from Providence that I should live 5 years longer.

I saw last week a gentleman who was lately at Hastings. I asked him where he lodged. He replied, at Polhill's. I next enquired after the poor man's wife, whether alive or dead. He answered, dead. So then, said I, she has scolded her last, and a sensible old man will go down to his grave in peace. Mr Polhill to be sure is of no great consequence either to you or to me; but having so fair an opportunity to inform myself about him, I could not neglect it. It gives me pleasure to learn somewhat of a man I knew a little of so many years since, merely for that reason and for that reason merely I mention the circumstance to you.

I find a single expression in your letter which needs correction. You say I carefully avoid paying you a visit at Wargrave. Not so—but connected as I happily am, and rooted where I am, and not having travelled these 20 years, being besides of an indolent temper and having spirits that cannot bear a bustle—all these are so many insuperables in the way. They are not however in yours, and if you and Mrs Hill will make the experiment, you shall find yourselves as welcome here both to me and to Mrs Unwin as it is possible you can be anywhere.

Yours affectionately,

Wm Cowper

Olney Nov. 11, 1782. Received of Mr Hill the sum of thirty pounds by draft on Child & Co.

£30. 0. 0.   Wm Cowper

TEXT: *Cowper Johnson MSS.*

TO THE REV. WILLIAM UNWIN

Nov. 18th, 1782

My dear William,

On the part of the poor, and on our part, be pleased to make acknowledgments such as the occasion calls for to our beneficent friend Mr Smith.[1] I call him ours, because having experienced his kindness to myself in a former instance, and in the present his disinterested readiness to succour the distressed, my ambition will be satisfied with nothing less. He may depend upon the strictest secrecy; no creature shall hear him mentioned either now or hereafter as the person from whom we have received this bounty. But when I speak of him or hear him spoken of by others, which sometimes happens, I shall not forget what is due to so rare a character. I wish, and your mother wishes it too, that he could sometimes take us in his way to Nottingham; he will find us happy to receive a person whom we must needs account it an honour to know. — We shall exercise our best direction in the disposal of the money, but in this town, where the Gospel has been preached so many years, where the people have been favoured so long with laborious and conscientious ministers, it is not an easy thing to find those who make no profession of religion at all, and are yet proper objects of charity. The profane are *so* profane, so drunken, dissolute and in every respect worthless, that to make them partakers of his bounty would be to abuse it. We promise however that none shall touch it, but such as are miserably poor, yet at the same time industrious and honest—two characters frequently united here, where the most watchful and unremitting labour will hardly procure them bread. We make none but the cheapest laces, and the price of *them* is fallen almost to nothing.

[1] Robert Smith, M.P. for Nottingham, had sent C. a sum of money for distribution among the poor of Olney. In accordance with Evangelical custom, the name of the donor was to be kept secret. See *The Task*, p. 477.

Thanks are due to yourself likewise, and are hereby accordingly rendered for waiving your claim in behalf of your own parishioners. You are always with them, and they are always, at least some of them, the better for your residence among them. Olney is a populous place, inhabited chiefly by the half-starved and the ragged of the earth, and it is not possible for our small party and small ability to extend their operations so far as to be much felt among such numbers. Accept therefore your share of their gratitude, and be convinced that when they pray for a blessing upon those who have relieved their wants, He that answers that prayer, and when He answers it, will remember His servant at Stock.

I little thought when I was writing the history of John Gilpin that he would appear in print.[2] I intended to laugh, and to make two or three others laugh, of whom you were one. But now all the world laughs, at least if they have the same relish for a tale ridiculous in itself and quaintly told, as we have. Well—they do not always laugh so innocently, or at so small an expense—for in a world like this, abounding with subjects for satire and with satirical wits to mark them, a laugh that hurts nobody has at least the grace of novelty to recommend it. Swift's darling motto was— *Vive la bagatelle*![3]— a good wish for a philosopher of his complexion, the greater part of whose wisdom, whencesoever it came, most certainly came not from above. *La bagatelle* has no enemy in me, though it has neither so warm a friend nor so able a one as it had in him. If I trifle, and merely trifle, it is because I am reduced to it by necessity. A melancholy that nothing else so effectually disperses, engages me sometimes in the arduous task of being merry by force. And strange as it may seem, the most ludicrous lines I ever wrote have been written in the saddest mood, and but for that saddest mood perhaps had never been written at all. To say truth, it would be but a shocking vagary,

[2] Lady Austen had told C. the story of John Gilpin. He turned it into a ballad for the private amusement of his friends. Unwin sent a copy to the *Public Advertiser*, where it was printed for the first time on Nov. 14, 1782— anonymously, no doubt because its frivolity would have offended Newton.

[3] C. probably had in mind a sentence in Johnson's *Lives of the Poets*: 'His favourite maxim was *vive la bagatelle*.'

should the mariners on board a ship buffeted by a terrible storm, employ themselves in fiddling and dancing. Yet sometimes, much such a part act I.

Your mother is delighted with your purchase and esteems it an excellent bargain. The 13s 6d included in Mr Smith's draft she [? sinks] in the same purpose, and gives it to the poor. On so laudable an occasion, we were not willing to be quite inactive.

I hear from Mrs Newton that some great persons have spoken with great approbation of a certain book. Who they are, and what they have said, I am to be told in a future letter. The Monthly Reviewers[4] in the meantime have satisfied me well enough,

Yrs. my dear William, with our love as usual,

Wm Cowper

TEXT: *BM. Add. MSS.* 24,155

TO JOSEPH HILL

[Dec. 7, 1782]

My dear friend,

At 7 o'clock this evening, being the 7th of December, I imagine I see you in your box at the coffee house. No doubt the waiter, as ingenious and adroit as his predecessors were before him, raises the teapot to the ceiling with his right hand, while in his left hand the teacup descending almost to the floor, receives a limpid stream; limpid in its descent, but no sooner has it reached its destination, than frothing and foaming to the view it becomes a roaring syllabub. This is the 19th winter since I saw you in this situation, and if 19 more pass over me before I die I shall still remember a circumstance we have often laughed at.

How different is the complexion of your evenings and mine! Yours spent amid the ceaseless hum that proceeds from

---

[4] Cowper's *Poems* were noticed in the *Monthly Review* for October 1782.

the inside of 50 noisy and busy periwigs;[1] mine by a domestic fireside, in a retreat as silent as retirement can make it, where no noise is made but what we make for our own amusement. For instance, here are two ladies and your humble servant in company; one of the ladies has been playing on the harpsichord, while I with the other have been playing at battledore and shuttlecock. A little dog in the mean time howling under the chair of the former, performed in the vocal way to admiration. This entertainment over, I began my letter, and having nothing more important to communicate, have given you an account of it. I know you love dearly to be idle when you can find an opportunity to be so. But as such opportunities are rare with you, I thought it possible that a short description of the idleness I enjoy might give you pleasure. The happiness we cannot call our own, we yet seem to possess, while we sympathise with our friends who can.

The papers tell me that peace is at hand, and that it is at a great distance; that the siege of Gibraltar[2] is abandoned, and that it is to be still continued. It is happy for me that though I love my country, I have but little curiosity. There was a time when these contradictions would have distressed me, but I have learnt by experience that it is best for little people like myself to be patient, and to wait till time affords the intelligence which no speculations of theirs can ever furnish.

I thank you for a fine cod with oysters, and hope that ere long I shall have to thank you for procuring me Elliot's medicines. Every time I feel the least uneasiness in either eye, I tremble lest my Æsculapius being departed, my infallible remedy should be lost for ever. Adieu! My respects to Mrs Hill.

Yrs faithfully,

Wm Cowper

TEXT: *Cowper Johnson MSS.*

[1] The 'sworn clerks' of the Chancery office.
[2] General Elliot held Gibraltar against a siege by French and Spanish forces from 1779 to September 1782, when Lord Howe relieved the garrison.

TO THE REV. JOHN NEWTON

Jan. 26, 1783

My dear friend,

It is reported among persons of the best intelligence at Olney—the barber, the schoolmaster, and the drummer of a corps quartered at this place, that the belligerent powers are at last reconciled, the articles of the treaty adjusted, and that peace is at the door.[1] I saw this morning, at nine o'clock, a group of about twelve figures very closely engaged in a conference, as I suppose, upon the same subject. The scene of consultation was a blacksmith's shed, very comfortably screened from the wind, and directly opposed to the morning sun. Some held their hands behind them, some had them folded across their bosom, and others had thrust them into their breeches pockets. Every man's posture bespoke a pacific turn of mind; but the distance being too great for their words to reach me, nothing transpired. I am willing however to hope that the secret will not be a secret long, and that you and I, equally interested in the event, though not perhaps equally well-informed, shall soon have an opportunity to rejoice in the completion of it. The powers of Europe have clashed with each other to a fine purpose; that the Americans, at length declared independent, may keep themselves so if they can; and that what the parties, who have thought proper to dispute upon that point, have wrested from each other in the course of the conflict, may be in the issue of it restored to the proper owner. Nations may be guilty of a conduct that would render an individual infamous for ever; and yet carry their heads high, talk of their glory, and despise their neighbours. Your opinions and mine, I mean our political ones, are not exactly of a piece, yet I cannot think otherwise upon this subject than I have always done. England, more perhaps

[1] The provisional articles of peace with America were signed on November 30, 1782, and with France and Spain on January 20, 1783.

through the fault of her generals, than her councils, has in some instances acted with a spirit of cruel animosity she was never chargeable with till now. But this is the worst that can be said. On the other hand, the Americans, who if they had contented themselves with a struggle for lawful liberty, would have deserved applause, seem to me to have incurred the guilt of parricide, by renouncing their parent, by making her ruin their favourite object, and by associating themselves with her worst enemy for the accomplishment of their purpose. France, and of course Spain, have acted a treacherous, a thievish part.[2] They have stolen America from England, and whether they are able to possess themselves of that jewel or not hereafter, it was doubtless what they intended. Holland appears to me in a meaner light than any of them. They quarrelled with a friend for an enemy's sake. The French led them by the nose, and the English have thrashed them for suffering it. My views of the contest being, and having been always such, I have consequently brighter hopes for England than her situation some time since seemed to justify. She is the only injured party. America may perhaps call her the aggressor; but is she were so, America has not only repelled the injury, but done a greater. As to the rest, if perfidy, treachery, avarice, and ambition can prove their cause to have been a rotten one, those proofs are found upon them. I think, therefore, that whatever scourge may be prepared for England on some future day, her ruin is not yet to be expected.

Acknowledge, now, that I am worthy of a place under the shed I described, and that I should make no small figure among the *quidnuncs* of Olney.

I wish the society you have formed may prosper.[3] Your subjects will be of greater importance, and discussed with more sufficiency. The earth is a grain of sand, but the spiritual interests of man are commensurate with the heavens.

Pray remind Mr Bull, who has too much genius to have a good memory, that he has an account to settle for Mrs Unwin with her grocer, and give our love to him. Accept for yourself

[2] Cf. *The Task*, p. 425.
[3] The Eclectic Society: an Evangelical discussion group.

and Mrs Newton your just share of the same commodity, with our united thanks for a very fine barrel of oysters. This, indeed, is rather commending the barrel than its contents. I should say therefore for a barrel of very fine oysters.

Yours, my dear friend, as ever,

Wm Cowper

We gain no advantage by a change of newsmongers. Our present one has already disappointed us twice. This is not excusable at such a time as this, or indeed at any time. We shall be obliged to you therefore if you will pay him off. We can furnish ourselves as well at Olney.

TEXT: *Private Correspondence* and *Barham Johnson MSS.*†

TO JOSEPH HILL

[Feb. 13, 1783]

My dear friend,

In writing to you I need never want a subject. Self is always at hand, and self with its concerns is always interesting to a friend. I am so perfectly at leisure that I am less excusable for not writing frequently to you, than you for not writing at all to me. It is not very probable that in the hurry of so much business you should form a wish to know in what manner I spend my time, and yet if that information should come, though uninvited by a wish, it may not be altogether unacceptable.

You may think perhaps that having commenced poet by profession, I am always writing verses. Not so—I have written nothing, at least finished nothing, since I published—except a certain facetious history of John Gilpin, which Mr Unwin would send to the *Public Advertiser*. Perhaps you might read it without suspecting the author. About two months since, and I believe since I wrote to you last, I received a visit from the Revd. Walter Bagot, whom I suppose, as his brother Mr Chester is in the number of your clients, you may know. It gave me great pleasure to see an old school-fellow whom I enrolled amongst my friends for many years after I left Westminster, and whom I had not seen for five and twenty. My book procured me this favour—it has procured me likewise other favours which my modesty will not permit me to specify except one, which modest as I am I cannot suppress, a very handsome letter from Dr Franklin at Passy. These fruits it has brought forth, but whether it has brought forth any money I know not, having never heard from my printer since he published. If I have any cash in your custody therefore, it will be as welcome as money usually proves to an author.

Pardon me, that run away with by such a darling subject I forgot the purpose I began with. To return therefore—My time passes partly in finding fault with a Peace which, deplorable as our condition is, I suppose nobody approves; and partly in quarrelling with a rainy season and a most dirty country. I raise cucumbers which I cannot eat, merely because it is difficult to raise them. And the conquest of difficulties is one of the most amusing things in the world because it is one of the most flattering to our pride. When I can, I walk—but always with a lady under my arm; which again is amusing, and for the same reason. For to extricate the ladies out of all the bogs into which I lead them is no small proof of ingenuity and prowess. Thus I spend my mornings, and my evenings in winding their silk and cotton, or reading history to the aforesaid ladies. Sigh now—and say—Happy creature! how I envy you. Envy me you must. It is

[The rest of the MSS is missing. According to Hayley the letter ends: 'I have been refreshing myself with a walk in the garden, where I find that January (who according to Chaucer was the mother of May) being dead, February has married the widow.

Yours, etc.

W.C.']

TEXT: *Cowper Johnson MSS.* * Some extracts from this letter were published by Hayley, and another fragment in the *Private Correspondence.*

TO THE REV. WILLIAM UNWIN

June 8, 1783

My dear William,

Our severest winter, commonly called the spring, is now over, and I find myself seated in my favourite recess, the greenhouse. In such a situation, so silent, so shady, where no human foot is heard, and where only my myrtles presume to peep in at the window, you may suppose I have no interruption to complain of, and that my thoughts are perfectly at my command. But the beauties of the spot are themselves an interruption; my attention is called upon by those very myrtles, by a double row of grass pinks just beginning to blossom, and by a bed of beans already in bloom. And you are to consider it, if you please, as no small proof of my regard that though you have so many powerful rivals, I disengage myself from them all, and devote this hour entirely to you.

You are not acquainted with the Revd. Mr Bull of Newport. Perhaps it is as well for you that you are not. You would regret still more than you do, that there are so many miles interposed between us. He spends part of the day with us tomorrow. A Dissenter, but a liberal one; a man of letters and of genius; master of a fine imagination, or rather *not* master of it; an imagination which, when he finds himself in the company he loves and can confide in, runs away with him into such fields of speculation as amuse and enliven every other imagination that has the happiness to be of the party. At other times he has a tender and delicate sort of melancholy in his disposition, not less agreeable in its way. No men are better qualified for companions in such a world as this, than men of such a temperament. Every scene of life has two sides, a dark and a bright one, and the mind that has an equal mixture of melancholy and vivacity, is best of all qualified for the contemplation of either. It can be lively without levity, and pensive without dejection. Such a man is Mr Bull. But he smokes tobacco.—Nothing is perfect—*nihil est ab omni parte beatum*.[1]

I find that your friend Mr Fytche has lost his cause; and more mortifying still, has lost it by a single voice. Had I been a Peer, he shd. have been secure of mine. For I am persuaded that if conditional presentations were in fashion, and if every minister held his benefice, as the judges their office, upon the terms of *Quamdiu bene se gesserit*,[2] it would be better for the cause of religion and more for the honour of the establishment. There ought to be discipline somewhere, and if the bishops will not exercise it I do not see why lay patrons should have their hands tied. If I remember your state of the case (and I never heard it stated but by you) my reflections upon it are pertinent. It is however long since we talked about it, and I may possibly misconceive it at present—if so—they go for nothing. I understand that he presented upon condition that if the parson proved immoral or negligent, he should have liberty to call upon him either for his resignation or the penalty. If I am wrong, correct me.

On the other side I send you a something, a song if you please, composed last Thursday. The incident happened the day before.

> The rose had been wash'd (just wash'd in a show'r)
> Which Mary to Anna convey'd,
> The plentiful moisture encumber'd the flow'r,
> And weighed down its beautiful head.
>
> The cup was all fill'd, and the leaves were all wet,
> And it seem'd to a fanciful view,
> To weep for the buds it had left with regret
> On the flourishing bush where it grew.
>
> I hastily seiz'd it, unfit as it was
> For a nosegay, so dripping and drown'd,
> And swinging it rudely, too rudely alas!
> I snapp'd it—it fell to the ground.

[1] Horace, *Odes*, II, xvi, 27.
[2] 'During his good behaviour.'

And such, I exclaim'd, is the pitiless part
Some act by the delicate mind,
Regardless of wringing and breaking a heart
Already to sorrow resign'd.

This elegant rose, had I shaken it less,
Might have bloom'd with its owner awhile,
And the tear that is wiped with a little address,
May be follow'd perhaps by a smile.

The muslin is found, the gown is admir'd:
Procure us some franks—adieu—I am tir'd.

W.C.

TEXT: *BM. Add. MSS.* 24,155

TO THE REV. JOHN NEWTON

July 27, 1783

My dear friend,

You cannot have more pleasure in receiving a letter from me, than I should in writing it, were it not impossible in such a place as this to find a subject. After having read a sheet full of nonsense or something nearly related to it, you learn indeed at last the state of our health, and are told that we are as well as usual; the only important matter to be found in four pages, important, because your friendship for us makes it so.

I live in a world abounding with incidents, upon which many grave, and perhaps some profitable observations might be made; but those incidents never reaching my unfortunate ears, both the entertaining narrative and the reflection it might suggest are to me annihilated and lost. I look back to the past week, and say, what did it produce? I ask the same question of the week preceding, and duly receive the same answer from both—nothing!—A situation like this, in which I am as unknown to the world, as I am ignorant of all that passes in it, in which I have nothing to do but to think, would exactly suit me, were my subjects of meditation as agreeable as my leisure is uninterrupted. My passion for retirement is not at all abated, after so many years spent in the most sequestered state, but rather increased—a circumstance I should esteem wonderful to a degree not to be accounted for, considering the condition of my mind, which, if not always melancholy, is yet never peaceful, did I not know, that we think as we are made to think, and of course approve and prefer, as Providence, who appoints the bounds of our habitation, chooses for us. Thus am I both free and a prisoner at the same time. The world is before me; I am not shut up in the Bastille though often as miserable as if I were, there are no moats about my castle, nor locks upon my gates but of which I have the key—but an invisible, uncontrollable agency, a local attachment, an inclination more forcible than I ever felt, even to the place of my birth, serves me for prison-walls, and for bounds which I cannot pass. In former years I have known sorrow, and before I had ever tasted of spiritual trouble. The effect was an abhorrence of the scene in which I had suffered so much, and a weariness of those objects which I had so long looked at with an eye of despondency and dejection. But it is otherwise with me now. The same cause subsisting, and in a much more powerful degree, fails to produce its natural effect. The very stones in the garden-walls are my intimate acquaintance. I should miss almost the minutest object, and be disagreeably affected by its removal, and am persuaded that were it possible I could leave this incommodious and obscure nook for a twelvemonth, I should return to it again with rapture, and be transported with the sight of objects which to all the world beside would be at least indifferent; some of them perhaps, such as the ragged thatch and the tottering walls of the neighbouring cottages, disgusting. But so it is, and it is so, because here is to be my abode, and because such is the appointment of *Him* that placed me in it. Here I spent 5 years in a state of warfare, and here I have spent almost eleven in a state of despair; nevertheless

> *Iste terrarum mihi praeter omnes*
> *Angulus ridet.*[1]

[1] 'That corner of the world has a smile for me before all others.' Horace, *Odes*, II, vi, 13–14. *Iste* should read *ille*.

It is the place of all the world I love the most, not for any happiness it affords me, but because here I can be miserable with most convenience to myself and with the least disturbance to others.

You wonder (and I dare say unfeignedly, because you do not think yourself entitled to such praise) that I prefer your style, as an historian,[2] to that of the two most renowned and admired writers of history the present day has seen. That you may not suspect me of having said more than my real opinion will warrant, I will tell you why. In your style I see no affectation. In every line of theirs I see nothing else. They disgust me always, Robertson with his pomp and his strut, and Gibbon with his finical and French manner. You are as correct as they. You express yourself with as much precision. Your words are ranged with as much propriety, but you do not set your periods to a tune. They discover a perpetual attention to exhibit themselves to advantage, whereas your subject engrosses you. They *sing*, and you *say*; which, as history is a thing to be *said*, and not *sung*, is, in my judgment, very much in your favour. A writer that despises their tricks, and is yet neither inelegant nor inharmonious, proves himself, by that single circumstance, a man of superior judgment and ability to them both. You have my reasons. I honour a manly character, in which good sense, and a desire of doing good, are the predominant features; but affectation is an emetic.

Mrs Unwin is well, and I ail nothing but as aforesaid. The weather is intensely hot, and I suppose will soon breed more thunder. Heavy rains would be very prejudicial to the corn, in its present state, and there is yet much hay uncarried. Accept our united love to you and yours. When Mrs Unwin expressed her sentiments on the subject of your journey she expressed mine—I add no more therefore but that I am ever, my dear friend,

Yours Wm Cowper

At one o'clock my glass in the shade is at 83.

TEXT: *Barham Johnson MSS.**†

[2] C. had praised Newton's *Review of Ecclesiastical History*, 1770.

TO THE REV. WILLIAM BULL

Aug. 23, 1783

My dear Bull,

I began to despair of you as a correspondent, yet not to blame you for being silent. I am acquainted with Rottingdean and all its charms, the downs, the cliff, and the agreeable opportunities of sauntering that the seaside affords. I knew, besides, that your preaching would be frequent, and allowed an especial force above all to the consideration of your natural indolence; for though diligent and active in your business, you know in your heart that you love your ease, as all parsons do: these weighty causes all concurring to justify your silence, I should have been very unreasonable had I condemned it.

I laughed, as you did, at the alarm taken by your reverend brother of the Establishment,[1] and at his choice of a text by way of antidote to the noxious tendency of your discourses. The text, with a little transposition and variation of the words, would perhaps have come nearer to the truth, and have suited the occasion better.

Instead of exhorting his hearers to hold fast the form of sound words, he should have said the sound of a form, which I take to be a just description of the sermons he makes himself, that have nothing but a sound and a form to recommend them. I rejoice that the bathing has been of use to you; the more you wash the filthier may you be, that your days may be prolonged, and your health more established. Scratching is good exercise, promotes the circulation, elicits the humours, and if you will take a certain monarch's word, of itching memory, is too great a pleasure for a subject.

I was always an admirer of thunder-storms, even before I knew whose voice I heard in them; but especially an admirer

[1] When staying at Rottingdean, Sussex, Bull preached from the window of a house hired for that purpose. He was denounced from the pulpit by the local parson, who took as his text 2 Timothy, i, 13: 'Hold fast the form of sound words, which thou has heard of me.'

of thunder rolling over the great waters. There is something singularly majestic in the sound of it at sea, where the eye and the ear have uninterrupted opportunity of observation, and the concavity above being made spacious reflects it with more advantage. I have consequently envied you your situation, and the enjoyment of those refreshing breezes that belong to it. We have indeed been regaled with some of these bursts of ethereal music. — The peals have been as loud, by the report of a gentleman who lived many years in the West Indies, as were ever heard in those islands, and the flashes as splendid. But when the thunder preaches, an horizon bounded by the ocean is the only sounding-board.

I have but little leisure, strange as it may seem: that little I devoted for a month after your departure to the translation of Madame Guyon.[2] I have made fair copies of all the pieces I have produced upon this last occasion, and will put them into your hands when we meet. They are yours, to serve as you please; you may take and leave as you like, for my purpose is already served. They have amused me, and I have no further demands upon them. The lines upon Friendship however, which were not sufficiently of a piece with the others, will not now be wanted. I have some other little things which I will communicate when time shall serve, but I cannot now transcribe them.

Mrs Unwin is well, and begs to be affectionately remembered to you and yours. I wish you many smugglers to shine in your crown of rejoicing[3] on a certain day that approaches, and would take the trade myself if I could suppose it might be the means of introducing me to a place amongst them; but I must neither wear a crown, nor help to adorn one.

Yours, my dear friend,

Wm Cowper

TEXT: *Southey*

[2] See p. 666 and pp. 163–64.
[3] 1 Thessalonians, ii, 19.

TO THE REV. WILLIAM UNWIN

August 4, 1783

My dear William,

I feel myself sensibly obliged by the interest you take in the success of my productions. Your feelings upon the subject are such as I should have myself, had I an opportunity of calling Johnson aside to make the enquiry you purpose. But I am pretty well prepared for the worst; and so long as I have the opinion of a few capable judges in my favour, and am thereby convinced that I have neither disgraced myself nor my subject, shall not feel myself disposed to any extreme anxiety about the sale. To aim with success at the spiritual good of mankind, and to become popular by writing on scriptural subjects, were an unreasonable ambition even for a poet to entertain in days like these. Verse may have many charms, but has none powerful enough to conquer the aversion of a dissipated age to such instruction. Ask the question therefore boldly, and be not mortified even though he should shake his head, and drop his chin, for it is no more than we have reason to expect. We will lay the fault upon the vice of the times, and we will acquit the poet.

I am glad you were pleased with my Latin ode[1] and indeed with my English dirge, as much as I was myself. The tune[2] laid me under a disadvantage, obliging me to write in alexandrines, which I suppose would suit no ear but a French one. Neither did I intend anything more than that the subject and the words should be sufficiently accommodated to the music. The ballad is a species of poetry, I believe, peculiar to this country, equally adapted to the drollest and the most tragical subjects. Simplicity and ease are its proper characteristics. Our forefathers excelled in it, but we moderns have lost the

---

[1] *In Submersionem Navigii, cui Georgius, Regale Nomen, inditum,* and the English version, *On the Loss of the Royal George,* (p. 76).

[2] Handel's March from *Scipio.*

art. It is observed that we have few good English odes. But to make amends, we have many excellent ballads, not inferior perhaps in true poetical merit to some of the very best odes that the Greek or Latin languages have to boast of. It is a sort of composition I was ever fond of, and if graver matters had not called me another way, should have addicted myself to it more than to any other. I inherit a taste for it from my father who succeeded well in it himself, and who lived at a time when the best pieces in that way were produced. What can be prettier than Gay's Ballad (or rather Swift's, Arbuthnot's, Pope's & Gay's) in the *What do ye call it*:[3] ' 'Twas when the seas were roaring.' I have been well informed that they all contributed, and that the most celebrated association[4] of clever fellows this country ever saw, did not think it beneath them to unite their strength and abilities in the composition of a song. The success however answered their wishes, and our puny days will never produce such another. The ballads that Bourne has translated,[5] beautiful in themselves, are still more beautiful in his version of them, infinitely surpassing in my judgment all that Ovid or Tibullus have left behind them. They are quite as elegant, and far more touching and pathetic than the tenderest strokes of either.

So much for ballads and ballad writers. A worthy subject, you will say, for a man whose head might be filled with better things. And *it is* filled with better things, but to so ill a purpose that I thrust into it all manner of topics that may prove more amusing. As for instance—I have two goldfinches which in the summer occupy the greenhouse. A few days since, being employed in cleaning out their cages, I placed that which I had in hand upon the table, while the other hung against the wall. The windows and the door stood wide open. I went to fill the fountain at the pump, and on my return was not a little surprised to find a goldfinch sitting on the top of the cage I had been cleaning, and singing to and kissing the

[3] *The What-d'ye-Call-it*, a 'tragi-comic pastoral farce', 1715, by John Gay.

[4] See *n.*, p. 295.

[5] The ballads translated into Latin by Vincent Bourne included Gay's *Black Ey'd Susan* and several by Prior.

goldfinch within. I approached him, and he discovered no fear; still nearer, and he discovered none. I advanced my hand towards him, and he took no notice of it. I seized him, and supposed I had caught a new bird, but casting my eye upon the other cage, perceived my mistake. Its inhabitant during my absence had contrived to find an opening where the wire had been a little bent, and made no other use of the escape it afforded him, than to salute his friend and converse with him more intimately than he had done before. I returned him to his proper mansion, but in vain. In less than a minute he had thrust his little person through the aperture again, and again perched upon his neighbour's cage, kissing him as at the first, and singing as if transported with the fortunate adventure. I could not but respect such friendship as for the sake of its gratification had twice declined an opportunity to be free, and consenting to their union, resolved that for the future one cage should hold them. I am glad of such incidents, for at a pinch and when I need entertainment, the versification of them serves to direct me.

I hope you will receive a very fine melon, which we send according to your last direction; it will leave this place on Wednesday. Accept my love and present it to all your family. Your mother is well and adds hers. I transcribe for you a piece of Madame Guyon, not as the best, but as being shorter than many and as good as most of them. It will give you an idea of her manner. When you write to or see Mr Smith, I beseech you to remember me to him as one that esteems him highly.

Yrs ever,

Wm C.

TEXT: *BM. Add. MSS.* 24,155

TO THE REV. WILLIAM UNWIN

Sept. 29, 1783

My dear William,

We are sorry that you and your household partake so largely of the ill effects of this unhealthy season. You are happy however in having hitherto escaped the epidemic fever, which has prevailed much in this part of the kingdom, and carried many off. Your mother and I are well. After more than a fortnight's indisposition, which slight appellation is quite adequate to the description of all I suffered, I am at length restored by a grain or two of emetic tartar. It is a tax I generally pay in autumn. By this time, I hope, a purer ether than we have seen for months, and these brighter suns than the summer had to boast, have cheered your spirits, and made your existence more comfortable. We are rational; but we are animal too, and therefore subject to the influences of the weather. The cattle in the fields show evident symptoms of lassitude and disgust in an unpleasant season; and we, their lords and masters, are constrained to sympathize with them: the only difference between us is, that they know not the cause of their dejection, and we do, — but, for our humiliation, are equally at a loss to cure it. Upon this account I have sometimes wished myself a philosopher.[1] How happy, in comparison with myself, does the sagacious investigator of nature seem, whose fancy is ever employed in the invention of *hypotheses*, and his reason in the support of them! While he is accounting for the origin of the winds, he has no leisure to attend to their influence upon himself; and while he considers what the sun is made of, forgets that he has not shone for a month. One project indeed supplants another. The *vortices*[2] of Descartes gave way to the gravitation of Newton, and this again is threatened by the electrical fluid of a modern.[3] One generation blows bubbles, and the next breaks them. But in the mean time your philosopher is a happy man. He escapes a thousand inquietudes to which the indolent are subject, and finds his occupation, whether it be the pursuit of a butterfly, or a demonstration, the wholesomest exercise in the world. As he proceeds, he applauds himself. His discoveries, though

[1] Natural scientist.

[2] The theory of the circular motion of matter. Descartes argued in *Le Monde*, 1664, that as matter is an extension, and as there is no vacuum, the movement of one body must set others in motion.

[3] The allusion may be to Galvani's important discoveries about the nature of electricity, in 1780.

eventually perhaps they prove but dreams, are to him realities. The world gaze at him, as he does at new phenomena in the heavens, and perhaps understand him as little. But this does not prevent their praises, nor at all disturb him in the enjoyment of that self-complacence to which his imaginary success entitles him. He wears his honours while he lives, and if another strips them off when he has been dead a century, it is no great matter; he can then make shift without them.

I have said a great deal upon this subject, and know not what it all amounts to. I did not intend a syllable of it when I began. But *currente calamo*,[4] I stumbled upon it. My end is to amuse myself and you. The former of these two points is secured. I shall be happy if I do not miss the latter.

By the way, what is your opinion of these air-balloons?[5] I am quite charmed with the discovery. Is it not possible (do you suppose) to convey such a quantity of inflammable air into the stomach and abdomen, that the philosopher, no longer gravitating to a centre, shall ascend by his own comparative levity, and never stop till he has reached the medium exactly *in equilibrio* with himself? May he not by the help of a pasteboard rudder, attached to his posteriors, steer himself in that purer element with ease; and again by a slow and gradual discharge of his aerial contents, recover his former tendency to the earth, and descend without the smallest danger or inconvenience? These things are worth inquiry; and (I dare say) they will be inquired after as they deserve. The *pennae non homini datae*[6] are likely to be less regretted than they were; and perhaps a flight of academicians and a covey of fine ladies may be no uncommon spectacle in the next generation. A letter which appeared in the

[4] 'Letting my pen run on.'

[5] On June 5, 1783, the brothers Montgolfier successfully launched a crude hot-air balloon near Lyons. On Sept. 19, they sent up a balloon carrying a sheep, a cock and a duck, thus inaugurating the age of air travel.

[6] 'Wings not given to man': Horace, *Odes*, I, iii, 34–5:
Expertus vacuum Daedalus aera
Pinnis non homini datis
('On wings not given to man Daedalus explored the void of air.')

public prints last week convinces me that the learned are not without hopes of some such improvement upon this discovery. The author is a sensible and ingenious man, and under a reasonable apprehension that the ignorant may feel themselves inclined to laugh upon a subject that affects himself with the utmost seriousness, with much good manners and management bespeaks their patience, suggesting many good consequences that may result from a course of experiments upon this machine, and amongst others, that it may be of use in ascertaining the shape of continents and islands, and the face of wide-extended and far distant countries; an end not to be hoped for, unless by these means of extraordinary elevation the human prospect may be immensely enlarged, and the philosopher, exalted to the skies, attain a view of the whole hemisphere at once. But whether he is to ascend by the mere inflation of his person, as hinted above, or whether in a sort of bandbox, supported upon balloons, is not yet apparent, nor (I suppose) even is his own idea perfectly decided.

Yours, my dear William,

W.C.

TEXT: *Southey*

TO JOSEPH HILL

Octr. 20, 1783

My dear friend,

I should not have been silent thus long, had I known with certainty where a letter of mine might find you. Your summer excursions however are now at an end, and addressing a line to you in the centre of the busy scene in which you spend your winter, I am pretty sure of my mark. I hear well of you, and of all that belongs to you. Our common friend Mr Small informs me that you have good health, that Mrs Hill is in health likewise, that your plantations thrive, and that your improvements at Wargrave do you honour. I congratulate you upon all these occasions, and wish the continuance of your prosperity. Mr Small, I believe, left the country this morning. He said he intended it. I had the pleasure of his company twice last week; once he dined with us, and once I met him at Lady Austen's, our near neighbour and friend.

I see the winter approaching without much concern, though a passionate lover of fine weather and the pleasanter scenes of summer. But the long evenings have their comforts too, and there is hardly to be found upon the earth, I suppose, so snug a creature as an Englishman by his fire-side in the winter. I mean however an Englishman that lives in the country, for in London it is not very easy to avoid intrusion. I have two ladies[1] to read to: sometimes more, but never less. At present we are circumnavigating the globe, and I find the old story with which I amused myself some years since, through the great felicity of a memory not very retentive, almost new. I am however sadly at a loss for Cook's second voyage, written by himself.[2] Lord Dartmouth furnished me with it once, but his books are all at Sandwell, the book in question at least is there, and he I suppose by this time in town. Besides, having no correspondence with his Lordship, I cannot fairly claim a right to trouble him. Can you help me at this plunge? Have you it, can you borrow it, or can you hire it, and will you send it? I shall be glad of Forster's[3] too. These together will make the winter pass merrily, and you will much oblige me.

I have nothing to say on political subjects for two reasons. First because I know none that at present would prove very amusing, especially to you who love your country, and 2ndly because there are none that I have the vanity to think myself qualified to discuss. I must beg leave however to rejoice a little at the failure of the *Caisse d'Escomptes*,[4] because I think

---

[1] Mrs Unwin and Lady Austen.

[2] *A Voyage towards the South Pole and round the World, performed in His Majesty's ships Resolution and Adventure, in the years 1772–5*, by James Cook, 1777.

[3] *A Voyage round the World in H.B.M. sloop Resolution, commanded by Captain Cook, during the years 1772–5*, by George Forster, F.R.S., 1777.

[4] A financial establishment set up to discount bills of exchange, to deal in precious metals, etc. It had to suspend payments for a time in October 1783.

the French have well deserved it. And to mourn equally that the 'Royal George' cannot be weighed. The rather because I wrote two poems, one Latin and one English, to encourage the attempt. The former of these only having been published, which the sailors would understand but little of, may be the reason perhaps why they have not succeeded.

My love to Mrs Hill.—Believe me my friend

Affectionately yours

Wm Cowper

TEXT: *Cowper Johnson MSS.**

TO THE REV. WILLIAM UNWIN

Nov. 10, 1783

My dear William,

I have lost and wasted almost all my writing time in making an alteration in the verses[1] I either enclose or subjoin, for I know not which will be the case at present. If prose comes readily I shall transcribe them on another sheet, otherwise, on this. You will understand before you have read many of them that they are not for the press. I lay you under no other injunctions. The unkind behaviour of our acquaintance, though it is possible that in some instances it may not much affect our happiness, nor engage many of our thoughts, will sometimes obtrude itself upon us with a degree of importunity not easily resisted, and then perhaps, though almost insensible of it before, we feel more than the occasion will justify. In such a moment it was that I conceived this poem, and gave loose to a degree of resentment which perhaps I ought not to have indulged, but which in a cooler hour I cannot altogether condemn. My former intimacy with the two characters alluded to was such that I could not but feel myself provoked by the neglect with which they both treated me on a late occasion. So much by way of preface.

[1] *The Valediction* (p. 90) addressed to Lord Thurlow and George Colman the elder. C. had sent to each a copy of his first volume of poems; neither acknowledged it.

You ought not to have supposed that if you had visited us last summer, the pleasure of the interview would have been all your own. By such an imagination you wrong both yourself and us. Do you suppose we do not love you? You cannot suspect your mother of coldness; and as to me, assure yourself I have no friend in the world with whom I communicate without the least reserve, yourself excepted. Take heart then, and when you find a favourable opportunity to come, assure yourself of such a welcome from us both as you have a right to look for. But I have observed in your two last letters somewhat of a dejection and melancholy that I am afraid you do not sufficiently strive against. I suspect you of being too sedentary. You cannot walk. Why you cannot is best known to yourself. I am sure your legs are long enough, and your person does not overload them. But, I beseech you, ride, and ride often. I think I have heard you say, you cannot even do that without an object. Is not health an object? Is not a new prospect, which in most countries is gained at the end of every mile, an object? Assure yourself that easy chairs are no friends to cheerfulness, and that a long winter spent by the fireside is a prelude to an unhealthy spring. Everything I see in the fields is to me an object, and I can look at the same rivulet or at a handsome tree every day of my life with new pleasure. This indeed is partly the effect of a natural taste for rural beauty, and partly the effect of habit, for I never in all my life have let slip the opportunity of breathing fresh air and of conversing with nature when I could fairly catch it. I earnestly recommend a cultivation of the same taste to you, suspecting that you have neglected it and suffer for doing so.

Last Saturday se'nnight, the moment I had composed myself in bed, your mother too having just got into hers, we were alarmed by a cry of fire on the staircase. I immediately rose, and saw sheets of flame above the roof of Mr Palmer's house, our opposite neighbour. The mischief however was not so near to him as it seemed to be, having begun in a butcher's yard at a little distance. We made all haste down stairs, and soon threw open the street door for the reception of as much lumber of all sorts as our house would hold, brought into it by several who thought it necessary to move their furniture.

In two hours' time we had so much that we could hold no more, even the uninhabited part of our building being filled. Not that we ourselves were entirely secure, an adjoining thatch on which fell showers of sparks being rather a dangerous neighbour. Providentially however the night was perfectly calm, and we escaped. By four in the morning it was extinguished, having consumed many outbuildings but no dwellinghouse. Your mother suffered a little in her health from the fatigue and bustle of the night but soon recovered; as for me, it hurt me not. The slightest wind would have carried the fire to the very extremity of the town, there being multitudes of thatched buildings and faggot-piles so near to each other that they must have proved infallible conductors.

We rejoice in the recovery of John and William. Thank you for the communication of the letters which I return, but have not time to comment upon them. I only applaud your feelings upon the occasion; it is a proper pride that resents an injury by conferring a favour. I cannot but wish you had had the means of doing it.—Your mother wishes you to take six pounds, due to her from your uncle, and pay Mrs Newton and yourself, when a convenient time shall offer.

The balloons prosper, and I congratulate you upon it. Thanks to Montgolfier[2] we shall fly at last.—Our sincere and affectionate good wishes attend you—

Yours ever my dear friend,

Wm Cowper

TEXT: *BM. Add. MSS.* 24,155

TO JOSEPH HILL

Olney, Nov. 23, 1783. Received of Mr Hill the sum of thirty pounds by draft on Child & Co.

£30. 0. 0. Wm Cowper

[2] The Marquis d'Arlandes and Pilâtre de Rozier made the first air journey in history on November 21, 1783, when they travelled five and a half miles in Montgolfier's balloon.

My dear friend,

Accept my many thanks for herrings and oysters, perfectly good, and the only ones I have seen this year.

Your opinion of voyages and travels would spoil an appetite less keen than mine. But being pretty much, perhaps more than any man who can be said to enjoy his liberty, confined to a spot, and being very desirous of knowing all that can be known of this same planet of ours, while I have the honour to belong to it, and having beside no other means of information at my command, I am constrained to be satisfied with narratives not always indeed to be implicitly depended upon, but which being subjected to the exercise of a little consideration, cannot materially deceive us. Swinburn's[1] is a book I had fixed upon and determined if possible to procure, being pleased with some extracts from it which I found in the *Review*. I need hardly add that I shall be much obliged to Mrs Hill for a sight of it, and that peevish as the author may be, he will yet be welcome. Not indeed in person, for such tempers are welcome nowhere, but in his volume where the more fretful I find him, I may perhaps find him the more diverting. I account myself truly and much indebted to Mrs Hill for the trouble she is so kind as to take upon my account, and shall esteem myself her debtor for all the amusement I meet with, in the Southern Hemisphere, should I be so fortunate as to get there.[2] My reading is pretty much circumscribed both by want of books, and the influence of particular reasons. Politics are my abhorrence, being almost always hypothetical, fluctuating, and impracticable. Philosophy, I should have said Natural Philosophy, mathematically studied, does not suit me; and such exhibitions of that subject as are calculated for less learned readers, I have read in former days and remember in the present. Poetry, English poetry, I never touch, being pretty much addicted to the writing of it, and knowing that much intercourse with those gentlemen betrays us unavoidably into a habit of imitation, which I hate and despise most cordially.

[1] Henry Swinburne wrote *Travels through Spain in 1775–67* and *Travels in the Two Sicilies in 1777–79*.

[2] See *n.*, p. 697.

I am glad my uncle is so well, and that he found new beauties in so old an acquaintance as the scene at Hastings. My most affectionate respects to him, if you please, when you see him next. — If *he* be the happiest man who has least money in the funds, there are few upon earth whom I have any occasion to envy. I would consent however to have my pounds multiplied into thousands, even at the hazard of all that I might feel from that tormenting passion. — I send nothing to the papers myself, but Unwin sometimes sends for me. His receptacle of my squibs is the *Public Advertiser*, but they are very few, and my present occupations of a kind that will still have a tendency to make them fewer.

Yrs my dear friend,

Wm Cowper

TEXT: *Cowper Johnson MSS.*

TO THE REV. JOHN NEWTON

Dec. 15, 1783

My dear friend,

I know not how it fares with you at a time when Philosophy has just brought forth her most extraordinary production, not exciting perhaps that prodigy a ship, in all respects complete, and equal to the task of circumnavigating the globe. My mind, however, is frequently getting into these balloons, and is busy in multiplying speculations, as airy as the regions through which they pass. The last account from France,[1] which seems so well authenticated, has changed my jocularity upon this occasion into serious expectation. The invention of these new vehicles is yet in its infancy, yet already they seem to have attained a degree of perfection which navigation did not reach, till ages of experience had matured it, and science had exhausted both her industry and her skill in its improvement. I am aware indeed that the first boat or canoe that was ever formed, tho' rude in its construction, perhaps not constructed at all, being only a hollow tree

---

[1] Professor Charles, and one companion, had made a flight of 27 miles in a much improved type of hydrogen balloon on Dec. 1.

that had fallen casually in the water, and which, tho' furnished with neither sails nor oars, might yet be guided by a pole, was a more perfect creature in its kind than a balloon at present; the single circumstance of its manageable nature giving it a clear superiority both in respect of safety and convenience. But the atmosphere, tho' a much thinner medium, we well know, resists the impression made upon it by the tail of a bird, as effectually as the water that of a ship's rudder. Pope, when inculcating one of his few useful lessons, and directing mankind to the providence of God as the true source of all their wisdom, says beautifully[1]

> Learn of the little Nautilus to sail,
> Spread the thin oar, and catch the driving gale.

It is easy to parody these lines, so as to give them an accommodation and suitableness to the present purpose.

> Learn of the circle-making kite to fly.
> Spread the fan-tail, and wheel about the sky.

It is certain at least that nothing within the reach of human ingenuity will be left unattempted to accomplish and add all that is wanting to this last effort of philosophical contrivance. The approximating powers of the telescope, and the powers by which the thunder-storm is delivered of its contents, peaceably and without mischief, were once perhaps in appearance more remote from discovery, and seemed less practicable, than we may now suppose it, to give direction to that which is already buoyant; especially possessed as we are of such consummate mechanical skill, already masters of principles which we have nothing to do with but to apply, of which we have already availed ourselves in the similar case of navigation, and having in every fowl of the air a pattern, which now at length it may be sufficient to imitate. Wings and a tail indeed were of little use, while the body, so much heavier than the space of air it occupied, was sure to sink by its own weight, and could never be held in equipose by any

---

[1] *An Essay on Man*, Ep. iii, 178–9.

implements of the kind which human strength could manage. But now we float; at random, indeed, pretty much, and as the wind drives us; for want of nothing however but that steerage which invention, the conqueror of many equal if not superior difficulties may be expected to supply.

Should the point be carried and man at last become as familiar with the air, as he has long been with the ocean, will it in its consequences prove a mercy, or a judgment? I think, a judgment—first, because if a power to convey himself from place to place like a bird would have been good for him, his Maker would have formed him with [such] a capacity. But he has been a groveller upon the earth for 6000 years, and now at last when the close of this present state of things approaches, begins to exalt himself above it. So much the worse for him; like a truant schoolboy, he forsakes his bounds, and will have reason to repent of his presumption. Secondly, I think it will prove a judgment because, with the exercise of very little foresight, it is easy to prognosticate a thousand evils which the project must necessarily bring after it; amounting at last to the confusion of all order, the annihilation of all authority, with dangers both to property and person, and impunity to the offenders. Were I an absolute legislator, I would make it death to a man convicted of flying, the moment he could be caught; and to bring him down from his altitudes by a bullet sent through his head should be no murder. Philosophers would call me a Vandal— the scholar would say that, had it not been for me, the fable of Dædalus would have been realized, and historians would load my memory with reproaches of phlegm and stupidity and oppression, but in the meantime the world would go on quietly, and if it enjoyed less liberty would at least be more secure.

I know not what are your sentiments upon the subject of the East India Bill.[3] This too has frequently afforded me matter of speculation. I can easily see that it is not without its blemishes; but its beauties, in my eye, are much predominant. Whatever may be its author's views, if he delivers so large a

<hr />

[3] Fox's Bill for the reform of the government of British India.

portion of mankind from such horrible tyranny as the East has so long suffered, he deserves a statue much more than Montgolfier, who, it seems, is to receive that honour. Perhaps he may bring our own freedom into jeopardy; but to do this for the sake of emancipating nations so much more numerous than ourselves, is at least generous, and a design that should have my encouragement, if I had any encouragement to afford it.

We are well, and love you. Remember us, as I doubt not you do, with the same affection, and be content with my sentiments upon subjects such as these, till I can send you, if that day should ever come, a letter more worthy of your reception.

Nous sommes les vôtres,

Guillaume et Marie.

TEXT: *Barham Johnson MSS.*† except for the last two paragraphs, where the text is Southey's.

TO THE REV. WILLIAM UNWIN

Jan. 3, 1784

My dear William,

Your silence began to be distressing both to your mother and me, and *had I not* received a letter from you last night, I should have written by this post to enquire after your health. —How can it be that you who are not stationary like me, but often change your situation and mix with a variety of company, should suppose me furnished with such abundant materials and yourself destitute? I assure you faithfully that I do not find the soil of Olney prolific in the growth of such articles as make letter-writing a desirable employment. No place contributes less to the catalogue of incidents or is more scantily supplied with anecdotes worth notice. We have one parson, one poet, one bellman, one crier, And the poor poet is our only squire. Guess then if I have not more reason to expect two letters from you, than you one from me. The principal occurrence and that which affects me most at present, came to pass this moment. The stairfoot door, being swelled by the thaw, would do anything better than it would open. An attempt to force it upon that office has been attended with such a horrible dissolution of its parts that we were immediately obliged to introduce a chirurgeon, commonly called a carpenter, whose applications we have some hope will cure it of a locked jaw and heal its numerous fractures. His medicines are powerful chalybeates and a certain glutinous salve which he tells me is made of the tails and ears of animals. — The consequences however are rather unfavourable to my present employment, which does not well brook noise, bustle, and interruption.

This being the case I shall not perhaps be either so perspicuous or so diffuse on the subject of which you desire my sentiments as I should be, but I will do my best. Know then that I learnt long since from the Abbé Raynal[1] to hate all monopolies, as injurious, howsoever managed, to the interests of commerce at large: consequently the Charter[2] in question would not at any rate be a favourite of mine. This however is of itself, I confess, no sufficient reason to justify the resumption of it. But such reasons I think are not wanting. A grant of that kind, it is well known, is always forfeited by the non-performance of the conditions. And why not equally forfeited if those conditions are exceeded, if the design of it be perverted and its operation extended to objects which were never in the contemplation of the donor? This appears to me to be no misrepresentation of their case whose Charter is supposed to be in danger. It constitutes them a trading company and gives them an exclusive right to traffic in the East Indies. But it does no more. It invests them with no sovereignty, it does not convey to them the royal prerogative of making war and peace, which the King cannot alienate if he would. But this prerogative they have exercised, and forgetting the terms of their institution have possessed them-

[1] Guillaume Raynal (1713–96) author of *Histoire philosophique et politique des établissements et du commerce des Européens dans les deux Indes*, 1772. The book was translated into English.

[2] The Charter of the East India Company was prolonged for ten years by the Charter Act of 1781.

selves of an immense territory, which they have ruled with a rod of iron, to which it is impossible they should ever have a right, unless such an one as it is a disgrace to plead, the right of conquest. The potentates[3] of this country they dash in pieces like a potter's vessel as often as they please, making the happiness of 30 millions of mankind a consideration subordinate to that of their own emolument, oppressing them as often as it may serve a lucrative purpose, and in no instance that I have ever heard, consulting their interest or advantage. That Government therefore is bound to interfere and to unking these tyrants is to me self-evident. And if having subjugated so much of this miserable world it is therefore necessary that we must keep possession of it, it appears to me a duty so binding upon the legislature to rescue it from the hands of those usurpers, that I should think a curse and a bitter one must follow the neglect of it. But suppose this were done, can they be legally deprived of their Charter? In truth I think so. If the abuse and perversion of a charter can amount to a defeasance of it, never were they so grossly palpable as in this instance, never was charter so justly forfeited. Neither am I at all afraid that such a measure should be drawn into precedent, unless it could be alleged as a sufficient reason for not hanging a rogue, that perhaps magistracy might grow wanton in the exercise of such a power, and now and then hang up an honest man for its amusement. When the Governors of the Bank shall have deserved the same severity, I hope they will meet with it. In the meantime I do not think them a whit more in jeopardy because a corporation of plunderers have been brought to justice.

We are sorry for Mrs Unwin's relapse. Half an ounce of senna boiled in half a pint of water, and wrung till it will yield no more, half an ounce of Epsom salts dissolved in it. Half the quantity taken an hour or two before rising, is Dr Kerr's prescription for the same disorder. He is a physician of great eminence at Northampton, and to my knowledge his remedy has been successful. Add to it a tea-spoonful of spirit

[3] Hasting's coercion of the Raja of Benares and of the Begums of Oudh. See also p. 938.

of lavender or grate nutmeg into it to prevent griping. — You are desired to keep the money till you hear further. We are well and love you all. I never wrote in such a hurry, nor in such a disturbance. Pardon the effects, and believe me

Your affectionate W. Cowper

TEXT: *BM. Add. MSS.* 24,155

TO THE REV. JOHN NEWTON

Jan. 13, 1784

My dear friend,

I too have taken leave of the old year, and parted from it just when you did but with very different sentiments and feelings upon the occasion. I looked back upon all the passages and occurrences of it, as a traveller looks back upon a wilderness through which he has passed with weariness and sorrow of heart, reaping no other fruit of his labour than the poor consolation that, dreary as the desert was, he has left it all behind him. The traveller would find even this comfort considerably lessened, if, as soon as he had passed one wilderness, another of equal length, and equally desolate, should expect him. In this particular, his experience and mine would exactly tally. I should rejoice indeed that the old year is over and gone, if I had not every reason to prophesy a new one similar to it. The new one is already old in my account. I am not, indeed, sufficiently second-sighted to be able to boast by anticipation an acquaintance with the events of it yet unborn, but rest convinced that, be they what they may, not one of them comes a messenger of good to me. If even death itself should be of the number, he is no friend of mine. It is an alleviation of the woes even of an unenlightened man, that he can wish for death, and indulge a hope, at least, that in death he shall find deliverance. But loaded as my life is with despair, I have no such comfort as would result from a supposed probability of better things to come when it once ended. For, more unhappy than the traveller with whom I set out, pass through what difficulties I may, through whatever dangers and afflictions, I am not a whit the nearer home, unless a dungeon may be called so. This is no very agreeable theme; but in so great a dearth of subjects to write upon, and especially impressed as I am at this moment with a sense of my own condition, I could choose no other. The weather is an exact emblem of my mind in its present state. A thick fog envelops every thing, and at the same time it freezes intensely. You will tell me that this cold gloom will be succeeded by a cheerful spring, and endeavour to encourage me to hope for a spiritual change resembling it—but it will be lost labour. Nature revives again; but a soul once slain lives no more. The hedge that has been apparently dead, is not so; it will burst into leaf and blossom at the appointed time; but no such time is appointed for the stake that stands in it. It is as dead as it seems, and will prove itself no dissembler. The latter end of next month will complete a period of eleven years in which I have spoken no other language. It is a long time for a man, whose eyes were once opened, to spend in darkness; long enough to make despair an inveterate habit; and such it is in me. My friends, I know, expect that I shall see yet again. They think it necessary to the existence of divine truth, that he who once had possession of it should never finally lose it. I admit the solidity of this reasoning in every case but my own. And why not in my own? For causes which to them it appears madness to allege, but which rest upon my mind with a weight of immovable conviction. If I am recoverable, why am I thus? why crippled and made useless in the church just at that time of life, when my judgment and experience being matured, I might be most useful? why cashiered and turned out of service till, according to the course of nature, there is not life enough left in me to make amends for the years I have lost,—till there is no reasonable hope left that the fruit can ever pay the expenses of the fallow? I forestall the answer—God's ways are mysterious, and He giveth no account of His matters—an answer that would serve my purpose as well as theirs that use it. There is a mystery in my destruction, and in time it shall be explained.

We are glad you have found so much hidden treasure; and

Mrs Unwin desires me to tell you that you did her no more than justice, in believing that she would rejoice in it. It is not easy to surmise the reason why the reverend doctor, your predecessor, concealed it. Being a subject of a free government, and I suppose full of the divinity most in fashion, he could not fear lest his great riches should expose him to persecution. Not can I suppose that he held it any disgrace for a dignitary of the church to be wealthy at a time when churchmen in general spare no pains to become so. But the wisdom of some men has a droll sort of knavishness in it, much like that of a magpie, who hides what he finds with a deal of contrivance, merely for the pleasure of doing it.

Mrs Unwin is tolerably well. She wishes me to add that she shall be obliged to Mrs Newton if, when an opportunity offers, she will give the worsted-merchant a jog. We congratulate you that Eliza[1] does not grow worse, which I know you expected would be the case in the course of the winter. Present our love to her. Remember us to Sally Johnson, and assure yourself that we remain as warmly as ever.

Yours,

W.C.
M.U.

TEXT: *Barham Johnson MSS.*†

TO THE REV. WILLIAM UNWIN

Mar. 21, 1784

My dear William,

I thank you for the entertainment you have afforded me. I often wish for a library, often regret my folly in selling a good collection, but I have one in Essex. It is rather remote indeed, too distant for occasional reference, but it serves the purpose of amusement, and a waggon being a very suitable vehicle

---

[1] Miss Cunningham, Mrs Newton's niece and Newton's adopted daughter.

for an author, I find myself commodiously supplied. Last night I made an end of reading Johnson's *Prefaces*. But the number of poets whom he has vouchsafed to chronicle being 56, there must be many with whose history I am not yet acquainted. These, or some of these, if it suits you to give them a part of your chaise when you come, will be heartily welcome. I am very much the biographer's humble admirer. His uncommon share of good sense, and his forcible expression secure to him that tribute from all his readers. He has a penetrating insight into character, and a happy talent of correcting the popular opinion upon all occasions where it is erroneous. And this he does with the boldness of a man who will think for himself, but at the same time with a justness of sentiment that convinces us he does not differ from others through affectation, but because he has a sounder judgement. This remark however has his narrative for its object rather than his critical performance. In the latter I do not think him always just when he departs from the general opinion. He finds no beauties in Milton's *Lycidas*, he pours contempt upon Prior to such a degree that were he really as undeserving of notice as he represents him, he ought no longer to be numbered among the poets. These indeed are the two capital instances in which he has offended me; there are others less important which I have not room to enumerate, and in which I am less confident that he is wrong. What suggested to him the thought that the *Alma*[1] was written in imitation of *Hudibras* I cannot conceive. In former years they were both favourites of mine and I often read them, but never saw in them the least resemblance to each other. Nor do I now, except that they are composed in verse of the same measure. After all, it is a melancholy observation, which it is impossible not to make after having run through this series of poetical lives, that where there were such shining talents there should be so little virtue. These luminaries of our country seem to have been kindled into a brighter blaze than others only that their spots might be more noticed. So much can Nature do for our intellectual part, and so little for our moral. What

---

[1] *Alma: or the Progress of the Mind*, by Matthew Prior, 1733.

vanity, what petulance in Pope. How painfully sensible of censure and yet how restless in provocation! To what mean artifices could Addison[2] stoop in hopes of injuring the reputation of his friend! Savage, how sordidly vicious and the more condemned for the pains that are taken to palliate his vices. Offensive as they appear through a veil, how would they disgust without one. What a sycophant to the public taste was Dryden! Sinning against his feelings, lewd in his writings though chaste in his conversation! I know not but one might search these eight volumes with a candle as the prophet[3] says, to find a man, and not find one, unless perhaps Arbuthnot were he.

I shall begin Beattie[4] this evening, and propose to myself much satisfaction in reading him. In him at least I shall find a man whose faculties have now and then a glimpse from heaven upon them. A man not indeed in possession of much evangelical light but faithful to what he has and never neglecting an opportunity to use it. How much more respectable such a character, than that of thousands who would call him blind and yet have not the grace to practice half his virtues! He too is a poet and wrote *The Minstrel*. The specimens which I have seen of it pleased me much. If you have the whole I should be glad to read it. I may, perhaps, since you allow me the liberty, indulge myself here and there with a marginal annotation, but shall not use this allowance wantonly so as to deface the volumes.

I understand that you did not ask my opinion of the style of your letter, and however I might express myself, had no design to give one. The general propriety of it was all that I had in view and to that I give my testimony.

Your mother wishes you to buy for her ten yards and a half of yard-wide Irish[5] from 2s. to 2s. 6d. per yard, and my head will be equally obliged to you for a hat, of which I enclose a

---

[2] Tickell's translation of the first book of the *Iliad*, revised by Addison, was published on the same day as Pope's first volume.

[3] Zephaniah, i, 12.

[4] James Beattie (1735–1803). The book which Unwin had lent to Cowper was probably *Dissertations Moral and Critical*, 1783.

[5] Irish worsted.

string that gives you the circumference. The depth of the crown must be four inches and one eighth. Let it not be a round slouch, which I abhor, but a smart well-cocked fashionable affair. A fashionable hat likewise for your mother. A black one if they are worn, otherwise chip.[6] If you have time she will be glad if you will pay her debts to Mrs Newton. She thinks they amount to about three pounds. If there be a balance on either side it shall be settled at our meeting.

Yrs my dear William,

W.C.

TEXT: *BM. Add. MSS.* 24,155

TO THE REV. JOHN NEWTON

March 29, 1784

My dear friend,

It being his majesty's pleasure that I should yet have another opportunity to write before he dissolves the parliament, I avail myself of it with all possible alacrity. I thank you for your last, which was not the less welcome for coming, like an extraordinary gazette, at a time when it was not expected. As when the sea is uncommonly agitated, the water finds its way into creeks and holes of rocks, which in its calmer state it never reaches, in like manner the effect of these turbulent times is felt even at Orchard side, where in general we live as undisturbed by the political element, as shrimps or cockles that have been accidentally deposited in some hollow beyond the water mark, by the usual dashing of the waves. We were sitting yesterday after dinner, the two ladies and myself, very composedly, and without the least apprehension of any such intrusion, in our snug parlour, one lady knitting, the other netting, and the gentleman winding worsted, when to our unspeakable surprise a mob appeared before the

[6] Made from wood fibre.

window; a smart rap was heard at the door, the boys halloo'd, and the maid announced Mr Grenville.[1] Puss[2] was unfortunately let out of her box, so that the candidate, with all his good friends at his heels, was refused admittance at the grand entry, and referred to the back door, as the only possible way of approach.

Candidates are creatures not very susceptible of affronts, and would rather, I suppose, climb in at a window than be absolutely excluded. In a minute, the yard, the kitchen, and the parlour, were filled. Mr Grenville advancing toward me shook me by the hand with a degree of cordiality that was extremely seducing. As soon as he and as many more as could find chairs were seated, he began to open the intent of his visit. I told him I had no vote, for which he readily gave me credit. I assured him I had no influence, which he was not equally inclined to believe, and the less, no doubt, because Mr Ashburner the draper addressing himself to me at this moment, informed me that I had a great deal. Supposing that I could not be possessed of such a treasure without knowing it, I ventured to confirm my first assertion by saying, that if I had any I was utterly at a loss to imagine where it could be, or wherein it consisted. Thus ended the conference. Mr Grenville squeezed me by the hand again, kissed the ladies, and withdrew. He kissed likewise the maid in the kitchen, and seemed upon the whole a most loving, kissing, kind-hearted gentleman. He is very young, genteel and handsome. He has a pair of very good eyes in his head, which not being sufficient as it should seem for the many nice and difficult purposes of a senator, he had a third also, which he wore suspended by a ribband from his buttonhole. The boys halloo'd, the dogs barked, Puss scampered, the hero, with his long train of obsequious followers, withdrew. We made ourselves very merry with the adventure, and in a short time settled into our former tranquillity, never probably to

---

[1] William Wyndham Grenville (1759–1834), a cousin and supporter of Pitt. He was Home Secretary in 1789, created a baron, 1790, Foreign Secretary, 1791, First Lord of the Treasury, 1806.

[2] One of C.'s hares.

be thus interrupted more. I thought myself, however, happy in being able to affirm truly that I had not that influence for which he sued; and which, had I been possessed of it, with my present views of the dispute between the Crown and the Commons, I must have refused him, for he is on the side of the former.[3] It is comfortable to be of no consequence in a world where one cannot exercise any without disobliging somebody. The town however seems to be much at his service, and if he be equally successful throughout the county, he will undoubtedly carry his election. Mr Ashburner perhaps was a little mortified, because it was evident that I owed the honour of this visit to his misrepresentation of my importance. But had he thought proper to assure Mr Grenville that I had three heads, I should not I suppose have been bound to produce them.

Mr Scott, who you say was so much admired in your pulpit, would be equally admired in his own, at least by all capable judges, were he not so apt to be angry with his congregation. This hurts him, and had he the understanding and eloquence of Paul himself, would still hurt him. He seldom, hardly ever indeed, preaches a gentle, well-tempered sermon, but I hear it highly commended: but warmth of temper, indulged to a degree that may be called scolding, defeats the end of preaching. It is a misapplication of his powers, which it also cripples, and teases away his hearers. But he is a good man and may perhaps outgrow it.

Many thanks for the worsted, which is excellent. We are as well as a spring hardly less severe than the severest winter will give us leave to be. With out united love, we conclude ourselves yours and Mrs Newton's affectionate and faithful

W.C.
M.U.

TEXT: *Barham Johnson MSS.*†

[3] Pitt's ministry, supported by the King, had clung to office despite frequent defeats in the Commons.

TO THE REV. WILLIAM UNWIN

[May, 1784][1]

My dear William,

It is hard upon us striplings who have uncles still living (N.B. I myself have an uncle still alive) that those venerable gentlemen should stand in our way even when the ladies are in question. That I, for instance, should find in one page of your letter a hope that Miss Shuttleworth would be of your party, and be told in the next that she is engaged to your uncle. Well—we may perhaps never be uncles, but we may reasonably hope that the time is coming, when others as young as we are now, shall envy us the privileges of old age, and see us engross that share in the attention of the ladies to which their youth must aspire in vain. Make our compliments if you please to your sister Elizabeth, and tell her that we are both mortified at having missed the pleasure of seeing her.

Balloons are so much the mode that even in this country we have attempted a balloon. You may possibly remember that at a place called Weston, little more than a mile from Olney, there lives a family whose name is Throckmorton.[2] The present possessor of the estate is a young man whom I remember a boy. He has a wife, who is young, genteel and

[1] The approximate date of this letter is established by the reference to the balloon, also mentioned in a letter to Newton of May 10, 1784.

[2] The Throckmortons (also called Throcks or Frogs) played a large part in C.'s life for the next decade. John Throckmorton (1753–1819) married in 1782 Maria, daughter of Thomas Giffard of Chillington Hall, Staffs. He succeeded in 1791 to the estate and baronetcy of his grandfather, Sir Robert, and went to live at Buckland House, Berks. Weston Hall continued to be occupied by the next brother, George (1754–1826) who in 1792 assumed the surname of Courtenay on inheriting through his mother that family's estate at Molland, Devon. In the same year he married 'Catharina', the daughter of Thomas Stapleton of Carlton, Yorks.

handsome. They are papists, but much more amiable than many protestants. We never had any intercourse with the family, though ever since we lived here we have enjoyed the range of their pleasure grounds, having been favoured with a key that admits us into all. When this man succeeded to the estate on the death of his elder brother, and came to settle at Weston, I sent him a complimentary card requesting the continuance of that privilege, having till then enjoyed it by the favour of his mother, who on that occasion went to finish her days at Bath. You may conclude that he granted it, and for about 2 years nothing more passed between us. A fortnight ago, I received an invitation in the civillest terms, in which he told me that the next day he should attempt to fill a balloon, and if it would be any pleasure to me to be present, should be happy to see me. Your mother and I went. The whole country were there, but the balloon could not be filled. The endeavour was I believe very philosophically made, but such a process depends for its success upon such niceties as make it very precarious. Our reception was however flattering to a great degree, in so much that more notice seemed to be taken of us than we could possibly have expected, indeed rather more than of any of his other guests. They even seemed anxious to recommend themselves to our regards. We drank chocolate and were asked to dine, but were engaged. A day or two after, Mrs U. and I walked that way and were overtaken in a shower. I found a tree that I thought would shelter us both, a large elm in a grove that fronts the mansion. Mrs T. observed us, and running towards us in the rain, insisted on our walking in. He was gone out. We sat chatting with her till the weather cleared up, and then at her instance took a walk with her in the garden. The garden is almost their only walk, and is certainly their only retreat in which they are not liable to interruption. She offered us a key of it in a manner that made it impossible not to accept it, and said that she would send us one. A few days after, in the cool of the evening, we walked that way again. We saw them going toward the house, and exchanged bows & curtsies at a little distance, but did not join them, In a few minutes, when we had passed the house and had almost reached the gate that opens out of the park into the adjoining field, I heard the iron gate belonging to the courtyard ring and saw Mr T. advancing hastily toward us. We made equal haste to meet him. He presented to us the key, which I told him I esteemed a singular favour, and after a few such speeches as are made upon such occasions, we parted. This happened about a week ago. I concluded nothing less than that all this civility and attention was designed on their part as the prelude to a nearer acquaintance. But here at present the matter rests. I should like exceedingly to be on an easy footing there, to give a morning call and now and then to receive one, but nothing more. For though he is one of the most agreeable men I ever saw, I could not wish to visit him in any other way, neither our house, furniture, servants or income being such as qualify us to make entertainments. Nor would I on any account be introduced to the neighbouring gentry, which must be the consequence of our dining there; there not being a man in the country except himself with whom I could endure to associate. They are squires, merely such, purse-proud and sportsmen. But Mr T. is altogether a man of fashion and respectable on every account.

I have told you a long story. Farewell. We number the days as they pass, and are glad that we shall see you and your sister soon.

Yours,

W.C.

TEXT: *BM. Add. MSS.* 24,155

TO THE REV. WILLIAM UNWIN

July 3, 1784

My dear William,

I was sorry that I could only take a flying leave of you. When the coach stopped at the door, I thought you had been in your chamber; my dishabille would not otherwise have prevented my running down for the sake of a more suitable parting. We rejoice that you had a safe journey, and though we should have rejoiced still more had you had no occasion for a physician, we are glad that having had need of one, you had the good fortune to find him. Let us hear soon that his advice has proved effectual, and that you are delivered from all ill symptoms.

Thanks for the care you have taken to furnish me with a dictionary. It is rather strange that at my time of life, and after a youth spent in classical pursuits, I should want one; and stranger still that being possessed at present of only one Latin author[1] in the world, I should think it worth while to purchase one. I say that it is strange, and indeed I think it so myself. But I have a thought that when my present labours[2] of the pen are ended, I may go to school again, and refresh my spirits by a little intercourse with the Mantuan and the Sabine Bard; and perhaps by a re-perusal of some others, whose works we generally lay by at that period of life when we are best qualified to read them, when the judgment and the taste being formed, their beauties are least likely to be overlooked.

This change of the wind and weather comforts me, and I should have enjoyed the first fine morning I have seen this month with a peculiar relish, if our new tax-maker[3] had not put me out of temper. I am angry with him, not only for the matter but for the manner of his proposal. When he lays his impost upon horses, he is even jocular and laughs; though considering that wheels[4] and miles and grooms were taxed before, a graver countenance upon the occasion would have been more decent. But he provokes me still more by reasoning as he does in justification of the tax upon candles. Some families, he says, will suffer little by it. Why? — Because they

[1] Horace.

[2] *The Task.*

[3] Pitt's budget, introduced on June 10, 1784, levied taxes on horses, hackney coaches and candles.

[4] In the eighteenth century turnpike companies were granted power to erect toll-bars and to exact fees from travellers in return for making and maintaining stretches of road.

are so poor, that they cannot afford themselves more than ten pounds in the year. Excellent! They can use but few, therefore they will pay but little, and consequently will be but little burthened: an argument which for its cruelty and effrontery seems worthy of a hero. But he does not avail himself of the whole force of it, nor with all his wisdom had sagacity enough to see that it contains, when pushed to its utmost extent, a free discharge and acquittal of the poor from the payment of any tax at all. A commodity, being once made too expensive for their pockets, will cost them nothing, for they will not buy it. Rejoice, therefore, O ye pennyless! the Minister will indeed send you to bed in the dark, but your remaining halfpenny will be safe; instead of being spent in the useless luxury of candlelight, it will buy you a roll for breakfast, which you will eat no doubt with gratitude to the man who so kindly lessens the number of your disbursements, and while he seems to threaten your money, saves it.—I wish he would remember that the halfpenny which government imposes, the shopkeeper will swell to twopence. I wish he would visit the miserable huts of our lace-makers at Olney, and see them working in the winter months by the light of a farthing candle from four in the afternoon till midnight. I wish he had laid his tax upon the ten thousand lamps that illuminate the Pantheon,[5] upon the flambeaux that wait upon ten thousand chariots and sedans in an evening, and upon the wax candles that give light to ten thousand card-tables. I wish in short that he would consider the pockets of the poor as sacred, and that to tax a people already so necessitous, is but to discourage the little industry that is left among us, by driving the laborious to despair.

A neighbour of mine in Silver End keeps an ass. The ass lives on the other side of the garden wall, and I am writing in the greenhouse. It happens that he is this morning most musically disposed, either cheered by the fine weather, or by some new tune which he has just acquired, or by finding his voice more harmonious than usual. It would be cruel to mortify so fine a singer, therefore I do not tell him that he

[5] See p. 848, n. 2.

interrupts and hinders me; but I venture to tell you so, and to plead his performance in excuse of my abrupt conclusion.

I send you the goldfinches,[6] with which you will do as you see good. We have an affectionate remembrance of your late visit, and of all our friends at Stock.

Believe me ever yours,

W. Cowper

TEXT: *BM. Add. MSS.* 24,155

TO THE REV. WILLIAM UNWIN

Augt. 14, 1784

My dear friend—I give you joy of a journey performed without trouble or danger. You have travelled 500 miles without having encountered either. Some neighbours of ours, about a fortnight since, made an excursion only to a neighbouring village, and brought home with them fractured skulls and broken limbs, and one of them is dead. For my own part I seem pretty much exempted from the dangers of the road. Thanks to that tender interest and concern which the Legislature takes in my security! having no doubt their fears lest so precious a life should determine too soon, and by some untimely stroke of misadventure, they have made wheels and horses so expensive that I am not likely to owe my death to either. Your mother and I continue to visit Weston daily, and find in those agreeable bowers such amusement as leaves us but little room to regret that we can go no farther. Having touched that theme, I cannot abstain from the pleasure of telling you that our neighbours in that place being about to leave it for some time, and meeting us there but a few evenings before their departure, entreated us during their absence to consider the garden and all its contents as our own, and to gather whatever we liked without the least scruple.

[6] A poem on two goldfinches: *The Faithful Bird*: see pp. 88, 692–3.

We accordingly picked strawberries as often as we went, and brought home as many bundles of honeysuckles as served to perfume our dwelling till they returned. I hear that Mr Throckⁿ. is making another balloon. A paper one, containing 16 quires. It is to fly upon the wings of ignited spirits, and will therefore I suppose be sent up at night. I take it for granted that we shall be invited to the spectacle, but whether we shall have the courage to expose ourselves to the inconveniences of a nocturnal visit is at present doubtful.

Once more, by the aid of Ld. Dartmouth, I find myself a voyager in the Pacific Ocean. In our last night's lecture[1] we were made acquainted with the island of Hapaee[2] where we had never been before. The French and Italians it seems have but little cause to plume themselves on account of their achievements in the dancing way; and we may hereafter, without much repining at it, acknowledge their superiority in that art. They are equalled, perhaps excelled, by savages. How wonderful! that without any intercourse with a politer world, and having made no proficiency in any other accomplishment, they should in this however have made themselves such adepts, that for regularity and grace of motion they might even be our masters. How wonderful too! that with a tub and a stick they should be able to produce such harmony, as persons accustomed to the sweetest music cannot but hear with pleasure. Is it not very difficult to account for the striking difference of character that obtains among the inhabitants of these islands? Many of them are near neighbours to each other, and their opportunities of improvement much the same. Yet some of them are in a degree polite, discover symptoms of taste and have a sense of elegance; while others are as rude as we naturally expect to find a people who have never had any communication with the Northern Hemisphere. These volumes furnish much matter of philosophical speculation, and often entertain me even while I am not employed in reading them.

I am sorry you have not been able to ascertain the doubtful

---

[1] C. had borrowed Captain Cook's account of his third voyage.
[2] Haabai: an island group in Tonga.

intelligence I have received on the subject of cork skirts and bosoms. I am now every day occupied in giving all the grace I can to my new production,[3] and in transcribing it; and shall soon arrive at the passage that censures that folly, which I shall be loth to expunge, but which I must not spare unless the criminals can be convicted. The world however is not so unproductive of subjects for censure, but that it may possibly supply me with some other that may serve as well. If you know any body that is writing, or intends to write an epic poem on the new regulation of franks, you may give him my compliments and these two lines for a beginning

> *Heu quot amatores nunc torquet epistola rara!*
> *Vectigal certum, perituraque gratia franki.*[4]

Our true love to all your family, yourself, you may be sure, included.

Yours faithfully

Wm Cowper

TEXT: *BM. Add. MSS.* 24,155

TO JOSEPH HILL

Olney, Nov. 6, 1784

Received of Joseph Hill Esq the sum of forty pounds by draft on Child & Co.

£40. 0. 0.   Wm Cowper

My dear friend,

I thank you for your attention to the state of my treasury, and for your readiness to supply it *par avance*. It is never so

---

[3] *The Task.*

[4] 'Alas, how many a lover suffers now from the letter that never comes! The tax is sure; the love of franking will not last.'

full but that there is room in it for more, and you did it no wrong when you supposed that at the time of your writing, it had need to be replenished.

To condole with you on the death of a mother aged 87 would be absurd. Rather therefore, as is reasonable, I congratulate you on the almost singular felicity of having enjoyed the company of so amiable and so near a relation, so long. Your lot and mine in this respect have been very different, as indeed in almost every other. Your mother lived to see you rise, at least to see you comfortably established in the world.—Mine, dying when I was six years old, did not live to see me sink in it. You may remember with pleasure while you live, a blessing vouchsafed to you so long; and I while I live must regret a comfort of which I was deprived so early. I can truly say that not a week passes, (perhaps I might with equal veracity say a day) in which I do not think of her. Such was the impression her tenderness made upon me, though the opportunity she had for showing it was so short. But the ways of God are equal, and when I reflect on the pangs she would have suffered had she been a witness of all mine, I see more cause to rejoice than to mourn that she was hidden in the grave so soon.

We have, as you say, lost a lively and sensible neighbour in Lady Austen. But we have been long accustomed to a state of retirement within one degree of solitude, and being naturally lovers of still life, can relapse into our former duality without being unhappy at the change. To me indeed a third is not necessary, while I can have the companion I have had almost these 20 years.

I am gone to the press again, and a volume of mine will greet your hands some time either in the course of the winter or early in the spring. You will find it perhaps on the whole more entertaining than the former, as it treats a greater variety of subjects, and those, at least the most of them, of a sublunary kind. It will consist of a poem in six books called *The Task*. To which will be added another which I finished yesterday, called I believe—*Tirocinium*—on the subject of education.

You perceive that I have taken your advice, and give the pen no rest.

I beg my respects to Mrs Hill and to your sisters and remain

Affectionately yrs

Wm Cowper

TEXT: *Cowper Johnson MSS.*

TO THE REV. JOHN NEWTON

Nov. 27, 1784

My dear friend,

All the interest that you take in my new publication, and all the pleas that you urge in behalf of your right to my confidence, the moment I had read your letter, struck me as so many proofs of your regard; of a friendship, in which distance and time make no abatement. But it is difficult to adjust opposite claims to the satisfaction of all parties. I have done my best, and must leave it to your candour to put a just interpretation upon all that has passed, and to give me credit for it as a certain truth, that whatever seeming defects, in point of attention and attachment to you, my conduct upon this occasion[1] may have appeared to be chargeable with, I am in reality as clear of all real ones as you would wish to find me.

---

[1] C. had not told Newton that he was engaged upon *The Task* until it was almost completed. He wrote to Unwin on December 18: 'I have had a letter from Mr Newton that did not please me, and returned an answer to it that possibly may not have pleased him. His was fretful and peevish; and mine, if not chargeable with exactly the same qualities, was however dry and unsavoury enough. We shall come together again soon, I suppose, upon as amicable terms as usual: but at present he is in a state of mortification. He would have been pleased, had the book passed out of his hands into yours, or even out of your hands into his, so that he had previously had opportunity to advise a measure which I pursued without his recommendation, and had seen the poems in manuscript. But my design was to pay you a whole compliment, and I have done it. If he says more on the subject, I shall speak freely, and perhaps please him less than I have done already.'

I send you enclosed, in the first place, a copy of the advertisement to the reader, which accounts for my title, not otherwise easily accounted for—secondly, what is called an argument, or a summary of the contents of each book, more circumstantial and diffuse by far than that which I have sent to the press. It will give you a pretty accurate acquaintance with my matter, though the tenons and mortises by which the several passages are connected, and let into each other, cannot be explained in a syllabus—and lastly, an extract, as you desired. The subject of it I am sure will please you; and as I have admitted into my description no images but what are scriptural, and have aimed as exactly as I could at the plain and simple sublimity of scripture language, I have hopes that the manner of it may please you too. As far as the numbers and diction are concerned, it may serve pretty well for a sample of the whole. But the subjects being so various, no single passage can in all respects be a specimen of the book at large.

My principal purpose is to allure the reader, by character, by scenery, by imagery, and such poetical embellishments, to the reading of what may profit him. Subordinately to this, to combat that predilection in favour of a metropolis, that beggars and exhausts the country by evacuating it of all its principal inhabitants: and collaterally, and as far as is consistent with this double intention, to have a stroke at vice, vanity, and folly, wherever I find them. I have not spared the Universities. Of those holds of every unclean & hateful thing, which pretend at the same time to be the nurseries of virtue, I cannot think even in prose without indignation. A letter which appeared in the *General Evening Post* of Saturday, said to have been received by a general officer, and by him sent to the press, as worthy of public notice, and which has all the appearance of authenticity, would alone justify the severest censure of those bodies, if any such justification were wanted. But their guilt is too notorious to need an accession of proof from any particular quarter. By way of supplement to what I have written on this subject, I have added a poem, called *Tirocinium*, which is in rhyme. It treats of the scandalous relaxation of discipline, that obtains in almost all schools universally, but especially in the largest, which are so negligent in the article of morals that boys are debauched in general the moment they are capable of being so. It recommends the office of tutor to the father, where there is no real impediment; the expedient of a domestic tutor, where there is; and the disposal of boys into the hands of a respectable country clergyman, who limits his attention to two, in all cases where they cannot be conveniently educated at home. Mr Unwin happily affording me an instance in point, the poem is inscribed to him. You will now I hope command your hunger to be patient, and be satisfied with the luncheon that I send, till dinner comes. That piecemeal perusal of the book, sheet by sheet, would be so disadvantageous to the work itself, and therefore so uncomfortable to me, that I dare say you will waive your desire of it. A poem, thus disjointed, cannot possibly be fit for anybody's inspection but the author's.

I just add by way of note to what is said above, that at Westminster a surgeon is kept, with the privity and under the connivance of the Master, whose chief business is to attend the boys *peste venerea contaminatos*; an anecdote which I learned last summer from unquestionable authority, and which indeed determined me to the subject. I have marked out none by name, nor even named the Universities.

Tully's rule — *nulla dies sine linea*[2] — will make a volume in less time than one would suppose. I adhered to it so rigidly, that though more than once I found three lines as many as I had time to compass, still I wrote; and finding occasionally, and as it might happen, a more fluent vein, the abundance of one day made me amends for the barrenness of another. But I do not mean to write blank verse again. Not having the music of rhyme, it requires so close an attention to the pause and the cadence, and such a peculiar mode of expression, as render it, to me at least, the most difficult species of poetry that I have ever meddled with.

I am obliged to you, and to Mr Bacon, for your kind

[2] 'Not a day without a line': a Latin proverb based on an anecdote in Pliny's *Historia Naturalis*, xxxv, 36, 12.

remembrance of me when you meet. No artist can excel as he does, without the finest feelings; and every man that has the finest feelings is, and must be, amiable. I almost wish for his sake that Russell's will may be set aside. His abilities ought not to be employed in an attempt to immortalize a curmudgeon; neither can he undertake the work with the enthusiasm that commands success. Our best love attends Mrs Newton, with the young ladies and all your family. Adieu, my dear friend.

Affectionately yours,

Wm Cowper

P.S. Many thanks for Equestrian John.[3] The engraver has given him an eye quite worthy of him. Thanks too for a barrel of oysters not yet open.

TEXT: *Barham Johnson MSS.*†*

TO JOSEPH HILL

Dec. 4, 1784

My dear friend,

   You have my hearty thanks for a very good barrel of oysters. Which necessary acknowledgment once made, I might perhaps show more kindness by cutting short an epistle, than by continuing one in which you are not likely to find your account either in the way of information or amusement. The season of the year indeed is not very friendly to such communications. A damp atmosphere and a sunless sky will have their effect upon the spirits, and when the spirits are checked, farewell to all hope of being good company, either by letter or otherwise. I envy those happy voyagers,[1] who with so much ease ascend to regions unsullied with a

---

[3] John Gilpin.
[1] Balloonists.

cloud, and date their epistles from an extra-mundane situation. No wonder if they outshine us who poke about in the dark below, in the vivacity of their sallies, as much as they soar above us in their excursions. Not but that I should be very sorry to go to the clouds for wit: on the contrary, I am satisfied that I discover more by continuing where I am. Every man to his business. Their vocation is to see fine prospects and to make pithy observations upon the world below. Such as these for instance. That the earth beheld from an height that one trembles to think of, has the appearance of a circular plain. That England is a very rich and cultivated country, in which every man's property is ascertained by the hedges that intersect the lands, and that London and Westminster seen from the neighbourhood of the moon make but an insignificant figure. I admit the utility of these remarks, but in the mean time as I say, *chacun à son goût*. And mine is rather to creep than fly, and to carry with me if possible an unbroken neck to the grave.

An article which I saw in the paper lately, gave me both pleasure and pain. I was hurt for the King, while the Chancellor's conduct pleased me. You guess that I allude to the application made in behalf of Dr Johnson.[2] Oh money ill-saved! Especially where the saving of money is in general so little attended to. Was it worth while to irritate, to grieve a man of Johnson's respectable character? to affront the Chancellor too? who I doubt not felt himself sufficiently mortified by the refusal. It was telling him in effect and emphatically too that he had urged an improper suit and had moved where he ought to have been still. I know him well enough to know what he would suffer from a rebuff of that sort. And indeed, though he is naturally liberal, yet his liberality in this instance seemed to have doubled its speed upon the spur of provocation.

[2] In June, 1784, Johnson's friends, alarmed by the state of his health, asked Lord Thurlow to apply for an increase in his pension, so that he might spend the winter in Italy. Thurlow approached the King, who refused. An offer by Thurlow to advance Johnson up to £600 out of his own pocket was politely declined. Johnson died on December 13th.

I hope that Mrs Hill is well, to whom I beg you will give my respects, and remain as ever

Yr affectionate

Wm Cowper

TEXT: *Cowper Johnson MSS.**

TO THE REV. WILLIAM UNWIN

Olney, Jan. 15, 1785

My dear William,

Your letters are always welcome. You can always either find something to say, or can amuse me and yourself with a sociable and friendly way of saying nothing. I never found that a letter was the more easily written because the writing of it had been long delayed. On the contrary, experience has taught me to answer soon, that I may do it without difficulty. It is in vain to wait for an accumulation of materials in a situation such as yours and mine, productive of few events. At the end of our expectations we shall find ourselves as poor as at the beginning.

I can hardly tell you with any certainty of information upon what terms Mr Newton and I may be supposed to stand at present. A month I believe has passed since I heard from him. But my *friseur* having been in London in the course of this week, whence he returned last night, and having called at Hoxton, brought me his love and an excuse for his silence, which he said had been occasioned by the frequency of his preachings at this season. He was not pleased that my MSS was not first transmitted to him, and I have cause to suspect that he was even mortified at being informed that a certain inscribed poem[1] was not inscribed to himself. But we shall jumble together again, as people that have an affection for each other at bottom, notwithstanding now and then a slight disagreement, always do.

[1] *Tirocinium* was dedicated to Unwin.

I know not whether Mr Smith has acted in consequence of your hint, or whether not needing one, he transmitted to us his bounty, before he had received it. He has however sent us a note for £20 with which we have performed wonders in behalf of the ragged and the starved. He is a most extraordinary young man, and though I shall probably never see him, will always have a niche in the museum of my reverential remembrance.

The death of Dr Johnson has set a thousand scribblers to work, and me among the rest. While I lay in bed, waiting till I could reasonably hope that the parlour might be ready for me, I invoked the Muse and composed the following:

EPITAPH

Here Johnson lies—a sage by all allowed
Whom to have bred may well make England proud;
Whose prose was eloquence by wisdom taught,
The graceful vehicle of virtuous thought;
Whose verse may claim, grave, masculine and strong,
Superior praise to the mere poet's song;
Who many a noble gift from heaven possessed,
And faith at last—alone worth all the rest.
Oh man immortal by a double prize,
By fame on earth, by glory in the skies!

It is destined I believe to the *Gentleman's Magazine*, which I consider as a respectable repository for small matters, which when entrusted to a newspaper can expect but the duration of a day. But Nichols[2] having at present a small piece of mine in his hands, not yet printed, (it is called *The Poplar Field*[3] and I suppose you have it) I wait till his obstetrical aid has brought that to light, before I send him a new one. In his last he published my epitaph upon Tiney[4] which I likewise imagine has been long in your collection.

Not a word yet from Johnson. I am easy however upon that subject, being assured that so long as his own interest is

[2] John Nichols (1745–1826), publisher of *The Gentleman's Magazine* and author of *Literary Anecdotes of the Eighteenth Century*, 1812–15.

731

at stake, he will not want a monitor to remind him of the proper time to publish.

You and your family have our sincere love. Forget not to present my respectful compliments to Miss Unwin, and if you have not done it already, thank her on my part for the very agreeable narrative of Lunardi.[5] He is a young man, I presume, of great good sense and spirit; his letters at least and his enterprising turn bespeak him such; a man qualified to shine not only among the stars, but in the more useful though humbler sphere of terrestrial occupation. I have been crossing the Channel in a balloon ever since I read of that achievement by Blanchard.[6] I have an insatiable thirst to know the philosophical reason why their vehicle had like to have fallen into the sea, when, for aught that appears, the gas was not at all exhausted. Did not the extreme cold condense the inflammable air and cause the globe to collapse? Tell me, and be my Apollo for ever.

Yours affectionately,

Wm Cowper

We love and thank you for your wishes to see us, and if we all live, we shall some time or other all meet together at Stock. But not just now. I could have filled another side, but the want of a frank has cramped me.

TEXT: *BM. Add. MSS.* 24,155

---

[3] p. 95.

[4] *Epitaph on a Hare*, p. 86.

[5] Vincenzo Lunardi, (1759–1806) by a balloon flight from Moorfields in London to Standon in Hertfordshire on September 15, 1784, became 'the first aerial traveller in the English atmosphere'. His description of the achievement was published in *Letters to his Guardian*, 1784. He was secretary to the Neapolitan Embassy in London.

[6] The first crossing of the English Channel by balloon was performed on the 7th January by a Frenchman, Jean-Pierre Blanchard, and an American physician, John Jeffries.

TO THE REV. WILLIAM UNWIN

Feb. 7th, 1785

My dear William,

Your letter reached me last night; consequently so late that the frank enclosed is useless, yesterday being the day of the date thereof. A mistake at the Newport Pagnel post office occasioned the delay; it had been returned from that place to London, or would have arrived at Olney a week sooner than it did.

We live in a state of such uninterrupted retirement, in which incidents worthy to be recorded occur so seldom, that I always sit down to write with a discouraging conviction that I have nothing to say. The event commonly justifies the presage, for when I have filled my sheet, I find that I have said nothing. Be it known to you, however, (that I may now at least communicate a piece of intelligence to which you will not be altogether indifferent) that I have received and revised and returned to Johnson the two first proof-sheets of my new publication. The business was dispatched indeed a fortnight ago, since when I have heard from him no further. From such a beginning, however, I venture to prognosticate the progress and in due time the conclusion of the matter.

In the last *Gentleman's Magazine* my *Poplar field* appears. I have accordingly sent up two pieces more: a Latin translation of it which you have never seen, and another on a rose-bud[1] the neck of which I inadvertently broke, which whether you have seen or not, I know not. As fast as Nichols prints off the poems I send him, I send him new ones. My remittance usually consists of two, and he publishes one of them at a time. I may indeed furnish him at this rate, without putting myself to any great inconvenience, for my last supply was transmitted to him in August and is but now exhausted.

[1] The Rose, p. 685.

I communicate the following anecdote at your mother's instance, who will suffer no part of my praise to be sunk in oblivion. A certain Lord Archibald Hamilton has hired the house of Mr Small at Clifton in our neighbourhood for a hunting seat. There he lives at present with his wife and daughter. They are an exemplary family in some respects and I believe an amiable one in all. The Revd. Mr Jones, the Curate of that parish, who often dines with them by invitation on a Sunday, recommended my volume to their reading. And his Lordship, after having perused a part of it, expressed to the said Mr Jones an ardent desire to be acquainted with the author, from motives which my great modesty will not suffer me to particularize. Mr Jones however like a wise man informed his Lordship that for certain especial reasons and causes I had declined going into company for many years, and that therefore he must not hope for my acquaintance. His Lordship most civilly subjoined that he was very sorry for it.

And is that all? say you. Now were I to hear you say so, I should look foolish and say: Yes. But having you at a distance I snap my fingers at you and say: No. That is not all. Mr Teedon,[2] who favours us now and then with his company in an evening as usual, was not long since discoursing with that eloquence which is so peculiar to himself on the many providential interpositions that had taken place in his favour. He had wished for many things, he said, which at the time when he formed those wishes, seemed distant and improbable; some of them indeed impossible. Among other wishes that he had indulged, one was, that he might be connected with men of genius and ability. And in my connexion with this worthy gentleman, said he, turning to me, that wish I am sure is amply gratified. — You may suppose that I felt the sweat gush out upon my forehead when I heard this speech, and if you do, you will not be at all mistaken. So much was I delighted with the delicacy of that incense.

Thus far I proceeded easily enough. And here I laid down

[2] Samuel Teedon (died 1798) the Olney schoolmaster. He believed himself to be especially favoured by Providence, and to be the recipient of personal messages from Heaven.

my pen, and spent some minutes in recollection endeavouring
to find some subject with which I might fill the little blank
that remains. But none presents itself. Farewell therefore, and
remember those who are mindful of you. Present our love to
all your comfortable fireside and believe me,

Ever affectionately yours

Wm Cowper

Do you like the cheese?
Ventorum is certainly good Latin. They that read Greek with
the accents would pronounce the ε in φιλέω, as an η. But I do
not hold with that practice, though educated in it. I should
therefore utter it just as I do the Latin word *filio*, taking the
quantity for my guide. Who wrote the Latin epigram and who
is the subject of it?

TEXT: *BM. Add. MSS.* 24,155

TO THE REV. WILLIAM UNWIN

April 30, 1785

My dear William,

I return you my thanks for a letter so warm with intelligence
of the celebrity of *John Gilpin*.[1] I little thought when I mounted
him upon my Pegasus that he would become so famous. I
have learned also from Mr Newton that he is equally renowned
in Scotland, and that a lady there, an acquaintance of Lady
Leven, the mother of Lord Balgonie, had undertaken to
write a second part on the subject of Mrs Gilpin's return to
London, but not succeeding in it as she wished, she dropped
it. He tells me likewise, that the headmaster of St Paul's
School (who he is I know not) has conceived in consequence

---

[1] *John Gilpin*, published in 1782 (see p. 677) achieved national celebrity
in the spring of 1785, when it formed the chief item in a series of recita-
tions given by the celebrated actor, John Henderson, at the Freemasons'
Hall in London. Henderson's success was repeated on provincial stages.
The ballad was reprinted in broadsheets and illustrated in prints.

of the entertainment that John has afforded him a vehement desire to write to me. Let us hope that he will alter his mind; for should we even exchange civilities upon the occasion, *Tirocinium* will spoil all. The great estimation however in which this knight of the stone-bottles is held may turn out a circumstance propitious to the volume of which his history will make a part. Those events that prove the prelude to our greatest success are often apparently trivial in themselves, and such as seemed to promise nothing. The disappointment that Horace mentions is reversed—we design a mug and it proves a hogshead.[2] It is a little hard that I alone should be unfurnished with a printed copy of this facetious story. When you visit London next you must buy the most elegant impression of it and bring it with you.

I thank you also for writing to Johnson. I likewise wrote to him myself. Your letter and mine together have operated to admiration. There needs nothing more but that the effect be lasting, and the whole will soon be printed. We now draw towards the middle of the 5th book of *The Task*. The man Johnson is like unto some vicious horses that I have known. They would not budge till they were spurred, and when they were spurred, they would kick. So did he. His temper was somewhat disconcerted; but his pace was quickened and I was contented.

I was very much pleased with the following sentence in Mr Newton's last: 'I am perfectly satisfied with the propriety of your proceedings as to the publication.' Now, therefore, we are friends again. Now he once more enquires after the work which, till he had disburthened himself of this acknowledgement, neither he nor I, in any of our letters to each other, ever mentioned. Some side-wind has wafted to him a report of those reasons by which I justified my conduct. I never made a secret of them, but both your mother and I have studiously

---

[2] Horace, *Ars Poetica*, 21:

> *Amphora coepit*
> *Institui: currente rota cur urceus exit?*

(It was a wine jar that was to be moulded; as the wheel runs round, why does it come out a pitcher?)

deposited them with those who we thought were most likely to transmit them to him. They wanted only a hearing, which once obtained, their solidity and cogency were such that they were sure to prevail.

You mention Bensley.[3] I formerly knew the man you mention, but his elder brother much better. We were school-fellows; and he was one of a club of seven Westminster men to which I belonged, who dined together every Thursday. Should it please God to give me ability to perform the poet's part to purpose, many whom I once called friends, but who have since treated me with a most magnificent indifference, will be ready to take me by the hand again. And some whom I never held in that estimation will, like Bensley (who was but a boy when I left London), boast of a connexion with me which they never had. Had I the virtues and graces and accomplishments of St Paul himself, I might have them at Olney and nobody would care a button about me, yourself and one or two more excepted. Fame begets favour; and one talent, if it be rubbed a little bright by use and practice, will procure a man more friends than a thousand virtues. Dr Johnson, I remember, in the life of one of our poets[4] (I believe of Savage) says that he retired from the world flattering himself that he should be regretted, but the world never missed him. I think his observation upon it is that the vacancy made by the retreat of any individual is soon filled up; that a man may always be obscure if he chooses to be so; and that he who neglects the world will be by the world neglected.

Your mother and I walked yesterday in the Wilderness. As I entered the gate, a glimpse of something white, contained in a little hole in the gate-post, caught my eye. I looked again and discovered a bird's nest, with two tiny eggs in it. By and by they will be fledged and tailed and get wing-feathers and fly. My case is somewhat similar to that of the parent bird. My nest is in a little nook. Here I brood and hatch, and in due time my progeny takes wing and whistles.

---

[3] See p. 557.

[4] In the life of Young, included in *The Lives of the Poets*, and contributed by Sir Herbert Croft.

We wait for the time of your coming with pleasant expectation. Accept our warm love and present it to all your family.
Yours truly,

Wm Cowper

Your mother has received a bill of charges attending admission into the Stuntney[5] estate. Your share of the expense amounts to about £13. She will be glad if you will send her a bank note for 10.

TEXT: *BM. Add. MSS.* 24,155

TO JOSEPH HILL

June 29, 1785

My dear friend,

I write in a nook that I call my *Bouderie*; it is a summerhouse not much bigger than a sedan chair, the door of which opens into the garden which is now crowded with pinks, roses and honey-suckles, and the window into my neighbour's orchard. It formerly served an apothecary, now dead, as a smoking-room, and under my feet is a trap-door which once covered a hole in the ground where he kept his bottles. At present however it is dedicated to sublimer uses. Having lined it with garden mats, and furnished it with a table and two chairs, here I write all that I write in summer-time, whether to the public or to my friends. It is secure from all noise, and a refuge from all intrusion; for intrusions sometimes trouble me even at Olney. I have never lived, I believe it is impossible to live, where they can be altogether evaded. At Berkhamsted I was haunted by the younger Harcourt, in the Temple by T. White, Esq., at Weymouth by Mr Foy, and at Olney I have a Mr Teedon to dread, who in his single person includes the disagreeables of them all. He is the most obsequious, the most formal, the most pedantic of all creatures, so civil that

---

[5] A village near Ely, where Mrs Unwin's father had owned property.

it would be cruel to affront him, and so troublesome that it is impossible to bear him. Being possessed of a little Latin, he seldom uses a word that is not derived from that language, and being a bigot to propriety of pronunciation, studiously and constantly lays the accent upon the wrong syllable. I think that Sheridan would adore him. He has formed his style (he told me so himself) by the pattern that Mr Hervey has furnished him with in his *Theron and Aspasio*;[1] accordingly he never says that my garden is gay, but that the flowery tribe are finely variegated and extremely fragrant. The weather with him is never fine, but genial, never cold and uncomfortable, but rigorous and frowning. If he cannot recollect a thing, he tells me that it is not within his recognizance, convincing me at the same time that the orthography of the word is quite familiar to him by laying a particular stress upon the *g*. In short he surfeits me whenever I am so unhappy as to encounter him, which is too often my lot in the winter, but thanks to my *Bouderie*, I can hide myself from him now. A poet's retreat is sacred. He acknowledges the truth of that proposition, and never presumes to violate it.

The last sentence puts me in mind to tell you that I have ordered my volume[2] to your door. My bookseller is the most dilatory of all his fraternity, or you would have received it long since. It is more than a month since I returned him the last proof, and consequently since the printing was finished. I sent him the manuscript at the beginning of last November, that he might publish while the town was full—and he will hit the exact moment when it is entirely empty. Patience, you perceive, is in no situation exempted from the severest trials; a remark that may serve to comfort you under the numberless troubles of your own.

I have to thank you for two baskets of very large and very fine mackerel since I thanked you for the first. Assure yourself that your many friendly offices and favours, though poorly

[1] James Hervey (1718–58): *Theron and Aspasio: or a series of dialogues and letters upon the most important subjects.* 3 vols., 1755. Its purpose was to recommend Calvin's theology 'to people of elegant manners and polite accomplishments'.

[2] *The Task.*

returned, are not thrown away upon the ungrateful, and believe me

    With my respects to Mrs Hill

                Your affectionate

                                Wm Cowper

TEXT: *Cowper Johnson MSS.*

TO THE REV. WILLIAM UNWIN

Thursday, July 27, [1785]

My dear William,

You and your party left me in a frame of mind that indisposed me much to company. I comforted myself with the hope that I should spend a silent day in which I should find abundant leisure to indulge sensations which, though of the melancholy kind, I yet wished to nourish. But that hope proved vain. In less than an hour after your departure, Mr Greatheed[1] made his appearance at the greenhouse door. We were obliged to ask him to dinner, and he dined with us. He is an agreeable, sensible, well-bred young man, but with all his recommendations I felt that on that occasion I could have spared him. So much better are the absent whom we love much, than the present whom we love a little. I have, however, made myself amends since, and nothing else having interfered, have sent many a thought after you.

You had been gone two days when a violent thunderstorm came over us. I was passing out of the parlour into the hall with Mungo[2] at my heels when a flash seemed to fill the room

---

[1] Samuel Greatheed had been an officer in the Engineers. When serving in Canada, a brother officer had converted him to a religious life. He resigned his commission to become a student at the 'Newport Pagnell Evangelical Institution for the Education of Young Men for the Christian Ministry', presided over by the Rev. William Bull. He was Bull's assistant from 1786–1789, when he became minister of Woburn, Bedfordshire. He was the author of *Memoirs of the Life and Writings of William Cowper*, 1814. He died in 1823.

[2] Cowper's bulldog.

with fire. In the same instant came the clap, so that the explosion was, I suppose, perpendicular to the roof. Mungo's courage upon the tremendous occasion constrained me to smile, in spite of the solemn impression that such an event never fails to affect me with. The moment that he heard the thunder, which was like the burst of a great gun, with a wrinkled forehead and with eyes directed to [the] ceiling whence the sound seemed to proceed, he barked. But he barked exactly in concert with the thunder. It thundered once, and he barked once, and so precisely in the very instant when the thunder happened, that both sounds seemed to begin and to end together.—Some dogs will clap their tails close and sneak into a corner at such a time, but Mungo it seems is of a more fearless family.—An house at no great distance from ours was the mark to which the lightning was directed. It knocked down the chimney, split the building, and carried away the corner of the next house in which lay a fellow drunk and asleep upon his bed. It roused and terrified him, and he promises to be drunk no more; but I have seen a woeful end of many such conversions. I remember but one such storm at Olney since I have known the place, and I am glad that it did not happen two days sooner for the sake of the ladies, who would probably, one of them at least, have been alarmed by it. You have left behind you Thomson's *Seasons* and a bottle of hartshorn. I will not promise that you shall ever see the latter again. Having a sore throat, I made free with part of it this morning, in the way of outward application and we shall probably find an use for the remainder. *The Seasons* you shall have again.

I have received since you went two very flattering letters of thanks, one from Mr Bacon, and one from Mr Barham, such as might make a lean poet plump and an humble poet proud; but being myself neither lean nor humble, I know of no other effect that they had than that they pleased me. And I communicate the intelligence to you, not without an assured hope that you will be pleased also.

We are now going to walk, and thus far I have written before I have received your letter.

Friday

I must now be as compact as possible. When I began, I designed four sides, but my packet being transformed into two single epistles, I can consequently afford you but three. I have fitted a large sheet with animadversions upon Pope, and shall send it by Sunday's post, indifferent whether Nichols detects me or not.[3] I am proceeding in my translation *velis et remis, omnibus nervis*[4] — as Hudibras has it and if God give me health and ability will put it into your hands when I see you next.

Your fish was good, perfectly good, and we did not forget you in our cups. — The money was found and not a farthing had eloped. My hat is come and we both admire it. But your mother's either was never sent or sent the wrong way, for it has not reached us. Tell John that I love him with all my heart for doing so much credit to his tutor and to my public recommendation of the very plan upon which he is educated.

Mr Teedon has just left us. He has read my book, and as if fearful that I had overlooked some of them myself, has pointed out to me all its beauties. I do assure you the man has a very acute discernment and a taste that I have no fault to find with. I hope that you are of the same opinion.

Be not sorry that your love of Christ was excited in you by a picture. Could a dog or a cat suggest to me the thought that Christ is precious, I would not despise that thought because a dog or a cat suggested it. The meanness of the instrument cannot debase the nobleness of the principle. He that kneels before a picture of Christ is an idolater; but he, in whose heart the sight of such a picture kindles a warm remembrance of the Saviour's sufferings, must be a Christian.

---

[3] C.'s remarks on Pope's translation of Homer were published in the *Gentleman's Magazine* for Aug. 1785 in a letter signed 'Alethes'.

[4] Samuel Butler 1613–80, *Hudibras*, Pt. I, canto II, lines 621–2:
> '*Velis et Remis, omnibus Nervis*,
> And all t'advance the *Cause's* Service.'

Velis et remis: 'with sails and oars (i.e. with all possible speed).'
Omnibus nervis: 'with might and main'.

Suppose that I dream as Gardiner[5] did, that Christ walks before me, that He turns and smiles upon me, and fills my soul with ineffable love and joy—will a man tell me that I am deceived, that I ought not to love or rejoice in Him for such a reason, because a dream is merely a picture drawn upon the imagination? I hold not with such divinity. To love Christ is the greatest dignity of man, be that affection wrought in him how it may.

Adieu, may the blessing of God be upon you all. It is your mother's hearty wish and mine.

Yours ever

Wm Cowper

P.S. You had hardly reached Emberton when Mr Teedon came to charge us with his thanks to Miss Unwin for her goodness to him. The poor man looked so humble and grateful that I forgave him all his past intrusions. I beseech you therefore that you transmit his acknowledgements to his kind benefactress.

P.P.S.—It happened that Mr Smith being gone to Hampstead when two of my *Task* packets were sent to his house, Johnson paid the postage of them. I entreat you at a fair opportunity to defray the debt, for I account it one.

TEXT: *BM. Add. MSS.* 24,155

TO THE REV. JOHN NEWTON

August 6, 1785

My dear friend,

I found your account of what you experienced in your state of maiden authorship very entertaining, because very natural. I suppose that no man ever made his first sally from the press

---

[5] Colonel James Gardiner (1688–1745) according to his own statement, led a life of extraordinary dissipation in Paris—until one day, happening to read a religious work, he saw what he believed to be a vision of Christ, and was instantly and permanently converted.

without a conviction that all eyes and ears would be engaged to attend him; at least, without a thousand anxieties lest they should not. But however arduous and interesting such an enterprise may be in the first instance, it seems to me that our feelings on the occasion soon become obtuse. I can answer, at least, for one. Mine are by no means what they were when I published my first volume. I am even so indifferent to the matter, that I can truly assert myself guiltless of the very idea of my book sometimes whole days together. God knows that my mind having been occupied more than twelve years in the contemplation of the most tremendous subjects, the world and its opinion of what I write is become as unimportant to me as the whistling of a bird in a bush. Despair made amusement necessary, and I found poetry the most agreeable amusement. Had I not endeavoured to perform my best, it would not have amused me at all. The mere blotting of so much paper would have been but indifferent sport. God gave me grace also to wish that I might not write in vain. Accordingly, I have mingled much truth with much trifle; and such truths as deserved, at least, to be clad as well and as handsomely as I could clothe them. If the world approve me not, so much the worse for them, but not for me. I have only endeavoured to serve them, and the loss will be their own. And as to their commendations, if I should chance to win them, I feel myself equally invulnerable there. The view that I have had of myself, for many years, has been so truly humiliating, that I think the praises of all mankind could not hurt me. God knows that I speak my present sense of the matter at least most truly, when I say, that the admiration of creatures like myself seems to me a weapon the least dangerous that my worst enemy could employ against me. I am fortified against it by such solidity of real self-abasement, that I deceive myself most egregiously if I do not heartily despise it. Praise belongeth to God; and I seem to myself to covet it no more than I covet divine honours. Could I assuredly hope that God would at last deliver me, I should have reason to thank him for all that I have suffered, were it only for the sake of this single fruit of my affliction, that it has taught me how much more contemptible I am in myself than I ever before suspected, and has reduced my former share of self-knowledge (of which at that time I had a tolerable good opinion) to a mere nullity, in comparison with what I have acquired since. Self is a subject of inscrutable misery and mischief, and can never be studied to so much advantage as in the dark. For as the bright beams of the sun seem to impart a beauty to the foulest objects, and can make even a dunghill smile, so the light of God's countenance, vouchsafed to a fallen creature, so sweetens him and softens him for the time, that he seems, both to others and to himself, to have nothing savage or sordid about him. But the heart is a nest of serpents, and will be such while it continues to beat. If God cover the mouth of that nest with his hand, they are hush and snug; but if he withdrew his hand, the whole family lift up their heads and hiss, and are as active and venomous as ever. This I always professed to believe from the time that I had embraced the Truth, but never knew it as I know it now. To what end I have been made to know it as I do, whether for the benefit of others or for my own, or for both, or for neither, will appear hereafter.

What I have written leads me naturally to the mention of a matter that I had forgot. I should blame nobody, not even my intimate friends, and those who have the most favourable opinion of me, were they to charge the publication of *John Gilpin*, at the end of so much solemn and serious truth, to the score of the author's vanity; and to suspect that, however sober I may be upon proper occasions, I have yet that itch of popularity that would not suffer me to sink my title to a jest that had been so successful. But the case is not such. When I sent the copy of *The Task* to Johnson, I desired, indeed, Mr Unwin to ask him the question, whether or not he would choose to make it a part of the volume. This I did merely with a view to promote the sale of it. Johnson answered, 'By all means.' Some months afterward, he enclosed a note to me in one of my packets, in which he expressed a change of mind, alleging that to print *John Gilpin* would only be to print what had been hackneyed in every magazine, in every shop, and at the corner of every street. I answered that I desired to be entirely governed by his opinion; and that if he chose to waive it, I should be better pleased with the omission. Nothing more passed between us upon the subject, and I concluded that I should never have the immortal honour of being generally known as the author of *John Gilpin*. In the last packet, however, down came John, very fairly printed, and equipped for public appearance. The business having taken this turn, I concluded that Johnson had adopted my original thought that it might prove advantageous to the sale; and as he had had the trouble and expense of printing it, I corrected the copy, and let it pass. Perhaps, however, neither the book nor the writer may be made much more famous by John's good company than they would have been without it; for the volume has never yet been advertised, nor can I learn that Johnson intends it. He fears the expense, and the consequence must be prejudicial. Many who would purchase will remain uninformed: but I am perfectly content.

My compliment to Mr Throckmorton[1] was printed before he had cut down the Spinney. He indeed has not cut it down, but Mr Morley the tenant, with the owner's consent, however, no doubt. My poetical civilities, however, were due to that gentleman, for more solid advantages conferred upon me in person. Without any solicitation on our part, or even hint that we wished it (it was indeed a favour that we could not have aspired to) he made us a present of a key of his kitchen garden, and of the fruit of it whenever we pleased. That key, I believe, was never given to any other person, nor is it likely that they should give it to many, for it is their favourite walk, and was the only one in which they could be secure from all interruption. They seem however to have left the country, and it is possible that he may never know that my Muse has noticed him.

I have considered your motto and like the purport of it: but the best, because the most laconic manner of it, seems to be—

'*Cum talis sis, sis noster*;'[2]

utinam being, in my account of it, unnecessary.

---

[1] *The Task*, p. 402.
[2] 'Since thou art such, thou shouldst be ours.'

Mrs Newton has our hearty thanks for the turbot and lobster, which were excellent. To her and to the young ladies we beg to be affectionately remembered.

Three weeks since, Mr Unwin and his late ward, Miss Shuttleworth, and John, called on us in their way from the North, having made an excursion so far as to Dumfries. Mr Unwin desired me to say that though he had been often in town since he had the pleasure of seeing you last, he had always gone thither on business, and making a short stay, had not been able to find an opportunity to pay his respects to you again.

Yours, my dear friend, most truly,

W.C.

TEXT: *Barham Johnson MSS.*†

TO LADY HESKETH

Octr. 12, 1785

My dear cousin,

It is no new thing with you to give pleasure, but I will venture to say you do not often give more than you gave me this morning, when I came down to breakfast and found a letter franked by my uncle and when opening that frank I found that it contained a letter from you, I said within myself, 'This is just as it should be: we are all grown young again, and the days that I thought I should see no more are actually returned.' You perceive therefore that you judged well when you conjectured that a line from you would not be disagreeable to me. It could not be otherwise than as in fact it proved a most agreeable surprise, for truly I can boast of an affection for you which neither years nor interrupted intercourse have at all abated. I need only recollect how much I valued you once, and with how much cause, immediately to feel a revival of the same value; if that can be said to revive which at the most has only been dormant for want of employment. But I slander it when I say that it has slept. A thousand

747

times have I recollected a thousand scenes, where our two selves have formed the whole of the drama, with the greatest pleasure; at times too when I had no reason to suppose that I should ever hear from you again. I have laughed with you at the *Arabian Nights Entertainment,* which afforded us as you well know a fund of merriment that deserves never to be forgot. I have walked with you to Netley Abbey! and have scrambled with you over hedges in every direction, and many other feats we have performed together, upon the field of my remembrance & all within these few years; should I say within this twelvemonth, I should not transgress the truth. The hours that I have spent with you were among the pleasantest of my former days, and are therefore chronicled in my mind so deeply as to fear no erasure. Neither do I forget my poor friend Sir Thomas; I should remember him indeed at any rate on account of his personal kindnesses to myself, but the last testimony that he gave of his regard for you endears him to me still more. With his uncommon understanding (for with many peculiarities he had more sense than any of his acquaintance), and with his generous sensibilities, it was hardly possible that he should not distinguish you as he has done. As it was the last so it was the best proof that he could give of a judgment that never deceived him, when he would allow himself leisure to consult it.

You say that you have often heard of me. That puzzles me. I cannot imagine from what quarter. But it is no matter. I must tell you however, my cousin, that your information has been a little defective. That I am happy in my situation is true, I live and have lived these 20 years with Mrs Unwin to whose affectionate care of me during the far greater part of that time, it is, under Providence, owing that I live at all. But I do not count myself happy in having been for 13 of those years in a state of mind that has made all that care and attention necessary. An attention and care that have injured her health, and which had she not been uncommonly supported, must have brought her to the grave. But I will pass to another subject; it would be cruel to particularize only to give pain, neither would I by any means give a sable hue to the first letter of a correspondence so unexpectedly renewed.

I am delighted with what you tell me of my uncle's good health. To enjoy any measure of cheerfulness at so late a day is much; but to have that late day enlivened with the vivacity [of] youth is much more, and in these postdiluvian times a rarity indeed. Happy for the most part are parents who have daughters. Daughters are not apt to outlive their natural affections, which a son has generally survived even before his boyish years are expired. I rejoice particularly in my uncle's felicity who has three female descendants from his little person who leave him nothing to wish for upon that head.

My dear cousin, dejection of spirits, which I suppose may have prevented many a man from becoming an author, made me one. I find constant employment necessary and therefore take care to be constantly employed. Manual employments do not engage the mind sufficiently as I know by experience, having tried many; but composition, especially in verse, absorbs it wholly. I write therefore generally three hours in a morning and in an evening transcribe. I read also but less than I write, for I must have bodily exercise, and therefore never pass a day without it. I have read the *Mirror* and many of the papers I admired, but not all. Dr Beattie is so great a favourite of mine, that where he shines I seem to have no eyes for the beauties of others, and I think that all the best papers are his.

You ask me where I have been this summer. I answer, at Olney. Should you ask me where I have spent the last 17 summers, I should still answer, at Olney. Aye and the winters also. I have seldom left it and except when I attended my brother in his last illness, never I believe a fortnight together.

My book is called *The Task*. I would order you one from the booksellers were the publication now my own, but being rather as you know of the least opulent of those who may be called gentleman rhymers, I cannot afford to print at my own expence, and am therefore forced to make a present of the copy.[1]

Adieu my beloved cousin. I shall not be always thus nimble in reply, but shall always have great pleasure in

[1] The copyright.

answering you when I can. I have several small matters in the *Gentleman's Magazines* for the last year or two, but I do not take it in, and therefore cannot refer you to them.

My poor Puss is in good health, except a cough which never troubled her till this day. Herself, a house dog & a small spaniel, were just now basking in the beams of our fireside, very comfortably in a group, but the great beast Mungo desired to be let into the kitchen just before I could tell you so. He is very fond of Puss, often salutes her with his black muzzle, and licks her face. The bread that she happens to leave is his constant perquisite, so that he may not be altogether disinterested in his attachment.

To me at Olney is direction enough. Mr Newton is now minister of St Mary Woolnoth's, and has been several years.

Yours my friend and cousin,

Wm Cowper

TEXT: *The Princeton University Library Chronicle*, XXIV, I: Autumn 1962. Charles Ryskamp: 'William Cowper and his Circle, a study of the Hannay Collection,' includes a transcription of this letter from a contemporary copy.

TO LADY HESKETH

Olney, Novr. 9, 1785

My dearest cousin,

Whose last most affectionate letter has run in my head ever since I received it and which I now sit down to answer two days sooner than the post will serve me, I thank you for it, and with a warmth for which I am sure you will give me credit, though I do not spend many words in describing it. I do not seek *new* friends, not being altogether sure that I should find them, but have unspeakable pleasure in being still beloved by an old one. — I hope that now our correspondence has suffered its *last* interruption, and that we shall go down together to the grave, chatting and chirping as merrily as such a scene of things as this will permit.

I am happy that my Poems have pleased you. My volume has afforded me no such pleasure at any time, either while I was writing it or since its publication, as I have derived from yours and my uncle's opinion of it. I make certain allowances for partiality, and for that peculiar quickness of taste with which you both relish what you like, and after all drawbacks upon those accounts duly made, find myself rich in the measure of your approbation that still remains. But above all, I honour John Gilpin, since it was he who first encouraged you to write. I made him on purpose to laugh at, and he served his purpose well; but I am now indebted to him for a more valuable acquisition than all the laughter in the world amounts to, the recovery of my intercourse with you, which is to me inestimable.

My benevolent and generous cousin, when I was once asked if I wanted anything, and given delicately enough to understand that the enquirer was ready to supply all my occasions, I thankfully and civilly, but positively declined the favour. I neither suffer, not have suffered any such inconveniences as I had not much rather endure than come under obligations of that sort to a person comparatively with yourself a stranger to me. But to you I answer otherwise. I know you thoroughly, and the liberality of your disposition; and have that consummate confidence in the sincerity of your wish to serve me, that delivers me from all awkward constraint, and from all fear of trespassing by acceptance. To you therefore I reply, Yes. Whensoever, and Whatsoever, and in what manner soever you please; and add moreover that my affection for the giver is such as will increase to me tenfold the satisfaction that I shall have in receiving. It is necessary however that I should let you a little into the state of my finances, that you may not suppose them more narrowly circumscribed than they are. Since Mrs Unwin and I have lived at Olney, we have had but one purse, although during the whole of that time, till lately, her income was nearly double mine. Her revenues indeed are now in some measure reduced, and do not much exceed my own; the worst consequence of this is that we are forced to deny ourselves some things which hitherto we have been better able to afford, but they are such things as neither life nor the well-being of life depend upon. My own income has been better than it is, but when it was best, it would not have enabled me to live as my connexions demanded that I should, had it not been combined with a better than itself, at least at this end of the kingdom. Of this I had full proof during three months that I spent in lodgings at Huntingdon. In which time by the help of good management and a clear notion of economical matters, I contrived to spend the income of a twelvemonth. Now, my beloved cousin, you are in possession of the whole case as it stands. Strain no points to your own inconvenience or hurt, for there is no need of it; but indulge yourself in communicating, no matter what, that you can spare without missing it, since by so doing you will be sure to add to the comforts of my life one of the sweetest that I can enjoy, a token and proof of your affection.

In the affair of my next publication, toward which you also offer me so kindly your assistance, there will be no need that you should help me in the manner that you propose. It will be a large work consisting, I should imagine, of six volumes at the least. The 21st of this month I shall have spent a year upon it, and it will cost me more than another. I do not love the booksellers well enough to make them a present of such a labour, but intend to publish by subscription. Your vote and interest therefore my dear cousin upon the occasion if you please, but nothing more. I will trouble you with some papers of Proposals when the time shall come, and am sure that you will circulate as many for me as you can. Now, my dear, I am going to tell you a secret. It is a great secret, that you must not whisper even to your cat. No creature is at this moment apprized of it but Mrs Unwin and her son. I am making a new translation of Homer, and am upon the point of finishing the twenty-first book of the *Iliad*. The reasons upon which I undertake this Herculean labour, and by which I justify an enterprise in which I seem to be so effectually anticipated by Pope, although in fact he has not anticipated me at all, I may possibly give you if you wish for them, when I can find nothing more interesting to say. A period which I do not conceive to be very near.

I have not answered many things in your letter, nor can do it at present for want of room. I cannot believe but that I should know you, notwithstanding all that Time may have done. There is not a feature in your face, could I meet it upon the road by itself, that I should not instantly recollect. I should say, That is my cousin's nose, or those are her lips and her chin, and no woman upon earth can claim them but herself. As for me, I am a very smart youth of my years. I am not indeed grown grey so much as I am grown bald. No matter. There was more hair in the world than ever had the honour to belong to me. Accordingly having found just enough to curl a little at my ears, and to intermix with a little of my own that still hangs behind, I appear if you see me in an afternoon, to have a very decent head-dress, not easily distinguished from my natural growth; which being worn with a small bag and a black riband about my neck, continues to me the charms of my youth, even on the verge of age.

Yours my dearest cousin,

William Cowper

Away with the fear of writing too often.

P.S. That the view I give you of myself may be complete, I add the 2 following items—that I am in debt to nobody, and that I grow fat.

TEXT: *The Princeton University Library Chronicle*, from C.'s MS.: see foregoing letter.

TO LADY HESKETH

Novr. 17 [1785]

My dearest cousin,

I am glad that I always loved you as I did. It releases me from any occasion to suspect that my present affection for you is indebted for its existence to any selfish considerations. No: I am sure that I love you disinterestedly and for your own sake, because I never thought of you with any other sentiments than those of the truest affection, even while I was under the influence of a persuasion that I should never hear from you again. But with my present feelings super-added to those that I always had for you, I find it no easy matter to do justice to my sensations. I perceive myself in a state of mind similar to that of the traveller described in Pope's *Messiah*, who as he passes through a sandy desert, starts at the sudden and unexpected sound of a waterfall. You have placed me in a situation new to me, and in which I feel myself somewhat puzzled to know how I ought to behave. At the same time that I would not grieve you by putting a check upon your bounty, I would be as careful not to abuse it, as if I were a miser and the questions were not about your money but my own. In the first place I thank you for your note. I should have taken it excessively ill of anybody but yourself who had called it a trifle. To me I assure you it is no such matter, whatever it may appear to you. Secondly, as to the writing-desk. It is certain that I have not one, and it is equally certain that I have gone on notably well these many years without one. Why therefore should I put you to expense for an article that I cannot be said to want?

My dear, we live you must know in a house that has two small parlours. The hare has entirely occupied one these 12 years, and has made it unfit to be the receptacle of anything better than the box in which she sleeps. The other which we ourselves occupy is already so filled with chairs, tables, &c, not forgetting our own proper persons, as absolutely to forbid the importation of anything more. I have indeed a small summer-house in our farthest garden (for we have two) that just affords room to myself, two chairs and a table. There I always write in summer, and there also in winter when the day is bright. Upon that table indeed such a desk might stand, but then this *séjour* is at such a distance from the house, and thieves are so numerous in the town, that in all probability it would be stolen. You know now, my dear, the whole state of the matter: therefore judge for yourself. As to Johnson's *Poets*, I have seen them and have read all his prefaces; Mr Unwin has them; consequently I have them whenever I please.—I have read extracts from Hayley's works in the *Review*, and have admired some of them, but I know that he has published now and then a performance which I have no curiosity to be better acquainted with than I am already by means of the aforesaid *Review*. Especially some dramatic pieces in verse. Why therefore should I put you to the expense of his works at large, in which perhaps are more things than his plays that I should at most but slightly run over and merely to satisfy curiosity? The quarto volume that you mention, in which he and Goldsmith who is a favourite of mine figure together, will suit me well. I want it, send it, I am impatient till it arrives.

Wine, my dearest cousin, is an article on which I have something to say that will not please you, and something that will. You must know that some years since, not many, when we began to feel ourselves a little pinched in our finances, I made an heroic resolution that I would drink no more. Accordingly I substituted half a pint of a certain malt liquor called ale instead of it, much against Mrs Unwin's will who opposed the innovation with all her might. But I was obstinate and had my own way as I generally have. The consequences were such a concert of music within, such squeaking, croaking and scolding of stomach and bowels denied their wonted comfort, and such perpetual indigestions withal, that I was constrained to return again to the bottle. I have a stomach that is good for little at the best, and that bids fair to be the first part of me that shall fail altogether in the performance of its functions; I find it necessary therefore to drink wine in order to keep it in tolerable humour, to the amount of three or four glasses after dinner and supper. A bottle accordingly serves me two days and sometimes two days and a half, which I mention principally with a view to commend my own sobriety. I drink nothing but port. The port therefore, my dear, which you offer me, I accept. It is to me a medicine which I cannot do without and yet a medicine, at times go, rather too costly for me. Shrub I never drink, for my quarrelsome stomach will bear neither the juice of orange or lemon; nor do I touch brandy more than twice in a twelvemonth. Brandy and Shrub therefore, my cousin, you shall send me none. Now I do assure you I have been [as][1] faithful and as explicit as if upon oath, and in all [that I hav]e said upon these subjects have not sacrificed a t[ittle o]f truth to false delicacy or to any such squeam[ish] impertinence. Now for the conveyance.—We have two. The Wellingborough coach passes through Olney on Tuesdays, Thursdays and Saturdays in its way from London. It sets out from Town at 5 in the morning on those days, and starts from the Cross Keys in St John Street, Smithfield. Rogers's waggon sets out every Wednesday and Saturday from the Windmill in St John Street. Rogers, the proprietor, lives at a village called Sherrington three miles short of Olney, but Olney is the goal he drives at. You are now in possession of the whole matter in detail.

Although I do not suspect that a secret to you, my cousin, is any burthen, yet having maturely considered that point since I wrote my last, I feel myself altogether disposed to release you from the injunction to that effect under which I laid you. I have now made such a progress in my translation that I need neither fear that I shall stop short of the end, nor that any other rider of Pegasus should overtake me. Therefore if at any time it should fall fairly in your way or you should feel yourself invited to say that I am so occupied, you have my poetship's free permission. My heart bounds at the thought of being introduced to Mrs Montagu; I have heard of her, and have heard of her all that you relate. You are certainly to be my introducer into notice. I have found by experience that without exactly such help as you will afford me, it is no easy matter to engage attention. Dr Johnson read and recommended my first volume, and the favourable account of it that appeared in the *Monthly Review* was written by a friend of his to whom he consigned that office. But your interest, my beloved cousin, will I doubt not promote that of my present publication far more.

Adieu! Bless you—so say we both—Yours,

Wm Cowper

[1] The words, which are missing because part of the manuscript was torn away in sealing and opening the letter, have been supplied from a contemporary copy. (Ryskamp).

P.S. They are just going to publish a new edition of Johnson's *Dictionary* revised by himself and much improved. It is to come out at first in weekly numbers, and will be completed in a year and half or little more, 2 vols. 4to. — At that time, therefore, I will beg you to send it to me — it is a work that every writer should be possessed of.

My dear, if I can produce a translation of the old Bard that the *literati* shall prefer to Pope's, which I have the assurance to hope that I may, it will do me more honour than anything that I have performed hitherto. At present they are all agreed that Pope's is a very inadequate representation of him.

TEXT: The *Princeton University Library Chronicle*, from C.'s MS.: see foregoing letter.

TO LADY HESKETH

Olney, Nov. 23, 1785

My dear cousin,

I am obliged to you for having allotted your morning to me, and not less obliged to you for writing when the opportunity you had set apart for that purpose had been almost entirely consumed by others. It cost me some little deliberation to decide whether I should answer by this night's post, or whether I should wait till I could tell you that the wine is arrived: but to say the truth, I had it not in my power to wait; so I cut the matter short at once by determining to believe that the frequency of my letters will not make them a burthen to you. I did not know or suspect that Providence had so much good in store for me in the present life, as I promise myself now from the renewal of our intimacy. But it seems that my calculations upon that subject were erroneous; it is renewed: and I look forward to the permanence of it with the pleasantest expectations, and resolve to do all I can to deserve your punctual correspondence, by being as punctual as possible myself. *How easily are resolutions made and kept, when the whole heart is in them!*

Fifty things present themselves to me that I want to say, and while each pleads for the preference, they all together so distract my choice that I hardly know with which to begin.

I thank you, my dearest cousin, for your medical advice. I have tried other wines, but never could meet with any that I could drink constantly but port, without being the worse for it. And with respect to the quantity, that is a point that habit so effectually decides, that after many years' practice, a limitation to a certain stint becomes in a manner necessary. When I have drank what I always drink, I can feel that more would disgust me. I have, indeed, a most troublesome stomach, and which does not improve as I grow older. I have eaten nothing for some time past that it has not quarrelled with, from my bread and butter in the morning down to the egg that I generally make my supper. It constrains me to deny myself some things that I am fond of, and some that are in a degree necessary to health, or that seem to be so. Green tea I have not touched these twenty years, or only to be poisoned by it: but bohea, which never hurts me, is so good a substitute, that I am perfectly well satisfied upon that head. Less easy, however, do I find it to reconcile myself to an almost total abstinence from all vegetables, which yet I have been obliged to practise for some time. But enough, and too much by half, upon a subject that shall never again engross so large a portion of the paper that I devote to you.

You supposed in a former letter that Mrs Cowper, of Devonshire Street, has written to me since I saw the rest of the family. Not so, my dear. Whatever intelligence she gave you concerning me, she had it from the Newtons whom she visits. Yourself were the last of my female relations that I saw before I went to St Albans. You do not forget, I dare say, that you and Sir Thomas called upon me in my chambers a very few days before I took leave of London: then it was that I saw you last, and then it was I said in my heart, upon your going out at the door, Farewell! there will be no more intercourse between us for ever. But Providence has ordered otherwise, and I cannot help saying once more, how sincerely I rejoice that he has. It were a pity that, while the whole world holds us, we, who were in a manner brought up together, should not love each other to the last. We do, however, and we do so in spite of a long separation; and although that separation should be for life, yet will we love each other.

I intended to have been very merry when I began, but I stumbled unawares upon a subject that made me otherwise; but if I have been a little sad, yet not disagreeably so to myself. That you admire Mr Pitt, my dear, may be, for aught I know, as you say it is, a very shining part of your character; but a more illustrious part of it, in my account, is your kindness and affection to me. Sweet self, you know, will always claim a right to be first considered—a claim which few people are much given to dispute. Upon the subject of politics you may make me just what you please. I am perfectly prepared to adopt all your opinions, for living when[1] and as I do, it is impossible that I should have any decided ones of my own. My mind, therefore, is as much a *carte blanche* in this particular as you can wish. Write upon it what you please. I know well that I honoured his father, and that I have cut capers before now for victories obtained under his auspices; and although capering opportunities have become scarce since he died, yet I am equally ready even now to caper for his son when a reasonable occasion should offer. As to the King, I love and honour him upon a hundred accounts; and have, indeed, but one quarrel with him in the world; which is, that after having hunted a noble and beautiful animal, till he takes it perhaps at last in a lady's parlour, he in a few days turns it up and hunts it again. When stags are followed by such people as generally follow them, it is very well: their pursuers are men who do not pretend to much humanity, and when they discover none, they are perfectly consistent with themselves; but I have a far different opinion of the character of our King: he is a merciful man, and should therefore be more merciful to his beast.

I admire and applaud your forgery,[2] but your last was performed in such haste that the date did not much resemble the direction. I imagine, however, that, all things considered,

[1] ? where
[2] The letter, no doubt, was franked in her father's name—*Southey*.

the Post Office, should they detect your contrivance, would not be much disposed to take notice of it. It is a common practice, but seldom so justifiably practised as by you.

My dearest cousin, if you give me wine, there is no good reason wherefore you should also be at the expense of bottles, of which we could not possibly make any other use than to furnish the rack with them, where the cats would break them. I purpose, therefore, to return the hampers charged with the same number that it brings, by your permission. The difference will be sixteen shillings in the price of the wine.

Our post comes in on Wednesdays, Fridays, and Sundays; on the two former days about breakfast time, and on Sundays, at this season at least, in the afternoon. Adieu, my dear; I am never happier, I think, than when I am reading your letters, or answering them,

Ever yours,

Wm. C.

P.S. The kindness of that concern you take in the affairs of my stomach calls upon me to be a little more particular. I have tried Madeira, and find that it heats me in the night. Sherry I understand to be a creator of appetite, which I do not want. I am taking bark and steel[3], from which I expect much. Mine is merely a case of relaxation.

TEXT: *Southey*

TO LADY HESKETH

Nov. 30 [1785]

My dearest cousin,

Your kindness reduces me to a necessity, (a pleasant one, indeed) of writing all my letters in the same terms: always thanks—thanks at the beginning, and thanks at the end. It is, however, I say, a pleasant employment when those thanks

---

[3] Peruvian, or cinchona, bark, and tincture of steel, a medicament containing iron.

are indeed the language of the heart: and I can truly add, that there is no person on earth whom I thank with so much affection as yourself. You insisted that I should give you my genuine opinion of the wine. By the way, it arrived without the least damage or fracture, and I finished the first bottle of it this very day. It is excellent, and though the wine which I had been used to drink was not bad, far preferable to that. The bottles will be in town on Saturday. I am enamoured of the desk and of its contents before I see them. They will be most entirely welcome. A few years since I made Mrs Unwin a present of a snuff-box—a silver one; the purchase was made in London by a friend; it is of a size and form that make it more fit for masculine than feminine use. She therefore with pleasure accepts the box which you have sent,—I should say with the greatest pleasure. And I, discarding the leathern trunk that I have used so long, shall succeed to the possession of hers. She says, Tell Lady Hesketh that I truly love and honour her. Now, my cousin, you may depend upon it, as a most certain truth, that these words from her lips are not an empty sound. I never in my life heard her profess a regard for any one that she felt not. She is not addicted to the use of such language upon ordinary occasions; but when she speaks it, speaks from the heart. She has baited me this many a day, even as a bear is baited, to send for Dr Kerr.[1] But, as I hinted to you upon a former occasion, I am as muleish as most men are, and have hitherto most gallantly refused; but what is to be done now?—If it were uncivil not to comply with the solicitations of one lady, to be unmoved by the solicitations of two would prove me to be a bear indeed. I will, therefore, summon him to consideration of said stomach, and its ailments, without delay, and you shall know the result.—I have read Goldsmith's *Traveller* and his *Deserted Village*, and am highly pleased with them both, as well for the manner in which they are executed, as for their tendency, and the lessons that they inculcate.

Mrs Unwin said to me a few nights since, after supper, 'I have two fine fowls in feeding, and just fit for use; I wonder

---

[1] C.'s physician. He lived at Northampton.

whether I should send them to Lady Hesketh?' I replied,
'Yes, by all means! and I will tell you a story that will at once
convince you of the propriety of doing so. My brother was
curate on a time to Mr Fawkes, of Orpington, in Kent: it was
when I lived in the Temple. One morning, as I was reading
by the fireside, I heard a prodigious lumbering at the door.
I opened it, and beheld a most rural figure, with very dirty
boots, and a great coat as dirty. Supposing that my great
fame as a barrister had drawn unto me a client from some
remote region, I desired him to walk in. He did so, and
introduced himself to my acquaintance by telling me that he
was the farmer with whom my brother lodged at Orpington.
after this preliminary information he unbuttoned his great
coat, and I observed a quantity of long feathers projected
from an inside pocket. He thrust in his hand, and with great
difficulty extracted a great fat capon. He then proceeded to
lighten the other side of him, by dragging out just such
another, and begged my acceptance of both. I sent them to a
tavern, where they were dressed, and I with two or three
friends, whom I invited to the feast, found them incomparably
better than any fowls that we had ever tasted from the
London coops. Now', said I to Mrs Unwin, 'it is likely that
the fowls at Olney may be as good as the fowls at Orpington,
therefore send them; for it is not possible to make so good a
use of them in any other way.'

My dear, I have another story to tell you, but of a different
kinf. At Westminster School I was much intimate with
Walter Bagot,[2] a brother of Lord Bagot.[3] In the course, as I
suppose, of more than twenty years after we left school, I saw
him but twice;—once when I called on him at Oxford, and
once when he called on me in the Temple. He has a brother[4]
who lives about four miles from hence, a man of large estate.
It happened that soon after the publication of my first
volume, he came into this country on a visit to his brother.

[2] The Rev. Walter Bagot (1731–1801), of Pipe Hall, Staffs, rector of
Blithfield and Leigh.

[3] William Bagot, M.P. for Staffs until 1780, when he was created Baron.

[4] Charles Chester, of Chicheley Hall, Bucks.

Having read my book, and liking it, he took that opportunity to renew his acquaintance with me. I felt much affection for him, and the more because it was plain that after so long a time he still retained his for me. He is now at his brother's; twice has he visited me in the course of the last week, and this morning he brought Mrs Bagot with him. He is a good and amiable man, and she a most agreeable woman. At this second visit I made him acquainted with my translation of Homer:[5] he was highly pleased to find me so occupied, and with all that glow of friendship that would make it criminal in me to doubt his sincerity for a moment, insisted upon being employed in promoting the subscription, and engaged himself and all his connexions, which are extensive, and many of them of high rank, in my service. His chariot put up at an inn in the town while he was here, and I rather wondered that at his departure he chose to walk to his chariot, and not to be taken up at the door; but when he had been gone about a quarter of an hour his servant came with a letter his master had written at the inn, and which, he said, required no answer. I opened it, and found as follows —

Olney, Nov. 30, 1785

My good friend,

You will oblige me by accepting this early subscription to your Homer, even before you have fixed your plan and price; which when you have done, if you will send me a parcel of your subscription papers, I will endeavour to circulate them among my friends and acquaintance as far as I can. Health and happiness attend you —

Yours ever,

Walter Bagot.

N.B. — It contained a draft for twenty pounds.

My dearest cousin, for whom I feel more than I can say, I once more thank you for all; which reminds me by the way of thanking you in particular for your offer of oysters. I am very fond of them, and few things agree better with me, when they are stewed without butter. You may perceive that I improve upon your hands, and grow less and less coy in the matter of acceptance continually.

In a letter of Mr Unwin's to his mother he says thus: 'I have been gratified to-day by the high character given of my friend's poem in *The Critical Review*.' So far, therefore, I have passed the pikes. The Monthly Critics have not yet noticed me.

Adieu! my faithful, kind, and consolatory friend!

Ever, ever yours,

Wm Cowper

TEXT: *Southey*

TO LADY HESKETH

Thursday, Dec. 15, 1785

Dearest cousin,

My desk is always pleasant, but never so pleasant as when I am writing to you. If I am not obliged to you for the thing itself, at least I am for your having decided the matter against me, and resolving that it should come in spite of all my objections. Before it arrived, Mrs Unwin had spied out for it a place that exactly suits it. A certain fly-table in the corner of the room, which I had overlooked, affords it a convenient stand when it is not wanted, and it is easily transferred to a larger when it is. If I must not know to whom I am principally indebted for it, at least let me entreat you to make my acknowledgements of gratitude and love. As to my frequent use of it, I will tell you how that matter stands. When I was writing my first volume, and was but just beginning to emerge from a state of melancholy that had continued some years, (from which, by the way, I do not account myself even now delivered) Mrs Unwin insisted on my relinquishing the pen, apprehending consequences injurious to my health. When ladies insist, you know, there is an end of the business; obedience on our part becomes necessary. I accordingly obeyed, but having lost my fiddle, I became pensive and unhappy; she therefore restored it to me, convinced of its utility, and from that day to this I have never ceased to scrape. Observe, however, my dear, that I scrape not always. My task that I assign myself is to translate forty lines a day; if they pass off easily I sometimes make them fifty, but never abate any part of the allotted number. Perhaps I am occupied an hour and a half, perhaps three hours; but generally between two and three. This, you see, is the labour that can hurt no man; and what I have translated in the morning, in the evening I transcribe.

Imagine not that I am so inhuman as to send you into the field with no coadjutor but Mr Bagot. He is indeed one of my great dependencies, but I have others, and not inconsiderable ones besides. Mr Unwin is of course hearty in my cause, and he has several important connexions. I have, by his means originally, an acquaintance, though by letters only, with Mr Smith, member for Nottingham. My whole intercourse with my bookseller has hitherto been carried on through the medium of his parliamentary privilege. He is pleased to speak very handsomely of my books, and, I doubt not, will assist my subscription with ardour. John Thornton the great, who together with his three sons, all three in parliament, has, I suppose, a larger sweep in the city than any man, will, I have reason to hope, be equally zealous in my favour. Mr Newton, who has a large influence in that quarter also, will, I know, serve me like a brother. I have also exchanged some letters with Mr Bacon, the statuary, whose connexions must needs be extensive, and who, if I may judge from the sentiments that he expresses towards me, will not be backward in my service. Neither have I any doubt but that I can engage Lord Dartmouth. These, my dearest cousin, except the last, (and I mention it for your greater comfort) are all, to a man, Pittites. Mr Smith, in particular, is one of the minister's most intimate friends, and was with him when the turnpikeman had like to have spoiled him for a premier for ever. All this I have said by way of clapping you on the back, not wondering that your poor heart ached at the idea of being almost a solitary Lady Errant on the occasion.

With respect to the enterprise itself, there are certain points

of delicacy that will not suffer me to make a public justification of it. It would ill become me avowedly to point out the
faults of Pope in a preface, and would be as impolitic as
indecent. But to you, my dear, I can utter my mind freely. Let
me premise, however, that you answered the gentleman's
inquiry, whether in blank verse or not, to a marvel. It is even
so: and let some critics say what they will, I aver it, and will
for ever aver it, that to give a just representation of Homer
in rhyme, is a natural impossibility. Now for Pope himself:—
I will allow his whole merit. He has written a great deal of
very musical and sweet verse in his translation of Homer, but
his verse is not universally such; on the contrary, it is often
lame, feeble, and flat. He has, besides, occasionally a felicity
of expression peculiar to himself; but it is a felicity purely
modern, and has nothing to do with Homer. Except the Bible,
there never was in the world a book so remarkable for that
species of the sublime that owes its very existence to simplicity, as the works of Homer. He is always nervous, plain,
natural. I refer to your own knowledge of his copyist for a
decision upon Pope's merits in these particulars. The garden
in all the gaiety of June is less flowery than his Translation.
Metaphors of which Homer never dreamt, which he did not
seek, and which probably he would have disdained if he had
found, follow each other in quick succession like the sliding
pictures in a show box. Homer is, on occasions that call for
such a style, the easiest and most familiar of all writers: a
circumstance that escaped Pope entirely, who takes most
religious care that he shall every where strut in buckram.[1]
The speeches of his heroes are often animated to a degree that
Pope no doubt accounted unmannerly and rude, for he has
reduced numbers of them that are of that character to the
perfect standard of French good-breeding. Shakespeare himself did not excel Homer in discrimination of character,
neither is he more attentive to exact consistence and preservation of it throughout. In Pope, to whatever cause it was
owing, whether he did not see it, or seeing it, accounted it an
affair of no moment, this great beauty is almost absolutely

[1] Stiffly.

annihilated. In short, my dear, there is hardly any thing in the world so unlike another, as Pope's version of Homer to the original. Give me a great corking pin that I may stick your faith upon my sleeve. There—it is done. Now assure yourself, upon the credit of a man who made Homer much his study in his youth, and who is perhaps better acquainted with Pope's translation of him than almost any man, having twenty-five years ago compared them with each other line by line throughout; upon the credit of a man, too, who would not for the world deceive you in the smallest matter, that Pope never entered into the spirit of Homer, that he never translated him, I had almost said, did not understand him: many passages it is literally true that he did not. Why, when he first entered on his task, did he (as he did, by his own confession) for ever dream that he was wandering in unknown ways, that he was lost upon heaths and forests, and awoke in terror? I will tell you, my dear, his dreams were emblems of his waking experience; and I am mistaken, if I could not go near to prove that at his first setting out, he knew very little of Greek, and was never an adept in it, to the last. Therefore, my beloved cousin, once more take heart. I have a fair opportunity to acquire honour; and if when I have finished the *Iliad*, I do not upon cool consideration think that I have secured it, I will burn the copy.

A hundred things must go unanswered, but not the oysters unacknowledged, which are remarkably fine. Again I leave space for Kerr,[2] not having seen him yet. I cannot go to him now, lest we *should meet in the midway between.*[3]

Saturday.

I must now huddle up twenty matters in a corner. No Kerr yet: a report prevails in our town that he is very ill, and I am very sorry if he is. I were not better than a beast could I forget to thank you for an order of oysters through the season. I love you for all your kindnesses, and for this among the rest. I wrote lately to Johnson on the subject of Homer. He

[2] C. had written about his state of health to Dr Kerr in Northampton, and awaited a visit.

[3] Cf. *Much Ado about Nothing*, II, i. [Act II, scene I].

is a knowing man in his trade, and understands booksellers' trap[4] as well as any man. He wishes me not to publish by subscription, but to put my copy into his hands. He thinks he can make me such proposals as I shall like. I shall answer him to-day, and not depart from my purpose. But I consider his advice as a favourable omen. The last post brought me a very obliging letter from the abovesaid Mr Smith. I shall answer it to-day, and shall make by intended application for his interest in behalf of my subscription. I always take care to have sufficient exercise every day. When the weather forbids walking, I ring a thousand bob-majors upon the dumb-bells. You would be delighted to see the performance. Again, I say that I love you, and I do so in particular for the interest that you took in the success of the passages that you say were read in the evening party that you mention. I know the friendly warmth of your heart, and how valuable a thing it is to have a share in it. The hare was caught by a shepherd's dog that had not the fear of the law before his eyes; was transferred by the shepherd to the clerk of the parish, and by him presented to us. Mrs Unwin is ever deeply sensible of your kind remembrances of her. Her son is sometimes in town, and if you permit him, will, I doubt not, rejoice to give a morning rap at your door, upon the first intimation of such permission from me, whenever opportunity shall offer.

Now farewell, my dearest cousin, and deservedly my most beloved friend, farewell.

With true affection yours,
Wm Cowper

TEXT: *Southey*

TO LADY HESKETH

Jan. 16, 1786

My dearest cousin,

I have sent, as I hope you have heard by this time, a

---

[4] *Understands booksellers' trap*: knows the publishing business.

specimen to my good friend the General.[1] To tell you the truth, I begin to be ashamed of myself that I had opposed him in the only two measures he recommended, and then assured him that I should be glad of his advice at all times. Having put myself under a course of strict self-examination upon this subject, I found at last that all the reluctance I had felt against a compliance with his wishes, proceeded from a principle of shame-facedness at bottom, that had insensibly influenced my reasonings, and determined me against the counsel of a man whom I knew to be wiser than myself. Wonderful as it may seem, my cousin, yet it is equally true, that although I certainly did translate the *Iliad* with a design to publish it when I had done, and although I have twice issued from the press already, yet I do tremble at the thought, and so tremble at it that I could not bear to send out a specimen, because, by doing so, I should appear in public a good deal sooner than I had purposed. Thus have I developed my whole heart to you, and if you should think it at all expedient, have not the least objection to your communicating to the General this interpretation of the matter. The specimen has suffered a little through my too great zeal of amendment; in one instance, at least, it will be necessary to restore the original reading. And by the way I will observe that a scrupulous nicety is a dangerous thing. It often betrays a writer into a worse mistake than it corrects, sometimes makes a blemish where before there was none, and is almost always fatal to the spirit of the performance.

You do not ask me, my dear, for an explanation of what I could mean by *anguish of mind*, and by *the perpetual interruptions* that I mentioned. Because you *do not* ask, and because your reason for not asking consists of a delicacy and tenderness peculiar to yourself, for that very cause I will tell you. A wish so suppressed is more irresistible than many wishes plainly uttered. Know then that in the year 73 the same scene that was acted at St Albans, opened upon me again at Olney, only covered with a still deeper shade of melancholy, and ordained

---

[1] Maj. Gen. Spencer Cowper, 1724–97, had commanded a brigade in the war of American Independence. He was promoted Lt. Gen. in 1787.

to be of much longer duration. I was suddenly reduced from my wonted rate of understanding to an almost childish imbecility. I did not indeed lose my senses, but I lost the power to exercise them. I could return a rational answer even to a difficult question, but a question was necessary, or I never spoke at all. This state of mind was accompanied, as I suppose it to be in most instances of the kind, with misapprehension of things and persons that made me a very untractable patient. I believed that every body hated me, and that Mrs Unwin hated me most of all; was convinced that all my food was poisoned, together with ten thousand megrims of the same stamp. I would not be more circumstantial than is necessary. Dr Cotton was consulted. He replied that he could do no more for me than might be done at Olney, but recommended particular vigilance, lest I should attempt my life—a caution for which there was the greatest occasion. At the same time that I was convinced of Mrs Unwin's aversion to me, I could endure no other companion. The whole management of me consequently devolved upon her, and a terrible task she had; she performed it, however, with a cheerfulness hardly ever equalled on such an occasion; and I have often heard her say, that if ever she praised God in her life it was when she found that she was to have all the labour. She performed it accordingly, but as I hinted once before, very much to the hurt of her own constitution. It will be thirteen years in little more than a week, since this malady seized me. Methinks I hear you ask—your affection for me will, I know, make you wish to do so—Is it removed? I reply, in great measure, but not quite. Occasionally I am much distressed, but that distress becomes continually less frequent, and I think less violent. I find writing, and especially poetry, my best remedy. Perhaps had I understood music, I had never written verse, but had lived upon fiddle-strings instead. It is better however as it is. A poet may, if he pleases, be of a little use in the world, while a musician, the most skilful, can only divert himself and a few others. I have been emerging gradually from this pit. As soon as I became capable of action, I commenced carpenter, made cupboards, boxes, stools. I grew weary of this in about a twelvemonth, and addressed myself to the making of birdcages. To this employment succeeded that of gardening, which I intermingled with that of drawing, but finding that the latter occupation injured my eyes, I renounced it, and commenced poet. I have given you, my dear, a little history in shorthand; I know that it will touch your feelings, but do not let it interest them too much. *In the year when I wrote* The Task, (for it occupied me about a year) *I was very often most supremely unhappy*, and am under God indebted in good part to that work for not having been much worse. You did not know what a clever fellow I am, and how I can turn my hand to any thing.

I perceive that this time I shall make you pay double postage, and there is no help for it. Unless I write myself out now, I shall forget half of what I have to say. Now therefore for the interruptions at which I hinted. — There came a lady into this country, by name and title Lady Austen, the widow of the late Sir Robert Austen. At first she lived with her sister, about a mile from Olney; but in a few weeks took lodgings at the vicarage here. Between the vicarage and the back of our house are interposed our garden, an orchard, and the garden belonging to the vicarage. She had lived much in France, was very sensible, and had infinite vivacity. She took a great liking to us, and we to her. She had been used to a great deal of company, and we, fearing that she would find such a transition into silent retirement irksome, contrived to give her our agreeable company often. Becoming continually more and more intimate, a practice obtained at length of our dining with each other alternately every day, Sundays excepted. In order to facilitate our communication, we made doors in the two garden-walls above-said, by which means we considerably shortened the way from one house to the other, and could meet when we pleased without entering the town at all, a measure the rather expedient, because in winter the town is abominably dirty, and she kept no carriage. On her first settlement in our neighbourhood, I made it my particular business, (for at that time I was not employed in writing, having published my first volume, and not begun my second) to pay my devoirs to her ladyship every morning at eleven. Customs very soon become laws. I began *The Task*—for she was the lady who gave me the Sofa for a subject. Being once engaged in the work, I began to feel the inconvenience of my morning attendance. We had seldom breakfasted ourselves till ten, and the intervening hour was all the time that I could find in the whole day for writing; and occasionally it would happen that the half of that hour was all that I could secure for the purpose. But there was no remedy: long usage had made that which at first was optional, a point of good manners, and consequently of necessity, and I was forced to neglect *The Task* to attend upon the Muse who had inspired the subject. But she had ill-health, and before I quite finished the work was obliged to repair to Bristol. Thus, as I told you, my dear, the cause of the many interruptions that I mentioned, was removed, and now, except the Bull that I spoke of, we have seldom any company at all. After all that I have said upon this matter, you will not completely understand me perhaps, unless I account for the remainder of the day. I will add therefore, that having paid my morning visit, I walked; returning from my walk, I dressed; we then met and dined, and parted not till between ten and eleven at night.

My cousin, I thank you for giving me a copy of the General's note, of which I and my publication were so much the subject. I learned from it better than I could have learned the same thing from any other document, the kindness of his purposes towards me, and how much I may depend on his assistance. I am vexed, and have been these three days, that I thwarted him in the affair of a specimen; but as I told you, I have still my gloomy hours, which had their share, together with the more powerful cause assigned above, in determining my behaviour. But I have given the best proof possible of my repentance, and was indeed in such haste to evince it, that I sent my despatches to Newport, on purpose to catch the by-post. How much I love you for the generosity of that offer which made the General observe that your money seemed to burn in your pocket, I cannot readily, nor indeed at all, express. Neither is Mrs Unwin in the least behind me in her sense of it. We may well admire and love you, for we have not met with many such occurrences, or even heard of many such, since we first entered a world where friendship is in every mouth, but finds only here and there a heart that has room for it.

I know well, my cousin, how formidable a creature you are when you become once outrageous. No sprat in a storm is half so terrible. But it is all in vain. You are at a distance, so we snap our fingers at you. Not that we have any more fowls at present. No, no; you may make yourself easy upon that subject. The coop is empty, and at this time of year cannot be replenished. But the spring will soon begin to advance. There are such things as eggs in the world, which eggs will, by incubation, be transformed, some of them into chickens, and others of them into ducklings. So muster up all your patience, for as sure as you live, if we live also, we shall put it to the trial. But seriously, you must not deny us one of the greatest pleasures we can have, which is, to give you now and than a little tiny proof how much we value you. We cannot sit with our hands before us, and be contented with only saying that we love Lady Hesketh.

The little item that you inserted in your cover, concerning a review of a certain author's work, in the *Gentleman's Magazine*,[2] excited Mrs Unwin's curiosity to see it in a moment. In vain did I expostulate with her on the vanity of all things here below, especially of human praise, telling her what perhaps indeed she had heard before, but what on such an occasion I thought it not amiss to remind her of, that at the best it is but as the idle wind that whistles as it passes by, and that a little attention to the dictates of reason would presently give her the victory over all the curiosity that she felt so troublesome. For a short time, indeed, I prevailed, but the next day the fit returned upon her with more violence than before. She would see it—she was resolved that she would see it that moment. You must know, my dear, that a watchmaker lives within two or three doors of us, who takes in the said *Magazine* for a gentleman at some distance, and as it happened it had not been sent to its proper owner. Accordingly the messenger that the lady dispatched, returned with it, and she was gratified. As to myself, I read the article

[2] Where C.'s second volume was reviewed in Dec., 1785.

indeed, and read it to her; but I do not concern myself much you may suppose about such matters, and shall only make two or three cursory remarks, and so conclude. In the first place therefore, I observe that it is enough to craze a poor poet to see his verses so miserably misprinted, and which is worse if possible, his very praises in a manner annihilated, by a jumble of the lines out of their places, so that in two instances, the end of the period takes the lead of the beginning of it. The said poet has still the more reason to be crazed, because the said *Magazine* is in general singularly correct. But at Christmas, no doubt your printer will get drunk as well as another man. It is astonishing to me that they know so exactly how much I translated of Voltaire. My recollection refreshed by them tells me that they are right in the number of books that they affirm to have been translated by me, but till they brought the fact again to my mind, I myself had forgotten that part of the business entirely. My brother had twenty guineas for eight books of English *Henriade*, and I furnished him with four of them. They are not equally accurate in the affair of the Tame Mouse. That I kept one is certain, and that I kept it as they say, in my bureau — but not in the Temple. It was while I was at Westminster. I kept it till it produced six young ones, and my transports when I first discovered them cannot easily be conceived — any more than my mortification, when going again to visit my little family, I found that mouse herself had eaten them! I turned her loose, in indignation, and vowed never to keep a mouse again. Who the writer of this article can be, I am not able to imagine, nor where he had his information of these particulars. But they know all the world and everything that belongs to it. The mistake that has occasioned the mention of Unwin's name in the margin would be ludicrous if it were not, inadvertently indeed, and innocently on their part, profane. I should have thought it impossible that when I spoke of One[3] who had been wounded in the hands and in the side, any reader in a Christian land could have been for a moment at a loss for the person intended.

[3] *The Task*, p. 444.

Adieu, my dear cousin; I intended that one of these should have served as a case for the other, but before I was aware of it, I filled both sheets completely. However, as your money burns in your pocket, there is no harm done. I shall not add a syllable more, except that I am and, while I breathe, ever shall be

Most truly yours,

Wm Cowper

Yes; one syllable more. Having just finished the *Iliad*, I was determined to have a deal of talk with you.

TEXT: *Southey*

TO LADY HESKETH

Mond. Feb. 27, 1786

My dearest cousin,

As I sat by the fire-side this day after dinner, I saw your chamber windows coated over with snow, so that the glass was hardly visible. This circumstance naturally suggested the thought that it will be otherwise when you come. Then the roses will begin to blow, and perhaps the heat will be as troublesome as the cold is now. The next thought of course was this—three long months must pass before we shall see her! I will, however, be as patient as I can, and comfort myself with the thought that we shall meet at last. You said in one of your letters that you had resolved to dream of nobody but of Homer and his translator. I hope you keep your resolution, for I can assure you that the last-mentioned dreams most comfortably of you. About three nights since I dreamed that, sitting in our summer-house, I saw you coming towards me. *With inexpressible pleasure I sprang to meet you, caught you in my arms, and said—Oh my precious, precious cousin may God make me thankful that I see thy face again!* Now, this was a dream, and no dream—it was only a shadow while it lasted; but if we both live, and live to meet, it will be realized hereafter. Yet alas! the passages and events of the day as well as of the night are little better than dreams. Poor Bagot! whom I love sincerely because he has a singular affection for me. Ten days since he wrote me a letter, by which it appeared he was cheerful and happy. Yesterday brought me another, consisting of only about six lines, in which he tells me that his wife is dead. I transcribe it, for it is impossible to do it justice any other way.

> Oh, my dear friend—Things are much altered with me since I wrote last. My harp is turned into mourning, and my music into the voice of weeping. Her whom you saw and loved,—her whom nobody ever yet saw and knew that did not love;—her have I lost. Pray to God for me, that for Christ's sake he would continue to comfort and support both me and mine under our great affliction. Yours ever,
>
> Walt. Bagot
>
> *Blithfield, Feb. 23, 1786*

Poor man! I can attest the truth of what he says from my own knowledge of her, however short. There are people whose characters we penetrate and fully comprehend in a moment: she was one of those. Her character was so strongly marked in the gentleness of her aspect, her voice, her carriage, that the instant she was seen she was beloved. My knowledge of her was two hours long, and no more; yet when I took leave of her, I could not help saying, God bless you, madam! Indeed, my cousin, I never felt so much for any man. His own sensibilities are naturally of the quickest, and he was attached to her in the extreme, as it was impossible but that he must be. Mr Madan's book[1] happened to be mentioned when he was here, when all he said of it was—'I know not how Mr Madan finds it, but the longer I know my wife, the more I love her.' At that time I had never seen her, but when I did I wondered not.

I hardly know how to leave this subject for another, but it is necessary that I should. So farewell, poor Bagot, for the present; may God comfort thee and thy seven children!—Now for Homer, and the matters to Homer appertaining.

[1] *Thelyphthora*, p. 581.

Sephus[2] and I are of opinions perfectly different on the subject of such an advertisement as he recommends. The only proper part for me is not to know that such a man as Pope has ever existed. I am so nice upon this subject that in that note in the specimen, in which I have accounted for the anger of Achilles (which, I believe, I may pay myself the compliment to say was never accounted for before) I have not even so much as hinted at the perplexity in which Pope was entangled when he endeavoured to explain it, nor at the preposterous and blundering work that he has made with it. No, my dear, as I told you once before, my attempt has itself a loud voice, and speaks a most intelligible language. Had Pope's translation been good, or had I thought it such, or had I not known that it is admitted by all whom a knowledge of the original qualifies to judge of it, to be a very defective one, I had never translated myself one line of Homer. Dr Johnson is the only modern writer who has spoken of it in terms of approbation, at least the only one that I have met with. And his praise of it is such as convinces me, intimately acquainted as I am with Pope's performance, that he talked at random, that either he had never examined it by Homer's, or never since he was a boy. For I would undertake to produce numberless passages from it, if need were, not only ill translated, but meanly written. It is not therefore for me, convinced as I am of the truth of all I say, to go forth into the world holding up Pope's translation with one hand as a work to be extolled, and my own with the other as a work still wanted. It is plain to me that I behave with sufficient liberality on the occasion if, neither praising nor blaming my predecessor, I go right forward, and leave the world to decide between us.

Now, to come nearer to myself. Poets, my dear, (it is a secret I have lately discovered) are born to trouble, and of all poets, translators of Homer to the most. Our dear friend, the General, whom I truly love, in his last letter mortified me not a little. I do not mean by suggesting lines that he thought might be amended, for I hardly ever wrote fifty lines together that I could not afterwards have improved, but by what appeared to me an implied censure on the whole, or nearly the whole quire that I sent to you. It was a great work, he said; it should be kept long in hand—years, if it were possible; that it stood in need of much amendment, that it ought to be made worthy of me, that he could not think of showing it to Maty,[3] that he could not even think of laying it before Johnson and his friend[4] in its present condition. Now, my dear, understand thou this: if there lives a man who stands clear of the charge of careless writing, I am that man. I might prudently, perhaps, but I could not honestly, admit that charge: it would account in a way favourable to my own ability for many defects of which I am guilty, but it would be disingenuous and untrue. The copy which I sent to you was almost a new, I mean a second, translation, as far as it went. With the first I had taken pains, but with the second I took more. I weighed many expressions, exacted from myself the utmost fidelity to my author, and tried all the numbers upon my own ear again and again. If, therefore, after all this care, the execution be such as in the General's account it seems to be, I appear to have made shipwreck of my hopes at once. He said, indeed, that the similes delighted him, and the catalogue of the ships surpassed his expectations: but his commendation of so small a portion of the whole affected me rather painfully, as it seemed to amount to an implied condemnation of the rest. I have been the more uneasy because I know his taste to be good, and by the selection that he made of lines that he thought should be altered, he proved it such. I altered them all, and thanked him, as I could very sincerely, for his friendly attention. Now what is the present state of my mind on this subject? It is this. I do not myself think ill of what I have done, nor at the same time so foolishly well as to suppose that it has no blemishes. But I am sadly afraid that the General's anxiety will make him extremely difficult to be

[3] P. H. Maty, assistant librarian at the British Museum, who had written a favourable review of *The Task*, and whose good opinion of C.'s Homer was now sought, unsuccessfully.

[4] Joseph Johnson's friend was Henry Fuseli (Johann Heinrich Füssli) a good classical scholar, and a poet as well as a painter.

pleased: I fear that he will require of me more than any other man would require, or than he himself would require of any other writer. What I can do to give him satisfaction, I am perfectly ready to do; but it is possible for an anxious friend to demand more than my ability could perform. Not a syllable of all this, my dear, to him, or to any creature.—Mum!

Your question, your natural, warranted, and most reasonable question concerning me and Mrs Unwin, shall be answered at large when we meet. But to Mrs Unwin I refer you for that answer; she is most desirous to give you a most explicit one. I have a history, my dear, belonging to me, which I am not the proper person to relate. You have heard somewhat of it—as much as it was possible for me to write; but that *somewhat* bears a most inconsiderable proportion to the whole.

All intercourse has ceased between us and Lady Austen almost these two years. This mystery shall also be accounted for when you come. She has left Bristol, and is at present settled within a mile of us with her sister. You are candid, and will give me credit when I say the fault is not with us.

I have disposed of thirty-three papers of Proposals[5]—even I. Mr Throckmorton has most obligingly given me his name, and has undertaken the disposal of twelve. Lord Archibald Hamilton has also subscribed, at the instance of a neighbour of mine, and does me the honour to say that he subscribes with pleasure. Adieu! my beloved cousin; thank you for all your welcome intelligence. I had need of it.

Yours most truly.

Wm Cowper

TEXT: *Southey*

TO ASHLEY COWPER

Olney, March 29, 1786

My dear Uncle,

Having so fair an opportunity I cannot let it pass without

---

[5] For a subscription to the translation of Homer.

writing a line or two just to tell you how much I rejoice that you have health and spirits. So my dear correspondent Lady Hesketh informs me. May you long enjoy them both! for without them, however willing we may be made to suffer what it shall please God to lay upon us, sufferers we must be, and in whatever situation, great sufferers too. Long silent as I have been, no considerable portion of my time has passed in which I have not often thought of you, for a more affectionate or kinder uncle, nephew never had. A gracious Providence is always working in behalf of Man, and under its direction, something is ever turning up in the course of human life to diversify a scene that would otherwise be at the best insipid and often insupportably irksome. It would have been impossible for me to have existed long the solitary creature I was when I first left St Albans, but God who watched over me there, did not forget me at Huntingdon; on the contrary, banished as I was from the sight of every face that I had ever seen, he yet made my life comfortable, both by his own immediate favour and by leading me after a few months into a family in which I have found nothing but friendship, affection and attention ever since.

And now appears a new scene again! How minute are the wheels on which turn often events the most important! In a fit of melancholy that I knew not how to support, I determined to make a bold push for better spirits and write the facetious *History of John Gilpin*. It answers its purpose, I laugh all the while I am about it, and in time the merry mood catches from one to another and others laugh too. So far so good; and had this been all, I had been well paid for writing it. But events of much greater importance than I could possibly dream of are connected with this trifle. My dear cousin, who knew that I could laugh *once*, but who, not without reason, supposed that I had altogether renounced the practice, on the authority of honest John takes heart and writes to me again after a silence of 15 years. — She was always as dear to me as relationship and friendship and all sorts of merit could make her; and the comforts that I have had in our revived correspondence, and the joy with which I look forward to an interview with her, are not to be expressed. By her means I am also introduced once more to an intercourse with the family from which I lately thought myself cut off for ever, and to her I owe this present opportunity of telling you, my dear Uncle, how sensible I am of your past goodness to me and how greatly I esteem and love you. I shall now and then have occasion to send you a packet addressed to Lady Hesketh, and as often as such occasion occurs, shall make the same use of it as at present. Now farewell. With every affectionate wish for the happiness of you and yours,

I remain, my dear Uncle,

Most truly and faithfully,

Wm Cowper

TEXT: *Panshanger MSS.***†* A copy: not in Cowper's hand.

TO LADY HESKETH

Monday, April 10, 1786

That's my good cousin! now I love you! now I will think of June as you do, that it is the pleasantest of all months, unless you should happen to be here in November too, and make it equally delightful. Before I shall have finished my letter, Mrs Unwin will have taken a view of the house concerning which you inquire, and I shall be able to give you a circumstantial account of it. The man who built it is lately dead. He had been a common sailor, and assisted under Wolfe and Amherst at the taking of Quebec. When we came hither he was almost pennyless, but climbing by degrees into the lace-business, amassed money, and built the house in question. Just before he died, having an enterprising genius, he put almost his whole substance to hazard in sending a large cargo of lace to America, and the venture failing, he has left his widow in penury and distress. For this reason, I conclude that she will have no objection to letting as much of her house as my cousin will have occasion for, and have therefore given you this short history of the matter. The bed is the best in the town, and the honest tar's folly was much laughed at, when it was known that he, who had so often swung in a hammock, had given twenty pounds for a bed. But now I begin to hope that he made a wiser bargain than once I thought it. She is no gentlewoman, as you may suppose, but she is nevertheless a very quiet, decent, sober body, and well respected among her neighbours.

But Hadley, my dearest cousin, what is to be said of Hadley? Only this at present, that having such an inhabitant as Mr Burrows, and the hope belonging to it of such another inhabitant as yourself, it has all charms, all possible recommendations. Yes; had I the wings that David[1] wished for, I would surely stretch them to their utmost extent that I might reach any place where I should have you to converse with perhaps half the year. But alas, my dear, instead of wings, I have a chain and a collar; the history of which collar and chain Mrs Unwin shall give you when you come; else I would fly, and she would fly also, with the utmost alacrity to Hadley, or whithersoever you should call us, for Olney has no hold upon us in particular. Here have we no family connexions, no neighbours with whom we can associate, no friendships. If the country is pleasant, so also are other countries; and so far as income is concerned, we should not, I suppose, find ourselves in a more expensive situation at Hadley, or anywhere, than here. But there are lets and hinderances which no power of man can remove, which will make your poor heart ache, my dear, when you come to know them. I will not say that they can never be removed, because I will not set bounds to that which has no bounds—the mercy of God; but of the removal of them there is no present apparent probability. I knew a Mr Burrows once; it was when I lived in the Temple; so far knew him that we simpered at each other when we met, and on opposite sides of the way touched hats. This Mr Burrows, though at that time a young man, was rather remarkable for corpulence, and yet tall. He was at the bar. On a sudden I missed him, and was informed soon after that he had taken orders. Is it possible that your Mr Burrows and

[1] Psalm iv, 6.

mine can be the same?[2] The imagination is not famous for taking good likenesses of persons and faces that we never saw. In general the picture that we draw in our minds of an *inconnu* is of all possible pictures the most unlike the original. so it has happened to me in this instance: my fancy assured me that Mr Burrows was a slim, elegant young man, dressed always to the very point of exactness, with a sharp face, a small voice, a delicate address, and the gentlest manners. Such was my dream of Mr Burrows, and how my dream of him came to be such I know not, unless it arose from what I seemed to have collected out of the several letters in which you have mentioned him. From them I learned that he has wit, sense, taste, and genius, with which qualities I do not generally connect the ideas of bulk and rotundity; and from them I also learned that he has numerous connexions at your end of the town, where the company of those who have anything rough in their exterior is least likely to be coveted. So it must have come to pass that I made to myself such a very unsuitable representation of him. But I am not sorry that he is such as he is. He is no loser by the bargain, in my account. I am not the less delighted with his high approbation, and wish for no better fortune as a poet, than always so to please such men as Mr Burrows. I will not say, my dear, that you yourself gain any advantage in my opinion by the difference; for to seat you higher there than you were always seated, is not possible. I will only observe in this instance, as always in all instances, I discover a proof of your own good sense and discernment, who finding in Mr Burrows a mind so deserving of your esteem and regard, have not suffered your eye to prejudice you against it; a *faux pas* into which I have known ladies of very good understanding betrayed ere now, I assure you. Had there been a question last year of our meeting at

[2] The Rev. John Burrows (1733–86) was C.'s contemporary in the Temple until he abandoned the law for the Church in 1760. He succeeded the topographer Pennant as rector of Hadley, Herts., and earned a reputation as a preacher in two London livings he held concurrently: St Clement Danes and Christ Church, Southwark. He 'found his chief happiness' in Mrs Montagu's Blue Stocking circle, which Lady Hesketh also frequented.

Olney, I should have felt myself particularly interested in this inattention of yours to the figure, for the sake of its contents; for at that time I had rather more body than it became a man who pretends to public approbation as a poet, to carry about him. But, thanks to Dr Kerr, I do not at present measure an inch more in the girth than is perfectly consistent with the highest pretensions in that way. Apollo himself is hardly less chargeable with prominence about the waist than I am.

I by no means insist upon making ladies of the Trojan women, unless I can reconcile you to the term. But I must observe in the first place, that though in our language the word be of modern use, it is likewise very ancient. We read in our oldest Bibles of the elect *Lady*,[3] and of Babylon the *Lady* of kingdoms.[4] In the next place, the Grecians, Homer at least, when a woman of rank is accosted, takes care in many instances that she shall be addressed in a style suited to her condition, for which purpose he employs a word more magnificent in its amount than even lady, and which literally signifies very little less than goddess. The word that I mean— that I may make it legible to you, is *Daimonie*. There were, no doubt, in Troy,— but I will say no more of it. I have that to write about to my English lady, that makes all the ladies of antiquity nothing worth to me.

We are this moment returned from the house above mentioned. The parlour is small and neat, not a mere cupboard, but very passable: the chamber is better, and quite smart. There is a little room close to your own for Mrs Eaton,[5] and there is room for Cookee and Samuel. The terms are half a guinea a week; but it seems as if we were never to take a step without a stumble. The kitchen is bad—it has, indeed, never been used except as a wash-house; for people at Olney do not eat and drink as they do in other places. I do not mean, my dear, that they quaff nectar or feed on ambrosia, but *tout au contraire*. So what must be done about this abominable kitchen? It is out of doors: that is not amiss. It has neither

[3] 2 John, i.
[4] Isaiah, xlvii, 5.
[5] Lady Hesketh's personal maid.

range nor jack: that is terrible. But then range and jack are
not unattainables; they may be easily supplied. And if it were
not—abominable kitchen that it is, no bigger than half an
egg-shell, shift might be made. The good woman is content
that your servants should eat and drink in her parlour, but
expects that they shall disperse themselves when they have
done. But whither, who can say? unless into the arbour in the
garden, for that they should solace themselves in said kitchen
were hardly to be expected. While I write this, Mrs U. is gone
to attempt a treaty with the linendraper over the way, which,
if she succeeds, will be best of all, because the rooms are
better, and it is just at hand. I must halt till she returns.—She
returns—nothing done. She is gone again to another place.
Once more I halt. Again she returns and opens the parlour
door with these tidings:—'I have succeeded beyond my
utmost hopes. I went to Maurice Smith's, (he you must know,
my dear, is a Jack-of-all-trades) I said, do you know if Mr
Brightman could and would let lodgings ready furnished to
a lady with three servants? Maurice's wife calls out, (she is a
Quaker) 'Why dost thee not take the vicarage?' I replied,
'There is no furniture.' 'Pshaw!' quoth Maurice's wife; 'we
will furnish it for thee, and at the lowest rate—from a bed to
a platter we will find all.'—'And what do you intend now?'
said I to Mrs Unwin. 'Why now,' quoth she, 'I am going to the
curate to hear what *he* says.' So away she goes, and in about
twenty minutes returns.—'Well, now it is all settled. Lady H.
is to have all the vicarage, except two rooms, at the rate of
ten guineas a year; and Maurice will furnish it for five guineas
from June to November, inclusive.' So, my dear, you and
your train are provided for to my heart's content. They are
Lady Austen's lodgings, only with more room, and at the
same price. You have a parlour sixteen feet by fourteen,
chamber ditto; a room for your own maid, near to your own,
that I have occupied many a good time; an exceeding good
garret for Cookee, and another ditto, at a convenient distance,
for Samuel; a cellar, a good kitchen, the use of the garden;—
in short, all that you can want. Give us our commission in
your next, and all shall be ready by the first of June. You will
observe, my beloved cousin, that it is not in all above eight

shillings a week in the whole year, or but a trifle more. And the furniture is really smart, and the beds good. But you must find your own linen. Come then, my beloved cousin, for I am determined that, whatsoever king shall reign, you shall be *Vicar* of Olney. Come and cheer my heart. I have left many things unsaid, but shall note them another time. Adieu!—

Ever yours,

W.C.

I am so charmed with the subject that concludes my letter that I grudge every inch of paper to any other. Yet must I allow myself space to say that Lord Dartmouth's behaviour to you at the concert has won my heart to him more than ever. It was such a well-timed kindness to me, and so evidently performed with an equal design of giving pleasure to you, that I love him for it at my heart. I have never, indeed, at any time, had occasion to charge him, as I know that many have done, with want of warmth in his friendship.—I honour you, my dear, for your constellation of nobles. I rejoice that the contents of my box have pleased you: may I never write anything that does not! My friend Bull brought me to-day the last *Gentleman's Magazine*. There your cousin is held up again.[6] Oh rare coz!

TEXT: *Southey*

TO LADY HESKETH

Olney, April 17, 1786

My dearest cousin,

If you will not quote Solomon, my dearest cousin, I will. He says, and as beautiful as truly—'Hope deferred maketh the heart sick, but when the desire cometh, it is a tree of life!'[1]

[6] In a review of *The Task*.
[1] Proverbs, xiii, 12.

I feel how much reason he had on his side when he made this observation, and am myself sick of your fortnight's delay.

* * * * *

The vicarage was built by Lord Dartmouth, and was not finished till some time after we arrived at Olney, consequently it is new. It is a smart stone building, well sashed, by much too good for the living, but just what I would wish for you. It has, as you justly concluded from my premises, a garden, but rather calculated for use than ornament. It is square, and well walled, but has neither arbour, nor alcove, nor other shade, except the shadow of the house. But we have two gardens, which are yours. Between your mansion and ours is interposed nothing but an orchard, into which a door opening out of our garden affords us the easiest communication imaginable, will save the roundabout by the town, and make both houses one. Your chamber-windows look over the river, and over the meadows, to a village called Emberton, and command the whole length of a long bridge, described by a certain poet,[2] together with a view of the road at a distance. Should you wish for books at Olney, you must bring them with you, or you will wish in vain, for I have none but the works of a certain poet, Cowper, of whom perhaps you have heard, and they are as yet but two volumes. They may multiply hereafter; but at present they are no more.

You are the first person for whom I have heard Mrs Unwin express such feelings as she does for you. She is not profuse in professions, nor forward to enter into treaties of friendship with new faces; but when her friendship is once engaged, it may be confided in even unto death. She loves you already, and how much more will she love you before this time twelvemonth! I have indeed endeavoured to describe you to her, but perfectly as I have you by heart, I am sensible that my picture cannot do you justice. I never saw one that did. Be you what you may, you are much beloved, and will be so at Olney, and Mrs U. expects you with the pleasure that

[2] *The Task*, p. 465.

one feels at the return of a long absent, dear relation; that is to say, with a pleasure such as mine. She sends you her warmest affections.

On Friday I received a letter from dear Anonymous,[3] apprizing me of a parcel that the coach would bring me on Saturday. Who is there in the world that has, or thinks he has, reason to love me to the degree that he does? But it is no matter. He chooses to be unknown, and his choice is, and ever shall be sacred to me, that if his name lay on the table before me reversed, I would not turn the paper about that I might read it. Much as it would gratify me to thank him, I would turn my eyes away from the forbidden discovery. I long to assure him that those same eyes, concerning which he expresses such kind apprehensions, lest they should suffer by this laborious undertaking, are as well as I could expect them to be, if I were never to touch either book or pen. Subject to weakness, and occasional slight inflammations, it is probable that they will always be; but I cannot remember the time when they enjoyed any thing so like an exemption from those infirmities as at present. One would almost suppose that reading Homer were the best opthalmic in the world. I should be happy to remove his solicitude on the subject, but it is a pleasure that he will not let me enjoy. Well then, I will be content without it; and so content that, though I believe you, my dear, to be in full possession of all this mystery, you shall never know me, while you live, either directly, or by hints of any sort, attempt to extort, or to steal the secret from you. I should think myself as justly punishable as the Bethshem-ites,[4] for looking into the ark, which they were not allowed to touch.

I have not sent for Kerr, for Kerr can do nothing but send me to Bath, and to Bath I cannot go for a thousand reasons. The summer will set me up again. I grow fat every day, and

---

[3] With the renewal of relations with Lady Hesketh, C. began to receive gifts from a wellwisher who insisted on remaining unidentified. 'Anonymous', as Lady Hesketh wrote in *Letters to the Rev. John Johnson*, 1901, was her sister Theodora Cowper (1731–1824). If C. guessed her identity, he did not reveal it.

[4] 1 Samuel, vi, 19.

shall be as big as Gog or Magog,[5] or both put together, before you come.

I did actually live three years with Mr Chapman, a solicitor, that is to say, I slept three years in his house; but I lived, that is to say, I spent my days in Southampton Row, as you very well remember. There was I, and the future Lord Chancellor, constantly employed from morning to night in giggling and making giggle, instead of studying the law. O fie, cousin! how could you do so? I am pleased with Lord Thurlow's enquiries about me. If he takes it into that inimitable head of his, he may make a man of me yet. I could love him heartily, if he would but deserve it at my hands. That I did so once is certain. The Duchess of ———, who in the world set her a-going? But if all the duchesses in the world were spinning, like so many whirligigs, for my benefit, I would not stop them. It is a noble thing to be a poet, it makes all the world so lively. I might have preached more sermons than ever Tillotson did, and better, and the world would have been still fast asleep; but a volume of verse is a fiddle that puts the universe in motion.

Yours, my dear friend and cousin,

W.C.

TEXT: *Southey*

TO [FANNY HILL][1]

Olney, Bucks, April 21, 1786

My dear [Fanny]

I do indeed well remember (and may therefore at the present late day conclude that I shall never forget) both yourself and your sister: always my esteemed and good friends, with whom I have spent I cannot tell how many cheerful

---

[5] The statues of two giants kept at Guildhall, London.

[1] Fanny was Joseph Hill's sister. Her name, wherever it occurs, and the address, are obliterated in the original.

hours, for I am not much better at calculation than I used to be, but so many that I might think myself happy indeed to spend with anybody hereafter half the number.

I return you many thanks for your well-written and elegant stanzas, for such they are without flattery, a fault with which I cannot charge myself in my conduct at any time toward any creature. May your prophecy prove as good as your verse; if it should, I shall get money enough and have no reason to regret that I have undertaken this Herculean labour. Labour in truth it is, but at the same time I must confess a most amusing one. My mornings and evenings are constantly devoted to it, for interruptions in this corner of the world I meet with none. In due time therefore I may hope to get through it. The encouragement that I receive in the mean-time both from my dear Lady Hesketh and from my zealous and good friend General Cowper is considerable. They are indefatigable in search of subscribers; nor am I a little indebted to your most friendly brother, who has ennobled my List with the the illustrious names of Rutland and Granby. All this, together with more of the same sort that has occurred in other quarters, looks well and makes me, though not naturally very sanguine, willing to hope that in due time the poet will be paid for his song.

There is much truth in the sentiment that Mr Hayley has translated. My father intended to beget a Chancellor, and he begat instead a translator of Homer. It is impossible for the effect to differ more from the intention. But it is no matter. At least, as we used to say, it will be all one a hundred years [hence.]

Since you desire to be anonymous,[2] though why you should desire it can be known only to yourself, you shall be so; unless I should betray you to Lady Hesketh, for which I will presume that I have your permission. She comes hither in June. We have taken the Vicarage for her, the whole of it that is not occupied by the curate and the mice; and here she will spend the summer. Guess how happy this makes me, and

[2] As the author of the verses already mentioned. They were in praise of C.: see the following letter and p. 801.

believe me my dear [Fanny] with my love to your sister most heartily given

Yours affectionately

Wm Cowper

TEXT: *Panshanger MSS.* **

TO LADY HESKETH

Olney, April 24, 1786

Your letters are so much my comfort, that I often tremble lest by any accident I should be disappointed; and the more because you have been, more than once, so engaged in company on the writing day, that I have had a narrow escape. Let me give you a piece of good counsel, my cousin: follow my laudable example — write when you can; take Time's forelock in one hand, and a pen in the other, and so make sure of your opportunity. It is well for me that you write faster than any body, and more in an hour than other people in two, else I know not what would become of me. When I read your letters I hear you talk, and I love talking letters dearly, especially from you. Well! the middle of June will not be always a thousand years off, and when it comes I shall hear you, and see you too, and shall not care a farthing then if you do not touch a pen in a month. By the way, you must either send me, or bring me some more paper, for before the moon shall have performed a few more revolutions I shall not have a scrap left — and tedious revolutions they are just now, that is certain.

I give you leave to be as peremptory as you please, especially at a distance; but when you say that you are a Cowper (and the better it is for the Cowpers that such you are, and I give them joy of you, with all my heart) you must not forget that I boast myself a Cowper too, and have my humours, and fancies, and purposes, and determinations, as well as others of

791

my name, and hold them as fast as they can. *You* indeed tell *me* how often I shall see you when you come! A pretty story truly. I am a *he* Cowper, my dear, and claim the privileges that belong to my noble sex. But these matters shall be settled, as my cousin Agamemnon[1] used to say, at a more convenient time.

I shall rejoice to see the letter you promise me, for though I met with a morsel of praise last week, I do not know that the week current is likely to produce me any, and having lately been pretty much pampered with that diet, I expect to find myself rather hungry by the time when your next letter shall arrive. It will therefore be very opportune. The morsel, above alluded to, came from—whom do you think? From [Fanny Hill], but she desires that her authorship may be a secret. And in my answer I promised not to divulge it except to you. It is a pretty copy of verses, neatly written, and well turned, and when you come you shall see them. I intend to keep all pretty things to myself till then, that they may serve me as a bait to lure you hither more effectually. The last letter that I had from [Fanny Hill] I received so many years since, that it seems as if it had reached me a good while before I was born.

I was grieved at the heart that the General could not come, and that illness was in part the cause that hindered him. I have sent him by his express desire, a new edition of the first book, and half the second. He would not suffer me to send it to you, my dear, lest you should post it away to Maty at once. He did not give that reason, but being shrewd, I found it.

The grass begins to grow, and the leaves to bud, and every thing is preparing to be beautiful against you come.—Adieu!

W.C.

You enquire of our walks, I perceive, as well as of our rides: they are beautiful. You enquire also concerning a cellar: you

---

[1] 'My cousin Agamemnon,' is a plausible, but elusive, fictional character. However, in C.'s translation of the *Iliad*, I, 172–3, Agamemnon says: 'But this concern Shall be adjusted at convenient time.' The words 'my cousin', are therefore addressed to Lady Hesketh.

have two cellars. Oh! what years have passed since we took the same walks, and drank out of the same bottle! but a few more weeks, and then!

TEXT: *Southey*

TO LADY HESKETH

May 1, 1786

You need not trouble yourself, my dearest cousin, about paper, my kind and good friend the General having undertaken of his own mere motion to send me all that I ever want, whether for transcript or correspondence. My dear, there is no possible project within the compass of invention, by which you can be released from the necessity of keeping your own nags at Olney, if you keep your carriage here. At the Swan they have no horses, or, which is equally negative in such a case, they have but one. At the Bull indeed, they keep a chaise; but not to mention the disagreeable of using one inn and hiring from another, or the extortionate demands that the woman of the Bull ever makes when anything either gentle or noble is so unhappy as to fall into her hands, her steeds are so seldom disengaged, that you would find the disappointments endless. The chaise of course is engaged equally, and the town of Olney affords nothing else into which you could put your person. All these matters taken together, and another reason with them, which I shall presently subjoin—it appeared to us so indispensable a requisite to your comfort here that you should have your own, both carriage and horses, that we have this day actually engaged accommodation for them at the Swan aforesaid.

Our walks are, as I told you, beautiful; but it is a walk to get at them; and though when you come, I shall take you into training, as the jockeys say, I doubt not that I shall make a nimble and good walker of you in a short time, you would find, as even I do in warm weather, that the preparatory steps are rather too many in number. Weston, which is our pleasantest retreat of all, is a mile off, and there is not in that whole mile to be found so much shade as would cover you. Mrs Unwin and I have for many years walked thither every day in the year when the weather would permit; and to speak like a poet, the limes and the elms of Weston can witness for us both how often we have sighed and said—'Oh! that our garden opened into this grove, or into this wilderness! for we are fatigued before we reach them, and when we have reached them, have not time enough to enjoy them.' Thus stands the case, my dear, and the unavoidable *ergo* stares you in the face. Would *I* could do so too just at this moment!— We have three or four other walks, which are all pleasant in their way; but except one, they all lie at such a distance as you would find heinously incommodious. But Weston, as I said before, is our favourite: of that we are never weary; its superior beauties gained it our preference at the first, and for many years it has prevailed to win us away from all the others. There was indeed some time since, in a neighbouring parish called Lavendon, a field, one side of which formed a terrace, and the other was planted with poplars, at whose foot ran the Ouse, that I used to account a little paradise: but the poplars have been felled, and the scene has suffered so much by the loss, that though still in point of prospect beautiful, it has not charms sufficient to attract me now. A certain poet wrote a copy of verses[1] on this melancholy occasion, which, though they have been printed, I dare say you never saw. When you come therefore you shall see them; but as I told you in my last, not before. No, my dear, not a moment sooner; and for the reason in my last given I shall disobey your mandate with respect to those of F. Hill; and for another reason also—if I copy them, they will occupy the rest of my paper, which I cannot spare; and if I enclose the original, I must send my packet to Palace Yard, and you finding that the postman passed your door without

[1] *The Poplar Field*: p. 95.

dropping a letter from me would conclude that I had neglected to write; and I will not incur such a suspicion in your mind for a moment.

On Saturday—for sooner than Saturday, we could not, on account of the weather—we paid our visit at Weston, and a very agreeable visit we found it. We encountered there, besides the family, four ladies, all strange to us. One of them was a Miss Bagot, a sister of my friend Walter's; and another of them was a Mrs Chester, his sister-in-law. Mr Chester, his brother, lives at Chicheley, about four miles from Olney. Poor Mrs Bagot was remembered with tears by Mrs Chester: she is by everybody's account of her a most amiable woman. Such also, I dare say, is Miss Bagot; but the room in which we were received was large, and she sitting at the side of it, exactly opposite to me, I had neither lungs nor courage to halloo at her; therefore nothing passed between us. I chatted a good deal with my neighbours; but you know, my dear, I am not famous for vociferation where there are ears not much accustomed to my voice. Nothing can be more obliging than the behaviour of the Throckmortons have ever been to us: they long since gave us the keys of all their retreats, even of their kitchen-garden. And that you may not suspect your cousin of being any other than a very obliging creature too, I will give you a stroke of his politesse. When they were here they desired to see the garden and greenhouse. I am proud of neither, except in poetry, because there I can fib without lying, and represent them better than they are. However, I conducted them to the sight, and having set each of the ladies with her head in a bush of myrtle, I took out my scissors and cut a bouquet for each of them. When we were with *them* Mrs Throckmorton told me that she had put all the slips into water, for she should be so glad to make them grow, and asked me if they would strike root. I replied, that I had known such things happen, but believed that they were very rare, and recommended a hot-bed rather, and she immediately resolved that they should have one. Now comes the period at which your cousin shines. In the evening I ordered my labourer to trundle up a wheelbarrow of myrtles and canary lavender (a most fragrant plant) to Weston, with which I sent a note to Mrs Throckmorton, recommending them to her protection. *Dites moi, ma chère, ne suis-je homme tout à fait poli?*

Weston, as I told you, is about a mile off, but in truth it is rather more. Gayhurst is five miles off: I have walked there, but I never walked thither. I have not these many years been such an extravagant tramper as I once was. I did myself no good I believe by pilgrimages of such immoderate length. The Chesters, the Throckmortons, the Wrightes, are all of them good-natured agreeable people, and I rejoice, for your sake, that they lie all within your beat. Of the rest of our neighbours I know nothing. They are not indeed many. A Mr Praed lives at a seat called Tyringham, which is also about five miles hence; but him I never saw, save once, when I saw him jump over a rail at Weston. There is a Mr Towers at a place called Astwoodberry, about seven miles off; but he is a foxhunter merely: and Lord Egmont dwelt in a hired house at a place called Woolaston, at the same distance; but he hired it merely by way of kennel to hold him during the hunting season, and by this time, I suppose, has left it.

The copper is going to work for you again. Fifty gallons of good beer, added to seventy, will serve to moisten your maidens' lips, and the throats of your lacqueys and your coachee's, till the season for brewing returns, for it does not succeed in warm weather.

Mrs Unwin sends you her affections; and the words that follow I take from her mouth as she delivers them: 'Tell Lady Hesketh that I have the sincerest complacency in the expectation of her; and in observing how all thing concur and coincide that can bid fair to make her stay at Olney agreeable, insomuch that she seems only to wave her pen and the thing she wants springs up in an instant.' May Heaven bless you, my ever dear, dear cousin.

Farewell. Yours,

Wm Cowper

I have heard that Dr Maty has criticized my specimen with asperity. Is there any truth in this, and how much? or is there none? It has vexed me.—I have a fine passion-tree in a green tub, that I destine to your parlour chimney: it will be full of flowers.

TEXT: *Southey*

TO LADY HESKETH

Olney, Mond. May 15, 1786

Dearest cousin, from this very morning I begin to date the last month of our long separation, and confidently and most comfortably hope that before the 15th of June shall present itself, we shall have seen each other. Is it not so? and will it not be one of the most extraordinary eras of my extraordinary life? A year ago, we neither corresponded, nor expected to meet in this world. But this world is a scene of marvellous events, many of them more marvellous than fiction itself would dare to hazard, and blessed be God! they are not all of the distressing kind; now and then, in the course of an existence whose hue is for the most part sable, a day turns up that makes amends for many sighs and many subjects of complaint. Such a day shall I account the day of your arrival at Olney.

Now, my dear, you have carried your point effectually. No more chickens from Olney, you may depend upon it. By this shrewd expedient of yours, you have as completely reduced us to submission as you could have done had you even been present and had lifted up your giant fist against us. I had rather be picked and pulled myself and thrust into a basket, than send you anything at the expence with which you threaten me. Yet were we not without a twinkling of thought that by a counter-expedient we might yet once more invade you with a parcel and at the same time elude the punishment. It was Mrs Unwin's proposal, for poor I had not presence of mind enough to start it. Your denunciation is that if we send a feather more, you will cease to write from that moment. At first we both acquiesced, and felt the necessity of obedience.

But presently Mrs U. brightened up and said, 'I can do it yet. They shall be picked to the last degree of nicety and shall be as featherless as the palm of my hand.' Having been bred a lawyer, you may be sure that I was fully sensible of all the beautiful ingenuity of this evasion; but my heart soon misgave me; I thought that perhaps some tiny featherling or other might escape us, and if not found upon the person of the chicken might yet be discovered in the basket, and I hear no more from my cousin for a month to come. So the victory is fairly yours, and we now turn our attack upon the General. He I suppose will lay us under a prohibition also, and from him the slightest negative must prevail, for he is a man and a warrior and we must not put him to his shifts as we have ventured to deal with you.

Now, my dear, touching this same bonnet. I blamed myself that I did not give you your cue in my last, for without it, I might have known that you would be at a loss. The lady says that she is not fond of black bonnets; the lady likewise says that she is not young and therefore does not wish for a very airy one. Something decent and yet smartish, neither Quakerly nor gay, will exactly suit her. You bid me, when I want wine, command you. I command you accordingly, for though I do not want now, I shall soon. I have had a friend from the North[1] to assist me, who though as sober as all parsons ought to be, has yet promoted somewhat the evacuation of bottles. This my command obeyed, I have none other to lay upon you, save that you make your own most desired appearance here, at the time appointed. Wherefore is it, canst thou tell me, that together with all those delightful sensations to which the sight of a long absent dear friend gives birth, there is a mixture of something painful? Flutterings and tumult and I know not what accompaniments of our pleasure that are in fact perfectly foreign from the occasion, and that will yet intrude themselves? Such I feel when I think of our meeting, and such, I suppose, feel you. And the nearer the crisis approaches the more I am sensible of them. I know before-hand that they will increase with every turn of the wheels

---

[1] No doubt Mrs Unwin's son-in-law, the Rev. Matthew Powley.

that shall convey me to Newport when I shall set out to meet you, and that when we actually meet, the pleasure and this unaccountable pain together will be as much as I shall be able to support. I am utterly at a loss for the cause, and can only resolve it into that appointment by which it has been foreordained that all human delights shall be qualified and mingled with their contraries. For there is nothing formidable in you. To me at least there is nothing such, no, not even in your menaces, unless when you threaten me to write no more. Nay. I verily believe that did I not know you to be what you are, and had I less affection for you than I have, I should have fewer of these emotions, of which I would have none if I could help it. But a fig for them all. Let us resolve to combat with, to conquer them. They are dreams: they are mere illusions of the judgment; some enemy that hates the happiness of humankind, and is ever industrious to dash it, works them in us, and their being so perfectly unreasonable as they are is a proof of it. Nothing that *is* such can be from a good agent. This I know too by experience, that like all other illusions they exist only by force of imagination, are indebted for their prevalence to the absence of their object, and in a few moments after its appearance cease. So then, this is a settled point, and the case stands thus. You will tremble as you draw near to Newport, and so shall I. But we will both recollect that there is no reason why we should, and this recollection will at least have some little effect in our favour. We will likewise both take the comfort of what we know to be true, that the tumult will soon cease, and the pleasure long survive the pain. Even as long, I trust, as we ourselves shall survive it.

What you say of Maty gives me all the consolation that you intended. We both think it highly probable that you suggest the true cause of his displeasure when you suppose him mortified at not having had a part of the translation laid before him, ere the Specimen was published. The General was very much hurt, and calls his censure harsh and unreasonable. He likewise sent me a consolatory letter on the occasion, in which he took the kindest pains to heal any wound that he supposed I might have suffered. I am not naturally insensible, and the sensibilities that I had by nature have been wonderfully enhanced by a long series of shock[s,] given to a frame of nerves that was never very athletic. I feel accordingly, on all occasions whether painful or pleasant, in the extreme. Am easily [el[1]]evated and easily cast down. The frown of a critic freezes [al[1]]l my poetical powers, and discourages me to a degree that makes me ashamed of my own weakness; yet I presently recover my confidence again; the half of what you so kindly say in your last, would at any time restore my spirits, and being said by you, is infallible. I am not asham[ed][2] to confess that having commenced as Author, I am most ardently desirous to succeed as such. *I have, what perhaps you little suspect me of, in my nature an infinite share of ambition.* But with it, I have at the same time, as you well know, an equal share of diffidence. To this combination of opposite qualities it has been owing that till lately I stole through life without undertaking anything, yet always wishing to distinguish myself. At last I ventured, ventured too in the only path that at so late a period was yet open to me, and am determined, if God have not determined otherwise, to work my way through the obscurity that has been so long my portion, into notice. Everything therefore that seems to threaten this my favourite purpose with disappointment affects me nearly. I suppose that all ambitious minds are in the same predicament. He that seeks distinction must be sensible of disapprobation exactly in the same proportion as he desires applause. And now my precious cousin, I have unfolded my heart to you in this particular, without one speck of dissimulation. Some people and good people too would blame me, but you will not, and they I think would blame without just cause. We certainly do not honour God when we bury or when we neglect to improve, as far as we may, whatsoever talent he may have bestowed on us, whether it be little or much. In natural things as well as in spiritual it is a never-failing truth, that to him who *hath*, that is to him who occupies what he hath diligently and so as to increase it—more shall be given.[3] Set me down therefore, my dear, for an industrious rhymer

[2] Readings uncertain owing to damage to MS. [Ryskamp].

[3] Matthew, xxv, 29.

so long as I shall have the ability, for in this only way is it possible for me, so far as I can see, either to honour God, or to serve man, or even to serve myself.

My critic's letter appeared in the *Public Advertiser* of the 1st of May and the General sent my answer to the printer of the same paper either on the 6th or 7th, he does not say which. But whether it has been printed, or on what day it was printed I cannot tell.—Probably either on the 7th 8th or 9th. It is signed 'A Well-wisher to the New Translation.'

Those lines of F.H.[4] to which I alluded are as follow:

> Better to sell the gourds he raises
> Than meanly purchase gold with praises
> Still Thurlow! Thurlow! has been tri[ed]
> And from the subject turn'd asid[e].

But never mind it, my dear, say nothing to her about it. She will thin[k] me more hurt than I was, and that will hurt *her*, and the pain I feel is little or none when my conscience tells me that I am clear.

I rejoice to hear that Mr T[hrockmorto]n wishes to be on a more intimate footing. I am shy, and suspect that he is not very much otherwise, and the consequence has been that we have eventually wished an acquainta[nce] without being able to accomplish it. Blessings on you! for the hint that you drop on the subject of the house at Weston, for the burthen of my song is, since we have met once again, let us never be separated, as we have been, more. Adieu, my dear, with Mrs. Unwin's love to you

Ever yours

Wm Cowper

TEXT: *Yale University Library Gazette, vol.* 34, 1959/60. Reproduced from the MS. letter owned by the Library, in Dr C. Ryskamp's *Cowper's Ambition: two documents.*

[4] Dr Ryskamp explains that Fanny Hill's verses were a reply to C.'s poem 'On the promotion of Edward Thurlow' (not this ed.) which she assumed had been written 'with a view to emolument' from the new Lord Chancellor. C. maintained that he had written it simply for his own amusement.

TO THE REV. JOHN NEWTON

Olney, May 20, '86

My dear friend,

Within this hour arrived three sets of your new publication,[1] for which we sincerely thank you. We have breakfasted since they came, and consequently, as you may suppose, have neither of us had yet an opportunity to make ourselves acquainted with the contents. I shall be happy, and when I say that, I mean to be understood in the fullest and most emphatical sense of the word, if my frame of mind shall be such as may permit me to study them. But Adam's approach to the Tree of Life, after he had sinned, was not more effectually prohibited by the flaming sword that turned every way,[2] than mine to its great Antitype has been now almost these 13 years[3]—a short interval of 3 or 4 days, which passed about this time twelvemonth, alone excepted. For what reason it is that I am thus long excluded, if I am ever again to be admitted, is known to God only. I can say but this: that if he is still my Father, his paternal severity has toward me been such, as that I have reason to account it unexampled. For though others have suffered desertion, yet few I believe for so long a time, and perhaps none a desertion accompanied with such experiences. But they have this belonging to them, that as they are not fit for recital, being made up merely of infernal ingredients, so neither are they susceptible of it; for I know no language in which they could be expressed. They are as truly things which it is not possible for man to utter, as those were which Paul heard and saw in the Third Heaven.[4] If the ladder of Christian experience reaches, as I suppose it does, to the very presence of God, it has nevertheless its foot in the

---

[1] *Messiah: Fifty...Discourses...on the...scriptural Passages...of the... Oratorio of Handel, 1786.*

[2] Genesis, iii, 24.

[3] See *n*, p. 629.

[4] 2 Corinthians, xii, 2–4.

abyss. And if Paul stood, as no doubt he did in that experience of his to which I have just alluded, on the topmost round of it, I have been standing, and still stand on the lowest, in this 13th year that has passed since I descended. In such a situation of mind, encompassed by the midnight of absolute despair, and a thousand times filled with unspeakable horror, I first commenced an author. Distress drove me to it, and the impossibility of subsisting without some employment still recommends it. I am not indeed so perfectly hopeless as I was, but I am equally in need of an occupation, being often as much and sometimes more worried than ever. I cannot amuse myself as I once could with carpenters' or with gardeners' tools, or with squirrels and guinea-pigs. At that time I was a child, but since it has pleased God whatever else he withholds to restore to me a man's mind, I have put away childish things.[5] Thus far therefore, it is plain that I have not chosen or prescribed to myself my own way, but have been providentially led to it. Perhaps I might say with equal propriety, compelled and scourged into it. For certainly, could I have made my choice, or were I permitted to make it even now, those hours which I spend in poetry, I would spend with God. But it is evidently his will that I should spend them as I do, because every other way of employing them, he himself continues to make impossible. If in the course of such an occupation, or by inevitable consequence of it, either my former connexions are revived, or new ones occur, these things are as much a part of the dispensation as the leading points of it themselves, the effect as much as the cause. If his purposes in thus directing me are gracious, he will take care to prove them such in the issue, and in the meantime will preserve me (for he is as able to do that in one condition of life as in another) from all mistakes in conduct that might prove pernicious to myself, or give unreasonable offence to others. I can say it as truly as it was ever spoken — Here I am, let him do with me as seemeth him good — .

At present, however, I have no connexions, from which either you, I trust, or any who love me and wish me well, have occasion to conceive alarm.[6] Much kindness, indeed, I have experienced at the hands of several, some of them near relations, others not related to me at all; but I do not know that there is among them a single person from whom I am likely to catch contamination. I can say of them all, with more truth than Jacob uttered when he called kid venison, 'The Lord thy God brought them unto me.'[7] I could show you among them two men, whose lives, though they have but little of what we call Evangelical light, are ornaments to a Christian country; men who fear God more than some who even profess to love him. But I will not particularize farther on such a subject. Be they what they may, our situations are so different, and we are likely to meet so seldom, that were they, as they are not, persons even of exceptionable manners, their manners would have little to do with me. We correspond, at present, only on the subject of what passed at Troy three thousand years ago; and they are matters that, if they can do no good, will at least hurt nobody.

Your friendship for me, and the proof that I see of it in your friendly concern for my welfare on this occasion, demanded that I should be explicit. Assure yourself that I love and honour you, as upon all accounts, so especially for the interest that you take, and have ever taken in me and in my welfare, most sincerely. I wish you all happiness in your new abode, all possible success in your ministry, and much fruit of your newly published labours; and am, with Mrs Unwin's love to yourself and Mrs Newton,

> Most affectionately yours, my dear friend,
>
> Wm Cowper

Many thanks for mackerel which we suppose came from you.

TEXT: *Barham Johnson MSS.*†

[6] An Olney neighbour had written to Newton that Cowper was consorting with worldly companions. See pp. 825–27.

[7] Genesis, xxvii, 20.

TO LADY HESKETH

Olney, May 25, 1786

I have at length, my cousin, found my way into my summer abode.[1] I believe that I described it to you some time since, and will therefore now leave it undescribed. I will only say that I am writing in a bandbox, situated, at least in my account, delightfully, because it has a window in one side that opens into that orchard, through which, as I am sitting here, I shall see you often pass, and which therefore I already prefer to all the orchards in the world. You do well to prepare me for all possible delays, because in this life all sorts of disappointments are possible, and I shall do well, if any such delay of your journey should happen, to practise that lesson of patience which you inculcate. But it is a lesson which, even with you for my teacher, I shall be slow to learn. Being sure however that you will not procrastinate without cause, I will make myself as easy as I can about it, and hope the best. To convince you how much I am under discipline and good advice, I will lay aside a favourite measure, influenced in doing so by nothing but the good sense of your contrary opinion. I had set my heart on meeting you at Newport. In my haste to see you once again, I was willing to overlook many awkwardnesses I could not but foresee would attend it. I put them aside so long as I only foresaw them myself, but since I find that you foresee them too, I can no longer deal so slightly with them. It is therefore determined that we meet at Olney. Much I shall feel, but I will not die if I can help it, and I beg that you will take all possible care to outlive it likewise, for I know what it is to be balked in the moment of acquisition, and should be loath to know it again.

Last Monday, in the evening, we walked to Weston,

[1] His summerhouse.

according to our usual custom. It happened, owing to a mistake of time, that we set out half an hour sooner than usual. This mistake we discovered, while we were in the Wilderness. So, finding that we had time before us, as they say, Mrs Unwin proposed that we should go into the village, and take a view of the house that I had just mentioned to you. We did so, and found it such a one as in most respects would suit you well. But Moses Brown our vicar, who, as I told you, is in his eighty-sixth year, is not bound to die for that reason. He said himself, when he was here last summer, that he should live ten years longer, and for aught that appears so he may; in which case, for the sake of its near neighbourhood to us, the vicarage has charms for me, that no other place can rival. But this, and a thousand things more, shall be talked over when you come.

We have been industriously cultivating our acquaintance with our Weston neighbours since I wrote last, and they on their part have been equally diligent in the same cause. I have a notion, that we shall all suit well. I see much in them both that I admire. You know perhaps that they are Catholics.

It is a delightful bundle of praise, my cousin, that you have sent me—all jasmine and lavender. Whoever the lady is, she has evidently an admirable pen, and a cultivated mind. If a person reads, it is no matter in what language; and if the mind be informed, it is no matter whether that mind belongs to a man or a woman: the taste and the judgement will receive the benefit alike in both. Long before *The Task* was published, I made an experiment one day, being in a frolicksome mood, upon my friend—we were walking in the garden, and conversing on a subject similar to these lines—

> The few that pray at all, pray oft amiss,
> And seeking grace to' improve the present good,
> Would urge a wiser suit than asking more.[2]

I repeated them, and said to him with an air of *nonchalance*, 'Do you recollect those lines? I have seen them somewhere, where are they?' He put on a considering face, and after some

[2] A misquotation from *The Task*, VI, p. 516.

deliberation replied—'Oh, I will tell you where they must be—in the *Night Thoughts.*' I was glad my trial turned out so well, and did not undeceive him. I mention this occurrence only in confirmation of the letter-writer's opinion; but at the same time I do assure you, on the faith of an honest man, that I never in my life designed an imitation of Young, or of any other writer; for mimicry is my abhorrence—at least in poetry.

Assure yourself, my dearest cousin, that both for your sake, since you make a point of it, and for my own, I will be as philosophically careful as possible that these fine nerves of mine shall not be beyond measure agitated when you arrive. In truth, there is much greater probability that they will be benefited, and greatly too. Joy of heart, from whatever occasion it may arise, is the best of all nervous medicines; and I should not wonder if such a turn given to my spirits should have even a lasting effect, of the most advantageous kind, upon them. You must not imagine neither, that I am on the whole in any great degree subject to nervous affections. Occasionally I am, and have been these many years, much liable to dejection; but at intervals, and sometimes for an interval of weeks, no creature would suspect it. For I have not that which commonly is a symptom of such a case belonging to me—I mean extraordinary elevation in the absence of Mr Bluedevil. When I am in the best health, my tide of animal sprightliness flows with great equality, so that I am never, at any time, exalted in proportion as I am sometimes depressed. My depression has a cause, and if that cause were to cease, I should be as cheerful thenceforth, and perhaps for ever, as any man need be. But, as I have often said, Mrs Unwin shall be my expositor.

Adieu, my beloved cousin! God grant that our friendship which, while we could see each other, never suffered a moment's interruption, and which so long a separation has not in the least abated, may glow in us to our last hour, and be renewed in a better world, there to be perpetuated for ever!

For you must know that I should not love you half so well, if I did not believe you would be my friend to eternity. There is not room enough for friendship to unfold itself in full bloom, in such a nook of life as this. Therefore I am, and must, and will be,

Yours for ever,

W.C.

TEXT: *Southey*

TO LADY HESKETH

Olney, May 29, 1786

Thou dear, comfortable cousin, whose letters, among all that I receive, have this property peculiarly their own, that I expect them without trembling, and never find anything in them that does not give me pleasure; for which therefore I would take nothing in exchange that the world could give me, save and except that for which I must exchange them soon (and happy shall I be to do so) your own company. That, indeed, is delayed a little too long; to my impatience at least it seems so, who find the spring, backward as it is, too forward, because many of its beauties will have faded before you will have an opportunity to see them. We took our customary walk yesterday in the wilderness at Weston, and saw, with regret, the laburnums, syringas, and guelder-roses, some of them blown, and others just upon the point of blowing, and could not help observing—all these will be gone before Lady Hesketh comes! Still however there will be roses, and jasmine, and honey-suckle, and shady walks, and cool alcoves, and you will partake them with us. But I want you to have a share of every thing that is delightful here, and cannot bear that the advance of the season should steal away a single pleasure before you can come to enjoy it.

Every day I think of you, and almost all the day long; I will venture to say, that even *you* were never so expected in your life. I called last week at the Quaker's to see the furniture of your bed, the fame of which had reached me. It is, I assure you, superb, of printed cotton, and the subject classical. Every morning you will open your eyes on Phaeton kneeling to Apollo, and imploring his father to grant him the conduct of his chariot for a day. May your sleep be as sound as your bed will be sumptuous, and your nights at least will be well provided for.

I shall send up the sixth and seventh books of the *Iliad* shortly, and shall address them to you. You will forward them to the General. I long to show you my workshop, and to see you sitting on the opposite side of my table. We shall be as close packed as two wax figures in an old-fashioned picture frame. I am writing in it now. It is the place in which I fabricate all my verse in summer time. I rose an hour sooner than usual this morning, that I might finish my sheet before breakfast, for I must write this day to the General.

The grass under my windows is all bespangled with dewdrops, and the birds are singing in the apple trees, among the blossoms. Never poet had a more commodious oratory in which to invoke his Muse.

I have made your heart ache too often, my poor dear cousin, with talking about my fits of dejection. Something has happened that has led me to the subject, or I would have mentioned them more sparingly. Do not suppose, or suspect that I treat you with reserve; there is nothing in which I am concerned that you shall not be made acquainted with. But the tale is too long for a letter. I will only add, for your present satisfaction, that the cause is not exterior, that it is not within the reach of human aid, and that yet I have a hope myself, and Mrs Unwin a strong persuasion of its removal. I am indeed even now, and have been for a considerable time, sensible of a change for the better, and expect, with good reason, a comfortable lift from you. Guess then, my beloved cousin, with what wishes I look forward to the time of your arrival, from whose coming I promise myself not only pleasure, but peace of mind—at least an additional share of it. At present it is an uncertain and transient guest with me; but the joy with which I shall see and converse with you at Olney, may perhaps make it an abiding one.

W.C.

TEXT: *Southey*

TO LADY HESKETH

Olney, June 4 and 5, 1786

You say, my dear, that it may perhaps be as well if the coachmaker *should* oblige you to stay in town a week longer than you otherwise would, because there will be time for rain to fall and to refresh and cool the air. But dost not consider that between the 5th and the 15th are 10 days? and that it required only 40 days to drown the world? Assure yourself that there will be time enough for rain between the present moment and that of your departure from Town, should it even take place exactly at the time appointed. The extreme sultriness of the present hour convinces me that a deluge is not far distant.

Ah my cousin! you begin already to fear and quake. What a hero am I compared with you! I have no fears of *you*; on the contrary am as bold as a lion. I wish that your carriage were even now at the door, you should soon see with how much courage I would face you. But what cause have *you* for fear? Am not I your cousin with whom you have wandered in the fields of Freemantle and at Bevis Mount?[1] who used to read to you, to laugh with you, till our sides have ached, at anything or at nothing? And am I in these respects at all altered? You will not find me so; but just as ready to laugh and to wander as you ever knew me. A cloud perhaps may cover me now and then for a few hours, but from clouds I was never exempted. And are not you the identical cousin with whom I have performed all these feats? The very Harriot whom I saw for the first time at de Grey's in Norfolk Street? (It was on a Sunday, when you came with my uncle and aunt to drink tea there, and I had dined there, and was just going back to Westminster.) If these things are so, and I am sure that you cannot gainsay a syllable of them

---

[1] At Southampton.

all, then this consequence follows; that I do not promise myself more pleasure from your company than I shall be sure to find; then you are my cousin in whom I always delighted, and in whom I doubt not that I shall delight even to my latest hour. But this wicked coach-maker has sunk my spirits. What a miserable thing it is to depend in any degree for the accomplishment of a wish and that wish so fervent, on the punctuality of a creature who I suppose was never punctual in his life! Do tell him, my dear, in order to quicken him, that if he performs his promise, he shall make my coach when I want one, and that if he performs it not, I will assuredly employ some other man.

As to the measles, you need not fear them here, either for yourself or for your maidens. And this I say boldly, because I doubt not that I say it truly. Much as I love and wish to see you, if I thought that you would incur the least danger by coming, since you are not sure that you have had them I would beg you by all means to postpone your journey. But our patient has been perfectly recovered these several days, and I know not that they are even in the town at present; let it be considered too that in the country, and especially at this season when windows and doors can be all set open, we soon grow sweet and wholesome. The Throckmortons took off our quarantine so long ago as last Tuesday when they sent a note to invite us to dinner the next day. We went, and a very agreeable day we had. They made no fuss with us which I was heartily glad to see, for where I give trouble I am sure that I cannot be welcome. The dinner was genteel and elegant, but not at all expensive, not more I suppose than they provide when they are alone; for though they are but two their train of domestics seems considerable. Themselves and their chaplain and we, were all the party. After dinner we had much cheerful and pleasant talk, the particulars of which might not perhaps be quite so entertaining upon paper, therefore all but one I will omit, and that I will mention only because it will of itself be sufficient to give you an insight into their opinion on a very important subject, their own religion. I happened to say that in all professions and trades mankind affect an air of mystery. Physicians, I observed, in particular were objects of that remark, who persist in prescribing in Latin, many times no doubt to the hazard of a patient's life through the ignorance of an apothecary. Mr T[hrockmorto]n assented to what I said, and turning to his chaplain, to my infinite surprise observed to him—'*That is just as absurd as our praying in Latin.*'—I could have hugged him for his liberality and freedom from bigotry, but thought it rather more decent to let the matter pass without any visible notice. I therefore heard it with pleasure and kept my pleasure to myself. The two ladies in the meantime were *tête-à-tête* in the drawing-room. Their conversation turned principally (as I afterwards learned from Mrs U.) on a most delightful topic, viz. myself. In the first place, Mrs T[hrockmorto]n admired my book, from which she quoted by heart more than I could repeat though I so lately wrote it.

In short, my dear, I cannot proceed to relate what she said of the book and the book's author for that abominable modesty that I have not even yet got rid of. Let it suffice to say that you who are disposed to love everybody who speaks kindly of your cousin, will certainly love Mrs T[hrockmorto]n when you shall be told what she said of him. And that you *will* be told is equally certain, because it depends on Mrs U. It is a very convenient thing to have a Mrs Unwin, who will tell you many a good and long story for me that I am not able to tell for myself. I am however not at all in arrear to our neighbours in the matter of admiration and esteem, but the more I know the more I like them, and have really an affection for them both.

I am delighted that *The Task* has so large a share of the approbation of your sensible Suffolk friend. This day's post brought a letter from Unwin in which he relates an occurrence almost as flattering. He stepped casually into a bookseller's shop in Bond Street with whom he never had any dealings, when the man thrust *The Task* into his hands supposing that he might not have seen it, enlarging much in commendation of it both to him and to another gentleman who came in. This, being praise voluntary and perfectly unbiassed by any considerations of connexion, I may venture to consider it as an unequivocal token for good. The bookseller doubtless meant to advance his own interest, not mine, who know not who even he was.

I forgot to mention it in the right place, yet because it ought to be mentioned I will do it here; that to Mrs T[hrockmorto]n I am indebted for Mr Wrighte's subscription, who laughingly told Mrs U. that she *made* him subscribe. Some little persuasion was probably requisite, for the productions of poets whether ancient or modern are, I fancy, not very alluring to him.

I am more and more concerned about the poor General. He now tells me that he has a complaint in his gums, which from his account of it, (for he says that it has loosened and will probably cost him all his teeth on one side) I suspect to be nearly related to the disorder that so terribly affects his eye. It is indeed a melancholy case. Oh that God would be pleased to heal him! I am at length almost obliged to despair of seeing him at Olney, after having hoped for it so long. I am thankful my cousin, that you at least have no distempers that threaten to deprive me of the great, great pleasure that I shall have in seeing you. Let me not omit here to say what I ought to have said above, that even if it were possible that the infection might yet cleave to our abode at the end of an whole month, your servants would be in no danger from such a cause. The distance between our respective mansions would effectually secure them from contagion.

We have already laid you in faggots to light your fires, and Mrs U. will this week order in your coals. If flat irons should not be found in the inventory, Mrs U. has some, and hers are yours; it will be easy to prevent a coincidence of washing times. We will if possible procure an inventory tomorrow. Any kind of tooth-brushes in the world, if they be but hard, will do as well as the Chinese. We hope that your beer will prove very good. According to the allowance of malt it ought to be so, and our brewer is a master of his art. You are already provided with butcher, baker, brewer, maltster and washerwoman, who are each in their kind the best in the town, and from whom you will have no need to fear the least imposition. Add to these a butterwoman, and your economical system must needs appear complete. Newport is exactly 5 miles from

Olney; two of them are turnpike, and 3 not, but all good. Mrs Scott had a mangle, but mangle we have none at Olney now. The review of my *Task* is announced in this last *Monthly Review* as designed for insertion in the next. You will read it I trust, with us.

I received yesterday from the General another letter of T. S.[2] An unknown auxiliary having started up in my behalf, I believe I shall leave the business of answering it to him, having no leisure myself for controversy. He lies very open to a very effectual reply.

As a cart can be so easily procured in your neighbourhood you will certainly find it less troublesome to hire such a one. What monster can he be who has spoiled your teeth that were in all respects so perfect? But I suspend my faith *sur cette article là*, till I shall see you.

My dearest cousin, adieu! I hope to write to you but once more before we meet. But oh! this coachmaker, and oh! this holiday week!

Yours, with impatient desire to see you,

Wm. Cowper

TEXT: *MSS. Cowper Museum, Olney**

TO LADY HESKETH

June 12, 1786

I am neither young nor superannuated, yet am I a child. When I had read your letter I grumbled—not at you, my dearest cousin, for you are in no fault, but at the whole generation of coach-makers, as you may suppose, and at yours in particular. I foresaw and foreknew that he would fail in his promise, and yet was disappointed; was, in truth, no more prepared for what I expected with so much reason, than

---

[2] The initials of a correspondent who had attacked C.'s *Proposals for a New Translation of Homer* in the *Public Advertiser*.

if I had not at all expected it. I grumbled till we went to dinner, and at intervals till we had dined; and when dinner was over, with very little encouragement, I could actually have cried. And if I had, I should in truth have thought them tears as well bestowed as most that I have shed for many years. At first I numbered months, then weeks, then days, and was just beginning to number hours, and now I am thrown back to days again. My first speech was, after folding up your letter (for I will honestly tell you all) I am crazed with Mondays, Tuesdays, and Wednesdays, and St Albans, and Totteridge, and Hadley. When is she to set out?—When is she to be here? Do tell me, for perhaps you understand it better than I. Why, says Mrs Unwin (with much more composure in her air than properly belonged to her, for she also had her feelings on the occasion) she sets out tomorrow se'nnight, and will be here on the Wednesday after. And who knows that? replied I; will the coach-maker be at all more punctual in repairing the old carriage, than in making the new one? For my part, I have no hope of seeing her this month; and if it be possible, I will not think of it, lest I should be again disappointed. And to say the truth, my dear, though hours have passed since thus I said, and I have had time for cooler consideration, the suspicion still sticks close to me, that more delays may happen. A philosopher would prepare himself for such an event, but I am no philosopher, at least when the comfort of seeing you is in question. I believe in my heart that there have been just as many true philosophers upon earth, as there have been men that have had little or no feeling, and not one more. Swift truly says—

> Indifference clad in reason's guise,
> All want of fortitude supplies.[1]

When I wake in the night, I feel my spirits the lighter because you are coming. When I am not at Troy, I am either occupied in the recollection of a thousand passages of my past life,

[1] 'Indifference Clad in Wisdom's Guise,
   All Fortitude of Mind supplies.'
   —Lines on the Death of Dr Swift.

in which you were a partaker with me, or conversing about you with Mrs Unwin. Thus my days and nights have been spent principally ever since you determined upon this journey, and especially, and almost without interruption from any other subject, since the time of your journey has seemed near at hand. While I despaired, as I did for many years, that I should ever see you more, I thought of you indeed, and often, but with less solicitude. I used to say to myself: Providence has so ordered it, and it is my duty to submit. He has cast me at a distance from her, and from all whom I once knew. He did it, and not I; it is He who has chosen my situation for me. Have I not reason to be thankful that, since he designed me to pass a part of my life, and no inconsiderable one neither, in a state of the deepest melancholy, he appointed me a friend in Mrs Unwin, who should share all my sorrows with me, and watch over me in my helpless condition, night and day? What, and where had I been without her? Such considerations were sufficient to reconcile me at that time to perpetual separation even from you, because perpetual I supposed it must be, and without remedy. But now every hour of your absence seems long, for this very natural reason, because the same Providence has given me a hope that you will be present with me soon. A good that seems at an immeasurable distance, and that we cannot hope to reach, has therefore the less influence on our affections. But the same good brought nearer, made to appear practicable, promised to our hopes, and almost in possession, engages all our faculties and desires. All this is according to the natural and necessary course of things in the human heart; and the philosophy that would interfere with it, is folly at least, if not frenzy. A throne has at present but little sensible attraction for me. And why? Perhaps only because I know that should I break my heart with wishes for a throne, I should never reach one. But did I know assuredly that I should put on a crown to-morrow, perhaps I too should feel ambition, and account the interposing night tedious. The sum of the whole matter, my dear, is this: that this villainous coach-maker has mortified me monstrously, and that I tremble lest he should do so again. From you I have no fears. I see in your letter, and all the way through it, what pains you take to assure me and give me comfort. I am and will be comforted for that very reason; and will wait still other ten days with all the patience that I can muster. You, I know, will be punctual if you can, and that at least is matter of real consolation.

I approve altogether, my cousin beloved, of your sending your goods to the waggon on Saturday, and cookee by the coach on Tuesday. She will be here perhaps by four in the afternoon, at the latest by five, and will have quite time enough to find out all the cupboards and shelves in her department before you arrive. But I declare and protest that cookee shall sleep that night at our house, and get her breakfast here next morning. You will break her heart, child, if you send her into a strange house where she will find nothing that has life but the curate, who has not much neither. Servant he keeps none. A woman makes his bed, and after a fashion as they say, dresses his dinner, and then leaves him to his lucubrations. I do therefore insist on it, and so does Mrs Unwin, that cookee shall be our guest for that time; and from this we will not depart. I tell thee besides, that I shall be more glad to see her, than ever I was in my life to see one whom I never saw before. Guess why, if you can.

You must number your miles fifty-six instead of fifty-four. The fifty-sixth mile ends but a few yards beyond the vicarage. Soon after you shall have entered Olney, you will find an opening on your right hand. It is a lane that leads to your dwelling. There your coach may stop and set down Mrs Eaton; when she has walked about forty yards she will spy a green gate and rails on her left hand; and when she has opened the gate and reached the house-door, she will find herself at home. But we have another manœuvre to play off upon you, and in which we positively will not be opposed, or if we are, it shall be to no purpose. I have an honest fellow that works in my garden, his name is Kitchener, and we call him Kitch for brevity. He is sober, and as trusty as the day. He has a smart blue coat, that when I had worn it some years, I gave him, and he has now worn it some years himself. I shall set him on horseback, and order him to the Swan at Newport, there to wait your arrival, and if you should not stop at that place, as perhaps you may not, immediately to throw himself into your suite, and to officiate as your guide. For though the way from Newport hither is short, there are turnings that might puzzle your coachman; and he will be of use too, in conducting you to our house, which otherwise you might not easily find, partly through the stupidity of those of whom you might inquire, and partly from its out-of-the-way situation. My brother drove up and down Olney in quest of us, almost as often as you up and down Chancery Lane in quest of the Madans, with fifty boys and girls at his tail, before he could find us. The first man, therefore, you shall see in a blue coat with white buttons, in the famous town of Newport, cry Kitch! He will immediately answer, My Lady! and from that moment you are sure not to be lost.

Your house shall be as clean as scrubbing and dry-rubbing can make it, and in all respects fit to receive you. My friend the Quaker, in all that I have seen of his doings, has acquitted himself much to my satisfaction. Some little things, he says, will perhaps be missing at first, in such a multiplicity, but they shall be produced as soon as called for. Mrs U. has bought you six ducks, and is fatting them for you. She has also rummaged up a coop that will hold six chickens, and designs to people it for you by the first opportunity; for these things are not to be got fit for the table at Olney. Thus, my dear, are all things in the best train possible, and nothing remains but that you come and show yourself. Oh, that moment! Shall we not both enjoy it?—That we shall.

I have received an anonymous complimentary Pindaric Ode from a little poet who calls himself a school-boy. I send you the first stanza by way of specimen. You shall see it all soon.

TO WM COWPER, OF THE INNER TEMPLE, ESQ

ON HIS POEMS IN THE SECOND VOLUME

In what high strains, my Muse, wilt thou
Attempt great Cowper's worth to show?
Pindaric strains shall tune the lyre,
And 'twould require
A Pindar's fire

To sing great Cowper's worth,
The lofty bard, delightful sage,
Ever the wonder of the age,
And *blessing to the earth*.

Adieu, my precious cousin, your lofty bard and delightful
sage expects you with all possible affection.—Ever yours,

Wm Cowper

I am truly sorry for your poor friend Burrows!

Our dinner hour is four o'clock. We will not surfeit you
with delicacies; of that be assured. I know your palate, and
am glad to know that it is easily pleased. Were it other than it
is, it would stand but a poor chance to be gratified at Olney. I
undertake for lettuce and cucumber, and Mrs U. for all the
rest. If she feeds you too well, you must humble her.

TEXT: *Southey*

TO EARL COWPER[1]

Olney, [?] *June 27, 1786*

My Lord,

Unknown as I am to your Lordship, except by the kind
mention of my friends, and especially of my dear cousin Lady
Hesketh, I should yet have been happy could I have found a
fair and warrantable pretext for writing to congratulate your
safe arrival in England. Your Lordship's great kindness to
me, the news of which arrived here yesterday in a letter from
Henry Cowper,[2] not only gives propriety to my congratula-
tions now, but even makes it necessary that I should not omit
them. I beg therefore that you will have the goodness to
accept both them, and the unfeigned thanks that I owe you

---

[1] George Nassau, 3rd Earl Cowper (1738–89), of Cole Green, Herts.

[2] Henry Cowper (1758–1840), Clerk Assistant of the House of Lords.
He was the son of Lt-Gen. Spencer Cowper and married Maria, daughter
of Major William and Maria Cowper.

for having doubled what you so liberally contributed before to the support of one whom you never saw. I can only assure your Lordship in return that you have not conferred this favour on a person insensible of your great generosity, or who will prove ungrateful.

Lady Hesketh, who is come to brighten the obscurest nook in the world with her presence, and to make me happy who have known and loved her from her childhood, but who had not seen her, till she arrived here last week, these 20 years, begs to be affectionately remembered to your Lordship, and adds her own thanks to mine on this occasion; for she deeply interests herself in all the good that befalls me.

Most sincerely wishing your Lordship all possible happiness, I remain your Lordship's

Most obliged and obedient humble servant

Wm Cowper

TEXT: *Panshanger MSS.*** This letter is dated 'July 27, 1786' in C.'s hand; the postmark and cover are missing. It states that Lady Hesketh has been in Olney for a week. Other, postmarked, letters show that she had arrived on or about June 19th. I therefore conjecture that that C. wrote 'July' in error.

TO THE REV. WILLIAM UNWIN

Olney, July 3, 1786

My dear William,

After long silence I begin again. A day given to my friends is a day taken from Homer, but to such an interruption now and then occurring, I have no objection. Lady Hesketh is as you observe arrived, and has been with us near a fortnight. She pleases every body, and is pleased in her turn with every thing she finds at Olney; is always cheerful and sweet-tempered, and knows no pleasure equal to that of communicating pleasure to us and to all around her. This disposition in her is the more comfortable, because it is not the humour of the day,

820

a sudden flush of benevolence and good spirits occasioned merely by a change of scene; but it is her natural turn and has governed all her conduct ever since I knew her first. We are consequently happy in her society, and shall be happier still to have you to partake with us in our joy. I can now assure you that her complexion is not at all indebted to art, having seen a hundred times the most convincing proof of its authenticity; her colour fading and glowing again alternately, as the weather or her own temperature have happened to affect it, while she has been sitting before me. — I am fond of the sound of bells, but was never more pleased with those of Olney than when they rang her into her new habitation. It is a compliment that our performers upon those instruments have never paid to any other personage (Ld Dartmouth excepted) since we knew the town. In short she is, as she ever was, my pride and my joy, and I am delighted with every thing that means to do her honour. — Her first appearance was too much for me. My spirits, instead of being greatly raised as I had inadvertently supposed they would be, broke down with me under the pressure of too much joy, and left me flat, or rather melancholy throughout the day to a degree that was mortifying to myself and alarming to her. But I have made amends for this failure since, and in point of cheerfulness have far exceeded her expectations; for she knew that sable had been my suit for many years.

And now I shall communicate intelligence that will give you pleasure. When you first contemplated the front of our abode, you were shocked. In your eyes it had the appearance of a prison, and you sighed at the thought that your mother dwelt in it. Your view of it was not only just, but even prophetic. It not only had the aspect of a place built for purposes of incarceration, but has actually served that purpose through a long, long period, and we have been the prisoners. But a gaol-delivery is at hand. The bolts and bars are to be loosed, and we shall escape. A very different mansion[1] both in point of appearance and accommodation expects us, and the expense of living in it not greater than we are subjected

[1] The Lodge, Weston Underwood.

to in this. It is situated at Weston, one of the prettiest villages in England, and belongs to Mr Throckmorton. We all three dine with him to-day by invitation, and shall survey it in the afternoon, point out the necessary repairs, and finally adjust the treaty. I have my cousin's promise that she will never let another year pass without a visit to us; and the house is large enough to contain us and our suite, and her also, with as many of hers as she shall choose to bring. The change will I hope prove advantageous both to your mother and me in all respects. Here we have no neighbourhood, there we shall have most agreeable neighbours in the Throck[morto]ns. Here we have a bad air in the winter, impregnated with the fishy-smelling fumes of the marsh miasma; there we shall breathe in an atmosphere untainted. Here, we are confined from September to March, and sometimes longer; there we shall be upon the very verge of pleasure-grounds in which we can always ramble, and shall not wade through almost impassable dirt to get at them. Both your mother's constitution and mine have suffered materially by such close and long confinement, and it is high time, unless we intended to retreat into the grave, that we should seek out a more wholesome residence. A pretty deal of new furniture will be wanted, especially chairs and beds, all which my kind cousin will provide, and fit up a parlour and a chamber for herself into the bargain. — So far is well, the rest is left to heaven.

I have hardly left myself room for an answer to your queries concerning my friend John & his studies. What the supplement of Hirtius[2] is made of, I know not. We did not read it at Westminster. I should imagine it might be dispensed with. I should recommend the *Civil War* of Cæsar, because he wrote it, who ranks I believe as the best writer as well as soldier of his day. There are books (I know not what they are but you do and can easily find them) that will inform him clearly of both the civil and military management of the Romans, the several officers, I mean, in both departments, and what was the peculiar province of each. The study of

---

[2] The 8th book of Caesar's *De Bello Gallico* is attributed to one of his generals, Aulus Hirtius.

some such book would, I should think, prove a good introduction to that of Livy, unless you have a Livy with notes to that effect. A want of intelligence in those points has heretofore made the Roman history very dark and difficult to me; therefore I thus advise.

Our love is with all your lovelies both great and small,

Yours, W.C.

TEXT: *BM. Add. MSS.* 24,155

TO THE REV. WILLIAM UNWIN

Olney, July 10, 1786

My dear William,

Having risen somewhat earlier than has been usual with me of late, and finding myself, in consequence of it, in possession of a vacant half-hour, I devote it, notwithstanding the indulgence granted me to be silent, to you, and the rather, because I have other good news to add to that which has already given you so much pleasure, and am unwilling that a friend who interests himself so much in my well-being should wait longer than is absolutely necessary for his share of my joy.

Within this twelvemonth my income has received an addition of a clear £100 per annum. For a considerable part of it I am indebted to my dear cousin now on the other side of the orchard. At Florence, she obtained me twenty pounds a year from Lord Cowper; since he came home she has recommended me with such good effect to his notice that he has added 20 more, 20 she has added herself, and 10 she has procured me from the William of my name whom you saw at Hertingfordbury. From my anonymous friend, who insists on not being known or guessed at, and never shall be by me, I have an annuity of £50.—All these sums have accrued within this year except the first, making together as you perceive an exact century of pounds annually poured into the replenished purse of your once poor poet of Olney. Is it possible to love such a cousin too much, who so punctually fulfils her promise that she made me at the first revival of our correspondence, to make it the chief comfort of her life to promote, as much as possible, mine?

The more I see of the Throckmortons the more I like them. He is the most accomplished man of his years that I remember to have seen, is always sensible in conversation and kind in his behaviour, and conducts himself handsomely and unexceptionably in the business of landlord and tenant. She is cheerful and good-natured to the last degree, and is, as you suppose, a niece of Lord Petre's.

Since we dined with them, I have dined with Lady H[esketh] at Gayhurst. It happened, and it hurt us all, the Throckmortons as well as ourselves, that your mother was not asked, consequently did not go. At first I was doubtful whether I would go myself, but thinking it the part of charity to suppose that obscurely as we have lived at Olney, a family 5 miles distant might not know that she existed, I went. To-day your mother will meet Mrs Wrighte at dinner at Lady H.'s and it will consequently no longer be a secret to said Mrs Wrighte that there is such a person as Mrs Unwin. We shall then see whether I am ever to visit again at Gayhurst or not.

Your mother's love with mine attends you all. She wishes that the fish may come on Thursday, else it must be eaten on Sunday, which is the only day when the trio do not meet.

I am summoned to breakfast.

Yours my dear William,

W.C.

We long for the 18th.

July 11. Your mother has been asked to Gayhurst, and will be of the party the next time we go. Lady H. sends her compliments; nobody now stands so fair as yourself for her chaplainship, you need only come and enter immediately on your office.

TEXT: *BM. Add. MSS.* 24,155

TO THE REV. WILLIAM UNWIN

Olney, Septbr. 24, 1786

My dear William,

So interesting a concern as your tutorship of the young gentleman in question cannot have been so long in a state of indecision, without costing you much anxiety. We have sympathized with you under it all, but are glad to be informed that the long delay is not chargeable upon Mr Hornby. Bishops are κακα θηρια, γαστερες ἀργοι.[1]— You have heard, I know, from Lady H[esketh,] and she has exculpated me from all imputation of wilful silence, from which indeed of yourself you are so good as to discharge me, in consideration of my present almost endless labour. I have nothing to say in particular on the subject of Homer, except that I am daily advancing in the work, with all the dispatch that a due concern for my own credit in the result, will allow.

You have had your troubles, and we, ours. This day three weeks your mother received a letter from Mr Newton, which she has not yet answered, nor is likely to answer hereafter. It gave us both much concern, but her more than me; I suppose, because my mind being necessarily occupied in my work, I had not so much leisure to browse upon the wormwood that it contained. The purport of it is a direct accusation of me, and of her an accusation implied, that we have both deviated into forbidden paths, and lead a life unbecoming the Gospel. That many of my friends in London are grieved, and the simple people of Olney, astonished. That he never so much doubted of my restoration to Christian privileges as now. In short, that I converse too much with people of the world, and find too much pleasure in doing so. He concludes with putting your mother in mind that there is still an intercourse between London and Olney; by which he means to insinuate that we cannot offend against the decorum that we are bound

---

[1] 'Evil beasts, idle bellies.'

to observe, but the news of it will most certainly be conveyed to him. We do not at all doubt it. We never knew a lie hatched at Olney that waited long for a bearer, and though we do not wonder to find ourselves made the subjects of false accusation in a place ever fruitful in such productions, we do and must wonder a little, that he should listen to them with so much credulity. I say this, because if he had heard only the truth, or had believed no more than the truth, he would not, I think, have found either me censurable or your mother. And that *she* should be suspected of irregularities is the more wonderful (for wonderful it would be at any rate) because she sent him, not long before, a letter conceived in such strains of piety and spirituality, as ought to have convinced him that she at least was no wanderer. But what is the fact, and how do we spend our [time] in reality? What are the deeds for which we have been represented as thus criminal? Our present course of life differs in nothing from that which we have both held these thirteen years, except that after great civilities shown us and many advances made on the part of the Throcks, we visit them. That we visit also at Gayhurst; that we have frequently taken airings with my cousin in her carriage; and that I have sometimes taken a walk with her on a Sunday evening, and sometimes by myself, which however your mother has never done. These are the only novelties in our practice, and if by these procedures so inoffensive in themselves, we yet give offence, offence must needs be given. God and our own consciences acquit us, and we acknowledge no other judges.

The two families with whom we have kicked up this astonishing intercourse are as harmless in their conversation and manners as can be found anywhere. And as to my poor cousin, the only crime that she is guilty of against the people of Olney is, that she has fed the hungry, clothed the naked, and administered comfort to the sick. Except indeed that by her great kindness, she has given us a little lift in point of condition and circumstances, and has thereby excited envy in some who have not the knack of rejoicing in the prosperity of others. And this I take to be the root of the matter.

My dear William, I do not know that I should have teased your nerves and spirits with this disagreeable theme, had not

Mr Newton talked of applying to you for particulars. He would have done it, he says, when he saw you last, but had not time. You are now qualified to inform him as minutely as we ourselves could of all our enormities. Adieu!

Our sincerest love to yourself and yours,

Wm C.

TEXT: *BM. Add. MSS.* 24,155

TO THE REV. JOHN NEWTON

Olney, Sepr. 30, 1786

My dear friend,

No length of separation will ever make us indifferent either to your pleasures or your pains. We rejoice that you have had so agreeable a jaunt, and (excepting Mrs Newton's terrible fall, from which, however, we are happy to find that she received so little injury) a safe return. We, who live always encompassed by rural scenery, can afford to be stationary; though we ourselves, were I not too closely engaged with Homer, should perhaps follow your example, and seek a little refreshment from variety and change of place, a course that we might find not only agreeable, but, after a sameness of 13 years, perhaps useful. You must undoubtedly have found your excursion beneficial, who at all other times endure, if not so close a confinement as we, yet a more unhealthy one, in city air and in the centre of continual engagements.

Your letter to Mrs Unwin, concerning our conduct and the offence taken at it in our neighbourhood, gave us both a great deal of concern; and she is still deeply affected by it. Of this you may assure yourself, that if our friends in London have been grieved, they have been misinformed; which is the more probable, because the bearers of intelligence hence to London are not always very scrupulous concerning the truth of their reports; and that if any of our serious neighbours have been astonished, they have been so without the smallest real occasion. Poor people are never well employed even when they judge one another; but when they undertake to scan the motives and estimate the behaviour of those whom Providence has exalted a little above them, they are utterly out of their province and their depth. They often see us get into Lady Hesketh's carriage, and rather uncharitably suppose that it always carries us into a scene of dissipation, which in fact it never does. We visit, indeed, at Mr Throckmorton's, and at Gayhurst; rarely, however, at Gayhurst, on account of the greater distance: more frequently, though not very frequently, at Weston, both because it is nearer, and because our business in the house that is making ready for us often calls us that way. The rest of our journeys are to Beaujeat turnpike and back again; or, perhaps, to the cabinet-maker's at Newport. As Othello says,

> The very butt and forehead of th'offence
> Hath this, no more.

What good we can get, or can do in these visits, is another question, which they, I am sure, are not at all qualified to solve. Of this we are both sure, that under the guidance of Providence we have formed these connexions; that we should have hurt the Christian cause, rather than have served it, by a prudish abstinence from them; and that St Paul himself, conducted to them as we have been, would have found it expedient to have done as we have done. It is always impossible to conjecture, to much purpose, from the beginnings of a providence, in what it will terminate. If we have neither received nor communicated any spiritual good at present, while conversant with our new acquaintance, at least no harm has befallen on either side; and it were too hazardous an assertion even for our censorious neighbours to make, that because the cause of the Gospel does not appear to have been served at present, therefore it never can be in any future intercourse that we may have with them. In the mean time I speak a strict truth, and as in the sight of God, when I say that we are neither of us at all more addicted to gadding than before. We both naturally love seclusion from company, and never go into it without putting a force upon our disposition. At the same time I will confess, and you will easily conceive, that the melancholy, incident to such close confinement as we have so long endured, finds itself a little relieved by such amusements as a society so innocent affords. You may look round the Christian world, and find few, I believe, of our station, who have so little intercourse as we with the world that is not Christian.

We place all the uneasiness that you have felt for us upon this subject to the account of that cordial friendship of which you have long given us proof. But you may be assured, that notwithstanding all rumours to the contrary, we are exactly what we were when you saw us last—I, miserable on account of God's departure from me, which I believe to be final; and she, seeking his return to me, in the path of duty and by continual prayer.

The soles which Mrs Newton was so kind as to order were transformed into an excellent turbot. She has our thanks; and our sincere love attends you both.

Yours my dear friend,

Wm Cowper

TEXT: *Barham Johnson MSS.*†

TO THE REV. JOHN NEWTON

Weston, Nov. 17, 1786

My dear friend,

My usual time of answering your letters having been unavoidably engrossed by occasions that would not be thrust aside, I have been obliged to postpone the payment of my debt for a whole week. Even now it is not without some difficulty that I discharge it; which you will easily believe, when I tell you that this is only the second day that has seen us inhabitants of our new abode. When God speaks to a chaos, it becomes a scene of order and harmony in a moment; but when his creatures have thrown one house into confusion by leaving it, and another by tumbling themselves and their goods into it, not less than many days' labour and contrivance is necessary to give them their proper places. And it belongs to furniture of all kinds, however convenient it may be in its place, to be a nuisance out of it. We find ourselves here in a comfortable dwelling. Such it is in itself; and my cousin, who has spared no expense in dressing it up for us, has made it a genteel one. Such at least it will be, when its contents are a little harmonized. She left us on Tuesday, and on Wednesday in the evening Mrs Unwin and I took possession. I could not help giving a last look to my old prison, and its precincts, and though I cannot easily account for it, having been miserable there so many years, felt something like a heart-ache when I took my last leave of the scene, that certainly in itself had nothing to engage affection. But I recollected that I had once been happy there, and could not without tears in my eyes bid adieu to a place in which God had so often found me.

The human mind is a great mystery; mine, at least, appeared to me to be such upon this occasion. I found that I not only had a tenderness for that ruinous abode, because it had once known me happy in the presence of God, but that even the distress I had suffered for so long a time on account of his absence, had endeared it to me as much. I was weary of every object; had long wished for a change, yet could not take leave without a pang at parting. What consequences are to attend our removal, God only knows. I know well that it is not in situation to effect the cure of melancholy like mine. The change, however, has been entirely providential; for much as I wished it, I never uttered that wish, except to Mrs Unwin. When I learned that the house was to be let, and had seen it, I had a strong desire that Lady Hesketh should take it for herself, if she should happen to like the country. That desire, indeed, is not exactly fulfilled; and yet, upon the whole, is exceeded. We are the tenants; but she assures us that we shall often have her for a guest; and here is room enough for us all. You, I hope, my dear friend, and Mrs Newton, will want no assurances to convince you that you will always be received here with the sincerest welcome. More welcome than you have been, you cannot be; but better accommodated you may and will be.

I have not proceeded thus far without many interruptions, and though my paper is small, shall be obliged to make my letter still smaller. Our own removal is I believe the only news of Olney. Concerning this you will hear much, and much I doubt not that will have no truth in it. It is already reported there, and has been indeed for some time, that I am turned Papist. You will know how to treat a lie like this which proves nothing but the malignity of its author. But other tales you may possibly hear that will not so readily refute themselves. This, however, I trust you will always find true, that neither Mrs Unwin nor myself shall have so conducted ourselves in our new neighbourhood, as that you shall have any occasion to be grieved on our account.

Mr Unwin has been ill of a fever at Winchester,[1] but by a letter from Mr Thornton we learn that he is recovering, and hopes soon to travel. His Mrs Unwin has joined him at that place.

Adieu, my dear friend. Mrs Unwin's affectionate remembrances and mine conclude me ever yours,

Wm Cowper

TEXT: *Barham Johnson MSS.*†

TO LADY HESKETH

The Lodge, Dec. 4, 1786

I sent you, my dear, a melancholy letter, and I do not know that I shall now send you one very unlike it. Not that anything occurs in consequence of our late loss more afflictive than was to be expected, but the mind does not perfectly recover its tone after a shock like that which has been felt so lately. This I observe, that though my experience has long since

---

[1] Where he died on November 29th

taught me, that this world is a world of shadows, and that it is the more prudent, as well as the more Christian course to possess the comforts that we find in it, as if we possessed them not, it is no easy matter to reduce this doctrine into practice. We forget that that God who gave them, may, when he pleases, take them away; and that perhaps it may please him to take them at a time when we least expect, or are least disposed to part from them. Thus it has happened in the present case. There never was a moment in Unwin's life, when there seemed to be more urgent want of him than the moment in which he died. He had attained to an age when, if they are at any time useful, men become useful to their families, their friends, and the world. His parish began to feel, and to be sensible of the advantages of his ministry. The clergy around him were many of them awed by his example. His children were thriving under his own tuition and management, and his eldest boy is likely to feel his loss severely, being by his years in some respect qualified to understand the value of such a parent; by his literary proficiency too clever for a schoolboy, and too young at the same time for the university. The removal of a man in the prime of life of such a character, and with such connexions, seems to make a void in society that can never be filled. God seemed to have made him just what he was, that he might be a blessing to others, and when the influence of his character and abilities began to be felt, removed him. These are mysteries, my dear, that we cannot contemplate without astonishment, but which will nevertheless be explained hereafter, and must in the mean time be revered in silence. It is well for his mother, that she has spent her life in the practice of an habitual acquiescence in the dispensations of Providence, else I know that this stroke would have been heavier, after all that she has suffered upon another account, than she could have borne. She derives, as she well may, great consolation from the thought that he lived the life, and died the death of a Christian. The consequence is, if possible, more unavoidable than the most mathematical conclusion, that therefore he is happy. So farewell, my friend Unwin! the first man for whom I conceived a friendship after my removal from St Albans, and for whom I cannot but still continue to feel a friendship, though I shall see thee with these eyes no more.

W.C.

TEXT: *Southey*

TO JOSEPH HILL

Weston Underwood, near Olney
Decr. 9, 1786

My dear friend,

You will think perhaps that I draw for money with a nimbleness and vivacity rather alarming, considering how lately I received your last remittances, but I find that whatever may be the case with a translation of Homer, a translation of person and property from one place to another is an expensive business. I have this day drawn on you for £20 payable at sight to Maurice Smith or order.

We had just begun to enjoy the pleasantness of our new situation, to find at least as much comfort in it as the season of the year would permit, when affliction found us out in our retreat, and the news reached us of the death of Mr Unwin. He had taken a western tour with Mr Henry Thornton, and in his return was seized at Winchester with a putrid fever which sent him to his grave. He is gone to it however, though young, as fit for it as age itself could have made him. Regretted indeed, and always to be regretted by those who knew him, for he had everything that makes a man valuable, both in his principles and in his manners, but leaving still this consolation to his surviving friends, that he was desirable in this world chiefly because he was so well prepared for a better.

I find myself, here, situated exactly to my mind. Weston is one of the prettiest villages in England, and the walks about it, at all seasons of the year, delightful. I know that you will rejoice with me in the change that I have made, and for which I am altogether indebted to Lady Hesketh. It is a change as great, as to compare metropolitan things with rural, from St Giles's to Grosvenor Square. Our house is in all respects commodious, and in some, elegant; and I cannot give you a better idea of that which we have left, than by telling you that the present candidates for it are a publican and a shoe-maker.

I am in no immediate want of them, but shall be obliged to you if you will send at your leisure Elliott's ointment and the dark-coloured eye-water.

With my affectionate respects to Mrs Hill,

I am, my dear friend, faithfully yours,

Wm Cowper

TEXT: *Cowper Johnson MSS.*

TO LADY HESKETH

Weston, Dec. 21, 1786

Your welcome letter, my beloved cousin, which ought by the date to have arrived on Sunday, being by some untoward accident delayed, came not till yesterday. It came however, and has relieved me from a thousand distressing apprehensions on your account.

The dew of your intelligence has refreshed my poetical laurels. A little praise now and then is very good for your hard-working poet, who is apt to grow languid, and perhaps careless without it. Praise I find affects us as money does. The more a man gets of it, with the more vigilance he watches over and preserves it. Such at least is its effect on me, and you may assure yourself that I will never lose a mite of it for want of care.

I have already invited the good Padre[1] in general terms, and

[1] The Rev. William Gregson, R.C. chaplain to the Throckmortons; 'pauperum medicus et amicus', according to a tablet in Weston church. He died in 1800, aged 68.

he shall positively dine here next week, whether he will or not. I do not at all suspect that his kindness to Protestants has anything insidious in it, any more than I suspect that he transcribes Homer for me with a view for my conversion. He would find me a tough piece of business I can tell him; for when I had no religion at all, I had yet a terrible dread of the Pope. How much more now!

I should have sent you a longer letter, but was obliged to devote my last evening to the melancholy employment of composing a Latin inscription for the tomb-stone of poor William, two copies of which I wrote out and enclosed, one to Henry Thornton,[2] and one to Mr Newton. Homer stands by me biting his thumbs, and swears that if I do not leave off directly, he will choke me with bristly Greek that shall stick in my throat for ever.

W.C.

TEXT: *Southey*

TO LADY HESKETH

The Lodge, Dec. 24, 1786

You must by no means, my dearest coz, pursue the plan that has suggested itself to you on the supposed loss of your letter. In the first place I choose that my Sundays, like the Sundays of other people, shall be distinguished by something that shall make me look forward to them with agreeable expectation, and for that reason desire that they may always bring me a letter from you. In the next place, if I know when to *expect* a letter, I know likewise when to *enquire after* a letter, if it happens not to come: a circumstance of some importance, considering how excessively careless they are at

[2] Henry Thornton, son of John Thornton (and great-grandfather of Mr E. M. Forster); banker, M.P. and philanthropist. The ally and friend of Wilberforce and Pitt, he was a leader of the anti-slavery movement and the chief organizer of the colony for liberated slaves, Sierra Leone.

the Swan, where letters are sometimes overlooked, and do not arrive at their destination, if no inquiry be made, till some days have passed after their arrival at Olney. It has happened frequently to me to receive a letter long after all the rest have been delivered, and the Padre assured me that Mr Throckmorton has sent notes three several times to Mrs Marriot,[1] complaining of this neglect. For these reasons, my dear, thou must write still on Saturdays, and as often on other days as thou pleasest.

The screens came safe, and one of them is at this moment interposed between me and the fire, much to the comfort of my peepers. The other of them being fitted up with a screw that was useless, I have consigned to proper hands, that it may be made as serviceable as its brother. They are very neat, and I account them a great acquisition. Our carpenter assures me that the lameness of the chairs was not owing to any injury received in their journey, but that the maker never properly finished them. They were not high when they came, and in order to reduce them to a level, we have lowered them an inch. Thou knowest, child, that the short foot could not be lengthened, for which reason we shortened the long ones. The box containing the plate and the brooms reached us yesterday, and nothing had suffered the least damage by the way. Every thing is smart, every thing is elegant, and we admire them all. The short candlesticks are short enough. I am now writing with those upon the table; Mrs U. is reading opposite, and they suit us both exactly. With the money that you have in hand, you may purchase, my dear, at your most convenient time, a tea-urn; that which we have at present having never been handsome, and being now old and patched. A parson once, as he walked across the parlour, pushed it down with his belly, and it never perfectly recovered itself. We want likewise a tea-waiter, meaning, if you please, such a one as you may remember to have seen at the Hall, a wooden one. To which you may add, from the same fund, three or four yards of yard-wide muslin, wherewithal to make neck-cloths for my worship. If after all these disbursements any

---

[1] The postmistress.

thing should be left in the bottom of the purse, we shall be obliged to you if you will expend it in the purchase of silk pocket-handkerchiefs. There, my precious—I think I have charged thee with commissions in plenty.

You neither must nor shall deny us the pleasure of sending to you such small matters as we do. As to the partridges, you may recollect possibly, when I remind you of it, that I never eat them; they refuse to pass my stomach; and Mrs Unwin rejoiced in receiving them only because she could pack them away to you—therefore never lay us under any embargoes of this kind, for I tell you beforehand, that we are both incorrigible. My beloved cousin, the first thing I open my eyes upon in a morning, is it not the bed in which you have laid me? Did you not, in our old dismal parlour at Olney, give me the tea on which I breakfast?—the chocolate that I drink at noon, and the table at which I dine?—the every thing, in short, that I possess in the shape of convenience, is it not all from you? and is it possible, think you, that we should either of us overlook an opportunity of making such a tiny acknowledgement of your kindness? Assure yourself that never, while my name is Giles Gingerbread,[2] will I dishonour my glorious ancestry, and my illustrious appellation, by so unworthy a conduct. I love you at my heart, and so does Mrs U., and we must say thank you, and send you a peppercorn when we can. So thank you, my dear, for the brawn and the chine, and for all the good things that you announce, and at present I will, for your sake, say no more of thanksgiving.

I have answered the Welshman's[3] letter, and have a hope that I shall hear no more of him. He desired my advice, whether to publish or not. In answer, I congratulated him on the possession of a poetical talent, with which he might always amuse himself when fatigued with the weightier matters of the law. As to publication, I recommended it to him by all means, as the principal incentive to exertion. And with

[2] As noted by Dr Ryskamp and Mrs Russell, this was the hero of *The Renowned History of Giles Gingerbread: A Little Boy who lived upon Learning*, a chapbook story published c. 1765.

[3] Walter Churchey, an attorney of Hay in Breconshire, who had sent his verses for criticism.

regard to his probability of success, I told him that, as he had, I understood, already made the experiment by appearing in print, he could judge how that matter stood, better than I or any man could do it for him. What could I say, my dear? I was really unwilling to mortify a brother bard, and yet could not avoid it but at the expense of common honesty.

The Padre is to dine with us on Thursday next. I am highly pleased with him, and intend to make all possible advances to a nearer acquaintance. Why he is so silent in company I know not. Perhaps he is reserved, like some other people; or perhaps he holds it unsuitable to his function to be forward in mixed conversation. Certain it is, that he has enough to say when he and I are together. He has transcribed the ninth book for me, and is now transcribing the twelfth, which Mrs Throckmorton left unfinished. Poor Teedon has dined with us once, and it did me good to stuff him.

We have heard from the poor widow[4] after whom you so kindly inquire. She answered a letter of Mrs Unwin's about a week since. Her answer was affectionate, tender, and melancholy to a great degree, but not without expressions of hope and confidence in God. We understand that she has suffered much in her health, as well as in her mind. It could not be otherwise, for she was attached to her husband in the extreme. We have learned by a sidewind, since I mentioned her last, that Billy left everything, or almost every thing, to the children. But she has at present one hundred pounds a year, and will have another hundred hereafter, if she outlives Mrs U., being jointured in her estate. In the meantime, her sister lives with her, who has, I believe, determined never to marry, from which circumstance she must doubtless derive advantage. She spent some time at Clapham,[5] after her return from Winchester, is now with Mr John Unwin at Croydon, and goes soon to her gloomy mansion, as she calls it, in Essex. We asked her hither, in hope that a little time spent at Weston might be of use to her, but her affairs would not suffer her to come. She is greatly to be pitied; and whether she will ever recover the stroke is, I think, very uncertain.

[4] Mrs William Unwin.

[5] In Henry Thornton's house, Battersea Rise.

I had some time since a very clever letter from Henry C[owper], which I answered as well as I could, but not in kind. I seem to myself immoderately stupid on epistolary occasions, and especially when I wish to shine. Such I seem now, and such to have been ever since I began. So much the worse for you. Pray, my dear, send me a bit of Indian glue, and an almanack.

It gives me true pleasure to learn that the General at least says he is better, but it would give me much more to hear others say the same. Thank your sister for her instructions concerning the lamp, which shall be exactly followed.

I am, my dearest, your most Gingerbread Giles, etc.

Wm Cowper

TEXT: *Southey*

TO LADY HESKETH

The Lodge, Jan. 8, 1787

It costs me no great difficulty, my dear, to read your letters; a strong inclination and a pretty deal of practice are excellent qualifications. It happens now and then that a word calls for closer attention than its neighbours and perhaps I am forced to wipe my spectacles before I can perfectly master it, but a handwriting so good as yours is, when you choose to write well, can never be inexplicable at the worst. At least I have never found it so.

I have had a little nervous fever lately, my dear, that has somewhat abridged my sleep, and though I find myself better today than I have been since it seized me, yet I feel my head lightish and not in the best order for writing. You will find me therefore perhaps not only less alert in my manner than I usually am when my spirits are good, but rather shorter. I will however proceed to scribble till I find that it fatigues me, and then will do as I know you would bid me do, were you here: shut up my desk and take a walk.

Trouble not thyself, my sweet coz, to ask any questions concerning the cardinal epistle. It is an affair of so little consequence that it would not be worth while to ask anybody's permission to do it, especially as it is probable, the letter being genuine and its fair authoress living, that it would be deemed improper.

The good General, who I find is still at Kingston, though through misapprehension of a passage in one of your late letters, I thought him settled in Town for the winter, writes me word that his eye is much better, and seems to express himself as confident of a cure: news which gave me the greatest pleasure. He tells me that in the 8 first books which I have sent him he still finds alterations and amendments necessary, of which I myself am equally persuaded. And he asks my leave to lay them before an intimate friend of his of whom he gives a character that bespeaks him highly deserving of the trust. To this I have no objection, desiring only to make the translation as perfect as I can make it; if God grant me life and health, I would spare no labour that might be necessary to secure that point. The General's letter is extremely kind and both for matter and manner like all the rest of his dealings with his cousin the poet.

I had a letter also yesterday from Mr Smith, Member for Nottingham. Though we never saw each other, he writes to me in the most friendly terms, and interests himself much in my Homer and in the success of my subscription. Speaking on this latter subject, he says that my *Poems* are read by hundreds who know nothing of my proposals, and makes no doubt that they would subscribe if they did. I have myself always thought them imperfectly, or rather insufficiently, announced, and shall send Johnson a line, I believe by this post, to desire him to bind up an advertisement of the Homer with the edition of my *Poems* that is just coming out. I blame myself that I did not think of this measure at the publication of the second edition, having lost, I fear, some advantage by the neglect. Johnson should indeed have thought of it himself; but the bookseller is almost as idle as his author is inattentive.

I could pity the poor woman who has been weak enough

[to claim][1] my song;[2] such pilferings are sure to be detected. I [wrote] it, I know not how long, but I suppose, 4 years ago. The rose in question was a rose given to Lady Austen by Mrs Unwin, and the incident that suggested the subject occurred in the room in which you slept at the Vicarage, which Lady Austen made her dining-room. Some time since, perhaps 2 years or more, Mr Bull going to London, I gave him a copy of it which he undertook to convey to Nichols, printer of the *Gentleman's Magazine*. He showed it to a Mrs Cardell, who begged to copy it and promised to send it to the printer's by her servant. Three or 4 months after, and when I had concluded that it was lost, I saw it in the *Gentleman's Magazine* with my signature, 'W.C.' Poor simpleton! She will find now perhaps that the rose had a thorn and that she has pricked her fingers with it.

A basket, my dear, that you announced some time since, containing crockery, is not yet arrived, and Rogers assures us that it is not in the warehouse in London. I mention it lest any accident should have befallen it.

Mrs Unwin begs me to mention her to you with affection. Our chairs are cushioned and my study is much indebted to them for neatness and smartness of appearance.

Adieu! my beloved cousin. I have done my possibles. That is to say, all that I can do without hurting my noddle, and I have a letter to write to the General beside. May God bless thee and preserve us both to another happy meeting!

Thine ever,

Wm Cowper

TEXT: *Panshanger MSS.**

P.S. Tuesday, Jan. 9.

You have our best love and thanks, my dear, for the basket and box which arrived last night and all the contents safe. Sir Giles's thanks in particular for the gingerbread. With the muslin came a puzzling. It measures just 2 yards and 3

---

[1] MS. damaged by the seal.
[2] *The Rose*: see p. 685.

quarters. Now as I always wear 3-cornered neckcloths which are cut across, a difficulty occurs: how to make the whole into neckcloths without waste. If there is any new fashion in the cutting of them, you can inform us.

The cups, saucers &c. are all very pretty & much admired. There being a whole dozen of cups, we suppose they are tea or coffee cups indiscriminately.

TO LADY HESKETH

The Lodge, Sunday, Jan. 14, 1787

My dearest cousin,

I have been so much indisposed in the course of the last week with the fever that I told you had seized me as not to be able to follow my last letter with another sooner, which I should otherwise certainly have done, because I know that you will feel some anxiety about me. My nights during the whole week may be said to have been almost sleepless, for waking generally about one in the morning I slept no more till toward the time when I commonly used to rise. The consequence has been that except the translation of about 30 lines at the conclusion of the 13th book, I have been forced to abandon Homer entirely. This was a sensible mortification to me, as you may suppose, and felt the more because, my spirits of course failing with my strength, I seemed to have peculiar need of my old amusement. It seemed hard therefore to be forced to resign it just when I wanted it most. But Homer's battles cannot be fought by a man who does not sleep well, and who has not some little degree of animation in the day time. Last night, however, quite contrary to my expectation, the fever left me entirely, and I slept quietly, soundly, and long. If it please God that it returns not, I shall soon find myself in a condition to proceed. I would now take the bark, but my stomach will not bear it, either the gross bark[1] or the tincture. Hoffman, and Duffy, and now and then

---

[1] See p. 760, n.; *Hoffman,* see p. 872, n.

a very small quantity of magnesia, are the only medicines that do not seem to poison me, and they in their turn have each of them done me service. I walk constantly, that is to say, Mrs Unwin and I together, for at these times I keep her continually employed, and never suffer her to be absent from me many minutes. She gives me all her time, and all her attention, and forgets that there is another object in the world.

I believe, my dear, I sent you very slovenly thanks for the contents of the box and basket. If I did, it was owing partly to want of room at the top of my letter and partly to a cause that always prevents my being very diffuse on that topic, which is that to a heart generous and kind as yours a great deal of acknowledgment is only another word for a great deal of trouble. I now however repeat my thanks for all in general, and for the green cloth I give my uncle thanks in particular. Present my love to him into the bargain, and tell him that I hope he will live to give me such another piece when this shall be worn out. The leaves for fruit and the baskets are beautiful, and we shall rejoice to see them filled with raspberries, strawberries, and cherries for you. Thanks also for the neat smart almanac. And now I am on the subject of thanksgiving, I beg that when you shall next see or write to my namesake of Epsom, you will mention me to him with much gratitude and affection, for him alone of all my benefactors I seem to forget, though, in fact, I do not forget him, but have the warmest sense of his kindness. I shall be happy if it please God to spare my life till an opportunity may offer to take him by the hand at Weston.

Mrs Carter thinks on the subject of dreams as everybody else does, that is to say according to her own experience. She has had no extraordinary ones, and therefore accounts them only the ordinary operations of the fancy. Mine are of a texture that will not suffer me to ascribe them to so inadequate a cause, or to any cause but the operation of an exterior agency. I have a mind, my dear (and to you I will venture to boast of it) as free from superstition as any man living, neither do I give heed to dreams in general as predictive, though particular dreams I believe to be so. Some very sensible persons, and I suppose Mrs Carter among them, will acknowledge that in old times God spoke by dreams, but affirm with much boldness that He has since ceased to do so. If you ask them, 'why?' they answer, because He has now revealed His will in the Scripture, and there is no longer any need that He should instruct or admonish us by dreams.

I grant that with respect to doctrines and precepts He has left us in want of nothing; but has He thereby precluded Himself in any of the operations of His Providence? Surely not. It is perfectly a different consideration; and the same need that there ever was of His interference in this way, there is still and ever must be while man continues blind and fallible and a creature beset with dangers which he can neither foresee nor obviate. His operations however of this kind are, I allow, very rare; and as to the generality of dreams, they are made of such stuff, and are in themselves so insignificant, that though I believe them all to be the manufacture of others, not our own, I account it not a farthing-matter who makes them.

As to my own peculiar experience in the dreaming way I have only this to observe. I have not believed that I shall perish because in dreams I have been told it, but because I have had hardly any but terrible dreams for 13 years. I therefore have spent the greatest part of that time most unhappily. They have either tinged my mind with melancholy or filled it with terrors, and the effect has been unavoidable. If we swallow arsenic we must be poisoned, and he who dreams as I have done, must be troubled. So much for dreams.

Tuesday.—I have always worn the three-cornered kerchiefs, and Mrs U. will easily find an use for the odd bit, therefore will not trouble you with the muslin again.

Thanks, my dear, for the very handsome turchas[2] dish, which arrived safe last night. My fever is not yet gone, but sometimes seems to leave me. It is altogether of the nervous kind and attended now and then with much dejection.

A young gentleman called here yesterday who came 6 miles out of his way to see me. He was on a journey to London from Glasgow, having just left the university there. He came I suppose partly to satisfy his own curiosity, but chiefly as it

[2] Turquoise.

seemed to bring me the thanks of some of the Scotch professors for my 2 volumes. His name is Rose,[3] an Englishman, and very genteel. Your spirits being good, you will derive more pleasure from this incident than I can at present, therefore I send it.

Adieu, dearest, dearest cousin.

Yrs Wm C.

TEXT: *BM. Add. MSS.* 39,673

TO SAMUEL ROSE

Weston, July 24, 1787

Dear Sir,

This is the first time I have written these six months,[1] and nothing but the constraint of obligation could induce me to write now. I cannot be so wanting to myself as not to endeavour at least to thank you both for the visits with which you have favoured me, and the poems that you sent me; in my present state of mind I taste nothing, nevertheless I read, partly from habit, and partly because it is the only thing that I am capable of.

I have therefore read Burns's poems,[2] and have read them twice; and though they be written in a language that is new to me, and many of them on subjects much inferior to the author's ability, I think them on the whole a very extraordinary production. He is I believe the only poet these kingdoms have produced in the lower rank of life since Shakespeare (I should rather say since Prior) who need not be indebted for any part of his praise to a charitable consideration of his origin, and the disadvantages under which he has

[3] Samuel Rose (1767–1804) had spent three years as a law student in Scotland. He was called to the bar in 1796, and was a trustee for the Crown pension granted to C. in 1794.

[1] C.'s fourth severe depression, in the course of which he twice attempted to commit suicide, lasted from January to June 1787.

[2] The first edition of *Poems, chiefly in the Scotch Dialect*, published at Kilmarnock in 1786.

laboured. It will be pity if he should not hereafter divest himself of barbarism, and content himself with writing pure English, in which he appears perfectly qualified to excel. He who can command admiration, dishonours himself if he aims no higher than to raise a laugh.

I am, dear sir, with my best wishes for your prosperity, and with Mrs Unwin's respects, your obliged and affectionate humble servant,

W.C.

TEXT: *Southey*

TO SAMUEL ROSE

Weston, Aug. 27, 1787

Dear Sir,

I have not yet taken up the pen again, except to write to you. The little taste that I have had of your company, and your kindness in finding me out, make me wish that we were nearer neighbours, and that there were not so great a disparity in our years; that is to say, not that you were older, but that I were younger. Could we have met in early life, I flatter myself that we might have been more intimate than now we are likely to be. But you shall not find me slow to cultivate such a measure of your regard, as your friends of your own age can spare me. When your route shall lie through this country, I shall hope that the same kindness which has prompted you twice to call on me, will prompt you again, and I shall be happy if, on a future occasion, I may be able to give you a more cheerful reception than can be expected from an invalid. My health and spirits are considerably improved, and I once more associate with my neighbours. My head, however, has been the worst part of me, and still continues so,—is subject to giddiness and pain, maladies very unfavourable to poetical employment; but a preparation of the bark, which I take regularly, has so far been of service to me in those respects, as to encourage in me a hope that by perseverance in the use of it, I may possibly find myself qualified to resume the translation of Homer.

When I cannot walk, I read, and read perhaps more than is good for me. But I cannot be idle. The only mercy that I show myself in this respect is that I read nothing that requires much closeness of application. I lately finished the perusal of a book which in former years I have more than once attacked, but never till now conquered; some other book always interfered before I could finish it. The work I mean is Barclay's *Argenis*;[1] and if ever you allow yourself to read for mere amusement, I can recommend it to you (provided you have not already perused it) as the most amusing romance that ever was written. It is the only one indeed of an old date that I ever had the patience to go through with. It is interesting in a high degree; richer in incident than can be imagined, full of surprises, which the reader never forestalls, and yet free from all entanglement and confusion. The style too appears to me to be such as would not dishonour Tacitus himself.

Poor Burns loses much of his deserved praise in this country through our ignorance of his language. I despair of meeting with any Englishman who will take the pains that I have taken to understand him. His candle is bright, but shut up in a dark lantern. I lent him to a very sensible neighbour of mine: but his uncouth dialect spoiled all; and before he had half read him through, he was quite *ramfuzled*.[2]

W.C.

TEXT: *Southey*

TO LADY HESKETH

The Lodge, Aug. 30, 1787

My dearest cousin,

Though it costs me something to write, it would cost me

---

[1] John Barclay: *Argenis*, 1621, a political satire in Latin.
[2] Exhausted.

more to be silent. My intercourse with my neighbours being renewed, I can no longer seem to forget how many reasons there are why you especially should not be neglected—no neighbour indeed, but the kindest of my friends, and ere long, I hope, an inmate.

My health and spirits seem to be mending daily: to what end I know not, neither will conjecture, but endeavour, as far as I can, to be content that they do so. I use exercise, and take the air in the park and wilderness: I read much, but as yet write not. Our friends at the Hall make themselves more and more amiable in our account, by treating us rather as old friends than as friends newly acquired. There are few days in which we do not meet, and I am now almost as much at home in their house as in our own. Mr Throckmorton, having long since put me in possession of all his ground, has given me possession of his library: an acquisition of great value to me, who never have been able to live without books since I first knew my letters, and who have no books of my own. By his means I have been so well supplied that I have not yet even looked at the *Lounger*, for which however I do not forget that I am obliged to you. *His* turn comes next, and I shall probably begin him to-morrow.

Mr George Throckmorton[1] is at the Hall. I thought I had known these brothers long enough to have found out all their talents and accomplishments; but I was mistaken. The day before yesterday, after having walked with us, they *carried* us up to the library (a more accurate writer would have said, *conducted* us) and then they showed me the contents of an immense port-folio, the work of their own hands. It was furnished with drawings of the architectural kind, executed in a most masterly manner, and among others contained outside and inside views of the Pantheon—I mean the Roman one.[2] They were all, I believe, made at Rome. Some men may be estimated at a first interview, but the Throckmortons must be seen often, and known long, before one can understand all their value.

[1] See n., p. 716.

[2] There was a Pantheon in Oxford Street, London, built by James Wyatt in 1772 as 'a winter Ranelagh.'

They often enquire after you, and ask me whether you visit Weston this autumn. I answer, yes; and I charge you, my dearest cousin, to authenticate my information. Write to me, and tell us when we may expect to see you. We were disappointed that we had no letter from you this morning. You will find me coated and buttoned according to your recommendation.

I write but little, because writing is become new to me; but I shall come on by degrees. Mrs Unwin begs to be affectionately remembered to you. She is in tolerable health, which is the chief comfort here that I have to boast of.—

Yours, my dearest cousin, as ever,

W.C.

TEXT: *Southey*

TO LADY HESKETH

The Lodge, Septbr. 4, 1787

My dearest coz,

Come when thou canst come, secure of being always welcome. All that is here, is thine, together with the hearts of those who dwell here. I am only sorry that your journey hither is necessarily postponed beyond the time when I did hope to have seen you; sorry too, that my uncle's infirmities are the occasion of it. But years *will* have their course and their effect; they are happiest, so far as this life is concerned, who, like him, escape those effects the longest, and who do not grow old before their time. Trouble and anguish do that for some, which only longevity does for others. A few months since, I was older than your father is now; and though I have lately recovered, as Falstaff says, some *smatch*[1] *of my youth*, I have but little confidence, in truth none, in so flattering

[1] Not quite: 2 *King Henry IV*, I, ii, 'Your Lordship, though not clean past your youth, hath yet some smack of age in you.' But cf. *Julius Caesar*, V,v, where Brutus says, 'Thy life hath had some smatch of honour in it.'

849

a change, but *expect, when I least expect it*, to wither again. The past is a pledge for the future.

Touching your retinue, my dear, you have nothing to consider but what will be most convenient to yourself. Here will be room for two menservants, and I imagine you will find occasion for your butler as well as for your coachman. Our servant sleeps always at his own house, and yours may sleep together. Mrs Eaton will occupy the chamber over my study, and when the bedstead arrives, the furniture for it which you know is now in our hands, shall be immediately made ready. As your arrival is likely to be in the winter, at least upon the verge of it, you will find your coach an indispensable. Mrs T[hrockmorto]n proposed to us, when we drank tea there last, to get a little covered cart and a little horse and a little boy to drive it, the days being now so short that before we can separate, it is dark. But you will probably like your own vehicle better. Some vehicle however you must have, for the passage from the Hall to the Lodge would be impracticable to you in an evening.

One thing more I will premise, my dearest coz, and by way of encouragement. It is suggested to me by the mention that you make of the house at the end of the village. That house, by the way, I hear is taken. No matter. There is no need of it. When you shall find yourself under this roof, you will find yourself under your own. From the time of your rising till the hour of dinner, your hours will be absolutely at your disposal. We engage for ourselves that we will never intrude upon you, and that it shall be a capital crime in anybody to give you the least disturbance. There is no danger of it indeed, for we were never in our lives so quietly served as now. Sam our lackey, and Molly our cook are never heard but when they answer a question. Sam's wife, by the way, has long been engaged to officiate in the scullery while you shall be with us, and she is the very counterpart of her husband for quietness and sobriety.— This being the case, I doubt not that we shall fadge notably together, my dear, and that you will find yourself perfectly at your ease.

Thanks for the waistcoat which I shall rejoice to receive. To give bulk to the parcel, you may send us if you please, some Bohea. We drink no other tea, either at the Hall, or here, and the Throcks always prefer ours, which is what you sent us, to their own. I think with reason.

Mr Giffard is here, Mrs Throck's uncle. He is lately arrived from Italy where he has resided several years, and is so much the gentleman that it is impossible to be more so. Sensible, polite, obliging, slender in figure, and in manner most engaging: every way worthy to be so nearly related to the Throckmortons.

I have read Savary's *Travels into Ægypt*, *Mémoires du Baron de Tott*, Fenn's *Original Letters*, *The Letters of Frederic of Bohemia*, and am now reading *Mémoires d'Henri de Lorraine*, *Duc de Guise*. I have also read Barclay's *Argenis*, a Latin romance, and the best romance that was ever written. All these, together with Madan's *Letters to Priestley* and several pamphlets within these 2 months. So I am a great reader.

Yours, my dearest, ever,

Wm Cowper

TEXT: *Panshanger MSS.**

TO SAMUEL ROSE

Weston, Oct. 19, 1787

My dear Sir,

A summons from Johnson, which I received yesterday, calls my attention once more to the business of translation. Before I begin I am willing to catch though but a short opportunity to acknowledge your last favour. The necessity of applying myself with all diligence to a long work that has been but too long interrupted, will make my opportunities of writing rare in future.

Air and exercise are necessary to all men, but particularly so to the man whose mind labours; and to him who has been all his life accustomed to much of both, they are necessary in the extreme. My time, since we parted, has been devoted entirely to the recovery of health and strength for this service, and I am willing to hope with good effect. Ten months have passed since I discontinued my poetical efforts; I do not expect to find the same readiness as before, till exercise of the neglected faculty, such as it is, shall have restored it to me.

You find yourself, I hope, by this time as comfortably situated in your new abode, as in a new abode one can be. I enter perfectly into all your feelings on occasion of the change. A sensible mind cannot do violence even to a local attachment without much pain. When my father died I was young, too young to have reflected much. He was Rector of Berkhamsted, and there I was born. It had never occurred to me that a parson has no fee-simple[1] in the house and glebe he occupies. There was neither tree, nor gate, nor stile, in all that country, to which I did not feel a relation, and the house itself I preferred to a palace. I was sent for from London to attend him in his last illness, and he died just before I arrived. Then, and not till then, I felt for the first time that I and my native place were disunited for ever. I sighed a long adieu to fields and woods, from which I once thought I should never be parted, and was at no time so sensible of their beauties, as just when I left them all behind me, to return no more.

W.C.

TEXT: *Southey*

TO LADY HESKETH

The Lodge, Nov. 10, 1787

The parliament, my dearest cousin, prorogued continually, is a meteor dancing before my eyes, promising me my wish only to disappoint me, and none but the king and his ministers can tell when you and I shall come together. I hope, however, that the period, though so often postponed, is not far distant, and that once more I shall behold you, and experience your power to make winter gay and sprightly.

---

[1] Absolute possession.

I have never forgotten (I never say forgot) to tell you the reason why Mr Bull did not fulfil his engagement to call on you on his return from the West. It was owing to an accident that happened to one of those legs of his. At Exmouth he chose to wallow in the sea and made use of a bathing machine for that purpose. It has a ladder, as you know, attached to its tail. On the lowermost step of that ladder he stood, when it broke under him. He fell of course, and with his knee on the point of a large nail which pierced it almost to the depth of two inches. The consequence was that when he reached London he could think of nothing but getting home as fast as possible. The wound has been healed some time but is occasionally still painful, so that he is not without apprehensions that it may open again, which, considering that he is somewhat gross in his habit, is not impossible. But I have just sent to invite him to dine with us on Monday.

I have a kitten, my dear, the drollest of all creatures that ever wore a cat's skin. Her gambols are not to be described, and would be incredible if they could. She tumbles head over heels several times together; she lays her cheek to the ground and presents her rump at you with an air of most supreme disdain; from this posture she rises to dance on her hind feet, an exercise that she performs with all the grace imaginable; and she closes these various exhibitions with a loud smack of her lips, which, for want of greater propriety of expression, we call spitting. But though all cats spit, no cat ever produced such a sound as she does. In point of size she is likely to be a kitten always, being extremely small of her age, but time I suppose, that spoils everything, will make her also a cat. You will see her I hope before that melancholy period shall arrive, for no wisdom that she may gain by experience and reflection hereafter, will compensate the loss of her present hilarity. She is dressed in a tortoise-shell suit, and I know that you will delight in her.

Mrs Throckmorton carries us to-morrow in her chaise to Chicheley.

Mr Chester has been often here, and Mrs Chester, as I told you, once; and we are glad and obliged to our neighbours for an opportunity to return their visits, at once so convenient and inviting. The event, however, must be supposed to depend on elements, at least on the state of the atmosphere, which is turbulent beyond measure. Yesterday it thundered, last night it lightened, and at three this morning I saw the sky as red as a city in flames could have made it. I have a leech in a bottle, my dear, that foretells all these prodigies and convulsions of nature: no, not as you will naturally conjecture by articulate utterance of oracular notices, but by a variety of gesticulations, which here I have not room to give an account of. Suffice it to say, that no change of weather surprises him, and that in point of the earliest and most accurate intelligence, he is worth all the barometers in the world. None of them all indeed can make the least pretence to foretell thunder—a species of capacity of which he has given the most unequivocal evidence. I gave but sixpence for him, which is a groat more than the market price, though he is in fact, or rather would be, if leeches were not found in every ditch, an invaluable acquisition.

Mrs Throck. *sola* dined with us last Tuesday. She invited herself; the particular reason of her so doing was that her husband and brother dined at Horton. The next day we dined at the Hall.

Mrs Wrighte's is still considered as a melancholy case, though we learn this evening that she has twice or thrice taken airings in the chaise, and must therefore I suppose be better. Pray, my dear, add to what I have already desired you to bring with you, a roll or two of green wax candle to go upon a spindle, spindle, spindle. I repeat it three times, having more than once experienced how apt that circumstance is to escape the memory. I have no room for any other addition than that of our best love, and to assure you how truly I am

Ever yours,

Wm Cowper

TEXT: *Wright*

TO LADY HESKETH

The Lodge, Novr 27, 1787

It is the part of wisdom, my dearest cousin, to sit down contented under the demands of necessity, because they are such. I am sensible that you cannot, in my Uncle's present state and of which it is not possible to expect any considerable amendment, indulge either us or yourself with a journey to Weston. Yourself, I say, both because I know it will give you pleasure to see *causidice mi*[1] once more, especially in the comfortable abode where you have placed him, and because after so long an imprisonment in London, you who love the country and have a taste for it would of course be glad to return to it. For my own part, to me it is ever new, and though I have now been an inhabitant of this village a twelve-month, and have during the half of that time been at liberty to expatiate and to make discoveries, I am daily finding out fresh scenes and walks which you would never be satisfied with enjoying. Some of them indeed are unapproachable by you either on foot or in your carriage. Had you twenty toes (whereas I suppose you have but ten) you could not reach them; and coach-wheels have never been seen there since the Flood. Before it indeed, Bishop Burnet[2] says, that the earth being perfectly free from all inequalities in its surface, they might be seen there every day. But *à l'heure qu'il est*, we are never the better for that. But then, my dear, we have other walks both upon hill-tops and in valleys beneath, some of which by the

---

[1] 'The appellation which Sir Thos. used to give him in jest when this excellent creature was of the Temple,' (marginal annotation on MS. by Lady Hesketh). The Italian words mean 'counsellor', or 'my legal adviser'.

[2] In *The Sacred Theory of the Earth*, or *Telluris Theoria Sacra*, 1681-9, Thomas Burnet argued that the Flood was caused by the drying and shrinking of the earth's crust, which on collapsing, forced subterranean waters to the surface.

help of your carriage, and many of them without its help, would be always at your command.

On Monday morning last, Sam brought me word into the study that a man was in the kitchen who desired to speak with me. I ordered him in. A plain, decent, elderly figure made its appearance, and being desired to sit, spoke as follows: 'Sir, I am Clerk of the Parish of All Saints in Northampton, brother of Mr Cox the upholsterer. It is customary for the person in my office to annex to a Bill of Mortality which he publishes at Christmas, a copy of verses. You would do me a great favour, Sir, if you would furnish me with one.' To this I replied—'Mr Cox, you have several men of genius in your town; why have you not applied to some of them? There is a namesake of yours in particular, Cox the statuary, who everybody knows is a first-rate maker of verses. He is surely the man of all the world for your purpose.' 'Alas Sir! I have heretofore borrowed help from him, but he is a gentleman of so much reading that the people of our town cannot understand him.' I confess to you, my dear, I felt all the force of the compliment implied in this speech, and was almost ready to answer: 'Perhaps, my good friend, they may find me unintelligible too for the same reason.' But on asking him whether he had walked over to Weston to implore the assistance of my Muse, and on his replying in the affirmative, I felt my mortified vanity a little consoled; and pitying the poor man's distress, which appeared to be considerable, promised to supply him. The waggon has accordingly gone this day to Northampton loaded in part with my effusions in the mortuary style.[3] A fig for poets who write epitaphs upon individuals; I have written *one* that serves *200* persons.

If you have not yet opened the parcel containing the *Loungers*, my cousin, you must do it now; for I have immediate occasion to know whether they are stitched only or bound, and if bound in what manner. Few days since, I received a second very obliging letter from Mr McKenzie,[4]

[3] Verses by Cowper were printed in the parish Bill of Mortality for the years 1787, 1788, 1789, 1790, 1792 (p. 130) and 1793 (p. 132).

[4] Henry Mackenzie, author of *The Man of Feeling*, and editor of *The Lounger*.

in which he accepts *avec beaucoup de politesse* an offer that I made him of my two volumes. I would therefore give him a Roland for his Oliver, and order Johnson to transmit to his bookseller Cadell just such a set in respect of binding as he has bestowed upon me. He tells me, in some sort confidentially (for as decently as I could I had asked him who were the authors of those papers) that Dr Beattie wrote but two, which are in the *Mirror* and on the subject of dreams and which he afterward extended into an essay. And that Dr Blair had nothing to do with it; also that his own papers, which are by far, he is sorry to say it, the most numerous, are marked V.I.Z. Accordingly, my dear, I am happy to find that I am at last engaged in a correspondence with Mr Viz, a gentleman for whom I have always entertained the profoundest veneration. But the serious fact is that the papers distinguished by those signatures have ever pleased me most and struck me as the work of a sensible man who knows the world well and has more of Addison's delicate humour than anybody.

A poor man begged food at the Hall lately. The cook gave him some vermicelli soup. He ladled it about some time with the spoon, and then returned it to her, saying—'I am a poor man, it is true, and I am very hungry, but yet I cannot eat broth with maggots in it.'

Once more, my dear, a thousand thanks for your box full of good things, useful things, and beautiful things, and with Mrs Unwin's affectionate remembrances,

Ever yours,

Wm Cowper

TEXT: *Panshanger MSS.* *

TO LADY HESKETH

Dec. 19, 1787 [in post mark]

Saturday, my dearest cousin, was a day of receipts. In the morning I received a box filled with an abundant variety of stationery ware, containing, in particular, a quantity of paper sufficient, well covered with good writing, to immortalize any man. I have nothing to do, therefore, but to cover it as aforesaid, and my name will never die. In the evening I received a smaller box, but still more welcome on account of its contents. It contained an almanack in red morocco, a pencil of a new invention, called an everlasting pencil, and a noble purse, with a noble gift in it, called a Bank note for twenty-five pounds. I need use no arguments to assure you, my cousin, that by the help of ditto note, we shall be able to fadge[1] very comfortably till Christmas is turned, without having the least occasion to draw upon you. By the post yesterday — that is, Sunday morning — I received also a letter from Anonymous, giving me advice of the kind present which I have just particularized; in which letter allusion is made to a certain piece by me composed, entitled, I believe, *The Drop of Ink*.[2] The only copy I ever gave of that piece, I gave to yourself. It is *possible*, therefore, that between you and *Anonymous* there may be some communication. If that should be the case, I will beg you just to signify to him, as opportunity may occur, the safe arrival of his most acceptable present, and my most grateful sense of it.

My toothache is in a great measure, that is to say, almost entirely removed; not by snipping my ears, as poor Lady Strange's ears were snipped, not by any other chirurgical operation, except such as I could perform myself. The manner of it was as follows: we dined last Thursday at the Hall; I sat down to table, trembling lest the tooth, of which I told you in my last, should not only refuse its own office, but hinder all the rest. Accordingly, in less than five minutes, by a hideous dislocation of it, I found myself not only in great pain, but under an absolute prohibition not only to eat, but to speak another word. Great emergencies sometimes meet the most effectual remedies. I resolved, if it were possible, then and there to draw it. This I effected so dexterously by a sudden twitch, and afterwards so dexterously conveyed it

---

[1] *fadge*: rub along.
[2] Published as *Ode to Apollo*.

into my pocket, that no creature present, not even Mrs Unwin, who sat facing me, was sensible either of my distress, or of the manner of my deliverance from it. I am poorer by one tooth than I was, but richer by the unimpeded use of all the rest.

When I lived in the Temple, I was rather intimate with a son of the late Admiral Rowley and a younger brother of the present Admiral. Since I wrote to you last, I received a letter from him, in a very friendly and affectionate style. It accompanied half a dozen books, which I had lent him five and twenty years ago, and which he apologized for having kept so long, telling me that they had been sent to him at Dublin by mistake; for at Dublin, it seems, he now resides. Reading my poems, he felt, he said, his friendship for me revive, and wrote accordingly. I have now, therefore, a correspondent in Ireland, another in Scotland, and a third in Wales. All this would be very diverting, had I a little more time to spare to them.

My dog, my dear, is a spaniel.[3] Till Miss Gunning begged him, he was the property of a farmer, and while he was their property had been accustomed to lie in the chimney corner, among the embers, till the hair was singed from his back, and till nothing was left of his tail but the gristle. Allowing for these disadvantages, he is really handsome; and when nature shall have furnished him with a new coat, a gift which, in consideration of the ragged condition of his old one, it is hoped she will not long delay, he will then be unrivalled in personal endowments by any dog in this country. He and my cat are excessively fond of each other, and play a thousand ganbols together that it is impossible not to admire.

Know thou, that from this time forth, the post comes daily to Weston. This improvement is effected by an annual subscription of ten shillings. The Throcks invited us to the measure, and we have acceded to it. Their servant will manage this concern for us at the Olney post office, and the subscription is to pay a man for stumping three times a week from Olney to Newport Pagnel, and back again.

[3] Beau.

Returning from my walk to-day, while I was passing by some small closes[4] at the back of the town, I heard the voices of some persons extremely merry at the top of the hill. Advancing into the large field behind our house, I there met Mr Throck, wife, and brother George. Combine in your imagination as large proportions as you can of earth and water intermingled so as to constitute what is commonly called mud, and you will have but an imperfect conception of the quantity that had attached itself to her petticoats: but she had half-boots, and laughed at her own figure. She told me that she had this morning transcribed sixteen pages of my Homer. I observed in reply, that to write so much, and to gather all that dirt, was no bad morning's work, considering the shortness of the days at this season.

Yours, my dear,

W.C.

TEXT: *Southey*

TO LADY HESKETH

The Lodge, Dec. 24, 1787

My dearest cousin,

The Throcks do not leave Weston till after Easter. But this I hope will have no effect upon your movements, should an opportunity present itself to you of coming sooner. We dined there last Saturday. After dinner, while we all sat round the fire, I told them, as I related it to you, the adventure of my tooth. This drew from Mrs Throck (singular as it must appear) a tale the very counterpart of mine. She, in like manner, had a tooth to draw, while I was drawing mine; and thus it came to pass (the world, I suppose, could not furnish such another instance) that we two, without the least intimation to each other of our respective distress, were employed in the same moment, sitting side by side, in drawing each a

[4] Enclosed fields.

tooth: an operation which we performed with equal address, and without being perceived by anyone.

This morning had very near been a tragical one to me, beyond all that have ever risen upon me. Mrs Unwin rose as usual at seven o'clock; at eight she came to me, and showed me her bed-gown with a great piece burnt out of it. Having lighted her fire, which she always lights herself, she placed the candle upon the hearth. In a few moments it occurred to her that, if it continued there, it might possibly set fire to her clothes, therefore she put it out. But in fact, though she had not the least suspicion of it, her clothes were on fire at that very time. She found herself uncommonly annoyed by smoke, such as brought the water into her eyes; supposing that some of the billets might lie too forward, she disposed them differently; but finding the smoke increase, and grow more troublesome (for by this time the room was filled with it) she cast her eye downward, and perceived not only her bed-gown, but her petticoat on fire. She had the presence of mind to gather them in her hand, and plunge them immediately into the basin, by which means the general conflagration of her person, which must probably have ensued in a few moments, was effectually prevented. Thus was that which I have often heard from the pulpit, and have often had occasion myself to observe, most clearly illustrated—that, secure as we may sometimes seem to ourselves, we are in reality never so safe as to have no need of a superintending Providence. Danger can never be at a distance from creatures who dwell in houses of clay. Therefore take care of thyself, gentle Yahoo! and may a more vigilant than thou care for thee.

On the day when we dined as abovementioned at the Hall, Mrs Throck had paid a morning visit at [Gayhurst]. When I enquired how she found Mrs [Wrighte] her account of her was as follows: 'They say she is much better, but to judge by her looks and her manner, there is no ground to think so. She looks dreadfully, and talks in a rambling way without ceasing.' If this be a just description of her, and I do not at all doubt it, I am afraid, poor woman! that she is far from well, notwithstanding all that the physician of minds has done for her. In effect there is but One who merits that title; and were all the frantic who have been restored to their reason to make a reasonable use of it, they would acknowledge that God, and not man, had cured them.

I thank you, my dear, for your intentions to furnish me, had I not been otherwise accommodated with one, with an everlasting pencil. You may yet perhaps, on some distant day, have an opportunity to fulfil those intentions, for 'everlasting,' as it is called, it is not such in point of duration; but claims the title on this account only, that in the using, it perpetually works itself to a point, and never wants cutting. Otherwise it wastes and wears, as every thing made of earthly materials must.

When the Throcks happen to mention the chairs again, your directions shall be pursued. As to the balance due on the plate account, it was, before the purchase of the silk handkerchiefs, etc., either six pounds or six guineas—we cannot recollect which. With the remainder, whatever it shall be found to be, Mrs Unwin will be obliged to you if you will give it in commission to Mrs Eaton, to buy for her some muslin for aprons, of the sort that you wore when you were at Olney, viz. with cross stripes. She thinks you called it an English muslin. They must be ell and nail long. But at the same time it does not appear probable to either of us, that there should be money remaining in your hands sufficient for this purpose.

I forgot to tell you that my dog is spotted liver-colour and white, or rather white and chestnut. He is at present my pupil as well as dog, and just before I sat down to write I gave him a lesson in the science of fetch and carry. He performs with an animation past all conception, except your own, whose poor head will never forget Tinker. But I am now grown more reasonable, and never make such a dreadful din but when Beau and I are together. To teach him is necessary, in order that he may take the water, and *that* is necessary in order that he may be sweet in summer. Farewell, my dearest coz.—I am, with Mrs U.'s affections,

Ever thine, most truly,

Wm Cowper

TEXT: *Southey*

TO LADY HESKETH

The Lodge, Feb. 1, 1788

Pardon me, my dearest coz, the mournful ditty that I sent you last.[1] There are times when I see every thing through a medium that distresses me to an insupportable degree, and that letter was written in one of them. A fog that had for three days obliterated all the beauties of Weston, and a north-east wind might possibly contribute not a little to the melancholy that indited it. But my mind is now easy; your letter has made it so, and I feel myself as blithe as a bird in comparison. I love you my cousin, and cannot suspect, either with or without cause, the least evil in which you may be concerned, without being greatly troubled. Oh trouble! the portion of all mortals, but mine in particular; would I had never known thee, or could bid thee farewell for ever; for I meet thee at every turn, my pillows are stuffed with thee, my very roses smell of thee, and even my cousin who would cure me of all trouble if she could, is sometimes innocently the cause of trouble to me.

I now see the unreasonableness of my late trouble, and would, if I could trust myself so far, promise never again to trouble either myself or you in the same manner, unless warranted by some more substantial ground of apprehension.

What I said concerning Homer, my dear, was spoken or rather written merely under the influence of a certain jocularity that I felt at that moment. I am in reality so far from thinking myself an ass and my translation a sand-cart, that I rather seem, in my own account of the matter, one of those flaming steeds harnessed to the chariot of Apollo of which we read in the works of the ancients. I have lately, I know not how, acquired a certain superiority to myself in this business, and in this last revisal have elevated the expression to a degree far

[1] C. had imagined that Lady Hesketh was ill, as she had not written for some time.

surpassing its former boast. A few evenings since, I had an opportunity to try how far I might venture to expect such success of my labours as can alone repay them, by reading the first book of my *Iliad* to a friend of ours. He dined with you once at Olney. His name is Greatheed. A man of letters and of taste. He dined with us, and the evening proving dark and dirty we persuaded him to take a bed: *pour passer le temps*, I entertained him as I tell you. He heard me with great attention, and with evident symptoms of the highest satisfaction, which when I had finished the exhibition he put out of all doubt by expressions which I cannot repeat; only this he said to Mrs Unwin while I was in another room, that he had never entered into the spirit of Homer before, nor had anything like a due conception of his manner. This I have said knowing that it [? must[2]] please you, and will now say no more except that [word obliterated] you set so little value on your sixpences, have [word obliterated]. I shall enclose what I wrote for the Clerk of All Saints Northampton, to convince you that I am not so squeamish on such occasions as to wait for [? asking[2]].

The brawn has been admired by all that have partaken of it as the best they ever saw or tasted. Nor has Mrs Unwin's gown, your present, been less admired, our neighbours with the long name having repeatedly paid that just tribute to its merits and Mr T[hrockmorton] in particular.

Adieu, my dear! Will you never speak of coming to Weston more?

Yours most affectionately

Wm C.

TEXT: *Panshanger MSS.*

TO LADY HESKETH

The Lodge, Feb. 7, 1788

My dearest cousin,

Thanks beforehand for the books which you give me to expect. They will all be welcome. Of the two editions of

---

[2] Readings uncertain owing to damage to MS.

Shakespeare I prefer that which is printed in the largest type, independent of all other considerations. *Don Quixote* by any hand must needs be welcome, and by Smollett's especially, because I have never seen it. He had a drollery of his own, which for aught I know, may suit an English taste as well as that of Cervantes, perhaps better, because to us somewhat more intelligible.

It is pretty well known (the clerk took care it should be so) both at Northampton and in this county, who wrote the Mortuary Verses. All that I know of their success is, that he sent a bundle of them to Maurice Smith at Olney, who sold them for threepence a piece—a high price for a *Memento Mori*, a commodity not generally in great request. The other small poem, addressed to Mrs Throck, has given, as I understand, great satisfaction at Bucklands.[1] The old baronet and his lady, having heard that such a piece existed, (Mrs Bromley Chester, I suppose, must have been their informant) wrote to desire a copy. A copy was sent, and they answered it with warm encomiums.

Mr Bull,[2] the lame curate, having been lately preferred to a living, another was of course wanted to supply his place. By the recommendation of Mr Romaine, a Mr Canniford came down. He lodges at Mr Socket's in this village, and Mr Socket lives in the small house to which you had once conceived a liking. Our lacquey[3] is also clerk of the parish. Canniford a day or two after his arrival had a corpse to bury at Weston. Having occasion to consult with the clerk concerning this matter, he sought him in our kitchen. Samuel entered the study to inform us that there was a clergyman without: he was accordingly invited in, and he came. We had but lately dined; the wine was on the table, and he drank three glasses while the corpse in question was getting ready for its last journey. The moment he entered the room, I felt myself incurably prejudiced against him: his features, his

[1] Buckland House, in Berkshire, seat of Sir Robert Throckmorton, grandfather of the two brothers of Weston Park. The poem was *The Poet's New Year's Gift*.

[2] The Rev. Thomas Bull, lately curate of Weston Underwood.

[3] Sam Roberts.

figure, his address, and all that he uttered, confirmed that prejudice, and I determined, having once seen him, to see him no more. Two days after he overtook me in the village. 'Your humble servant, Mr Cowper! a fine morning, sir, for a walk. I had liked to have called on you yesterday morning to tell you that I had become your near neighbour. I live at Mr Socket's.' I answered without looking at him, as drily as possible,— 'Are you come to stay any time in the country?'— He believed he was.—'Which way,' I replied, 'are you going? to Olney?'—'Yes.'—'I am going to Mr Throckmorton's garden, and I wish you a good day, sir.'—I was in fact going to Olney myself, but this rencontre gave me such a violent twist another way that I found it impossible to recover that direction, and accordingly there we parted. All this I related at the Hall the next time we dined there, describing also my apprehensions and distress lest, whether I would or not, I should be obliged to have intercourse with a man to me so perfectly disagreeable. A good deal of laugh and merriment ensued, and there for that time it ended. The following Sunday, in the evening, I received a note to this purport: 'Mr Canniford's compliments,' etc. Understanding that my friends at the Hall were to dine with me the next day, he took the liberty to invite himself to eat a bit of mutton with me, being sure that I should be happy to introduce him. Having read the note, I threw it to Mrs Unwin. 'There,' said I, 'take that and read it; then tell me if it be not an effort of impudence the most extraordinary you ever heard of.' I expected some such push from the man; I knew he was equal to it. She read it, and we were both of a mind. I sat down to my desk, and with a good deal of emotion gave it just such an answer as it would have deserved had it been genuine. But having heard by accident in the morning that he spells his name with a C, and observing in the note that it was spelt with a K, a suspicion struck me that it was a fiction. I looked at it more attentively and perceived that it was directed by Mrs Throck. The inside I found afterwards was written by her brother George. This served us with another laugh on the subject, and I have hardly seen, and never spoken to, Mr Canniford since. So, my dear, *that's the little story I promised you.*

Mr Bull called here this morning: from him I learn what follows concerning Postlethwaite.[4] He waited on the Bishop of London, like a blundering ignoramus as he is, without his canonicals. The Bishop was highly displeased, as he had cause to be; and having pretty significantly given him to know it, addressed himself to his chaplain with tokens of equal displeasure, enjoining him never more to admit a clergyman to him in such attire. To pay this visit he made a journey from Clapham to town on horseback. His horse he left at an inn on the Lambeth side of Westminster Bridge. Thence he proceeded to the Bishop's, and from the Bishop's to Mr Scott. Having finished this last visit he begged Mr Scott's company to the inn where he had left his horse, which he said was at the foot of *London* Bridge. Thither they went, but neither the inn nor the horse were there. Then, says Postlethwaite it must be at Blackfriars Bridge that I left it. Thither also they went, but to as little purpose. Luckily for him there was but one more bridge, and there they found it. To make the poor youth amends for all these misadventures, it so happened that the incumbent, his predecessor, died before the crops of last year were reaped. The whole profits of that year, by consequence, go into P.'s pocket, which was never so stuffed before.

Good night, my dearest coz. Mrs Unwin's love attends you.

Affectionately yours,

Wm Cowper

TEXT: *Wright*

TO LADY HESKETH

The Lodge, Feb. 16, 1788

I have now three letters of yours, my dearest cousin, before me, all written in the space of a week, and must be indeed insensible of kindness did I not feel yours upon this occasion.

[4] The Rev. Richard Postlethwaite, curate of Olney.

I cannot describe to you, neither could you comprehend it if I should, the manner in which my mind is sometimes impressed with melancholy on particular subjects. Your late silence was such a subject. I heard, saw and felt a thousand terrible things which had no real existence, and was haunted by them night and day till they at last extorted from me the doleful epistle which I have since wished had been burned before I sent it. But the cloud has passed and as far as you are concerned my heart is once more at rest.

Before you gave me the hint, I had once or twice, as I lay on my bed watching for the break of day, ruminated on the subject which in your last but one you recommend to me. Slavery, or a release from slavery such as the poor negroes have endured, or perhaps both those topics together, appeared to me a theme so important at the present juncture and at the same time so susceptible of poetical management that I more than once perceived myself ready to start in that career, could I have allowed myself to desert Homer for so long a time as it would have cost me to do them justice. While I was pondering these things, the public prints informed me that Miss More was on the point of publication, having actually finished what I had not yet begun. The sight of her advertisement convinced me that my best course would be that to which I felt myself most inclined: to persevere without turning aside to attend to any other call, however alluring, in the business that I have in hand. It occurred to me likewise that I have already borne my testimony in favour of our black brethren, and that I was one of the earliest, if not the first, of those who have in the present day expressed their detestation of the diabolical traffic in question. On all these accounts I judged it best to be silent, and especially because I cannot doubt that some effectual measures will now be taken to alleviate the miseries of their condition, the whole nation being in possession of the case, and it being impossible also to allege an argument in behalf of man-merchandise that can deserve a hearing. I shall be glad to see Hannah More's poem;[1] she is a

[1] Hannah More, (1745–1833), the most formidable blue-stocking of the age. She belonged to the Thornton circle. Her long propagandist poem, *Slavery*, was published in 1788, as was *Thoughts on the Manners of the Great.*

favourite writer with me, and has more nerve and energy both in her thoughts and language than half the rhymers in the kingdom. The *Thoughts on the Manners of the Great* will likewise be most acceptable. I want to learn as much of the world as I can, but to acquire that learning at a distance, and a book with such a title promises fair to serve that purpose effectually.

For poor Hannah's[2] sake I thank you, as does Mrs Unwin, heartily, for your kind intentions to send her Mrs Trimmer's publication.[3] She is at present a very good girl, affectionate and studious to please, and will I verily believe turn that lady's instructions to as good account as any of her little disciples.

I recommend it to you, my dear, by all means to embrace the fair occasion, and to put yourself in the way of being squeezed and incommoded a few hours, for the sake of hearing and seeing what you will never have opportunity to see and hear hereafter, the trial[4] of a man who has been greater and more feared than the Mogul himself, and of his myrmidon Sir Elijah. Whatever we are at home, we have certainly been tyrants in the East; and if these men have, as they are charged, rioted in the miseries of the innocent, and dealt death to the guiltless with an unsparing hand, may they receive a retribution that shall make all future governors and judges of ours in those distant regions tremble. While I speak thus, I equally wish them acquitted. They were both my schoolfellows and for Hastings I had a particular value. As to our friends at the Hall, whether on this subject or any other, I never find them violent. If they dispute, as they do sometimes, it is with each other, never with me. To me and to mine they are always equally obliging, kind and friendly. Poor Mrs Throg is doing Lent penance at this time, a discipline which I assure you does not at all agree with her. A

[2] Hannah Wilson: p. 630, *n*.

[3] *Fabulous Histories: Designed for the Instruction of Children, respecting their Treatment of Animals.* 1786.

[4] The trial of Warren Hastings, first governor-general of British India, began in Westminster Hall on February 13, 1788, and ended with his acquittal in 1795. Thurlow was the presiding judge until 1792. The attempt to impeach Sir Elijah Impey, Chief Justice of the Supreme Court, broke down.

diet differing so much from that which she allows herself in common affects both her looks and her spirits. The gentlemen, the Padre excepted, are less scrupulous than she, and consequently fare better. Mr Throg goes to town tomorrow, but designing to stay there only till Thursday next, he will hardly have time to call upon you.

I have lately had a letter from a lady unknown to me, though she tells me she was intimate with my brother. Her name is Margaret King, and she lives at Perton Hall near Kimbolton. I answered it 2 or 3 days ago, and shall probably hear from her again. The consequence will be that I shall have a new correspondent: an acquisition that I can hardly afford to make.

The terrible curate, of whom I told you, is become to me less terrible, having left Weston and taken up his abode at Ravenstone. I have had the good hap to see him but once, and may now hope that I shall see him no more.

Farewell, my dearest cousin, with Mrs Unwin's affectionate respects, I conclude myself

Ever yours,

Wm Cowper

All advertisements that you may see in the name of Andrew Fridge are my compositions.

The letter that you mention, of which Padre Postlethwaite was so much the subject, came safe to hand.

TEXT: *Panshanger MSS.* *

TO LADY HESKETH

The Lodge, Feb. 22, 1788

I thank you, my dearest coz, for the bank-note which I received this morning, and for your letter which accompanied it. I send my answer sooner by one post than the usual time, that you may be apprised of its safe arrival as early as possible.

I do not wonder that your ears and feelings were hurt by Mr Burke's severe invective. But severe as it was, I am told that they who are to follow him threaten to bear still harder upon the culprit than he. So that whatever be the event of the trial, whether Hastings be condemned or acquitted, unpunished he cannot be; for perhaps there is not so much difference as one would at first imagine, between being pilloried and pelted with addled eggs, and placed at the bar of such a court, a mark for all eyes and the theme of the most unmerciful reproaches. The main difference seems to be that in the former case the mob are the agents and the spectators, and in the latter, persons of consideration, quality and fashion. Otherwise I do not know but that the tongue of a great orator may be as formidable as the hoot of an Irish chairman, and a rhetorical flourish finely turned and pointed at least as painful in its effects as a handful of *boue de Londres*. But you are to know, my dear, or probably you know it already, that the prosecution of public delinquents has always, and in all countries, been thus conducted. The style of a criminal charge of this kind has been an affair settled among orators from the days of Tully to the present, and like all other practices that have obtained for ages, this in particular seems to have been founded originally in reason and in the necessity of the case. He who accuses another to the state must not appear himself unmoved by the view of the crimes with which he charges him, lest he should be suspected of fiction, or of precipitancy, or of a consciousness that after all he shall not be able to prove his allegations. On the contrary, in order to impress the minds of his hearers with a persuasion that he himself at least is convinced of the criminality of the prisoner, he must be vehement, energetic, rapid; must call him tyrant and traitor and everything else that is odious; and all this to his face, because all this, bad as it is, is no more than he undertakes to prove in the sequel; and if he cannot prove it, he must himself appear in a light very little more desirable and at the best to have trifled with the tribunal to which he has summoned him. Thus Tully, in the very first sentence of his first oration against Catiline, calls him a monster: a manner of

address in which he persisted till said monster, unable to
support the fury of his accuser's eloquence any longer, rose
from his seat, elbowed for himself a passage through the
crowd and at last burst from the Senate House in an agony,
as if the Furies themselves had followed him.

And now, my dear, though I have thus spoken, and have
seemed to plead the cause of that species of eloquence which
you and every creature who has your sentiments must necessarily dislike, perhaps I am not altogether convinced of its
propriety. Perhaps, at the bottom, I am much more of opinion
that if the charge, unaccompanied by any inflammatory matter
and simply detailed, being once delivered into the court and
read aloud, the witnesses were immediately examined and
sentence pronounced according to the evidence, not only the
process would be shortened, much time and much expense
saved, but Justice would have at least as fair play as now she
has. Prejudice is of no use in weighing the question—Guilty
or Not Guilty— and the principal aim, end and effect of all
such introductory harangues is to create as much prejudice
as possible. When you and I therefore shall have the whole and
sole management of such a business entrusted to us, we will
order it otherwise.

I have not quarrelled with Hoffman[1]—on the contrary I
admire him as much as ever. But I am become a better
economist in that particular than I was. Last year I took his
anodyne till it had ceased to be one. I now only take it
occasionally, and find the benefit of it. When I dine at the
Hall, which we generally do twice a week, I talk five times
more than at any other time. The consequence is a flurry of
spirits which a spoonful of Hoffmann presently composes.
My health is, in the main, better than it has been these 30
years. I know not now what it is to have a disordered stomach.
A fever of the nervous kind indeed attends me Spring and
Fall, for which I take a decoction of bark that never fails to
remove it and which I am now taking. Except that when that
fever prevails, I sleep as well as any man.

I was glad to learn from the papers that our Cousin Henry

---

[1] Hoffmann's Anodyne: a compound of ether, alcohol and ethereal oil.

shone as he did in reading the charge.[2] This must have given much pleasure to the General. Yet alas! a thought comes across me that had he pursued his first career, he might have lived to press the Woolsack himself, instead of addressing it in the humbler capacity of a reader. — Mr Throg returned from London yesterday. He arrived just at dinner time and found Uzz in his Hall ready to dine with him. — What shall I say? How shall I tell it you? Making a general sweep of loose papers out of my desk, I unwittingly threw into the fire along with them your birthday copy of verses by our friend Frances. I would with all my heart that thou wert here to box my ears for doing it.

Mrs Unwin's love attends thee with that of thy ever affectionate

W.C.

TEXT: *Panshanger MSS.**

TO LADY HESKETH

The Lodge, March 3, 1788. Monday

My dearest coz,

He who can sit up all night at a gaming table, knowing that he is to spend the next day in the accusation of another at the bar of the first Court of Judicature in the world, is not a jot more innocent than he whom he accuses.[1] If he has not committed the same offences it is only because he never had the same opportunity, for profligate he must be to a degree that no Governor of Fort St George past, present, or to come can possibly surpass. This may look like an assertion built upon grounds too slight to bear it, but if I were not writing to my cousin whom I would not entertain merely with logical

[2] 'The charges and the answers of Hastings were first read. The ceremony occupied two whole days, and was rendered less tedious than it would otherwise have been by the silver voice and just emphasis of Cowper, the clerk of the court.' (Macaulay's Essay on Hastings.)

[1] C. J. Fox was one of the prosecutors in the trial of Warren Hastings.

deductions, I think I could make it appear probable at least, if not absolutely certain.

One day last week, Mrs Unwin and I having taken our morning walk, and returning homeward through the Wilderness, met the three Throckmortons. A minute after we had met them, we heard the cry of hounds at no great distance, and mounting the broad stump of an elm which had been felled, and by the aid of which we were enabled to look over the wall, we saw them. They were at that time in our orchard. Presently we heard a terrier belonging to Mrs Throg, which you may remember by the name of Fury, yelping with much vehemence, and saw her running through the thickets within few yards of us at her utmost speed as if in pursuit of something which we doubted not was the fox. Before we could reach the other end of the Wilderness the hounds entered also; and when we arrived at the gate which opens into the Grove, there we found the whole dirty and weary cavalcade assembled. The huntsman dismounting begged leave to follow his hounds on foot, for he was sure, he said, that they had killed him. A conclusion which I suppose he drew from their profound silence. He was accordingly admitted, and with a sagacity that would not have dishonoured the best hound in the world, pursuing precisely the track which the fox and the dogs had taken, though he had never had a glimpse of either after their first entrance through the rails, soon arrived where he found the slaughtered prey, videlicet in the pit of a certain place called Jessamy Hall, into which both the fox and the dogs had entered by a large aperture in the brickwork at the bottom of it. Being himself by far too staunch to boggle at a little filth contracted in so honourable a cause, he soon produced dead Reynard, and rejoined us in the Grove with all his dogs about him. Having an opportunity to see a ceremony which I was pretty sure would never fall in my way again, I determined to stay and to notice all that passed with the most minute attention. The fox's tail, or brush as I ought to call it, was given to one of the Hall foot-boys who, bearing it in his hat-band, ran with it to his mistress, and in the height of his transport offered it to her fair hand, neither so clean nor so sweet as it had been while the fox possessed it. Happily however for Mrs Throg, not being quite so enraptured, she had the presence of mind to decline the offer. The boy therefore, for aught I know, remains to his hour in possession both of the tail and the stink that belongs to it. The huntsman having by the aid of a pitchfork lodged Reynard on the arm of an elm at the height of about 9 feet from the ground, there left him for a considerable time. The gentlemen sat on their horses contemplating the fox for which they had toiled so hard, and the hounds assembled at the foot of the tree with faces not at all less expressive of the most rational delight, contemplated the same object. The huntsman re-mounted. He cut off a foot and threw it to the hounds. One of them swallowed it whole like a bolus. He then once more alighted, and drawing down the fox by his hinder legs, desired the people who were by this time rather numerous to open a lane for him to the right and left. He was instantly obeyed; when, throwing the fox to the distance of some yards, and screaming like a fiend as he is—'Tear him in pieces'—at least six times repeatedly, he consigned him over absolutely to the pack, who in a few minutes devoured him completely. Thus, my dear, as Virgil says,[2] what none of the gods could have ventured to promise me, time itself pursuing its accustomed course has of its own accord presented me with.—I have been in at the death of a fox—and you now know as much of that matter as I, who am as well informed as any sportsman in England.

A thousand thanks, my dear, for your kind intention to furnish me not only with books but with shelves also to set them on. I am in reality equally in want of both, having no shelf in the world but an encoignure which holds a lexicon and a dictionary.

My dog[3] turns out a most beautiful creature but is at present apt to lift up his leg in the house, on which subject he and I had a terrible quarrel this morning. My cat is the most affectionate of all her kind, and in my eyes a beauty also.— The Throgs, with whom we walked this morning, enquired

[2] *Aeneid* IX, 6–7.
[3] Beau.

after you as they often do, when I made your remembrances as you desired.

Adieu, my dearest coz, with Mrs Unwin's very best and warmest respects, I remain ever yours,

Wm Cowper

I often think of my Uncle though I do not always mention him. Few days pass in which he is not in my thoughts—Give my love to him.

TEXT: *Panshanger MSS.**

TO MARGARET KING[1]

Weston Underwood, March 3, 1788

I owe you many acknowledgments, dear madam, for that unreserved communication, both of your history and of your sentiments, with which you favoured me in your last. It gives me great pleasure to learn that you are so happily circumstanced, both in respect of situation and frame of mind. With your view of religious subjects, you could not indeed, speaking properly, be pronounced unhappy in any circumstances; but to have received from above not only that faith which reconciles the heart to affliction, but many outward comforts also, and especially that greatest of all earthly comforts, a comfortable home, is happiness indeed. May you long enjoy it! As to health or sickness, you have learned already their true value, and know well that the former is no blessing, unless it be sanctified, and that the latter is one of the greatest we can receive, when we are enabled to make a proper use of it.

There is nothing in my story that can possibly be worth your knowledge; yet, lest I should seem to treat you with a reserve which, at your hands, I have not experienced, such as it is, I will relate it.—I was bred to the law; a profession to

[1] Mrs King (1735–95) was the wife of the Rev. John King, rector of Pertonhall, Beds., a friend of C.'s brother John.

which I was never much inclined, and in which I engaged rather because I was desirous to gratify a most indulgent father, than because I had any hopes of success in it myself. I spent twelve years in the Temple, where I made no progress in that science, to cultivate which I was sent thither. During this time my father died. Not long after him, died my mother-in-law;[2] and at the expiration of it, a melancholy seized me, which obliged me to quit London, and consequently to renounce the bar. I lived some time at St Albans. After having suffered in that place long and extreme affliction, the storm was suddenly dispelled, and the same day-spring from on high which has arisen upon you, arose on me also. I spent eight years in the enjoyment of it; and have ever since the expiration of those eight years, been occasionally the prey of the same melancholy as at first. In the depths of it I wrote *The Task*, and the volume which preceded it; and in the same deeps am now translating Homer. But to return to Saint Albans. I abode there a year and half. Thence I went to Cambridge, where I spent a short time with my brother, in whose neighbourhood I determined, if possible, to pass the remainder of my days. He soon found a lodging for me at Huntingdon. At that place I had not resided long, when I was led to an intimate connexion with a family of the name of Unwin. I soon quitted my lodging, and took up my abode with them. I had not lived long under their roof, when Mr Unwin, as he was riding one Sunday morning to his cure at Gravely, was thrown from his horse; of which fall he died. Mrs Unwin having the same views of the gospel as myself, and being desirous of attending a purer ministration of it than was to be found at Huntingdon, removed to Olney, where Mr Newton was at that time the preacher, and I with her. There we continued till Mr Newton, whose family was the only one in the place with which we could have a connexion, and with whom we lived always on the most intimate terms, left it. After his departure, finding the situation no longer desirable, and our house threatening to fall upon our heads, we removed hither. Here we have a good house, in a most beautiful

[2] His stepmother, Rebecca Cowper.

village, and, for the greatest part of the year, a most agreeable neighbourhood. Like you, madam, I stay much at home, and have not travelled twenty miles from this place and its environs, more than once these twenty years.

All this I have written, not for the singularity of the matter, as you will perceive, but partly for the reason which I gave at the outset, and partly that, seeing we are become correspondents, we may know as much of each other as we can, and that as soon as possible.

I beg, madam, that you will present my best respects to Mr King, whom, together with yourself, should you at any time hereafter take wing for a longer flight than usual, we shall be happy to receive at Weston; and believe me, dear madam, his and your obliged and affectionate,

W.C.

TEXT: *Southey*

TO MRS HILL

Weston Underwood, March 17, 1788

My dear Madam,

A thousand thanks to you for your obliging and most acceptable present which I received this evening. Had you known my occasions you could not possibly have timed it more exactly. The Throckmorton family, who live in our near neighbourhood, and who sometimes take a dinner with us, were by engagement made with them two or three days ago appointed to dine with us just at the time when your turkey will be in perfection. A turkey from Wargrave, the residence of my friend, and a turkey, as I conclude, of your breeding, stands a fair chance, in my account, to excel all other turkeys; and the ham its companion will be no less welcome.

I have to thank you likewise for an excellent piece of cod with oysters, which however singular it may seem, came also just in due season to furnish out a smart entertainment for the very same neighbours of ours, the Throckmortons.

I shall be happy to hear that my friend Joseph has recovered entirely from his late indisposition, which I was informed was gout, a distemper which however painful in itself, brings at least some comfort with it, both for the patient and those who love him, the hope of length of days, and an exemption from numerous other evils. I wish him just so much of it as may serve for a confirmation of this hope, and not one twinge more.

Your husband, my dear Madam, told me, some time since that a certain library of mine concerning which I have heard no other tidings these five and twenty years, is still in being. Hue and cry have been made after it in Old Palace Yard, but hitherto in vain. If he can inform a bookless student in what region or in what nook his long-lost volumes may be found, he will render me an important service.

I am likely to be furnished soon with shelves, which my cousin of Norfolk Street is about to send me, but furniture for those shelves I shall not presently procure unless by recovering my stray authors. I am not young enough to think of making a new collection, and shall probably possess myself of few books hereafter but such as I may forth put myself, which cost me nothing but what I can better spare than money—time and consideration.

I beg, my dear Madam, that you will give my love to my friend, and believe me with the warmest sense of his and your kindness,

Your most obliged and affectionate

Wm Cowper

TEXT: *Cowper Johnson MSS.*

TO LADY HESKETH

The Lodge, March 21, 1788

My dearest coz,

I am, after all, become a contributor to the poetical effusions at this time produced on the subject of the slave trade. Since

I wrote last the following reached me enclosed in a letter from Mr Newton to whom it was addressed.

My dear Sir,

We had some gentlemen employed about the abolition of the slave-trade with us the other day. They are very desirous of some good ballads to be sung about the streets on that subject, which they mean to print and distribute, and think they might be of use to the cause. If you think Mr Cowper could by your means be prevailed on to do this for them, they would be extremely obliged to him, and nobody could do it so well.

Yrs in haste

J. Balgonie[1]

Thus assailed, what could I do less than surrender all my resolutions to the contrary? Accordingly, I have sent up two pieces. One a serious ballad to the tune of Hosier's Ghost, called *The Negro's Complaint*[2] — the other in a different strain and entitled *Sweet Meat has Sour Sauce or the Slave-trader in the Dumps*. This I tell you my dear, that if they should happen to be sung within your hearing, you may pull your bell and send for them, because they are your cousin's. I have not however yet heard, nor has there been time for it, whether they have been approved or not. You know, I doubt not, that Lady Balgonie is Mr Thornton's daughter. To the family of the Thorntons I have had particular obligations, and they are all subscribers to my Homer. So that the application was on every account irresistible. I am, in fact, not sorry to have been constrained to abandon for a few hours the business of translation, that I might lend my shoulder, however insignificant, to this honourable attempt. I do not perfectly discern, at present, the probable utility of what I have done, for it

[1] Jane, daughter of John Thornton, and the wife of Lord Balgonie, later 8th Earl of Leven.

[2] Printed on p. 95. The Society for the Abolition of the Slave Trade circulated thousands of copies under the title 'A subject for Conversation at the Tea-Table.' It was set to music and sung in the streets of London and other cities. See T. Clarkson: *History of the Abolition of the Slave Trade*, 1808, I, 108.

seems an affair in which the good pleasure of King Mob is not likely to be much consulted; but at least it can do no harm, and I may perhaps hereafter have the comfort of flattering myself that I helped a little.

A house-breaker lately apprehended at Olney is to be executed at Aylesbury on Wednesday. About a week since, 3 of the principal inhabitants of Olney called on me just at dinner-time, and put into my hand a letter addressed to one of them by the prisoner. He begged hard that intercession might be made for him by petition to the judge, and their business with me was to entreat that I would draw it. I confess that I was rather averse to the employment for two reasons. First, because I knew the man to have been an offender for many years, and the fittest that could be to be made an example of, which was nowhere more wanted than at Olney. And secondly, because his case afforded not a single plea for mercy, or anything which at all resembled one. On these grounds I remonstrated against the measure. But they still continuing to press it upon me, and I foreseeing that if the matter should hitch with me, the death of the prisoner would be charged on my refusal, I accordingly bent myself to this work also. I sent them a sheetful of what might be called a petition, that evening; it seemed to say something but in fact said nothing, for nothing was there to be said. When, however, they came to offer it to their neighbours for attestation, nobody would sign it. [So] this exercise of my ingenuity came to nothing. I hear that the poor wretch is very penitent and reconciled now to his fate, which makes the miscarriage an affair not at all to be regretted.

When I first began to think seriously of addressing myself to Homer again, (it is about 9 months since) Mrs Unwin received a letter from Johnson enquiring after my health, in which he discovered some anxiety to know if the work proceeded. In order to satisfy him and Fuseli of the sincerity of my intentions to finish it, I immediately sent up the 12th and 13th books for Fuseli's revisal, which otherwise I should have sent to you as I had used to do, with a desire that you would transmit them to the General. From Johnson I have heard nothing since; so that had I not learned by a sidewind that the parcel actually reached him, I must have concluded that it had miscarried. But a friend of mine saw it on his counter within few hours after its arrival. I am now in the 16th Book and my share of the business proceeding so much faster than that of Fuseli, am likely to be ready for the press before he will have had leisure to criticize the remainder.

Looking back on what I have written I observe that the transitions in this letter are truly Pindaric. To finish it therefore in the same strain, I will just tell you that I have received this week a basket including a turkey and ham from the amiable Mrs Hill. It comes just in time to make a dinner for the Throcks, who next week take leave of Weston which I suppose they will see no more till Midsummer. — Mrs Unwin reads Mrs Trimmer to me after supper, with whose little books I am charmed.

So now, my dear, good night to thee. Adieu. Not Peter, but
William Pindar[3]

TEXT: *Panshanger MSS.* **

TO LADY HESKETH

The Lodge, March 31, 1788

My dearest coz,

I have received from the General six dozen of Oporto, four ditto of sherry, and Madeira, he says, shall follow soon. My thanks are due to *you* for thanking *him*, because it proves the interest that you take in my emoluments. — The hen, I find, has hatched, and we have another cousin. The Throgs gave me this intelligence, having found it in their paper, which as it happened I did not see. They leave Weston on Wednesday, and we dine with them tomorrow for the 3rd time within the week. I shall regret their going, but regret is vain. London has attractions irresistible by those who have youth and

---

[3] 'Peter Pindar' was the pseudonym of John Wolcot, a contemporary satirist.

money. I shall amuse myself in their absence with raising cucumbers in their garden which will be sent after them, and melons on which they will regale themselves at their return. I have some thoughts, but have not absolutely resolved on it, that I shall charge Monsieur their valet with as much of my Homer as has been copied fair, to be consigned to you, and by you, when you have done with it, to the General. My doubts are occasioned only by the smallness of the quantity, four books or five at most being all that are in travelling order. But the General groans to see them, and you perhaps will not be sorry; I think therefore that I shall send them.

One day last week, on Thursday it might be, we met in the Grove Mrs Throg in company with two young ladies and a lady not so young as they. I soon learned that they were the Miss Knaps. One of them, the eldest as I believe, addressing herself to me, gave me to understand that she had seen you lately, and spoke of you in terms that proved she knew you. The poor thing had walked from Gayhurst that morning, and was at that moment setting out on her return by the same conveyance. When I saw her she was completely fagged, or as the Scots poet Burn[s] calls it, *ramfuzled*. Therefore in what condition she reached Gayhurst, or whether she be still living, I neither know nor can conjecture. You are likely to be first informed, for if she still draws vital air, she goes to Town tomorrow. When you see her I beg that you will present her with my compliments and assure her from me, that such journeys are not for a frame like hers. Her sister, who more prudently had committed herself to the back of an horse, fared better, and their friend Mrs Roberts who likewise performed on foot, seemed not to suffer much fatigue from doing so. Yet even she perhaps, for she is thin and delicate, might have migrated by means of a carriage or quadruped with more advantage.

Mrs Throg has promised to write to me. I beg that as often as you shall see her you will give her a smart pinch and say: 'Have you written to my cousin?' I build all my hopes of her performance on this expedient, and for so doing these my letters not patent shall be your sufficient warrant. You are thus to give her the question till she shall answer: 'Yes.'—I have written one more song and sent it. It is called *The Morning Dream*, and may be sung to the tune of Tweedside or any other tune that will suit it, for I am not nice on that subject. I would have copied it for you, had I not almost filled my sheet without it, but now, my dear, you must stay till the sweet sirens of London shall bring it to you. Or if that happy day should never arrive, I hereby acknowledge myself your debtor to that amount. I shall now probably cease to sing of tortured negroes, a theme which never pleased me, but which in the hope of doing them some little service, I was not unwilling to handle. What you tell me concerning the disposition of our great folks in this matter is truly mortifying. It had been less dishonourable for England never to have stirred in it, than after having done so, to fall asleep again. Till now, we were chargeable perhaps only with inattention, but hereafter, if the poor creatures be not effectually redressed, and all buying and selling of them prohibited for ever, we cannot be wronged by the most opprobious appellations. Call us who will deliberately cruel and tyrants upon principle, we are guilty and must acknowledge it.

If anything could have raised Miss More to a higher rank in my opinion than she possessed before, it could only be your information that after all, she and not Mr Wilberforce is author of that volume. How comes it to pass, that she being a woman, writes so little like one? With a force, and energy, and a correctness hitherto arrogated by the men, and not very frequently displayed even by the men themselves? Adieu, my dearest coz! Mrs U. sends affectionate remembrances.

Ever thine

Wm Cowper

P.S. Your account of the Chancellor's behaviour makes me wish you would touch the porcupine with more caution.

TEXT: *Panshanger MSS.* *

TO LADY HESKETH

The Lodge, April 7, 1788

My dearest coz,

I begin to scribble, but I do not say that I shall be able to fill the sheet. Interruptions have occurred and the evening is far spent. But I will do my best.

We waited with the impatience that belongs to the love we feel for the donor, for the case announced in your last.[1] But whether it did not reach the inn in due season, which was probably the cause, or whether it were owing to any other less obvious reason, it came not. All that I can say therefore at present is that when it comes it will be most entirely welcome, and in the meantime I must be content to bestow my lumber where I can, which is in every nook and cranny that can be made to contain it. My very dressing-table is filled with Homer, not to mention my drawer in the secretary, and my desk.

I sent you, my dear, by the Throcks, the four first books of the *Iliad*, which I hope have by this time reached you. This last edition of it differs so much from that which you have seen that I can venture to say you will at least find novelty in it. When you shall have seen enough of it, I will beg the favour of you by the safest means to convey it to the General. I have also this day written to Johnson, and have sent him a civil hue and cry after Fuseli, who has now been in possession of the 12th and 13th books not less than nine months and for aught that appears has done little or nothing to them. I have likewise suggested to him that having finished eleven books for the press and advanced in my translation as far as to the 17th, I cannot but suppose that it would be a good time to begin printing, and that I should be glad of his opinion upon that matter.

---

[1] Lady Hesketh had sent him two chiffoniers: see *Gratitude*, p. 97.

What is the state of the subscription I know not nor am at all able to conjecture, but I suppose it is such as may vindicate such a noble enterprise, as that of going to press immediately, from the imputation of rashness. You perhaps can inform me, my coz, whether the General and Henry have yet sent in their quotas. To me it appears doubtful, because in a letter which I received from Henry once on a time, he spoke of his list as not at that time delivered, saying that he had procured upwards of thirty Rt.Honble. names, and hoped at the meeting of Parliament to procure many more. The time indeed of which I speak has been long since past, but having never heard a syllable of the matter either from him, the General or Johnson, I naturally suppose that the matter may rest where it did. All this I mention to you, as I do everything that interests me, because it does so, knowing that whatever falls under that description interests you likewise, and because I know that if I desire it, when you see Henry next you will ask him the question.

In the aforesaid letter sent to Johnson by this post, I have also desired him, as I did before, to send the 12th and 13th books to you, when Fuseli shall have revised them; which books I will also beg of you to send to the General at your own best leisure. Thou hast been, my dearest coz, from the first a principal mover of the wheels on which the business of my subscription has rolled, to which kindness of yours you are indebted for the additional trouble with which this letter saddles you.— Having made the progress that I have mentioned, I begin to feel a wish that the printers' share of the labour were begun. I know them to be as tedious as asses, and that having proceeded as far as I have, I shall have finished *Iliad* and *Odyssey* too, long enough before they will have come up with me, should they even set off tomorrow. There is therefore no reason why they should not, or at least as soon as possible.

Mr Bean, the new vicar, drank tea with us this evening, whom I like much. I like his wife also. I have seen her, but Mrs Unwin has not. Dirty ways or high winds or rain or snow have hindered her walking to Olney ever since they have been settled there. As to Postlethwaite, of him I have heard nothing farther than that he never was so happy in his life, which is enough in all reason, and is probably all that I shall ever hear of *him*. I have the comfort to find, on comparing notes with Mr Bean, that the newly arrived parson, so much my terror once, was equally his. It is plain therefore that I was not frightened for nothing. Adieu! If you see the Throcks, any or all, give my love to them, and remember your commission. I am, with Mrs Unwin's best remembrances,

Ever thine,

W.C.

P.S. Rogers has this day had a particular charge to be careful of the case, and to bring it by the next waggon, all which he has promised.

TEXT: *Panshanger MSS.* **

TO JOSEPH HILL

Weston Underwood, May 8, 1788

My dear friend,

You judge well, as of other things, so especially concerning poets and their occasions, and I am obliged to you for anticipating mine by your draft for 30£ which I received yesterday and not the day before as I ought to have done, your letter being addressed to me in Northamptonshire, whereas my residence is in Bucks.

Walter Bagot wrote me word that he had seen you and that you look well, which I was heartily glad to hear. His brother Chester called on me a few days since, who if we did not live 5 miles asunder would be more my comfort than under that predicament he can be. His carriage however is to waft us to Chicheley as soon as we can meet to settle a day for dining with him. These trips are practicable at this season, but in the winter the roads forbid them.

Alas! my library—I must now give it up for a lost thing

887

for ever.[1] The only consolation belonging to the circumstance is or seems to be that no such loss did ever befall any other man, or can ever befall me again. As far as books are concerned I am

Totus teres atque rotundus,[2]

and may set fortune at defiance.[3] Those books which had been my father's had, most of them, his arms on the inside cover, but the rest, no mark, neither his name nor mine. I could mourn for them like Sancho for his Dapple,[4] but it would avail me nothing.

You will oblige me much by sending me a Crazy Kate. A gentleman last winter promised me both her and the Lace-maker,[5] but he went to London, that place in which as in the grave— All things are forgotten[6]— and I have never seen either of them.

I begin to see some prospect of a conclusion, of the *Iliad* at least, now opening upon me, having reached the 18th book. Your letter found me yesterday in the very fact of dispersing the whole host of Troy, by the voice only of Achilles.[7] There is nothing extravagant in the idea, for you have witnessed a similar effect attending even such a voice as mine, at midnight, from a garret window, on the dogs of a whole parish whom I have put to flight in a moment.

I must beseech you if possible to send me a box of Elliott's ointment, for with all its present faults, it is the only medicine that renders me any effectual service. My last box was made by this Irish bungler, successor to Elliott, and has nevertheless restored me to eyesight a thousand times. If Kate be not

[1] When C. was removed to St Albans in 1763, he left his books behind in the Temple. In March 1788 Hill had heard a rumour that they were still around, and C. had asked him to find them.

[2] Horace, *Satires*, II, vii, 86: '(in myself) complete, like a sphere, perfectly round.'

[3] Ibid: 88.

[4] *Don Quixote*, Part I, xxxiii.

[5] Prints, by Stothard, illustrating *The Task* (see p. 410) and *Truth*, pp. 230–31.

[6] Psalm lxxxviii, 12, in the version of the Book of Common Prayer.

[7] *Iliad*, xviii, 217.

on the road before this reaches you, perhaps you can contrive to send them together.

Present my very best respects to Mrs Hill, and believe me, my dear friend,

Most truly yours,

Wm Cowper

TEXT: *Cowper Johnson MSS.**

TO LADY HESKETH

The Lodge, May 12, 1788

It is probable, my dearest coz, that I shall not be able to write much, but as much as I can, I will. The time between rising and breakfast is all that I can at present find, and this morning I lay later than usual.

I rejoice as much as you that you set me to work, and that my labours have seemingly sped so well. It may be a good thing to have caught a *Lady* of Mrs Montagu's eminence in literary accomplishments and of her influence in the literary world, by *the right ear*. My subscription perhaps may feel the benefit of it. But I have learned not to be over-sanguine in expectation, and recommend it to thee to guard against it. The rather too, because thy natural temper is that way inclined. What we much wish we believe in proportion, and nobody I think has warmer wishes for my prosperity than thou. In the style of this lady's note to you, I can easily perceive a smatch of her character. Neither men nor women write with such neatness of expression, who have not given a good deal of attention to language, and qualified themselves by study. At the same time it gave me much more pleasure to observe that my coz, though not standing on a pinnacle of renown quite so elevated as that which lifts Mrs Montagu to the clouds, falls in no degree short of her in this particular; so that should she make you a member of her Academy she will do it honour. Suspect me not of flattering *you*, for I abhor the thought. Neither *will* you suspect it, when you recollect that it is an invariable rule with me never to pay compliments to those I love.

Two days *en suite* I have walked to Gayhurst. A longer journey than I have performed on foot these 17 years. The first day I went alone, designing merely to make the experiment, and choosing to be at liberty to return, at whatsoever point of my pilgrimage I should find myself fatigued. For I was not without suspicions that years and some other things not less injurious than years, viz. melancholy and distress of mind, might by this time have unfitted me for such achievements. But I found it otherwise. I reached the church, which stands as you know in the garden, in 55 minutes, and returned in ditto time to Weston. The next day, I took the same walk with Mr Powley, having a desire to show him the prettiest place in the country. I not only performed these two excursions without injury to my health, but have by means of them gained indisputable proof that my ambulatory faculty is not yet impaired. A discovery which, considering that to my feet alone I am likely, as I have ever been, to be indebted always for my transportation from place to place, I find very delectable. My little dog was on the point of killing a most beautiful pheasant there, but fortunately the gardener caught him in his arms time enough to prevent it. Beau, the handsomest creature in the world were it not for the extreme brevity of his tail, observing the pheasant's felicity in that respect whose tail was of a length unexampled, conceived envy at the sight and would have slain him. Foolish creature, could he by killing him have made that tail his own, who would not have laughed at a dog's rump adorned with a pheasant's tail! So little do we sometimes understand our own true advantage.

I forgot when I wrote last, and had almost forgotten now, to acquit your servants from all imputation of neglect in the affair of letters. Though yours have twice been long delayed, they have never been charged. A proof that the fault has been in the Olney post-office. Mrs Marriott indeed sent me an apology in the first instance, and told me that the letter had been overlooked. Which how it should possibly happen is to me unintelligible, though it has often been produced to me as the reason of similar delay.—You will find in the last *Gentleman's Magazine* a Sonnet addressed to Henry Cowper, signed 'T.H.' I am the writer of it. No creature knows this but yourself. You will make what use of the intelligence you shall see good. But since I affronted Sephus[1] by praising him in print, I am become timorous and wary.

Ever thine,

W.C.

P.S. Mrs U. being woman is consequently curious, and impatient of course to see the list; you being woman too, will know how to pity her infirmity and to consult her case. —She sends you her best affections.—Johnson desires me not to print till the whole is finished.—The affair is therefore settled.

TEXT: *Panshanger MSS.* *

TO LADY HESKETH

The Lodge, May 27, 1788

My dearest cuzwuzz,

The General in a letter which came yesterday sent me enclosed a copy of my sonnet, thus introducing it.—'I send you a copy of verses somebody has printed in the *Gentleman's Magazine* for April last. Independent of my partiality towards the subject, I think the lines themselves are good.'

Thus it appears that my poetical project has succeeded to my wish, and I write to him by this post on purpose to inform him that the somebody in question is myself. I send him also a copy of the Montagu lines with a short history of that matter.—As Barebones says,[2] they will amuse him—

I like your proposed method well. Begin therefore and

[1] In *An Epistle to Joseph Hill, Esq.* (p. 93).
[2] *On Mrs Montagu's Feather-Hangings.*

exhibit away to right and left as fast as possible. You will have 5 weeks complete for the exercise of your distributory function, for it is too late to get them inserted in the *Magazine* for May. The first week in June I shall send them to my trumpeter Mr Urban, who will sound them forth to purpose.

I no longer wonder that Mrs Montagu stands at the head of all that is called learned, and that every critic vails his bonnet to her superior judgment. I am now reading and have reached the middle of her *Essay on the Writings and Genius of Shakespear*, a book of which, strange as it may seem, though I must have read it formerly, I had absolutely forgot the existence. The learning, the good sense, the sound judgment and the wit displayed in it, fully justify not only my compliment but all compliments that either have been already paid to her talents, or shall be paid hereafter. Voltaire I doubt not rejoiced that his antagonist wrote in English, and that his countrymen could not possibly be judges of the dispute. Could they have known how much she was in the right, and by how many thousand miles the Bard of Avon is superior to all their dramatists, the French critic would have lost half his fame among them.

This book I brought home with me on Friday from Mr Chester's. He gave me a morning call in the beginning of last week, and appointed with us that day for a jaunt to Chicheley. Mrs and Miss Chester accordingly rendered themselves at the Lodge between 12 and 1 and carried us to the place of our destination. We spent a most agreeable day, and in the evening were sent home right honourably in his chaise and four. They are a most amiable family and I am only sorry that we live seven miles asunder, and seven of the dirtiest miles, in winter, that can be found in all the country. At present, and while summer lasts, they are as good as any.

Those pieces of Burns which you mentioned with approbation, in your letter before the last, are exactly the pieces which I should have recommended to your notice in particular. Could a nightingale be so unhappy as to acquire the scream of a jay, she would furnish an instance somewhat resembling the case of a good poet writing in a detestable language. A man may whistle well, but if his breath be offensive one would [not wish][2] to sit within the wind of him. Poor Burns [is rather] in this predicament.

Once more our post goes every day. A poor [man for] the small sum of a shilling per day undertakes to walk 90 miles per week. A London porter would disdain such wages for such labour, neither do I imagine that our Mercury will long prove equal to it. When he gives it up I will tell you.

I saw at Mr Chester's a head of Paris. An antique of Parian marble. His uncle who left him the estate brought it, as I understood Mr Chester, from the Levant. You may suppose that I viewed it with all the enthusiasm that belongs to a translator of Homer. It is in reality a great curiosity and highly valuable.

Our friend Sephus has sent me two prints. The Lacemaker and Crazy Kate. These also I have contemplated with pleasure, having, as you know, a particular interest in them. The former of them is not more beautiful than a lacemaker once our neighbour at Olney, though the artist has assembled as many charms in her countenance, as I ever saw in any countenance, *one* excepted. Kate is both younger and handsomer than the original from which I drew, but she is in a good style and as mad as need be.

How does this hot weather suit thee my dear in London? As for me, with all my colonnades and bowers I am quite oppressed by it. With Mrs Unwin's best love

I am ever thine

Wm Cowper

TEXT: *Panshanger MSS.* *

TO JOSEPH HILL

Weston Underwood, June 8, 1788

My dear friend,

Your letter brought me the very first intelligence of the event[1] it mentions. My last letter from Lady Hesketh gave

[2] Readings uncertain owing to damage to MS.
[1] Ashley Cowper's death.

me reason enough to expect it, but the certainty of it was unknown to me till I learned it by your information. If gradual decline, the consequence of great age, be a sufficient preparation of the mind to encounter such a loss, our minds were certainly prepared to meet it: yet to you I need not say that no preparation can supersede the feelings of the heart on such occasions. While our friends yet live, inhabitants of the same world with ourselves, they seem still to live to *us*; we are sure that they sometimes think of us; and, however improbable it may seem, it is never impossible that we may see each other once again. But the grave, like a great gulf, swallows all such expectations, and in the moment when a beloved friend sinks into it, a thousand tender recollections awaken a regret, that will be felt in spite of all reasonings, and let our warnings have been what they may. Thus it is I take my last leave of poor Ashley, whose heart toward me was ever truly parental, and to whose memory I owe a tenderness and respect that can never leave me.

Every letter of yours bring me some proof of your friendship, and lays me under some new obligation. Before I close this, I must remember to thank you for the ointment, which could not have arrived more seasonably; our late violent changes of weather from extreme heat to the opposite degree of cold having inflamed my eyes exceedingly. By the same basket I received a very fine turbot and lobster, for which-Thanks also. I beg you to present my affectionate regards to Mrs Hill, and to believe me,

> My dear friend,
>> Ever yours,
>>> Wm Cowper

TEXT: *Cowper Johnson MSS.* *

TO LADY HESKETH

The Lodge, June 10, 1788

My dearest coz,

Your kind letter of precaution to Mr Gregson sent him hither as soon as chapel service was ended in the evening, but he found me already apprised of the event that occasioned it by a line from Sephus received a few hours before. My dear uncle's death awakened in me many reflections, which for a time sunk my spirits. A man like him would have been mourned had he doubled the age he reached; at any age his death would have been felt as a loss that no survivor could repair. And though it was not probable that, for my own part, I should ever see him more, yet the consciousness that he still lived was a comfort to me. Let it comfort us now that we have lost him only at a time when Nature could afford him to us no longer, that as his life was blameless so his death was without anguish, and that he is gone to heaven. I know not that human life in its most prosperous state can present anything to our wishes half so desirable as such a close of it.

Not to mingle this subject with others that would ill sort with it, I will add no more at present than a warm hope that you and your sister will be able effectually to avail yourselves of all the consolatory matter with which it abounds. You gave yourselves, while he lived, to a father whose life was doubtless prolonged by your attentions and whose tenderness of disposition made him always deeply sensible of your kindness. In this respect, as well as in many others, his old age was the happiest that I have ever known, and I give you both joy of having had so fair an opportunity, and of having so well used it, to approve yourselves equal to the calls of such a duty in the sight of God and man.

Adieu! my dearest coz—I am with Mrs Unwin's affectionate compliments on the occasion,

Ever thine,

Wm Cowper

TEXT: *Panshanger MSS.*

TO LADY HESKETH

The Lodge, June 15, 1788

Although I know that you must be very much occupied on the present most affecting occasion, yet, not hearing from you, I began to be uneasy on your account, and to fear that your health might have suffered by the fatigue, both of body and spirits, that you must have undergone, till a letter that reached me yesterday from the General set my heart at rest, so far as that cause of anxiety was in question. He speaks of my uncle in the tenderest terms, such as how how truly sensible he was of the amiableness and excellence of his character, and how deeply he regrets his loss. We have indeed lost one who has not left his like in the present generation of our family, and whose equal, in all respects, no future of it will probably produce. My memory retains so perfect an impression of him, that, had I been painter instead of poet, I could from those faithful traces have perpetuated his face and form with the most minute exactness; and this I the rather wonder at because some with whom I was equally conversant five-and-twenty years ago, have almost faded out of all recollection with me. But he made an impression not soon to be effaced, and was in figure, in temper, and manner, and in numerous other respects, such as I shall never behold again. I often think what a joyful interview there has been between him and some of his contemporaries, who went before him. The truth of the matter is, my dear, that they are the happy ones, and that we shall never be such ourselves till we have joined the party. Can there be any thing so worthy of our warmest wishes as to enter on an eternal, unchangeable state, in blessed fellowship and communion with those whose society we valued most, and for the best reasons, while they continued with us? A few steps more through a vain, foolish world, and this happiness will be yours. But be not hasty, my dear, to accomplish thy journey! For of all that live thou art one whom I can least spare; for thou also art one who shalt not leave thy equal behind thee.

W.C.

TEXT: *Southey*

TO LADY HESKETH

The Lodge, June 27, 1788

For the sake of a longer visit, my dearest coz, I can be well content to wait. The country, this country at least, is pleasant at all times, and when winter is come, or near at hand, we shall have the better chance for being snug. I know your passion for retirement indeed, or for what we call *deedy* retirement, and the F[rog]s intending to return to Bath with their mother, when her visit at the Hall is over, you will then find here exactly the retirement in question. I have made in the orchard the best winter-walk in all the parish, sheltered from the east, and from the north-east, and open to the sun, except at his rising, all the day. Then we will have Homer and *Don Quixote*: and then we will have saunter and chat, and one laugh more before we die. Our orchard is alive with creatures of all kinds; poultry of every denomination swarms in it, and pigs, the drollest in the world!

I rejoice that we have a cousin Charles[1] also, as well as cousin Henry, who has had the address to win the good-likings of the Chancellor. May he fare the better for it! As to myself, I have long since ceased to have any expectations from that quarter. Yet if he were indeed mortified as you say (and no doubt you have particular reasons for thinking so) and repented to that degree of his hasty exertions in favour of the present occupant, who can tell? he wants neither means nor management, but can easily at some future period redress the evil, if he chooses to do it. But in the mean time life steals away, and shortly neither he will be in circumstances to do me a kindness, nor I to receive one at his hands. Let him make haste therefore, or he will die a promise in my debt, which he will never be able to perform. Your communications on this subject are as safe as you can wish them. We divulge nothing

---

[1] Maria Cowper's son Charles was called to the bar on Nov. 29, 1788.

but what might appear in the magazine, nor that without great consideration.

I must tell you a feat of my dog Beau.[2] Walking by the river side, I observed some water-lilies floating at a little distance from the bank. They are a large white flower, with an orange coloured eye, very beautiful. I had a desire to gather one, and, having your long cane in my hand, by the help of it endeavoured to bring one of them within my reach. But the attempt proved vain, and I walked forward. Beau had all the while observed me very attentively. Returning soon after toward the same place, I observed him plunge into the river, while I was about forty yards distant from him; and, when I had nearly reached the spot, he swam to land with a lily in his mouth, which he came and laid at my foot.

Mr Rose, whom I have mentioned to you as a visitor of mine for the first time soon after you left us, writes me word that he has seen my ballads against the slavemongers, but not in print. Where he met with them, I know not. Mr Bull begged hard for leave to print them at Newport Pagnel, and I refused, thinking that it would be wrong to anticipate the nobility, gentry, and others,[3] at whose pressing instance I composed them, in their design to print them. But perhaps I need not have been so squeamish; for the opportunity to publish them in London seems now not only ripe, but rotten. I am well content. There is but one of them with which I am myself satisfied, though I have heard them all well spoken of. But there are very few things of my own composition, that I can endure to read, when they have been written a month, though at first they seem to me to be all perfection.

Mrs Unwin, who has been much the happier since the time of your return hither has been in some sort settled, begs me to make her kindest remembrance.

Yours, my dear, most truly,

W.C.

TEXT: *Southey*

---

[2] See *The Dog and the Water Lily*, p. 101.

[3] The Committee for the Abolition of the Slave Trade.

TO LADY HESKETH

The Lodge, July 5, 1788

Not *emetic tartar*, my coz, but the *soluble salt of tartar*, has been of such sovereign use to me. I have not ceased to take it since the time when Dr Ash[1] prescribed it, and believe myself indebted to it in a great degree for the measure of health that I have enjoyed. But with all its virtues it has not superseded the necessity of now and then (once or twice in a year perhaps) a dose of its namesake the emetic. My stomach is much improved since the last operation, and yet is in all respects a troublesome, and in one, a very singular stomach. For you must know, my dear, to carry on the *Johnsonianism* a little farther, that take what I will of the emetic kind, I could not absolutely swear when the operation is over that I have *spuked* at all. The only effect of it seems to be that it disturbs certain air-bubbles contained in the *organ* of *digestion*, which as they escape out of said organ through the gullet or throat, bring with them a part of what I wish to be rid of. But your true roaring vomit that pumps up the very dregs from the bottom, is an exploit to which I am by no means equal. Accordingly much is left where it was.

I have seen no more of Mrs Piozzi's *Letters*[2] than the *Magazine* and *Review* have afforded. If I remember right, the letters of Johnson pleased me chiefly on this account, that though on all other occasions he wrote like nobody, in his letters he expresses himself somewhat in the style of other folks. For I hate triplets in prose, and can hardly think even *his* good sense a sufficient counterpoise for his affectation. I admire your new way to pay off old scores, and to save yourself from the Royal Durance alias the King's Bench,

---

[1] A London physician, and a friend of Joseph Hill, who left him his Cowper MSS.

[2] *Letters to and from the late Samuel Johnson.*

by printing my letters. You have my free permission to do it, but not till I am dead. No. Nor even then till you have given them a complete revisal, erasing all that the critics in such matters would condemn. In which case, my dear, thou wilt reduce thy noble to ninepence, and must take thy seat in a gaol at last.

I shall be as happy in the arrival of my Solander[3] as he whose name it bears was to arrive once more in England after his circumnavigation. To be the proprietor of anything that was once my uncle's will make me rich. A mere trifle acquires value by having been the property of such a man; but his watch will be a vade mecum with which I shall hold a thousand conversations when I am in the woods alone; nor will his snuff-box fall a whit short of it as a most desirable companion. The love I bore him, and the honour I have for his memory, will make them both inestimable to me. The box therefore charged with these treasures will both for its own sake and for the sake of its contents, be an addition not to my convenience only but likewise to my real comfort. Not forgetting the Dean's[4] toothpick. For the Dean also was justly one of the principal boasts of our family, and a man whom I loved and honoured most devoutly. I have not words to tell you how much I feel myself obliged by the distinction made in my favour on this occasion, and I beg you will tell your sister so, giving her at the same time my sincerest thanks and acknowledgements. With respect to the conveyance of them hither, I think I shall be easier if they come by the Wellingbro' coach, having more confidence in it than in the waggon. The passage is quicker, the quantity of lumber less, and the chances of damage are fewer in proportion. It is also an established law that the trusty Kitch meets always the coach at its arrival, and brings hither our parcels immediately. Whereas we wait sometimes 2 or 3 days, and sometimes longer, for a parcel sent by the waggon. Thanks too for the chocolate.

Beau's performance was exactly such as I represented it,

[3] Ashley Cowper's repeating watch. Solander was the Swedish botanist who accompanied Captain Cook on his voyage of 1768-71.
[4] The Hon. Spencer Cowper, Dean of Durham.

without any embellishment. I may now add that the next time we walked to the same place together, he repeated it. With respect to his diet it is always of the most salutary kind: lights he never eats, and liver, having observed that it makes him sick, we never give him now. Bread he eats in abundance, and it is the only thing for which he begs with much importunity. He is regularly combed, and his ears, which are remarkably handsome, are my own particular care. They gather burrs while he threads all the thickets in his way, from which I deliver them myself as soon as we get home. But having taught him to take the water, and even to delight in it, I never give him a forced washing, lest he should contract an hydrophobia and refuse the river. I have observed too that dogs often washed get rheumatisms, because they do not dry themselves by exercise, but lie down in their damp coats which is hurtful to every thing but a Highlander.

The Frogs are to come home this day by dinner.

I want much to see what resolution the Chancellor moved against Mr Rose. At least he will give him a trimming, and a good one, I doubt not.

Ever yours, my dear!

Wm Cowper

P.S. I forgot to tell you that my watch is no repeater, neither good for much in its kind. It was made at Cambridge for my brother and brought home the day after his death. A metal one, for which I paid 6 guineas. It has been one of my chief employments to wish for a better.

TEXT: *MSS. Coll., Cowper Museum, Olney*

TO MARGARET KING

Weston Underwood, Aug. 28, 1788

My dear Madam,

Should you discard me from the number of your correspondents, you would treat me as I seem to deserve, though I do not actually deserve it. I have lately been engaged with company at our house, who resided with us five weeks, and have had much of the rheumatism into the bargain. Not in my fingers, you will say:—True. But you know as well as I, that pain, be it where it may, indisposes us to writing.

You express some degree of wonder that I found you out to be sedentary, at least much a stayer within doors, without any sufficient data for my direction. Now if I should guess your figure and stature with equal success, you will deem me not only a poet but a conjurer. Yet in fact I have no pretensions of that sort. I have only formed a picture of you in my own imagination, as we ever do of a person of whom we think much, though we have never seen that person. Your height I conceive to be about five feet five inches, which, though it would make a short man, is yet height enough for a woman. If you insist on an inch or two more, I have no objection. You are not very fat, but somewhat inclined to be fat, and unless you allow yourself a little more air and exercise, will incur some danger of exceeding in your dimensions before you die. Let me, therefore, once more recommend to you to walk a little more, at least in your garden, and to amuse yourself occasionally with pulling up here and there a weed, for it will be an inconvenience to you to be much fatter than you are, at a time of life when your strength will be naturally on the decline. I have given you a fair complexion, a slight tinge of the rose in your cheeks, dark brown hair, and, if the fashion would give you leave to show it, an open and well-formed forehead. To all this I add a pair of eyes not quite black, but nearly approaching to that hue, and very animated. I have not absolutely determined on the shape of your nose, or the form of your mouth; but should you tell me that I have in other respects drawn a tolerable likeness, have no doubt but I can describe them too. I assure you that though I have a great desire to read him, I have never seen Lavater,[1] nor have availed myself in the least of any of his rules on this occasion. Ah, madam! if with all that sensibility of yours, which exposes you to so much sorrow, and necessarily must expose you to it,

[1] J. K. Lavater's *Physiognomy*.

in a world like this, I have had the good fortune to make you smile, I have then painted you, whether with a strong resemblance, or with none at all, to very good purpose.

I had intended to have sent you a little poem, which I have lately finished, but have no room to transcribe it. You shall have it by another opportunity. Breakfast is on the table, and my time also fails, as well as my paper. I rejoice that a cousin[2] of yours found my volumes agreeable to him, for, being your cousin, I will be answerable for his good taste and judgment.

When I wrote last, I was in mourning for a dear and much-valued uncle, Ashley Cowper. He died at the age of eighty-six. My best respects attend Mr King; and, I am, dear madam,

Most truly yours,
W.C.

TEXT: *Southey*

TO LADY HESKETH

The Lodge, Sepr. 13, 1788

My dearest coz—Beau seems to have objections against my writing to you this morning that are not to be overruled. He will be in my lap, licking my face and nibbling the end of my pen. Perhaps he means to say, I beg you will give my love to her, which I therefore send you accordingly.

There cannot be, this hindrance excepted, a situation more favourable to the business I have in hand than mine at this moment. Here is no noise, *save* (as we poets always express it) that of the birds hopping on their perches and playing with their wires, while the sun glimmering through the elm opposite the window falls on my desk with all the softness of moonshine. There is not a cloud in the sky nor a leaf that moves, so that over and above the enjoyment of the present

[2] The Rev. Thomas Martyn, Regius Professor of Botany at Cambridge University.

calm, I feel a well-warranted expectation that such as the day is, it will be to the end. This is the month in which such weather is to be expected, and which is therefore welcome to me beyond all others, October excepted, which promises to bring you hither. At your coming, you will probably find us and us only, or to speak more properly, *uzz*. The Frogs, as I believe I told you, hop into Norfolk soon, on a visit to Lord Petre's, who beside his palace in Essex, has another in that county. All the brothers are now at the Hall, *save* the physician,[1] who is employed in prescribing medicine to the Welsh at Cardiff. There lives he with *Madame son épouse*, with an income of 300*l* a year, all happiness and contentment. The mother is also here, and here is also our uncle Giffard, a man whom if you know, you must love, and if you do not, I wish you did. But he goes this morning, and I expect every minute to see him pass my window. In volubility, variety, and earnestness of expression, he very much resembles your father, and in the sweetness of his temper too, so that though he be but a passenger, or rather a bird of passage, for his headquarters are in France and he only flits occasionally to England, he has much engaged my affections. I walked with him yesterday on a visit to an oak[2] on the borders of Yardley Chase, an oak which I often visit, and which is one of the wonders that I show to all who come this way and have never seen it. I tell them all that it is a thousand years old, verily believing it to be so, though I do not know it. A mile beyond this oak stands another which has for time immemorial been known by the name of Judith, and is said to have been an oak when my namesake the Conqueror first came hither. And beside all this, there is a good coachway to them both, and I design that you shall see them too.

A day or two before the arrival of your last letter we were agreeably surprised by that of a hamper stuffed with various articles in the grocery way corresponding exactly with a bill of parcels which accompanied them. Though we had received no advice of the same, we were not at all at a loss for the

---

[1] Charles Throckmorton, 1757–1840, later 7th baronet.
[2] The subject of *Yardley Oak*, p. 121.

sender, and hereby, my dear, make you our very best acknowledgements for your kind present. Having had company this
summer, and being also obliged now and then to feed the
Frogs, our stock of hams and tongues is not, at present, much.
One of the former and two of the latter making up our whole
store in that way.

I have, as yet, no news from the Chancellor.[3] It is possible
that none I may have till he can send me good. For to me it
seems that after having expressed for me so much warmth of
friendship still subsisting, he has laid himself under pretty
strong obligations to do something for me, if anything can be
done. But though, in my time, my rest has been broken by
many things, it never was yet by the desire of riches or the
dread of poverty. At the same time I have no objection to all
that he can do for me be it ever so much.

I am going this morning with the Dowager Frog to
Chicheley on a visit to the Chesters, which obliges me to
shorten my scribble somewhat. Unless I finish my letter first,
you will not get it by this post. Therefore farewell my dear!
May God keep thee and give us a joyful meeting. So pray we
both. Amen.

Ever thine

Wm C.

TEXT: *MSS. Coll., Cowper Museum, Olney*

TO MARGARET KING

Weston Underwood, Oct. 11, 1788

My dear Madam,

You are perfectly secure from all danger of being overwhelmed with presents from me. It is not much that a poet
can possibly have it in his power to give. When he has

---

[3] Lady Hesketh had written to Thurlow to remind him of his promise,
many years earlier, that if he should become Lord Chancellor, he would
provide for C. Thurlow's answer had encouraged C. to write himself on
August 26th.

presented his own works, he may be supposed to have exhausted all means of donation. They are his only superfluity. There was a time, but that time was before I commenced writer for the press, when I amused myself in a way somewhat similar to yours; allowing, I mean, for the difference between masculine and female operations. The scissors and the needle are your chief implements; mine were the chisel and the saw. In those days you might have been in some danger of too plentiful a return for your favours. Tables, such as they were, and joint stools such as never were, might have travelled to Pertonhall in most inconvenient abundance. But I have long since discontinued this practice, and many others which I found it necessary to adopt, that I might escape the worst of all evils, both in itself and in its consequences—an idle life. Many arts I have exercised with this view, for which nature never designed me; though among them were some in which I arrived at considerable proficiency, by mere dint of the most heroic perseverance. There is not a 'squire in all this country who can boast of having made better squirrel-houses, hutches for rabbits, or bird-cages, than myself; and in the article of cabbage-nets, I had no superior. I even had the hardiness to take in hand the pencil, and studied a whole year the art of drawing. Many figures were the fruit of my labours, which had, at least, the merit of being unparalleled by any production either of art or nature. But before the year was ended, I had occasion to wonder at the progress that may be made, in despite of natural deficiency, by dint alone of practice; for I actually produced three landscapes which a lady[1] thought worthy to be framed and glazed. I then judged it high time to exchange this occupation for another, lest by any subsequent productions of inferior merit I should forfeit the honour I had so fortunately acquired. But gardening was of all employments that in which I succeeded best; though even in this I did not suddenly attain perfection. I began with lettuces and cauliflowers: from them I proceeded to cucumbers; next to melons. I then purchased an orange-tree, to which, in due time, I added two or three myrtles. These

[1] Lady Austen.

served me day and night with employment during a whole severe winter. To defend them from the frost, in a situation that exposed them to its severity, cost me much ingenuity and much attendance. I contrived to give them a fire heat; and have waded night after night through the snow, with the bellows under my arm, just before going to bed, to give the latest possible puff to the embers, lest the frost should seize them before morning. Very minute beginnings have sometimes important consequences. From nursing two or three little evergreens, I became ambitious of a green-house, and accordingly built one; which, verse excepted, afforded me amusement for a longer time than any expedient of all the many to which I have fled for refuge from the misery of having nothing to do. When I left Olney for Weston, I could no longer have a greenhouse of my own; but in a neighbour's garden I find a better, of which the sole management is consigned to me.

I had need take care, when I begin a letter, that the subject with which I set off be of some importance; for before I can exhaust it, be it what it may, I have generally filled my paper. But self is a subject inexhaustible, which is the reason that though I have said little, and nothing, I am afraid, worth your hearing, I have only room to add that I am, my dear Madam,

Most truly yours,

W.C.

Mrs Unwin bids me present her best compliments, and say how much she shall be obliged to you for the receipt to make that most excellent cake which came hither in its native pan. There is no production of yours that will not be always most welcome at Weston.

TEXT: *Southey*

TO SAMUEL ROSE

The Lodge, Feb.[1] 19, 1789

My dear Sir,

If I were not the most industrious man alive, and if I were not sure that you know me to be so, I should think a long apology necessary for so long a silence; but I will spare myself and you that trouble, assured that in consideration of my various employments you will excuse me.

It gave me much pleasure to hear of Mrs Rose's complete recovery. May she long be continued to you. The loss of a good mother is irreparable; no friend can supply her place.

You mention your visit at Lady Hesketh's with much pleasure, and I can assure you (for I have it under her own hand) that you were not the only person much pleased on that occasion. Continue what you are, and I will ensure you a welcome among all persons of her description.

I have taken, since you went, many of the walks which we have taken together, and none of them, I believe, without thoughts of you. I have, though not a good memory in general, yet a good local memory, and can recollect by the help of a tree or a stile, what you said on that particular spot. For this reason I purpose, when the summer is come, to walk with a book in my pocket. What I read at my fireside I forget, but what I read under a hedge or at the side of a pond, that pond and that hedge will always bring to my remembrance; and this is a sort of *memoria technica* which I would recommend to you, did I not know that you have no occasion for it. But though I do not often find my fireside assistant to my memory on other subjects, there is one on which it serves me faithfully at the present moment. We are indebted not only to your uncle's kindness for the coals by which we warm ourselves, but to his purse also. If that account be not already liquidated, you may settle it when you please with my cousin, who will be responsible for the amount, and left me a commission to tell you so.

[1] Dated Jan. 19th, in error, by Southey.

I am reading Sir John Hawkins[2] and still hold the same opinion of his book as when you were here. There are in it undoubtedly some awkwardnesses of phrase, and, which is worse, here and there some unequivocal indications of a vanity not easily pardonable in a man of his years; but on the whole I find it amusing, and to me at least, to whom everything that has passed in the literary world within these five and twenty years, is news, sufficiently replete with information. Mr Throckmorton told me about three days since, that it was lately recommended to him by a sensible man, as a book that would give him more insight into the history of modern literature, and of modern men of letters than most others. A commendation which I really think it merits. Fifty years hence perhaps the world will feel itself obliged to him.

I say nothing about politics, persuaded that it becomes me more, situated as I am, to be a hearer on that subject than a speaker. But this I may and will say, that I rejoice in the fairer prospect that now seems to open on us of the King's recovery.

Mrs Unwin's restoration is slow, but I hope sure. She cannot walk at all without support, nor long, with any; yet she walks better than she did a week ago. She must certainly have received some greater hurt than we were aware of, but what hurt we shall never know. It is sufficient that he knows who is able to heal the worst. With her best compliments, I remain, my dear friend, truly yours

Wm Cowper

TEXT: *MS. Victoria and Albert Museum, Catalogue No.* 126, 48 *G*4/8 (Dyce Coll.)

TO LADY HESKETH

The Lodge, Wednesday Feb. 25, 1789

My dearest coz,

You dislike the crossing of letters, and so do I, yet though

[2] *The Life of Samuel Johnson, LL.D,* by Sir John Hawkins, London, 1787.

I write at the hazard of that inconvenience, I feel that I must write this evening. My hands are at present less full than usual. Having lately sent Johnson as much Review-work[1] as will serve to satisfy him for a time, I allow myself a little vacation from those labours, which, however, I must soon resume.

The King's recovery is with *us* a subject of daily conversation and of continual joy. It is so providentially timed, that no man who believes a providence at all, can say less of it than that *This is the finger of God*! Never was a hungry faction so mortally disappointed, nor the integrity of an upright administration more openly rewarded.[2] It is a wonderful era in the history of this country; and posterity will envy us the happiness of having lived at such a period. We who are loyal subjects and love our monarch, may now take up the old Jacobite ditty and say— *The King shall enjoy his own again*. An application which I fear we should never have had an opportunity to make, had his recovery been delayed but a little longer. The faction at home have driven too fast, and the Irish will feel that they have made a blunder. Now let us listen to the raptures that will be pretended on this occasion. Sheridan, I expect, will soar in rhetorical ecstasies: Burke will say his prayers are answered, and Fox will term it the happiest event that he has ever witnessed; and while they thus speak, they will gnash their teeth and curse inwardly. Oh they are a blessed Junto; may opposition to Ministry be their business while they live!

You must not yet, my dear, felicitate me on the double recovery of the King and Mrs Unwin too. I rather think it

---

[1] Reviews of books for the *Analytical Review*, published by Joseph Johnson.

[2] The Prince of Wales had advanced the claim that he should be Regent as of right when the King was unfit to rule: a claim supported by Fox and his friends, who believed that the Prince would bring them into power, but successfully resisted by Pitt on the constitutional ground that the right to appoint a Regent lay with Parliament. An appropriate Bill had almost reached the end of its passage through both Houses when the King's doctors announced on February 12th 'a progressive state of amendment,' and on the 26th, 'the cessation of the illness.'

probably that the King will be able to rule us, before she will be able to walk. She boasts indeed that she is as active as old Farmer Archer, but she would find few hardy enough to bet on her head were a trial to take place between them. My hopes are chiefly in the approach of a gentler season, for the progress of her amendment now is almost imperceptible.

About a fortnight since I received six bottles of rum from Henry, who might, according to what the General told me, have sent seven had he pleased, no law forbidding it. I have written twice to the General and have had no answer. Is he ill? or can you tell me what else it is that occasions his silence?

When you were here we told you a long story about my brother's mare and the money due for her keeping. Almost two years ago, when Mr Heslop[3] wrote to me on that subject expressing a desire to have the account settled, I referred him to Mr Hill as to my agent in all money-matters, who I told him would settle it with him and discharge the balance. Nothing however ensued on this reference, and he never called on Mr Hill for the purpose. The day before yesterday I received a letter from him sent hither from Adstock by a messenger who came on foot, requiring again a liquidation of the account, and threatening me with legal coercion if I delayed to settle it any longer. This being rather a strange procedure and somewhat ungentlemanlike made me very angry, and the next day, that is yesterday, I wrote to him signifying as much, reminding him of my letter of reference, and referring him to Mr Hill again. What course he will deign to take now is in his own bosom, but he is an unreasonable man, if being at this moment in town he will rather choose to trouble me with farther demands than to go to Great Queen Street to have them satisfied.

Mr Newton writes me word that Martin Madan on his way to London, where he intended to have spent a day or two with his sister whom he has not seen these 4 years, was seized with an asthma and obliged to return to Epsom. His illness continued a fortnight and he was judged to be in great

[3] Archdeacon of Bucks.

danger; he, however, recovered, but by the report of his physician is not likely to last long.

I dined yesterday at the Hall, where, notwithstanding the difference of our political sentiments, we were perfectly at peace with each other. Religion and politics both excluded, we are sometimes threatened with a dearth of topics, but in general make a tolerable shift without them. They are always kind and friendly.

Mrs Unwin's best compliments attend you.

I am my dear most truly yours
Wm Cowper

TEXT: *BM. Add. MSS.* 39,673

TO SAMUEL ROSE

The Lodge, July 23, 1789

You do well, my dear sir, to improve your opportunity. To speak in the rural phrase, this is your sowing time, and the sheaves you look for can never be yours unless you make that use of it. The colour of our whole life is generally such as the three or four first years, in which we are our own masters, make it. Then it is that we may be said to shape our own destiny, and to treasure up for ourselves a series of future successes or disappointments. Had I employed my time as wisely as you in a situation very similar to yours, I had never been a poet perhaps, but I might by this time have acquired a character of more importance in society and a situation in which my friends would have been better pleased to see me. But three years mis-spent in an attorney's office were almost of course followed by several more equally mis-spent in the Temple, and the consequence has been, as the Italian epitaph says—'*Sto qui.*'[1]—The only use I can make of myself now, at least the best, is to serve *in terrorem* to others when occasion

---

[1] 'Here I am.'

may happen to offer, that they may escape, so far as my admonitions can have any weight with them, my folly and my fate. When you feel yourself tempted to relax a little the strictness of your present discipline, and to indulge in amusements incompatible with your future interests, think on your friend at Weston.

Having said this, I shall next with my whole heart invite you hither, and assure you that I look forward to approaching August with great pleasure because it promises me your company. After a little time (which we shall wish a longer) spent with us, you will return invigorated to your studies and pursue them with the more advantage. In the mean time, in point of season, you have lost little by being confined to London. Incessant rains and meadows under water have given to the summer the air of winter, and the country has been deprived of half its beauties.

We begin to be seriously alarmed for the harvest. The hay has most of it already perished, and the corn having spired into a stalk of uncommon length, will consequently be productive of little. A very intelligent neighbour assured me two days ago, that the present wet weather continuing another fortnight will certainly cause a great dearth, if not a famine. The moulders and bakers even now find it difficult to procure wheat, and a lean crop succeeding will reduce us to a penury in the article of bread, such as is seldom felt in England.

It is time to tell you that we are all well and often make you our subject. Lady Hesketh desires to be kindly remembered to you, as does Mrs Unwin. We comfort ourselves as well as we can under all these threatening appearances with cheerful chat and the thought that we are once more together. This is the third meeting that my cousin and we have had in this country; and a great instance of good fortune I account it in such a world as this, to have expected such a pleasure thrice without being once disappointed. Add to this wonder as soon as you can, by making yourself of the party.

I am truly yours,

Wm Cowper

TEXT: *Pierpont Morgan Library MSS.*

TO SAMUEL ROSE

Weston, Aug. 8, 1789

My dear friend,

Come when you will, or when you can, you cannot come at a wrong time, but we shall expect you on the day mentioned.

If you have any book that you think will make pleasant evening reading, bring it with you. I now read Mrs Piozzi's *Travels* to the ladies after supper, and shall probably have finished them before we shall have the pleasure of seeing you. It is the fashion, I understand, to condemn them. But we who make books ourselves are more merciful to book-makers. I would that every fastidious judge of authors were himself obliged to write; there goes more to the composition of a volume than many critics imagine. I have often wondered that the same poet who wrote the *Dunciad* should have written these lines:[1]

> The mercy I to others show,
> That mercy show to me.

Alas! for Pope, if the mercy he showed to others was the measure of the mercy he received! he was the less pardonable too, because experienced in all the difficulties of composition.

I scratch this between dinner and tea; a time when I cannot write much without disordering my noddle, and bringing a flush into my face. You will excuse me therefore if, through respect for the two important considerations of health and beauty, I conclude myself,

Ever yours,

W.C.

TEXT: *Southey*

[1] From *The Universal Prayer*.

TO LADY HESKETH

The Lodge, Feb. 26, 1790

You have set my heart at ease, my cousin, so far as you were yourself the object of its anxieties. What other troubles it feels can be cured by God alone. But you are never silent a week longer than usual without giving an opportunity to my imagination (ever fruitful in flowers of a sable hue) to tease me with them day and night. London is indeed a pestilent place, as you call it, and I would, with all my heart, that thou hadst less to do with it; were you under the same roof with me, I should know you to be safe, and should never distress you with melancholy letters.

I feel myself well enough inclined to the measure you propose, and will show to your new acquaintance with all my heart a sample of my translation, but it shall not, if you please, be taken from the *Odyssey*. It is a poem of a gentler character than the *Iliad*, and as I propose to carry her by a *coup de main*, I shall employ Achilles, Agamemnon, and the two armies of Greece and Troy in my service. I will accordingly send you in the box that I received from you last night the two first books of the *Iliad*, for that lady's perusal; to those I have given a third revisal; for them therefore I will be answerable, and am not afraid to stake the credit of my work upon *them* with her, or with any living wight, especially one who understands the original. I do not mean that even they are finished, for I shall examine and cross-examine them yet again, and so you may tell her, but I know that they will not disgrace me; whereas it is so long since I have looked at the *Odyssey* that I know nothing at all about it. They shall set sail from Olney on Monday morning in the Diligence, and will reach you I hope in the evening. As soon as she has done with them, I shall be glad to have them again, for the time draws near when I shall want to give them the last touch.

I am delighted with Mrs Bodham's[1] kindness, in giving me the only picture of my own mother that is to be found, I suppose, in all the world.[2] I had rather possess it than the richest jewel in the British crown, for I loved her with an affection that her death, fifty-two years since, has not in the least abated. I remember her too, young as I was when she died, well enough to know that it is a very exact resemblance of her, and as such it is to me invaluable. Every body loved her, and with an amiable character so impressed upon all her features, every body was sure to do so.

I have a very affectionate and a very clever letter from Johnson,[3] who promises me the transcript of the books[4] entrusted to him in a few days. I have a great love for that young man; he has some drops of the same stream in his veins that once animated the original of that dear picture.

W.C.

TEXT: *Southey*

TO MRS BODHAM

Weston Underwood near Olney, Bucks.
Feb. 27, 1790

My dearest Rose,

Whom I thought withered and fallen from the stalk, but who I find are still alive: nothing could give me greater

---

[1] Anne Bodham (1784–1846), a daughter of C.'s uncle, the Rev. Roger Donne, had married the Rev. Thomas Bodham, rector of Mattishall, Norfolk. The Bodhams figure in James Woodeforde's Diaries.

[2] The gift which inspired *On the Receipt of my Mother's Picture out of Norfolk*: p. 108.

[3] John Johnson (1769–1833), a grandson of Roger Donne, was at this time at Caius College, Cambridge. After a visit to C., he had suggested to Mrs Bodham the gift of the portrait. In 1793 he was ordained, and two years later, when C. and Mrs Unwin had become incapable of looking after themselves, he took them into his own household, at great personal inconvenience, until they died. In 1800 he became rector of Yaxham with Welborne in Norfolk. He edited the 1815 text of the *Poems*, for which he wrote a 'Sketch of Cowper's Life', and *The Private Correspondence*.

[4] Homer.

pleasure than to know it and to learn it from yourself. I loved you dearly when you were a child and love you not a jot less for having ceased to be. Every creature that bears any affinity to my own mother is dear to me, and you, the daughter of her brother, are but one remove distant from her; I love you therefore and love you much, both for her sake and for your own. The world could not have furnished you with a present so acceptable to me as the picture which you have so kindly sent me. I received it the night before last, and viewed it with a trepidation of nerves and spirits somewhat akin to what I should have felt had the dear Original presented herself to my embraces. I kissed it and hung it where it is the last object that I see at night, and, of course, the first on which I open my eyes in the morning. She died when I had completed my sixth year, yet I remember her well and am an ocular witness of the great fidelity of the copy. I remember too a multitude of the maternal tendernesses which I received from her and which have endeared her memory to me beyond expression. There is in me, I believe, more of the Donne that of the Cowper, and though I love all of both names and have a thousand reasons to love those of my own name, yet I feel the bond of nature draw me vehemently to your side. I was thought in the days of my childhood much to resemble my mother, and in my natural temper, of which at the age of 58 I must be supposed a competent judge, can trace both her and my late uncle your father. Somewhat of his irritability, and a little, I would hope, both of his and of her—I know not what to call it without seeming to praise myself which is not my intention, but speaking to *you*, I will e'en speak out and say— good nature. Add to all this, that I deal much in poetry as did our venerable ancestor the Dean of St Paul's, and I think I shall have proved myself a Donne at all points. The truth is that whatever I am, I love you all.

I account it a happy event that brought the dear boy your nephew to my knowledge, and that breaking through all the restraints which his natural bashfulness imposed on him, he determined to find me out. He is amiable to a degree that I have seldom seen, and I often long with impatience to see him again.

My dearest cousin, what shall I say in answer to your affectionate invitation? I *must* say this, I cannot come now, nor soon, and I wish with all my heart I could. But I will tell you what may be done perhaps and it will answer to us just as well. You and Mr Bodham can come to Weston, can you not? The summer is at hand, there are roads and wheels to bring you, and you are neither of you translating Homer. I am crazed that I cannot ask you all together for want of house room, but for Mr Bodham and yourself we have good room, and equally good for any third in the shape of a Donne, whether named Hewitt, Bodham, Balls or Johnson,[1] or by whatever name distinguished. Mrs Hewitt has particular claims upon me; she was my playfellow at Berkhamsted and has a share in my warmest affections. Pray tell her so. Neither do I at all forget my cousin Harriot. She and I have been many a time merry at Catfield and have made the parsonage ring with laughter. Give my love to her. Assure yourself, my dearest cousin, that I shall receive you as you were my sister, and Mrs Unwin is for my sake prepared to do the same. When she has seen you she will love you for your own.

I am much obliged to Mr B. for his kindness to my Homer, and with my love to you all and with Mrs Unwin's kind respects, am, my dear, dear Rose—

Ever yours,

Wm Cowper

P.S.—I mourn the death of your poor brother Castres whom I should have seen had he lived, and should have seen with the greatest pleasure. He was an amiable boy and I was very fond of him.

P.S.—Your nephew tells me, that his sister in the qualities of the mind resembles you; that is enough to make her dear to me, and I beg you will assure her that she is so. Let it not be long before I hear from you.

---

[1] Mrs Bodham's siblings included Catherine, who married John Johnson the elder: Elizabeth (Mrs Thomas Hewitt); Harriot (Mrs Richard Balls); and the Rev. Castres Donne, rector of Loddon, who had died recently.

Still another P.S.—I find on consulting Mrs Unwin that I have underrated our capabilities and that we have not only room for you and Mr Bodham, but for two of your sex, and even for your nephew into the bargain. We shall be happy to have it all so occupied.

TEXT: *Barham Johnson MSS.*

TO JOHN JOHNSON

Weston, March 23, 1790

Your MSS. arrived safe in New Norfolk Street, and I am much obliged to you for your labours. Were you now at Weston I could furnish you with employment for some weeks, and shall perhaps be equally able to do it in summer, for I have lost my best amanuensis in this place, Mr George Throckmorton, who is gone to Bath.

You are a man to be envied, who have never read the *Odyssey*, which is one of the most amusing storybooks in the world. There is also much of the finest poetry in the world to be found in it, nothwithstanding all that Longinus has insinuated to the contrary. His comparison of the *Iliad* and *Odyssey* to the meridian, and to the declining sun, is pretty, but I am persuaded, not just. The prettiness of it seduced him; he was otherwise too judicious a reader of Homer to have made it. I can find in the latter no symptoms of impaired ability, none of the effects of age; on the contrary, it seems to me a certainty, that Homer, had he written the *Odyssey* in his youth, could not have written it better: and if the *Iliad* in his old age, that he would have written it just as well. A critic would tell me, that instead of *written*, I should have said *composed*. Very likely—but I am not writing to one of that snarling generation.

My boy, I long to see thee again. It has happened some way or other that Mrs Unwin and I have conceived a great affection for thee. That I should, is the less to be wondered at (because thou art a shred of my own mother); neither is the wonder great that she should fall into the same predicament: for she loves every thing that I love. You will observe, that your own personal right to be beloved makes no part of the consideration. There is nothing that I touch with so much tenderness as the vanity of a young man, because I know how extremely susceptible he is of impressions that might hurt him in that particular part of his composition. If you should ever prove a coxcomb, from which character you stand just now at a greater distance than any young man I know, it shall never be said that I have made you one; no, you will gain nothing by me but the honour of being much valued by a poor poet, who can do you no good while he lives, and has nothing to leave you when he dies. If you can be contented to be dear to me on these conditions, so you shall; but other terms more advantageous than these, or more inviting, none have I to propose.

Farewell. Puzzle not yourself about a subject when you write to either of us; every thing is subject enough from those we love.

W.C.

TEXT: *Southey*

TO LADY HESKETH

The Lodge, May 28, 1790

My dearest coz,

I thank thee for the offer of thy best services on this occasion. But Heaven guard my brows from the wreath you mention,[1] whatever wreath beside may hereafter adorn them! It would be a leaden extinguisher clapped on all the fire of my genius, and I should never more produce a line worth reading. To speak seriously, it would make me miserable, and therefore

[1] The wreath of Poet Laureate, following Warton's death. It was offered to, and declined by, Hayley.

I am sure that thou of all my friends wouldst least wish me to wear it.

Adieu! thine in a Homer-hurry,

Wm Cowper

Let me hear from thee again soon for it is long since I had thy last.—All best wishes from this place attend thee.

TEXT: *Panshanger MSS.*

TO JOHN BACON

Weston Underwood, Sep. 7, 1790

Dear Sir,

I have no need to make a new inscription, your own being in respect of the matter of it unimprovable. The alterations that I have made in the expression I have made merely on this principle, that the merit of all monumental writing consists in a strict adherence to classical neatness of phrase and connection, that the members of which the whole consists may slide handsomely into each other, and that there may not be one syllable redundant.

You will find my labours on the other side, for which I can say nothing but that I have done my best, which *best* is always most readily at your service. I am, with Mrs Unwin's respects,

Yours dear Sir, very affectionately,

Wm Cowper

Sacred to the Memory of
JOHN HOWARD,
who
Devoted Life and Fortune
to the service of his fellow-creatures,
Author of many merciful regulations
In the Gaols of his own native England.
He compassed Europe

That he might communicate them
To other countries also.
Prompted forth a second time
By the desire and hope
Of alleviating that dreadful calamity the Plague
He terminated his course of Benevolence
At this place,[1]
Jan. 9. 1790, aged 58.
He united in his character
Many virtues,
Each worthy of a Memorial,
All springing from the Faith and animated by the Charity
Of a Christian.
He refused a Statue at home,
But has here a Monument
That posterity may share with us the benefit of his example.

TEXT: *Correspondence of John Howard*, ed. J. Field, London, 1855. This letter has not hitherto been collected.

TO JOHN JOHNSON

Weston, Decr. 18, 1790

My dearest Johnny,

I address you with a new pen, a great rarity with me, and for which I am indebted to my Lady Cousin. And this I do, the very day after the receipt of your letter, having an ardent desire to tell you in legible characters, how much I, and how much we all love and are obliged to you. The oysters, like those you sent first, surpass all encomium, and the Cottenham cheeses were especially welcome, being always cheeses that deserve to be numbered among the best in the world, and cheeses beside, which we have not tasted for many years.

---

[1] Khersones, in the Crimea, where a monument designed by Bacon was being planned at this time. The date and age given by C. are inaccurate.

We thank you with no common thanks, but with such as your kindness merits.

But what thanks can I render you proportioned to your zeal exerted in favour of my Subscription? Be assured that I shall never forget it, speed as it may, and in order to immortalize it will record it immediately in verse, which must be of the extemporare kind, because I have no time for anything better.

> There was no market-town in all
>   The land of the Iceni
> Where Johnny did not loudly call
>   For ev'rybody's guinea.
>
> But gold was scarce; and we regret
>   That folks were grown so wise
> That few thought Homer half so sweet
>   As sausage and mince-pies.

I fear my Johnny that this will prove the case, but whether it should or not, my obligation to thee is equal. In the mean time I perceive myself so flattered by the instances of illustrious success mentioned in your letter that I feel all the amiable modesty, for which I was once so famous, sensibly giving way to a spirit of vainglory. The King's College subscription makes me proud, the effect that my verses have had on your two young friends, the mathematicians, makes me proud, and I am, if possible, prouder still of the contents of the letter that you enclose. You must give my most respectful compliments to Mr Reeve the writer of it, and you must tell him how much I feel obliged to him for his own subscription so handsomely given, and for the readiness with which he gives me also his interest with others. I know not what Mr Cowper that gentleman can have met with at Saffron Walden, and whom he supposes me. A cousin of mine he must have been, but which of my cousins I cannot even conjecture. For my own part I was never there, nor ever had the happiness to be in his company.

You complained of being stupid, and sent to me one of the

cleverest letters. I have not complained of being stupid, and have sent you one of the dullest. But it is no matter; I never aim at anything above the pitch of everyday scribble when I write to those I love.

Homer proceeds—my boy—we shall get through in time, and I hope by the time appointed. We are now in the 10th Iliad. I expect the ladies every minute to breakfast, and will be responsible to you for a letter in due time from each. You have their best love. Mine attends the whole army of Donnes at Mattishall Green assembled. How happy should I find myself were I but one of the party! My capering days are over, but do you caper for me, that you may give them some idea of the happiness I should feel were I in the midst of them.—

I am my dearest Johnny, Yours,

Wm C.

You will remember, I hope, your promised call here in January, or at whatever time you leave Norfolk.

Mrs Hewitt, Mrs Balls, Mrs Bodham, and Kate! May God bless you all together, and yours with you—Amen!

I admire your advertising-boards; that which you sent hither is gone to Newport Pagnel to catch as many gudgeons there as will bite, and then it will go to catch others at Woburn. I shall insist on defraying the cost.

Remember to thank Mr H. for pheasants and *The gods go a-hunting*.

TEXT: *Barham Johnson MSS.*

TO JOHN JOHNSON

Weston, Jan. 21, 1791

I know that you have already been catechized by Lady Hesketh on the subject of your return hither before the winter shall be over, and shall therefore only say that if you CAN COME, we shall be happy to receive you. Remember also that nothing can excuse the non-performance of a promise, but absolute necessity! In the mean time my faith in your veracity is such, that I am persuaded you will suffer nothing less than necessity to prevent it. Were you not extremely pleasant to us, and just the sort of youth that suits us, we should neither of us have said half so much, or perhaps a word on the subject.

Yours, my dear Johnny, are vagaries that I shall never see practised by any other; and whether you slap your ankle, or reel as if you were fuddled, or dance in the path before me, all is characteristic of yourself, and therefore to me delightful. I have hinted to you indeed sometimes that you should be cautious of indulging antic habits and singularities of all sorts, and young men in general have need enough of such admonition. But yours are a sort of fairy habits, such as might belong to Puck or Robin Goodfellow, and therefore, good as the advice is, I should be half sorry should you take it.

This allowance at least I give you:—continue to take your walks, if walks they may be called, exactly in their present fashion, till you have taken orders. Then indeed, forasmuch as a skipping, curvetting, bounding divine might be a spectacle not altogether seemly, I shall consent to your adoption of a more grave demeanour.

W.C.

TEXT: *Southey*

TO LADY HESKETH

[c. 7 April 1791]

My dear cousin,

Mrs Harcourt's strange and unaccountable story has now proved to me an occasion of false hope for the last time; hang me if ever I build anything on it more. When the General sent me news of an unclaimed dividend, that story immediately struck into my mind, and I said to myself and to Mrs Unwin, the lost money is at length come to light. The more we thought and the more we reasoned about the matter the more we were convinced it must be so, till at last I gave myself up without reserve to all the agreeable speculations that such a prospect was likely to suggest. This dream was of two days' continuance; then came Sephus's letter and told me that it *was* a dream. As to Mrs Unwin, she was sure to behave on the occasion as she behaves on all others, calmly and wisely. She only said: 'Well, the Lord will provide in his own time — Should it ever be good for you to be rich, he will make you so'. But how do you think I behaved myself? Better, I can tell you, than there was any reason to suppose that I should. I folded up the letter that had just undeceived me, laid it on the fire-side shelf with much deliberation, and opening a sheet of Homer that came by the same post, proceeded immediately to the perusal of it. Thus, she behaved like a good Christian as she is, and I like a philosopher as I am. I had indeed promised my friend Sephus that I would do so, and it was necessary that I should keep my word.

We had a great curiosity to receive from you some account of your *cognoscenti*, and how your entertainment of that party was conducted. Not that we had or could have any doubt that they would find themselves agreeably situated under your roof, but the manner of managing such an assembly, so unlike all other assemblies, was the circumstance on which I especially wanted to be informed. You have gratified us much by your description of the evening. It is no wonder that it proved a pleasant one, for they must of course be qualified to entertain each other, and you I am sure were equally well qualified to entertain them all. I have much real respect for Mrs Carter, whom I have always been accustomed to consider not only as a learned lady, but as a good one. Blessings on her that she has a friendship for you, which is evident by her giving you counsel.

You have done just the very thing I wished you to do in leaving Horace W[alpole] without any farther solicitation. Assure yourself, my dear, that Johnson has been in no fault. Had he been king of these realms he could not have been attended and danced after more assiduously, insomuch that I should feel myself hurt should any foot of man, woman or child dance another step in that service; hurt, not only, nor so much, for my own sake, as for yours. Mind it not, my coz. As you say yourself, we shall do excellently well without him, and when he shall see the List, as some time or other it is probable that he will, he will find that for once in his life at least he has missed an opportunity of being in the best company.

Johnny, my dear Johnny, will be here, I expect, on Friday. He has given you I presume an account of his success at Cambridge; success with which he is dissatisfied, but I should be unreasonable indeed were I so. He has sent me a list of as many names as amount to a 100 guineas, not to mention the honour that I shall receive from most of them. I thank you for subscribing to his country-woman's poems; I knew you would and told him so.

I have drawn on thee for a Cheshire cheese, value I know not what. Mr Rose is to send it and thou must make thy payment to him. You do not mention him, for which reason I presume that he was not at your *coterie*. I have been close.

I like Barbara's verses well, except that the 4 first are dreadfully ungrammatical. But still I think the manner of these cruel poets, as you justly call them, might be better hit, and were I not a fellow-craft myself, should perhaps attempt it. These are rather too intelligible, and too good; in short there is too much thought in them.

Our alterations proceed with the greatest success, and two beautiful rooms are forming out of desolation and the old store-room. Mr Frog does his part nobly, gives new deal flooring, new doors, and new and larger windows.

Mrs U. bids me say, forasmuch as she knows that you interest yourself in her well-being, that she has got rid of the fever that hung on her all the winter, and is better in every respect. With her best affections I remain, my dear, every yours —

W.C.

P.S. Our cousin of Totteridge's[1] letter is a most kind one,

[1] The former Penelope Madan, wife of Gen. Sir Alexander Maitland.

and I sent her a most kind answer. She will perhaps make you acquainted with the contents of it. It accompanies this, to Henry that he may frank it.

Tell the Minister I can't afford to go to war, especially for the sake of an airy nothing called the Balance of Europe. God is able to save us, even though the Russian should eat up the Turk tomorrow.

TEXT: *Panshanger MSS.***. The original is undated. The evidence for my dating is as follows: a letter to Joseph Hill dated 6 April 1791 may well be the answer to 'Sephus's letter'; a letter to Johnson (the cousin) of the same date thanks him 'for your splendid assemblage of Cambridge luminaries'—i.e. subscribers to Cowper's translation of Homer —and anticipates Johnson's arrival at Weston: and a letter to Rose of 7 April 1791 orders a Cheshire cheese, to be paid for by Lady Hesketh, who will be advised 'in my next'. A letter dated 25 March 1791 asked Lady Hesketh to stop canvassing Horace Walpole in view of the failure of approaches made by Johnson (the publisher).

TO JOSEPH JOHNSON

Weston, July 3, 1791

Dear Sir,

This moment returned from my walk and obliged to prepare for dinner, I have only time to tell you that I have read your letter attentively, yet suspect that I do not perfectly understand it.

Do you mean that the whole subscription money, both first and second payment, shall be yours, except the sums beyond the price of a copy? Out of this money to pay the printer, &c and take the remainder as your own?

This seems, by the manner in which your proposals are expressed, to be the purport of them, and yet I cannot believe it to be so. Because in that case I should have no other reward of my labours than the thousand pounds which you propose to give for the copyright. A recompense short of what I have been taught to look for, judging by the sums which have been given not long since for works of much less length and difficulty and, if I am well informed, even by yourself.

I shall wish your speedy answer, and remain in the meantime, dear Sir,

Yours, Wm Cowper

TEXT: *Panshanger MSS.*:** a copy in Cowper's hand.

TO THE REV. WILLIAM BULL

Weston, July 27, 1791

My dear Mr Bull,

Mindful of my promise I take the pen, though fearing, and with reason enough, that the performance will be hardly worth the postage. Such as it is however, here it comes, and if you like it not, you must thank yourself for it.

I have blest myself on your account that you are at Brighton and not at Birmingham, where it seems they are so loyal and so pious that they show no mercy to dissenters.[1] How can you continue in a persuasion so offensive to the wise and good! Do you not perceive that the Bishops themselves hate you not more than the very blacksmith of the establishment, and will you not endeavour to get the better of your aversion to red-nosed singing men and organs? Come—be received into the bosom of mother-church, so shall you never want a jig for your amusement on Sundays, and shall save perhaps your academy from a conflagration.

[1] The 'Church and King' riots, described by Pitt as the 'effervescence of the public mind'. Joseph Priestley tells the story in his *Memoirs*: '...On the occasion of the celebration of the anniversary of the French Revolution, on July 14, 1791, by several of my friends, but with which I had little to do, a mob encouraged by some persons in power, first burned the Meeting-house in which I preached, then another Meeting-house in the town, and then my dwelling-house, demolishing my library, apparatus, and, as far as possible, every thing belonging to me'.

As for me, I go on at the old rate, giving all my time to Homer, who I suppose was a Presbyterian too, for I understand that the Church of England will by no means acknowledge him as one of hers. He, I say, has all my time, except a little that I give every day to no very cheering prospects of futurity. I would I were a Hottentot, or even a dissenter, so that my views of an hereafter were more comfortable. But such as I am, hope, if it please God, may visit even me; and should we ever meet again, possibly we may part no more. Then, if Presbyterians ever find the way to heaven, you and I may know each other in that better world, and rejoice in the recital of the terrible things that we endured in this. I will wager sixpence with you now, that when that day comes, you shall acknowledge my story a more wonderful one than yours—only order your executors to put sixpence in your mouth when they bury you, that you may have wherewithal to pay me.

I have received a long letter from an unknown somebody, filled with the highest eulogiums on my Homer. This has raised my spirits and is the true cause of all the merriment with which I have greeted you this morning. Pardon me, as Vellum[2] says in the comedy, for being jocular. Mrs Unwin joins me in love to yourself and your very good son, and we both hope and both sincerely wish to hear of Mrs Bull's recovery.

Yours affectionately,

Wm Cowper

TEXT: *Southey*

TO SAMUEL ROSE

Weston, Dec. 21, 1791

My dear friend,
    It grieves me, after having indulged a little hope that I

---

[2] Addison's comedy, *The Drummer*, II, i.

might perhaps have the pleasure to see you in the holidays, to be obliged to disappoint myself. The occasion too is such as will ensure me your sympathy.

On Saturday last, while I was at my desk near the window, and Mrs Unwin at the fireside, opposite to it, I heard her suddenly exclaim, 'Oh! Mr Cowper, don't let me fall!' I turned and saw her actually falling, together with her chair, and started to her side just in time to prevent her. She was seized with a violent giddiness, which lasted, though with some abatement, the whole day, and was attended too with some other most alarming symptoms. At present however she is relieved from the vertigo, and seems in all respects better, except that she is so enfeebled as to be unable to quit her bed for more than an hour in a day.

She has been my faithful and affectionate nurse for many years, and consequently has a claim on all my attentions. She has them, and will have them as long as she wants them; which will probably be, at the best, a considerable time to come.

I feel the shock, as you may suppose, in every nerve. God grant that there may be no repetition of it. Another such a stroke upon her would, I think, overset me completely; but at present I hold up bravely.

Lady Hesketh is also far from well. She has ventured these last few days to dine in the study, else she has kept her chamber above this fortnight. She has suffered, however, by this first sally, and has taken cold, as I feared she would.

Thus we are a house of invalids, and must wait for the pleasure of receiving you here till it shall please God to restore us to health again. With my best compliments to Mrs Rose, and with those of the two ladies, I remain, dear friend, most sincerely yours,

Wm Cowper

TEXT: *Wright*

TO LADY HESKETH

The Lodge, April 5, 1792

My dearest coz,

I knew that you would be charmed with Hayley's[1] letter, and since I sent it to you I have received from him two more, which when you see them will delight you not less than that which is in your hands already. He invites me to Eartham, which for the beauty of the place he longs to show me, and being told that I cannot move, which is a truth that I tell to all who give me occasion, he affords me a hope that I shall see him here in the course of the ensuing summer. But it will grieve you to think that at 47 years of age he has the infirmities that belong to a much more advanced period, has a disorder in one hip which almost cripples him, and has not for years been able to put on his shoes and stockings himself. All this, and eyes subject to inflammation besides, is the consequence of a fever ill-managed when he was a boy. Nevertheless, fond as he is of his home, both for its own sake and for the inconvenience that he finds in travelling, I have so bewitched him by some means or other, I cannot tell how, that he determines to surmount all difficulties and to push his way to Weston. And his letters are in truth so affectionate, his desires to assist me so earnest, and there is even such a tenderness in his whole manner toward me, that terrified as I always am at the thought of a stranger, and terrified as I doubtless shall be even at the sight of him, I yet long to see him. What you say on the subject of his sonnet, I mean about the publication of it, this moment occurs to me. No, my dear, that must not be. If I publish his compliment to me, I shall feel myself bound to answer it with another to him, which he

---

[1] William Hayley (1745–1820), author of *The Triumphs of Temper*, 1781, and of other once popular, now unreadable, effusions in verse and prose; the friend and helper of Blake and other artists and writers. 'Everything about that man is good,' said Southey, 'except his poetry.' See also p. 25.

will in his turn hold it necessary to publish also, and thus we shall coax and wheedle each other in rhyme to the annoyance of all discreet persons and to our own utter confusion. Let it rest therefore for the present. If I live, I will have all the honour of it in due time and will do equal honour to him, but I will secure both these points in a way that shall expose neither him nor me to the sneers of the wicked.

Mr Rose tells me that he has seen Mr Mackenzie (you know whom I mean, the author of *The Lounger* etc.) who has reported to him the favourable opinion of the great Dr Robertson concerning my Homer. I shall not however recite it to you; let it suffice you to know that it is all that either you or I could wish. I have also desired said Mr Rose to buy me a Cheshire cheese, for which you know who is to be account-able—This hangs well together, does it not? The cause of this confusion however is the hurry that I am in to take thee to task for speaking so irreverently of the letter of my friend the Quaker. He heard me aspersed,[2] he wished to be able to contradict the aspersion by authority from myself, and there-fore though a perfect stranger to me, gave me an opportunity, and the only one I could have had, to furnish him with the means of doing it. See the matter in this light, and thou will approve his conduct as much as I do.

The slave trade is now at last, I hope, in a fair way to be abolished.[3] This day's paper has brought us the news, and now I begin to feel some pride again at the thought that I am an Englishman.

Lady Throg has disappointed us and comes not. George too is a renegade and no better than she. I expected that he would have come yesterday, and now learn that he is not to be expected at all. Tell me if thou canst—is he about to be married? If so, I excuse him, but can excuse him on no other consideration.

I have dined 3 times with the Giffards who are extremely kind and obliging, but the Hall makes me melancholy

[2] Represented as a supporter of the slave trade.

[3] The House of Commons had passed Wilberforce's motion, 'that the slave trade ought to be gradually abolished.'

wanting the Hall faces.—Molly Peers still wastes and declines, and I suppose must die of her present illness, but she may last a long time.—Mrs U. sends her warmest thanks for all favours and her best respects. Bids me tell you that at last our family is arranged. Sam is house-steward &c., his wife, cook and housekeeper. Hannah, *her* maid, and colleague with Nanny, and M. Brown takes part of the household work. Thus the affair is settled whether M. Peers lives or dies.

[Unsigned]

TEXT: *Panshanger MSS.***

TO WILLIAM HAYLEY

Weston-Underwood, April 6, 1792

My dear friend,

God grant that this friendship of ours may be a comfort to us all the rest of our days in a world where true friendships are rarities, and especially where, suddenly formed, they are apt soon to terminate. But, as I said before, I feel a disposition of heart toward you that I never felt for one whom I had never seen, and that shall prove itself, I trust, in the event a propitious omen.

You tell me a tale of woes that move my compassion much, and my sorrow both for your past and present sufferings. I remember indeed to have seen it pathetically related in a poem of yours, many years ago. From that poem I took my first impressions of you, and more favourable impressions of you I could not have taken from anything. Horace says somewhere[1] though I may quote it amiss perhaps, for I have a terrible memory

> *Utrumque nostrum incredibili modo*
> *Consentit astrum—*

I have been all my life subject to inflammations of the eye, and in my boyish days had specks on both that threatened to

[1] *Odes* II, xvii, 21–22: 'our stars agree in a marvellous way.'

cover them. My father, alarmed for the consequences, sent me to a female oculist of great renown at that time, in whose house I abode two years, but to no good purpose. From her I went to Westminster School where at the age of 14 the small-pox seized me and proved the better oculist of the two, for it delivered me from them all. Not however from great liableness to inflammation, to which I am in a degree still subject, though much less than formerly, since I have been constant in the use of a hot foot-bath every night, the last thing before going to rest. If you have never tried it I will earnestly recommend it to you.—But *our stars consent*, at least have had an influence somewhat similar, in another and more important article. I cannot indeed say that I have ever been actually deprived of understanding, but near thirty years ago I had a disorder of mind that unfitted me for all society, and was in fact during many months sequestered from it. In sufferings therefore we are brethren, brethren too in occupation, and brethren I hope we shall be hereafter in heart and affection.— So much for our respective infirmities; and now as you see I have made myself a proper object of my own satire, and if I have not inspired you with the wish of a *peevish hearer*, it is owing more to your good nature than to my prudence.

It gives me the sincerest pleasure that I may hope to see you at Weston, for as to any migrations of mine they must I fear, notwithstanding the joy I should feel in being a guest of yours, be still considered in the light of impossibles. Come then, my friend, you and your good handmaid of 40, and be as welcome, as the country people say here, as *the flowers in May*. I am happy as I say in the expectation, but the fear or rather the consciousness that I shall not answer on a nearer view, makes it a trembling kind of happiness, and a doubtful.

After my escape into the world again out of that privacy which I have mentioned above, I went to Huntingdon. Soon after my arrival there I took up my quarters at the house of the Revd. Mr Unwin. I lived with him while he lived, and ever since his death have lived with his widow. Her therefore you will find mistress of the house, and I judge of you amiss, or you will find her just such as you would wish. To me she has been often a nurse, and invariably the kindest friend, through a thousand adversities that I have had to grapple with in the course of almost 30 years.—I thought it better to introduce her to you thus, than to present her to you at your coming, quite a stranger.—Bring with you any books that you think may be useful to my commentatorship, for, with you for an interpreter, I shall be afraid of none of them. And in truth if you think that you shall want them, you must bring books for your own use also, for they are an article with which I am *heinously unprovided*,[2] being much in the condition of the man whose library Pope describes as

> no mighty store
> His own works neatly bound, and little more.[3]

You shall know how this has come to pass hereafter.

Tell me, my friend, are your letters in your own handwriting? If so, I am in pain for your eyes, lest by such frequent demands upon them I should hurt them. I had rather write you three letters for one, much as I prize your letters, than *that* should happen.

And now for the present adieu! I am going to accompany Milton into the lake of fire and brimstone,[4] having just begun my annotations, which I suppose will turn out but a poor business, for all the bushes had been well beaten before I took the field.

Yours very affectionately

Wm Cowper

TEXT: *Panshanger MSS.* *

TO LADY HESKETH

The Lodge, May 5, 1792.—A January storm

I rejoice, my dearest coz, as thou reasonably supposest me to do, in the matrimonial news communicated in thy last.

---

[2] Shakespeare, 1 *King Henry IV*, III, iii, 212.
[3] Not traced in Pope.
[4] *Paradise Lost*, I, 50–74.

Not that it was altogether news to me, for twice I had received broad hints of it from Lady Frog by letter, and several times *viva voce* while she was here. But she enjoined *me* secrecy as she did *you*, and you know that all secrets are safe with me, safer far than the winds were in the bags of Aeolus. I know not in fact the lady whom it would give me more pleasure to call Mrs Courtenay than the lady in question, partly because I know her, but especially because I know her to be all that I can wish in a neighbour.

I have often observed that there is a regular alternation of good and evil in the lot of all men, so that a favourable incident may be considered as the harbinger of an unfavourable one, and vice versa. Dr Madan's[1] experience witnesses to the truth of the observation. One day he gets a broken head, and the next, a mitre to heal it. I rejoice that he has met with so effectual a cure, though my joy is not unmingled with concern, for till now I had some hope of seeing him, but since I lie in the north, and his episcopal call is to the west, that is a gratification, I suppose, which I must no longer look for.

My sonnet,[2] which I sent you, was printed in the Northampton paper last week, and this week it produced me a complimentary one in the same paper, which served to convince me at least by the matter of it, that my own was not published without occasion, and that it had answered its purpose.[3]

My correspondence with Hayley proceeds briskly, and is very affectionate on both sides. I told him (for I thought it best to confess what he could not fail to discover) that I was very little acquainted with his works, having seen only his volume of dramatic pieces; but that to make him amends I had a cousin called Lady Hesketh who loved the very sound of his name, and had often almost scolded me for not reading him. To her expostulations, I said, I had always replied, that if Hayley were a poet even more divine than she thought him, yet, having Homer to translate, he must continue to be

[1] Spencer Madan (1729–1813) C.'s first cousin, brother of Maria C. and of Martin Madan. He was elected Bishop of Bristol on May 12th, and was translated two years later to Peterborough.

[2] To William Wilberforce.

[3] See p. 933, and n.2.

divine in vain for me.—Here follows his answer—'If I had at *any time the power of shining*, I believe the season is over and I am "shorn of my beams". They are not however worth regretting; for had they been shorn like a sheep's coat, at their full growth, they would not have made a golden fleece large enough to have loaded a mouse. So tell your fair cousin Hesketh, whom I hope to have one day an opportunity of *scolding* in my turn, for having praised me to you so abominably above my deserts.' Such are this good man's humble thoughts of himself, while me he exalts above measure. You, I know, will love him for both.—I expect him here in about a fortnight, and wish heartily with Mrs Unwin that you would give him a meeting. I have promised him indeed that he shall find us alone, but you are one of the family.

I wish much to print the following lines in one of the daily papers. Lord Stormont's clear vindication of the poor culprit in the affair of Cheit Sing[4] has confirmed me in the belief that he has been injuriously treated, and I think it an act merely of justice to take a little notice of him.

To Warren Hastings Esq.
By an old schoolfellow of his at Westminster
—

Hastings! I knew thee young, and of a mind,
While young, humane, conversible and kind,
Nor can I well believe thee, gentle *then*,
Now grown a villain and the *worst* of men,
But rather some suspect, who have oppressed
And worried thee, as not themselves the *best*.

If thou wilt take the pains to send them to thy newsmonger I hope thou wilt do well.

I wait with patience for the beneficial consequences of my late hateful and miserable disorder, but none such have I found yet either in mind or body; on the contrary I was much better in many respects than I have been at any time since, before it seized me. This is one of my sablest days, which

---

[4] The Raja of Benares, whom Hastings had heavily fined.

perhaps this letter would not have led you to suspect. But no more of that.—Adieu my dear—with Mrs Unwin's love

.I remain ever yours

Wm Cowper

Mr Newton lives in Coleman's Buildings, No 6 Royal Exchange.—But he is at present, and will be all this month and part of the next, in the country. There is a Sir John Fenn[5] in Norfolk, who collects names and handwritings as Patty More does; he wished for mine, and, at Johnny's request, I shall send it him thus accompanied. But before I transcribe the lines, it is necessary I should tell you that Lady Fenn has published a book in which she makes large citations from *The Task*.

To Sir John Fenn

Two omens seem propitious to my fame,
Your spouse embalms my verse, and you my name;
A name which, all self-flatt'ry far apart,
Belongs to one who ven'rates in his heart
The *wise and good*, and, therefore, of the few
Known by those titles, Sir, both *yours and you*.

TEXT: *Panshanger MSS.* *

TO LADY HESKETH

The Lodge, May 24, 1792

I would with all my heart, my dearest Coz, that I had not ill news for the subject of the present letter, but when, so far as myself am concerned, shall I be able to send thee any better? My friend, my Mary, in whom thou knowest that I live and have my being far more than in Him from who I received

---

[5] Fenn was an antiquary who acquired the Paston Letters and first edited them for publication.

that being, has again been attacked by the same disorder that threatened me last year with the loss of her, and of which you were yourself a witness. Gregson would not allow that first stroke to be paralytic, but this he acknowledges to be so, and with respect to the former I never had myself any doubt that it was, but this has been much the severest. Her speech has been almost unintelligible from the moment when she was struck, it is with difficulty that she opens her eyes and she cannot keep them open, the muscles necessary to the purpose being contracted, and as to self-moving powers from place to place, and the use of her right hand and arm, she has entirely lost them.

It has happened well, that of all men living the man most qualified to assist and comfort me, is here, though till within these few days I never saw him, and a few weeks since had no expectation that I ever should. You have already guessed that I mean Hayley. Hayley, the most benevolent and amiable of his kind, and who loves me as if he had known me from my cradle. When he returns to Town, as he must alas! too soon, he will pay his respects to you; and you will then find him to deserve all that could be said to his advantage in many words, and I have used but few.

I will not conclude without adding that our poor patient is beginning I hope to recover from this stroke also. But her amendment is slow, as must be expected at her time of life, and in such a disorder. I am as well myself as you have ever known me in a time of much trouble, and even better.

It was not possible to prevail on Mrs Unwin to let me send for Dr Kerr, but Hayley has written to his friend Dr Austin a representation of her case, and we expect his opinion and advice tomorrow. In the meantime we have borrowed an electrical machine[1] from our neighbour Socket, the effect of which we tried yesterday and the day before, and we think it has been of material service.

She was seized while Hayley and I were walking, and while Mr Greatheed, who called while we were abroad, was with her.

---

[1] A contrivance for passing a static electricity through the human body.

I forgot in my last to thank thee for the proposed amendments of thy friend. Whoever he is, make my compliments to him and thank him. The passages to which he objects have been all altered, and when he shall see them new-dressed I hope he will like them better.

As to the lines I sent you of which Hastings was the subject, trouble not thyself about them.

Mrs. U.'s love and Mr H.'s best compliments attend thee.

Thine ever

Wm Cowper

She was taken ill last Tuesday. I have no need to trouble thee for viands of any sort on H.'s account. He drinks only water, and eats little beside mustard.

TEXT: *Panshanger MSS.* *

TO WILLIAM HAYLEY

Weston, June 10, 1792

My dear Hayley and such most deservedly,

I received your Huzza[1] with great pleasure, and am happy that you at last found your way into the presence of my great friend and yours. But happy chiefly because I know what would have been your bitter mortification on my account if you had not; for I have still a most obstinate and provoking backwardness to hope well of my own fortunes, notwithstanding the warm impressions which your zeal accompanied with your manners, and both exerted in my behalf, must necessarily have made upon him. It is my happiness however to have no anxious thoughts about your success, except for your sake. I do indeed anxiously wish that every thing you do

---

[1] The first word of a note sent from London by Hayley, reporting a visit to Lord Thurlow, whom he thought he had persuaded to do something for C.

may prosper, and should I at last prosper by your means shall taste double sweetness in prosperity for that reason.

I rose this morning as I usually do with a mind all in sables, having been whispered into the deepest melancholy by my nocturnal monitor. My evil one I mean, for as I told you I have two, and the good one was silent as he generally is. In this mood I presented myself at Mary's bedside, whom I found, though after many hours lying awake, yet cheerful and not to be infected with my desponding humours. It is a great blessing to us both that, poor feeble thing as she is, she has a most invincible courage and a trust in God's goodness that nothing shakes. She is now in the study, and is certainly in some little degree better than she was yesterday, but how to measure that little I know not, except by saying that it is just perceptible. Could she sleep more, her amendment would be more discernible. You are always dear to her, and so she bids me tell you.

I am glad that you saw—but I forget. I have still more to say about Mary. She has constantly used the embrocation since we received it, night and morning, and always feels a glow after it, and the electuary answers better than anything of the kind she has taken. We continue our sparkling operations[2] and never without good effect, and the result of all is, that though as I have said, the difference between day and day is small, she is on the whole so much improved that she now and then takes a turn in the study supported by me only, and even with very little help of mine. But still she rides to bed, and rides down again between Samuel and Molly.

And now I will say what I was going to say. I am glad that you saw my Johnny of Norfolk, because I know it will be a comfort to you to have seen your successor. He arrived to my great joy yesterday, and not having bound himself to any particular time of going, will I hope stay long with us.

You are now once more snug in your retreat, and I give you joy of your return to it after the bustle in which you have lived since you left Weston. Weston mourns your absence, and will mourn it till she sees you again. What is to become of

_____
[2] With the 'electrical machine.'

Milton I know not. I do nothing but scribble to you, and seem to have no relish for any other employment. I have however, in pursuit of your idea to compliment Darwin, put a few stanzas together which I shall subjoin. You will easily give them all that you find they want, and match the song with another.

TO DOCTOR DARWIN[3]

Two poets (poets by report
　Not oft so well agree)
Sweet Harmonist of Flora's Court!
　Conspire to honour thee.

They best can judge a poem's worth
　Who oft themselves have known
The pangs of a poetic birth
By ${ \text{labours of} \atop \text{bringing forth} }$ their own.

The verse that kindles, meets a fire,
　A kindred fire in them,
The numbers live that they admire,
　And die, that they condemn.

Live thou—well pleas'd alike, thy song
　With that award we greet,
Rich in embellishment as strong,
　And learn'd as it is sweet.

No envy mingles with our praise,
　Though could our hearts repine
At any poet's happier lays—
　At whose so soon as thine?

But we in mutual bondage knit
　Of friendship's closest tie
Can gaze on even Darwin's wit
　With an unjaundic'd eye.

[3] Erasmus Darwin, author of *The Botanic Garden*. The third stanza, and the variant first couplet of the fourth, are published for the first time.

And deem the bard, whoe'er he be,
   And howsoever known,
Who would not twine a wreath for thee
   Scarce worthy of his own.

Rose was greatly mortified that he missed you both at your house and at his own. A thousand thanks for the favour you have obtained for him.

I have received at last a letter of thanks from Tom Clio,[4] to whom Johnson gave my Homer 5 months ago. He is a violent overturner of thrones and kingdoms, and foolishly thinks to recommend himself to me by telling me that he is so. He adds likewise that Mr Paine often dines with him.— Will it not be best to leave his letter unanswered?

I have this moment one of the kindest letters that ever was from Carwardine—I will give you the contents in shorthand in my next.

My love to yr. dear boy; hope you found him well.[5]

I am now going to my walk with Johnny. Much cheered since I began, by writing to you, by reading Carwardine, and by Mary's looks and good spirits.

         Adieu, *mi charissime*!

                    Wm Cowper

Our patient goes on rarely.

TEXT: *BM. Add. MSS.* 39,673

TO WILLIAM HAYLEY

Tuesd. June 19, 1792

I began to suspect that all was not right at Eartham, and

---

[4] 'Clio' was originally the nickname, then the pseudonym, of Thomas Rickman (1761–1834), bookseller and political reformer.
[5] His son, Tom.

even to be distressed in my sleep about you. Therefore I rejoice more and more that you are once again snug at home, and that, being there, you will have nothing to do but to recruit your strength and spirits wasted in London. Wasted indeed—do you see what has come to pass? Our Knight of the great black eye-brows[1] is displaced, and though his will be good, his power to serve me is reduced to a nullity. Will you believe at last that I have some skill in my own destiny, or will nothing convince you? I tell you that could you have let the poor man alone, he would have been Chancellor to the day of his death; but you must needs inspire him with a purpose to enrich *me*, and from that moment there was an end of his office. But fear not. You shall never see me dejected for any such reason. After living 60 years in the world without money, it would be strange indeed if I should now at last begin to find it an essential. I am as rich at this moment as I ever was since I was born, and having no good reason to suppose that I shall yet live other 60 years to an end, have no need to care whether I add to my present stock or not. Such as it is, it will be sure to serve me till, if all turn out well at last,—the sun shall no more rise to light me, neither for brightness shall the moon give light unto me, but the Lord shall be unto me an everlasting light, and my God my glory.[2]

Thus have I filled a whole page talking to my dear William of Eartham about money, and have not said a syllable yet about my Mary. A sure sign that she goes on well. Be it known to you that we have these 4 days discarded our sedan with two elbows. Here is no more carrying or being carried, but she walks upstairs boldly with one hand upon the balustrade and the other under my arm, and in like manner she comes down in a morning. Still I confess she is feeble, and misses much of her former strength; the weather too is sadly against her; it deprives her of many a good turn in the orchard, and 50 times I have wished this very day that Dr Darwin's scheme of giving rudders and sails to the ice-

---

[1] Lord Thurlow had been dismissed from office.
[2] Cf. Isaiah, lx, 19.

islands[3] that spoil all our summers were actually put in practice. So should we have gentle airs instead of churlish blasts, and those everlasting sources of bad weather being once navigated into the Southern Hemisphere, my Mary would recover as fast again.

We are both of your mind respecting the journey to Eartham, and think that July, if by that time she have strength for the journey, will be better than August. We shall have more long days before us, and them we shall want as much for our return as for our going forth. This however must be left to the Giver of all Good. If our visit to you be according to His will He will smooth our way before us, and appoint the time of it, and I thus speak, not because I wish to seem a saint in your eyes, but because my poor Mary is actually one, and would not set her foot over the threshold to save her life, unless she had, or thought she had, God's free permission. With that, she would go through floods and fire, though without it she would be afraid of everything. Afraid even to visit you, dearly as she loves and much as she longs to see you.

The same post that brought me your last brought me one from Lady H., which serves to prove that if I have the art of making myself irresistibly winning, you are not a whit behind me. She calls you the *astonishing Hayley*, and calls you so on account of your uncommon kindness to me, for the sake of which it is easy to see that she loves you entirely. You have in short the true key to her heart, and the more you love me the

[3] *Ice islands*: the Arctic ice-pack. Erasmus Darwin's *The Loves of the Plants*, 1789, canto 1, lines, lines 527–30:

> There, NYMPHS! alight, array your dazzling powers,
> With sudden march alarm the torpid Hours,
> On ice-built isles expand a thousand sails,
> Hinge the strong helms, and catch the frozen gales.

Part of Darwin's lengthy footnote reads: 'If the nations who inhabit this hemisphere of the globe, instead of destroying their seamen and exhausting their wealth in unnecessary wars, could be induced to unite their labours to navigate these immense masses of ice into the more southern oceans, two great advantages would result to mankind: the tropic countries would be much cooled by their solution, and our winters in this latitude would be rendered much milder for perhaps a century or two, until the masses of ice became again enormous.'

dearer you will be to her. She is charmed with your offer of an asylum for me under your own roof, should it please God to take my Mary home and to leave me in the wilderness; and in truth there is no corner of the earth where I could be so well disposed of; but you would find me a woeful inmate and one who would put both your friendship and your patience to the severest trials. But more than enough of this. Mary, thank God! is not going home yet. My afflictions are not at an end, and He knows that they would be insupportable to me without her.

Thank you for the extract from Pye. I have many times been mortified and made sick by my own praises; they have come from such bunglers in the art. But now I feel myself flattered indeed, since I have been praised by you the best of our poets, and not by you only but by this commentator on the king of critics. If all this do not make me vain I must be the very Phoenix of humility. There is a Mr Polwhele too from whom I have received a compliment in verse within this week. He is a clergyman of the West who has lately published 2 volumes of Devonshire and Cornish poetry. He sent me the books with one of the blank leaves devoted to my sublime self. But I have not had time to read any of his verses yet, except his verses to me, and therefore know not at present whether to be proud or not, or to what degree upon the occasion.

We will talk more about an Anglo-Grecian Homer when the time comes. My bookseller says it will be bought only by idle folks who are at a loss to know what to do with their money. My chief fears are from the blockheadism of the printers, lest they should craze me with their blunders. But let it rest for the present. I never have room to write myself half out.

My Johnny sends his best compliments and thanks for your kind invitation which he shall be happy, he says, to accept if he can. I have good hopes of him that in time he will be equal to the task you assign him of perpetuating our remembrance together with his own. I have already seen of his doings in the poetical way, and they have only one fault which in time will be a beauty, a redundance of wild imagination; but of a very original cast.

947

Adieu my dear friend and crony-bard. I can never tell you how much I missed you for many days, or indeed how much I miss you still. But at first, I seemed to feel my Mary's illness a concern too heavy for me without your presence and assistance, and was terrified at the thought of your absence. But now I make shift and am pretty well content with hearing from you often, and with the hope of seeing you soon again. I ask Mary what I shall say for her, and she replies, give my true love to him and his boy. It is now Wednesday. She has had a good night and is cheerful and well this morning — Adieu.

Ever yours,

Wm Cowper

TEXT: *Panshanger MSS.**

TO *LADY HESKETH*

June 21, 1792

My dearest coz,

I have indeed found a most extraordinary friend in Hayley, who interests himself as much in my welfare as if he were not only my brother-bard, but my brother in truth, the son of my own mother. His offer to receive me into his habitation, should I be obliged to abandon this by an event which would leave me forlorn indeed, is, like all the rest of his dealings with me, friendly and generous in the extreme. But whether I would or would not accept that offer, and whither I should betake me if I declined it, are matters about which I will not speculate at present, both because they are subjects that give me pain, and because I trust that there is just now no need to do it. Equally indebted I am to thyself for thy hospitable offer, but thou judgest like one who knows me well in supposing that a London abode would little suit me after so many years spent in the country, which has been my delight too and the *sine qua non* of terrestrial comfort with me ever since I knew the difference. But as I say, these are themes which a kind Providence seems at present to permit me to set at a distance. Mrs Unwin's health is so far restored, that if it please God to continue this mercy to us a few weeks longer,

948

I shall hope by that time to see her at least in as good health
as she enjoyed before this last illness. She now takes a turn or
two in the orchard walk supported slightly by Johnny and
me, and every day grows stronger. She bids me give her best
love to you and tell you that she is *herself* persuaded that there
is nothing paralytic in her disorder, but that it is a complex
case consisting entirely of bile, spasm and rheumatism.
Whatever it be, it has been dreadfully alarming, and the next
immediate cause of it I believe was an accident that befell
John Britain, who guiding his broad-wheeled waggon
through our gateway, was first squeezed between the wheel
and the post, and than thrown under the wheel, or rather
right before it on his back, so that had the horses moved
another step he must have been killed infallibly. She was in
the servants' hall when this happened, and consequently
within hearing of the outcry made by those who saw his
danger, and though she saw it not herself, yet being immediately told that he was much hurt and how narrowly he had
escaped, she was so much agitated in her spirits that she never
recovered the effects of that emotion, and three days after
was struck with this illness. Such have always been the effects
of surprise and terror upon her; she endures them for a few
days as if she would completely get the better of them, and
then sinks under them. John himself has pretty well recovered
from his bruises, and yesterday evening drove the same
waggon into our yard with better success. Not but that he is
still lame, and by a considerable swelling of the limbs is
supposed to have had both his thigh-bones injured.

I was shocked yesterday by a story which could not but be
true, because Archer received it in a letter from one of his
fellow-servants in town, that poor Lady Frog had been
terribly cut and bruised by an overturn of her carriage as she
was going to Ranelagh. At first she was supposed to be killed.
I immediately on hearing the news gave Ranelagh and all its
allurements to those who invented them, that is to say,
à tous les diables.

But let us call a more agreeable subject. Thou has seen and
hast a copy of the sonnet with which Hayley accompanied
his first letter, but thou hast not seen another sonnet written

in a blank leaf of his poems presented to Mrs Unwin. This last therefore shall occupy the rest of my paper, and here it is:

SONNET TO MRS UNWIN

Mary! whose friendship, like a seraph's wings,
Formed the bright shield of Cowper, in whose guard
Rescued from fiends, and now no more ill-starr'd
From woe's dark waste to glory's field he springs,
And with celestial animation sings
Of hallow'd themes, by meaner poets marr'd,
But now applauded by the world, that rings
With the blest music of thy blameless Bard:
How must thy soul exult in his renown,
Proud of a tutelary angel's part!
On this my homage to his laureate crown,
Nor less to thee, his muse! Thou wilt not frown;
For me thou see'st no rival of his art,
But of his fame the friend, the brother of his heart.

I have other fine verses also sent me in the blank leaf of certain poems published lately by the Revd. Mr Polwhele, and purporting to be the works of Devonshire and Cornish bards. The verses to me are good, the rest I have had no time to examine.

I have likewise at last had a letter of thanks from Tom Clio, to whom Johnson gave my Homer. He is a red-hot Paine-ite, and thinking me such also, boasts that his namesake Tom dines often with him. He commends my Homer and hopes for my correspondence, but I shall not answer him.

I shall do as you advise respecting Mr Newton, that is to say, I shall keep Hayley as much out of sight as possible. It may be easy perhaps to do it entirely, for he will be here only a day or two.

Johnny sends love; you will perhaps see him soon. He goes to town tomorrow, but returns next week.

Adieu—thine W.C.

The Chancellor Medicean-Venused[1] must be a droll figure.

[1] 'The Chancellor is seen in all the print-shops naked and in the attitude of the Medicean Venus:' C. to Hayley, June 23, 1792.

But why they have given him that form I cannot conjecture. He will laugh as heartily as anybody if he hears of it. — Thanks for the Ode.

Johnny is happy that you are pleased with his sister.

TEXT: *Panshanger MSS.* * *

TO WILLIAM HAYLEY

Weston Underwood, June 27, 1792

> Compared with Thurlow's Genius I begin
> To fancy mine more valiant far and stout;
> For when his own had put him in,
> Mine put him out.

There's poetry for you and in a stanza of a new construction! You have hung me upon the hooks of conjecture and there I must dangle till you shall take me down again. *That* you say you will not do till we come together at Eartham. Well then — let us talk about this journey to Eartham. You wish me to settle the time of it, and I wish with all my heart to be able to do so, living in hopes meanwhile that I shall be able to do it soon. But some little time must necessarily intervene. Our Mary must be able to walk alone, to cut her own food and to feed herself, and to wear her own shoes, for at present she wears mine. When she is so far restored as to be mistress of all these qualifications once again, then we will appoint a time for this formidable but pleasing enterprise. I have sent you always accounts of amendment and of still more amendment, and these so often that you will wonder, I doubt not, at being told that she is still so feeble as to be insufficient for these purposes. You will wonder when I inform you that she walked yesterday, at two journeys, twenty times the length of the orchard-gravel, and that I am just now returned after walking with her 12 times that length at once. But these feats she performs between me and Sam. Not that we support her much, but for security's sake, for she has rather a tottering step, and should she stumble it would hardly be in the power of one to prevent her falling. She walks in my shoes too, her ankle being so much weakened by this illness that in her own it cannot support her, but comes sideway to the ground, causing her great pain and indeed making it impossible for her to walk at all. Thus at least it was when she attempted to wear her own shoes about 9 days since, and from that time we have made no new experiment.—All these things considered, my friend and brother, you will see the expedience of waiting a little before we set off for Eartham; we mean indeed, before that day arrives, to make a trial of the strength of her head, how far it may be able to bear the motion of a carriage, a motion that it has not felt these 7 years. I grieve that we are thus circumstanced, and that we cannot gratify ourselves in a delightful and innocent project without all these precautions, but when we have leaf-gold to handle we must do it tenderly.

I thank you, my brother, both for presenting my authorship to your friend Guy, and for the excellent verses with which you have inscribed your present. There are none neater or better turned. With what shall I requite you? I have nothing to send you but a gimcrack which I have prepared for my bride and bridegroom neighbours[1] who are expected tomorrow. You saw in my book a poem entitled *Catharina*,[2] and which concluded with a wish that we had her for a neighbour. This therefore is called

CATHARINA
THE SECOND PART

Believe it or not, as you chuse,
   The doctrine is certainly true,
That the future is known to the Muse,
   And poets are oracles too.

[1] George Courtenay, formerly Throckmorton, married Miss Catharine Stapleton on June 29.
[2] See p. 106.

I did but express a desire
　　To see Catharina at home
At the side of my friend George's fire,
　　And lo! she is actually come.

Such prophecy some may despise,
　　But the wish of a poet and friend
Perhaps is approved in the skies,
　　And therefore attains to its end.
'Twas a wish that flew ardently forth
　　From a bosom effectually warm'd
With the virtue I saw and the worth
　　In the person for whom it was form'd.

No want of such motives I found
　　When I wish'd Catharina a bride,
So richly in her they abound,
　　With accomplishments many beside,
And therefore I wished as I did,
　　And therefore this union of hands
Not a whisper was heard to forbid,
　　But all cry—Amen!—to the bands.

Since therefore I seem to incur
　　No danger of wishing in vain
When making good wishes for her,
　　I will e'en to my wishes again.
With one I have made her a wife,
　　And now I will try with another
Which I cannot suppress for my life—
　　How soon I can make her a mother.

Let me have your improvements upon them, for which they shall wait. All that I write is so much better for passing through your hands, that you are likely to be plagued with every scrap of it in future.

Our dear Mary wants me to lead her about a little, weary as she is of one posture and of sitting so long. She sends you her most affectionate remembrances. God bless you and reward

you for all your projects formed for her good and mine—
Adieu—Ever yours

Wm Cowper

TEXT: *Panshanger MSS.** More than half the letter, including
the epigram on Thurlow, is unpublished. Hayley's extract
substituted C.'s final version of the poem addressed to
'Catharina'; the original draft in the MS. letter, as printed
here, gives a hitherto unpublished variant of lines 17–20.

TO WILLIAM HAYLEY

Weston, July 4, 1792

The Chancellor once was a tree full of fruit,
    A tree in the summer and fanned by the south,
He was great at the top and moist at the root,
    And the good things he bore would drop into your mouth.

But since that his Lordship has quitted his place
    Steriles numerandus est arbores inter,[1]
And *now* to solicit his favours and grace
    Is searching your boughs for plums in the winter.

But these are only my jocular sentiments, for in reality I
think with you, my dear indefatigable friend, that though his
Lordship, unofficed as he is, may have little to give, he may
have much within the reach of his influence, and I am certain
if that influence be not exerted in my favour, it will not be
because I have not the warmest advocate in the world to
actuate it.

I know not how you proceed in your life of Milton, but I
suppose not very rapidly, for while you were here, and since
you left us, you have had no other theme but me. As for

---

[1] He is to be numbered among the barren trees.

myself, except my letters to you, and the nuptial song I inserted in my last, I have literally done nothing since I saw you. Nothing I mean in the writing way, though a great deal in another; that is to say, in attending my poor Mary, and endeavouring to nurse her up for a journey to Eartham. In this I have hitherto succeeded tolerably well, and had rather carry this point completely, than be the most famous editor of Milton that the world has ever seen, or shall see.

Your humorous descant upon my art of wishing made us merry, and consequently did good to us both. There is much wit in it, and could we produce between us a volume of scribblements as sprightly and smart as that, we should be rich in a hurry. I sent my wish to the Hall yesterday and nearly in the form that you recommended. The fifth stanza, to which I knew you would object because I disliked it myself, I expunged, and substituted one in its stead, partly of your own matter and partly of other matter of my own—namely this:

> Maria would leave us, I knew,
>   To the grief and regret of us all,
> Yet less to our grief, might we view
>   Catharina the Queen of the Hall.

This led me to wish as I did, etc.

The second stanza remains as it was, because Mary observed, the poor husband would otherwise be quite out of the question. They are excellent neighbours, and so friendly to me that I wished to gratify them. When I went to pay my first visit, George flew into the court to meet me, and when I entered the parlour Catharina sprang into my arms.

What a wonder it will be should I continue poor much longer. Here is my Johnny as industrious as a bee, writing letters every day and all day long, and sending them round the world with a zeal to do me service. What service I know not, nor shall know, it seems, till Sunday or Monday next, nor should I have known that I am the subject of them had not *so* much of the secret escaped Lady Hesketh.

I return you many thanks for the letter you sent to the

Chancellor, and for giving me a copy of it. With the poetical parts of it he must be pleased because he has good taste, and with the prose because it is exactly suited to his honest and manly character. Having no longer any excuse for silence, I suppose he will give you an answer, and that answer can hardly fail to teach us once for all what we have to expect from him.

What a mysterious creature you are! Since you have known me you say the delightful hope that you have conceived of being instrumental to my peace and comfort is a source of comfort to yourself and of inexpressible gratification, and at the same time explains to you many wonderful things in your own destiny which you could never comprehend till now. I love you for all this in my heart, but the latter part I understand not a word of, but, with all my soul, rejoice if by any means I may be of use to you, either by alleviating the sorrows or solving the enigmas of your lot.

I write in a fidgeting hurry of spirits and seem to have connected no two ideas. This has been owing to the fear of being hindered every minute by Mr Newton, who is to be with us to-day, and I know not at what hour. Mary continues to mend but still walks between two. She loves my Hayley and I hers. — Adieu,

Wm Cowper

TEXT: *Wright*

TO LADY HESKETH

Weston Underwood, July 21, 1792

My dearest coz,

I am crazed with having much to do and doing nothing. Everything with me has fallen into arrear to such a degree that I almost despair of being able by the utmost industry to redeem the time that I have lost. With difficulty it is that I can steal even now a moment to address a few lines to thee. They must be as few as I can make them. Briefly therefore I say thus—

My portrait is nearly finished.[1] An excellent one in my mind and in the opinion of all who see it, both for drawing and likeness. It will be completed I believe on Monday. I shall keep it a short time after Abbot is gone, that my 2 or 3 friends in this neighbourhood may be gratified with a sight of it, and shall then send it to his house in Caroline Street, Bloomsbury, where it will remain some time. Should it be your wish to view it, you will then have an opportunity, and trust me I think it will afford you as much pleasure, nay perhaps even more, than a sight of the original myself; for you will see it with this thought in your mind, that whether I live or die, while this picture subsists my charming lineaments and proportions can never be forgotten.

We have not even yet determined absolutely on our journey to Eartham, but shall I believe in 2 or 3 days decide in favour of it. Hayley interests himself so much in it, and I am persuaded that it bids fair to do us both so much good, that I am sincerely desirous of going. A thousand lions, monsters, and giants are in the way, but perhaps they will all vanish if I have but the courage to face them. Mrs Unwin, whose weakness might justify her fears, has none. Her trust in the Providence of God makes her calm on all occasions.

Should Anonymous have consigned his half year's remittance to your hands and my namesake William his annual one, thou canst not do better than send them, for I hear a flying rumour that travelling is costly, and that consequently money will be wanted.—This moment I receive yours. Many thanks for it and for the draft contained in it.

I learned lately from Sephus that you are not very well, and know too well not to know that you hide from me the worst half of your malady let it be what it may. God preserve thee, restore thy health and give us a comfortable meeting once more in the winter.

---

[1] This portrait of Cowper by Lemuel Abbott (1760–1803) was commissioned by Mrs Bodham. It now hangs in the National Portrait Gallery.

Sam's wife shall be paid. Mrs Unwin sends her best love. Johnny goes to Eartham, but not with us, because Sam will be more useful by the way. Johnny therefore and Nanny Roberts will jog together in the stage. You shall hear from me as soon as I can after my arrival.

Adieu—must go to be painted—can't add another syllable except that I am ever thine,

Wm Cowper

My dear Johnny sends his affectionate compliments. He goes with us. All in a coach together which Abbot will send us from town. To-morrow will be my last sitting, and I verily think the portrait, exclusive of the likeness which is the closest imaginable, one of the best I ever saw. You will see by this P.S. that the journey is already determined on. Would to heaven that you could join us!

TEXT: *MSS. Cowper Museum, Olney*

TO WILLIAM HAYLEY

Weston Underwood, July 22, 1792

This important affair, my dear brother, is at last decided, and we are coming. Wednesday se'nnight, if nothing occur to make a later day necessary, is the day fixed for our journey. Two days it will certainly cost us, and it is not possible to say till we make the trial that it will not cost us a third. This is unpleasant, because it leaves you at an uncertainty when to look for us and will therefore worry your spirits; but there is no remedy. Our rate of travelling must depend on Mary's ability to bear it.—How foolish I am to represent a thing as uncertain which in fact ascertains itself! I forgot that our mode of travelling will occupy three days unavoidably, for we shall come in a coach. Abbot finishes my picture tomor-

row, on Wednesday he returns to town, and is commissioned
to order one down for us with four steeds to draw it,

> Hollow pamper'd jades of Asia
> That cannot go but forty miles a day.[1]

Send us our route, for I am as ignorant of it almost as if I
were in a strange country. We shall reach St Albans I suppose
the first day. Say where we must finish our second day's
journey and at what inn we may best repose? As to the end of
the third day, we know where that will find us— viz. in the
arms and under the roof of our beloved Hayley. General
Cowper having heard a rumour of this intended migration
desires to meet me on the road, that we may once more see
each other. He lives at Ham near Kingston. Shall we go
through Kingston, or near it? for I should wish to give him
as little trouble as possible, though he offers very kindly to
come as far as Barnet for that purpose. Nor must I forget
Carwardine,[2] who so kindly desired to be informed what way
we should go. On what point of the road will it be easiest to
him to find us? On all these subjects you must be my oracle.

My friend and brother, we shall overwhelm you with our
numbers; this is all the trouble that I have left. My Johnny of
Norfolk, happy in the thought of accompanying us, would
be broken-hearted to be left behind. Sam and Sam's wife also
will be part of your burthen, but they, being one flesh, will
occupy one bed only. Four beds therefore will serve us all,
and fewer will not. Tell me if you can supply them without
miserable inconvenience, for to distress you would make
me miserable, and I would leave Sam behind though I foresee
that he will be everything to us upon the road. These are
questions that you must answer by the return of the post,

---

[1] Shakespeare, 2 *King Henry IV*, II, iv. 163–4:
> ... And hollow pamper'd jades of Asia,
> Which cannot go but thirty mile a day ...

Almost identical lines occur in Marlowe's *Tamberlaine the Great*, second
part, lines 3980–81.

[2] The Rev. Thomas Carwardine, of Earls Colne Priory, Essex, a friend
of Hayley.

otherwise I shall hardly have time to give General Cowper and Carwardine sufficient notice. In the midst of all these solicitudes I laugh to think what they are made of, and what an important thing it is for me to travel. Other men steal away from their homes silently and make no disturbance, but when I move, houses are turned upside down, maids are turned out of their beds, and all the counties through which I pass appear to be in an uproar. Surrey greets me by the mouth of the General, and Essex by that of Carwardine. How strange does all this seem to a man who has seen no bustle and made none for 20 years together!

You already perceive that, escorted as we shall be, there is no need to trouble your Mary to assist mine. She gives her love to you and thanks you for the offer. God bless you my dear brother and afford us the blessing of a happy meeting! I have had this week past a rheumatism in my back, commonly called the lumbago, which has sometimes almost crippled me. I am now better, but feel that this writing posture increases my pain again. Adieu therefore. With Johnny's best bow and Mary's best love to you and yours, I remain

Yr affectionate

Wm Cowper

Hannah is mending fast, sends her duty and goes to her school on Wednesday.

TEXT: *Panshanger MSS.**

TO THE REV. WILLIAM BULL

July 25, 1792

My dear Mr Bull,

Engaged as I have been ever since I saw you, it was not possible that I should write sooner; and busy as I am at present, it is not without difficulty that I can write even now: but I promised you a letter, and must endeavour, at least, to be as good as my word. How do you imagine I have been occupied these last ten days? In sitting, not on cockatrice eggs nor yet to gratify a mere idle humour, nor because I was too sick to move; but because my cousin Johnson has an aunt who has a longing desire of my picture, and because he would, therefore, bring a painter from London to draw it. For this purpose I have been sitting, as I say, these ten days; and am heartily glad that my sitting time is over. You have now, I know, a burning curiosity to learn two things, which I may choose whether I will tell you or not. First, who was the painter; and secondly, how he has succeeded. The painter's name is Abbot. You never heard of him, you say. It is very likely; but there is, nevertheless, such a painter, and an excellent one he is. *Multa sunt quae bonus Bernardus nec vidit, nec audivit.*[1] To your second enquiry I answer, that he has succeeded to admiration. The likeness is so strong, that when my friends enter the room where my picture is, they start, astonished to see me where they know I am not. Miserable man that you are, to be at Brighton instead of being here, to contemplate this prodigy of art, which, therefore, you can never see; for it goes to London next Monday, to be suspended awhile at Abbot's; and then proceeds into Norfolk, where it will be suspended for ever.

But the picture is not the only prodigy I have to tell you of. A greater belongs to me; and one that you will hardly credit, even on my own testimony. We are on the eve of a journey, and a long one. On this very day se'nnight we set out for Eartham, the seat of my brother bard, Mr Hayley, on the other side of London, nobody knows where, a hundred and twenty miles off. Pray for us, my friend, that we may have a safe going and return. It is a tremendous exploit, and I feel a thousand anxieties when I think of it. But a promise, made to him when he was here, that we would go if we could, and a sort of persuasion that we can if we will, oblige us to it. The journey and the change of air, together with the novelty to us of the scene to which we are going, may, I hope, be useful to us both; especially to Mrs Unwin, who has most need of

[1] '*Bernardus non vidit omnia*. I could not come to the knowledge of every particular.' Thomas Fuller, *Appeal of Injured Innocence*, 1659.

restoratives. She sends her love to you and to Thomas, in which she is sincerely joined by your affectionate

W.C.

TEXT: *Southey*

TO WILLIAM HAYLEY

Weston, July 29, 1792

> Through floods and flames to your retreat
> I win my desperate way,
> And when we meet, if e'er we meet,
> Will echo your huzza![1]

You will wonder at the word *desperate* in the second line, and at the *if* in the third; but could you have any conception of the fears I have had to battle with, of the dejection of spirits that I have suffered concerning this journey, you would wonder much more that I still courageously persevere in my resolution to undertake it. Fortunately for my intentions it happens, that as the day approaches my terrors abate; for had they continued to be what they were a week since, I must after all have disappointed you; and was actually once on the verge of doing it. I have told you something of my nocturnal experiences, and assure you now, that they were hardly ever more terrific than on this occasion. Prayer has, however, opened my passage at last, and obtained for me a degree of confidence that I trust will prove a comfortable viaticum to me all the way. On Wednesday, therefore, we set forth.

The terrors that I have spoken of would appear ridiculous to most; but to you they will not, for you are a reasonable creature, and know well that to whatever cause it be owing (whether to constitution, or to God's express appointment), I am hunted by spiritual hounds in the night season. I cannot

[1] See n., p. 941.

help it. You will pity me, and wish it were otherwise; and though you may think there is much of the imaginary in it, will not deem it for that reason an evil less to be lamented. So much for fears and distresses. Soon I hope they shall all have a joyful termination, and I, my Mary, my Johnny, and my dog, be skipping with delight at Eartham.

Well! this picture is at last finished, and well finished, I can assure you. Every creature that has seen it has been astonished at the resemblance. Sam's boy bowed to it, and Beau walked up to it wagging his tail as he went, and evidently showing that he acknowledged its likeness to his master. It is a half-length, as it is technically, but absurdly called; that is to say, it gives all but the foot and ankle. Tomorrow it goes to town, and will hang some months at Abbot's when it will be sent to its due destination in Norfolk.

I hope, or rather wish, that at Eartham I may recover that habit of study which—inveterate as it once seemed, I now seem to have lost—lost to such a degree, that it is even painful to me to think of what it will cost me to acquire it again.

Adieu! my dear, dear Hayley; God give us a happy meeting! Mary sends her love. She is in pretty good plight this morning, having slept well, and for her part, has no fears at all about the journey.

Ever yours,

W.C.

TEXT: *Southey*

TO LADY HESKETH

Eartham, Augt. 11, 1792

My dearest coz,

I would gladly have devoted to you my first hours after breakfast, while my mind was fresh and unfatigued with study, but Hayley, who is never so happy as when he can render me some service, insisted on my passing the time with him till eleven o'clock in the revisal of my Miltonic labours.

Now therefore I can give you nothing but the vapid lees of an imagination already jaded, and in no condition to describe what I felt in this memorable journey. Much anxiety I felt before it, and much in the course of it, fearful of its effects on Mrs Unwin, and that she would want strength to endure the fatigue of it. We reached Barnet on the evening of the first day where, though she boasted herself unwearied, I suffered inconceivable dejection on her account, finding her power of articulation and even her voice almost entirely lost through weariness, and the inn so noisy that she seemed to have no chance of sleep. The next morning however I found her sufficiently refreshed, and with Mr Rose added to our party who had kindly walked from London the evening before to meet us, we began our second day's journey.

I passed through London, as he I suppose has told you, less affected by the scene than I had hoped I should be. Him we dropped at the Surrey end of Westminster Bridge, and proceeded to Kingston. There, as you have learned, we met the good General, whom we found already at the Sun expecting us. So altered indeed was he, that neither his face, his person, nor the sound of his voice announced him to me, who had not seen him almost 30 years. But I guessed him, or rather found him out by inference, and hasting to embrace him soon learned that I was not mistaken. We passed somewhat more than an hour together, when he went home to dinner, having first made me promise, if possible, to dine with him on my return. From Kingston we proceeded to Ripley, where if we did not find the most splendid of all receptacles for travellers, we found at least what was more valuable to us, tolerable chambers and a silent house. Mrs Unwin slept better than the preceding night, and when she rose appeared so well and in such good spirits that I had no fears left respecting her ability to perform the remainder of the journey. Accordingly she performed it well, and between nine and ten, having passed some of the Sussex hills by moonlight with more terror to myself than her, we arrived safe at the gate of our beloved Hayley. Here we inhabit a paradise. His pleasure-ground is a hill about 3 quarters of a mile in circuit, beautiful beyond my power or opportunity to describe at present, and commanding a noble view of both sea and land from the summit. Mrs Unwin, I thank God, seemed already somewhat the better for the journey, the fine air and the exercise that this delightful place affords her. She has slept almost twice as much every night since we came as she did at Weston, and has had twice the appetite, for at Weston she has for some time hardly eaten enough to sustain her. Her amendment in short has been such that I could not expect a single week to do more for her even at Eartham, and as to myself, I was never better. So much for our journey, and such consequences of it as we have at present experienced.

I have filled my paper and said nothing in answer to yours. —Yet not so, for I have told you on recollection what you chiefly desired to know. I can at present only add that you are every day affectionately remembered by us all, and every day wished for, and that Hayley, who always speaks of you with delight, challenged me yesterday to drink your health in a bumper, which was done accordingly. Johnny (once Sir John Croydon, but now better known by the title of the Reverend Doctor Palbarto) desires to live always in your remembrance and good opinion, as does our host the benevolent Hayley; and Mrs Unwin, who has just joined me in the library, sends her best love. How long we shall stay I know not, but I already see that to depart will be an affair of some difficulty.

> Adieu, my dear, I am
> Ever thine
>
> Wm Cowper

TEXT: *Panshanger MSS.***

TO LADY HESKETH

Eartham, Sund., Augt. 26, 1792

I know not how it is, my dearest coz, but in a new scene, and surrounded by strange objects, I find my powers of thinking dissipated to a degree that makes it difficult to me even to write a letter, and even a letter to you. But such a letter as I can, I will, and have the fairer chance to succeed this morning, Hayley and Romney and Hayley's son and Beau being all gone to the sea together for bathing. The sea, you must know, is nine miles off, so that unless stupidity prevent, I shall have opportunity to write not only to you but to poor Hurdis[1] also, who is broken-hearted for the loss of his favourite sister lately dead, and whose letter giving an account of it and which I received yesterday, drew tears from the eyes of all our party. My only comfort respecting even yourself is that you write in good spirits, and assure me that you are in a state of recovery, otherwise I should mourn not only for Hurdis but for myself, lest a certain event should reduce me and in a short time too, to a situation as distressing as his; for though nature designed you only for my cousin, you have had a sister's place in my affections ever since I knew you. The reason is, I suppose, that having no sister the daughter of my own mother, I thought it proper to have one the daughter of yours. Certain it is that I can by no means afford to lose you, and that unless you will be upon honour with me to give me always a true account of yourself, at least when we are not together, I shall always be unhappy, because always suspicious that you deceive me.

Now for ourselves. I am, without the least dissimulation, in perfect health. My spirits are about as good as you have ever seen them, and if increase of appetite and a double portion of sleep be advantages, such are the advantages that I have received from this migration. As to that gloominess of mind which I have had these 20 years, it cleaves to me even here, and could I be translated to paradise, unless I left my body behind me, would cleave to me there also. It is my companion for life and nothing will ever divorce us. So much for myself. Mrs Unwin is evidently the better for her jaunt, though by no means as well as she was before this last attack, still wanting help when she would rise from her seat and a support in walking. Neither can she use her knitting needles, nor read

[1] The Rev. James Hurdis, 1763–1801, author of *The Village Curate*, was at this time curate of Burwash, Sussex.

with ease, or long together. But she is able to use more exercise than she could at home, and moves with rather a less tottering step. God knows what He designs for me, but when I see those who are dearer to me than myself, distempered and enfeebled, and myself as strong as in the days of my youth, I am shocked to my very heart and tremble for the solitude in which a few years may place me. I wish her and you to die before me indeed, but not till I am more likely to follow you immediately. Enough of this.

Charlotte Smith's last novel I have not read, therefore can say nothing of its merits, but it seems to have the fate of all writings tinged with politics, to be censured or commended according to the political opinions of her readers. I advise you however to read it, and the rather because I know that she has bestowed in it high encomiums on the British constitution. She will soon publish another which I believe you will find excellently written and not exceptionable on the same account.[1]

Romney has drawn me in crayons, and in the opinion of all here, with his best hand and with the most exact resemblance possible.—But I must remember that I am near the end of my paper.

The 17th of September is the day on which I intend to leave Eartham. We shall then have been six weeks resident here, a holiday-time long enough for a man who has much to do, and who can do nothing except at home.

I have made both Hayley and Romney acquainted with the flattering things you say of them, and they are at least as much flattered by them as wise men ought to be.—Each presents his best thanks and compliments. Hayley, who knows you, never mentions you but with admiration—. And now farewell, my dearest coz; let me soon hear from you, and if it please God have a favourable account of you. Tell me too, that soon after our return to Weston, we shall have the happiness to see you there. Farewell—with Mrs U.'s sincere and affectionate best wishes, I remain ever thine

Wm Cowper

[1] See *n.*, p. 987.

P.S. Hayley, whose love for me seems to be truly that of a brother, has given me his picture drawn by Romney about 15 years ago. An admirable likeness, and which you will rejoice the more to see, because it will effectually displace a certain Hobowchin[2] that you wot of.

TEXT: *Panshanger MSS.* *

TO LADY HESKETH

Eartham, Sepr. 9, 1792

My dearest coz,

I determine if possible to send you one more letter, or at least, if possible, once more to send you something like one, before we leave Eartham. But I am in truth so unaccountably local in the use of my pen that, like the man in the fable who could leap well nowhere but at Rhodes, I seem incapable of writing at all except at Weston.—This is, as I have already told you, a delightful place; more beautiful scenery J have never beheld, nor expect to behold hereafter. But the charms of it, uncommon as they are, have not in the least degree alienated my affections from Weston. The genius of that place suits me better; it has an air of snug concealment in which a disposition like mine feels itself peculiarly gratified; whereas here I see from every window woods like forests and hills like mountains, a wildness in short that rather increases my natural melancholy, and which were it not for the agreeables that I find within doors, would soon convince me that mere change of place can avail me little. I feel too already, and so does Mrs Unwin, that the winters here must be cruelly cold and such as would be ill endured by persons accustomed to live under a hill and not on the summit, amidst small enclosures and not within view of the ocean. Accordingly I

[2] 'Hoborchin': owl. The new picture, as C. later wrote to Hayley, would displace one of himself, the 'theme of many an angry remark.'

have not looked out for a house in Sussex, nor shall. The enquiry indeed would be vain, and has already proved such to Mrs Smith, much better acquainted with the country than I am, having been born within a few miles of Eartham. Having mentioned that lady I will just add that about 3 nights since I opened the 3rd volume of her *Desmond*; and though I began at the wrong end, was so much pleased with it that I could not lay it down till supper interrupted me. I read half the volume, found much in it of a political kind, and nothing to which I could not heartily subscribe, or to which you would not subscribe as heartily. I mention this, lest through the prejudices you may have received from others you should deprive yourself of a real pleasure.

The intended day of our departure continues to be the 17th.—I hope to reconduct Mrs Unwin to the Lodge with her health considerably mended; but it is in the article of speech chiefly and in her powers of walking that she is sensible of much improvement. Her sight and her hand still fail her, so that she can neither read nor work—mortifying circumstances both, to her who is never willingly idle.

On the 18th I purpose to dine with the General and to rest that night at Kingston. But the pleasure I shall have in the interview will hardly be greater than the pain I shall feel at the end of it, for we shall part probably to meet no more.

Johnny, I know, has told you that Mr Hurdis is here. Distressed by the loss of his favourite sister, he has renounced the place where she died for ever, and is about to enter on a new course of life at Oxford. You would admire him much. He is gentle in his manners and delicate in his person, resembling our poor friend Unwin both in face and figure more than any one I have ever seen. But he has not, at least he has not at present, his vivacity.

I have corresponded since I have been here with Mrs Courtenay and had yesterday a very kind letter from her. Sir John and Lady Throg[1] she tells me were so fortunate as to leave Paris just two days before the terrible 10th of August.[2]

---

[1] John Throckmorton had succeeded to a baronetcy.

[2] The day when the mob sacked the Tuileries, massacred the Swiss Guard, and took the King and Queen prisoners.

Adieu my dear, may God bless you. Write to me as soon as you can after the 20th. I shall then be at Weston, and indulging myself in the hope that I shall e'er long see you there also. With the best compliments of our host and Johnny, and the best affections of Mrs Unwin—I remain

Ever thine

Wm Cowper

TEXT: *Panshanger MSS.* *

TO MRS COURTENAY

Eartham, Sepr. 10, 1792

My dear Catharina,

I am not so uncourteous a knight as to leave your last kind letter, and the last I hope that I shall receive for a long time to come, without an attempt at least to acknowledge and to send you something in the shape of an answer to it; but having been obliged to dose myself last night with laudanum, on account of a little nervous fever to which I am always subject, and for which I find it the best remedy, I feel myself this morning particularly under the influence of Lethean vapours, and consequently in danger of being uncommonly stupid.

You could hardly have sent me intelligence that would have gratified me more than that of my two dear friends[1] having departed from Paris two days before the terrible 10th of August. I have had many anxious thoughts on their account; and am truly happy to learn that they have sought a more peaceful region while it was yet permitted them to do so. They will not I trust revisit those scenes of tumult and horror while they shall continue to merit that description. We are here all of one mind respecting the cause in which the Parisians are engaged; wish them a free people and as happy as they can wish themselves. But their conduct has not always pleased us; we are shocked at their sanguinary proceedings,

---

[1] Sir John and Lady Throckmorton.

and begin to fear, myself in particular, that they will prove themselves unworthy, because incapable of enjoying it, of the inestimable blessings of liberty. My daily toast is Sobriety and Freedom to the French—for they seem as destitute of the former as they are eager to secure the latter.

We still hold our purpose of leaving Eartham on the 17th, and again my fears on Mrs Unwin's account begin to trouble me; but they are now not quite so reasonable as in the first instance. If she could bear the fatigue of travelling then, she is more equal to it at present; and supposing that nothing happens to alarm her, which is very probable, may be expected to reach Weston in much better condition than when she left it. Her improvement however is chiefly in her looks, and in the articles of speaking and walking; for she can neither rise from her chair without help, nor walk without a support, nor read, nor use her needles. Give my compliments to the good doctor and make him acquainted with the state of the patient, since he of all men seems to have the best right to know it.

I am proud that you are pleased with the Epitaph[2] I sent you, and shall be still prouder to see it perpetuated by the chisel. It is all that I have done since here I came, and all that I have been able to do. I wished indeed to have requited Romney for his well-drawn copy of me, in rhyme; and have more than once or twice attempted it: but I find, like the man in the fable who could leap only at Rhodes, that verse is almost impossible to me, except at Weston. Tell my friend George that I am every day mindful of him, and always love him, and bid him by no means to vex himself about the tardiness of Andrews.[3] Remember me affectionately to William[4] and to Pitcairn, whom I shall hope to find with you at my return; and should you see Mr Buchanan,[5] to him also. I have now charged you with commissions enow, and having

[2] On Fop, Lady Throckmorton's spaniel: see p. 129.

[3] James Andrews, a monumental sculptor, of Olney.

[4] William Throckmorton, barrister, a younger brother of Sir John: Pitcairn, his friend.

[5] The curate of Weston Underwood.

added Mrs Unwin's best compliments and told you that I long to see you again, will conclude myself,

My dear Catharina,

Most truly yours,

Wm Cowper

TEXT: *Panshanger MSS.*†

TO WILLIAM HAYLEY

The Sun at Kingston,
Tuesday, Sepr. 18, 1792

My dear Brother,

With no sinister accident to retard or terrify us, we find ourselves, at a quarter before one arrived safe at Kingston. I left you with a heavy heart and with a heavy heart took leave of our dear Tom[1] at the bottom of the chalk-hill. But soon after this last separation my troubles gushed from my eyes and then I was better.

At the descent of the first hill one of the horses belonging to the servants' chaise fell, but no harm ensued; and we, leading the way, knew it not till we came to Petworth.

We must now prepare for our visit to the General. I add no more therefore than our dearest remembrances and prayers that God may bless you and yours and reward you an hundred-fold for all your kindness. Tell Tom I shall always hold him dear for his affectionate attentions to Mrs U[nwin]: from her heart the memory of them can never be erased— Johnny loves you all, and has his share in all these acknowledgements.— Adieu—my dear Hayley—

Ever yours

Wm Cowper

TEXT: *Panshanger MSS.*

[1] Hayley's son.

TO WILLIAM HAYLEY

Weston, Thursday Sepr. 21, 1792

My dear Hayley,

Chaos himself, even the Chaos of Milton, is not surrounded with more confusion nor has a mind more completely in a hubbub than I experience at the present moment. At our first arrival after long absence, we find a hundred orders to servants necessary, a thousand things to be restored to their proper places, and an endless variety of *minutiae* to be adjusted, which though individually of little importance, are most momentous in the aggregate. In these circumstances I find myself so indisposed to writing that, save to yourself only, I would on no account attempt it. But to you I will give such a recital as I can of all that has passed since I sent you that short note from Kingston, knowing that if it be a perplexed recital, you will consider the cause and pardon it. I will begin with a remark in which I am inclined to think you will agree with me; that there is sometimes more true heroism passing in a corner and on occasions that make no noise in the world, than has often been exercised by those whom that world esteems her greatest heroes and on occasions the most illustrious. I hope so at least—for all the heroism I have to boast, and all the opportunities I have of displaying any, are of a private nature. After writing that note, I immediately began to prepare myself for my appointed visit to Ham; but the struggles that I had with my own spirit, labouring as I did under the most dreadful dejection, are never to be told. I would have given the world to have been excused, sensible that I was unfit for company, and fearing lest I should unavoidably discover that unfitness by a countenance too faithful to my feelings. I went however, and carried my point against myself, assuming a cheerful aspect and behaving cheerfully, with a heart riven asunder. I had reasons for all this anxiety which I cannot relate now, and you would hardly deem me in my senses if you knew them. The visit however passed off well, and we returned in the dark to Kingston; I with a lighter heart than I had known since my departure from Eartham, and Mary too; for she had suffered hardly less than myself, and chiefly on my account. That night we rested well in our inn, and at 20 minutes after eight next morning set off for London. Exactly at 10 we reached Mr Rose's door, and as *we* drove up to it one way, the chaises he had ordered to meet us drove up to it the other. We drank a dish of chocolate with him which cost us about 20 minutes, and proceeded, Mr Rose riding bodkin[1] with us as far as St Albans where his mother is, and Johnny riding ditto with the servants. From this time forth we met with no impediment; at every inn we found horses and chaises as ready as if they had been provided, and saving another downfall of one of our servants' horses, which however was attended with no mischief, met with nothing worth recording. In the dark, and in a storm, and at eight at night, we found ourselves at our own back door. Mrs Unwin was very near slipping out of the chair in which she was taken from the chaise, but at last was landed safe.

We have all had a good night and are all well this morning. Johnny having recovered from a violent colic which tormented him all the way from Woburn to Weston. God bless you my dearest brother! Mrs Unwin joins me in most affectionate remembrances to yourself and our dearest Tom, and Johnny sends a thousand thanks for all your kindness. It grieves me much to learn from him, that when we parted from you at the end of the wood, you had great uneasiness in your hip and talked of going to bed at your return. Let me hear from you and tell me that you are better.

Ever yours,

Wm Cowper

Socket's letter is delivered and his parents are well.

TEXT: *Panshanger MSS.* *

---

[1] Wedged between C. and Mrs Unwin, making a third where there was only room for two.

TO WILLIAM HAYLEY

Weston, Octr. 28, 1792

Nothing done, my dearest brother, nor likely to be done at present. Yet I purpose in a day or two to make another attempt, to which however I shall address myself with fear and trembling, like a man who having sprained his wrist, dreads to use it. I have not indeed like such a man injured myself by any extraordinary exertion, but seem as much enfeebled as if I had. Nor is my own unaccomplished task my only trouble; I have a variety of other labours upon my hands, as yet untouched. Poetry to revise in abundance, volume after volume, and the authors I suppose already wondering at my delay. These, I at last discover, are great sources of my dismay and trouble. The consciousness that there is so much to do and nothing done, is a burthen that I am not able to bear. Milton especially is my grievance, and I might almost as well be haunted by his ghost, as goaded with such continual self-reproaches for neglecting him. I will therefore begin. I will do my best. And if after all, that best prove good for nothing, I will even send the notes, worthless as they are, that I have made already. A measure very disagreeable to myself, and to which nothing but necessity shall compel me. I shall rejoice to see those new samples of your biography which you give me to expect, yet I doubt if they will have a good effect on my rascally spirits, and whether, instead of animating me as they ought with an ambition to do as well, they will not, by driving me to despair of that, disqualify me to do anything at all. I am a pitiful beast, and in the texture of my mind and natural temper have three threads of despondence for one of hope.

Allons! Courage! Here comes something however, produced after a gestation as long as that of a pregnant woman, and *vix vi expressum*[1] at last. It is the debt long unpaid, the compliment due to Romney, and if it has your approbation I will

[1] 'Hardly and painfully delivered.'

send it, or you may send it for me. I must premise however that I intended nothing less than a sonnet when I began. I know not why, but I said to myself, it shall not be a sonnet. Accordingly I attempted it in one sort of measure, then in a second, then in a third, till I had made the trial in half a dozen different kinds of shorter verse, and behold it is a sonnet at last. — The Fates would have it so.

TO GEORGE ROMNEY, ESQR.

Romney— expert infallibly to trace
   On chart or canvas, not the form alone
   And semblance, but, however faintly shown,
The mind's impression too on ev'ry face
With strokes that Time ought never to erase—
   Thou hast so pencill'd mine, that though I own
   The subject worthless, I have never known
The artist shining with superior grace.

But this I mark—that symptoms none of woe
   In thy incomparable work appear.
Well—I am satisfied it should be so,
   Since, on maturer thought, the cause is clear;
For in my looks what sorrow couldst thou see,
While I was Hayley's guest, and sat to thee?

The passage of Milton corrected according to your excellent observation, exceptionable enough before, becomes beautiful indeed. I thank you heartily for it, and sure as I live to comment on those lines will avail myself of it.

We are all alone. Johnny of Norfolk is gone to his own county, but gives us hope that we shall have him again in about six weeks. Lady Hesketh is gone to Bath, where a line from you will I dare say do her as much good as the waters. Dr Madan is a cousin of mine, and we were school-fellows. He is an amiable man and was a most agreeable one. What he may be now he is mitred I cannot say; we have not seen each other almost these 30 years, and though we love each other, have in all that time exchanged but one letter.

Adieu—my dearest brother. Mary is purely well this morning, and sends her best love.—Remember us to dear Tom and his playfellow.

Yrs ever

Wm C.

When I called yr nerves invincible, I meant by weather. In all other nervous respects I think myself, in the bruisers' phrase, as good a man as you.—When I have seen you here again, then we will talk about another journey to Eartham.

TEXT: *Panshanger MSS.**

TO GEORGE ROMNEY, ESQ.

Weston Underwood, Novr. 28, 1792

My dear Romney,

Since I left Eartham nothing has occurred that has given me so much pleasure as the arrival of your fine picture of our most amiable friend Hayley; and your kindness in sending me what the box contained beside gratifies me in the highest degree, convincing me that I am not forgotten by one whom I shall myself always remember with affection. All arrived safe, and for all I thank you.—My young cousin[1] has told me by letter how kindly you behaved to him when he called on you. For this I thank you likewise, for I love him and have great reason to do so. It was a very sensible mortification to me that I could not have the pleasure of seeing you at your own house in my way through London but the danger of offending others whom I should have been obliged to pass unvisited, deterred me. The happy day I hope will come when you will make me amends for what I lost by that severe necessity by giving us your company at Weston. Happy indeed should I be to see you here, and the hope of it which you gave me encouragement to entertain is too pleasant to be slightly

---

[1] John Johnson.

parted with. Hayley will be called to London some time in the course of the coming year, and a chaise will bring you easily in seven hours. A little relaxation will be good for you, and your enjoying it here will be equally good for me. I have been a poor creature ever since I saw you; dispirited to the greatest degree and incapable of all mental exertion; a state from which I do not expect deliverance till the buds shall peep and less sullen skies revive me. Mrs Unwin is at least as well as she was at Eartham—perhaps a little better. She desires me to say how kindly she remembers you, and how much she shall rejoice to see you. Adieu,—God bless you!

Believe me affectionately yours

Wm Cowper

TEXT: *Pierpont Morgan Library MSS.*

TO LADY HESKETH

Decr. 1, 1792

I am truly glad, my dearest coz, that the waters of Cheltenham have done thee good, and wish ardently that those of Bath may establish thy health and prove the means of prolonging it many years; even till thou shalt become what thou wast called at a very early age, an old wench indeed. I have been a *pauvre misérable* ever since I came from Eartham, and was little better while there, so that whatever motive may incline me to travel again hereafter, it will not be the hope that my spirits will be much the better for it. Neither was Mrs Unwin's health so much improved by that frisk of ours into Sussex as I had hoped and expected. She is however tolerably well, but very far indeed from having recovered the effects of her last disorder. My birthday (the 61st that I have numbered) has proved for once a propitious day to me, for on that day my spirits began to mend, my nights became less hideous, and my days have been such of course.

I have heard nothing from Joseph, and having been always used to hear from him in November, am reduced to the dire necessity of supposing with you that he is heinously offended. Being in want of money however, I wrote to him yesterday and a letter which ought to produce a friendly answer; but whether it will or not is an affair, at present, of great uncertainty. Walter Bagot is offended too, and wonders that I would have any connection with so bad a man as the author[1] of the *Essay on Old Maids* must necessarily be. Poor man! he has five sisters I think in that predicament, which makes *his* resentment rather excusable. Joseph by the way has two, and perhaps may be proportionably influenced by that consideration. Should that be the case, I have nothing left to do but to wish them all good husbands, since the reconciliation of my two friends seems closely connected with that contingency.

In making the first advances to your sister[2] you have acted like yourself, that is to say, like a good and affectionate sister, and will not I hope lose your reward. Rewarded in another world you will be no doubt, but I should hope that you will be not altogether unrecompensed in this. Thou hast a heart I know that cannot endure to be long at enmity with any one, and were I capable of using thee never so ill, I am sure that in time you would sue to me for a pardon. Thou dost not want fire, but meekness is predominant in thee.

I was never so idle in my life and never had so much to do. God knows when this will end, but I think of bestirring myself soon and of putting on my Miltonic trammels once again. That once done, I shall not I hope put them off till the work is finished. I have written nothing lately, but a sonnet to Romney, and a mortuary copy of verses for the town of Northampton, having been applied to by the new clerk for that purpose.

Johnson designs handsomely. You must pardon Johnson and receive him into your best graces. He purposes to publish together with my Homer a new edition of my 2 volumes of poems, and to make me a present of the entire profits. They are to be handsome quartos with an engraving of Abbot's picture of me prefixed.—I have let myself neither time nor room for politics.

[1] Hayley.
[2] Lady Croft, whose husband was dying.

The French are a vain and childish people, and conduct themselves on this grand occasion with a levity and extravagance nearly akin to madness; but it would have been better for Austria and Prussia to have let them alone.[3] All nations have a right to choose their own mode of government, and the sovereignty of the people is a doctrine that evinces itself; for whenever the people choose to be masters they always are so, and none can hinder them. God grant that we may have no revolution here, but unless we have a Reform we certainly shall. Depend upon it my dear, the hour is come when power founded in patronage and corrupt majorities must govern this land no longer. Concessions too must be made to Dissenters of every denomination. They have a right to them, a right to all the privileges of Englishmen, and sooner or later, by fair means or by force, they will have them.

Adieu my dearest coz. I have only time to add Mrs U.'s most affectionate remembrances, and to conclude myself.

Ever thine,

Wm Cowper

Mr and Mrs Rose come on the 22nd., and Johnny with them. The former to stay ten days.

It is strange that anybody should suspect Mrs Smith of having been assisted by me. None writes more rapidly or more correctly. 20 pages in a morning, which I have often read and heard read at night, and found not a word to alter.—This moment comes a very kind letter from Joseph. Sephus tells me I may expect to see very soon the strongest assurances from the people of property of every description to support the King and present Constitution. In this I do most sincerely rejoice, as you will. He wishes to know my political opinions, and he shall most truly.

TEXT: *MSS. Cowper Museum, Olney*

[3] The Austrian Netherlands had been occupied by the French after the victory of Jemappes. On November 15 the National Convention offered its support to all peoples striving for liberty. 'All governments are our enemies', said its president, 'all peoples are our allies.'

TO WILLIAM HAYLEY

[postmarked Dec. 8], *1792*

My dearest brother,

The picture is arrived and safe in the place to which I had destined it. There is no fear now that I shall not often think of you, seeing that you are always before my eyes:

> In language warm as could be breathed or penned,
> Thy portrait speaks th'original, my friend—
> Not by those looks that indicate thy mind,
> They only speak thee friend of all mankind;
> Expression here more soothing still I see,
> That friend of all a partial friend to me.

I sent Romney a letter of warm thanks for his kind remembrance of me, and was too much gratified by his present to mortify him by a refusal. Attention is always charming, and his had all the charms that attention could possibly have. I little thought he would remember so long the slight mention that was made one morning, at breakfast in your billiard-room, of the articles in question, and had indeed so completely forgot it myself, that concluding they came by Lady Hesketh's orders given to Johnny, I intended to have thanked *her* for them in my next letter. But my good angel, from whom you know I sometimes receive seasonable advice, whispered me in the ear on the second morning after I received them, thus—

> 'Since Romney has made me so handsome a present, let me not delay to deal as handsomely with him.'

Having no doubt that the intelligence was authentic, I wrote my acknowledgments immediately. My hope is, and so I told him, that the good day will come, when I shall receive you here both together.

I fully purposed writing to you yesterday morning, but rose

so miserable that Mary would not suffer it. Indeed I almost
constantly descend into the study such a wretch, that my little
dog's joy to see me is almost insupportable, and to return his
caresses impossible. This being the case, how shall I take your
friendly advice and jump at once *in medias res*? I have had a
mere trifle in hand a fortnight, not in verse but in prose, nor
for myself but for my bookseller, and trifle as it is have found
it too arduous for me. Nevertheless I have hope. My monitor
above-mentioned has not been silent on this subject, and
from him I understand that the propitious moment, tardy as it
seems, will yet arrive, when I shall not only begin but finish.
Mark the confidence I place in you. I dare not say so much to
any other man, lest he should despise me as a fool and a fanatic.
But true it is, that all the grand incidents of my life have been
previously announced to me in this way. The moment I start,
you shall know it. In the meantime be beloved and honoured
as you ought by me for all the generosity, the unexampled
generosity of your offers. I will tell you what you shall do for
me, and what I shall want at your hands when once I shall have
begun in earnest.

Lady Hesketh is at Bath; in good health I believe, and I am
sure in good spirits. Warm as ever on the side of monarchy
and ministry, and hating the French most perfectly, but droll
and humorous in her manner of expressing that hatred to a
degree that forces me, even me, to laugh heartily.—When
you turn all the cocks that water you, think of those lines of
Milton, *Ad Patrem*:

> *nunc mea Pierios cupiam per pectora fontes*
> *irriguas torquere vias, totumque per ora*
> *volvere laxatum gemino de vertice rivum*[1]

Repeat those lines and you will seem to receive an immediate
answer to your supplication.

Adieu my dearest brother—Mary loves you, is much as

[1] 'Oh that Pieria's spring would thro' my breast
  Pour its inspiring influence, and rush
  No rill, but rather an o'erflowing flood!'
(Cowper's own translation).

982

usual, and with me affectionately remembers you and her two griffins.[2]

Yrs ever

Wm Cowper

TEXT: *Panshanger MSS.*** The verses on Hayley's portrait, and the two sentences at the end referring to Lady Hesketh, have been published separately.

TO LADY HESKETH

The Lodge, December 18th, 1792

I like nobody's politics but yours, my dearest coz: and yours I like because they make me merry. I have laughed I believe but 4 times since I came out of Sussex, and each time at your laudable and extreme abhorrence of the French. I do in truth detest them as much as you. They had a good cause in the beginning but have spoiled it by their excessive folly, and disgraced it indelibly by their unexampled barbarity. They will probably pay dear by and by for the pleasant sport they are taking now; not that I think the Austrians and Prussians will ever prevail against them, but in due time we shall see them tearing themselves in pieces; an employment in which they would have been long since occupied had not their attention been called another way.

With respect to our own affairs likewise you and I are pretty much of a mind. We are both as loyal as any of his Majesty's subjects, and perfectly satisfied with our present constitution, which is surely a more respectable mode of Government and worthier of a great nation than any dirty republic ever was or will be. But certain vices have infected it which more than anything else threaten its dissolution, and which therefore I wish to see eradicated. You on the other hand are fearful of

[2] Mrs Unwin's name for Tom Hayley and his companion, Thomas Socket, who had pulled her in a garden chair round the grounds of Eartham.

meddling with them, at least in the present crisis. The times are turbulent, and you think a calm would be a more proper season. Now here we differ. My opinion is that this is the favourable moment. A State alarmed will make concessions, but a State in perfect peace and security will not even think of doing it. We shall soon see how the friends of Reform will act, but I think if they sleep now, and I hear that they intend to do so, they will miss their opportunity.

You think otherwise of my neighbours than they deserve. They are no Democrats, you may take my word for it, and you may assure yourself I believe, without the least danger of self-deception, that no man of considerable landed property will ever be so. They only wish, as I do, a parliamentary reform, and having had the happiness to be born in England, to have also the free enjoyment of all English privileges.[1] You think that Government having granted them something, though in truth very little, they are bound in gratitude to be quiet. But no gratitude is due, because there is no obligation conferred. Had they received their whole demand they would have had no cause to say 'Thank you,' for to give a man what is his own is no bounty, but merely an act of justice.

These I am persuaded are their views of the matter, and if it were not for a little film of prejudice against all Dissenters from our Church Establishment, I am equally persuaded they would be yours.

I have reason in particular to lament the death of poor Sir Archer,[2] and shall have annual cause to do so. On Sunday evening I received hat-band and gloves from the undertaker I suppose, by order of the executors: a useless donation to me who have not a scrap of mourning and can now less than ever afford to purchase it. The loss of a worthy man is always matter of concern; and one's grief for the loss of a benefactor, whether expressed by a black coat or not, may always be trusted for sincerity.

Mrs Unwin, all Foxite as she is, loves you dearly, and often testifies it by her manner of speaking of you. She is as well as the season will permit, which too much confines her. As for

[1] The Throckmortons were Roman Catholics.

[2] Sir Archer Croft was the husband of Lady Hesketh's younger sister.

me, I continue idle, having neither spirits, nor ability, nor leisure for writing. But today and yesterday have found myself a little better than usual.—Adieu, my dear, God bless you.—When shall we read romances again in an evening? Mr and Mrs Rose will be here in a day or two but their stay will be short.

Ever thine, W.C.

Whether thou knowest it or not, my translations of Milton lie and have long lain at your house in N[ew] N[orfolk] S[treet], whither the General sent them. I honour his zeal that carried him to court.

TEXT: *Panshanger MSS.* **

TO WILLIAM HAYLEY

Weston, Jan. 8, 1793

My dearest Hayley,

Your silence alarms me. I cannot account for it but by supposing that you are ill and too ill to write. If this be the case I beseech you to order somebody to send me a line, since certainty, however unpleasant, is always better than conjecture. My little friend Tom will write with all his heart, or if he be too much engaged, Socket. I have received letters today which have rather distressed me, but the receipt of none from you is at present my chief distress, and I cannot be satisfied to let the quarter of an hour pass which is now passing and which is the only opportunity I shall have today without dispatching these few lines of enquiry after you. I am now going into the walk with my poor Mary, who encounters almost the worst weather for the sake of a little air and exercise. Adieu, therefore, and unless we should be writing at the same time and our letters cross each other, let me hear from you or of you immediately after the receipt of this.

Ever yours

Wm Cowper

TEXT: *Panshanger MSS.* **

TO WILLIAM HAYLEY

Weston, Jan. 29, 1793

My dearest Hayley,

I truly sympathise with you under your weight of sorrow for the loss of our good Samaritan.[1] But be not broken-hearted my friend! Remember: the loss of those we love is the condition on which we live ourselves, and that he who chooses his friends wisely, from among the excellent of the earth, has a sure ground of hope concerning them when they die, that a merciful God has made them far happier than they could be here, and that he shall join them soon again. This is solid comfort, could we but avail ourselves of it, but I confess the difficulty of doing so. Sorrow is like the deaf adder that hears not the voice of the charmer, charm he never so wisely,[2] and I feel so much myself for the death of Austin, that my own chief consolation is that I had never seen him. Live yourself, I beseech you, for I have seen so much of you, that I can by no means spare you. And I will live as long as it shall please God to permit me. I know you set some value upon me, therefore let that promise comfort you, and give us not reason to say like David's servants — We know that it would have pleased thee more if all we had died than this one for whom thou art inconsolable.[3] You have still Romney and Carwardine and Guy and me my poor Mary, and I know not how many beside; as many I suppose as ever had an opportunity of spending a day with you. He who has the most friends, must necessarily lose the most, and he whose friends are numerous as yours, may the better spare a part of them. It is a changing transient scene: yet a little while and this poor dream of life will be over with all of us.

The living, and they who live unhappy, they are indeed

---

[1] Dr Austin, a London physician who had prescribed, at Hayley's request, for Mrs Unwin.

[2] Psalm lviii, 4–5.

[3] A paraphrase of 2 Samuel, xix, 6.

subjects of sorrow. And on this account poor Mrs Smith[4] has engrossed much of my thoughts and my compassion. I know not a more pitiable case. Chained to her desk like a slave to his oar, with no other means of subsistence for herself and her numerous children, with a broken constitution, unequal to the severe labour enjoined her by necessity, she is indeed to be pitied. It is easy to foresee that notwithstanding all your active benevolence, she will and must ere long die a martyr to her exigencies. I never want riches except when I hear of such distress.

This has been a time in which I have heard no news but of the shocking kind, and the public news is as shocking as any. War I perceive—war in procinct[5]—and I cannot but consider it as a prelude to war at home. The national burthen is already nearly intolerable, and the expenses of a war will make it quite so. We have many spirits in the country eager to revolt and to act a French tragedy on the stage of England. Alas poor Louis![6] I will tell you what the French have done. They have made me weep for a King of France, which I never thought to do, and they have made me sick of the very name of liberty, which I never thought to be. Oh, how I detest them! coxcombs as they are on this occasion as they ever are on all. Apes of the Spartan and the Roman character, with neither the virtue nor the good sense that belonged to it.— Is this treason at Eartham? I hope not. If it is, I must be a traitor.

Adieu, my beloved friend. Mary drinks tar-water and is the better for it though she has lately begun. I write in the greatest haste and remain ever yours,

W.C.

TEXT: *BM. Add. MSS.* 39,673

[4] Charlotte Smith (1749–1806), the novelist, had been at Eartham at the time of C.'s visit. Separated from an extravagant husband, she supported twelve children by her writings.

[5] *Paradise Lost*, VI, 19–21:

> Warr he perceav'd, warr in procinct, and found
> Already known what he for news had thought
> To have reported.

[6] Louis XVI had been executed on January 23.

TO LADY HESKETH

Weston Lodge, Feb. 10, 1793

My dearest coz—

> My pens are all split, and my ink-glass is dry,
> Neither wit, common sense, nor ideas have I.

In vain has it been that I have made several attempts to write since I came from Sussex; not politics, but what concerns me even more than they (though they concern me much) the work for which I stand already engaged to the public. My love therefore to Mrs Matthews and bid her expect nothing from me, but rather slake her anger with drops of pity for a poor miserable author worn to the stumps. Seriously, unless more comfortable days arrive than I have the confidence to look for, there is an end of all writing with me. I have no spirits. When the Rose came I was obliged to prepare for his coming by a nightly dose of laudanum. While he stayed I kept myself in heart by no other means. When he went, I discontinued it; but have been obliged to call it to my aid again. Twelve drops suffice; but without them I am devoured by melancholy.

Apropos of the Rose. His wife is a very sensible woman, good-tempered and agreeable. She has an understanding well-matched to his own, and a manner of expressing herself so similar to his, that but for the tone of voice your ear would hardly distinguish them. Imitation is a natural effect of admiration. In her political notions she is a pretty exact counterpart of yourself; loyal in the extreme and hates the French most cordially. Therefore if you find her thus principled and thus inclined when you become acquainted with her, should that ever happen, you must not place her resemblance of yourself in these particulars to the account of her admiration of you, for she is your likeness ready-made. In fact, we were all of one mind about Government matters and about their playing the devil in France, and notwithstanding your opinion that the Rose is himself a Democrat, I can assure

988

you that he is nothing less. He is a Whig, and I am a Whig, and you, my dear are a Tory, and all the Tories nowadays call all the Whigs Republicans. How the deuce you came to be a Tory is best known to yourself; you have to answer for this novelty to the shades of your ancestors, who were always Whigs ever since we had any.

I am sorry for this war[1] that comes thundering at such a terrible rate. It may be necessary, but of that I am no competent judge. I am sure it will starve us all, and of that I can judge pretty well, being cruelly pinched already. Why should we show the French any mercy? A mercy it would be to beat them, since there is no other chance that they can ever be brought to their senses; and mercy they deserve none, being perfectly merciless themselves. Were they not so, would they suffer such a monster to exist among them as Mr Equality?[2] Oh how consummately wicked must that country be, where assassination is the mode, where murder costs no remorse, and yet where that villain without a likeness upon earth is permitted to live, and to live a member of their national Council!

I admire the Duchess of Gordon's answer to Ld L— and say Amen to it with all my heart. May he be hanged before the day comes for which he wishes![3]

Your approbation of my picture pleases me much. There is another at Eartham which you would approve equally. The painters having made two good hits, it would be folly to try them again, therefore I purpose never to do it. You have heard that Johnson gives me the profits of an edition of my poems, and £200 for a new edition of Homer. What think you of my little bookseller now?

[1] France had declared war on February 1st, 1793.

[2] In September 1792 the Paris Commune had voted to give Philippe, Duke of Orleans, the surname of Egalité, and the electors had appointed him a delegate to the Convention. In this capacity he had voted for the death sentence on his cousin, Louis XVI.

[3] C. probably meant James, 8th Earl of Lauderdale, 1759–1839, who at this time styled himself 'Citizen Maitland', and turned up at the House of Lords 'in the rough costume of Jacobinism'. His uncle had married Penelope Madan, C.'s cousin and Lady Hesketh's.

Adieu my dearest coz—with Mrs U.'s best love

Ever thine

Wm Cowper

Thanks for *Village Politics*[4]—it is perfectly well conceived for the purpose.

TEXT: *Panshanger MSS.**

TO WILLIAM HAYLEY

Weston, Feb. 24, 1793

My dear Hayley,

Your letter, so full of kindness and so exactly in unison with my own feelings for you, should have had, as it deserved to have, an earlier answer, had I not been perpetually tormented with inflamed eyes, which are a sad hindrance to me in everything. But to make amends, if I do not send you an early answer, I send you at least a speedy one, being obliged to write as fast as my pen can trot, that I may shorten the time of poring upon paper as much as possible. Homer too has been another hindrance, for always when I can see, which is only during about 2 hours in a morning and not at all by candle-light, I devote myself to him, being in haste to send him a second time to the press, that nothing may stand in the way of Milton. By the way, where are my dear Tom's remarks[1] which I long to have, and must have soon or they will come too late.

Oh you rogue! What would you give to have such a dream about Milton as I had about a week since? I dreamed that being in a house in the city and with much company, looking toward the lower end of the room from the upper end of it, I descried a figure which I immediately knew to be Milton's. He was very gravely but very neatly attired in the fashion of his day, and had a countenance which filled me with those

[4] A tract by Hannah More.

[1] Tom Hayley's 'Observations on Cowper's Homer.'

feelings that an affectionate child has for a beloved father. Such for instance as Tom has for you. My first thought was wonder where he could have been concealed so many years, my second a transport of joy to find him still alive, my third, another transport to find myself in his company, and my fourth a resolution to accost him. I did so, and he received me with a complacence in which I saw equal sweetness and dignity. I spoke of his *Paradise Lost* as every man must who is worthy to speak of it at all, and told him a long story of the manner in which it affected me when I first discovered it, being at that time a schoolboy. He answered me by a smile and a gentle inclination of his head. I told him we had poets in *our* days, and no mean ones, and that I was myself intimate with the best of them. He replied—I know Mr Hayley very well by his writings. He then grasped my hand affectionately and with a smile that charmed me said—Well, you, for your part, will do well also. At last, recollecting his great age, for I understood him to be about 200 years old, I said that I might fatigue him by much talking and took my leave, and he took his with an air of the most perfect good breeding. His person, his features, his dress, his manner, were all so perfectly characteristic, that I am persuaded an apparition of him could not represent him more completely. This may truly be said to have been one of the dreams of Pindus,[2] may it not?

How truly I rejoice that you have recovered Guy! That man won my heart the moment I saw him, give my love to him and tell him I am truly glad he is alive again.

There is much sweetness in those lines from the Sonneteer of Avon, and not a little in dear Tom's. An earnest, I trust, of good things to come.

My friend Hurdis is encouraged to stand for the poetry professorship at Oxford, a vacancy being expected to happen soon. Can you do him any service? I know if you can you will.—With Mary's kind love, I must now conclude myself, my dear brother, ever yours

Lippus[3]

TEXT: *Panshanger MSS.*

[2] A mountain sacred to Apollo and the Muses.
[3] A man with inflamed eyes.

TO WILLIAM HAYLEY

Weston, March 19, 1793

My dearest brother,

I wrote to your dear little boy, and hope that you have accepted that letter in part of payment, for I am so busy every morning before breakfast (my only opportunity), stalking and strutting in Homeric stilts, that you ought to account it an instance of marvellous grace and favour that I condescend to write even to you. Sometimes I am seriously almost crazed with the multiplicity and magnitude of the matters before me, and the little or no time that I have for them; and sometimes I repose myself after the fatigue of that distraction on the pillow of despair; a pillow which has often served me in time of need, and is become, by frequent use, if not very comfortable, at least convenient. So reposed, I laugh at the world, and say, 'Yes, you may gape and expect both Homer and Milton from me, but I'll be hanged if ever you get them.'

In Homer, you must know, I am advanced as far as to the 15th of the *Iliad*, leaving nothing behind me that can reasonably offend the most fastidious; and I design him for public appearance in his new dress as soon as possible, for a reason which any poet may guess if he will but thrust his hand into his pocket. Johnson gives me £200 for this second edition, which is to consist of 750 copies only, and the copyright still remains in me. But I suppose I have told you this six times already. Repetition is a vice that I begin to perceive myself rather in danger of.

Three days ago I received a swingeing packet by the post. Oh ho, says I, it is come at last. This can be nothing less than an appointment to some good place under government. Here are the Royal arms, and the bulk of it is promising to a degree that may fairly encourage the most flattering expectations. It must be so, says Mary, and certainly comes from Lord Thurlow. So I opened it and found Mrs Smith's poem. Now you may imagine that I was mortified by this discovery, but I can assure you that I was not. For since, had it actually been what I supposed, and I had seen it with these eyes, I should not have believed it, I found myself very easily let down from my imaginary exaltation into the vale of poverty again. I have told you that it arrived three days ago, and now I must tell you that I have not yet had time to read it, but must tell you also that I will read it as soon as I can, and should anything in the shape of a feasible improvement offer, will be sure to suggest it. That is to say, I will suggest the matter of it, but am inclined to think that it will be unversified, both because I have no time at all for anything but my own business, and because I have always found it impracticable to patch my own upon another's, so as to give satisfaction.

You forbid me to tantalize you with an invitation to Weston, and yet, with almost a Frenchman's barbarity, invite me to Eartham—No, no, there is no such happiness in store for me at present. Had I rambled at all, I was under promise to all my own dear mother's kindred to go to Norfolk, and they are dying to see me; but I have told them that die they must, for I cannot go; and ergo, as you will perceive, can go nowhere else.

Thanks for Mazarin's epitaph. It is full of witty paradox, and is written with a force and severity which sufficiently bespeak the author. I account it an inestimable curiosity, and shall be happy when time shall serve, with your aid, to make a good translation of it. But that will be a stubborn business. Adieu!—my dearest Hayley—Mary sends her best love. The clock strikes eight; and now for Homer.

Ever yours,

Wm C

Johnson has not yet sent me the wished-for parcel from Mr Smith. He keeps everything of the sort as he did your letter. Hang him.

P.S. I have always forgot to tell you that Mr Newton is not the man who almost quarrelled with me for connecting myself with your antivirginityship.[1] The feud, however, is

[1] See p. 979.

composed. Still another P.S.—Have this moment received yours. Your little man was well entitled to all the pleasure my praise could yield him. I left off fencing when one of my eyes had been almost poked out, and hope that you will now do the same. Mr B. sent me a very obliging note telling me that he does not frank, but that his friend Mr Freeling has offered the use of his name.

TEXT: *BM. Add. MSS.* 30,805

TO JOSEPH HILL

Weston Underwood, March 29, 1793

Received of Joseph Hill Esq. the sum of forty pounds by draft on Child & Co.

Wm Cowper

My dear friend,

Your tidings concerning the slender pittance yet to come, are as you observe, of the melancholy cast. Not being gifted by nature with the means of acquiring much, it is well however that she has given me a disposition to be contented with little. I have now been so many years habituated to small matters, that I should probably find myself incommoded by greater, and may I but be enabled to shift, as I have been hitherto, unsatisfied wishes will never trouble me much. My pen has helped me somewhat, and after some years' toil I begin to reap the benefit. Had I begun sooner, perhaps I should have known fewer pecuniary distresses; or, who can say? it is possible that I might not have succeeded so well. Fruit ripens only a short time before it rots; and man in general arrives not at maturity of mental powers at a much earlier period. I am now busied in preparing Homer for his second appearance. An author should consider himself as bound not to please himself but the public; and so far as the good pleasure of the public may be learned from the critics, I design to accommodate myself to it. The Latinisms, though employed by Milton and numbered by Addison[1] among the arts and expedients by which he has given dignity to his style, I shall render into plain English; the rougher lines, though my reason for using them has never been proved a bad one so far as I know, I shall make perfectly smooth, and shall give body and substance to all that is in any degree feeble and flimsy; and when I have done all this and more, if the critics still grumble, I shall say the very deuce is in them. Yet that they will grumble I make little doubt, for unreasonable as it is to do so, they all require something better than Homer, and that something they will certainly never get from me.

As to the canal[2] that is to be my neighbour I hear little about it. The Courtenays of Weston have nothing to do with it, and I have no intercourse with Tyringham. When it is finished the people of these parts will have to carry their coals 7 miles only, which now they bring from Northampton or Bedford, both at the distance of 15. But, as Balaam says,[3] who shall live when these things are done? It is not for me, a sexagenarian already, to expect that I shall. The chief objection to canals in general seems to be, that multiplying as they do, they are likely to swallow the coasting trade.

I cannot tell you the joy I feel at the disappointment of the French;[4] pitiful mimics of Spartan and Roman virtue, without a grain of it in their whole character!

Remember me most kindly to your sisters, and make my best compliments to Mrs Hill.

Ever yours,

Wm C.

Many thanks for a barrel of fine oysters.

TEXT: *Cowper Johnson MSS.*

[1] *Spectator*: No. 285: '...Another way of raising the language, and giving it a poetical turn, is to make use of the idioms of foreign tongues.'

[2] A section of the Grand Junction Canal.

[3] Numbers, xxiv, 23: '...Alas, who shall live when God doeth this.'

[4] The French on March 18th were defeated at Neerwinden, and retreated.

TO JOHN JOHNSON

The Lodge, April 11, 1793

My dearest Johnny,

In the first place, as a most important article, which I would not willingly forget, I wish you to send us another keg of Geneva, that excellent liquor of which we both take a tablespoonful every day after dinner. This laudable practice, together with the gift of a bottle to the Courtenays, has pretty much reduced our quantity, so that we are in danger of being left ginless unless soon supplied.

The long muster-roll of my great and small ancestors I signed, and dated, and sent up to Mr Blue-mantle, on Monday, according to your desire. Such a pompous affair, drawn out for my sake, reminds me of the old fable of the mountain in parturition, and a mouse the produce. Rest undisturbed, say I, their lordly, ducal, and royal dust![1] Had they left me something handsome, I should have respected them more. But perhaps they did not know that such a one as I should have the honour to be numbered among their descendants! Well! I have a little bookseller that makes me some amends for their deficiency. He has made me a present—an act of liberality which I take every opportunity to blazon, as it well deserves. But you, I suppose, have learned it already from Mr Rose.

Fear not, my man. You will acquit yourself very well, I dare say, both in standing for your degree, and when you have gained it. A little tremor, and a little shamefacedness in a stripling, like you, are recommendations rather than otherwise; and so they ought to be, being symptoms of an ingenuous mind rather unfrequent in this age of brass.

What you say of your determined purpose, with God's help, to take up the Cross, and despise the shame, gives us

[1] See n.2, p. 111.

both real pleasure.[2] In our pedigree is found one[3] at least who did it before you. Do you the like, and you will meet him in heaven, as sure as the Scripture is the word of God.

The quarrel that the world has with evangelic men and doctrines, they would have with a host of angels in the human form: for it is the quarrel of owls with sunshine; of ignorance with divine illumination.

Adieu, my dear Johnny! We shall expect you with earnest desire of your coming, and receive you with much delight.

W.C.

TEXT: first paragraph, *Bailey*, *p. xxvi*; otherwise *Southey*.

TO LADY HESKETH

The Lodge, May 7, 1793

My dearest cousin,

You have thought me long silent and so have many others. In fact, I have not for months written punctually to any but yourself and Hayley. My time, the little time that I have, is so engrossed by Homer that I have at this moment a bundle of unanswered letters, and letters likely to be so. Another evil consequence of this engrossment is, that when I do make shift to write to anybody, I omit always what I most wish to insert, and what I remember I express so clumsily that the scribble is hardly intelligible even to myself. And in addition to all this, I am obliged to be short; an effect of which you I know will complain as much as any. Thou knowest, I dare say, what it is to have a head weary with thinking. Mine is so fatigued by breakfast-time that 3 days in 4 I am utterly incapable of sitting down to my desk again for any purpose whatever.

I have not yet, though ardently desirous to do it, complied with thy request concerning the stanzas to be sent to Lady

[2] John Johnson was ordained deacon on July 7, 1793.

[3] Cowper believed that his mother's family descended from the poet Donne, Dean of St Paul's.

Jane;[1] and the delay has been merely owing to want of opportunity and power to transcribe them. I will find one as soon as possible, or my kind Johnny who is here and as busy almost as myself preparing for his degree, shall copy them for me. The Queen however is no such favourite with me as once she was, and had the verses never have been written perhaps it had been as well.

I am glad I have convinced thee at last that thou art a Tory. Your friend's definition of Whig and Tory may be just for aught I know so far as the latter are concerned, but respecting the former I think him mistaken. There is no *true* Whig who wishes all the power in the hands of his own party. The division of it which the lawyers call tripartite is exactly what he desires, and he would have neither King, Lords nor Commons unequally trusted, or in the smallest degree predominant. Such a Whig am I, and such Whigs are the real friends of the Constitution.

I thank thee for the cuttings of newspaper, which because they came from thee I read. Otherwise I never read an article either for or against the Minister,[2] sensible that both the praise and the blame are bought and paid for, and at a price far greater than they are worth. For which reason, if I see a paragraph of either sort coming and have timely notice, I always get out of the way.

I find thee still unconvincible respecting my neighbours. Yet thou art misinformed. They are, as I have told thee, no Jacobins, but abhor the whole fraternity. The very book you recommend to me [as a[3]] proper antidote to partiality in [favour[1]] of French politics, has been lent me long since by Mr Courtenay and I am now in the middle of it.

Mr Buchanan returns every respectable acknowledgement for your kind letter which it is possible for a well-bred little man to imagine.

I am sorry that thou art bound to Cheltenham again,

[1] Possibly Lady Balgonie. The verses were probably 'On the Queen's Visit to London'.

[2] Pitt.

[3] Words obliterated in MS.

having hoped that we should have had thee here. You go I trust only to confirm your cure, for Mrs Cowper tells me your health seems perfectly restored. She has been mauled, and I suppose I too as her revisor, by the Critical Reviewers.[4] There was no chance, considering her subjects, that either she or I should escape it.

Mrs Unwin is neither better nor worse than usual. She sends her best love and Johnny his most affectionate obeisances. Adieu, my dear—I am dead with weariness and ever thine

Wm Cowper

TEXT: *Panshanger MSS.* *

TO LADY HESKETH

Augt. 29, 1793

My dearest coz,

The day with me seems too short for the business of it, and often it happens that I can hardly find time even for a short letter. This is pretty much my case at present, so that I will not absolutely promise to fill my sheet, but I will do what I can toward it. I might wait indeed for a fairer opportunity, but am unwilling to do so, lest my longer silence should retard your decision to what point of the compass you shall first direct your course. Your question, at what time your coming to us will be most agreeable, is a knotty one and such as had I the wisdom of Solomon I should be puzzled to answer. I will, therefore, leave it still a question, and refer the time of your journey Westonward entirely to your own election; adding this one limitation however, that I do not wish to see you here exactly at present, on account of the unfinished state of my study; the wainscott of which still

---

[4] Maria C. was the author of *Original Poems on various Occasions*. Written by a Lady. Revised by William Cowper, Esq. 1792.

smells of paint, and which is not yet papered. I intended indeed not to have papered it at all, and in that intention sent for a man from Northampton to stain it with water-colours. He has indeed stained it, and made such a blotched and unsightly piece of work of it that I am now obliged to paper it, as the only means of hiding its deformities. The paper we expect, and have long expected Mr Andrews to procure for us from London. The man with whom he deals for that commodity is gone I suppose to some of the watering-places, and thinks of nothing so little as his proper business.

But to return; though as I have already insinuated, thy pleasant company is the thing which I always wish, and as much at one time as another, I believe if I examine myself minutely, since I despair of ever having it in the height of summer, which for your sake I should desire most, the depth of the winter is the season that would be most eligible to me. For then it is that in general I have most need of a cordial, and particularly in the month of January. I am sorry that I have departed so far from my first purpose, and am answering a question which I declared myself unable to answer. Choose thy own time, secure of this, that whatever time that be, it will always to us be a welcome one.

I rejoice that our troops on the continent act worthily of themselves, since there they are; but cannot help wishing vehemently that they were all at home again. I know that discontent is breeding fast, and that no victories will satisfy our merchants, our manufacturers, and the persons employed by the latter, for the losses they sustain by the injury done to commerce. The principals have a money-getting habit, and abhor naturally a season when there is none to be got; and the poor folks who serve them are idle, and consequently not hungry only but angry also. The war therefore is daily engendering a spirit amongst us that prosecutions will by and by prove insufficient to control. A spirit the more dangerous because it is not Jacobinism, which may be kept in awe, but the effect of real evils the stimulus of which is hourly felt, and which unavoidably makes those who feel it murmur.

What shall we do with Dunkirk when we have won it? Shall we attempt to keep it? Heaven make us wiser.

I thank you for your pleasant extract from Miss Fanshaw's letter—

> Her pen drops eloquence as sweet
> As any Muse's tongue could speak
> Nor needs a scribe like her regret
> Her want of Latin or of Greek.

And now my dear, adieu—I have done more than I expected and begin to feel myself exhausted with so much scribbling at the end of four hours' close application to study.

Cousin Tom paid us a short visit lately and enquired much after you.

With Mrs U.'s best remembrances I remain

Ever thine

Wm Cowper

TEXT: *Panshanger MSS.* *

TO LADY HESKETH

Septr. 26, 1793

My dearest coz,

I sit down to write this moment fresh from a scolding-bout, and in some hope that while I converse with you I may recover a little of the sweetness of my temper. A labourer whom I have employed to transplant some of my laurels, and who was ordered to take them up with as much earth about the roots as possible, very punctually obeyed and did so, but having done so, shook it all away before he planted them again. This I had the ill hap to discover at the latter end of his job, and when it was too late to prevent the greater part of the mischief. Can you wonder that my equanimity has been disturbed? I think not. And to make it the more provoking, the fellow has spent all his life in a garden.

I am not sorry, as thou seemest to be, that in your new maid you have a new piece of stuff to work upon. The chance of having a servant to suit you, is so much the more in your favour. Your true hackneyed Nab[1] is, as I take it, one of the most pestilent beings in the creation, and I have been tempted even to parody two lines of my own on this subject, which contain Homer's opinion of servants in general; but applied to this denomination of servants in particular the sentiment to me seems juster:

> Jove, when he dooms a woman to the place
> Of lady's maid, takes half her worth away.

But enough of both these subjects; perhaps my murdered laurels have made me more severe than I ought to have been on the nymphs in question. If so, they will I hope have the goodness to consider it and forgive me.

I now recollect that it is incumbent on me to thank thee for thy letter so comfortably and delightfully long, and which made me merry more than once or twice while I read it. Would that I could send thee one in return that would do as much for thee!

Sunday's post brought me a very long poetical epistle from the curate of Pershore, calling himself by the name of Wm Russel. It is rather a silly business, yet the man is a better versifier too than our whilom cousin Tom Clio. You shall see it at a convenient time. The same post brought me also a letter from a schoolmaster in Oxfordshire who wishes me to stand forth as editor of a volume of poetical extracts which he purposes to give to the public. He seems a very good sort of man and even a pious one, but I shall not comply. It is sufficient to be responsible for what I write myself. I cannot afford to be so for the writings of others.

Johnny was always a good boy, sober, gentle and in all respects well-disposed. Ordination therefore has made no difference in him. You must direct to him at East Dereham, Norfolk; but I expect him here on the eleventh of next month to spend a fortnight or thereabout with us. —I was astonished the other day to see a sundial sprung in the walk; a handsome one and handsomely mounted on a stone pedestal. Johnny had given orders to Andrews for the purpose, and to intro-

[1] Abigail: lady's maid.

duce it without my knowledge, which was done accordingly. The rogue in short is always stealing upon me some kindness or other.

I admire your idea of the French trap for admirals and, though you enjoined me not to mention it, have already mentioned it to Mr Buchanan who admires it too. An English sentinel I am sure should always be coupled with a French one, lest monsieur should throw open the gate in the night and admit an army to murder all our countrymen in their sleep.

Miss Fanshaw's verses are safe, and you shall have them when you come. Adieu. May you have a good journey to Bath, a pleasant time there, and smooth and dry roads when you cross to Weston!

Ever thine

Wm Cowper

Mr Bean[1] is well, still very young and handsome and sends his compliments.

TEXT: *Panshanger MSS.***

TO THE REV. JOHN JOHNSON

Weston Underwood, November 30, 1793

My dearest Johnny,

That I may begin my Sabbath pleasantly at least, though not so piously as yourself, I begin it with a letter to you. To pay a debt that has been long owing cannot be a bad deed on any day. Time was when on Sabbath mornings in winter I rose before day, and by the light of a lanthorn trudged with Mrs Unwin, often through snow and rain, to a prayer-meeting at the Great House, as they call it, near the church at Olney. There I always found assembled 40 or 50 poor folks who preferred a glimpse of the light of God's countenance and

---

[2] The vicar of Olney.

favour to the comforts of a warm bed, or to any comforts that the world could afford them; and there I have often myself partaken that blessing with them. If I live a different life now, it is not because I have found, or think that I have found a better way of living, but because for reasons too long and too unpleasant to be enumerated here, I have been constrained to do so, God knows with how much sorrow and misery to myself, on account of the loss of His presence which is better than life. I will not tell you how I lost it, and probably I never shall, and there merely because it would do you no good to know it, the story being absolutely incredible; but I know the truth of it, and have for 20 years suffered things not to be expressed, in consequence. The instruction however to be collected from it I will give you, and it is this. Never shut your eyes against a known duty, nor close your ears to an express providential call, however uncommon and even unprecedented it may be, and however difficult the service that it enjoins. This, my dear Johnny, without intending it when I began, I have preached to you, who are now preparing to preach to others. God help you to profit by the lesson, which I am sure is a good one, and heal the wounds that I have incurred and long time languished under, because I neglected it. Amen.

It is of no consequence that you had not time to see Johnson, for Hayley has seen him, and conferred with him much to my satisfaction. Diverse matters, all very agreeable to me, were the subjects of it, but the most agreeable of all, in the result of it, was this new edition of Milton; on which subject I learn that the publication is postponed on account of the war, which leaves the world no leisure for literary amusements; Johnson accordingly thinks it would be too hazardous to send forth so expensive a work at present. I have therefore leisure, when Homer is finished, which will soon be the case, instead of acting the dull part of a commentator, to perform the poet's part, far pleasanter and more adapted to my natural propensity. You will not be displeased to learn that Lawrence's sketch of me is to be engraved by Bartolozzi; though for private use only, and that a new edition of my poems with embellishments by Lawrence is in contemplation.

You do kindly and like yourself to gratify your sister's preference of landed honours to vile cash, though your compliance is certainly an expensive one. Her pride in this instance is of a kind that I have no quarrel with.

Adieu—We are as well as usual. Lady Hesketh is here. Hers and Mrs Unwin's best love attends you.

Yrs ever,

Wm Cowper

Give my best love to your sister, whose likeness to my mother ensures to her always my tenderest attachment—and my love to all friends.

I hope you have by this time heard from Mr Newton. I have nothing more to do with Homer now but to go over the last book of the *Iliad* with Clarke's notes, to write a new preface, and to transcribe the alterations.

TEXT: *Barham Johnson MSS.*

TO LADY HESKETH

[Sept. 5, 1795][1]

Mr Johnson is again absent; gone to Mattishall, a circumstance to which I am indebted for an opportunity to answer your letter as soon almost as I have received it. Were he present, I feel that I could not do it.—You say it gives you pleasure to hear from me, and I resolve to forget for a moment my conviction that it is impossible for me to give pleasure to any body. You have heard much from my lips that I am sure has given you none; if what comes from my pen be less

[1] This letter is undated in Southey's edition. But according to John Johnson's Diary (*Times Literary Supplement* Oct. 5 and 12 1951) the expedition to Happisburgh took place on Aug. 31, 1795. Internal evidence shows that the letter was written shortly afterwards. A letter by Johnson, published in the *Letters of Lady Hesketh*, dated Sept. 6, 1795, states that Cowper had written to Buchanan and Lady Hesketh on the previous day.

unpalatable, none has therefore so strong a claim to it as yourself.

My walks on the sea-shore have been paid for by swelled and inflamed eyelids, and I now recollect that such was always the condition of mine in the same situation. A natural effect I suppose, at least upon eyelids so subject to disorder as mine, of the salt spray and cold winds, which on the coast are hardly ever less than violent. I now therefore abandon my favourite walk, and wander in lanes and under hedges. As heavy a price I have paid for a long journey, performed on foot to a place called Hazeborough. That day was indeed a day spent in walking. I was much averse to the journey, both on account of the distance and the uncertainty of what I should find there; but Mr Johnson insisted. We set out accordingly, and I was almost ready to sink with fatigue long before we reached the place of our destination. The only inn was full of company; but my companion having an opportunity to borrow a lodging for an hour or two, he did so, and thither we retired. We learned on enquiry, that the place is eight miles distant from this, and though, by the help of a guide, we shortened it about a mile in our return, the length of the way occasioned me a fever, which I have had now these four days, and perhaps shall not be rid of in four more; perhaps never. Mr J. and Samuel, after dinner, visited the light-house. A gratification which would have been none to me for several reasons, but especially because I found no need to add to the number of steps I had to take before I should find myself at home again. I learned however from them that it is a curious structure. The building is circular, but the stairs are not so, flight above flight, with a commodious landing at every twentieth stair, they ascend to the height of four stories; and there is a spacious and handsome apartment at every landing. The light is given by the patent lamp, of which there are two ranges: six lamps in the upper range, and five in the lower; both ranges, as you may suppose, at the top of the house. Each lamp has a broad silver reflector behind it. The present occupant was once commander of a large merchant-man, but, having chastised a boy of his crew with too much severity, was displaced and consequently ruined. He had, however, a friend in the Trinity-House, who, soon after this was built, asked him if he would accept the charge of it; and the cashiered captain, judging it better to be such a lamp-lighter than to starve, very readily and very wisely closed with the offer. He has only the trouble of scouring the silver plates every day, and of rising every night at twelve to trim the lamps, for which he has a competent salary (Samuel forgets the amount of it) and he and his family a pleasant and comfortable abode.

I have said as little of myself as I could, that my letter might be more worth the postage. My next will perhaps be less worth it, should any next ensue; for I meet with little variety, and shall not be very willing to travel fifteen miles on foot again, to find it. I have seen no fish since I came here, except a dead sprat upon the sands, and one piece of cod, from Norwich, too stale to be eaten. — Adieu.

W.C.

TEXT: *Southey*

TO THE REV. JOHN BUCHANAN

Mundsey near North Walsham,
Septr. 5, 1795

...to interpose a little ease
Let my frail thoughts dally with false surmise.[1]

I will forget for a moment that to whomsoever I may address myself, a letter from me can no otherwise be welcome than as a curiosity; rendered such by the desperate condition of the writer. To you, Sir, I therefore address this, urged to it by extreme penury of employment, and the desire I feel to learn something of what is doing, and has been done at Weston, my beloved Weston, since I left it, hopeless of ever seeing it again. Mr Johnson being absent from our present

[1] Adapted from *Lycidas*, 152-3.

home at this place, I have an opportunity to trouble you, which otherwise you would have been so fortunate as to have escaped.

I live a mere animal life, which to a man of a mind naturally active is of itself a misery nearly insupportable. I walk. That is my only occupation, and of that I have had rather too much, having by a walk of 15 miles[2] and upward induced a fever which I have now suffered by these 5 days. No day indeed has passed since my arrival here, in which I have not walked about eight. A degree of exercise so far beyond what I used even in my best health at Weston, that I might have foreseen the consequence. The winds, I suppose, on all our shores, are almost always violent. Here at least they are such, and many degrees colder than even in the fields adjoining; so that an ascent through the road that intersects the cliff, though it measures not more than 50 paces, seems at once to gain another and a much warmer climate. The coldness of these blasts even in the hottest days has been such, that added to the irritation of the salt spray with which they are always charged, they have occasioned me an inflammation in the eyelids which threatened a few days since to confine me entirely; but by absenting myself as much as possible from the beach, and guarding my face with an umbrella, that inconvenience is in some degree abated. My chamber commands a very near view of the ocean, and the ships at high water approach the coast so closely, that a man furnished with better eyes than mine might I doubt not discern the sailors from the window. No situation, at least when the weather is clear and bright, can be pleasanter; which you will easily credit when I add that it imparts something a little resembling pleasure even to me. Regret however is the predominant sensation. Regret that neither this pleasure nor any other, if other I had, will be allowed me long. Alas! I tread a shore

[2] An annotation by Johnson reads: 'Dear soul! The 15 miles were in reality only 8 — the walk, to which he alludes, being from Mundsley to Happisburgh, which are 4 miles asunder. We went below-cliff, on a fine level sand, as hard as marble, and after dining at Happisburgh, returned by the pathway across the fields. It was on Monday, Augt. 31.'

within few miles, within sight indeed, of a place[3] where I passed some of the happiest days of my youth, in company with those whom I loved and by whom I *was* beloved. That pleasure I must know no more for ever.

I beg, Sir, if you favour me with any answer to this, that you will not waste ink and paper in attempting to console me. A labour that must be lost on me. You will gratify me much more by confining yourself to the news of Weston as I said in the beginning. In what has passed there I feel some interest; in topics of consolation, none. If Mr Gregson and your neighbours the Courtenays are there, mention me to them in such terms as you see good. Tell me if my poor birds are living. I never see the herbs I used to give them without a recollection of them, and sometimes am ready to gather them, forgetting that I am not at home.

Pardon this intrusion from your miserable correspondent

W.C.

Mrs U. continues much as usual. She knows not that I write or would send her compliments.

TEXT: *Panshanger MSS.**†: a copy in the hand of, and annotated by, John Johnson.

TO WILLIAM HAYLEY

[June, 1797]

Ignorant of everything but my own instant & impending misery, I know neither what I do, when I write; nor can do otherwise than write; because I am bidden to do so. Perfect despair, the most perfect that ever possessed any mind, has had possession of mine, you know how long, and knowing that, will not need to be told, who writes.

[3] Annotation by Johnson: 'Catfield, a parish of which his uncle, the Rev. Roger Donne, was Rector.'

TEXT: *BM. Add. MSS.* 38,887, *f.*126, where Hayley wrote: 'It was on Tuesday, the 20th of June 1797, that after long lamenting the calamitous suspension of our correspondence, I received in Sussex a letter with the postmark of Dereham, combining the following words, in the handwriting of Cowper, but with no signature, "To William Hayley Esq: Eartham, near Chichester" [then the text as above, written in Hayley's hand].

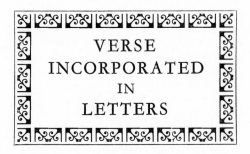

VERSE
INCORPORATED
IN
LETTERS

COWPER'S CIRCLE

The names of many of Cowper's relatives, friends, acquaintances and neighbours recur throughout this volume. This index gives the pages where the footnote references will be found.